Paul M. Og̶
— Creviewed for faith & History

The Forerunners

The Forerunners

Dutch Jewry in the North American Diaspora

Robert P. Swierenga

Wayne State University Press   Detroit

AMERICAN JEWISH CIVILIZATION SERIES

Editors
Moses Rischin, San Francisco State University
Jonathan D. Sarna, Brandeis University

Books in this series

Jews of the American West, edited by Moses Rischin and John Livingston, 1991

An Ambiguous Partnership: Non-Zionists and Zionists in America, 1939–1948, Menahem Kaufman, 1991

Hebrew in America: Perspectives and Prospects, edited by Alan Mintz, 1992

A Credit to Their Community: Jewish Loan Societies in the United States, 1880–1945, Shelly Tenenbaum, 1993

Judaism Faces the Twentieth Century: A Biography of Mordecai M. Kaplan, Mel Scult, 1993

The Forerunners: Dutch Jewry in the North American Diaspora, Robert P. Swierenga, 1994

Copyright © 1994 by Wayne State University Press,
Detroit, Michigan 48202. All rights are reserved.
No part of this book may be reproduced without formal permission.
Manufactured in the United States of America.
99 98 97 96 95 94   5 4 3 2 1

Library of Congress Cataloging-in-Publication Data
Swierenga, Robert P.
    The forerunners : Dutch Jewry in the North American diaspora /
Robert P. Swierenga.
        p. cm. — (American Jewish civilization series)
    Includes bibliographical references and index.
    ISBN 0-8143-2433-9 (alk. paper)
    1. Jews, Dutch—United States—History. 2. Jews—Netherlands—
History. 3. Immigrants—United States—History. 4. United States
—Emigration and immigration. 5. United States—Ethnic
relations. 6. Netherlands—Ethnic relations. I. Title. II. Series.
E184.J5S9 1994
973′.049240492—dc20   93-26128

Designer: Mary Primeau

Grateful acknowledgment is made to the Lucius N. Littauer Foundation for
financial assistance in the publication of this volume.

To My Father
John R. Swierenga
A "Yiddischer Goy"

CONTENTS

LIST OF FIGURES

LIST OF TABLES

PREFACE

The Dutch Jews in North America have been virtually invisible to historical scholarship. The prevailing categories of Sephardic and Ashkenazic, or Portuguese, German, and Russian, have masked the distinctive Dutch, no less than the French, Hungarian, and other smaller subethnic Jewish identities. Yet both in the colonial era and in the early nineteenth century, Dutch Jews were conspicuous among the forerunners. Nevertheless, the immigration and life of Dutch Jews in the United States is a subject entirely unexplored. Apart from a pro forma reference to the first Jewish arrivals in New Amsterdam in the 1650s, scholars typically make no mention of the Dutch Jews. One Jewish historian stated that there are "very few known cases of [Jewish] emigration from Holland itself," although many German Jews passed through Rotterdam harbor via the Rhine River.

There are several plausible reasons why knowledgeable historians have overlooked the Dutch Jewish stream. First, they arrived in the early years, 1790–1840, before the writing of even rudimentary Jewish histories. It was after the mass German wave that the first historical accounts were written, and these carried the story directly from the Sephardic beginnings to the German era, overlooking the Dutch. Moreover, the period when the Dutch held the ascendancy was relatively short-lived and their numbers were not large. Even at its peak in the 1820s and 1830s, Holland Jews comprised a plurality but not a majority of Jewish immigrants. Finally, the Dutch as Yiddish speakers readily adopted the English language and rapidly assimilated into an amorphous American Jewry, so that they had become "invisible" by the end of the nineteenth century when the first

12

chroniclers and filiopietists sketched the outlines of American Jewish history.

Historians are not entirely to blame for the omission. Netherlands government officials also overlooked Jewish emigrants. Between 1847 and 1880, when official records on emigration are supposedly complete, they include only 572 Jews, but the actual number can be estimated at more than ten times that number. Between 1800 and 1880, 6,500 Dutch Jews emigrated to the United States. The Jews were in fact the most overrepresented religious group among Netherlands overseas emigrants compared to Reformed and Roman Catholic emigrants. Perhaps one should not fault the Dutch officials either. Dutch Jews began migrating in substantial numbers during the Napoleonic era (1790–1815), which was long before the Dutch registration system for overseas emigration began in 1847 when the Calvinists and Catholics began departing en masse. Moreover, more than ten thousand Dutch Jews went to England, whereas Dutch Calvinists and Catholics emigrated directly to the United States. Such cross-Channel movement was a longtime component of Dutch-English trading activity and Dutch officials therefore did not consider it to be "overseas" emigration. Hence it went unreported in the emigration records even though England became a primary American staging area for Dutch Jews in the nineteenth century. Jews in the Netherlands were also entirely an urban people and such emigrants were notorious for emigrating clandestinely, that is, leaving without first registering at the city hall, as the 1847 law required. All the more was this the practice among single young men, who comprised fully one-quarter of all the Dutch Jewish emigrants to America.

Despite the fact that Jews made up barely 2 percent of the Netherlands population and a similarly small portion of the overseas emigrants, nevertheless Dutch blood runs thick in the veins of the first American Jewish families. More than 10 percent of the six hundred genealogies in Rabbi Malcolm H. Stern's exhaustive compilation of pioneer Jewish families included at least one Dutch-born head and often both parents were Dutch. Familiar names are Abrahams, Barnett, Content, Cromelien, DaCosta, Davies, DeLucena, DeSolla, Ezekiel, Haas, Hays, Hendricks, Hyneman, Isaacs, Israels, Joseph, Jones, Levy, Kokernot, Lyons, Moses, Myers, Peixotto, Pereira, Phillips, Pike, Pinheiro, Pinto, Polock, Solis, Solomons, Tobias, Touro, Van Blitz, Van Veen, and Workum. The several Sephardic families on the list were among the very earliest arrivals from Amsterdam in the seventeenth and eighteenth centuries. The Ashkenazic families came primarily after the American Revolution, many

13

by way of England. Out of all proportion to their relatively small population, the Dutch forerunners were thus truly prominent in the founding of American Judaism.

At the beginning of the nineteenth century the total Jewish population in the United States had grown to twenty-five hundred. Most were Ashkenazim, although leadership still remained in the hands of the descendants of the founding Sephardic families. All of the pioneer congregations in New York; Charleston, SC.; Newport, RI; Philadelphia; Richmond; and Lancaster, PA, followed the Sephardic ritual in the arrangement of the prayer book and pronunciation of the Hebrew language in worship. Increasingly after the Revolution German, Dutch, and Polish Jews came to dominate culturally and religiously as well as numerically. They founded Ashkenazic congregations based on their own prayers and pronunciations, beginning with Philadelphia's Rodeph Shalom in 1795 and New York's Bnai Jeshurun in 1825. Hollanders comprised approximately one-quarter of the new arrivals, and by 1830 first-generation Dutch families made up one-half of the Jewish families both in New York City's Lower East Side and in New Orleans as well as one-third in Philadelphia's northern and southern periphery wards and in Baltimore's Fells Point district.

Dutch Jews provided leadership for American Jewry in the early national period. Jewish scholars have given passing notice to their role, but none considered them in their totality or recognized the scope and intensity of their activities. The Dutch played an integral part in every pioneer Jewish congregation, educational endeavor, and charitable organization in America until at least midcentury when German Jews gradually overwhelmed them by sheer numbers. Abraham and Judah Touro, Dr. Daniel L. M. Peixotto, Reverend Samuel Myer Isaacs, Rabbi Jacob Voorsanger, Moses Dropsie, and department store magnate Isaac Magnin cut a wide swath through American Jewry.

The story of Dutch Jewry in America is complex and compelling. It deserves to be told in detail and in all its richness. The purpose of this book is to provide the first history of the Dutch Jews in the United States. The story begins in the homeland with the constricted place of Jews in Dutch society and the stresses and strains of the Napoleonic era that spawned the immigration. Economic hardships prompted them to look abroad, and the promise of American life with its freedoms, equality, and opportunities was a strong allure. Like all Jews, they sought both success and survival, even if these goals were often in conflict. Success came with a price—assimilation, intermarriage, conversion, or even atheism in a pluralistic society. But the Dutch clung to Orthodox traditionalism, even if fossilized, within their Dutchness and later within their Jewishness. Eventually they became hyphenates, Jewish-Americans. But this was not until the first generation had passed away and the second generation was swamped by German Jewry. In the intervening years Dutch Jewish settlement deserves to be recognized as a distinct epoch in American Jewish history.

Since the Dutch were an urban populace, even more urban than German and Polish Jews, their story revolves around the major eastern seaboard centers of New York, Philadelphia, Boston, Baltimore, and New Orleans. A chapter is devoted to each of these cities, beginning with the most prominent center of New York City. Then the narrative follows the Dutch to the Great Lakes frontier cities of Buffalo, Pittsburgh, Cincinnati, Cleveland, Toledo, Detroit, Chicago, and Saint Louis. Finally, they move across the continent to San Francisco. In three eastern cities—New York, Philadelphia, and Boston—Dutch Jews had a sufficient population mass to establish ethnic synagogues in the 1840s and 1850s. In other places such as Baltimore and New Orleans, they comprised up to one-third of mixed English, German, and Polish congregations. None of the pure Dutch congregations survived the second generation and by 1905 all had closed. Several of their cemetery and benevolent associations, however, continued for generations and at least one New York City organization, the Netherland Israelitisch Sick Fund (NISF), continues to the present day. After the ethnic institutions disappeared, Dutch Jewish families continued to intermarry, even when matching families lived in distant cities. Dutch with Dutch was preferred, or Dutch with English. But in the end Dutch with German became common.

Economically, the Civil War was the great divide. Until then most Dutch Jewish immigrants were petty merchants, retail storekeepers, and dealers in the clothing business. But after that war, wage earners—cigarmakers, diamond cutters, and tailors—became predominant. The shift reflected structural changes in the homeland following the Jewish emancipation law of 1796. For centuries Jews had been barred from the guilds of artisans and forced to earn a precarious living as street vendors of old clothes, food items, and sundries. Only after midcentury did the Jews begin to enter the skilled trades in tobacco, clothing, and gems—all practiced in the ghetto, in the Yiddish tongue, and with respect of the holy days.

The major reference group for Dutch Jews was their coreligionists and not their fellow Gentile countrymen. There is no evidence in any American city of Dutch Jewish contacts with Dutch Reformed or Roman Catholic immigrants. Nevertheless, comparisons are drawn in the text from time to time between these groups. For example, Jewish and Gentile assimilation rates differed because many Dutch Jews migrated via England where they lived for a time and adapted to English culture, while Dutch Calvinists and Catholics came directly to the United States. The really important Dutch Jewish contacts were with other European Jewish immigrant groups, especially the Germans. In the antebellum decades, the strongly Orthodox Dutch opposed Reform Judaism brought to America by the German Jews. But in the postwar decades, the second-generation Dutch gradually espoused Reform, and then they more readily blended into the German Jewish community.

Scholars always accumulate more debts than they can ever repay for the selfless assistance of librarians, archivists, and other specialists. I wish to acknowledge the valuable aid of Nancy Schwartz of the Western Reserve Historical Society (WRHS), Cleveland; Ida Cohen Selavan of Hebrew Union College (HUC) Library, Cincinnati; Fanny Zelcer of the American Jewish Archives (AJA), Cincinnati; Daniel Sharon of the Spertus College of Judaica, Chicago; Charles Bernstein of the Chicago Jewish Historical Society; and Michael Cole of the interlibrary loan staff of Kent State University libraries. With Cole's assistance I heavily mined via their interlibrary loan departments the excellent collections of HUC and AJA of Cincinnati. I thank the staffs for their cooperation and patience. Rabbi Abraham Leibtag of Akron's Temple Israel, Herbert Hochhauser and Adriaan de Wit of Kent State University, and Marc Lee Raphael of the College of William and Mary offered advice and technical assistance. Cartographers Howard D. F. Veregin, Kristyn R. Liddington, and Charles T. Magruder of the Kent State University geography department prepared the graphics, and Stephen C. Tapp of the university's computer services willingly asssisted in data processing. The secretaries in the Kent State history department, Carolyn Brothers and especially Bette Sawicki, with endless patience and great skill transformed my ragged copy and cluttered tables into legible text. Finally, I am indebted to Helga Kaplan of Kent State University, Jonathan D. Sarna of Brandeis University, Aubrey Newman of the University of Leicester, England, and Moses Rischin of San Francisco State University, who read virtually the entire manuscript, and to the late Robert Cohen of Haifa University and Rabbi Malcolm H. Stern of New York City, who read extensive sections. They not only saved me from countless errors, oversights, and muddled statements, but their probing questions forced me to rethink larger points. Sarna's vast bibliographic knowledge of Ameri-

16

can Jewry opened many closed doors and his enthusiastic response to early drafts stimulated me to press on with the writing. I trust that all of those named and others who assisted me will find their efforts here rewarded. Of course, any errors that remain are mine alone.

Chapter 1

⌖

NETHERLANDS JEWRY

Sephardim and Ashkenazim

Organized Jewish life in the Netherlands began in the early seventeenth century, which was relatively late compared to the rest of Europe, and it coincided with the onset of Holland's Golden Age. This was the 150 years from 1590 to 1740, following the heroic Calvinist revolt against Catholic Spain, when the young republic glittered in the "solid gold of prosperity" and its culture "shone with dazzling brilliance," studded by such men as the Jewish philosopher Baruch Spinoza (1632–1677) and the Gentile artist Rembrandt van Rijn (1606–1669). Dutch merchantmen plied the seven seas and planted colonies first in the East Indies and then in the West. Dutch trade and shipping within Europe, particularly in the Baltic, was even more spectacular. Holland suddenly emerged as an economic colossus with Amsterdam as the hub. The city became "the world's warehouse," conveying goods from all continents financed by its powerful money and banking houses.[1]

The Netherlands at the time was unique in Europe for its tolerance. Although it was a powerful empire driven by a dynamic Calvinism that yielded not an inch to Catholic Spain, Catholic France, or Protestant England, it allowed freedom of conscience and minimal civil rights to Jews and other persecuted minorities. Amsterdam's emergence as an international trade center attracted Sephardic merchants from the Iberian Peninsula, men who learned of its irenic spirit and came to take advantage of its economic promise. These Portuguese Jews were known as Marranos or New Christians, because they had been forced to convert on pain of death by the Spanish Inquisition. Between 1590 and 1610 about four hundred Sephardic Jews settled in the Netherlands. By 1635 the first persecuted Ashkenazic Jews arrived from German and Polish centers.[2]

Although the number of Jews in Holland did not equal those in England, Germany, and France, Amsterdam by 1650 became the "Little Jerusalem," the largest center of Jewish culture in western Europe, and for the next three hundred years Dutch Jews generally fared better than Jews elsewhere. They found it "pleasant to wait for redemption" in the tolerant Netherlands, where virulent antisemitism, pogroms, and calls for expulsion were unknown. Nevertheless, the national and city governments imposed restrictions from the outset and Jews remained second-class citizens until 1796, excluded from government posts and the guilds and forced to live by peddling and trade. When they openly adopted Judaism in Amsterdam, the city leaders only reluctantly granted permission to buy a cemetery and build a synagogue. As Moses Asher observed wryly; "They allow us to sing psalms and to die of hunger."[3]

It was unique to Holland that Sephardic and Ashkenazic communities developed simultaneously, although the Sephardim arrived a few decades earlier and initially in larger numbers. The first Sephardi were generally well-to-do merchants and culturally assimilated, but in the eighteenth century the number of poor increased to the breaking point and the Amsterdam synagogue leaders dispatched many to the Dutch West Indies and elsewhere. The Ashkenazi community had as many poor but fewer wealthy elite to finance deportations. They spoke only Yiddish and were wholly Jewish in culture. The two communities lived in close proximity within the Jewish quarters of Amsterdam, Rotterdam, The Hague, and other lesser urban centers. They gradually became a more amalgamated group, but Dutch authorities frequently distinguished the two groups in administrative reports.[4]

Dutch Jews maintained contact with the larger Jewish community of western Europe. It remained common for Dutch Jews to intermarry with German, English, and Polish Jews, and the Amsterdam Jewish Quarter ("Jodenbuurt") always depended on Germany and Poland for its spiritual leaders. Most of the chief rabbis and rabbinical teachers until the twentieth century were born outside of

Holland. This influx of foreign Ashkenazic leadership kept Dutch Jewry very Yiddish. Except for the earliest beginnings, the Sephardic Jews drew their leadership from the Dutch-born or at least Dutch-raised. The Ashkenazim, therefore, always felt inferior and the more cosmopolitan Sephardim felt superior, even in the mid-twentieth century.[5] Although the Ashkenazim followed humbler occupations and were less aristocratic, they brought to the Netherlands a zest for scholarship, and their libraries, schools, and printing shops established the reputation of Amsterdam Jewry for broad learning. They kept as many printing shops busy as did the Sephardim during the seventeenth and eighteenth centuries, which made Amsterdam a principal center of printing in Europe. Nevertheless, it was the second-generation Sephardi, Spinoza, who rose to the intellectual pinnacle as the great rationalistic philosopher of the seventeenth century, for which the embarrassed Sephardim excommunicated him; he lies buried in a Lutheran cemetery.[6]

Mokum and *Mediene*

The Jewish population increased slowly in the first half of the nineteenth century and more rapidly thereafter. It numbered an estimated 40,000 in 1795, reached 59,000 by 1850, and then nearly doubled to 115,000 by 1920. Ashkenazic Jews, who were called "Hoogduitse Joden" (later "Nederlandsch Israelieten"), comprised 95 percent and Sephardic Jews, called "Portugese Joden," totaled only 5 percent after 1850.[7]

Europe's Jews, historically, lived in the largest cities. They rarely could own land and were restricted by law to urban occupations in trade and commerce. Their communal religious life dictated settlement close to the synagogues. Dutch city governments also granted favorable social and economic privileges to Jews in order to attract them and spur economic growth. As a result, Jews were overrepresented in the large cities in every province (Table 1.1). They comprised 1.8 percent of the national population in 1839 but 4.0 percent of the urban population and only 0.6 percent of the rural population. Compared to a national urban population of 37 percent, the Jews were 81 percent urban, for an overshot of 44 percent.[8]

Traditionally, Dutch Jews were divided between those of *Mokum* (Amsterdam) and those of the *Mediene* (the provinces). Although Jews lived in every province, two-thirds in 1830 lived in Noord Holland and Zuid Holland. However, only one-third of the total

Table 1.1
Jewish Population per Province, City and Country, 1839

Province	N	Total Population % All	Total Population % Urban	Total Population % Rural	% Urban All	% Urban Jews	% Urban Over-shot
Drenthe	1,401	1.9	5.6	1.2	16	46	30
Friesland	1,945	0.9	2.8	0.2	26	85	59
Gelderland	3,667	1.1	2.6	0.5	27	66	39
Groningen	3,184	1.8	3.6	1.4	19	38	19
Limburg	1,107	0.6	1.4	0.3	25	62	37
Noord Brabant	1,951	0.5	1.3	0.3	22	56	34
Noord Holland	25,632	5.8	8.7	0.6	87	96	9
Overijssel	2,758	1.4	2.7	1.1	20	39	19
Utrecht	1,528	1.1	1.7	0.4	50	80	30
Zeeland	597	0.4	1.1	0.1	31	82	51
Zuid Holland	8,475	1.6	2.6	0.6	52	83	31
Total	52,245	1.8	4.0	0.6	37	81	44

Sources: Compiled from J. A. de Kok, *Nederland op de breuklijn Rome-Reformatie* (Assen, Neth., 1964), 294–99; *Staten van de Bevolking der Steden en Gemeenten van het Koningrijk der Nederland, 1 January 1840* (The Hague, 1841).

Dutch population lived in these populous provinces. In 1849, 56 percent resided in large cities, while the general population was not even 25 percent urban. Over time the Jewish concentration in the two urban provinces became all the more pronounced, reaching 82 percent by 1930. Likewise by 1930 over 80 percent of Dutch Jews lived in cities over one hundred thousand inhabitants. Jews were an urban populace par excellence and concentrated in the largest cities. While the general population became more urban, the Jews "metropolized," specifically in Mokum-Amsterdam. Already in 1849, 43 percent of all Dutch Jews lived there and by 1880 half lived in Amsterdam. This city and London were clearly the two preeminent Jewish cities of western Europe.[9]

In 1829 Amsterdam's Jews, who had increased by 18 percent since 1812, comprised 10.7 percent of the city's population. All but a handful lived on the crowded east bank of the Amstel River—the Old Side, and not in the fashionable Jordaan on the West Side, as is often supposed. Conditions in the overcrowded "Jodenbuurt" were atrocious, compared to elsewhere in the city. Indeed, Amsterdam's Jewish Quarter had the worst slums in all of Europe. The row houses were small, dark, and unhealthy. Trachoma, an eye disease carried from North Africa, was particularly rampant, affecting 40 percent of all Jewish children in the city by 1880, and a whopping 75 percent of students in the ghetto charity school. The Jews tolerated such coarse conditions in order to live within the religious and social community. Suffering engendered a sense of solidarity and mutuality. Only after the revolution of 1848 spawned a rising middle class did the "atmosphere of gloom" gradually lift and the life of the proletariate improve.[10]

The diamond trade brought increased prosperity to Dutch Jews after 1860. The Sephardi minority were heavily involved in the diamond industry, which was centered in their neighborhood (the "Weesperstraat") on the fringe of the Jewish Quarter. Free public schooling under the liberal 1862 education law also opened the future for Jews. Most were street vendors and petty merchants, dealers in old clothes and rags, cattle traders, and butchers. They virtually monopolized secondhand clothing, which before the introduction of ready-made clothing was a vital business. They also peddled fruits and vegetables, potatoes, pickles, fish, flowers, and raffle tickets. Jews were greatly underrepresented in manufacturing and the professions throughout the nineteenth century. Only medicine and brokering were open to them. Except for diamond workers, their home industries of cigar, dress, and shoe making were low paying. Jews peddled out of necessity and preference. Although their occupational choices were limited by government regulations and guild restrictions, they enjoyed the freedom of selling, which was compatible with their segregated living, Yiddish speaking, Sabbath and festival observances, and the desire to pass their businesses from father to son.[11]

While Amsterdam had ten times as many Jews as any other Dutch city in 1840, and its Jewish ghetto numbered nearly 11 percent of the city population, other regional trade centers also had sizable Jewish communities. In Hoorn, an international harbor on the Zuider Zee about 25 miles north of Amsterdam, 7.7 percent of the population was Jewish. During the Golden Age Hoorn was a center of Dutch colonial trade with the East and West Indies, and in the eighteenth century it became the marketplace of West-Friesland. Lesser Jewish clusters were in the eastern textile centers of Meppel, Zwolle, and Zutphen; the northern capitals and market hubs of Leeuwarden and Groningen; the government center of The Hague; and the port city of Rotterdam.[12] Very few lived in the southern Catholic provinces or in rural areas. Those in the Mediene resembled their compatriots in Mokkum and they flowed back and forth freely. Thus Holland's Jews were geographically dispersed if not culturally assimilated.

The French Era and "Dutchification"

One of the primary challenges of Dutch Jewish history is to explain the impact on Jewish legal rights of the Napoleonic "liberation" and creation of the Batavian Republic. Napoleon Bonaparte liberated German and Polish Jews from their political and religious feudalism and promoted *égalité*, so German Jews welcomed the French "rights of man." But Dutch Jews, except for a minority of secular liberals, were "greatly grieved" by the French conquest in 1795; they had long been fervent supporters of the House of Orange. Although they lacked full civil rights and had been segregated socially, culturally, and economically, they had enjoyed full religious liberty and many other freedoms. Dutch Jews were never officially ghettoized as in the remainder of Europe.[13] Dutch historian Ivo Schöffer describes the pre-Napoleonic system as a milder form of apartheid, whereas Simon Schama more positively calls it "benign pluralism." Jews could not marry Gentiles, join craft guilds, or move freely to the inland provinces. This forced them to concentrate in certain trades such as merchandising. But their synagogue leaders (*parnassim*) had almost complete control over religious laws and customs. Thus, by design and by preference, the "Jewish nation" was a people apart, an "alien community."[14]

French liberals would jeopardize this comfortable situation and force the Jewish nation to become merely a religious congregation of assimilated individual citizens in a unified state. Understandably, therefore, most Jews chose unconditionally for the Dutch Orange monarchy, which had safeguarded their autonomy, and against the Francophile Protestant liberals (known as Patriots) who, in turn, were hostile to Jews for this reason. A few Jewish liberals in Amsterdam formed a separate club, Felix Libertate (Happiness through Freedom), because the Patriots did not accept them. But the Jewish liberals, mostly drawn from the German community, met with opposition within the Jewish camp as well as outside of it. The synagogue authorities considered expelling them, but they forestalled disciplinary action by separating and founding their own congregation.[15]

The Protestant Patriots and Jewish People's Society in 1795 welcomed French troops as liberators who would topple the conservative Orange monarchy and impose democratic reforms. Indeed, the National Convention of the Batavian Republic proclaimed full emancipation of all Jews on September 2, 1796, even before the first Constitution of 1798. This famous and controversial decree opened all guilds and government offices to Jews and made them eligible for general poor-law relief. They also became subject to compulsory military service. The Jews thus gained what the benign Orange rulers had not granted, namely, legal recognition as a separate faith community equal with Protestants, Catholics, and Secularists.

Orthodox leaders and their followers viewed the French reforms as a ruse that would eventually destroy their autonomous community by forced integration. They would become a mere religion, the Dutch Israelitic Congregation. In 1806 these fears became real when Napoleon changed the Batavian Republic into the kingdom of Holland and put his brother Lodewijk (Louis) Napoleon on the throne as king of Holland (1806–1810). The liberators had become occupiers. The enlightened King Louis was determined to raise the Jews' socioeconomic standing and to integrate them into the larger society. He terminated congregational authority and for the first time brought the Sephardic and Ashkenazic communities together under one organization by a royal decree in 1808, which instituted a Supreme Consistory for the Dutch High-German Jews. This decree, based on the French consistorial system, marked a radical centralization in Jewish religious life. It removed one of the pillars of Jewish communal life, the autonomous power of the congregations; it forced the *parnassim* to surrender all authority to the Amsterdam Consistory, now dominated by radical democrats. Louis additionally required the chief rabbi to be Dutch-born or a resident of Holland for a minimum of six years, and he promoted the Dutch language in synagogue worship by ordering the use of a Dutch instead of Hebrew Bible and by requiring all religious instruction in the Dutch tongue. Moreover, rabbis could no longer consecrate marriages outside the synagogue, or face dismissal. The traditional Jewish leaders understandably resisted these organizational and language changes of the new regime. They particularly objected when King Louis suppressed Yiddish, the language of Dutch Jews, and tried to replace it with the Dutch language.[16]

This "Dutchification" was worrisome enough, but there were other forced changes. An 1808 decree compelled all Netherlanders who did not yet possess an official surname to select surnames and register them with civil authorities.[17] The Supreme Consistory subsequently *required* Jews to use the new family names in all religious ceremonies on pain of being jailed or branded for refusal.[18] In 1810

24

when Holland was fully incorporated into the French Empire, the new centralized bureaucracy was strengthened by a host of intrusive laws, taxes, and military conscription. In 1811, for example, the French regime required all Dutch citizens to register with the government by name, stating their occupation, the rental value of their home, and the names of all members living in the household. All this was to levy taxes and conscript young men for the French army.[19]

Not all bureaucratic changes gave Jews cause for concern. Louis Napoleon tried to encourage Jewish legal equality and he opened a few government positions to the Jewish Patriots. He abolished special oaths for Jews. Markets held on Saturday were changed to another weekday. Jews, like other religions, were permitted to collect money to care for their own poor, and they were allowed for a brief period in 1809 to form their own infantry battalions complete with Jewish officers and kosher foods as another way to maintain their identity. But Jews never warmed to this military corps and King Louis had to abandon his plan within a year. The men were distributed among the French regiments.[20]

All of the legal and religious "reforms" had less adverse effects on the Dutch Jews than did the Napoleonic war, which pitted England against French expansionism. Because of the war the years from 1793 to 1813 were very difficult economically. The French occupation and British blockade of 1807 brought trade and shipping to a halt. The staple market in Amsterdam dried up and the harbor of Rotterdam virtually closed. Many trading companies shut and international merchants, such as Dutch Jews who traded heavily with London, were devastated economically. By 1810 many were ruined and faced bankruptcy. The economic hardships of this severe depression extended to all segments of the Dutch population owing to widespread unemployment, inflation in food prices, and the shortages of poor relief monies. The Jewish poor suffered more than most because they had long experienced extreme poverty due to discrimination.[21]

The Emigrant Stimulus

The net result of these myriad economic and religious problems resulting from the Napoleonic conquest and wars was that Dutch Ashkenazic Jews began to emigrate to the United States in the first decades of the nineteenth century.[22] German Jews,

25

by contrast, did not begin emigrating for another fifteen to twenty years, until after the end of the Napoleonic war in 1815 when French revolutionary ideals were crushed. In the conservative reaction to Napoleon's defeat in Germany, the ideal of religious freedom also collapsed. Germany was impoverished and exhausted by the wars and the authorities moved to strengthen traditional institutions, raise taxes, and abridge the rights of Jews. There were even Jewish pogroms and riots in 1818 and 1819 in Frankfurt, Heidelberg, and elsewhere.[23]

In the Netherlands Jews enthusiastically welcomed the restored monarch King Willem (William) I. But Willem was also an enlightened despot, who continued the "Dutchification" begun during the French era, which further increased government demands, including regulation of the Jewish denominations. He required that all synagogue announcements and publications on behalf of the government, as well as the synagogue minutes, be written in Dutch. An 1817 decree mandated that lessons in the Jewish charity schools must be given in pure Hebrew and Dutch "to the exclusion of the bastard Jewish language." However, he placated the Orthodox *parassim* by abolishing the odious French creation, the Supreme Consistory, whose arbitrary actions had finally caused riots in 1813 in the Amsterdam Jewish Quarter and other centers, and by restoring the autonomy of the ten (eventually twelve) main synagogues throughout the country. Most important, the legal emancipation decree of 1796 remained intact in the revised Constitution of 1814. It forbade traditional discrimination by the guilds, abolished all special fees on Jews as Jews, and guaranteed that Jews would be eligible for public poor-relief. However, the new government in 1814 created the Israelitisch Kerkgenootschap (Jewish Church Society), which was a centralized, hierarchical body to control both Sephardic and Ashkenazic congregations. The objective was to end religious independence and integrate Jews (and all religious groups) into Dutch society.[24]

This latter goal was aimed at elevating the Jewish poor who remained among the poorest of the poor despite French égalité. Alms statistics in 1799 reveal that over 80 percent of Amsterdam's Ashkenazic Jews and 54 percent of her Sephardic Jews had to rely on the public dole for food and fuel. Housing conditions were equally atrocious. Except for a few wealthy merchants who lived in stately mansions, Amsterdam Jews were crowded into their old *jodenhoek* where the average dwelling housed 2.9 families with 12.5 persons (compared to 2.1 families with 7.9 persons in Christian dwellings). The French period made conditions even worse, owing to the economic dislocations caused by the abolition of the United East India

Company, the imposition of new taxes, and the sharp cuts in government spending to reduce the national debt. By 1805, 82 percent (19,600 out of 24,000) of Amsterdam Jews were classified as poor. In the face of such extreme deprivation, the few prosperous merchants were unable to provide the customary philanthropy to their brethren.[25]

King Louis's creation in 1808 of the Supreme Consistory inadvertently contributed to the collapse of the Jewish relief system. One of the new rules abolished the monopoly of the communal meat market of the Amsterdam congregation and allowed the faithful to buy kosher meat (at lower prices) from private butchers. This was catastrophic for the congregation's Poor Relief Fund because profits from the meat market largely funded the relief system. The 18,000 persons dependant on the relief fund saw their monthly stipend reduced by 90 percent! As historian J. Michman aptly noted: The bill for the "liberal" reforms was "paid by the paupers of Amsterdam."[26] Indeed, despite the new liberal rules, the Jews received very little poor-relief until 1825 when the government created the Dutch Israelitic Charity Board to house the infirm and ailing, pay unemployment relief, and provide fuel and bread to the indigent.[27]

The impoverishment of already poor Amsterdam Jews was the chief reason, in H. Daalder's view, for their mass exodus from the city in the first decades of the nineteenth century. As many as a quarter of the Ashkenazim and 15 percent of the Sephardim sought work in the interior provinces, in England, and even in the distant United States. In 1859, 53 percent of the Ashkenazim and 62 percent of the Sephardim in Amsterdam were still on the public dole. As late as 1879, 37 percent of the Ashkenazim lived on the dole, 20 percent at full assistance. This put a great strain on benevolent funds. In 1868 when 50 percent of the Jews in the city were unable to support themselves, the poor board budget totaled ƒ57,000; the government provided ƒ48,000 (84 percent) and the city's eight synagogues had to contribute the remaining ƒ9,000 (16 percent). Conditions only improved after new industries developed in diamond manufacturing, cigar making, and the needle trades, all of which offered Jews job opportunities.[28]

From Nation to Congregation

Dutch Jewish religious and cultural life fragmented in the nineteenth-century era of emancipation and integration. The emancipation law of 1796 and French occupation began a process of secularization and "Dutchification" that was speeded up by the forces of centralization, urbanization, democratization, and segmentation (*verzuiling*) of Dutch society.[29] Intimacy and face-to-face contacts, which had always characterized life in the Jewish quarters of Amsterdam and other cities, gradually lessened. The Jews were a close-knit minority, a separate subculture, tied by their religion to each other and to the great talmudic centers of eastern Europe, from which their religious leaders came. But by the end of the century, Jews had transformed themselves into a "disparate people with little affinity to either each other or to world jewry," according to Netherlands historian H. Daalder. Secularism was rampant and Dutch Jews were alienated from the centers of Jewry in Europe and America. As one man declared: "I am a Dutchman of the jewish faith, who does not care about the jewish faith." Clearly, such Jews were well along the path of assimilation; they had been successfully "Netherlandized," transforming themselves from a Jewish nation into Jewish Netherlanders.[30]

The marker of the assimilation of Ashkenazic Jewry in Holland was the gradual loss of the Yiddish language, which for centuries was the social glue of the community. Yiddish gave way to vernacular Dutch during the nineteenth century. The process began during the Revolutionary era. Leaders of the Dutch Jewish Enlightenment, such as Moses Cohen Belinfante and Jonas Daniel Meijer, viewed Yiddish with "disgust" as a "mixed-language" jargon, and promoted Dutch in religious instruction and Bible translation. In 1787 young Portuguese Jews in The Hague first translated the Hebrew prayers of the Portuguese worship rite into the Dutch language. In 1808 Belinfante headed an Amsterdam educational society that began to translate the Hebrew Bible into Dutch. Meijer, the president of the new Central Consistory in 1809, worked to bring the project to completion. Although the French conquest in 1810 stalled their efforts, King Louis Napoleon encouraged the use of the national language in religious education. Belinfante in 1806 had launched the first Dutch-language periodical in the Netherlands, published in Amsterdam.[31]

In 1813 the French-created Amsterdam Consistory, acting on instructions from Paris, decided in the interest of promoting national unity that in all synagogue services and record keeping, only the French or Dutch language, and not Yiddish or Portuguese, must be used exclusively. Both Sephardic and Ashkenazic communities objected, but the Ashkenazim were especially angered. Most Sephardim at least spoke Dutch, but few Ashkenazim could do so. They could not understand announcements in Dutch or read Dutch

Scriptures. Since it was often necessary to communicate, synagogue authorities repeatedly had to obtain permission to issue publications in Yiddish. The language rulings so angered the *Hoogduitse* that when French troops hastily withdrew from Amsterdam in late 1812, riots broke out against the Consistory, which finally yielded on the French language but kept the requirement of Dutch for official government announcements and synagogue minutes. Yiddish and Portuguese were permitted, however, in the worship rites.[32]

The restored monarch Willem I continued the pressure to introduce Dutch. In 1814 he decreed that all synagogue minutes and official correspondence be in Dutch and that all leaders must know the language. The chief rabbi must be completely fluent, but the cantor (*hazan*) need only be able to read Dutch. Later, in 1827, a government decree offered rewards for the best translation into Dutch of Jewish sermons and educational materials. But the Jews resisted. Until 1842 the Sephardic Synagogue of Amsterdam held its proceedings mainly in Portuguese. Yiddish did not fully disappear from Jewish synagogue schools until the 1870s. The Leeuwarden Synagogue did not drop Yiddish until 1886, and when they did so, older members seceded in anger.[33]

The greatest pressure to jettison Yiddish in favor of the Dutch language came in the last quarter of the nineteenth century under Chief Rabbi Dr. Joseph Hirsch Dünner. During his lengthy and domineering rabbinate (1872–1911), Dünner banned Yiddish and made Dutch compulsory in the synagogue schools. This hastened assimilation from within because the denominational schools were the only place to learn Yiddish. Previously, many youth had attended private Jewish day schools taught in Yiddish, but these schools disappeared rapidly after the 1859 educational reform under which the government established free public schools that were religiously neutral. Even more of a detriment, the law ordered all denominational schools to close by the end of 1861. While the more cultured Jews began to speak Dutch thereafter, the masses only gradually interspersed Dutch words in their Yiddish conversations.[34]

The enthusiastic espousal by Jews of secular public schools in the 1850s and 1860s speaks volumes. This was at the same time that Calvinists and Catholics were successfully obtaining public monies to build separate Christian schools. Dutch society was being restructured at midcentury into confessionally distinct institutional pillars with Calvinist, Catholic, socialist, and liberal (or neutral) schools, newspapers, and labor organizations. Indeed, one could live from the cradle to the grave within a religious bloc. But Jewish leaders missed the boat by refusing to accept the challenge of pillarization.

They rejected as "reactionary" the advice of a few leaders to establish state-subsidized Jewish denominational schools and instead sent their children to the so-called neutral or mixed schools where socialist philosophies gained ground. Rabbi Dünner only belatedly in the late 1890s suddenly changed his views about state schools and called for more denominational Talmud Torah schools such as the lone one in Amsterdam that had survived, but it was too late. By then, many of their youth were lost to the faith and blended into the increasingly pluriform Dutch society. Jews "never coalesced into a real pillar" as did the other religious communities in the Netherlands.[35]

The Jewish failure to meld into a single religious bloc may have been exacerbated by a lack of leadership. From 1838 to 1874 the Ashkenazim had no chief rabbi, and the Sephardim had none from 1822 to 1900. As the Ashkenazim lost control of the Yiddish language they also became cut off from the nourishment of eastern European thought. The synagogues became secularized and increasingly elitist, and this caused the poorer working classes to gradually drift away. The result was that Jews were successfully integrated into Dutch society and they came to share the general provincialism of the Netherlands in world affairs. By the end of the nineteenth century, they found socialism more attractive than Zionism and many could no longer speak Yiddish. Even among the proletariate in the Amsterdam "Jodenbuurt," the physical center of Dutch Jewry, the transition to Dutch was well underway.[36]

Thus, in the first half of the nineteenth century the liberal and prosperous bourgeois component of Netherlands Jewry was weakened, at least temporarily, by the wars and political centralization. Then in the second half-century its proletarian members left Orthodox Judaism behind for new ideologies. No longer did the synagogue and Yiddish language bind the community together as it had before the Napoleonic era, although Jewish community life continued to flourish, especially outside of Amsterdam. "No to Palestine, Vote Red" proclaimed an election poster in the Amsterdam Jewish Quarter in 1912.[37] It was a sign of the times.

Sigmund Seeligmann, the leading intellectual of Dutch Jewry in the early twentieth century, praised his countrymen for their adaptation to the national culture in his famous article "Die Juden in Holland, eine Charakteristik" (1923).[38] Seeligmann coined the phrase "species hollandia judaica" to describe this single essence of Dutch Jews—their assimilative nature. But contemporary Netherlandic scholars such as Jozeph Michman and Robert Cohen disagree. Michman notes that Dutch Jews and especially those of Amsterdam in the decades before the Holocaust maintained stronger ties with their Jewish tradition than did German, French, and Italian Jews, as is evidenced by their much lower rate of mixed marriages. These same data show that the Dutch Jewish sense of identity was stronger than among their Gentile compatriots. While the Dutch Jews had become more secular and acculturated, they had not amalgamated with their non-Jewish neighbors.[39]

Michman credits the survival of the Jewish "essence" to the strong commitment of Amsterdam Jews to a traditional and even "petrified" Orthodoxy throughout the middle decades of the nineteenth century. Only in the 1870s and 1880s was Orthodoxy finally destroyed by economic modernization, particularly the expansion of the diamond trade during the "Cape Time," which ruptured traditional institutions such as the synagogue and undermined religious observances such as the Sabbath. A "revolutionary secularization process" destroyed Orthodoxy suddenly within one generation. Jews in the higher social strata had slowly been assimilating for some time, but now the masses suddenly in a few decades experienced a rising prosperity that lured them to abandon their traditional values and pious living for a new-found freedom and materialism. They desecrated the Sabbath by doing business rather than going to the synagogue. Thereafter, Jewish social solidarity rested primarily on secular bases such as Zionism and socialism.[40]

Whether the diamond trade caused the sudden break with tradition rather than the earlier surrender of Jewish leaders to secular public education is debatable. But, in any case, if the religious declension provided the context for emigration, the cause was primarily economic. Political and religious freedoms were at stake in the Napoleonic years. But historic Jewish poverty was worsened by the French conquest with its economic dislocations and increasing government demands on Dutch citizens. Following the American Civil War, a second Jewish immigrant wave developed because the belated industrialization in the Netherlands left artisans without adequate work and hope for the future.

31

Chapter 2

THE DUTCH ERA: IMMIGRATION BEFORE 1830

The earliest Dutch Jews in the New World were part of the great Iberian dispersion fleeing persecution from the Inquisition. Some Marranos (supposedly Christianized Jews) settled in Catholic regions, but most were driven out or martyred. Only the Protestant colonies begrudgingly offered Jews the possibility of founding open communities so that is where they went.

Brazil and the Caribbean Cockpit

Dutch Jewish immigration to the Western Hemisphere was initially centered in Dutch Brazil and the Caribbean colonies of Surinam and Curaçao.[1] By 1630 the Dutch with the help of Amsterdam and Brazilian Jewry had conquered the northern Brazilian province of Pernambuco and held it for twenty-five years. About one thousand Sephardi Jews from Amsterdam, all already reconverted or officially educated in Judaism, emigrated to the leading city of Recife under the benevolent Dutch West India Company (WIC) policy of religious toleration, and they quickly dominated the carrying trade with Holland. As the first open Jewish community in the New World, Recife soon boasted a thriving community and synagogue, Tsur Israel (Rock of Israel), the latter under the parental eye of the Amsterdam Sephardi body. The first rabbi to serve in America, Isaac Aboab da Fonseca, arrived in Recife from Amsterdam in 1642 along with a large group of settlers. A total of 1,450 Jews lived in the Dutch territory of Brazil in the mid-1640s, fully one-half of the white civil population. North America did not have as large a Jewish population until more than a century later. In 1645 the States-General in Amsterdam, with prodding from influential Sephardi merchants, granted Jews in Brazil the first New World charter, according them "equality" with "other inhabitants of the United Netherlands themselves."[2]

But the Brazil boomlet was short-lived. Between 1648 and 1654 the Portuguese recaptured Recife and the Jesuits reestablished the Inquisition. Some six hundred *relapsi*, now considered heretics, were given three months to flee for their lives. Most returned to their native Holland, where they were cordially received. But a substantial minority went to the WIC colonies of Curaçao, Surinam, and Saint Eustatius; others settled in British and French islands. They maintained tenuous links with the mother community at Amsterdam or for the British colonies with the London counterpart of Bevis Marks Synagogue. A small group of twenty-three managed to find safe if unwelcome harbor at New Amsterdam, where they are considered the founding fathers of the Jewish community of North America, even though most left before the British conquest in 1664.[3] The Recife diaspora of 1654 comprised experienced sugar planters, brokers, and agents who laid the basis for Jewish communities from the Guianas and Surinam to New Netherland.

Throughout the seventeenth and eighteenth centuries, the cockpit of Western Hemisphere Jewry remained in the Caribbean during the heyday of the West Indian sugar trade. Jews in these outposts of Amsterdam and London merchant companies, notably the WIC, led the way economically, culturally, and politically. Here wealthy families emerged and legal and religious rights and freedoms were won for those expelled from Christian Europe by persecution and prejudice. Victories in the Caribbean hastened further legal gains for Jews in British North America. The Nova Zeelandia charter of 1657, granted by the WIC to the Zeelander colony of David Nassy (alias Joseph Nunez de Fonseca) on the Wild Coast (as the Guianas were then called), promised Jews "libertie of conscience," freedom of worship and schools, political representation, and the right to own land. This charter, in turn, became the model for the Surinam charter of 1665, which together with successive laws granted

Surinam's Jews greater rights and liberties than anywhere else. Liberated Marranos enjoyed the status as an ethnic minority equal to that of Dutch burghers. In 1694, five hundred Jewish sugarcane planters lived in Surinam, Holland's most prosperous colony, and by 1730 Jews owned more than one-fourth of the colony's four hundred sugar plantations, concentrated along the upper Surinam River in a region known as "Joden Savannah." This Plain of the Jews became the first all-Jewish locality in the Americas.[4]

Curaçao, "the Mother-City of all the islands in America," rivaled Surinam in Jewish influence and became the largest Sephardi colony in the entire Caribbean basin. The Jewish community began in 1651 when the Netherlands government sent out a dozen families to open agricultural plantations. They were given a tract of land near the fortress, now Willemstad, in what became the Jewish Quarter. To induce emigration, the West India Company gave a limited charter of privileges—perhaps the first in the New World—granting the right to own slaves, select lands, and be exempt from taxes for ten years. Local authorities refused to recognize all of these rights and the colony languished and almost was abandoned, until 1659 when Isaac da Costa led some seventy Brazilian refugees from Amsterdam to Curaçao under an expanded grant of economic and religious privileges.[5]

These pioneers of Curaçaon Jewry established Congregation Mikvé Israel (Hope of Israel) the year they arrived and the young community flourished for two hundred years. In 1674 the congregation called Josiau Pardo (c. 1626–1692) of Amsterdam as the first *haham* (Sephardi rabbi). Pardo, descended from a line of Amsterdam rabbis, had served as rector of the famed Amsterdam academy Yeshibah de los Pintos and then as rabbi of Rotterdam's Sephardi synagogue. He led Mikvé Israel until 1683 and helped to consolidate the community by promulgating detailed regulations that governed religious customs and practices.[6]

Many Curaçaon Jews became large plantation owners and farmers. They owned one-third of the plantations, which ranged up to 4,000 hectares and included the "best tillable lands," and held 16 percent of the slaves in 1764–1765. But most Jews specialized in trade and shipping, where they had a comparative advantage, given their excellent connections in the New World and the Old. Curaçao's large natural harbor provided a stepping-stone to the islands of the Caribbean and the Spanish Main. As early as 1686 the Curaçaon Jews also began trading with coreligionists in New Netherland and Barbados as well as in Amsterdam. The Curaçao-New Amsterdam exchange "was extremely serviceable in leading to the commercial development of both colonies." During the first sixty years, 1650–

1710, Curaçao Jewish merchants owned some two hundred vessels and Jewish brokers outnumbered Gentiles by four to five times. The success of the Curaçao Jewish merchants derived from the practice of sending to their far-flung trading posts capable representatives or partners, usually relatives—sons, brothers, brothers-in-law, cousins.[7]

The British West Indies also attracted a substantial share of Dutch Sephardim from Brazil, Curaçao, the Guianas, and Holland itself. Isaac Pinheiro, a sugar planter, distiller, and export merchant, was one of the notable settlers at Charleston, the capital of Nevis in the Leeward Islands. Pinheiro traded regularly at New York and other North American ports and even became a freeman there in 1695. After his death in 1710 his widow Esther carried on his far-flung enterprises, visiting New York and Boston regularly in 1716–1718 aboard the family's small sloop *Neptune*, exchanging salt, sugar, and molasses for fish, soap, timber, and European goods. Widow Pinheiro aptly exemplifies the Biblical proverb of the "virtuous woman."

> She is like the ship of the merchant
> She brings her food from afar . . .
> She looks well to the ways of her household,
> And does not eat the bread of idleness.
> Her children rise up and call her blessed.
>   (Proverbs 31:14, 27–28)

More Dutch Jews could be found in Barbados, Jamaica, and every other British possesion in the Caribbean. Their knowledge of the sugar industry, slave trade, merchant shipping, and shopkeeping made them highly desirable. Indeed, in religion and culture the Jewish communities in the islands, although under British rule, were offshoots not of London but of Amsterdam, whose synagogue supplied the Torah scrolls and ornaments. The Caribbean and even the London Jewish communities, Jacob Marcus perceptively observes, "represented attempts on the part of the Dutch Jews to cope with England's new and restrictive navigation laws."[8]

The Caribbean Dutch Sephardim faced Amsterdam but they also turned in business and religious life to Jewish communities in North America. The numerous European wars of the seventeenth and eighteenth centuries that spilled into the Americas, including the American War of Independence, provided great opportunities to the neutral Dutch traders in the Caribbean. They extended their hegemony throughout the Atlantic world and even into the eastern

35

Mediterranean. Despite the great risks from English, French, and Spanish privateers, the Dutch Jews prospered, including the blockade runners of Saint Eustatius. These ex-Iberians in the Caribbean borderlands occupied a "half-way house between the Anglo-Saxon frontier and the new metropolises of Western Europe," which gave them a status and dignity unimagined in Europe and equipped them to survive among the warring empires.[9] These experiences such Jewish merchants as the Touros and Pinheiros brought to North America in the course of their business ventures.

At the birth of the United States in 1787 the Jews of the slave islands outnumbered those in North America by five times and may have equaled those in England. Surinam had fourteen hundred Jews and Curaçao fifteen hundred—both nearly one-half of the total white population. By contrast, the entire United States in 1790 numbered less than fifteen hundred Jews.[10] But the balance shifted gradually after the American Revolution when Dutch Jews came to the United States instead of the Caribbean because the Latin American economies stagnated. The WIC was liquidated in 1791 and Curaçao, Surinam, and all former colonies under company jurisdiction became part of the Netherlands government. The European naval blockades and counterblockades in the years from 1795 to 1802 prevented a single European ship from anchoring in the Curaçao harbor.[11]

In contrast to the Caribbean, North American Jewry grew slowly until the 1830s. Between 1800 and 1830 about 3,000 Jews arrived, of which an estimated one-quarter (750) were Dutch. The census marshals in 1830 numbered about 4,000 Jews. British, Dutch, and Danish colonies in the Caribbean by comparison counted 5,000 Jews; and the most Jewish city in the Western Hemisphere in 1830 was not New York with 1,150 Jews but Paramaribo, the capital and major port of Surinam, with more than 1,200. Willemstad in Curaçao had nearly 1,000 Jews in 1830.[12]

In the colonial period most Jews were Sephardim who came to North America through Amsterdam and London. Yet Ashkenazim also comprised a substantial part of the Jewish community from the earliest days, and by the mid-eighteenth century the vast majority of newcomers were Ashkenazim from Holland, Germany, and England. All followed the Sephardic rite in the arrangement of the prayer book and pronunciation of the Hebrew language in worship because their synagogues were "daughters" of the Sephardic synagogues in Amsterdam, London, and the Caribbean and because the more dignified service, led by a reader, was better adapted to a Protestant society and appealed to upwardly mobile Jews. Unlike Europe, where the two groups maintained distinct communities, in frontier North America they had to learn to live and worship together.[13]

Colonial New York and Joseph Jesurun Pinto

New York has always been the focal point of North American Jewry ever since the Sephardi-Netherlandic colonization of New Amsterdam. The first Jews to arrive in the city in 1654 were Dutch citizens, much to the chagrin of Governor Peter Stuyvesant and the local Calvinist clergy who wanted to throw the "godless rascals" out. This "deceitful race," the governor declared, "are hateful enemies and blasphemers of the name of Christ," and they must not be allowed to "infect and trouble this new colony."[14]

While the ardently antisemitic Stuyvesant waited for the expected authority from the directors of the WIC to ban all Jews, the Reverend Johannes Megapolensis, the leading cleric in the colony, likewise urged the Dutch Reformed church leaders in Amsterdam to press the directors for a favorable decision. More Jews had arrived in the meantime and they talked alarmingly of founding a synagogue! "This causes among the congregation here a great deal of grumbling and murmuring." Moreover, some Jewish poor require alms from the church, and their merchants "have no other God but the unrighteous Mammon, and no other aim than to get possession of Christian property and to ruin all other merchants by drawing all trade toward themselves." Megapolensis went on to request urgently of "the Messrs. Directors, that these godless rascals, who are of no benefit to the country, but look at everything for their own profit, may be sent away from here."[15]

Amsterdam's Jewish merchants sprang into action to defend their harassed brethren in New Amsterdam. In a bold petition to the WIC directors, they declared that the refugees had risked "their possessions and their blood" to defend Dutch interests in Brazil until hounded out by the Inquisition, that the French and British allowed Jews to settle in their Caribbean colonies, and that "yonder land is extensive and spacious. The more of loyal people that go live there, the better."

To the shock of Stuyvesant and the clerics, who may not have realized that seven of the company's "principal shareholders" were rich and influential members of the Sephardic community of

New Netherland

Amsterdam, the "Messrs. Directors" permitted the Jewish settlers to remain in the Dutch Reformed stronghold, along with Lutherans, Catholics, and Baptists, "provided that they shall not become a charge upon the deaconry or Company." Profits were more important than the principle of religious uniformity. The Calvinist authorities must tolerate heretics, atheists, and "various other servants of Baal" and "connive" at their private worship services.[16] In this way, Dutch Jews gained an early foothold in this major port city where they remained an integral part of its growing Jewish community. More Dutch Jews eventually came to live in New York than in any American city, and they disproved the prediction that they would be of "no benefit." These first twenty-three led to the seminal Jewish community in North America and they were the vanguard of some three million who eventually followed in the next three centuries.

N.Y.

The first contingent in the 1650s included the merchant Abraham de Lucena, who brought the first Torah scroll and became a leading spokesperson for the Jewish community, and Joseph da Costa (d'Acosta), past president of the Amsterdam synagogue and a large shareholder in the WIC. De Lucena and Da Costa worked assiduously in the first years to obtain legal and property rights for Jews from the recalcitrant New Amsterdam burgomasters. And long before Stuyvesant's rule came to an abrupt end in 1664, New York's Jews had won more civil and economic rights than their coreligionists anywhere except in Amsterdam itself. In the eighty years from 1690 to 1770, about one in seven Jewish merchants who gained burgher rights (were freedmen) were Dutch. This is probably also a good estimate of the Dutch proportion of the Jewish population of colonial New York City.[17]

The Dutch also provided religious leadership. From 1700 to 1720 Abraham Haim de Lucena (possibly a relative of the elder De Lucena) served as the second minister (*hazan*) of Congregation Shearith Israel. By 1720 the congregation had outgrown its synagogue and solicited contributions to build a new one from the wealthy Curaçao community. New arrivals in these years were the distinguished merchants Isaac Pinheiro and his son Abraham, and Michael (Jechiel) Hays and his son Judah. The impoverished merchant Hyam Myers of Amsterdam arrived in the 1740s and found work as the ritual slaughterer (*shohet*) of Congregation Shearith Israel. Around 1755 came Uriah Hendricks, scion of a large and increasingly influential line, who outfitted privateers and supplied the army during the French and Indian War. During the American Revolution he was one of sixteen Jews (out of one thousand signers) of an Address of Loyalty to the Crown during the British occupation of New York

City. Described as a "Loyalist in politics and a loyally-conforming Jew in religious practice," Hendricks was able to stay in New York after the war and became president of Shearith Israel in 1791. Lesser lights, all patriots, were Benjamin I. Jacobs, Myer Myers the famed goldsmith, the medical doctor Andrew Judah, and the merchant Isaac Adolphus from Amersfoort, who also became the synagogue president. In advertising his wares in the *New York Journal*, Adolphus appealed to consumers' patriotism to buy American rather than British goods. Myers used his metalworking skills to make bullets during the American Revolution and Jacobs distinguished himself in military service. Myers's son Samuel served in the Virginia militia and his youngest daughter Rachel Moses was killed by a cannonball in the British siege of Charleston, SC, "apparently the only Jewish female casualty of the Revolution."[18]

Two Dutch immigrants held the honored position of *hazan* in the second half of the eighteenth century. They were the renowned Joseph Jesurun Pinto, minister of Shearith Israel from 1758 until 1765, and Isaac Touro, who served twenty years in Rhode Island at Newport's synagogue (1760–1780) and then briefly in 1781–1782 at Shearith Israel. Pinto received excellent rabbinic training in his native Amsterdam and earned the title of Learned Scholar (*Hamaskil Venabon*). He then emigrated to London with his parents in 1757 and began preparing himself for a synagogue post in British North America. In 1758 the trustees of London's Spanish and Portuguese Congregation highly recommended him to Shearith Israel (then seeking a young minister) as one "very well versed in the Reading of the Pentateuch" and with the ability to teach Hebrew. The congregation responded favorably, offering Pinto a yearly salary of £50 sterling.

Pinto served the New York congregation for seven years and his ministry marked an apex in the congregation's spiritual development, although he encountered some difficulties owing to differing expectations between the leaders of the synagogue and himself. Of all the ministers until modern times who served Shearith Israel, Pinto was one of the most knowledgeable in Hebrew and rabbinic literature. He taught Spanish and Portuguese as well as Hebrew, and he spoke English and native Dutch. Early in 1766 he and his family permanently returned to Europe, first to London and then back to Amsterdam. Later he became *hazan* of the Sephardi congregation in Hamburg, where he died in 1782.

Pinto's writings began at age twenty-one when he prepared a lengthy guide (entitled *Seder Hazanut*) for young synagogue clerics. The guide, written in Portuguese, included numerous Hebrew and

Spanish quotations from Jewish authorities and amply demonstrated his grasp of Amsterdam's Sephardic liturgical traditions and customs. In New York Pinto expanded the book to include annotations on the practices of Shearith Israel Congregation that differed from those of London and Amsterdam. Pinto also wrote the first English-language "Form of Prayer," which he read at a public celebration at Shearith Israel on the occasion of the fall of New France to the British in 1770. Thus, Pinto was the first Jewish minister to lead an American congregation in a Thanksgiving Day service. He also preached the first sermon in an American synagogue. In 1759 Pinto finished his compendium and calendar, a systematic compilation of all traditions, customs, and ceremonies of the New York congregation, including a religious calendar for the specific times of divine services adapted from the Amsterdam timetable. Shearith Israel used the famed Pinto Calendar to set its Sabbath eve services for several centuries until recent times.[19]

Despite Pinto's leadership and that of other colonial Dutch Jews, not many of their countrymen immigrated to New York in the Revolutionary era. The New York Jewish community remained quite small until after 1820 when the city became the largest center of Jewry, including the Dutch Jews, in America. In 1790, 6 of 40 (15 percent) Jewish households in New York City were of Dutch birth or ancestry and all came before 1760. In rural New York State another 3 of 7 Jewish households were Dutch (Table 2.1). After thirty years, in 1820, 12 of 74 Jewish households, or 16 percent, were Dutch (Table 2.2). The 97 persons in these households, excluding blacks, comprised 18 percent of the total Jewish population of the city. During the 1820s the Dutch community nearly doubled in size, but it still did not keep pace with the rapidly expanding Jewish settlement. In 1830 the 24 Dutch households (out of 157) containing 185 persons were only 15 percent of all Jews (Table 2.3). Although they were a declining proportion overall, the Dutch ranked second only to English Jews in 1830 among New York's Jewish ethnic groups.[20]

The Jewish population in the United States in the years from 1770 to 1815 was extremely mobile, largely because of the turmoil and trade disruptions caused by the two wars with England. Newport had the largest Jewish community before the American Revolution. Philadelphia then became the premier city when it swelled with war refugees from British-occupied Newport and New York. By 1790, however, New York City still held its lead with 242 Jews, compared with 188 in Charleston, 112 in Philadelphia, 76 in Newport, and 30 in Baltimore (Table 2.1).

From 1800 to 1815 during the Napoleonic wars and the Second

Table 2.1

Dutch Jewish Households as a Percentage of All Jewish Households in Major Cities, 1790 Census

City or Region	All Jews*			Dutch Jews				
	House-holds	Per-sons	Pers./ house.	House-holds	Per-sons	Pers./ house.	% All	% Persons
Baltimore	5	30	6.0	1	8	8.0	20	27
Charleston, SC	52	188	3.6	5	18	3.6	10	10
Georgetown, SC	9	37	4.1	1	5	5.0	11	14
Newport, RI	10	76	7.6	0	0	0	0	0
New York City	40	242	6.0	6	26	4.3	15	11
Philadelphia	18	112	6.2	1	3	3.0	6	3
Other MD	2	12	6.0	0	0	0	0	0
Other New England	5	29	5.8	1	15	15.0	20	52
Other New York	7	31	4.4	3	13	4.3	43	42
Other PA	10	72	7.2	1	3	3.0	10	4
Other SC	5	28	5.6	1	4	4.0	20	14
Totals	163	857	5.3	20	95	4.8	12	11

*Rosenwaike's data is about 90 percent complete for the entire nation, but the Virgina and Georgia 1790 census schedules have not survived, so Richmond and Savannah are omitted.

Source: Compiled from Ira Rosenwaike, "An Estimate and Analysis of the Jewish Population of the United States in 1790," *PAJHS* 50 (Sept. 1960), 36–42.

Anglo-American War, Charleston attracted many Jewish merchants and was the largest center until New York regained the lead permanently upon the opening of the Erie Canal.[21] In 1820 the ranking was as follows: Charleston 674, New York 528, Philadelphia 402, Richmond 191, Baltimore 120, and Savannah 94. Newport was down to only one family (Table 2.2). By 1830, Philadelphia, New Orleans, and Baltimore moved up, and Savannah slipped. The major cities ranked as follows: New York, 1,150, Philadelphia 750, Charleston 650, New Orleans 160, Baltimore and Richmond 150 each, Cincinnati 140, Savannah 80, and Columbia, SC, 70.[22]

Newport and Isaac Touro

Besides New York City, pioneer Dutch Jews were prominent in the eighteenth century in Newport, Charleston, Richmond, Norfolk, and Philadelphia.

Table 2.2
Dutch Jewish Households as a Percentage of All
Jewish Households in Major Cities, 1820 Census

City or Region	All Jews*			Dutch Jews				
	House- holds	Per- sons	Pers./ house.	House- holds	Per- sons	Pers./ house.	% All	% Persons
Baltimore	21	120	5.7	6	33	5.5	29	27
Charleston	109	674	6.2	10	66	6.6	9	10
Georgetown, SC	15	80	5.3	4	17	4.3	27	21
Norfolk	4	20	5.0	2	13	6.5	50	65
New Orleans	10	42	4.2	4	13	3.2	40	31
New York	74	528	7.1	12	97	8.1	16	18
Philadelphia	58	402	6.9	12	75	6.3	21	19
Richmond	32	191	6.0	5	26	5.2	16	14
Savannah	21	94	4.5	0	0	0	0	0
Westchester, NY	5	30	6.0	0	0	0	0	0
Other	29	204	7.0	0	0	0	0	0
Totals	378	2,385	6.3	55	340	6.2	15	14

*Excludes nonwhites

Source: Compiled from Ira Rosenwaike, "The Jewish Population of the United States as Estimated from the Census of 1820," *American Jewish Historical Quarterly* 53 (Dec. 1963), 153–77.

The first Jews in the merchant port of Newport on the Narragansett Bay were Marrano refugees from Brazil. The Habib Ben-Am family of Amsterdam and six others arrived as early as 1652 or 1653.[23] The liberal spirit of Roger Williams made Rhode Island very appealing. "This is the place for Jews," Habib wrote to relatives in Amsterdam. "Every inhabitant will be able to erect a Temple to his God. Our family will remain here. We are sure more Jews will gather here, as sure as we are that day follows night." At Habib's request, a relative from Amsterdam emigrated to Newport with *matzoh* (unleavened bread) and a *Haggadah* (order of service for the Passover Seder) and together they celebrated the first Seder in Newport.

Whether Habib remained in Newport is unknown, but between 1658 and 1677 when a group came from Barbados and the Jewish cemetery was purchased, a number of traders came and went. The 1677 contingent prospered for a few years but subsequent restrictions on the civil liberties and economic rights of Jews caused many to leave, and a permanent community did not develop until the

Table 2.3
Dutch Jewish Households as a Percentage of All
Jewish Households in Major Cities, 1830 Census

City	Jewish Households	Dutch Households	%
Augusta, GA	7	1	14
Baltimore	30	13	43
Charleston	104	4	4
Cincinnati	16	2	12
Columbia, SC	11	1	9
Georgetown, SC	14	3	21
New Orleans	36	16	44
New York	157	24	15
Philadelphia	105	24	23
Richmond, VA	28	8	29
SC (other)	18	0	0
VA (other)	25	1	4
Washington, DC	1	1	100
Other places	78	3*	4
Total	630	101	16

*Bloomfield Tp., NJ, 1; Westchester Co., NY, 1; Berks County, PA, 1.

Source: Ira Rosenwaike, *On the Edge of Greatness: A Portrait of American Jewry in the Early National Period* (Cincinnati, 1985), 112–64.

1740s. Newport mercantile enterprises were closely tied to New York businessmen such as the Hollander Judah Hays, and merchants moved back and forth. Newport's Jews monopolized the West Indies shipping traffic and contributed to the city's flourishing commerce, which rivaled New York in intercoastal and foreign trade by the mid-eighteenth century.[24]

The most famous Dutch Jews in Newport, the "metropolis of the United Colonies" were the Reverend Isaac Touro and the merchant Moses Michael Hays. The young Touro arrived in 1759 via Curaçao and New York after completing his theological training at the Portuguese seminary in Amsterdam. He came in response to a "call" from Congregation Yeshuat Israel (Salvation of Israel) of Newport to be its *hazan*. Its Sephardi rite was solely in Hebrew and most of the city's sixty to seventy Jewish families at the time were Sephardic.[25]

The congregation had already determined to build its first synagogue. The Reverend Touro quickly took charge and guided the planning process and actual construction. To fund the building the fledgling group sent appeals to congregations in New York, Jamaica, Surinam, Curaçao, London, and Amsterdam. All responded favorably. The imposing building, completed and dedicated in 1763, was modeled after the mother Sephardic synagogue in Amsterdam. One of its three sacred scrolls was a gift from the Amsterdam congregation. For twenty years Touro sparked the spiritual vitality of the Jewish community. He also personally directed religious education and established a Talmud Torah school under the auspices of the synagogue. Touro's ministry is described in great detail in the diaries of his close friend Dr. Ezra Stiles (minister of the Congregational Church of Newport and future president of Yale University) who he instructed in elementary Hebrew. Touro conducted all the services and chanted the Scriptures in his sonorous voice, but did not preach. Cantors seldom did. Preaching was done in Newport by occasional visiting rabbis fluent in Spanish, Portuguese, and Dutch, such as Rabbi Tobiah ben Jehuda, a native of Poland, who pursued Hebrew studies for eighteen years in Amsterdam and immigrated to Newport in 1773.[26] When Jehuda soon moved on to New York and elsewhere, the sizable Holland group in the synagogue was doubtless disappointed. Touro was a central cog at the Newport synagogue for twenty years, and he also supervised the education of Jewish youth.

Another Dutch member was Touro's brother-in-law, the merchant Moses Michael Hays, a second-generation immigrant who was born in New York City in 1739. Moses was a son of the New York merchant and watchmaker Judah Hays of Amsterdam, who was one of the earliest Jewish shipowners in the West Indies Trade; he also did business in Newport and later settled there. Moses Hays left New York for Newport in 1769 to build and freight ships with Myer Polock and to enter the lucrative China trade. He pursued shipping and banking businesses until the British conquest in 1776 shut down the thriving seaport. Earlier that year he had, under protest of discrimination and after an initial refusal, taken the loyalty oath required by the Rhode Island legislature. Moses temporarily carried on his enterprises from South Kingston, RI, but returned to Newport in 1780 after the British departed. He remained until at least 1783 when he resettled permanently in Boston as a maritime insurance underwriter.[27]

Moses Michael Hays did not leave Newport, however, before one final contribution to the city. While still in New York, he had introduced into American Masonry the "Ancient Accepted Scottish Rite" and in 1768 he was appointed deputy inspector general of masonry for North America. Using the authority of this exalted position, Hays in 1769 constituted the King David's Lodge in New

York. In 1780 he removed this lodge to Newport and became its master. Almost every Jew in the city joined, including the Reverend Isaac Touro. In 1781 Hays as lodge master welcomed General George Washington to Newport.[28]

But neither the lodge nor the synagogue could save the Jewish community, which at its height exceeded one thousand residents. The American Revolution not only destroyed Moses Hays's shipping business, but it dealt a death blow to the city's entire economy. All but seven Jewish families left the city by December 1776 when the British occupied it. The Reverend Touro was one of those who remained and endured the privations, but the synagogue could not function with so few men. In 1780 Touro left for New York where he served as interim *hazan* at the equally deserted Shearith Israel synagogue. Just as in Newport, New York's Jews had also fled the British occupation, going to Philadelphia and other safe places. Touro's Loyalist leanings helped keep the synagogue open. Shortly thereafter, he went to the British colony of Kingston, Jamaica, where in failing health he died at the youthful age of forty-six in 1784. The inscription on his tombstone reads: "Rev'd, the able and faithful Minister of Congregation Yeshuat Israel."[29]

The Touro name remains honored forever in Newport and New York because the Reverend Touro's sons Abraham of Swansea (near Boston) and Judah of New Orleans gave generously of their great wealth to create permanent endowments for Jewish cemeteries and synagogues. For Newport specifically, Abraham Touro at his death in 1822 bequeathed $10,000 "to revive the Jewish religion there, and in such way & manner as to induce some of that nation to settle & keep up a worship." His remains were interred in the old cemetery near his mother. In 1824 the Rhode Island legislature and Newport town council established the Abraham Touro Fund. These reserves permitted repairs to the synagogue and ensured its upkeep, which remained under the legal control of New York's Congregation Shearith Israel until the 1890s. Thus, the synagogue continued to operate at a minimal level for special events—bar mitzvahs, weddings, and funerals.[30]

Brother Judah Touro (see Fig. 2.1) also kept Newport in mind and in 1842 he provided funds to completely restore the cemetery and enclose it with an iron railing built on a granite base. At his death in 1854 Judah Touro's will provided money for a minister and his remains were interred in the Newport cemetery following one of the longest processions in the city's history. The Dutch-born *hazan*, Samuel Myer Isaacs of New York, was one of many clerics who participated in the funeral ceremonies. Isaacs threw the

Fig. 2.1. Judah Touro (1775–1854) of New Orleans, LA. Daguerreotype reprinted by permission of the American Jewish Historical Society, from Bertram Wallace Korn, *The Early Jews of New Orleans* (Waltham, MA, 1969).

traditional handful of dirt from Jerusalem over the lowered coffin and offered a prayer at the committal service. Eventually, in 1881, a century after regular services ceased, the Touro brothers' endowments bore fruit. The synagogue was completely refurbished, rededicated, and reopened as the Touro Synagogue upon the influx of eastern European Jews to the city.[31]

Charleston and Abraham Azuby

As in New York and Newport, Sephardi Dutch were also among the earliest Jewish settlers in Charleston, SC. Simon Valentine van der Wilden, an early Brazilian refuge to New Amsterdam, shifted his prosperous merchant business there from New York by 1696. In 1703 he was a police comissioner and in 1715 he and a partner, Mordecai Nathan, were shipping many hogsheads of kosher beef out of Charleston to the West Indian markets from their five-hundred acre cattle ranch. In the 1740s, when Charleston Jewry took form, came the merchants Jacob Lopez and David Lopez de Oliveira, and Joseph Tobias, the first president of Congregation Beth Elohim (House of God) in 1750. At least twelve more merchants arrived before 1800, most notably Abraham de Ely Azuby of Amsterdam, who emigrated in 1764 and served as *hazan* of Beth Elohim for more than twenty years from 1784 until his death in 1805. The congregation had 107 members in 1800. In 1789 Azuby requested a donation for his flock from Congregation Mikveh Israel of Philadelphia, a body that at least ten Charleston Jews joined during the American Revolution after being expelled from Charleston following the British conquest.[32]

The other pioneer Dutch Jews in Charleston were Frances Hart, daughter of Moses Hart of The Hague; Nathan Levy, a physician; Lyon Moses of Amsterdam, who served in the Philadelphia militia during the American Revolution; Samuel da Costa; Isaac Canter; Joseph and his brother Emanuel Abraham(s); Solomon Moses, a shopkeeper; Joseph Solomon(s) of Amsterdam, a merchant; Hyam Harris; Jacob Harris and his son Jacob, Jr.; Joseph Tobias and his son Jacob; and Isaac Cohen D'Avezedo. During the war the Abraham brothers were Loyalists who continued to do business in occupied Charleston. But Jacob Tobias served in the South Carolina militia until his premature death in 1775.[33]

In the period 1800 to 1825 Charleston boasted as the center of Jewish life and culture in North America. As a result, it attracted many Dutch families. Joshua Canter and his son Emanuel came in 1800, as did Israel Solomon(s) of Amsterdam, followed by Benjamin Cohen D'Alzado (1807) and his son Moses (1819), Isaac M. Goldsmith of Rotterdam (1809), Moses H. de Young (1819), J. de Jong(h) (by 1820), Samuel A. Waterman of Amsterdam (1823), and Henry Nathan (by 1830). In the Georgetown District (County) were Levi J. Myers (1805) who moved to Charleston in 1814; Israel's brother, Sampson Solomon(s) (1817); John Barnett and Saul Boaz (by 1820); and Chapman Solomon (by 1830) who died in New

Orleans in 1849. Most of the practicing Dutch Jews in Charleston worshiped at Synagogue Beth Elohim. At the founding of the Reformed Society of Israelites in 1825, only one first-generation immigrant, Jacob Harris, and possibly several sons of immigrants were among the charter members.[34]

Philadelphia's Transient Merchants

As early as the mid-1650s Jewish traders from the New Netherland colony carried goods down the Delaware (then South) River to scattered settlements in the newly subjugated territory of New Sweden that later grew into the city of Philadelphia. Jews thus lived in the Pennsylvania country at least twenty-five years before the landing of William Penn and his Quaker colonists.[35] In the next century Jewish newcomers slowly filtered in and formed the nucleus of a small community within the dominant English Quaker colony and city. In the 1730s and 1740s, particularly, several dozen New York Jewish families arrived, making Philadelphia, like Newport, an offshoot of the Shearith Israel Congregation.

A few Dutch Jews were drawn to Pennsylvania in the decades immediately prior to the American Revolution. The most renowned was Aaron Levy (1742–1815), who was born in western Poland but lived for some years in Amsterdam before emigrating in 1760.[36] Immediately after his arrival he plunged into frontier land investments on a vast scale in the central region around Northumberland. During the Revolution he sold supplies to the Pennsylvania troops and purchased government bonds issued by the Continental Congress. He also became involved in the land schemes of Philadelphians Robert Morris, the head of the Confederation's Treasury Department, and James Wilson, an attorney and member of Congress. After the war, Aaron continued to buy and sell interior Pennsylvania land totaling in the hundreds of thousands of acres, and in 1786 he platted and founded the town of Aaronsburg some thirty miles west of Northumberland. In 1794 he moved back to Philadelphia, where he had first settled for a time, and remained there until his death in 1815. The merchant Aaron Levy stood foursquare in his Jewish tradition and also was one of the Jewish heroes of the American Revolution.

Three other Dutch Jews, the Levy brothers and Eleazer Lyons, emigrated to Philadelphia in the eighteenth century. Five years before Aaron's arrival, in 1755, one Isaac Levy, perhaps a relative, came from Rotterdam and was naturalized in Philadelphia in 1763. Nothing is known of his life except for the notable act of his divorce and remarriage about 1770. The other Levy was Aaron's nephew and namesake Aaron Levy, Jr. (1774–1852), who arrived in Philadelphia in 1796 from Holland and went into business with his uncle. The year of Eleazer Lyons's (1729–1816) immigration is unknown, but from 1772 he operated businesses in Harrisburg, Lancaster, and Philadelphia. In 1776 he married Hannah Levy, also a Hollander. In the 1780s he moved his operations to Baltimore and then in the 1790s he was in the Dutch colony of Surinam. He died in Philadelphia in 1816.[37]

During the American Revolution Cushman Polock, a young man from Amsterdam who had lent the government money and fought with the Patriot forces in Georgia, fled to Charleston and later to Philadelphia as a refugee. He had suffered the loss of his property, for which Congress later compensated him $1,287. Polock was active in Congregation Mikveh Israel.[38]

Early in 1783, just before the Revolution officially ended, two Dutch business partners, Lazarus Barnett and Lyon Moses, arrived fresh from Amsterdam and established "the business of a Dutch Broker." The firm dissolved within six months, however, owing to financial difficulties; Barnett fled his creditors for London in 1784, leaving Lyon Moses to reestablish his credit and reputation, which he did by 1785. Barnett applied for membership in the city's only synagogue, Mikveh Israel, but did not remain in Philadelphia long enough to complete the process. By 1790 he was living in Charleston, SC.[39]

When peace was restored after General Washington's victory at Yorktown, refugees returned to their homes and Philadelphia's swollen Jewish community quickly declined. But newcomers came to take their places and the city again reached its prewar level of about five hundred persons by 1820 and quickly surpassed it thereafter. Many Dutch Jews were among the community builders, and their story is told in the chapter on Philadelphia.

Richmond and the Myers and Levy Families

Richmond had virtually no Jewish community until after the Revolution when one formed quickly. In 1790 the approximately one hundred Jews composed 4 percent of the white population, which was a much greater proportion than in New York and Philadelphia. The next year Congregation Beth Shalome (House of Peace) was founded with twenty-six members, none of whom were Dutch.[40] The only Dutch Jews in the entire state of Virginia at the time were three young men, all born in New York City, who lived in the seaport of Norfolk, which was a lesser Jewish center than Richmond, the capital. These were the cousins Joseph A. Myers, son of Asher; Samuel Myers, son of Myer; plus Moses Myers, son of Hyam (not related). Joseph was in business in Richmond by 1787, in partnership with his brother Moses A., and was active in the Masons until his death in 1827. Samuel (1755–1836) and Moses (1753–1835) were partners in the large trading firm of Isaac Moses & Company, centered in New York and Amsterdam. Moses was born in 1752, the son of Hyam Myers, New York's kosher butcher. Samuel Myers' father, Myer Myers, was the famed colonial New York silversmith and his grandfather was Solomon Myers of Amsterdam.[41]

During the American Revolution Moses Myers became a major in the Virginia militia, which was the highest rank attained by a Jew in that state. He witnessed Lord Charles Cornwallis's surrender at Yorktown after the Tories had pillaged and burned his home. The firm of Isaac Moses & Company prospered greatly during the war by running the English blockade of American seaports, but after the Revolution the economic disruptions in Anglo-American trade bankrupted the firm and the partnership dissolved in early 1786. This forced the partners to seek other opportunities and both cousins went to Virginia where Joseph already lived. Moses married in 1789 and took his bride to the rising port of Norfolk where he opened a prosperous import-export business and served as the Virginia agent for the wealthy Philadelphian Stephen Girard. In 1792 he became superintendent of the new Norfolk branch of the Bank of Richmond. His son Samuel matriculated in 1808 at the College of William and Mary, likely the first Jew to do so.[42]

Meanwhile, Myers's trading firm had spread its operations to nearly every seaport in the Atlantic world, which made it vulnerable to the shipping disruptions of the Anglo-French wars, the U.S. embargo of 1807, and ultimately the War of 1812 itself. By 1818 Moses was again driven into bankruptcy by a crushing $75,000 of indebtedness, and his oldest son John, who had joined the firm as a full partner, went to debtor's prison. A $5,000 legacy from his old friend Abraham Touro helped Moses recover. He served many years in the city council, including a stint as president (1795–1797), and he represented as consular agent the governments of France, the Batavian

Republic (Netherlands), and the Scandinavian countries. In 1802 he declined President Thomas Jefferson's appointment as commissioner of bankruptcy, but late in life in 1827 he secured from President John Quincy Adams the plum patronage post of collector of the port of Norfolk, but political difficulties forced him to resign after three years. Religiously, Norfolk had no organized Jewish congregation during Moses Myers's lifetime, but while isolated from formal Judaism, he preserved the ancestral faith by circumcising his eight sons, joining in buying a Hebrew cemetery, and meeting for informal worship.

Samuel Myers moved around the State of Virginia: Norfolk (1787), Petersburg (1789), and Richmond, where he finally settled permanently in 1796. By 1800 he was a prominent merchant and city alderman. He was a lifelong member of Congregation Beth Shalome and was one of the founders of the Richmond Amiable Society, a purely social club. He donated to the Virginia Historical Society a colonial business receipt book of his wife's father and grandfather Judah Hays of New York and Moses Michael Hays of Newport and Boston. Samuel's wife Judith Hays was a daughter of Moses Michael Hays and Rachel Myers. Rachel was a daughter of Solomon Myers, the grandfather of Samuel Myers; thus Samuel married his first cousin.

Samuel and Judith Myers had three sons and three daughters, all of whom became prominent in Richmond. Samuel H. Hays and Gustavus Adolphus were lawyers, Henry was a physician. Daughter Rachel married her Dutch-American cousin, U.S. Naval Commander Joseph Myers, who was reared by his uncle Moses Mears Myers, Samuel's youngest brother. Moses had married in New York in 1796 to another daughter of Moses Michael Hays, Sarah (Sally) Hays, and in 1798 the young couple settled in Richmond where Moses became an auctioneer or vendue master. Judith and Sally Hays's sisters, Catherine and Slowey Hays of Boston, also joined the clan in Richmond and affiliated with Beth Shalome. At his death in 1836, Samuel Myers left the largest estate in Richmond up to that time; his executor had to give security bond for $354,000.[43] Samuel's achievements allowed his son Gustavus to reach the pinnacle of prominence among Richmond's elite in the antebellum decades. An attorney and businessman, Gustavus patronized the arts and became a leading politician and Mason. He was a founder of the Virginia Historical Society, active in the Richmond Athenaeum (later Forum), contributor to literary journals, and a member of the Richmond Library Society. As an active Mason, perennial Richmond city councilman, and Virginia state representative (1859–1861) at the outset of the Confederacy, Myers was acquainted with all the leading men of the South, including Chief Justice John Marshall and Confederate President Jefferson Davis. Although he was an active supporter of Congregation Beth Shalome, he eventually married a prominent Gentile widow, the daughter of Virginia Governor William B. Giles, and is buried in a Christian cemetery.[44]

During the antebellum decades many Dutch Jews came to Virginia's capital city. In 1820 five of thirty-two Jewish families in Richmond and two of four families in Norfolk were Dutch. Dutch and German families largely dominated Richmond's Beth Shalome Congregation when its new synagogue was dedicated in 1822.[45] Besides the Myers clan, those in the capital city included the Ezekiel, Levy, Pyle, and Solomon families.

Tobias Jacob Ezekiel, a Sephardi of Amsterdam and an outfitter of sailing ships, emigrated to Philadelphia in 1804 and married into the pioneer New York Isaaks family. In 1807 he arrived in Richmond and immediately joined the Richmond Blues in the defense of the city against the British vessel HMS *Leopard*, which had fired on the USS *Chesapeake* in Chesapeake Bay and threatened to take the port of Portsmouth by force. The Richmond Light Infantry Blues, formed in 1793, was one of the oldest military companies in the United States and it included many Jews during its illustrious history. Tobias Ezekiel's grandson and namesake, Herbert Tobias Ezekiel, became a Richmond city official and was president of several Jewish lodges, B'nai B'rith, and the Young Men's Hebrew Association (YMHA). He also coauthored the detailed chronicle, *The History of the Jews of Richmond from 1769 to 1917*, published in 1917. Tobias Ezekiel's son established retail stores in Boston, New York, Philadelphia, and Richmond.[46]

The Levy family, like that of the Ezekiels and Myers, cut a wide swath through Richmond Jewry. The patriarch was Abraham Levy (1769–1852), a dry goods merchant, who became the leader of the Jewish community. Levy was born in Amsterdam and after marrying Rachel Cornelia Bernard and having several children, the family emigrated to London late in the Napoleonic wars, where Isaac A. was born in 1816. The growing family crossed the ocean to Richmond in 1818. Jacob A., who was born in Amsterdam in 1804, and Abraham, Jr., followed their father into the family dry goods store on Main Street. Another son, Moses Albert, graduated from the University of Pennsylvania Medical School; three years later in 1835 he enlisted as a surgeon in General Sam Houston's volunteer army and navy in the Texas war for independence and then lived out his life in Matagorda, Texas.[47] A sister Rebecca, who was married in Amsterdam to Wolf B. Pyle (1798–1840), also came to Richmond with her husband. In 1825 Pyle filed his declaration of intent to become a citizen and in 1831 became the first Jew to be naturalized in Richmond. He died in the city in 1840. The couple's oldest daughter Mary married in Richmond in 1846 to another Hollander, her cousin Isaac A. Isaacs, of the Boston Aaron Isaacs family. Aaron Isaacs (Van Brunt) had married in Richmond in 1824 to Esther Levy, the youngest daughter of Abraham Levy. Their son D. Hardy Pyle was born in 1835, was married in Beth Shalome, and served in the Confederate army. Wolf Pyle's brother, Louis B. Pyle, also lived in Richmond by 1831 when court records show he was fined for Sunday breaking.[48]

The entire family was active in Beth Shalome. Isaac A. Levy was president of the congregation in 1849 when he died at the young age of 33; older brother Jacob A. succeeded him for the next eighteen years. Abraham, Sr., and son Jacob were the prime movers in the successful petition of 1846 to the Richmond city council requesting exemptions for Jews from Sunday closing laws. Like all Orthodox Jews, retail merchants such as the Levys made great financial sacrifices to observe both the Jewish Sabbath and Christian Sunday. Jacob and his wife Martha, who was a daughter of Tobias Ezekiel, raised ten children, several of whom also worked in the family business and were members of the Blues or married Jewish men who were Blues. After the Civil War Jacob became a city councilman and boasted of being the oldest Jewish resident of Richmond until his death in 1878 at 74 years of age. His tombstone bears this testimony: "A good man and pious Israelite."[49]

Other early arrivals were the Solomon brothers Simon and Ezekiel, who were in Richmond by 1805 when they obtained peddler's licenses, and Tobias Jacob Ezekiel. Simon Solomon was listed as a merchant in the first city directory of 1819, he paid a fine for public drunkenness in 1826, and died in 1844. Ezekiel Solomon's son Isaac (1796–1881) also was a peddler and streetstall vender who in the course of his long career in Richmond became a sort of unofficial Jewish politician. He petitioned the city council on numerous occasions on behalf of himself and fellow merchants.[50]

In the 1830s several Dutch Jews from Philadelphia migrated to Richmond to take advantage of growing economic opportunities. Family members already there enticed them. Jacob Ezekiel (1812–1899), a son of Ezekiel Jacob Ezekiel and Hannah Rebecca Israel of Amsterdam and a brother-in-law of Jacob A. Levy, came in 1834 after apprenticing in the bookbinding trade in Philadelphia for seven years. A year later Jacob Ezekiel married in Richmond to Catherine

Myers de Castro (also Dutch) and the couple raised fourteen children, notably the eminent sculptor Sir Moses Jacob Ezekiel of Richmond, who studied in Rome and was the only American Jew knighted by King Umberto I of Italy. Jacob Ezekiel became a prosperous dry goods merchant from 1834 to 1869, in partnership with another Dutch brother-in-law, Isaac Hyneman, under the firm name of Ezekiel and Hyneman. An advertisement in the *Richmond Compiler* in 1838 noted that they had purchased the store formerly occupied by Jacob A. Levy and "they are determined to sell to the ladies better bargains than ever." Moses described his father as a "good writer and well-read man . . . , [who] possessed the complete works of Maimonides, who is called the second Moses." These literary gifts qualified him as the longtime secretary-treasurer of Congregation Beth Shalome and a power in the wider Jewish community. Ezekiel opposed all sectarianism in public life. He and Levy succeeded in pushing through the Virginia legislature in 1849 a law exempting Jews from Sunday closing laws. In 1851 Ezekiel effectively petitioned the U.S. government against ratifying a treaty with the Swiss Republic because of its alleged antisemitic policies. Three years later he protested the Swiss contribution of a block of granite for the Washington Monument. During the Civil War he served in the Confederate military patrol around Richmond. Ezekiel moved to Cincinnati in 1869 where he helped establish Hebrew Union College. He also participated in forming the Union of American Hebrew Congregations in 1873.[51]

Ezekiel's partner, Isaac Hyneman, arrived from Philadelphia in 1836 and shortly thereafter married Adeline Levy, Jacob A. Levy's sister. They raised at least five sons, one of whom (Jacob Ezekiel) distinguished himself in the Confederate army. Isaac Hyneman was one of the charter subscribers in Richmond to Isaac Leeser's periodical the *Occident*, along with fellow Hollanders Jacob and Isaac Levi and Jacob Ezekiel. In the mid 1840s Hyneman returned to Philadelphia.[52]

Emanuel Semon (Seamon) of Amsterdam also moved from Philadelphia in the 1830s and became a customs collector. He too joined Beth Shalome and in 1840 became a U.S. citizen, having filed his first papers in Philadelphia in 1835. His unit of the Blues helped capture John Brown following Brown's Harpers Ferry raid in 1859. Semon died in 1871 in Philadelphia. His son Jacob S. Semon also joined the Blues and served in the Confederate forces until he was captured and imprisoned in Philadelphia.[53]

Other Richmond Dutch Jews in the 1830s and 1840s included Emanuel J. Myers, Levi J. Workum, Julia Blitz, Isaac Pepper, and

Isaac van Vort. Myers, a Napoleonic soldier, was related to the Norfolk Myers and Richmond Ezekiel families. He arrived in 1833 with his wife and son and joined Beth Shalome. In 1836 he ran afoul of the Richmond Sunday closing ordinance. His wife Edel (Adeline) Waterman was a sister of Amsterdam natives Samuel A. Waterman of Charleston and Baltimore and Moses A. Waterman, who came to Richmond with his family and operated a dry goods store for many years. Myers died in Richmond in 1871. Another Amsterdammer was Levi J. Workum, son of Jacob L. Workum who settled in Cincinnati and married Hannah Ezekiel in Richmond's Beth Shalome synagogue in the 1850s. Workum later returned to Cincinnati. Mark Blitz also married in the Richmond synagogue in the 1840s. He was a son of Julia Blitz, who was born in Amsterdam in 1802 and died in Richmond in 1858.[54] Isaac Pepper (1762–1822) was a teacher and linguist in The Hague who emigrated with his family to Richmond in the early 1820s and died about 1822. Son Louis J., a dry goods merchant, was a Napoleonic soldier and never married. He returned to Amsterdam after the Civil War. His wife Catherine lived on to 1848 and his son Louis to 1881. Two daughters married in Richmond in the 1830s.[55]

In the antebellum decade, around 1856, Isaac van Vort, a cigar-maker from Holland, settled in Richmond. He applied for U.S. citizenship in 1859, but the Civil War delayed the process until 1868. Van Vort initially joined the Ashkenazi congregation Keneseth Israel but later he affiliated with the pioneer congregation Beth Shalome. His daughter Rachel became a city public schoolteacher and his daughter Rosa superintended one of Richmond's two leading hospitals.[56]

Dutch Jews were clearly well entrenched in Richmond Jewry from the 1780s. Most were active throughout the nineteenth century in the Beth Shalome congregation. Their marriage alliances formed a network of interrelated families which linked far-flung Dutch Jewish families and formed a pattern that became typical throughout the nineteenth century. And most remarkably, Richmond's Dutch Jews were members of the local military band, the Richmond Blues, and fought wholeheartedly for the Confederacy during the Civil War. Later, for fifty-four years (1891–1945), Rabbi Edward Nathan Calisch, a son of Amsterdammers, led Richmond Jewry into the American mainstream, but his story has been told elsewhere.[57]

England as a "Way Station"

England was an immigration country and staging area for Dutch Jewry as well as for European Jews generally. Indeed, Dutch Jews first arrived in London in 1654, which was the same year they first settled in New Amsterdam. More Dutch, German, and Polish Jews settled in England than anywhere else in the second half of the eighteenth century and in the nineteenth century. The Jewish population of England climbed from 6,000 in 1740 to more than 20,000 by 1810, 35,000 by 1850, and 60,000 by 1880. These Ashkenazi newcomers quickly overwhelmed the historic Sephardi community of London, and in 1803, less than 2,000 out of 15,000 Jews in England were Sephardi.[58] Of the much smaller number of Sephardim who arrived in England in the second half of the eighteenth century, Hollanders were the most numerous. Most were poor people, old clothes men and peddlers, who sought and eventually found greater economic opportunities across the Channel.[59]

But a notorious gang of international thieves and fences from Amsterdam, who carried their nefarious practices to London in the mid-eighteenth century met with anything but success—several were executed on the gallows. The Sephardi elite of the Great Synagogue tried unsuccessfully to check the influx of the Ashkenazi rabble from Holland by refusing poor relief, but the English packet boats from Hellevoetsluis continued to disgorge their cargoes. By 1800 the German-Dutch Synagogue numbered 12,000 to 15,000 (including Polish, Russian, and Turkish Jews), or three-fourths of all Jews in London.[60]

An exception to the disreputable Dutch was the Goldsmid family, a long-established Dutch Jewish family in London. In the 1790s the brothers Benjamin and Abraham Goldsmid, as financiers and brokers, became the principal bond salesmen for the city of London and advisors to the Crown during the Napoleonic wars. The Goldsmids were the first Jews since the Middle Ages to play a significant part in English financial history at a time when finance was crucial to national survival. Subsequently, Isaac Lyon Goldsmid led the fight for Jewish emancipation and in 1837 helped establish the University of London, for which he became the first Jew to be awarded a hereditary title. His son Francis became the first Jewish barrister (1833) and was also given a title.[61]

So many Dutch Jews emigrated to England between 1750 and 1860 "as to give a pronounced Dutch cast to a large part of English Jewry." The era of the Napoleonic wars (1793–1815) accelerated the

Dutch Ashkenazi emigration of businessmen to London. By 1803 Dutch-born persons comprised nearly one-third of the alien members of London's big Bevis Marks Synagogue. Dutch Jews served as rabbis, teachers, and lay leaders. The London Board of Guardians annual report in 1861 stated, "Holland continues to supply most of the foreign poor."[62] England was only a few hours by ship from Holland across the English Channel and Dutch Jewish merchants had long traded there.[63] The country offered more economic opportunities as well as religious liberty to the desperately poor Dutch Jews. As a result, Dutch Jews formed the main body of Jewish immigrants in England. In 1860 the industrial East End districts of Whitechapel and Saint George's contained 2,294 Dutch. The influence of Dutch Jews in tobacco manufacturing in London became so dominant that it gained the reputation of being a Dutch Jewish trade. The entertainment industry also attracted many Dutch Jews.[64]

The focal point of the Dutch community was the Tenter Ground in London, a dull and squalid area located along Tenter Street in the Spitalfields subdistrict of the East End.[65] Israel Zangwill vividly portrayed "The Dutch Tenters" in his novel *Children of the Ghetto* (1892):[66]

> They eat voraciously, and almost monopolize the ice cream, hot pea, diamond-cutting, cucumber, herring, and cigar trades. They are not so cute as the Russians. Their women are distinguished from other women by the flaccidity of their bodices; some wear small wollen caps and sabots. When Esther [Ansell—a main character] read in her school-books that the note of the Dutch character was cleanliness, she wondered. She looked in vain for the scrupulously scoured floors and the shining caps and faces. Only in the matter of tobacco-smoke did the Dutch people she knew live up to the geographical "Readers."

Although everyone spoke Yiddish, the lingua franca, the polyglot Jewish ghetto had its usual ethnic pecking order: English, German, Polish, Dutch, Russian, and Lithuanian (from top to bottom). According to Zangwill, the long-established Dutch Sephardi despised the newer Ashkenazi Dutch and Poles who likewise looked down on each other. While a Dutchman pitied a Pole as a "poor creature," Belcovitch swears, "'I always said no girl of mine should marry a Dutchman,'" to which his wife replies, "'I would not trust a Dutchman with my medicine-bottle, much less with my Alte or my Becky. Dutchmen were not behind the door when the Almighty gave out noses, and their deceitfulness is in proportion to their noses.' The company murmured assent." Zangwill

Table 2.4
Dutch Jewish Couples with English and German
Jewish Spouses, 1850, 1860, 1870

Year	N	English Spouse		German Spouse	
		N	%	N	%
1850	157	20	13	23	15
1860	385	40	10	70	18
1870	668	72	11	131	20

Source: Compiled from Robert P. Swierenga, comp., *Dutch Households in U.S. Population Censuses, 1850, 1860, 1870: An Alphabetical Listing by Family Heads*, 3 vols. (Wilmington, DE, 1987).

continues, "One gentleman, with a rather large organ, concealed it in a red cotton hankerchief, trumpeting uneasily. 'The Holy One, blessed be He, has given them larger noses than us,' said the *Maggid*, 'because they have to talk through them so much. . . . They oughtn't to call it the Dutch tongue, but the Dutch nose.' "[67] Zangwill's witty caricature of the Dutch itself illustrates the superciliousness of the English Jews.

England was also an ideal staging area for American-bound Jews. It provided the opportunity to learn the English language and become oriented toward English law and social and religious institutions.[68] Thus, hundreds of Dutch Jews lived for a time in London, often marrying and beginning a family, and then moving on to the United States. The full extent of two-stage immigration via England and the rate of intermarriage there is unknown, but it increased over time. In 1850, 13 percent of all Dutch Jewish couples in the United States had English-born spouses (Table 2.4) and 5.2 percent of all their children were born there. By 1870, however, more children were born in England than in the Netherlands—13.7 percent compared to 10.6 percent. Only ten years earlier, in 1860, Dutch-born children outnumbered English-born by four to one—19.4 and 4.6 percent, respectively (Table 2.5). An 1846 report from New York by a knowledgeable German Jew concurs with the statistical data, "Some individual English Jews can be found here, but the majority are Dutch and Polish Jews who have come here after living for a long time in England, where they adopted English customs and manners."[69]

58

Table 2.5
Birthplaces of Dutch Jewish Children: 1850, 1860, 1870

Year	N	England		Netherland		USA		Other	
		N	%	N	%	N	%	N	%
1850	539	28	5.2	72	13.4	424	78.7	15	0.3
1860	1,173	54	4.6	228	19.4	876	74.7	15	1.3
1870	2,012	276	13.7	213	10.6	1,497	74.4	26	1.3
1850–70	3,724	358	9.6	513	13.8	2,797	75.1	56	1.5

Source: Compiled from Swierenga, *Dutch Households in U.S. Population Censuses.*

The Dutch Era, 1800–1830

In the early republic, Jews of all backgrounds were so few that one could hardly have predicted the future growth. New York City in 1806 had only 279 Jews, Philadelphia in 1811 had some 30 families, and Savannah's Jewish congregation in 1820 numbered 80 to 100. Charleston, SC, in 1811 had 600 to 700 Jews, which was the largest settlement by far in North America. The historic Jewish colonies in Newport, RI, and Lancaster, PA, had disappeared by 1800. Baltimore, New Orleans, and Cincinnati had only a few dozen Jews in 1820. The aggregate Jewish population nationally in 1820 is estimated at 2,750, or barely 0.03 percent of the total population.[70]

A careful tally by Ira Rosenwaike of the 1820 census, which suffers from normal underenumeration, identified 378 known Jewish households, totaling 2,385 persons, in the seven states of New York, Pennsylvania, Maryland, Virginia, South Carolina, Georgia, and Louisiana (Table 2.2). Charleston easily led with 674 Jews, followed by New York City with 528, Philadelphia 402, Richmond 191, and Baltimore 120. The 55 Dutch Jewish households with 340 persons comprised 14 percent of the total Jewish households and population in the seven states. Only about 10 percent of the Dutch families were Sephardi in ancestry.[71] The localities with the highest percentage of Dutch households in 1820 were Norfolk, New Orleans, Baltimore, the Georgetown district of South Carolina, and Philadelphia, which ranged from 50 percent in Norfolk to 40 percent in New Orleans, 29 percent in Baltimore and 27 percent in Georgetown. These were all secondary centers. In the primary cities the Dutch comprised 21 percent in Philadelphia and 16 percent in both New York and

Richmond. Charleston, the premier Jewish city, only had 9 percent Dutch. No Dutch Jews were identified in Savannah or the outlying counties of South Carolina, Virginia, and New York.

The Dutch households in 1820, in toto, were about the same size as Jewish households generally, except in New York City. Dutch-headed families averaged 6.2 persons, compared to 6.3 persons for other Jews. But in New York the Dutch households were larger—8.1 persons in average, compared to 7.1 persons for other Jews.

Most of the Jewish immigrants to the states in the early nine-teenth century came from Holland and England. Although roughly equal in number, in some cities one or the other nationality was dominant. Dutch Jews were more numerous in New Orleans and Baltimore, and English Jews were in the vast majority in Charleston and Cincinnati. In New York and Philadelphia, the two groups were more equally represented, although the English had a slight edge in New York and the Dutch in Philadelphia.[72]

Dutch Jews in 1830 were more concentrated than Jews generally. At least 101 families have been identified in the 1830 census, of which 77 lived in only four cities: Philadelphia 24, New York 24, New Orleans 16, and Baltimore 13 (Table 2.3).[73] As a percentage of the total Jewish population in these cities, New Orleans and Baltimore had the highest proportion—44 and 43 percent Dutch, while 23 percent of Philadelphia's Jews were Dutch, and 15 percent in New York. Most of the remaining 24 families lived in southern cities: Charleston, Columbia, Richmond, and Augusta. As in 1820, the Dutch influence was greater in secondary Jewish commercial centers, particularly in the South.

Death records of these Dutch Jews of 1830 show that Baltimore residents were most mobile. Of Baltimore's thirteen Dutch families, eight family heads died elsewhere in the next decade (three in Philadelphia, two in New Orleans, and one each in New York, Richmond, and Galveston, TX). With some exceptions, Dutch residents of the other cities lived out their lives in the same city. Besides the Baltimore-Philadelphia-New Orleans links in the early decades, there is evidence that after midcentury Dutch Jews were linked in the cities of western New York and the states of the Old Northwest.

Occupations

The occupational profile of the Dutch Jews in 1830 mirrored that of Jews generally. Most were engaged in retail or

60

wholesale trade or as shopkeepers.[74] They were clothing and dry goods merchants, brokers and traders, and a few skilled craftsmen. Of sixty-two heads of households whose occupations are known, forty-one had clothing, fancy goods, and food shops, eleven were brokers and traders, six were skilled craftsmen, and four were professionals, including two in medicine and a synagogue sexton.[75]

Each city had its own characteristics. In New Orleans and Baltimore the Dutch Jews were largely in the dry goods trade, but those in Philadelphia and New York were more diverse, including fancy goods and clothiers (new and secondhand); pawnbrokers; and craftsmen such as gilders, watchmakers, a spectacle maker, quill pen maker, tailor, carder, and a doctor.[76] Dutch Jews did not enter the professions until the second and third generations. In brief, compared to the general work force, Jews (including the Dutch) were overrepresented in trade and commerce and underrepresented in manufacturing, construction, crafts, and the professions. Overall, it is a rosy picture of growing prosperity. Jews were not among the enormously wealthy of their day, but they did have their fair share among the richest five hundred in the large cities. As Rosenwaike concluded, "Jews generally resembled their neighbors in their economic status."[77] Given their poverty for generations in European ghettos, this was quite an accomplishment.

Urban Concentrations

American Jews, including the Dutch, did not live in closely confined ghettos as in Europe, but they did tend to congregate in the vicinity of their synagogues and places of business. In New York City in 1830, for example, Jews lived in all but two of the city's fourteen wards, but over half (55 percent) were concentrated in three contiguous uptown wards (5, 6, and 8) near their synagogues, Bnai Jeshurun and Anshe Chesed, which were in the center of the district. In Philadelphia, similarly, Jewish families lived in all fifteen wards save one, and in all adjacent communities except Kensington. Since Philadelphia was a walking city, this dispersal is not surprising. The main concentrations were in New Market and Dock to the south (around Synagogue Rodeph Shalom) and in Lower Delaware and High Street to the north, around the original synagogue, Mikveh Israel. All these wards were along the Delaware River.[78]

By 1830, Jewish congregations had been established in seven out of eleven major eastern cities. New York had three congregations;

Philadelphia two; and the cities with single congregations were Charleston, New Orleans, Baltimore, Richmond, Cincinnati, Savannah, and Columbia.[79] Two-thirds of U.S. Jews lived in only three cities: New York, Philadelphia, and Charleston. At least 90 percent lived in large cities at a time when 90 percent of the American populace was rural!

The first big wave of German Jews arrived in the 1830s when the Jewish population in the United States jumped from 4,000 to 17,000. In this decade 6,000 Jews came from Germany, compared to only 300 in the 1820s. Dutch Jewish immigration, by contrast, increased only slightly after 1830, from 300 in the 1820s to 450 in the 1830s, and 500 in the 1840s.[80] Increasingly, the Dutch were swamped by new German arrivals.

Conclusion

Amsterdam was the cockpit of Dutch Jewry in America. Via Brazil, the Caribbean, or London they came, beginning in the 1650s to New Amsterdam. All were Sephardi until the mideighteenth century when Ashkenazi became predominant. The migration was a natural outgrowth of WIC trade, linked to plantation sugarcane production. Jews followed their ships and markets to the New World and established their base of operation in thriving Atlantic coastal cities facing Europe. Throughout the colonial period the Dutch Caribbean colonies attracted more Jews than the British North American colonies. But the age of revolutions (1776–1815) disrupted, and in many cases abolished, traditional trade patterns and caused economic stagnation. After 1780 the rising United States, particularly New York City, became the magnet for European and Caribbean Jewry. As late as 1830, however, more Jews lived in Paramaribo, Surinam, than in New York, and more lived in Willemstad than in Philadelphia.

Jews in colonial North America were an infinitesimal minority of less than one-half of 1 percent, except in the southern cities of Charleston, Richmond, and Savannah. Their minority status forced them to connive, compromise, and concede in order to survive. Like highly mobile Jews in Europe, some worshiped Mammon rather than Jahweh and they violated religious rules and regulations with impunity. They ignored dietary laws, prayers, observance of Sabbath and Passover, and intermarried with Gentiles and saw their children baptized. Most, however, against all odds clung to their

Jewishness. With great determination and financial sacrifice, they purchased cemeteries, founded congregations, and performed religious offices even when untrained and often unqualified. Malcolm Stern's detailed intergenerational family trees of six hundred pioneer American Jewish families reveals a high degree of in-group marriage. Admittedly, Stern's list ignores Jews totally lost to the faith, but it does show that few children and grandchildren of Jewish pioneers married Gentiles or were baptized. There are also examples of Jewish proselytes.

The Dutch comprised 15 to 20 percent of colonial American Jewry, but their proportion declined in the eighteenth century, reaching a low of 9 percent in 1790. Then the Napoleonic and Anglo-American wars spawned more Dutch emigration, so that the Dutch proportion rose to 14 and 16 percent by 1820 and 1830, respectively (Tables 2.1, 2.2, 2.3). In every Jewish center at least one Dutch family or group of related families made a major impact in synagogue life and general mercantile affairs. In New York City Abraham Haim de Lucena and Joseph Jesurun Pinto served as *hazan* of Congregation Shearith Israel and Judah Hays and Uriah Hendricks were leading merchants. In Newport the leaders were *Hazan* Isaac Touro and Moses Michael Hays, the China trader and Master Mason. In Charleston Abraham Azuby was *hazan* of Congregation Beth Elohim in the immediate postwar decades. The Myers families in Richmond were prominent bankers, traders, and city officials. Dutch Jews held elective office in Richmond and Norfolk.

During the Revolution Jews divided between Loyalists and Patriots in much the same proportion as other Americans. Those of Sephardi extraction were wholehearted Patriots, while the Ashkenazim joined both sides in roughly equal proportions. Jews in New York City and throughout the South, who lived under British occupation for years, were most prone to profess loyalty to the Crown. Ashkenazim who had lived in England or had strong commercial connections with the mother country and its West Indies colonies also were Loyalists or fence sitters. Among Dutch Jews, Isaac Moses and Rachel Pinto of New York and Aaron Levy of Philadelphia were Patriots, while Uriah Hendricks and Isaac Touro of New York and Isaac da Costa of Boston are examples of Loyalists or crypto-Loyalists.[81]

Dutch Jews particularly used England as a staging area for immigration in the nineteenth century. In the Civil War era more Dutch Jewish children in America had been born in England than in the Netherlands.

Occupationally, Dutch Jews were merchants prior to the Revolution and shopkeepers and traders in the early nineteenth century. They were underrepresented among craftsmen until after the Civil War, and few became professionals. In 1830 they were on the brink of being inundated by the first massive German Jewish immigration. But the Dutch continued to be leaders in the Jewish community, despite being a minority. The years before 1830 can truly be called the Dutch era in American Jewry.

Chapter 3

NEW YORK CITY: THE BASTION

The Rise of the Jewish Community

In the 1820s New York took pride of place as the bastion of Jewry in the United States. Dutch Jews continued to be an integral part of that community throughout the nineteenth century. New York City rose to Jewish prominence with the German Jewish surge following Napoleon's defeat in 1815 and the opening of the Erie Canal in 1825, which assured its economic ascendancy. By 1824 the city already boasted the largest Jewish settlement in the United States. Population growth was exceptional thereafter, reaching 1,000 Jews in 1826, 2,000 in 1836, 12,000 in 1846, 30,000 in 1856, and 40,000 by 1859. At that time 5 percent of the city's population was Jewish. The high point of German Jewry was 1878 when the population reached 60,000. Thereafter, the eastern European wave from Russia and Austria-Hungary doubled and tripled the size of the Jewish community to 175,000, pushing it over 10 percent of the city's population by 1890. By then New York was the largest Jewish city in the world. From 1910 to 1960 its Jewish populace never accounted for less than 25 percent, although it is now below 15 percent and declining.[1]

Table 3.1

Dutch Jewish Household Heads in New York City, 1790 and 1820

Head of Household	N in House-hold	Birth	Death	Place of Death	Occupation
1790					
David Hays (Bedford, NY)	9	1732	1812	Mt. Pleasant, NY	merchant
Michael Hays (Jacob)	4	1753	1799	Bedford, NY	merchant
Uriah Hendricks	8	1731	1797	NYC	merchant
Benjamin Jacobs	3	1744	1824	NYC	merchant
Myer Myers	6	1723	1795	NYC	merchant
Joseph Pinto	3	?	1798	NYC	silversmith
Rachel Pinto	2	1722	1815	NYC	—
	35				
1820					
A. Canter	4	?	?	?	?
David Cromelien	12	1789	1843	Phil.	?
Tobias Ezekiel	8	c.1750	1832	NYC	merchant
Harmon Hendricks	17	1771	1838	NYC	merchant
Samuel M. Isaacs	9	?	?	?	?
Benjamin Jacobs	2	1744	1824	NYC	merchant
Abraham Levy	5	1776	1834	NYC	carder
David Levy	8	1770	1855	Cinc.	spectacle maker
Jacob Levy	9	1753	1837	NYC	?
Moses L. Moses	8	1744	1843	NYC	grocer
Moses L. M. Peixotto	7	1767	1828	NYC	merchant
Alexander Ruden	8	1772	1848	NYC	merchant, tailor
	97				

Sources: Ira Rosenwaike, "An Estimate and Analysis of the Jewish Population of the United States in 1790," *PAJHS*, 50 (Sept. 1960): 37–38; Ira Rosenwaike, "The Jewish Population of the United States as Estimated from the Census of 1820," *American Jewish Historical Quarterly* 53 (Dec. 1963): 153–57; Joseph R. Rosenbloom, *A Biographical Dictionary of Early American Jews; Colonial Times Through 1800* (Lexington, 1960); Malcolm H. Stern, comp., *First Jewish American Families: 600 Genealogies, 1654–1977* (Cincinnati, 1978), passim.

Republican New York

At the time of the first federal census in 1790 six Dutch Jewish family heads lived in the city and one, David Hays, was a merchant in Bedford, Westchester County, near the Connecticut border to the north (Table 3.1). Two were born in the Netherlands, Uriah Hendricks and Benjamin Jacobs, and the others were second-generation immigrants born in New York. The most notable were the iron magnate Hendricks, the renowned silversmith Myer Myers, and the social activist Rachel Pinto.

Uriah Hendricks (1731–1798) of Amsterdam came to New York around 1755 after living for a time in London. His rise to success was meteoric due to his business acumen and two fortuitous marriages. As David De Sola Pool noted, Uriah "was the founder of a large and ramifying line in the United States." His first wife Eve Esther was a daughter of one of the city's wealthiest import merchants Mordecai Gomez and Rebecca de Lucena (also of Dutch ancestry). Uriah's dowry to his wife was an astounding £1000 sterling. This marriage produced ten children, most notably son Harmon. After Eve's death, Uriah married Rebecca, daughter of Newport's leading merchant Aaron Lopez. Uriah founded a metal business, Hendricks & Co., that remained in the family for four generations until 1928. Uriah was a Loyalist in politics and a "loyally conforming Jew" in religion. He and fellow Hollander Myer Myers superintended the cemetery of Congregation Shearith Israel after the Revolution and in 1791 he served as president of the synagogue. A yellow fever epidemic carried off the "Ironmonger" in 1798.[2]

Myer Myers (1723–1795) was born in New York as son of Solomon Myers of Amsterdam. He became a famed gold- and silversmith and also rose to prominence in the Shearith Israel congregation, serving as president in 1759 and again in 1770. His ecclesiastical pieces such as silver scroll bells, alms plates, and baptismal bowls were highly prized. During the British occupation of New York City, Myers fled to Norwalk, Connecticut, and then to Philadelphia, where he worshiped at the Mikveh Israel synagogue. In 1883 he returned to New York with his family settling in the Dock Ward near Federal Hall, the first national capitol. The Gold and Silver Smith's Society in 1886 honored him as its chairman for plying his craft with exceptional skill for more than fifty years. In the fine arts, Myers is one of the "early American immortals."[3]

Rachel Pinto (1722–1815) was the unmarried daughter of Abraham and Sarah Pinto of Amsterdam who emigrated sometime before 1725. She was one of seven children of this illustrious family that included Isaac, *hazan* of Newport's congregation, and Joseph, a New York silversmith. Mother Sarah earned the description Virtuous Mother of Israel, and Rachel's tombstone bears the epitaph "The aged and virtuous virgin of Israel." Rachel earned this honor by her life of charity. She was a major benefactor of the Polonies Talmud Torah School, the Hebra Hased Va-amet Benevolent Society (the oldest in New York), and of a home for poor children.[4]

In 1820, when New York was on the brink of explosive growth, eleven Dutch Jewish families resided in the city (Table 3.1). Most were Dutch-born and had come after the Revolution ended. As in 1790 most were petty merchants except for Harmon Hendricks. Most illustrious were Moses L. Moses and Moses Levy Maduro Peixotto. The former served eleven years as president of Shearith Israel (1827–1829, 1834–1841) and was a trustee of the Talmud Torah School and the Hebra. Peixotto's illustrious Sephardic background in the Netherlands began in 1599 when his merchant ancestor Moses fled from Portugal. Peixotto was an Atlantic shipping magnate who moved his base from Curaçao to New York in 1807 to try to escape from the trade embargoes of the Anglo-French wars that were crippling his operations. He set up a mercantile house on Front Street. In 1816 on the death of his friend Gershom Mendes Seixas, longtime *hazan* of Shearith Israel, Peixotto agreed to succeed Seixas as *hazan*, which he did from 1816 until his own death in 1828. Gifted with a fine singing voice, his biggest challenge was to learn English. He managed in 1825 to give his first public address (sermon) in English, doubtless with a thick Dutch brogue, since he was then fifty-eight years old. His children and grandchildren intermarried with the oldest and most prominent American Jewish families— Cardozo, Hays, Seixas, Gomez, Davis, Nathan, Naar, and Phillips. His son Dr. Daniel L. M. Peixotto became a noted physician and professor of medicine, and his grandchildren were leaders in Cleveland, San Francisco, and New York.[5]

Between 1820 and 1830 the number of Dutch Jewish families doubled from eleven to twenty-four (see Table 3.2), and all but five or six were newcomers from the Netherlands. These fresh arrivals were not the leading merchants of earlier immigrations, but petty tradesmen—clothiers, pawnbrokers, and skilled craftsmen. They settled in the older districts on the Lower East Side and Lower Midtown (Table 3.3; Fig. 3.1). In 1830 Dutch Jews made up one-half of the Jewish households on the Lower East Side in Wards 4 and 7, about a fifth of the families in the Lower Midtown section in Wards 6 and 10, and less than 5 percent in the Central and Upper Midtown area in Wards 8 and 14. Only five Dutch families lived in the new center of the Jewish community east of Broadway uptown, where two-thirds of all Jews in the city resided.

By 1850, 178 first-generation Dutch Jews lived in the city. With their spouses and children, the Dutch households totaled 429 persons. The greatest concentrations were in Wards 4 and 6 east of Broadway in the Lower Midtown area. The Holland Jews increased to 356 in 1860, and the total community reached 792 persons, or 2

Table 3.2
Dutch Jewish Household Heads in New York City, 1830 Census

Birth Year	Name	N in House- hold	Ward	Occupation	Death	
?	Andrew Cohen*	2	7	?	?	?
1789	David Cromelien	17	8	?	Phil. 1843	
1799	John M. Davies	8	4	clothier	New York 1879	
1786	Tobias Ezekiel	12	14	quill manufacturer	New York 1832	
1800	Leonard Garrets	8	4	clothier	New York 1872	
1768	Gompert S. Gomperts	7	7	?	New York 1831	
1771	Harmon Hendricks*	12	1	merchant	New York 1838	
1779	Andrew A. Jones	8	8	?	New York 1850	
1792	Moses Joseph	10	6	clothier	Baltimore 1850	
1776	Abraham Levy	4	7	carder	New York 1834	
?	Alexander Levy*	2	4	?	?	?
1770	David Levy	8	8	spectacle maker	Cinc. 1855	
1782	Hart Levy	10	6	porterhouse	New York 1866	
1753	Jacob Levy, Jr.	6	8	?	New York 1837	
1804	Levy Lyons	6	10	grocer	New York 1835	
1774	Moses L. Moses*	8	10	grocer	New York 1843	
1799	Daniel L. M. Peixotto	13	6	medical doctor	New York 1843	
1798	Elias L. Phillips	8	8	merchant	New York 1845	
1762	Moses S. Pike	8	6	pawnbroker	New York 1851	
1783	William N. Polack	7	7	?	New York 1854	
1772	Alexander Ruden	4	10	broker	New York 1848	
1797	Lewis Simmons	2	7	merchant tailor	New York 1874	
1785	Benedict Solomon	11	4	?	New York 1867	
1798	Marcus van Gelderen	4	14	kosher butcher	New York 1871	
		185				

*Birthplaces of Cohen and Alexander Levy are given by Rosenwaike as "?"; Hendricks and Moses were born in New York.

Source: Ira Rosenwaike, *On the Edge of Greatness: A Portrait of American Jewry in the Early National Period* (Cincinnati, 1985), 112–64.

percent of the Jewish population in the city. The Dutch were spread out widely over the city by then, with concentrations in Wards 6, 8, and 14. By 1870 there were 628 first-generation Dutch Jews and a total group, including wives and children, of 1,675 persons. One-third were then concentrated in Ward 11 with other substantial groups in Wards 7, 10, and 13.

Table 3.3
Dutch Jews in New York City by Ward, 1830–1870*

Ward	1830 N	1830 %	1850 N	1850 %	1860 N	1860 %	1870 N	1870 %
1	12	6.5	22	5.1	0	0.0	1	0.0
2	0	0.0	8	1.9	0	0.0	1	0.0
3	0	0.0	0	0.0	0	0.0	1	0.0
4	29	15.7	123	28.7	58	7.3	15	0.9
5	0	0.0	1	0.2	8	1.0	0	0.0
6	41	22.2	94	21.9	92	11.6	23	1.4
7	22	11.9	11	2.6	69	8.7	143	8.5
8	47	25.4	18	4.2	84	10.6	54	3.2
9	0	0.0	36	8.4	61	7.7	21	1.3
10	18	9.7	30	7.0	56	7.1	120	7.2
11	0	0.0	7	1.6	58	7.3	550	32.8
12	0	0.0	1	0.2	16	2.0	40	2.4
13	0	0.0	2	0.5	0	0.0	210	12.5
14	16	8.6	34	7.9	94	11.9	44	2.6
15			6	1.4	0	0.0	18	1.1
16			12	2.8	36	4.6	90	5.4
17			16	3.7	43	5.4	89	5.3
18			8	1.9	25	3.2	14	0.8
19					2	0.2	46	2.8
20					53	6.7	63	3.8
21					33	4.2	43	2.6
22					4	0.5	90	5.4
City Totals*	185	100.0	429	100.0	792	100.0	1,676	100.0

*The totals include non-Dutch spouses and American-born children.

Sources: Compiled from Rosenwaike, *Edge of Greatness*, 112–38; Robert P. Swierenga, comp., *Dutch Households in U.S. Population Censuses, 1850, 1860, 1870: An Alphabetical Listing by Family Heads*, 3 vols. (Wilmington, DE, 1987); see note on sources for methodology.

The number of newcomers dwindled after 1860.[6] In that year over half of the first generation had arrived in the United States after 1850, but by 1870 only one-quarter (27 percent) had lived in America ten years or less; more than half (53 percent) had arrived in the 1850s, and 20 percent came before 1850. As with other Dutch Jewish immigrants, a lengthy sojourn in London was common. Seven families in New York in 1850 had children born in London, and judging from the ages of the children, these families stayed in England an average of ten years. In 1860, twelve Dutch Jewish families

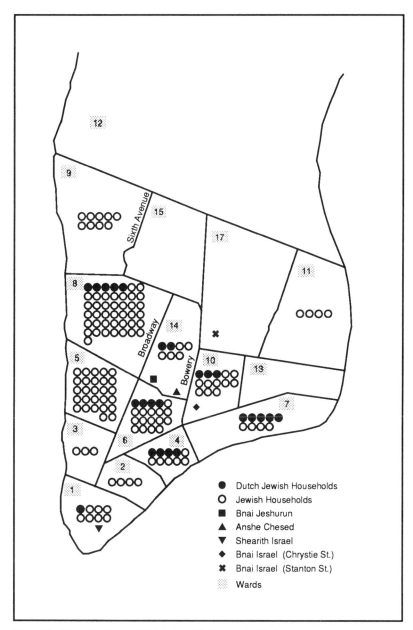

Fig. 3.1. Distribution of Dutch Jewish Households by Ward, New York City, 1830. Adapted by permission from Ira Rosenwaike, *On the Edge of Greatness: A Portrait of American Jewry in the Early National Period* (Cincinnati, 1985).

had English-born children, but the average residence in London was only four years. One family each had children born in France and Belgium. In the 1860s there was a great swell in Dutch Jews immigrating from London to New York. Seventy families had 171 children born in England, and the average sojourn was nearly twelve years. There were also five families with children born in Germany, Belgium, France, Ireland, and Austria. Clearly the Amsterdam-London-New York connection was a strong and growing one, especially in the years immediately following the American Civil War.

The London stopover also led to a high incidence of Dutch-English and Dutch-German marriages. In 1850, nearly one-half (29 of 64) of all Dutch Jewish couples in New York who were married before reaching American shores had non-Dutch spouses. The proportion declined to one-third in 1860 and to one-quarter in 1870. Unlike the years before 1850 when English mates were preferred, after 1850 German mates increasingly outnumbered English. The 1860 federal census showed 21 Dutch Jews married to Germans, and 16 to English. The corresponding 1870 figures are twice as large but in similar proportions: 48 German and 33 English. Thus, Dutch immigrants in London tended to marry English in the early decades before 1850, but after the large influx of German Jews to London in the 1840s, Dutch Jews increasingly chose Germans as mates. More important than the outmarriage is the sharply rising rate of in-group marriages; by 1870 three-quarters of Dutch Jewish couples in New York were both Dutch.[7]

The sex of the non-Dutch spouse is also remarkable. Before 1850 Dutch women married English and German husbands twice as often as Dutch men married English and German wives. But after 1850 the reverse was the case. By 1860 Dutch men were twice as likely to marry German or English spouses as vice versa; by 1870 they were five times as likely. It is possible that before 1850 Dutch women became upwardly mobile by marrying English husbands. But after 1850 Dutch men in London more and more selected nonDutch mates, probably for the same reason. The large number of such marriages was because the pool of eligible Dutch-born was limited. The same forces were at work in America among the second generation. In almost every instance of a Dutch marrying an American, the wife was non-Dutch. Dutch Jewish women in America married Dutch husbands, but Dutch men increasingly selected American-born mates. This would seem to be rooted in cultural more than demographic factors, but the causes are not clear.

Religious Life

The Jewish community of New York, like that in North America generally, but unlike Europe, blended Sephardi and Ashkenazi in one synagogue under the Sephardic *minhag* (worship rites) until the early nineteenth century.[8] As a religious minority in a new land, the Jews also had to live by the old adage, "The law of the land is the law to be observed." Thus, their religious life was affected by colonial and (later) state laws on marriage, burial, incorporation of religious societies, separation of church and state, poor relief, and even occupational restrictions. At first, the Dutch authorities in New Netherland did not permit Jews to establish a synagogue; as a result, they worshiped in private homes until about 1692 when they rented quarters for a synagogue. It was 1729 before they could afford their own synagogue, Shearith Israel. The first Jews also had to care for their own poor and promise not to proselytize. The most important impact in the eighteenth and nineteenth centuries was the intrusion of democracy and freedom of religion into traditional Jewish practice. Although Shearith Israel held the line against lawbreakers, individual Jews could live outside the covenant community and ignore ritual requirements and dietary laws; they could even with impunity marry Christians.[9]

For more than 150 years New York Jews maintained relative unity within the pioneer synagogue of Shearith Israel. But in 1825 it suffered the first of many schisms when recent immigrants, who could not "accustom" themselves to the predominantly "Portuguese" liturgy, broke away and formed a second synagogue, Bnai Jeshurun, based on the Ashkenazic rite. Mainly English in background, the seceders also included German, Dutch, and Polish Jews.[10] Soon each nationality group wanted its own synagogue and secession followed secession. The result was a state of near anarchy in the Jewish community. The traditional weapon of excommunication had lost its sting by the early nineteenth century. In 1828 a number of Dutch, Germans, and Poles left Bnai Jeshurun to form Congregation Anshe Chesed (People of Loving Kindness), which adopted Minhag Amsterdam. In 1845 Bnai Jeshurun suffered yet another schism when its charter members left and formed the Shaaray Tefila congregation. The mother synagogue, Shearith Israel, still retained its mixed character. More than half the membership at mid century was German, Dutch, and Polish. By 1847 there were ten synagogues, including one Portuguese, four "Polish" (eastern European), four German, and one "Nederdutch." These ten by 1860 had grown to 27 synagogues, one for every nationality group and religious taste.[11] Not every new congregation was born in schism. Population growth required more synagogues, even without strife. Nationalism only made the growth process more painful and disjointed.

The pace of assimilation was retarded only by the steady arrival of immigrants from Europe who brought a commitment to Judaism and included ministers and teachers to serve the American community, which as yet had not generated an indigenous leadership. These steady contacts with European Jewry were strengthened by appeals for aid from Jews in Palestine and elsewhere in Europe to which New York Jews responded generously.[12]

Reverend Samuel Myer Isaacs

Dutch Jews served leadership roles in the New York synagogues and none carried greater weight than the Reverend Samuel Myer Isaacs (1804–1878), "rabbi" of Shaaray Tefila for thirty-three years (see Fig. 3.2). Isaacs was born on January 4, 1804, in Leeuwarden—the capital city of the province of Friesland in the far northern Netherlands—the son of a prominent merchant-banker, Meyer Samuel Isaacs (Isaks) and Rebecca Samuels, his wife. This devout family had five sons and four became ministers. The Leeuwarden synagogue seated six hundred and was one of the largest congregations outside the main Jewish centers in Amsterdam, Rotterdam, and The Hague.[13]

The Napoleonic wars, which pitted England against French expansionism, and especially the British Orders-in-Council of 1805 that effectively blockaded the European continent, severely hurt international merchants such as the Dutch Jews who traded largely with London. Meyer Isaacs fell into debt after 1805 and by 1810 he had borrowed 6,300 florins from family and friends.[14] After Napoleon formally annexed the Netherlands in 1810 and sent in French occupation forces, Meyer Isaacs and other merchants, already financially strapped and increasingly fearful of the loss of their historic liberties and property, fled in 1814 to England, leaving behind their property and debts.

The Isaacs family settled in the Spitalfields section of East London, which became a Dutch Jewish center. Here Meyer Isaacs entered the rabbinate and gave early training to his sons, including Samuel, who was 10 years old when the family moved to London. This age was young enough for Samuel to learn to speak English

Fig. 3.2. Reverend Samuel M. Isaacs (1804–1878) of Congregation Shaaray Tefila, New York, NY. Reprinted from Simon Cohen, *Shaaray Tefila: A History of Its Hundred Years: 1845–1945* (New York, 1945).

without a Dutch accent. This ability later earned him many speaking engagements in America, where sermons and public addresses in English were much preferred to the customary Yiddish or German tongue.

Samuel attended public school, but as an orthodox Jewish teenager he also studied Hebrew, the Talmud, and Jewish history in the synagogue school and under the tutelage of his father. After completing his education Samuel taught Hebrew for a time at the Jewish Orphanage of London and then in the 1830s he became principal of a Jewish day school. This position enabled the young man to become well connected in the wider Jewish community. He developed a lifelong friendship with the famed Anglo-Jewish banker Sir Moses Montefiore, who shared his devotion to Palestine. He also became acquainted with Solomon Hirschel (Herschel, Herschell), the chief rabbi of the Great Synagogue of London and the leading rabbi in the entire British Empire.

The year 1839 marked the major turning point for the 35-year-old Hebrew educator. He was married in the Great Synagogue by Rabbi Hirschel himself; but shortly before this he had decided to emigrate to America with his bride in response to a call from the newly founded Ashkenazi congregation Bnai Jeshurun (Sons of Israel) of New York to be its first preacher and cantor. The congregation, an offshoot of Shearith Israel, was located in the midtown area on Elm Street at this time. The synagogue trustees had offered Isaacs the position without an interview but only after a "scrutinizing vigilance" of his credentials and on the recommendation of Solomon Cohen, a trusted intermediary in London. Undoubtedly, Isaacs's unique ability to preach in perfect English was a major factor in his appointment. A few days after his wedding, Isaacs and his new wife, Jane Symmons (1824–1884) of London, took their "honeymoon" trip to New York aboard the Brig *Emery*, arriving on September 10, 1839, after a lengthy two-month voyage on stormy seas.[15]

At his installation at Bnai Jeshurun on the last Saturday in September, Isaacs preached the first English sermon by a regular minister in any New York synagogue. His title was *hazan*, which signified the chief religious leader who acted as reader (cantor) at the services and conducted weddings and funerals. The *hazan* was recognized by the Gentile community as the "minister" of the congregation. Isaacs also preached on special holidays and every Sabbath service before the new moon. Regular preaching in the vernacular, following the model of Protestant ministers, was just entering the synagogue at this time. Isaacs had likely learned the innovative practice of weekly vernacular preaching (as compared with the traditional formal preaching on only two Sabbaths per year) from the London synagogue, which began English-language preaching in 1817.[16]

Bnai Jeshurun grew rapidly under Isaacs's leadership despite several secessions rooted in nationality sentiments. New immigrants more than made up for the defections. By 1839 Polish and German

76

Jews had withdrawn to form a new congregation, and in 1843 another German group seceded. But the major schism occurred in 1844 when a dissenting faction of young, antiestablishment German members, who disputed the outcome of elections for synagogue trustees controlled by the reigning leadership oligarchy, seized control of the Elm Street synagogue by force. Rather than fight, the leaders chose to withdraw quietly, along with *Hazan* Isaacs, the sexton (*shammas*) Benjamin M. Davis, also a Hollander, and at least ten other Holland families.[17]

The new congregation, organized formally in 1845, primarily by English and Dutch Jews, chose the name Shaaray Tefila (Gates of Prayer). Immediately before the split, Isaacs had declined a "flattering call" with a liberal salary from the growing Baltimore Hebrew Congregation.[18] His decision to remain perhaps led the unhappy faction to take direct action. Old World differences were too strong for harmony. Each nationality group and even people from particular localities demanded their own forms of worship among their own brethren. By 1860 the Portuguese, English, German, Polish, Dutch, and even regional subgroups worshiped separately, and the city counted twenty-seven synagogues.[19]

Isaacs's long tenure at Shaaray Tefila marked the high point of Orthodoxy in New York Judaism. In 1847 when the congregation dedicated its new Wooster Street synagogue (at 110–112 Wooster Street, between Spring and Prince streets), Isaacs's friend Rabbi Isaac Leeser of Philadelphia gave the major address. Leeser was the acknowledged leader of American Orthodox Judaism, and Isaacs was his associate and collaborator.[20] Isaacs devoted his pulpit to the defense of pure religion undefiled, calling the faithful to observe the full Mosaic law, the Levitical dietary rules and purification rites, and especially to keep the Sabbath. Honoring the Sabbath was difficult for Jewish retail merchants and clerks because Saturday was the major American shopping day, and state and local Sunday-closing laws often kept Jewish businesses closed on that day as well —until they won legal exemptions.[21]

Reverend Isaacs's second theme was to uphold Orthodoxy against the new Reform Judaism that German Jews were bringing to America in the 1840s. Among other worship practices, Reform introduced mixed choirs and instrumental music, integrated seating, prayers in English, abolition of head coverings and calling men up to the Torah, and confirmation for young women as well as young men. Reform congregations also were lax in enforcing religious discipline and Sabbath-keeping.

Isaacs challenged these new ideas "from the fertile fields of

Germany, where everything grows fast, although not always wholesome." What is at issue, he warned, is that Jews are "assimilating our system to that of Christianity. . . . Shame on those Rabbis who have A.D. in their thoughts." In 1840, within a year of his arrival, Isaacs led a movement to exclude nonobserving Jews from membership in Bnai Jeshurun. But the majority favored benign tolerance and Isaacs could only wield his pen. He lamented, "In the days of yore, violators were . . . publicly stoned to death, . . . but now . . . we court their society, give them the first honors in the Synagogue, [and] call them up to hear that law recited which anathematizes the Sabbath-violator. We behold the hands of sacrilege destroying the ten commandments." There is no place for a doctrine of "the *minimum* God, the *maximum* man," he thundered. Such strong sentiments led historian Hyman Grinstein to declare that Isaacs was "without doubt the most ardent exponent of Sabbath observance in New York City prior to the Civil War."[22]

Isaacs also admonished the women of his congregation for not washing in the ritual pool (*mikveh*), which he had carefully constructed according to the guidelines of Rabbi Abraham Rice of Baltimore. He even attributed the recent deaths of several young married women in the congregation to God's anger at their direct disregard of the law of purity.[23]

Isaacs's goal was to safeguard the rank and file of American Jewry from Reform: "My object is . . . to prove, from facts, that our system of worship, apart from its *temporalities*, is the best of all systems; and to adduce evidence that adding or diminishing, abrogating, or altering our form of prayers, handed down to us from the Men of the Great Synod, . . . at the will or caprice of men, who, however well-intentioned, are yet tinctured with the spirit of the age and are not capable of judging correctly or dispassionately—that reforms so instituted—will lead to inevitable ruin in our polity, and tend to unfetter the chain by which we have ever been riveted in union and in love."[24] Clarion calls such as this put Isaacs at the forefront of the defense of Orthodoxy in New York and throughout the country.

Shaaray Tefila prospered under Reverend Isaacs. The liturgy, ritual, and physical arrangement of seating all conformed to the requirements of Orthodoxy. But the worship services were tempered by such "Protestantizing" practices as regular vernacular preaching from English-language Jewish Bibles. Also, Isaacs's expanded role as minister of the congregation was more akin to an Episcopal priest than a traditional cantor. The appreciative congregation increased their rabbi's salary regularly from $1,200 in 1845 to $3,500 by the end of his tenure in the 1870s. The congregation also showed their high regard for his services by buying a $5,000 insurance policy on the life of their leader. In 1851 when Shaaray Tefila gave their "worthy minister" permission to return to England for a three-month visit, his student, Aaron S. Solomon, also a Hollander, served as Reader for the congregation. On the Isaacs's silver wedding anniversary in 1864 the grateful congregation celebrated at a Sabbath service and presented them with a cash gift of $2,900! Nine years later, in 1873, at the gala celebration of Isaacs's seventieth birthday, the congregation's gift was an amazing $4,250.[25]

In the 1860s, the Uptown movement of Jews directly affected the synagogue. Orthodox Jews who lived Uptown would not ride on the Sabbath, so they transferred to nearby synagogues. In the face of declining membership and a growing indebtedness, Shaaray Tefila was forced to relocate Uptown. More than two-thirds of its contributing members lived above Fourteenth Street in 1863. In 1863 and 1864 the congregation discussed a proposed merger with the mother synagogue, Bnai Jeshurun, that also planned to move Uptown, but in the end Shaaray Tefila decided to build on their own. The spirit of rivalry was too great to overcome.[26] Shaaray Tefila sold its Wooster Street synagogue in 1864, and after worshiping for five years in a rented building on Broadway at Thirty-sixth Street, in 1869 they dedicated a newly built $150,000 synagogue on Forty-fourth Street at Sixth Avenue, about two miles to the north, where they worshiped until 1894.[27] Barnett L. Solomon, another Hollander, was president of Shaaray Tefila during this relocation, and the longtime sextons, also Dutch, were Benjamin M. Davis, Isaac Bildersee, and Isaac's son Barnett. Davis held the post from 1847 until his death in 1858; Isaac Bildersee then served until his death in 1872. Both funerals were "largely attended." Isaacs's sons Myer and then Isaac served as clerk of the congregation for many years. Because of the "flourishing condition" of the congregation, their minister's workload was so heavy that the trustees in 1865 hired an assistant "to conduct the service according to the ancient liturgy with the accepted tunes, leaving the duties of Preacher more especially to the veteran of the New York pulpit."[28]

In 1857 Samuel Isaacs carried the fight against Reform to the wider Jewish community by launching a periodical, the *Jewish Messenger*, which he made an effective organ for Orthodoxy (see Fig. 3.3). He set the tone and established his themes in the initial ringing editorials, "Mammon Worship," which condemned materialism; "Our Divine Law," which commended true religion as the "boon and boast of Israel throughout the dispersion"; and "The Want of Union," which advocated a super board to safeguard Judaism in

Fig. 3.3 The *Jewish Messenger* (New York), first edition masthead, January 2, 1857.

democratic America. The *Jewish Messenger* also promoted unified Jewish charities, day schools and seminaries, and orphan asylums. The rabbi turned journalist enlisted in the struggle his sons Myer, Abram, and Isaac as writers and assistant editors.[29]

A few years before his death, Isaacs took yet another bold step to save historic Judaism. To stem the growing secularization among the young, he agreed somewhat reluctantly to support a radical plan proposed by Reverend Sabato Morais of Philadelphia's Mikveh Israel Congregation to prepare a liberalized and simplified Ashkenazic worship rite acceptable to all American synagogues. The time for nationality synagogues with distinctive rites had passed, Isaacs believed,

Portuguese and German, Polish and Hollander, in connection with the manner of worshipping Israel's God, are names that should, long ere this, have been erased from our nomenclature. . . . The badge we all should have proudly worn is that of "American Jews;" . . . signifying that the circumstances which had given origin to marked differences in ritual had ceased to exist, and that the necessity for reconstructing another, perfectly uniform, and more conformable to our changed condition, had arrived.[30]

Isaacs in 1875 published the revolutionary proposal and warmly endorsed it in his *Jewish Messenger*, but the plan was stillborn, even though it stimulated widespread debate. It pleased neither the ardent Orthodox nor the Reform wings who were rallying behind Isaac M. Wise's successful prayer book *Minhag America*. And Isaacs's declining health and approaching retirement made it impossible for him to carry the crusade. Apart from a universal worship rite, he opposed any change in law or custom that deviated from the traditional ritual of worship, and he especially opposed any plans to remove Hebrew from the prayer book. Judaism, he insisted, was a religion based on traditional law that could only change slowly with the authority of generations and it must keep its link to the ancient land of Israel.[31]

In addition to his ministerial and journalistic work, Isaacs promoted the customary Jewish tenets of charity, Palestinian relief, and religious education. His motto was, "Not to touch the worship, but to improve the worshippers." Morais aptly characterized him as a "humble Jew to whom the needy turned with confiding looks; with affection." His early editorials in the *Jewish Messenger* advocated the founding of an orphanage in New York by harping on the disgraceful case of a Jewish orphan placed in a Christian institution and converted there, all because no Jewish asylum existed. With the famous Mortara affair (the supposed child stealing and baptism of a Jewish child by Italian Catholics) fresh in the minds of world Jewry in 1858–1859, this appeal brought immediate action. The Hebrew Benevolent Society established the Hebrew Orphan Asylum of New York in 1859. Subsequently, Isaacs worked assiduously to combine all Jewish charities in the city by organizing the United Hebrew Charities in 1873. He also helped establish Mount Sinai Hospital (1852) and served as its first vice president.[32]

Internationally, Isaacs crusaded for Palestinian relief and as early as 1849 began long-term fund-raising efforts. In 1853 he became treasurer of the North American Relief Society for Indigent Jews in Palestine, a position he held for many years. When news came of a massive famine in Palestine in 1853–1854, Isaacs was the "first to take action; the other ministers followed his lead." He mounted the first national campaign in the United States for the relief of Jews overseas. Reverend Isaacs's exceptional efforts earned him the accolade "champion of charitable institutions."[33]

In Palestinian relief, the Dutch Jews in New York also responded to appeals from the Amsterdam Relief Committee, Pekidim and Amarkalim, headed by the Dutch merchant banker and religious leader Zevi Hirsh Lehren (1784–1853), to help Holy Land famine victims. Funds raised among the more prosperous New Yorkers were channeled through a newly formed New York branch Hebrah (1832) to the committee in Amsterdam. This cooperative effort shows the continuing links between Dutch American Jews and their homeland.[34]

These ties were of long standing. Already in the seventeenth century, the Amsterdam Synagogue mothered North American Jews by sending prayer books, bibles, and sacred scrolls. The worship services of Shearith Israel from the earliest days followed the Sephardic ritual of Amsterdam; but later in the eighteenth century London rites were introduced and blended with those of Amsterdam. By the nineteenth century Bnai Jeshurun and other Ashkenazic synagogues in New York recognized the primary authority of the Great Synagogue in London and its chief rabbi, but they also maintained close relations with Amsterdam. Thus, London gained the ascendancy and Amsterdam had a secondary role.[35]

Isaacs also promoted Jewish education, decrying the fact that Jewish children sat under Gentile teachers in the public schools. "We betray a culpable negligence in the proper religious training of our children," he charged. In 1842 Isaacs converted his congregation's afternoon school into an all-day English and Hebrew school, the New York Talmud Torah and Hebrew Institute, with the Dutch-born Henry Goldsmith as teacher of Hebrew. Although the school began strongly with 80 boys and was one of only three in the entire country, it failed within five years because of financial difficulties. Isaacs was not easily discouraged. In 1852 his congregation again founded a day school, the Bnai Jeshurun Educational Institute, which boasted an enrollment of 177 pupils within a year; but it too had to close after three years (1855) because of insufficient students.[36]

The Hebrew free school movement struggled because the New York State legislature had secularized all public schools by eliminating Protestant textbooks and by allowing local school boards, whether in Catholic or Jewish hands, to choose daily Scripture readings. In Jewish neighborhoods only Old Testament passages were read. Jewish children began flooding to the public schools thereafter and all Jewish synagogue schools had closed by 1860. Isaacs considered this an unmitigated tragedy, since the 30,000 Jews in the city surely provided the potential pupils for many religious schools. The rabbi did succeed, however, in 1857 in establishing the Hebrew High school, and he acted as principal and Hebrew teacher for many years. The school thrived as a boarding institution and offered a college preparatory curriculum.[37]

Isaacs finally in 1864 gained support to establish the all-day Hebrew Free School No. 1, which was soon followed by three evening schools that taught only Hebrew. Isaacs's fellow Hollanders, *Hazan* M. R. de Leeuw and associates of the Dutch congregation Bnai Israel, spearheaded the effort. The schools enrolled five hundred students by 1869 and provided a "sound religious education" for many decades. Nevertheless, Isaacs described the battle for religious education as "uphill work"; advocates faced a constant battle against the "hostility and indifference of the community."[38]

The Dutch rabbi particularly decried the lack of Hebrew seminaries and colleges to provide educated leaders, "Synagogues are crying aloud for ministers," he said, "and there are none to respond to the call. Jewish children are hungering for religious food . . . and there is none to supply the desideratum; and this in free and happy America! Where are our collegiate establishments? Where our theologian institutes?" In 1867 Isaacs achieved his goal by helping establish Maimonides College of Philadelphia, the first theological seminary for Jews in the United States. Unfortunately, the college failed after a few years through no fault of Isaacs. In 1872 the *Jewish Messenger* sadly lamented the fact that "there is not a single Jewish pulpit in America occupied by a minister instructed on our soil."[39] This had to await the founding of Hebrew Union College in Cincinnati in 1875.

Besides his religious activities, Isaacs also involved himself in political issues, especially in efforts to defend Jews worldwide against antisemitic outbursts and to unify Judaism in America. Only a year after his own immigration, the famous Damascus Affair of 1840 provided the first opportunity. This international crusade, which aimed to rescue a number of Jews imprisoned in Syria, is sometimes considered the beginning of modern Jewish history because it aroused a latent national consciousness and identity. Isaacs and Henry I. Hart, another Hollander at Bnai Jeshurun, served on a seven-member committee of correspondence to coordinate a petition drive calling on the American government to intervene. Out of this effort, Isaacs joined with Rabbi Isaac Leeser, the conservative leader of Philadelphia, to help unify all American Jews. In 1849 and 1850 Isaacs sent out numerous appeals for an all-Jewish convention or synod to promote the "welfare of Israel" by developing a uniform synagogue government and by establishing Hebrew seminaries and colleges to provide educated leaders for the future. Reform leaders refused to cooperate and the unity movement failed.

At the outset of the Civil War Isaacs made yet another attempt to restore law and order to the disjointed and religiously confused Jewish community. He proposed through the pages of the *Jewish Messenger* that the learned and esteemed Orthodox Rabbi Abraham Rice of Baltimore be elected chief rabbi of the United States since American Judaism was a body without a head to guide it. The proposal met with a storm of criticism from independent-minded Jewish leaders and Isaacs was forced to abandon his plan.[40]

Isaacs also joined the Jewish protest chorus in the Mortara affair through the columns of the *Jewish Messenger* and by chairing a combined committee of all twelve synagogues in New York City.[41] The committee sponsored a mass meeting of two thousand persons, both Jews and Protestants, to petition the American president to intervene with the Vatican. When this effort proved unsuccessful, because American Jewry was too disorganized, Isaacs in 1859 led in the founding of the Board of Delegates of American Israelites in New York. Again he used his paper to generate enthusiasm and overcome resistance from independent-minded rabbis. This board, under the leadership of Isaac Leeser of Philadelphia, expanded into a national organization of all Orthodox congregations with the goal of becoming a type of national synod or general governing board. But the Reform Jews, taking their cue from Rabbis David Einhorn and Isaac M. Wise, refused to affiliate. The board worked to secure and maintain Jewish civil and religious rights at home and abroad. Samuel Isaacs's son, Myer Samuel Isaacs, served as secretary of the board until 1876 when he became president. He was one of the key men on the board during its history. A fellow Hollander Henry Hart, also of Shaaray Tefila, served as the first president until his death in 1863.[42]

Reverend Isaacs's public activities and unusual facility in the English language gave him a high visibility. Jews and nonJews alike greatly esteemed him, and Protestant intellectuals and clerics particularly respected him. In 1845 several professors at Yale College and the mayor of New Haven, CT, invited him to lecture on the topic, "On the Present Condition and Future Spiritual and Temporal Hopes of Jews." When Shaaray Tefila dedicated their new Wooster Street synagogue in 1847 many Protestant clergymen attended and several spoke to the congregation. When a steam engine exploded at a large factory in New York City in 1849, killing several Gentile husbands and fathers, Isaacs's congregation raised $230 for the families. Although many Christian churches joined in the collection, Wooster Street was the only Jewish synagogue to participate and the act of charity did not go unnoticed.[43] In 1850 Isaacs raised $150 for Saint Vincent's Hospital of Detroit in response to a personal appeal from the Sisters of Charity who had provided care to several indigent Jews because there was as yet no Jewish congregation in the city. This may be the first public Jewish contribution to a Christian charity. Three years earlier Isaacs had convened a special meeting that raised $80 for Irish famine relief.[44]

Isaacs believed that Jews as Jews "have no politics" and he steadfastly refused to comment on political questions, even when readers during the developing crisis demanded to know his views. "We have no wish or inclination to meddle in politics," he declared in October of 1860. "Religion and politics have little in common; American Israelites, most decidedly, object to hold identical political opinions, as they do doctrinal matters." For Isaacs, theological unity was as right as political unity was wrong. But when his beloved Union began to break apart after Abraham Lincoln's election, he could hold back no longer. "Stand by the Flag!" he cried after the shelling of Fort Sumter brought on the Civil War. Thereafter, Isaacs endeared himself to the northern public by using the pages of the *Jewish Messenger* ardently to defend the Union and the war effort, even at the expense of losing his Southern readership. "We want subscribers," he editorialized, "for without them we cannot publish a paper, and Judaism needs an organ; but we want much more truth and loyalty." By June 1861 the *Jewish Messenger* had lost so many Southern subscribers that Isaacs had to revert to a bi-weekly publication schedule to stem the red ink.[45]

Isaacs ranked the survival of the Union far above the abolition of slavery. He was well acquainted with prominent antislavery leaders such as Professor Calvin E. Stowe, husband of Harriet Beecher Stowe and a prominent philosemite, and in 1856 Isaacs campaigned for the antislavery candidate, John Charles Frémont. But Isaacs refrained from preaching antislavery sermons by claiming that he did not want to "broach Biblical arguments for or against slavery [that are] calculated to enflame the violence of either section." Like Lincoln at first, he strongly defended the Union cause "with or without slavery." But as the president and Congress moved toward emancipation, Isaacs began bitterly to denounce slavery. After President Lincoln's assassination he was one of two ministers selected to give prayers at the public memorial services in Union Square.[46]

The *Jewish Messenger* was the only Jewish periodical that wholeheartedly supported the Union and thereby gained the approbation of the abolitionist weekly the *Independent*, which noted that Isaacs's stance "might well be imitated by certain professedly Christian Editors, who . . . by continually discoursing the evils of war, passively sympathize with those who would overthrow the Union." The Hebrew congregation of Shreveport, Louisiana, adopted a stinging resolution denouncing the *Jewish Messenger* as "a black Republican paper" that had abandoned religion for politics. Isaacs replied that it was not a political issue to be "loyal citizens of that great republic, which has even extended a welcome to the oppressed, and has ever protected Israel."[47]

Although never formally ordained, Isaacs was one of the leading Jewish ministers in the United States in the mid-nineteenth century. One of his colleagues called him the "father of the American Jewish clergy." His funeral service at Temple Shaaray Tefila in 1878 was the largest Jewish funeral of the century. Every synagogue and Jewish organization in the country sent representatives. Isaacs was a religious leader of major influence, a renowned journalist, and a mover and shaker in Jewish affairs. He was the first Jewish cleric to preach regularly in English in Ashkenazic synagogues, and he was much in demand as a guest speaker because of this ability.[48] Throughout his long career he was the featured speaker at some 47 synagogue dedication ceremonies across the country. He officiated at 812 weddings and not one was a mixed marriage, or "as far as my knowledge extends," ended in divorce. Isaacs was also the first to reach his seventieth year while in office.[49]

But he was most honored for his defense of Orthodoxy. Colleagues eulogized him as "a faithful proponent" of Judaism who "lamented the increasing defection amidst our ranks; the prevailing disloyalty to the sinaitic covenant." An eminent Christian clergyman in a glowing tribute sent to Isaacs's sons described their father as "a bulwark of strength against the infidelity and godlessness that are growing upon us in this great city. His firm devotion to God's holy word brought him into direct and cordial sympathy with us Christians. . . . May his mantle rest on his children. Your father's death is a public calamity. Who shall fill his place? Our city could better spare millions of its money than one such resolute watchman and soldier in its moral defense."[50]

Ironically, within two years of Isaacs's death, Congregation Shaaray Tefila began going over to Reform led by the new minister, Rabbi Dr. Frederic de Sola Mendes, Isaacs's assistant since 1874, who ungraciously described his predecessor as "rigidly, obstinantly orthodox." The conservative Dutch contingent along with their

English and Polish compatriots resigned in the face of this revolution. Most of the German Jews, who tended toward Reform, remained. Thus the end of Dutch leadership marked a crucial turning point in the history of the Shaaray Tefila Congregation.[51] More broadly it signaled the waning influence in American Jewish life of the traditional British-Dutch-Polish amalgam, which had succumbed to the overwhelming numbers of German immigrants.

Reverend Isaacs, like his Dutch Calvinist counterparts in the Midwest, was a fiery champion of the old ways in religion. He was largely responsible for shaping unorganized New York Jewry into a coherent, articulate and respectable community. As the first English preacher in Ashkenazic congregations, Isaacs used the pulpit to preserve historic Judaism through strict religious observance, Hebrew education, and community self-help organizations. In the early years he was second only to Isaac Leeser of Philadelphia as the most influential Orthodox rabbi in America. This son of Friesland, whose family fled the oppression of Napoleon, cut a wide swath within American Judaism. He placed pulpit, pen, and podium in the service of Orthodoxy and valiantly fought against the forces of secularism and liberalism that were rotting the roots of the Jewish faith in the rising age of unbelief.

Bnai Israel, the "Netherdutch" Congregation

Several dozen Dutch Jewish families, mainly well-established pre-1830 immigrants, continued to worship at Shaaray Tefila as well as at the Bnai Jeshurun and Anshe Chesed synagogues. But all were mixed congregations and newer Dutch immigrants of the 1840s wanted to worship "according to the custom of the Jews of Holland." On April 1, 1847 about fifteen men, led by renowned restauranteur Leonard Gosling, met in the parlour of the old Shakespeare Hotel and organized a Netherland congregation. Gosling was chosen president and L. Fellerman vice-president. The sum of $98 was collected to defray the preliminary expenses. There were about one hundred Dutch Jewish families in New York City at this time, mostly Ashkenazi in background, and eventually at least sixty joined the Dutch congregation. On April 25 the group adopted the name Bnai Israel (Sons of Israel) and appointed as a building committee Myer S. Cohen, Simon Cohen Noot, and Joseph Samson.

One month later, on May 20, the congregation dedicated their first synagogue at 258 Williams Street, and on May 24 the members assembled again in the first congregational meeting to adopt a constitution and by-laws and elect Noot as minister and Emanuel de Young as secretary.[52]

A first hand report of the May 20 consecration service, published in the *Occident*, states bluntly: "The object of the founders of this Congregation was to have a Synagogue where they can worship according to the Amsterdam Minhag." The language of the Amsterdam rite was Yiddish (i.e., the Judeo-German idiom of eighteenth-century European Jewry) since the mother Ashkenazi synagogues in Amsterdam did not adopt the vernacular until the 1870s and virtually no Dutch Sephardi emigrated after 1790.[53] Secondarily, the seceders wanted to preserve Orthodoxy. Editor Leeser of the *Occident* observed with obvious approval: "Many of the members are anxiously endeavoring to induce others to a more strict observance of religion."[54] No records survive and the congregation apparently never published the customary souvenir historical booklet on its twenty-fifth anniversary; however, the occasion was reported extensively in the *Jewish Messenger*.[55]

Although they could not boast for several years of their own synagogue, the congregation did own all the necessary furniture and liturgical works, including a miniature Torah scroll that one of its members had brought from Holland. They borrowed regular Torah scrolls from Shearith Israel for the consecration service, but soon purchased two of their own.[56] The congregation also immediately purchased a cemetery on Seventy-first Street. Shortly after they added a second on Ninety-fifth Street and in 1885 bought a plot in the Washington cemetery, Parkville, Long Island. The cemeteries were administered by the Burial and Mutual Aid Society (Hebrah Ahavat Achim) organized in 1847, and a second society (Hebrah Etz Haim) formed in 1852. The congregation's finances in the first year were modest: $1,333 in receipts and $1,240 in expenses.[57]

It took the congregation thirteen years before they owned their own building. In 1850, after renting facilities on Williams Street and then at 154 Pearl Street (both in the Chatham Square area on the Lower East Side), they purchased land and cast a wide appeal for synagogue funds. But as a small group of recent immigrants, their plans were stymied by a lack of monies. Editor Leeser of the *Occident* reported:

Notwithstanding the good intentions of the members, they have not been able to afford the outlay to erect a proper building for themselves. They have, however, resolved to begin the work in earnest, and have already purchased a suitable piece of ground, but they lack the means to defray the expenses of the building. They have accordingly requested us to make a public appeal for them to the various congregations of America to aid them in their pious work, which we now cheerfully do.

Leeser urged the "pious-minded" to support this "worthy object" and to send their contributions to Abraham Leon, vice president of Bnai Israel, or to members Philip Lichtenstein, Philip Levy, and Moses S. Cohen who "are authorized to receive donations and subscriptions." Unfortunately, the appeal was in vain and the best the congregation could do was move in 1851 to a more "commodious" building at 63 Chrystie Street, between Walker and Hester streets, also on the Lower East Side and just across the street from Temple Emanu-El. The interior of the new synagogue was refurbished "at considerable expense" under the direction of the architect of the new synagogue in Charleston, SC. With much pride in their "handsome" new home, the congregation consecrated the synagogue on the "eve of passover," April 16, 1851.[58]

The first minister of Bnai Israel from 1847 until 1854 was the noted Dutch Hebrew scholar Simon Eliazer Cohen Noot. Noot was followed in rapid succession by David Davidson, Myer S. Cohen, Philip Levy, Joshua de Leon, Emanuel L. Goldsmith, M. R. de Leeuw (who served twelve years), and Noot's son Isaac C. (who served more than twenty years). When Gosling, the first president (*parnass*), moved temporarily to Poughkeepsie in late 1847, Henry de Boer took his place. De Boer then moved to Philadelphia shortly thereafter. So the congregation had each of the trustees beginning with Emanuel Pike serve in turn as *parnass*, one month at a time, until the next election when Moses S. Cohen was selected. Abraham Leon was the first vice president and treasurer. Cohen provided able leadership until his untimely death in 1852, from which loss the congregation did not recover for some time. His successor, A. Pakker, also died in office. Pakker's replacement was Aaron S. van Praag, a dental surgeon and relative of Cohen who had been treasurer of Bnai Israel. On taking office, Van Praag declared, "The spiritual condition of the congregation must be raised, if they wish not to become disorganized altogether." Van Praag's comment touches on the problems of high geographical mobility of New York Jews and also the informal organization of Bnai Israel.[59]

In the 1860s E. M. Ezekiel, Myer S. Cohen, Jacob Davis, and Solomon L. Gerrits served as presidents of the congregation. Cohen worked as well in the broader Jewish community, notably as Bnai Israel's representative and an officer of the Board of Delegates of American Israelites. Cohen occasionally addressed the congregation as reader and lecturer, as in the Thanksgiving Day service of 1860, and he taught Hebrew in its innovative Free Sunday School. He was also the Hebrew teacher at the Hebrew Free School until his untimely death in 1866. Jacob Gelder, Kasper Kese, and R. de Leeuw were the sextons in the 1860s.[60]

The Reverend Simon Noot had a crucial part in guiding Bnai Israel in its first decade, but, unlike Rabbi Isaacs, his heart was in teaching more than in the ministry. Thus he did not remain with the congregation until his death, as Rabbi Isaacs did at Shaaray Tefila. Noot was a teacher in the Jewish School of Amsterdam who emigrated in 1843 with his wife and four children. He came in response to a call by the Polish-Dutch congregation of Philadelphia, Beth Israel (House of Israel), to become its first regular minister. This new congregation, founded in 1840, elected Noot just before Passover in April 1843. A fellow Hollander David A. Phillips was sexton. Noot served for four years until the new "Netherdutch" synagogue of New York called him. Noot was technically a reader and teacher, he was not an ordained rabbi, but the perennial shortage of ordained clergymen in the early years made it necessary to use laymen. Noot's voice was "exceedingly harmonious, and his manner of reading exquisitely correct and impressive" according to one of his parishioners. The congregation also hired guest rabbis to fill the pulpit. Dr. W. Schlesinger, a recent arrival from Sulzbach, Germany, preached at various New York synagogues in 1849 and 1850 and was "frequently" at Bnai Israel.[61]

Reverend Noot had obtained an excellent Hebrew education in the Netherlands. As early as 1844 he advertised his *Hebrew Grammar* for sale for $6. As Editor Leeser of the *Occident* commented in 1852, "He is known as one of the best Hebraists in the country; and it is saying but little to assert, that those trained in Amsterdam, in the knowledge of the sacred languages, are excelled by none all over the world." Leeser added that Noot's "style of writing Hebrew is both pure and elegant."[62] Noot had demonstrated these skills in 1849 when the New York synagogues engaged him as one of only two professional scribes to write new Torah scrolls that were always in short supply in the American Jewish community. Noot later sold gilded bibles and other religious books purchased on consignment from Leeser.[63]

In addition to serving as a lay rabbi and reader of the Dutch synagogue, Noot devoted his considerable energies to Hebrew education, which he believed to be an indispensable requirement for every congregation. The small, young Bnai Israel congregation took on the "sacred cause of Education" from the outset and in 1847 established its first Hebrew school, the Academy of the Beginning of Wisdom. They appointed Noot as principal and teacher of Hebrew literature, language, and the Talmud.[64] This venture prompted Bnai Jeshurun, whose Talmud Torah Institute had been dissolved, to join the Bnai Israel venture and establish a combined institution. The Green Street Hebrew School (officially the Bnai Jeshurun Educational Institute) opened with 8 teachers and 88 pupils on January 2, 1852, with Noot as headmaster and Hebrew teacher. Attendance quickly climbed to 142, and in 1854 the school erected its own building on a vacant lot adjacent to the Bnai Jeshurun Synagogue on Green Street.[65]

Before leading the Green Street Hebrew School, Noot had held a part-time appointment in a secular school as teacher of Hebrew, Chaldean, and Talmud at Professor J. Sedgwick's academy on Sixth Avenue. Men preparing for the Christian ministry also sat under his tutelage there.[66] As a condition of Bnai Jeshurun's appointment to head its Green Street School, Noot resigned from Sedgwick's academy as well as reader at Bnai Israel.[67]

Two years later, in 1854, the Reverend Noot left New York City; his talents were needed elsewhere. First, the Dutch-Polish congregation of Ohabei Shalom, Massachusetts's first synagogue, called him to establish a Hebrew school for the Boston Jewish community. Noot went gladly and got the school fully underway within two years. Then late in 1855 he accepted a call to return to Philadelphia to become *hazan* of the recently established Dutch synagogue, Bnai Israel, founded in 1852.[68] Noot labored in the City of Brotherly Love for six years until 1862, serving as principal of the Hebrew Education Society school, which Isaac Leeser had conceived in 1847 and established in 1848. The school, which actually opened its doors first in 1851, grew to 170 pupils and became a fully accredited private school. In 1857 Simon Noot appointed his son, Isaac C., only seventeen years of age, as assistant Hebrew teacher at the school. Isaac was his father's assistant until 1864.[69]

In 1862 Simon Noot accepted a second call from Boston's Ohabei Shalom Synagogue to be its rabbi. He led the congregation in the construction of its second synagogue in 1863 and worked there until his death in 1867. Surely the Reverend Simon Eliazer Cohen Noot deserves careful study as one of the pioneer Hebrew educators and scholars of the nineteenth century in the United States. He served the Dutch synagogues of New York and Philadelphia, assisted the

Boston Dutch congregation, and built strong Hebrew schools in all three major centers of American Jewry.

The Bnai Israel Congregation enjoyed steady growth under Noot's successor, the Reverend M. R. de Leeuw, who became *hazan* in 1855 and ministered until 1867 when he became the sexton at Bnai Jeshurun. With his energetic and effective leadership, the congregation finally realized its dream of owning its own synagogue. By 1860 the group had grown very large, numbering more than 150 (male) members, and they again needed more space. A number of Germans affiliated in these years and rose to leadership positions, but the Dutch remained dominant. In June 1860 the trustees were fortunate to be able to purchase a large but unpretentious Presbyterian church building at 41 Stanton Street for $11,000. The edifice at the desirable corner of Forsythe Street was fifty feet wide and sixty feet in depth; it seated over six hundred. In two months the alterations were completed at a cost of $2,000, which included the purchase of some used synagogue furniture—a large reading desk, chandeliers, and an ark—from the recently renovated Crosby Street Synagogue of Shearith Israel. After repainting and redecorating the furniture, it was said to be "equal to new." The entire interior of the synagogue was "fitted up in a style at once simple and elegant" and "presented a brilliant appearance," especially the richly carved and elaborately ornate altar. A "superb chandelier" hung from the center of the ceiling. Solomon Gerrits donated a fine clock.[70]

On Sunday, August 5, 1860, the congregation consecrated their new synagogue before a "large and influential audience" of visiting dignitaries. Reverend De Leeuw began the ceremonies by appearing at the entrance door and proclaiming, "Open the gates of righteousness for me, that I may enter and praise the Lord." The male choir, which he conducted, responded: "This is the gate of the Lord, into which righteousness shall enter." At the ceremonial opening of the ark, De Leeuw sang a song composed by E. M. Lowenstamm, Chief Rabbi of Rotterdam, for the 1844 consecration of a new synagogue in The Hague. Jonas Solomon then lit the perpetual lamp. Several of the leading rabbis of New York participated. Rabbi Morris J. Raphall of Bnai Jeshurun, the first speaker, recalled the day eleven years ago when he spoke at the dedication of the Pearl Street synagogue. He said: "Though your beginning is but small, your program will be sure as long as you pursue the right." Raphall also remembered the consecration of the Chrystie Street synagogue, which was a "shrine superior to the original place of worship in Pearl Street as a palace [is] to a shanty." And now the fine new synagogue! Certainly the congregation "deserved the success. . . . Union and adherence to principle had occasioned their prosperity."[71]

Samuel M. Isaacs of Shaaray Tefila, a fellow Hollander, then took the lead role by giving the dedication address also in English. Isaacs used the opportunity, as always, to defend Orthodoxy. "No dissimulation must tarnish our sanctuary," he admonished. He reminded the hearers that "although they had built those strong walls within which to rest secure in the worship of the Most High, yet that hydra-headed monster, whose name is Reform and whose approach is destruction, is even now battering at the gates to enter and steal away the faith." The Rabbi adjured them "not to alter the prayers composed by their ancestors." In Holland, he reminded them, they had been "steadfast adherents to the Judaism of their ancestors." Therefore, he concluded, "reform your hearts—but touch not the tree that stood firmly three thousand years. Let not the smallest inroad be made in the landmarks of our faith." Donations received after Isaacs's discourse totaled $500. Rabbi Jonah Bondi of Congregation Anshe Chesed then spoke briefly in German, after which Rev. De Leeuw closed the service in a "beautiful prayer" in Hebrew and chanted Psalm 150 with the choir.[72] The Stanton Street Synagogue certainly enjoyed an auspicious beginning.

Within months of the dedication service, the ambitious Netherlandic congregation launched a Hebrew Free Sunday School "for the education of young Israelites of both sexes, in the Jewish religion." This was the pioneer of such schools in the city. Several "talented and pious ladies" of the congregation did the teaching. Attendance reached 250 after one year and included children from nearby congregations and from families with no affiliation. Editor Isaacs of the *Jewish Messenger* applauded the efforts and urged "older Kehilas" (congregations) to emulate the young congregation. He also suggested contributing funds for supplies and books since Bnai Israel is "not a very wealthy congregation, and cannot be expected unaided to supply the scholars who are instructed gratuitously, in books, etc." Isaacs's only lament was that the curriculum included no Hebrew instruction and very little Jewish history. In 1863 Bnai Israel staff led in the formation of the Hebrew Free Sunday School Teacher's Association of New York; all but two of the initial officers were Dutch. But the next year all resigned en masse in a policy dispute.[73]

For the next years Reverend De Leeuw took his place among the leaders of New York Jewry. He delivered timely sermons at special services such as the National Fast Day in October of 1861, annual Thanksgiving Day services, and the memorial service after President Lincoln's assassination in 1865. With the synagogue "very tastefully draped in mourning emblems," De Leeuw spoke eloquently of the fallen leader, equating him with Moses who also saw the Promised Land but could not enter it.[74]

De Leeuw's hallmarks were his fervent prayers and excellent choirs. His Bnai Israel choir participated in dedication services at several city synagogues and his Sunday School choirs performed regularly at school programs. "It is delightful to hear them intone in concert, the beautiful Hebrew melodies," remarked editor Isaacs in the *Jewish Messenger.*[75]

Hazan De Leeuw represented Congregation Bnai Israel at meetings of city-wide Orthodox Jewish organizations—the Association of United Hebrew Congregations, the Shecheetah convention (which licensed ritual slaughterers), and the New York Mutual Protective Matzoh Association (which licensed ritual bakers). He spoke in 1866 at a meeting of the Hebrew Benevolent Society demanding that Jewish orphans under their care must be raised Orthodox. As the newly appointed principal of the Hebrew Free School No. 1, De Leeuw's words carried clout.[76]

The Reverend Isaac C. Noot succeeded De Leeuw as school principal and reader of the Dutch congregation. Noot had returned to New York in 1864 to succeed Myer Cohen as Hebrew instructor at the Hebrew Free school. A theological conservative like his father, Noot joined the ministerial profession in 1871 by accepting the post of regular reader at Congregation Darech Amuno. He quickly proved himself and a year later, the Dutch congregation claimed their native son. Bnai Israel enjoyed "quite a revival" under the able Noot, together with the popular synagogue president M. S. Cohen and vice-president Abraham Leon. Remarkably, the fathers of all three officers had held the very same posts in the pioneer years. In 1874 the *Jewish Messenger* reported, concerning Noot's reappointment to a three-year term: "The Rev. Mr. Noot lectures smoothly in English, and enjoys the favor and esteem of his congregation." The fact that Noot lectured only in English dates the congregation's transition away from the Dutch language to the early 1870s. At this time only three synagogues in New York (out of thirty) had rabbis able to lecture in English.

The twenty-fifth anniversary of Bnai Israel on June 16, 1872 was a festive occasion, with the synagogue at 41 Stanton Street decorated lavishly in bunting and flowers. The ladies' auxiliary presented Rev. Noot an "elegant" cap and robe, President Cohen recounted a brief history of the congregation, and the Rev. Isaacs of Shaaray Tefila fondly recalled his Dutch roots in the sermon. Rev. Noot closed with expressions of gratitude and amazement that he should be "filling the father's place." At the conclusion of the service, the congregation surprised the aged Rev. Isaacs with the gift of a gold-handled, ebony cane to guide his steps "in the down hill of life." Isaacs had always supported and encouraged his fellow Hollanders.[77]

94

In charitable endeavors, the Dutch congregation in its early years tended to act independently. In 1848 Reverend Noot raised Palestine relief funds by selling at a public auction thirty-two kegs of kosher wine that a Palestinian missionary had brought to America. In 1853 the congregation responded to a request from New Orleans to New York Jewry for help to buy a new burial ground for fever victims in the epidemic of 1853. Although the amount of the Dutch contribution ($70) compared favorably with that of other congregations, they met separately at their synagogue chambers on Chrystie Street to raise the funds and they forwarded the monies directly.[78]

By the late 1850s the Dutch cooperated in wider Jewish efforts. In the campaign to raise funds for Jewish relief in Palestine, all of the New York synagogues combined their efforts in 1832 in the Society for Offerings of the Sanctuary (Hebrah Terumat Hakodesh) and pledged a fixed yearly contribution. But the Hollander Sons of Israel, faithful to Amsterdam's Rabbi Zevi Hirsch Lehren, organized their own relief society (Hebrah Herumat) in 1848 and contributed funds as needed to Palestinian emissaries through Amsterdam. It is not known if they ever affiliated with this combined organization, which dissolved in the early 1850s. However, the Stanton Street Synagogue did participate from the outset in 1859 in the Board of Delegates of American Israelites, the national organization of Orthodox congregations, which had continuing ties with the Amsterdam committee. In 1878 the Dutch body also joined the Board's successor organization, the Union of American Hebrew Congregations. They contributed to the Alliance Israélite Universelle for the relief of Russian Jews and in 1886 they sent delegates to the organizational meeting of the Jewish Theological Seminary.[79]

In local benevolence the Dutch always worked cooperatively. During the 1857 economic crisis the Reverend Isaacs in the *Jewish Messenger* called on the city's congregations to create a united benevolent society to combat the rising poverty. Bnai Israel delegated its president, Myer S. Cohen, and trustee Lyon Berhard to join an ad hoc board of representatives of nine Orthodox congregations. Throughout 1858 and 1859 the board aided the Jewish poor. Similarly, before Passover in 1861 and again at Rev. Isaacs's behest, Bnai Israel hosted representatives from seven congregations to raise funds to supply the poor with passover bread. From its formation in 1865 the Bnai Israel Ladies' Benevolent Society raised funds for the poor and needy by staging charity balls and other social events. The congregation also contributed its share to the Hebrew Free Burial Society.[80]

The Dutch Jews also organized their own health insurance and burial society. On December 10, 1859, twelve men formed the "Tree of Life" Society, which was officially incorporated as the Netherland Israelitisch Sick Fund (Nederland Israelitisch Ziekenfonds).[81] NISF stated in its provisional regulations: "Let us then unite so that this tree will produce the best fruit and so that its roots will never cease to exist." The names of only seven of the brothers are known; these were the trustees Benjamin S. de Young (who served as president for more than thirty years), Joseph Polak, Simon Winkel (long time secretary), Louis Polak, Abraham van der Poorten, Wolf van Praag, and Lewis Benjamin. These first members, five of whom were citizens of the United States, lived on the Lower East Side near the present Brooklyn Bridge.[82]

The NISF statement of purpose is typical of ethnic associations that provide insurance against catastrophic expenses. "The object of this Society shall be to provide services of doctors for members, their wives, and their children; to pay its members sick benefits; to pay death benefits upon the death of either a member or his wife; to provide burial for a member, his wife or their children; and such other benefits as are set forth and in accordance with the laws provided in the Constitution or amendments thereto." The mottos of the association were the proverb *Eendracht maakt macht* (Union is strength) and the English dictum "Utility is our aim." The NISF initially purchased two cemeteries at the Bayside Cemetery near Ozone Park in Queens, known as Acacia Cemetery and Bayside Cemetery.[83] At some time in the nineteenth century, one group of Dutch, who took the name United Brethren, seceded and bought their own cemetery near the Acacia Cemetery of the NISF, under the motto *Sjewet Achiem* (Brethren Who Dwell Together). This splintering is another example of the proverb "One Dutchman—a theologian. Two Dutchmen—a church. Three Dutchmen—a schism." In July of 1873 the large and prosperous NISF held its "first annual excursion" up the Hudson River on two commodious steamers replete with a fine band for the occasion. The NISF exists to the present day, although the average age of its board members is over eighty years.[84]

The depression of 1873 took its toll on the Dutch congregation and the synagogue mortgage went into default in 1878. To save the building, the body considered accepting an offer to consolidate from a 135-member Hungarian congregation, but the majority "did not wish to lose its nationality" and rejected the merger, much to the chagrin of the minority. So the beautiful Stanton Street Synagogue was sold under duress for $20,000 to the Roman Catholic Church and the Dutch rented the Golden Rule Hall at 125 Rivington Street. In January the Hollanders purchsed for $600 a building lot in a dense Jewish neighborhood two miles northeast at 289 East Fourth Street near Avenue C, and they began construction of a smaller $10,000 brick two-story ediface to seat three hundred.[85]

The cornerstone-laying ceremony in June drew "a large assemblage." *Hazan* Noot admonished his congregants to "defend their holy faith" and strengthen the "fraternal bond," after which Dr. Berhard, the oldest member, handled the silver trowel. In September the Fourth Street Synagogue was dedicated in another dramatic ceremony. Reverend Noot led the Torah circuit to the historic and impressive Ark that had originally graced the Portuguese Synagogue on Crosby Street. Trustee Michael E. Goodhart lit the Perpetual Lamp and the Reverend Abram S. Isaacs, the late Samuel's son, urged the congregation to launch a Sabbath afternoon children's service. "Too many synagogues have become asylums for the aged and infirm, in which the child's face is rarely seen, the child's prayer rarely heard," declared Isaacs. For the congregation "to make their orthodoxy more than a name and a memory, they must observe the great unwritten commandment, honor thy children, that their spiritual life be prolonged."[86]

The Reverend Noot, an educator by profession, heartily endorsed the proposal and within months he had three to four hundred neighborhood youth regularly attending the Children's Synagogue. Nearly six hundred came to the Hanukkah service in 1881, 1882 and 1883; more had to be turned away, the "throng being so great." Dr. David Brekes and Benjamin S. de Young assisted in the work, which gave Bnai Israel a very visible presence in their community. The flourishing congregation in 1881 rewarded Noot with a salary increase and another three-year term as *hazan*. The Dutch synagogue had not only survived the fiscal crisis and kept its identity, but it found its niche in an active youth ministry.[87]

The good times did not last, however, and the Dutch synagogue dwindled in membership as families moved uptown to more affluent districts. In 1897, Bnai Israel also moved to East Seventy-ninth Street. Sometime after 1902 the congregation disbanded and the group continued only as the NISF funeral association.[88] The day of the nationality congregation had passed for the Dutch.

Other Dutch Notables

In addition to the Reverends Samuel Isaacs and Simon Noot, Dutch laymen provided leadership for the New York

97

Jewish community. Van Praag served for over thirty-six years—beginning in 1837 as president of the Hebrew Mutual Benefit Society (Hebrah Gemilut Hesed)—along with fellow Hollanders Simon Noot, Alexander Canter, Jonas Solomon, Henry Goldsmith, Emanuel de Young, and John and Mark Levy. The society, founded in 1826 by Bnai Jeshurun, was the first mutual aid society in New York. It helped Jews in distress by providing health and accident insurance, burial rites, food for the indigent, care for widows and orphans, and immigrant aid. Representatives also met newly arrived Jewish immigrants at the docks and found them lodging, jobs, and religious fellowship.[89] This organization represented the pride inherent in Jews who refused to solicit aid from public charities; rather, they took care of their own as a religious obligation.[90]

Associated with Van Praag in Jewish charities and education was Henry Goldsmith, a noted Hebrew scholar cast in the same mould as Simon Noot. Goldsmith taught Hebrew in Isaacs's Talmud Torah School in the early 1840s and was an assistant *hazan* and clerk of Bnai Jeshurun in the 1840s and 1850s. Goldsmith became secretary of the Hebrew Benevolent Society in 1843 and continued for more than twenty-five years. He frequently wrote for the *Jewish Messenger* and the *Occident* in defense of Orthodoxy and of the necessity of teaching Hebrew to Jewish youth. As the able Hebrew teacher at Bnai Jeshurun's day school, Goldsmith was "highly praised for his fine work." In 1845 his class "could translate most of the Pentateuch, and two of its members were able to read and translate *Rashi*, an accomplishment which was unheard of in the city at that time." Goldsmith's salary was $6 a week, according to a letter of his father, for which he taught "Rashi, Bioer, Eben Ezer and Gemore [Talmud], he now teaches Sanhedren, is very big in Hebrew, is a pupil of [Heinrich F. H.] Gesenius." Subsequently, Goldsmith practiced law in New York City.[91]

Other Dutch lay leaders in synagogue life, besides those in the Shaaray Tefila and Bnai Israel congregations, were the Reverend Moses L. M. Peixotto of Shearith Israel; Marcus van Gelderen, the first kosher butcher of Bnai Jeshurun in the 1820s and 1830s and later president of Anshe Chesed Synagogue (Van Gelderen was certified by the *hakum* in Amsterdam); Eleazer Metz, *shohet* and *hazan* at Anshe Chesed from 1829 to 1834; Mayer M. Cohen, *shohet* in the 1840s; Henry Goldsmith, clerk of Bnai Jeshurun (1845–1854); Emanuel de Young, assistant *hazan* and secretary-clerk of Bnai Jeshurun (1854–1894); and Jacob Lewis, president of Congregation Beth El. In the late 1850s Dutch Jews led the Hebrah Brotherly Love Mutual Benefit Society of Congregation Anshe Chesed, including Barnett Levy, president; Moses Fellerman, vice president; and directors Solomon Gerrits, Louis Korper, and Isaiah Goldsmith. There are many other Hollanders who were active in the Jews' Hospital of New York, the Young Men's Hebrew Benevolent and Fuel Association, the Bachelor's Hebrew Benefit and Loan Association, the Board of Delegates of American Israelites, and other religious and civil societies.[92]

Second-generation Dutch Jews continued to provide leadership. Harmon Hendricks, Uriah's son, presided over Shearith Israel from 1824 to 1826. Simon Noot's son, Isaac, taught Hebrew in the New York Hebrew Free School. Moses Peixotto's son Daniel, a physician and medical professor trained at Columbia, was editor of the *Medical and Physical Journal* of New York from 1827 to 1830. In 1829 he became a fellow of the College of Physicians and Surgeons, and from 1830 to 1832 he served as president of the New York Medical Society. From this bully pulpit, he defended the emerging medical profession against quack doctors, even petitioning the state legislature for medical licensing laws. He particularly worked to require smallpox vaccinations only by "regular" doctors. In 1830 he helped organize a great democratic rally in New York of thirty thousand Jacksonians to celebrate the triumph of the July Revolution in France. As a practicing Jew, Dr. Peixotto also promoted Hebrew benevolent and educational societies such as the Hebrew Literary and Religious Library Association, and on occasion he gave "public discourses" or sermons at Synagogue Shearith Israel such as one in 1830 that lauded the rabbinic contributions of his father to the congregation. From 1835 to 1839, Dr. Peixotto was the first president and professor of medicine at the Willoughby (Ohio) Medical College. His wife Rachel was a daughter of the prominent New York merchant Benjamin Seixas, one of the founders of the New York Stock Exchange, and a member of one of the pioneer Jewish families in America.[93]

Reverend Isaacs's three sons, Myer S., Abram S., and Isaac S., all born in New York City, also became community leaders. Myer, the eldest son, graduated from New York University Law School, specialized in real estate law, and was appointed judge of the Marine (later City) Court of New York City. He was vice president of the New York Real Estate Exchange and took an active part in Republican politics. In benevolence he served as vice president of the Hebrew Free School Association, trustee of Maimonides College of Philadelphia, helped establish the Montefiore Home, held the posts of secretary (1859–1868) and then president (1868–1878) of the Board of Delegates of American Israelites, and was president of the

Baron de Hirsch Fund. In 1867 Myer traveled to London and Paris on behalf of the board to confer with his counterparts there about the condition of Jews in Palestine. In his absence, his brother Isaac was secretary to the board. For twenty years Myer worked with his father and brother Isaac as editors of the *Jewish Messenger* but stepped down after his father's death. Abram, the second son, graduated from New York University, earned a doctorate from the University of Breslau (Poland), and became professor of Semitic languages at New York University. He was also an ordained minister of the East Eighty-sixth Street Synagogue in the 1880s and later (1896–1905) of the Bnai Jeshurun congregation in Paterson, NJ. He succeeded his father as editor of the *Jewish Messenger* until it merged with the *American Hebrew* in 1903. He used pulpit and pen to promote religious tolerance. Isaac, the youngest son was a lawyer and editor and a prime mover in organizing the YMHA.[94]

Morris Goodhart (Goedhart) was born in Amsterdam in 1838 and migrated to New York in 1846 with his parents. His family moved two years later to Hartford, Connecticut, where Goodhart attended Yale College and became the first Hebrew admitted to the Connecticut bar. He practiced law in New Haven and served as clerk of the City Court until moving back to New York in 1869 to continue in the profession of law. He was active in benevolent and fraternal societies and served as president of the Hebrew Mutual Benefit Society and B'nai B'rith Benevolent Society.[95] In the arts, Rose Eytinge, born in 1835 in Philadelphia and the daughter of Simon Eytinge, became an actress in New York City, working in the 1860s with both Edwin Booth's and James William Wallack's acting companies. In religious education, Louisa R. Bildersee of Bnai Jeshurun, daughter of Isaac Bildersee, was the first principal of the synagogue's Sunday school, which commenced in 1862. She was an English teacher in the Hebrew Free School.[96]

A third-generation leader was Jacques Judah Lyons, *hazan* of Shearith Israel from 1840 until the late 1850s. Lyons's grandparents had left Holland for Surinam, but eventually settled in Lancaster, Pennsylvania, before the American Revolution. The Lyons family was influential in Philadelphia where Jacques's uncle Mordecai had a stationery business on Chestnut Street about 1836.[97]

The community involvements of these second- and third-generation Hollanders do not suggest a Dutch network. The efforts are too individualistic for that. Rather, they show the continuation of a commitment to the faith. The children walked in the footsteps of their parents, the forerunners, who had built Judaism in the early republic.

Social Adjustments

New York Jewry was never homogeneous, but a house divided against itself. There were from the beginning Sephardim and Ashkenazim, native-born and immigrant, rich and poor. Later, ethnic and nationality groups emerged, and finally the religious division between Orthodoxy and Reform. The pecking order in nineteenth-century New York began with the descendants of the first families, followed by the English and their close allies, the Dutch, who began arriving in the first decades of the nineteenth century. Then in the 1830s and 1840s Germans and Poles came.[98]

A German Jew in New York in 1846 explained the finely drawn social gradations among these predominantly lower classes:

> The Portuguese regards himself to be the aristocrat among the Jews and his bearing is in complete accordance with his conceitedness. He is a gentleman. Some individual English Jews can be found here, but the majority are Dutch and Polish Jews who have come here after living for a long time in England, where they adopted English customs and manners. He [*sic*] belongs to the genteel class. The local Pole is the dirtiest creature of all classes, and he is responsible for the disparagement of the name "Jew" even here. The Dutch Jew is by far better, an honest fellow despite his coarse clumsiness. . . . The German is haughty toward the Pole, who in turn hates him. The Dutch competes with the German, and though the English deems himself superior to the German he associates with him on quite friendly terms.[99]

The Dutch Jews felt a natural affinity to the English because the Amsterdam and London Jewish centers had long been linked commercially and the synagogues shared nearly identical rituals and liturgy. In the United States, English and Dutch Jews constituted the bulk of the early membership in the mother synagogue Shearith Israel, and also in the first daughter, Bnai Jeshurun. The two groups also composed the main body of the Hebrew Mutual Benefit Society in 1826.

In the opinion of historian Hyman Grinstein, the English and Dutch Americanized more rapidly than the Germans. They had no language problems since the Dutch had learned English during their sojourn in London. Most English and Dutch also spoke Yiddish, the international Jewish language, whereas the German Jews had become Germanized in the old country and as the dominant group in the new country by 1860 they continued to use German in worship and at home. While the Dutch readily gave up Yiddish, which as a mongrel tongue had little respect in America, the Germans clung to their native tongue, which was a respectable language in New York among both Jews and Gentiles. The Dutch of Bnai Israel kept their synagogue records in English from its beginnings in 1847, as did the Anshe Chesed congregation, which had many Dutch and Polish members. As already noted, a Dutch rabbi, Samuel Isaacs, preached sermons in English beginning in 1839. Because the Dutch readily adopted English, even in the Dutch synagogues in New York, they became Americanized more quickly.[100] But it is unlikely that this language accommodation in preaching and record keeping carried over into mixed seating, bareheaded worship, choirs, organs, and other trappings of Gentile practice.

The only surviving firsthand account of life among the New York Dutch Jews in the early years is a letter of Emanuel L. Goldsmith (Goudsmit) of New York to S. L. Kyser of Amsterdam, dated April 4, 1848, of which Meyer Roest printed fragments on April 30, 1886 in his *Nieuwe Israëlitische Nieuwsbode* (*Israelitish New Messenger*), under the title, "Letter from New York, 1848: Americans Are Ignorant." The Reverend Goldsmith was a respected educator, Jewish scholar and Talmudist well-versed in modern languages who in the 1840s and 1850s frequently was called upon to judge in religious disputes in New York congregations. That he held no clerical office gave him a respected independence.[101]

Goldsmith's letter begins by describing the favorable reaction among New York immigrants to the Revolution of 1848 in France: "Every day there is rejoicing and merriment, illuminations and music, particularly among the French and Germans." The next sentence shows Goldsmith's liberalism:

> I personally believe that the whole world will become a single republic. The world is now too enlightened to want to be suppressed any longer by the despotic kings and to pay all kinds of taxes for all of humanity. Anyhow, one does not know what the future will bring, but hopefully everything will turn out for the public good.

Goldsmith next commented on the adverse economic conditions brought on by the Mexican War, noting also that the revolution in France in 1848 had bankrupted a few French companies in America, "But since peace with Mexico is in sight, people think things will clear up."

Goldsmith's personal circumstances were favorable, judging from his letter.

> As far as we ourselves are concerned, with God's aid we have an honorable income; but that's all. To "put by" anything is impossible, be-

cause although there are hardly any taxes here, one nevertheless needs quite a lot of money. House rents are terribly expensive here. We spend *f*1,375 [$550] on it per year, but we have sub-leased. Clothing is expensive, and one has to dress neatly, otherwise one cannot visit any respectable people. Food is not expensive and there is plenty. We need *f*50 [$20] per week and live no more than middle class. . . . The area here is overflowing with milk and honey. And in the western country [the Midwest] where there are now Killes [congregations] everywhere, everything costs nearly nothing, cheaper than it ever was in Haaksbergen and Ochtrup [inland towns, the former in Overijssel Province and the latter in Germany]. People are making a good living. If you apply yourself you can subsist on *f*50 [$20], that is to say, as a poor man. The only thing that bothers me is the great heat in summer and the insects, which make sleeping impossible. Nevertheless, we all are as healthy as in Europe, because it matters a great deal how one lives and takes care of oneself.

Goldsmith's grown children were also prospering:

My son Henry [Goldsmith] has G.d. [thank God] a good income and an honorable one at that. He is held in high esteem by Jews and Christians. My daughter Betje and her husband have G.d. also a good income. He has a boarding house, and year after year he has more than 20 people who eat, drink and sleep at his place, like a college, where every day many people are together.

The Reverend Henry Goldsmith, as noted earlier, was in the 1840s a Hebrew teacher and part-time *hazan* for the Bnai Jeshurun Congregation. When the school closed in 1847 he temporarily took up the skilled trade of cigarmaker. The family in 1850 had two Irish maids, which was a sure sign of upward mobility. In 1860 Henry was a prosperous attorney, owning a house valued at $8,000, and with an Irish maid to assist his wife in household chores and attend their four daughters. By 1870 attorney Goldsmith's property had increased substantially: his home in the Uptown district was worth $20,000, and he owned $12,000 in personal property. His 21-year-old son was also an attorney and his aged father Emanuel, then 83 years old and a widower, lived in. Ten years earlier, Emanuel and his wife had boarded with a married daughter. Betje [Elisabeth] Goldsmith married a fellow Hollander, Myer S. Cohen—Reverend Isaacs officiated—and they operated a boarding house that catered to Dutch Jewish single men. In the mid-1860s Cohen was elected president of Congregation Bnai Israel. By 1870 he was still running the boarding house but his primary occupation was that of lace importer. The value of his inventory and personal property totaled $10,000. He had also moved Uptown with his wife and children.

Clearly, Emanuel Goldsmith had reason to be optimistic in 1848 about the future prospects of his family in New York City. His children and grandchildren had prospered beyond his fondest dreams and he relished them all. In a big family celebration on his fiftieth wedding anniversary in 1862, the couple's progeny presented them with a massive gold medal that contained in genealogic order the names of every one of the branches. As a mark of Goldsmith's wide respect, Samuel M. Isaacs and other rabbis spoke at the gathering and the *Jewish Messenger* carried a full account.[102]

The remainder of Goldsmith's letter provides interesting insights into synagogue life in New York City, from the viewpoint of an orthodox but mildly progressive Jew who was appalled at the laxity among his fellow religionists: "As far as the situation of the Jews is concerned, it is terrible in matters of religion. As you write from Holland, so it is here also; it's either Koggel [a pastry] . . . with barley soup and 3-year-old wormy smoked beef [a kosher food dish] or else ham and oysters." This is Goldsmith's unique way of describing the split among American Jews between those who observe the traditional rituals and those who do not. He continues: "The Americans, overall, are ignorant just like the English Jews and devout, or not Jews at all."

Goldsmith continues by criticizing Dr. Max Lilienthal, the second ordained rabbi in New York, who began serving three Orthodox German congregations in 1845 after immigrating from Munich. Lilienthal tried to introduce a few features of Reform Judaism and within three years was discharged by his largest congregation. "I suggested to him," Goldsmith opined, "to introduce no innovation whatsoever, since his congregations are too ignorant and not amenable to any reform. But he told me that he would arrange everything as he wanted. He introduced a few innovations in the synagogue and made enemies on the spot; they said that he was newfangled."

Goldsmith himself belonged to the "English" synagogue, Bnai Jeshurun, along with other Dutch Jews. As already noted, Rabbi Isaacs served this congregation from 1839 to 1844 and Simon Noot, Aaron van Praag, M. R. de Leeuw, and Goldsmith's son, Henry, held leadership positions in the synagogue and its Hebrew school.[103]

Emanuel Goldsmith reserved his most biting criticism for his fellow Hollanders. He writes at length: "The Dutch Jews living here are all of the old nobility, of the Barnevelds and De Witts [patrician families founded in the Golden Age] and more of that class. That is really the worst kind from Amsterdam. There are certainly more than a 100 families. But I swear to you that as long as I have lived here, I have not been in the home of three of them. They provide for themselves honestly but they are absolutely without any moral standard for themselves." Elsewhere in the letter Goldsmith laments this moral indifference when he says, "The non-Jews teach 'Torah' [the Ten Commandments, etc.] and the Jews eat 'ham'." Goldsmith explains:

[These Dutch Jews] built a synagogue for themselves and introduced in it "Minhag Amsterdam". Their Chazzan and minister is a certain S. Noot [Simon Eliazer Cohen Noot] from Amsterdam. They absolutely wanted to have me as a member of their congregation. However, I have said that I will stay at my congregation, but that if I could be of service to them, I will do so with pleasure. Thereupon they have made me an honorary member and I will "paskenen" [judge in religious matters] for them, and on "jontev" [holy day] I will give a "droosje" [a brief sermon] for them with everything that goes with it, which I have promised to do, without wishing, however, for the slightest service in return.

This "sjewoees" [Pentecost] they inaugurated their synagogue. I gave a "droosje" there and Henry [Goldsmith] gave an English reading with which they have made a lot of money. Subsequently we have made L. P.[104] (whom you certainly know) a "parnes" [synagogue president] because now he is a rich man. On the fast day of "Seliches" [prayers of penance before Rosh Hashana] they went to the cemetery where S. N. [Simon Eliazer Cohen Noot] said something. After that D. P. pronounced a kind of "hesped" [funeral oration], and after that he left and openly ate stewed oysters (in front of the board and the members of the congregations). In addition all year long he eats "treife" [non-kosher foods] and transgresses the Sabbath. After this they also let him act as speaker in the synagogue. When I heard this, I was mad at them and informed them that I didn't want to have anything more to do with them and would never come to their synagogue and that I will proclaim their behavior in all Killes (congregations). That I have done on "sjabbes sjoewe" [the Sabbath between Rosh Hashana and Yom Kippur] and on "sjabbes bereisjies" [the first Sabbath of the New Year] when I gave a "droosje" in one of the Polish synagogues, where I exposed them in their true light. . . . You can imagine how the Netherlanders liked this.

Although Goldsmith's letter demonstrates his continuing ties with the homeland, his exasperation with his fellow countrymen in New York for being too *religiously* nationalistic is clear.

Goldsmith undoubtedly applauded Rabbi Leeser's essays in the 1850s in the *Occident* that lamented the "*Shibboleth* of clannishness" by which we "fritter away our strength in boyish and frivolous contentions."[105] Individual nationality synagogues lead to "rivalry," "bitterness of feeling," and "disunity," said Leeser: "The German will not unite with the Pole, the Pole with the Portuguese, the Portuguese with the Hollander or Bohemian, and so to the end of the chapter."[106]

Dutch Jews were not only nationalistic in religion but in politics. Late in the Civil War young patriots led by Benjamin de Young—one of the founders of the NISF insurance society—formed the New York Union Memorial Association. At the group's fourth annual picnic in 1867 at Frinke's Grove, a "very large" crowd gathered to unfurl the "first Holland flag in New York" amidst "great cheering and innumerable huzzahs." Dockworth's band "delightfully rendered" appropriate national aires and a forty-voice male chorus sang a special song written by member A. Berlyn. De Young, a prosperous secondhand clothier, donated the silk flag trimmed in silver. Morris Goodhart of Hartford, CT, delivered the keynote address at the flag's inaugural. Editor S. M. Isaacs and his sons attended and reported on the grand display of Dutch-American patriotism in the *Jewish Messenger*.[107]

Occupations

In the nineteenth-century Dutch Jews in New York were equally made up of peddlers and petty traders, merchants and brokers, and craftsmen (shoemakers, tailors, butchers, and cigarmakers). There were only a smattering of professionals. Newer immigrants turned to peddling or drew upon their craft skills while more established settlers moved up to shopkeeping, trade, and commerce. Although not well off, the Dutch rose above poverty. Their relative status is indicated by the admissions reports covering the years 1856–1858 of the Jews' Hospital, which treated charity cases. Of 662 patients only 1.9 percent (13) were Dutch, compared to 47 percent Germans, 37 percent Poles, and 3.2 percent English. The Dutch percentage was exactly equivalent to their share of the Jewish population in the city in these years.[108] The Dutch Jews also had a high literacy rate of 97 percent according to the 1850–1870 federal censuses.

No Dutch Jews in New York City or County worked in agriculture between 1850 and 1870. But in the late 1830s, several had a leading part in an attempt to plant an agricultural colony in Ulster County, New York. The Sholem Colony—the first concerted effort to found a Jewish agricultural colony—originated in 1837 when a committee of Anshe Chesed Synagogue selected a large tract of land in Ulster County. Three of the four committee members were Dutch —Moses S. Cohen, Marcus van Gelderen, and William N. Polack. In all, twelve families bought land, including Cohen, Van Gelderen, Polack, and another Dutchman, Joseph Davies. Van Gelderen, born in the Netherlands in 1798, had come to New York in 1822. Davies was also born in Holland, educated in England, and came to the United States in 1798. Polack immediately conveyed his land to fellow Hollander Moses Content at his purchase price and left the colony. The timing of the venture was inopportune; the panic of 1837 struck just as the colony began. In addition their land was stony ground unsuitable for farming.

Sholem Colony failed within a few years (in 1841) when nine mortgages were foreclosed and the remaining three were refinanced. The project was then abandoned and all but a few settlers returned to New York City. The colonists were not recent immigrants but trustees and leaders in New York synagogues. Van Gelderen was the kosher butcher at Bnai Jeshurun and Shearith Israel and later became president of Anshe Chesed. Cohen became president of Bnai Israel and Polack was one of the founders and trustees of Anshe Chesed. The colonists' goal was clearly to establish a pilot project that would attract new immigrants who were genuine farmers. Although there is an atmosphere of mystery about this colony, initiated largely by Dutch Jews, the reasons for its failure are obvious. Urban Jews, however sagacious, had misjudged the difficulties of opening farms in an isolated frontier area with poor-quality land.[109]

At least one Jew of Dutch ancestry in New York, however, lived a life in farming. He was Benjamin Etting Hays (1778–1858) of Pleasantville, Westchester County, some six miles north of Tarrytown and 25 miles north of Manhattan. At his death in 1858 the obituary in the *Occident* supposed that Hays was "perhaps" the "last Jewish farmer in the United States." His forefathers had emigrated from Holland with the first Jewish settlers, carrying their own capital and agricultural implements. They settled first near New Rochelle at the neck of Long Island Sound, just north of The Bronx. As faithful Jews, they "remained plain, unassuming farmers, adhering rigorously to the Jewish laws, highly esteemed for their wealth, industry, and integrity. . . . Far removed from every religious influence, they never forgot the God of Israel, nor ceased to obey the Law of Moses." It is no surprise, therefore, to find Benjamin E. Hays listed among the charter subscribers to the *Occident*, the first national Jewish periodical begun in 1843.[110] The Hays family was deeply involved in the American Revolution. David and Michael Hays (Benjamin's father and uncle, respectively) were patriots who sold livestock to the Colonial army; another uncle, Reuben Etting of New York, fought at Charleston, SC, where he was captured and died from mistreatment in a British prison. Benjamin Hays's body was sent to New York City for burial in the family plot of the Shearith Israel cemetery.[111] One would like to know more about the life of this unique Jewish farming family living among the Dutch Calvinists of Tarrytown and Pleasantville.

In the first half of the nineteenth century, most Dutch Jews in New York, like their brethren elsewhere, were shopkeepers and merchants. In 1830, when the picture is complete for the first time, of the sixteen household heads for which occupation is known, 80 percent (13) were proprietors, merchants, and manufacturers—compared to 50 percent for all employed Jews (Table 3.4).[112] There were three clothiers and a merchant tailor, a broker and a pawnbroker, four shopkeepers (including two grocers and a kosher butcher), a quill manufacturer, a medical doctor, a spectacle maker, and a carder (Table 3.2). The city directories of 1831 to 1835 show the continuing preponderance of proprietors. Of twelve Hollanders who were identified, eight owned stores (two fancy stores, two unspecified merchants, a merchant tailor shop, porterhouse, kosher butcher shop, and a quill manufacturer), one was a broker, one a doctor and a teacher, and one an upholsterer (Table 3.5). The four most prevalent occupations among Jews in these years were merchant (29 percent), clothier (7 percent), broker (5 percent), and manufacturer (5 percent).

The Dutch were clearly overrepresented among merchants and professionals and underrepresented among skilled craftsmen and unskilled workers. They were mainly self-employed retailers selling consumer products. One notable exception was the Hendricks Brothers Metals Company established by Uriah Hendricks before the Revolution (in 1764), which continued for at least four generations into the twentieth century as the oldest Jewish business concern in the United States. In 1812 son Harmon as president of the firm opened the first copper-rolling mill in America. Harmon Hendricks, who lived in fashionable Greenwich Village, was probably the richest Jew in the city in the early nineteenth century. At his death in 1838 he left an estate, reportedly of three million dollars plus valuable real estate. Bonds of the Hendricks company were as gilt-edged as government securities and its common stocks were "blue chip."[113]

By 1850 the biggest change in the Dutch job profile among first-generation immigrants was the sharp increase in clerks and crafts-

Table 3.4
Dutch Jewish Occupation Groups in New York, 1830–1870*

	Occupational Group						
	Merchant and Professional		Skilled		Semi- and Unskilled		Total
Period	N	%	N	%	N	%	N
1830	13	81.2	2	12.5	1	6.3	16
1831–1835	11	91.7	1	8.3	0	0.0	12
1850	98	68.5	38	26.6	7	4.9	143
1860	98	44.7	94	42.9	27	12.3	219
1870	343	54.9	228	36.5	54	8.6	625
1850–1870	539	54.6	360	36.5	88	8.9	987

*The totals include children of Dutch stock in the workforce.

Sources: Compiled from Beverly Hyman, "New York Businessmen, 1831–1835" (unpublished paper, HUC, Cincinnati, 1977), 5–12; Rosenwaike, *Edge of Greatness*, 112–38; Swierenga, *Dutch Households in U.S. Population Censuses*; see note on sources for methodology.

men, although petty proprietors and merchants still predominated. The breakdown of the 143 employed Dutch Jews in the 1850 census was: 68 percent proprietors, clerks, merchants, and peddlers; 27 percent skilled craftsmen; and only 5 percent semiskilled and unskilled workers. The largest single category was clerks (20), followed by peddlers (17), clothiers (15), and cigarmakers (10). Clerking, peddling, and cigar making were entry level jobs for the new immigrants of the 1840s.

The immigration of the 1840s clearly lowered the overall economic status of Dutch Jewry in the Empire City, but this only signaled greater changes to come. The next twenty years brought a dramatic decline in the status of the Dutch. Blue-collar workers, especially cigarmakers, came to dominate the labor force. In 1860 only 45 percent of Dutch Jews were merchants and professionals; this was a 33 percent decline since 1850. In this same period skilled craftsmen increased more than twofold and unskilled workers increased fourfold. During the 1860s, when immigration slowed, the pre-war Dutch in New York improved their economic lot. By 1870 the proportion of merchants and professionals had risen to 55 percent and blue-collar workers were less numerous at 36 percent skilled and 9 percent unskilled (Table 3.4).

Table 3.5
Dutch Jews in New York City, 1831–1835 City
Directories

Name	Occupation	Address*
Mayer Cohen	fancy store	20 Division
Moses Cohen	quill manufacturer	386 Grand
Rowland Cromelien	upholsterer	463 Broadway, h. 492 Broome
Benjamin F. Hart	teacher	Grove at Hudson, h. 68 Canal, (later) 40 Renwick
Henry Hart	fancy store	297 (later 127) Broadway
Uriah Hendricks	merchant	85 Water, h. 77 Greenwich
Washington Hendricks	merchant	85 Water, h. 61 Greenwich
Hart Levy	porterhouse	h. 103 Cedar, (later) 8 Elizabeth, 208 Broadway
Eleazer Metz	kosher butcher	167 Mott, (later) 22 Spring
Daniel L. M. Peixotto, M.D.	doctor	94 Elm, (later) 22 White
Lewis Simmons	merchant tailor	3 Division, (later) 28 Pell, 203 Chrystie
Solomon B. Solomon	broker	18 Wall, h. 41 Clinton

*h. indicates house; otherwise business address.

Source: Beverly Hyman, "New York Businessmen, 1831–1835," 5–12.

In no other city were Dutch cigarmakers so dominant as they became in New York after 1850. In that year only 10 Jewish Hollanders made their living in the cigar sweatshops. In 1860 the number grew to 44, but in 1870, 136 were cigarmakers, plus 21 strippers, manufacturers, tobacconists, and other workers with the weed. In twenty years, cigarmakers as a proportion of employed Dutch Jews rose from 7 percent to 25 percent. If not tobacco, the Dutch turned to the garment trade that German Jews monopolized. In 1870 there were 38 Dutch tailors, dressmakers, capmakers, cutters, sewing machine operators, dyers, and the like. Another 26 were retailers operating fancy goods stores, clothing and dry goods houses, and secondhand clothing shops.

The concentration of the lower-class Dutch immigrants in the cigar industry is clearly exemplified in the family of Samuel Gompers, the famed American labor leader and founder of the American Federation of Labor (AFL).[114] Gompers is the quintessential Dutch Ashkenazic Jewish immigrant of the second half of the nineteenth century (see Fig. 3.4). Although Samuel was born on the East Side of London of Dutch parents, Solomon Gompers and Sara Rood, the

110

Fig. 3.4. Samuel Gompers (1850–1924) of New York, NY. Courtesy of George Meany Memorial Archives.

Gompers family had lived in Amsterdam for generations. Samuel's grandfather and namesake, Samuel Moses Gompers, was an import-export merchant who traveled five or six times a year between Amsterdam and London. The Dutch economy at the time was closely tied to that of England, providing mainly foodstuffs in exchange for manufactured goods.[115]

The family fortunes had shrunk to a level of genteel poverty by the 1840s, and they lived in the poorest of Amsterdam slums, the Rood Leeuwengang (Red Lion Passage). In 1845 Samuel decided to move with his wife and six children to the Spitalfields subdistrict of London's East End, which had a large Dutch Jewish ghetto. Many relatives of the Gompers family already resided in London.[116] Samuel's oldest son Solomon, in 1847 married Sara Rood, daughter of a Dutch family of "well-to-do tradesmen," who Samuel had brought from Amsterdam as a live-in family maid. Solomon was a cigarmaker and his wife kept a Dutch kitchen and maintained the mother tongue. As Samuel recalled with nostalgia in his autobiography, "Our home preserved many of the customs of the Dutch community from which father and mother came. In our big room was a large fireplace in which mother had a Dutch oven that produced what seemed to us children marvelously delicious things to eat. All mother's cooking utensils were of the squat, substantial Dutch make, necessary for old-fashioned Dutch cooking that nourished us youngsters three times a day."[117]

Samuel Gompers was born in 1850, the first of five sons and grew up in the mixed Dutch and English culture of the East End ghetto. From age six to ten he went to a Jews' Free School and then his father apprenticed him to a cigarmaker. He continued to study the Talmud and the Hebrew language in the Jews' School at night and learned English on the streets and a smattering of Dutch at home.[118]

In 1863 Solomon Gompers decided to move his family to New York City, where many friends had gone and a brother-in-law had emigrated six months before. As Samuel remembered, "My father found it extremely difficult to support a family of six children on his scanty wages earned at the cigarmaking trade. . . . Emigration to America promised relief." Members of the Cigarmaker's Society (Union) of England had established an emigration fund to provide passage money to America, and Solomon borrowed from that fund.[119] Samuel was thirteen years old at the time. Thus, the Gompers family followed the typical chain migration pattern, first following family to the staging area in London and then on to the East Side of New York.

After landing at Castle Garden following an arduous seven week voyage, relatives and friends met the Gompers and shepherded them to a little four-room flat in a tenement on Houston Street, among the "Holland Dutchmen" as Samuel put it.[120] Solomon and his oldest son Samuel resumed their cigar making trade in the flat and established their Dutch-English household in the midst of dire poverty and squalor. Their home stood between a slaughterhouse and a brewery. Within a year Samuel joined the Cigarmaker's Local and went to work in a cigar factory. Within ten years, by the mid-1870s, Samuel became a labor leader who went on to great fame.[121]

The economic advancement after the Civil War of Dutch Jews such as the Gompers family is difficult to measure. One indicator, although notoriously unreliable, is the value of real estate and personal property reported in the federal censuses. In 1850 the census marshals in New York rarely recorded this information and only 3 of 152 Dutch households reported any property. These were very wealthy individuals who owned $4,000, $7,000, and $10,000, respectively. In 1860 when the data are more complete, 100 of 152 families reported property, primarily personalty. Only ten families owned real estate (ranging up to $40,000), but ninety families owned reportable personalty ranging from $25 to $50,000, with the average per household being $1,741. In 1870, 180 of the 327 Dutch Jewish households (55 percent) had wealth to report; 17 owned realty ranging from $4,000 to $60,000 (average $22,412) and 176 owned personalty ranging from $100 to $150,000 (average $2,444). This was an average increase in wealth in one decade of $700 per household in unweighted dollars, although the extreme wealth of one individual distorted the average. The wealthiest Dutch Jew in the city in 1870 was Morris J. Leon, owner of a clothing store, where his eldest son also worked as a clothier and his middle son served as clerk. Leon owned realty valued at $45,000 and personal property valued at $150,000. Leon and his wife had immigrated in the early 1840s, only twenty-five years earlier. His rise to the upper level of the New York wealthy in such a short time is remarkable.

Although tobacco employed more Dutch, they made the greatest impact on the diamond industry in New York. Since the late sixteenth-century Jewish firms—first in Amsterdam and later in Antwerp and London—had dominated the international diamond trade, especially to Asia, Latin America, and South Africa in the famous "Cape Time" of the 1870s. Thus Dutch craftsmen, 70 percent of whom were Jewish, were in a solid position to introduce diamond cutting and polishing in the United States, and they came to dominate the gem trade in the early decades of the twentieth century.

The diamond industry in America was a direct result of the overseas expansion of Amsterdam diamond houses and their craftsmen in response to international trade pressures. In the 1860s the

Dutch diamond trade suffered from depressed conditions, and this prompted a few cutters and polishers to emigrate to the United States where they opened shops, primarily in New York City but also in the early years in Boston and Detroit. Boston actually became the first center of the Dutch diamond industry. But New York supplanted Boston as the diamond center because its importers maintained closer ties with Amsterdam and London diamond dealers who had gained a monopoly in the South African trade in uncut stones.

The Amsterdam Jewish immigrants J. H. Groen and P. de Bruyn established the pioneer diamond workshop in New York City in October of 1860. In a major technology transfer, they brought all the necessary specialized tools with them. Editor S. M. Isaacs of the *Jewish Messenger* proudly announced the "New Commercial Enterprise" of "our co-religionists." He boasted: "We wish the beginners every success, of which we feel assured when we consider that the art is now almost exclusively in the hands of the Israelites of Amsterdam." The firm of Groen and De Bruyn specialized in repairs and setting stones for the city's wealthy women. De Bruyn was a particularly skilled master craftsman whose shop was full of apprentices and journeymen. He earned the reputation as the best polisher in New York and gradually established the diamond industry in New York City.[122]

New York City gained the absolute supremacy as the American diamond center in the 1890s after London came to monopolize the trade in uncut South African gems and the U.S. government passed protective tariffs. The McKinley Tariff of 1890 brought the first dislocation and triggered a massive shift to New York of Dutch diamond houses. In response to the nascent American gem industry, Congress sharply increased the import tax on polished diamonds or set stones from 10 percent (the rate since the tariff bill of 1883) to 25 percent. The rate for cut, unset diamonds remained at 10 percent, and uncut stones were admitted duty free.[123] In one stroke, Netherlands diamond manufacturers were priced out of their major market. The only answer was to open shops in the United States and transfer their skilled craftsmen there.

The Wilson-Gorman Tariff of 1894 gave New York City yet another boost by increasing duties to 30 percent on cut diamonds and 25 percent on cut but unset stones. Uncut stones, which had been duty free, were now taxed at 10 percent. These tariff rates, especially the prohibitive tax on manufactured gems, induced importers to open cutting and polishing shops in America, and they offered high wages to Dutch and Belgian craftsmen. Several Amsterdam firms opened branch factories in New York and by 1894 three hundred Amsterdam diamond craftsmen worked in New York.[124]

Dutch diamond imports grew rapidly after 1894; by 1908 the United States bought 90 percent of Amsterdam's production. The American consumer market had an insatiable appetite for diamonds. In 1925 the total value of raw and polished diamonds sent from Amsterdam to America totaled $30 million. Most went initially to New York City and were distributed from there. Because U.S. wages were so high, the purest and most expensive stones were processed in New York; the average quality gems were manufactured in Amsterdam and the poorest stones were cut and polished in Antwerp where wages were the lowest.

Dutch diamond workers dominated the New York industry. In 1908, 70 percent were Dutch-born. By 1919 the industry employed seven hundred diamond workers, of which two hundred were Hollanders. The Dutch contingent grew to three hundred by 1926. Most lived in Brooklyn, with a smaller nucleus in New York City on Nassau Street's jewelry row. A Dutchman, Andries Meyer, was president of the Diamond Workers Protective Union in 1908.[125]

The major Amsterdam firms to set up houses in New York were Eduard van Dam, the Zilver Brothers, and the Van Wezel Brothers. The Van Dam firm also had a branch in Antwerp. The Van Wezel firm became the largest diamond house in New York City by the 1920s, employing more than seventy workers. A. S. van Wezel, the founder, had come to New York early in the twentieth century, and his brother, S. M. van Wezel, continued the firm. D. S. Granaat, J. Hoedenmaker, and S. Konijn were other Dutch firms in New York, but of brief duration. Other Dutch diamond polishers in small firms were located in Cincinnati, Chicago, and Los Angeles. All diamond workers earned very high wages and were the aristocrats of the crafts.

The Dutch diamond craftsmen in America were slow to assimilate. They had constant contact with the Netherlands and lived and worked together in small colonies of elite craftsmen. The New York Jewish diamond workers held on to their language and customs and were a "typical Dutch colony," as Jacob van Hinte aptly noted. They even influenced the American language by introducing the Dutch technical terms of their industry. This is remarkable and did not happen among Grand Rapids, MI, Dutch furniture workers or Paterson, NJ silk workers.[126]

Conclusion

Dutch Jews in New York in the middle decades of the nineteenth century exercised an influence far exceeding their relatively small numbers. This was a result of their clannishness and commitment to religious orthodoxy, education, and charity. Led by devout and able clerics and scholars such as Samuel Myer Isaacs and Simon Cohen Noot and by laymen like Henry Goldsmith and Aaron van Praag, they organized synagogues, schools, periodicals, and benevolent societies, and they participated in the life of Jewry generally. But their Dutchness was always close to the surface and religious nationalism prompted the majority to organize Dutch cemeteries, societies, and a synagogue in the 1840s and 1850s. Their religious conservatism also set them apart. Dutch Jews in the United States, especially in the first generation, were staunchly Orthodox. They valued tradition and custom, as did their fathers and grandfathers in Holland, who had opposed the new French revolutionary ideals, even though the Napoleonic regime offered emancipation.

Socially, the Dutch compared favorably to the English at the top of the status pyramid. Their command of the English language, gained during the customary stopover in London and their association with English Jews in New York, led to a rapid Americanization. But, if possible, they preferred to marry fellow Hollanders and they kept up contact even with Dutch Gentiles. In 1862 when a number of prominent Netherlanders in New York City formed an immigrant aid society, the New Amsterdam Association, Dutch Jews attended the organizational meetings and were gratified that the society decided that "no distinction should be made with regard to creed."[127] In the 1870s and 1880s, when a flood of poorer laborers and craftsmen such as the Gompers family arrived, the Dutch blended more with the majority German and Polish Jews. They simply became Jews rather than Holland Jews, although a Dutch cultural veneer remained, such as Mrs. Gompers's Dutch kitchen.

Economically, in the early decades of the nineteenth century, the Dutch of New York were overrepresented among Jewish shopkeepers and merchants, mostly in retail consumer goods, and they were underrepresented among skilled craftsmen and unskilled workers. In manufacturing the Hendricks family copper rolling mill was an exceptional success. During the middle decades, the proportion of immigrants who were clerks, peddlers, and cigarmakers increased sharply, and the first generation Dutch Jews experienced a decline in

116

social status. Independent businessmen gave way to skilled wage earners such as cigarmakers, as exemplified by Samuel Gompers. In the early twentieth century, the elite Dutch diamond craftsmen came to dominate their highly specialized industry on the Nassau Street diamond row. By 1930 a few cemeteries were the only institutional remnants of Dutch Jewry in the city, but their leaven remains in New York City Jewry.

Chapter 4

PHILADELPHIA: AN EARLY BASE

The Beginning

When the American Revolution began, Philadelphia had about three hundred Jewish inhabitants and was third behind New York City and Charleston. Jewish businessmen sold military supplies of all kinds to the Continental army, subscribed to government bonds, lent funds, and served in the army. Jewish patriots considered the Revolution "our cause."[1] At the immediate outset of the war, Jonas Phillips, a Hessian immigrant and the ritual slaughterer for New York's Shearith Israel Congregation, saw an incredible opportunity for trade with his Amsterdam kinsman, the merchant Gumpel Samson, who was the agent for many American Jewish importers. Phillips sent a letter to Samson via the Dutch Caribbean colony of Saint Eustatius, dated July 28, 1776, in which he ordered a long list of consumer goods. "As no English goods can come over at all, and much money can be earned with Holland goods if one will venture, . . . I can assure you that four hundred per cent is to be earned thereby." The letter is also of historical interest because Phillips reported that the American army already totaled 100,000 men, and he enclosed a copy of the Declaration of Independence. The riskiness of Phillips's venture is apparent from the fact that his letter never reached Amsterdam; the British intercepted it and eventually it ended up in the British Public Records Office.[2]

After the British troops departed Philadelphia in 1778, the city swelled with Jewish refugees from other occupied cities—Charleston, Savannah, New York, and Newport—and became the Jewish capital of the infant Unites States for many decades. With as many as two hundred families in the city, the pews of Congregation Mikveh Israel (Hope of Israel) filled to overflowing and in 1782 the congregation built its first authentic synagogue. The original members included several Dutch, judging solely from the names.[3] But when peace came in 1783 and the refugees returned to their homes, the city's Jewish population, including the suburb of Northern Liberties, dwindled by 1790 to only 25 families containing about 150 persons. This was barely a quarter of the prewar total and roughly half that of New York City. The congregation struggled to pay its building indebtedness and minister's salary and other expenses. They devised a legalized lottery to raise funds among the members and in 1788 they even made a general appeal for donations to the Gentile community to stave off foreclosure on their synagogue. Benjamin Franklin, among others, donated £5 sterling. Happily, they saved the synagogue.[4]

Religious freedom in America created discipline problems for Jewish immigrants who were accustomed to "tightly circled" communal living in European ghettos. Besides sabbath-breaking, Gentile intermarriages, and sporadic synagogue attendance, conflicts that derived from differing Old World worship liturgies led to schism along nationality lines. Mikveh Israel tried to hold the community together in 1792 by enacting membership requirements, with the ultimate punishment being the denial of a religious burial, a ban with eternal consequences.[5] Throughout the nineteenth century, Mikveh Israel, although "distinctively American," remained markedly conservative in character and its worship adhered closely to the Orthodox Sephardic rites, "allowing no modern innovations in its services."[6]

German, Dutch, and Polish newcomers, who were dissatisfied with the Sephardic rite (*minhag*) because it was foreign to them, remained members only until they could muster the required quorum (*minyan*) of ten men aged thirteen years and above for an Ashkenazic service. This happened in 1795, only thirteen years after the founding of Mikveh Israel, when the Dutch grocer Leon (Louis) van Amring (Amringe) and several German Jews organized separate services. The German Hebrew Society that grew out of this division founded the first Ashkenazic synagogue in North America, Rodeph

Shalom (Seekers of Peace). It antedated by thirty years a similar secession in New York of Bnai Jeshurun from Shearith Israel. In 1795 there were no more than thirty or forty Ashkenazic families in Philadelphia.[7]

In 1801 the new group had enough members to purchase a cemetery in the Kensington district of Northern Liberties, and in 1802 they established an independent German Shul, where they could read their prayers "according to the German and Dutch Rules," which were "not to be altered." This agreement spelled out in the Articles of Incorporation in 1810 was clearly a compromise between the German and Dutch members. Of the twenty-five signatories of the bylaws drafted in 1810 (and written in Yiddish), ten (40 percent) were Dutch-born.[8]

In keeping with the spirit of the City of Brotherly Love, the German synagogue grew without the bitter internecine conflicts that occurred at Bnai Jeshurun and in almost all other cities. The German Hebrew Society of Philadelphia at first depended on its Portuguese predecessor for kosher services and sacred scrolls. For many years the German and Dutch congregants continued to contribute and maintain formal ties with the mother synagogue. Both congregations were strictly Orthodox and every Jew settling in the city was asked to decide which of the two bodies he desired to join.[9] Most of the Dutch, who began to arrive in large numbers after 1800, joined Congregation Rodeph Shalom.

Napoleonic Era Immigrants

In the early national period the Jewish community resumed its steady growth, reaching about 450 (58 households) in 1820 and 730 (105 households) in 1830. New York's Jewish settlement surpassed 550 in 1820 and was 1,150 in 1830. Philadelphia's major growth spurt came in the 1840s when the Jewish community quadrupled from 1,500 to 6,000 and reached 10,000 by 1860.[10]

Dutch Jews were a significant component of this growth. Some of the pioneers, who deserve special mention, are Abraham Eleazer Israel (1773–1852), who took passage on the *Atlantic* and arrived on September 15, 1804; Joseph de Young (de Jong) of Rotterdam, who took cabin passage with his wife and son on the *America* from Amsterdam, arriving August 16, 1805; Abraham Cohen (c. 1765–1836), who sailed on the *Frederick Augustus* and arrived on April 29, 1807; and Daniel Goodman, who crossed on the *Ocean*, arriving June 16,1808. Goodman lived in New Orleans in 1830.[11]

Joseph de Young (1776–1851), who Napoleon had appointed Dutch diamond agent for the French government, settled first in Newark, NJ, but by 1809 he lived in New Hanover township, Montgomery County, PA, immediately north of Philadelphia. Probably he was peddling. By 1811 he had opened a general merchandise store in Philadelphia and joined the Ashkenazic congregation Rodeph Shalom. Both of his aged parents, who had also emigrated, died that year and their burials are recorded in the congregation's burial book. By 1830 Joseph was widowed and had moved again to Berks County, PA, near Reading, where he owned a country store. His works of charity earned him the accolade "a true friend of the poor." His oldest son, Isaac, who was born in Rotterdam in 1795, after serving in the New Jersey Regulars during the War of 1812, became a successful fancy goods merchant in Philadelphia and briefly (1828–1832) in Baltimore in partnership with his younger brother Michael. Another son Philip, graduated from the University of Pennsylvania Medical College in 1838 and practiced in Philadelphia, helping many Jewish charity patients. One would like to know more about this very Jewish Dutch family of Pennsylvania.[12]

Two interrelated families who made a major mark on the Jewish communities and synagogue life of Philadelphia, Richmond, and Cincinnati in the early years were Ezekiel Jacob Ezekiel (1781–1831) and his father-in-law Eleazar Joseph Israel (1751–1817) whose Hebrew name was Rabbi Isaac Eleazer.[13] Ezekiel's wife, Hannah Rebecca, was Israel's oldest daughter. Both families immigrated from Amsterdam, led by Israel's oldest son, Abraham Eleazer Israel who arrived in 1804.[14] The rest of the families migrated in 1810. Ezekiel Ezekiel's brother, Tobias Ezekiel, also immigrated, as did his sister Sarah, who married Mordecai B. Cohen in Philadelphia. Cohen was also Dutch. The Ezekiel family had lived in Utrecht in 1809 where the oldest daughter, Martha, was born. She married Dutch-born Jacob A. Levy of Richmond. The second child, Jacob (1812–1899), was born in Philadelphia. Adeline, the third child who was also born in Philadelphia in 1815, married Isaac Hyneman of Richmond, also of Dutch birth. All three children were orphaned young in 1818 when Hannah died—Eleazer had died a year earlier; Hannah's two brothers and married sister each adopted one of the children. Jacob, and perhaps the whole family, worshiped at the Rodeph Shalom congregation.[15]

Eleazer Israel (1751–1817) was a Hebrew scribe who wrote scrolls of the holy law (Sepher Torah), which he presented to the Congregation Mikveh Israel. He immigrated in 1810 with his married daughter, Hannah Rebecca, and four of his other children, to join his oldest son Abraham, who had left already in 1804 and married Sarah Barnett at Philadelphia. The Israel children were Michael E. (Cohen) Israel, who was a member of the Philadelphia School Board in 1829; Isaac E. Israel, who died prematurely in Philadelphia in 1818; Rosetta Israel (1786–1854), who married Levi M. Goldsmit (Goudsmit), and Martha. Abraham's wife, Sarah Barnett, was a sister of Rebecca Barnett, Mrs. Hyman Polock.[16] The latter had been married by the famous Solomon Hirschel (Herschel, Herschell), chief rabbi of the Great Synagogue of London, and two weeks later, the newlyweds emigrated to Philadelphia. These intermarriages among Dutch Jewish families speak volumes about the glue of national identity, language, and culture among Dutch Jewish émigrés. That Rabbi Hirschel married the Polocks also attests to the social prominence of some of the Dutch in London and Philadelphia.[17]

Other Dutch Jews in Philadelphia before 1810 were Leon van Amring, Benedict Nathan, Isaac Stuttgart, Moses Spyers, Aaron Stork, Elias Hyneman, Levi Goldsmit, and Moses I. Goldkop. All were merchants. The grocer Van Amring was in the city by 1795 when he helped organize Rodeph Shalom. Benedict Nathan was an import merchant in 1806 in partnership with a French Jew, Lyon Cadet, who were heard to speak together in "Low Dutch, French, and High French." Isaac Stuttgart (1785–1830) arrived in Philadelphia from Amsterdam in 1807 and established a fancy goods store. He was a member of Rodeph Shalom until 1824, when he joined Mikveh Israel. Moses Spyers (1763–1837), also an Amsterdammer, settled in London sometime before 1806 and then emigrated to New York. By 1810 he resided in Philadelphia and was a dealer and later a watchmaker. Aaron Stork (1764–1842), a grocer and wine merchant, arrived from Holland in 1807. At his death in 1842, he was buried in the Spruce Street Cemetery along with Stuttgart and other Dutch Jews. Elias Hyneman (1765–1845), a grocery merchant, arrived in Philadelphia before 1806 from Montgomery County, PA, where his oldest son Leon was born. Second son Benjamin was born in Philadelphia in 1806. Son Isaac went to Richmond in 1838 but returned within a decade. In the 1820s and 1830s, Hyneman operated a grocery in partnership with his sons.[18] Levi Goldsmit (1781–1849) came from the Netherlands before 1810 and by 1815 owned a dry goods store with Moses I. Goldkop, who was born in Amsterdam in 1798 and immigrated to Philadelphia in 1815.[19]

Hyman Polock (1786–1870), was another Amsterdammer who "occupied a very prominent position in Jewish communal circles" in Philadelphia. Like Spyer, he went to London during the economic crisis of the Napoleonic wars and was married there by Rabbi Hirschel. In 1811 he emigrated to Philadelphia and opened a jewelry store. Polock participated in 1830 in a three-person committee, along with fellow Dutchman, Goldsmit, to revise the constitution of the first Hebrew burial and aid society in Philadelphia, the Society for the Visitation of the Sick and Mutual Assistance, founded in 1813. Polock later served as president of the society and in 1863 was honored at its fiftieth anniversary as the only surviving founder. His sponsor for membership in Mikveh Israel aptly described Polock as a man of "right honest Industry and religious" and his eulogist declared that he was "an honorable, upright man . . . of varied and deep learning." That he was. When his daughter Sarah died in the city in 1899 at age 87, the oldest native Philadelphian of the Jewish community, she was also praised as a devout adherent of the Jewish religion.[20]

The Dutch Jews who reached Philadelphia in the Napoleonic era were émigrés rather than immigrants. Families such as the Ezekiels, Israels, De Youngs, and Polacks were petty merchant capitalists in Amsterdam or Rotterdam involved in the export trade. The seemingly endless European wars and trade disruptions from blockades and embargoes threatened economic disaster and prompted them to take ship, either directly or via London, for the "First New Nation" where opportunities were unlimited.

These families were cut from the same cloth. Several were previously tied by marriage or business and they forged more links in America. Devout and learned in religion, active in synagogue life and benevolence, and adept in business and the professions, they helped lay the foundations for the rising Jewish communities in Philadelphia, New York, Baltimore, Richmond, and New Orleans in the early republic.

Post-Napoleonic Arrivals, 1816–1820

In the post-Napoleonic years several more Dutch families arrived from the Netherlands and made major contributions to American Jewry. Aaron Moses Dropsie (1794–1839) took passage on the *Dido* from Amsterdam to Philadelphia, arriving September 27, 1819, at twenty-five years of age, with the occupation of packer. He opened a pawnshop and became a man of means. Like most of his fellow Hollanders, he joined Rodeph Shalom, even though he married a Christian. In 1826 when the synagogue tightened its membership rules to exclude Jews who intermarried,

Dropsie was granted the only exception. The agreement was even more unusual in requiring that Dropsie's young son, Moses Aaron, be given no religious education until he was old enough to make his own choice. Presumably Dropsie's wife concurred in this arrangement. Young Moses eventually made his choice for Judaism and became a leader in Philadelphia Jewry. Dropsie College was the result of his benevolence.[21]

The David Eytinge family of Amsterdam similarly left their mark. David (1764–1855) first sent several of his four sons to Philadelphia in the years between 1816 and 1820 before emigrating himself in 1826. He landed first in New York and then joined his sons in Philadelphia. He was a merchant, as were his sons. The eldest, Barnet (1782–1863), emigrated first in 1816. Philip came sometime before 1820 and with Barnet operated a wholesale fancy goods business in Lower Delaware Ward for many years. Solomon (b.1792) emigrated in 1820 and was a merchant on High Street. Simon (1790–1869) left in 1828, sailing from Antwerp to New York on the *Heroine* with his wife and five children. A merchant in Amsterdam, he became a jeweler in Philadelphia in partnership with Benjamin I. Philips. Simon moved to Baltimore by 1850 and was a pawnbroker. His son Samuel, born in Amsterdam in 1819, was a furniture dealer in Baltimore by 1850. In 1822 Barnet Eytinge was a member of Rodeph Shalom, and it is likely that the entire clan joined the German Shul.[22]

Herman van Beil (1799–1865) of Amsterdam also cut a wide swath through the Philadelphia Jewish community. He immigrated to the city in 1820 at age twenty-one, arriving on the ship *Enterprise* from Amsterdam on November 6. Although trained as a bookbinder, he became a secondhand clothes dealer and later a pawnbroker. He joined Mikveh Israel initially and served as a cantor on a rotating basis. He then transferred to Rodeph Shalom and was its secretary in 1827 and president in 1831. In 1858 Van Beil transferred yet again to Isaac Leeser's new congregation, Beth-El Emeth, and served as trustee and vice president (1860–1861). The small, traditionalist congregation followed the Sephardic rite. When Herman van Beil died at his home on Franklin Street in 1865, his obituary proclaimed, "In his life he was an honorable, upright man . . . of varied and deep learning. He was the oldest member of the Eastern Star Lodge, in Philadelphia, of the Masonic Order." Lodge membership was typical of successful Dutch Jewish businessmen and indicates the extent of acculturation, but Van Beil's philanthropic activities, which are discussed later, show that he remained very Jewish.[23]

The man who rose to the highest pinnacle in Philadelphia was

Abraham Hart, a second-generation Jew, whose father was German and mother Dutch.[24] His father Abraham was born in Hanover in 1781, came to Philadelphia in 1804, and married Sarah Stork (1791–1863), daughter of Aaron Stork, who was born in Amsterdam and brought to Philadelphia by her parents in 1807. Abraham Hart, Sr., had a number of business partnerships: in groceries with Elias Hyneman (also Dutch) until 1811 and in dry goods with Michael Nisbet (nativity unknown) until 1815. In 1816, Abraham, Sr., went bankrupt and his father-in-law Aaron Stork took charge of his affairs and saved the store located on the southwest corner of Third and Race streets. After Abraham's untimely death in 1823, his widow Sarah Hart, with the help of her teenaged son Abraham, Jr., born in Philadelphia in 1810, continued the business, and with unstinting effort and ability she built up a successful book and stationery store and operated it until her death in 1863. Young Abraham thus came under the influence of his Dutch mother and grandfather more than his German father.

In 1829 Abraham Hart, Jr., received the opportunity that launched his career as "the leading Philadelphia Jew of his generation." Matthew Carey, owner of the city's leading book publishing firm, Carey, Lea and Carey, was so impressed with the young bookseller, then only nineteen years old, that Carey took young Abraham as a junior partner. As the historians Edwin Wolf 2nd and Maxwell Whiteman describe it, "Within a week, one of James Fenimore Cooper's popular novels appeared in bookstores bearing the new imprint, Carey & Hart. Hart became one of the most successful and highly esteemed book publishers in the country." Wolf and Whiteman continue, "and in the next generation he was without question the leading Jewish layman of Philadelphia." Abraham Hart, Jr., along with Moses Aaron Dropsie whose career is discussed later, represented the epitome of success for second-generation Dutch Jewish immigrants in Philadelphia. Other Holland-born Jews in Philadelphia before 1820 are Benjamin I. Philips, Jacob S. Jacobs, and Abraham Lazarus, but biographical details are lacking, except that Lazarus in 1820 was a dealer at 246 North Second Street.

To a lesser extent than the New York Dutch who settled for a time in London, the Philadelphia Dutch came directly from Amsterdam, except in three known instances. In the 1850 census and again in 1860, only two Dutch Jewish families in Philadelphia had children born in England, and these families had lived there from 8 to 43 years. Four families in 1850 and eight in 1860 had English-born wives but all their children were born in the United States. Whether these marriages took place in England or America is not known, but if there was a London stopover it was very brief. In the 1870 census only six families had children born in England and the average stay, judging from the children's ages, was 7.3 years. These were several cigarmakers' families, and a peddler and an agent. Four families in 1870 had English spouses, but no children were born in England. This compares with 75 Dutch Jewish families in New York in 1870 who had English-born children, and with an average sojourn of 12 years. Only four New York Dutch with English spouses had no children born in England. Clearly, the Dutch Jews in Philadelphia had been better off economically in the Netherlands, and they immigrated earlier than those settling in New York who, out of economic necessity, spent a longer sojourn in London. For the Philadelphia Dutch Jews, a London stopover or two-stage migration, was not as necessary or desirable.

Once established, these differing migration traditions persisted for decades. Relatives in London followed family and friends to New York while Philadelphia relatives in the Netherlands came direct. The origin of these traditions probably lies in Atlantic trade patterns that linked Amsterdam with Philadelphia during the American Revolution. Philadelphia remained the commercial and financial center of the infant nation until New York City supplanted it in the Jacksonian era after the completion of the Erie Canal. Then London and Amsterdam trade were both funneled into New York.

Religious Life

As already noted, many Dutch initially joined the more familiar Rodeph Shalom Congregation. Leon van Amring was a founder of Rodeph Shalom in 1795.[25] Van Amring, Stuttgart, Spyers, Stork, Hyneman, Goldsmit, and Goldkop were original signers of the 1810 constitution. Dutch members who served as trustees and officers were Jacob de Lange, Abraham Israel, Spyers, Stork, Abraham B. Cohen, Stuttgart, and Van Beil. De Lange, a dry goods merchant in Upper Delaware, was the first secretary of the congregation in 1810–1811. Stuttgart held the post in 1817–1818 and was president in 1821–1822.[26]

In the years 1813–1815 a "large portion" of the charter members, who were unhappy with the lack of a regular reader and the inadequate rented quarters, returned to the well-established Congregation Mikveh Israel, which had a beautiful building and enjoyed a higher status in the community. At least five of the original ten Dutch sign-

Table 4.1
Dutch in Congregation Rodeph Shalom Subscriber's
List, 1811–1840

S. (or L.) Cantor 1811–1833	Elias Solomon Lens 1835
Abraham B. Cohen 1811–1837	S. Myers 1820–1838
Moses Content 1825	Benedict Nathan 1811
Abraham Cuyk 1820–1830	A. H. Pachter 1818
Morris de Bruin 1832	Abraham Schoyer 1815–1818
Jacob de Lange 1811	R. Schoyer 1823
A. H. de Young 1822–1824	E. Semon 1833
Joseph de Young 1814–1816	Jacob Semon 1832
Aaron M. Dropsie 1822–1837	Moses Semon (Siemon) 1827–1835
Barnet Eytinge 1822–1823	S. Semon 1834
L. Fellerman 1836	Moses Shoyer 1820, 1822
Moses Fellerman 1835	Myer Shoyer 1821
A. Garritson 1822	Moses Spyers 1811–1812
F. Garritson 1821	Aaron Stork 1811–1812
I. Garritson 1823–1827	H. F. Stork 1823
Isaac Goldsmit 1838	Henry Stork 1822
L. M. Goldsmit 1811–1812	I. Stuttgart 1822
Elias Hyneman 1811–1815	Isaac Stuttgart 1812–1825
Abraham E. Israel 1811–1812, 1833	Herman van Beil 1822–1834
Jacob S. Jacobs 1833	Moses Isaac vander Slice 1835–1839
Abraham Lazarus 1816–1834	S. A. Waterman 1837

Source: Edward Davis, *The History of Rodeph Shalom Congregation, Philadelphia, 1802–1926* (Philadelphia, 1926), app. 3, 141–45.

ers of Rodeph Shalom transferred, including De Lange, Goldsmit, Hyneman, Israel, and Spyers.[27] Trustee Abraham B. Cohen joined them and became a sexton at Mikveh Israel. It appears that these membership transfers had more to do with a desire for upward social mobility than with any changes in personal circumstances.

Throughout the nineteenth century at least one-quarter of the member families of Mikveh Israel were Dutch or of Dutch ancestry and many held office there.[28] Dutch leaders at Mikveh Israel included the sextons Cohen and Israel, the latter held the post almost thirty years from 1824 until his death in 1852. Van Beil served as cantor on a rotating basis. Benjamin I. Philips was president from 1811 to 1815.[29]

Despite the defections to Mikveh Israel, most Dutch remained in the German congregation and they were joined by newcomers. In its first twenty-five years, Dutch members comprised one-third to one-half of the yearly subscribers and were among the largest contributors (see Table 4.1 for a list of the Dutch subscribers, 1811–1840).

Abraham B. Cohen, a carver and gilder, remained in the congregation without interruption for at least a decade, as did his son Moses Cohen. Newcomers in the late 1810s and early 1820s were Abraham Lazarus (a dealer in North Liberties), Abraham Cuyk, Dropsie, Van Beil, and Dr. Alexander Wertheim, a Dutchman who came from Baltimore to be clerk of the Philadelphia Board of Health and served as circumcizer until his sudden death in 1830.[30] Van Beil was secretary in 1827 and president in 1831. Dropsie was a financial mainstay of Rodeph Shalom until his death in 1839. His son Moses was one of the few Dutch who remained active in the congregation until the 1880s and later. S. A. Waterman, formerly of Baltimore, was elected treasurer in 1837. In 1839 Elias Solomon, "an estimable Israelite" who had immigrated from the Netherlands around 1834 or 1835, was elected as the third *hazan*. He was also the sexton. Solomon read the services for two years, during which time another Dutchman, Moses Shoyer, was president.[31]

Throughout the 1820s and 1830s the struggling immigrant congregation rented various buildings, costing no more than $250 per year, in the southern district bordered by Cedar and Vine streets and Second and Eighth streets. Between 1815 and 1824 the annual subscription list nearly doubled from twenty to thirty-seven members and in 1819 they hired the first regular minister, Jacob Lippman of London. "Rabbi Jacky" had many inadequacies and his tenure was stormy. He finally resigned in 1833 and by 1836 the list of subscribers had shrunk to a low of eight. The congregation was nearly bankrupt and plagued by constant bickering and frustration over the inability to afford their own synagogue. To remain viable the officers even rescinded the rule barring those who married "contrary to the Jewish Rite," provided that they agreed to raise their children as Jews. This allowed Abraham Cuyk, who had married a Gentile, to remain a synagogue leader along with Aaron Dropsie who was exempted in the original rule.[32]

Although Rodeph Shalom experienced its ebb tide in the 1830s, a fresh tide of German immigrants in the next decade soon restored its fortunes. In 1847 after years of waiting, the congregation finally could afford its own synagogue, which was located on the north side of Philadelphia on Julianna Street above Callowhill. The few Dutch Jews who still lived in the northern wards continued to worship at Rodeph Shalom, but it had truly become a German congregation. The lists of officers and members in 1867 and 1881, published in Davis's synagogue history, contain no known Dutch members. The opening of the Julianna Street synagogue thus marked the emergence of Rodeph Shalom from its first fifty years of struggles and sent a signal that the German congregation was ready to take its place among the major synagogues of Philadelphia.[33]

In addition to Rodeph Shalom, the Dutch had yet another option with the founding in 1840 of a second Ashkenazic synagogue, Beth Israel, commonly called the Polish congregation. The worship rites were those of the Great Synagogue of London. A number of Dutch immigrants joined Beth Israel, and one, Hyman Polock, helped found the congregation and served many years as a trustee and was the fourth president. Myer A. van Collem, a tailor, was a trustee and David A. Philips the sexton.[34]

The first regular minister of Beth Israel was also Dutch. In April 1843, the congregation sent a call to a young educator and reader in Amsterdam, the Reverend Simon E. Cohen Noot, who was born in 1810. Noot accepted the call, emigrated to Philadelphia, and served the congregation as reader for four years. In 1847 he took a position as reader in the newly formed Dutch synagogue of New York, Bnai Israel.[35] The Philadelphia congregation grew rapidly and in 1848 under Noot's successor, the Reverend Gabriel Papé, they broke ground for a "really beautiful" synagogue, which they consecrated with much fanfare on the Great Sabbath immediately before Passover 1849. The Dutch minister Samuel Myer Isaacs of New York's Sharaay Tefila Congregation delivered the dedicatory address in his customary English tongue. The "new and imposing building" was located on the north end near Mikveh Israel.[36]

Despite the accolades, Beth Israel was neither distinguished nor wealthy. It appealed frequently to the wider Jewish community to tide it over financial difficulties. New immigrants joined, however, and the congregation slowly grew under Papé's leadership until his death in 1872. But it did not remain the home of very many Dutch.[37] In 1852 the Dutch immigrants had sufficient strength to form their own nationality congregation, Bnai Israel (Sons of Israel), as they had done in New York in 1847 and would do in Boston in 1859.

Bnai Israel, the Netherlands Synagogue, 1852–1879

As in New York and elsewhere, the Dutch Jews of Philadelphia formed a nationality synagogue as soon as they had a sufficient number of men to sustain a congregation. But, unlike the New York congregation who openly admitted that their primary motive was to worship according to the Amsterdam *minhag*, the Philadelphia Dutch justified their decision to organize on the basis of geographical convenience. According to Isaac Leeser, editor of the *Occident* and rabbi of neighboring Beth-El Emeth Synagogue, the Dutch synagogue "has sprung into being from the necessity there exists, almost, of having a place of worship nearer to those living in the lower part of town, than the Synagogues hitherto existing, which are all four to the North."[38]

If nothing else, this reason for existence blunted the charge of selfish nationalism leveled by Reverend Leeser a few months earlier in his editorial in the *Occident* entitled "Thoughts on the Jewish Ministry." In this strident editorial, Leeser condemned nationality synagogues in the strongest terms:

> All this produces rivalry, and consequently, often bitterness of feeling, which prevents all unison for the common good. The German will not unite with the Pole, the Pole with the Portuguese, the Portuguese with the Hollander or Bohemian, and so on to the end of the chapter. Every little knot of settlers has thus its own fancies, its own faults, as well as its own good traits to guard and watch over. And what is gained by this separation, this isolated standing aloof? We will whisper in your ear, kind reader, "Nothing at all." The result is a waste of money and source of contention and estrangement.

Different pronunciations of the Hebrew language, poems originating from different parts of Europe, and even different ceremonies and prayers are all minor, Leeser declared. "America is different from Europe. As a mixed culture, various nationality groups must give up their customs," he concluded.[39]

The Dutch ignored this sober advice and proceeded to begin a nationality synagogue on grounds of convenience. On July 25, 1852, some thirty Dutch males, many of whom were among the earliest Jewish settlers in the city, organized the Netherlands Bnai Israel Congregation. Henry de Boer, a dealer in old clothes who had helped organize the Dutch congregation in New York five years earlier, again took the lead and served as the first president of the congregation. This doubtless explains why the Philadelphia Dutch chose the same name for their congregation as did the New York Dutch synagogue. De Boer was succeeded by Moses A. van Collem, a tailor, who was already living in Philadelphia in 1830. The congregation consecrated its first synagogue in a rented hall on the third floor of a building on the southeast corner of George Street (now Guilford) and Cedar (now South) Street, between Second and Third streets. This was on the border between the New Market and Southwark wards.

Besides the inauspicious meeting place, the congregation could not at first afford their own clergyman. So the Reverend Lippman of Rodeph Shalom offered his services free of charge for two years, with the occasional assistance of Feist Bachman, a layman, on high holy days and festivals. During Lippman's tenure, the Netherlanders kept their official membership uptown at Rodeph Shalom in order to obviate the need for Bnai Israel to purchase its own burial ground or have a kosher butcher. All of these characteristics of the early years indicate that the members of the Dutch synagogue were not well-off. Most, indeed, were recent immigrants.[40]

From this tenuous beginning the congregation made "strenuous efforts to obtain a permanent footing" among the three older synagogues of Philadelphia: Mikveh Israel (Portuguese), Rodeph Shalom (German), and Beth Israel (Polish).[41] The Dutch synagogue, like its counterparts in New York and in Boston, was strictly Orthodox. Rare, indeed, was the Dutch Jew in America who was not Orthodox, at least until the 1870s.

Bnai Israel grew rapidly and enjoyed its greatest success from 1855 to 1862 during the tenure of the Reverend Simon E. Cohen Noot.[42] Noot, a teacher in the Jewish School in Amsterdam, emigrated in 1843 to become the reader of Philadelphia's Dutch-Polish synagogue, Beth Israel. After four years, he transferred to the Dutch synagogue, Bnai Israel of New York, where he was reader and Hebrew teacher for eight years, 1847–1854. Then for one year, 1854–1855, he went to Boston as reader of the Dutch-Polish synagogue Ohabei Shalom and particularly to organize and open a new Hebrew school for the Warren Street congregation. Noot in 1855 thus returned to Philadelphia where he had served his first congregation, but his second ministry was in a wholly Dutch congregation. He again taught Hebrew at the Philadelphia Education Society School, which was founded in 1857.[43]

Within months after Noot's arrival, his energetic leadership and that of the trustees enabled the infant congregation to purchase their own building on the east side of South Fifth Street above Catherine Street, which they converted into a synagogue and dedicated with great fanfare on January 8, 1857. The location was less than a mile southwest of Cedar Street in the Southwark district, in the heart of the Dutch Jewish settlement. This was the fulfillment of a dream. As Leeser reported: "This Congregation have made strenuous efforts since their first organizing, to obtain a permanent footing among the older bodies in the city." Only six months later, on July 3, 1857, a malicious attempt was made to set fire to the synagogue building and the culprits were never found.[44] Whether this overt antisemitism was an isolated act or endemic in the community is unknown.

The Reverend Noot served the congregation for six years and was an "ardent and zealous advocate" who on many occasions "extracted it from its financial difficulties."[45] In early 1862 affairs reached such a critical state that the congregation faced an imminent decision to sell its synagogue. In desperation Noot appealed to his friend and countryman Samuel M. Isaacs of New York City to help raise contributions. Isaacs reported the "deplorable" situation in his prominent journal, the *Jewish Messenger*: "[We] trust that we need but call attention to the fact in order that the benevolence of our co-religionists may be aroused, to extend the desired aid." Isaacs offered to receive and forward all donations.

The appeal saved the day, but Noot decided several months later to accept the call of Boston's Ohabei Shalom Congregation. The Dutch body at Philadelphia could no longer afford his salary, although they reelected him as their reader by acclamation in 1861 and again in 1862. At his farewell on September 7, 1862, Bnai Israel adopted a resolution praising their departing leader for helping establish the congregation. "We miss a devout minister and a profound scholar, universally admired for his mental endowments and for his gentleness and benevolence in social and private life."[46]

Hazan Noot had not built the congregation single-handedly. His second son Isaac, who was assistant teacher of Hebrew at the Philadelphia Education Society School, occasionally preached "with permission" at Bnai Israel (and other city synagogues as well) "in order to qualify himself gradually for the office of a teacher of religion."[47] Henry de Boer, the president and acting treasurer of the congregation in 1857 and following years, was credited "for his great efforts to reduce the debts incurred in the purchase of the new Synagogue." He was a dealer in secondhand clothes in 1850 and 1860 and a dry goods jobber in 1870. Another key individual was the longtime sexton and collector John M. Davis, also Dutch, who lived with his family in a private apartment in the synagogue and also served as caretaker and watchman. He was so respected that at his death in 1866 the congregation agreed to pay for his funeral expenses and to maintain his widow and family for five months until they could complete their planned move to New York.[48]

Others holding leadership positions in the 1860s, in addition to President De Boer who was reelected "by acclamation" in January 1861, were his successors Simon Alexander and Joseph Sanson, merchant and Philadelphia court interpreter, respectively; treasurer E. Wolters, a dealer in secondhand clothes and his successor Isaac Goldsmit; secretary H. J. Hunt (Hond), son of Jacob Hond, a clothier; and trustees Simon Alexander; Eleazer Gerrit Boutelje, a tobacconist; George Fellerman, a dealer and peddler; and Abraham de Bruin, another dealer.[49] Several Germans and Poles held offices in Bnai Israel, which was not as exclusively Dutch as its counterpart in New York. This could be expected since it was the only synagogue on the south end for a number of years and non-Dutch Jews found it convenient to worship there.

Hazan Simon Noot served the wider Jewish community in numerous ways while ministering at Bnai Israel. Most important was his work in education, as senior teacher of Hebrew in the school of the Hebrew Education Society of Philadelphia, for which he was paid $500 per year.[50] Noot and Congregation Bnai Israel also reached out to the community in 1856 by founding the Jewish Foster Home of Philadelphia for orphans who would otherwise go to Gentile institutions. Noot considered the Hebrew orphanage and school to be intertwined, the first to provide "order, cleanliness, and every comfort" and the second "to cultivate our tender minds, and furnish us with information, instruction both in religious and moral duties."[51] The congregation was a regular contributor to the foster home to the extent that its meager finances allowed.

Late in his tenure, in March 1861, Noot as a staunch defender of Orthodoxy sought to organize a council of all of Philadelphia's *hazans*. The council was to serve as a "consulting body to devise such rules and regulations as [might] benefit the cause of Judaism, and prevent in future any abuse in marriages; *Halizah* [the ceremony of "taking off" or "untying" shoes];[52] divorces; examination of *shochetim* [kosher butchers, etc.]; by persons not duly qualified to act in these matters." In the absence of a legally established ecclesiastical body to maintain the purity of the faith in an open, pluralistic society, Noot clearly hoped to organize a quasi-official body to encourage congregations to practice stricter discipline. Editor Leeser published Noot's proposal in the *Occident* and "heartily" endorsed it, citing lamentable examples of breakdowns in synagogue authority. To the chagrin of Leeser, Noot's proposed council of *hazans* collapsed with his departure a year later for Boston.[53]

When Reverend Noot left for the position in Boston in 1862, the Reverend Samuel B. Breidenbach replaced him and served the small Dutch congregation for twelve years until 1874. Under Reader Breidenbach the congregation continued to promote Hebrew education. In November 1864 the president of Bnai Israel joined in a concerted effort with all the chief officers of the city's synagogues to found a Hebrew college, actually a high school, to prepare young men for rabbinical education. The Hebrew Education Society coordinated the effort.[54]

During the summer of 1866 the congregation completely renovated and improved their synagogue building. On September 6 the building was rededicated in a solemn service in which Reverend Isaac Leeser, the leader of Orthodox Jewry in America, gave an address exhorting the people "to remain faithful to orthodox Judaism," and the choir, directed by merchant Henry de Boer, sang psalms of praise.[55] De Boer's choir was more than a simple synagogue choir. Earlier in 1866 the forty-seven-voice group had formed the Musical Harmony Association of Philadelphia, and they offered to provide public entertainment "for any Jewish benevolent association in the state of Pennsylvania."[56] Although Breidenbach was German, the Dutch continued to dominate the ruling body. The "noted Hebrew," George Fellerman, a peddler, served as president in 1868–1869; Abraham Levy was treasurer; George M. Goldsmit, sexton; George's brother Isaac M., secretary; and the trustees were Moses and Henry Simons, M. de Boer, S. Pauwse, and Joseph Sanson.[57]

The congregation tended to go it alone in many matters. For example, they did not contribute to the United Hebrew Relief Association as did six other synagogues, nor did they send delegates to the New York-based association, the Board of Delegates of American Israelites, which was conceived by Samuel Isaacs, a fellow Hollander. When Rabbi Leeser died in 1868, however, Bnai Israel's officers attended the funeral and sent a glowing resolution, calling Leeser "a true champion of Israel, at home and abroad who, on many occasions, extended his courtesies and friendliness toward us. This congregation has lost a friend."[58] Under Breidenbach's leadership the congregation seemed to have a promising future, but this was not to be. The next minister, while Dutch-born, was the last to serve before the congregation disbanded.

The Reverend Jacob Voorsanger (1852–1908), who was born in Amsterdam, arrived in Philadelphia in January 1873 after a three-months' stay in London. Although the word *voorsanger* in Dutch means fore-singer or cantor, Jacob's father was a diamond cutter and the family had no rabbinical roots. Jacob had no rabbinical training or ordination either, but a few months after his arrival in America Bnai Israel appointed him assistant cantor to Breidenbach. In the pioneer years of Judaism in America such a practice was acceptable and even necessary. Voorsanger married in 1873 and also secured a position as librarian of the YMHA of Philadelphia.[59] Voorsanger succeeded his mentor as reader in 1874 at an inadequate salary of $400 per year. To improve his preaching skills and reach his goal of being a rabbi Voorsanger took elocution lessons from a private tutor and began a self-study program in the Talmud, in Jewish history and world culture, and in languages. Voorsanger is described as a "big" man in every sense, a person of imposing stature who expressed his views forcibly and eloquently, yet with a genial spirit.

Reverend Voorsanger served Bnai Israel for three years until September 1876 when the floundering congregation could no longer afford his salary. Why the synagogue lost members during the 1870s is not entirely clear. One reason was the declining rate of Dutch Jewish immigration to Philadelphia after the Civil War era. Another was the relocation of members from the south end to more prestigious uptown districts. Perhaps the forces of Americanization had weakened the need for a separate Dutch synagogue, especially one committed to Orthodoxy when the tide was running to Reform Judaism. In any case, a lay member, George Goldsmit, acted as reader for two years.

During this time the congregation gained one last goal. On March 3, 1878, it opened a Hebrew school, using its vestry room on Fifth Street above Catharine Street to provide instruction for children of downtown Israelites.[60] But in 1879 Congregation Bnai Israel disbanded and its members transferred to other synagogues. The last president of the congregation was Joseph Sanson, who became a Philadelphia court interpreter in the 1890s; George Fellerman had preceded Sanson as president. Philadelphia's Dutch Jewish community, like that in Boston, was too small and scattered to maintain a nationality synagogue for more than a single generation.

Dutch Jewish Acculturation, 1820–1870

In 1820 there were at least 22 Dutch Jewish households in Philadelphia, totaling about 108 persons (Table 4.2). This was more than one-third of all Jewish households and one-quarter of all Jewish persons in the city. In 1830 the number of Dutch households grew by two to 24, and family members totaled more than 160 (Table 4.3). This was 23 percent of all Jewish households, or about the same proportion as in 1820 (see Table 4.4).[61]

There were two areas of Dutch concentration in 1830; one was around the mother synagogue Mikveh Israel, which was the center of the entire Jewish community, and one was in the southern wards (see Fig. 4.1).[62] In the synagogue area of Lower Delaware, Upper Delaware, and Ward 1 of Northern Liberties, the Dutch comprised 45 percent of all Jewish households, while in the southern wards of

Table 4.2
Dutch Jewish Household Heads in Philadelphia and Northern Liberties, 1820

Name	N	Occupation
Abraham B. Cohen	3	carver and gilder
Jacob de Lange	6	dry goods store
Aaron Dropsie	3	pawnbroker
Barnet Eytinge	3	wholesale fancy goods store
Philip Eytinge	1 (?)	wholesale fancy goods store
Solomon Eytinge	3	merchant
Ezekiel Jacob Ezekiel	4	
Moses I. Goldkop	7	dry goods store
Levi M. Goldsmit	5	dry goods store
Widow Esther Hart	10	runs boarding house
Elias Hyneman	8	grocery merchant
Abraham E. Israel	5	Hebrew sexton, manufacturer
Jacob A. Jacobs	6	
Abraham Lazarus	4	dealer
Benedict Nathan	2 (?)	import merchant
Benjamin I. Philips	8	jewelry store
Hyman Polock	8	jewelry store
Moses Spyers	2	dealer
Aaron Stork	10	grocer, wine merchant
Isaac Stuttgart	2 (?)	fancy goods store
Leon van Amring(e)	7	grocery merchant
Herman van Beil	1	secondhand clothing dealer

Sources: Ira Rosenwaike, "The Jewish Population of the United States as Estimated from the Census of 1820," *American Jewish Historical Quarterly* 53 (Dec. 1963), 158–61; Edwin Wolf 2nd and Maxwell Whiteman, *The History of the Jews of Philadelphia from Colonial Times to the Age of Jackson* (Philadelphia, 1956); Henry Samuel Morais, *The Jews of Phiadelphia: Their History from the Earliest Settlements to the Present Time* (Philadelphia, 1894).

New Market and Southwark, they totaled 42 percent. In the eastside city wards (High Street, Chestnut, Walnut, Dock, and Pine), the Dutch comprised 20 percent, but not one Dutch household resided in these city wards west of Seventh Street.

As a proportion of the Jewish population, the Dutch ranged from 100 percent in the periphery Southwark district, 67 percent in Upper Delaware Ward, 60 percent in Ward 1 of Northern Liberties (a northern periphery district), 33 percent in Lower Delaware in the heart of the city center, to only 11 percent in Dock and none in the seven westside wards. Thus, the Dutch Jews lived among their countrymen along the west bank of the Delaware River, but tended

Table 4.3
Dutch Jewish Household Heads in Philadelphia, 1830

Name	N	Birth	Death	Place of Death	Occupation	Ward
Abraham B. Cohen	2	c.1765	1836	Phil.	carver and gilder	New Mark.
Jacob de Lange	7	1777	1837	New Orleans	dry goods merchant	Up. Dela.
Aaron Dropsie	7	1794	1839	Phil.	pawnbroker	N. Lib. 5
Barnet Eytinge	6	1778	1863	Phil.	wholesale fancy store	Low. Dela.
David Eytinge	5	1764	1855	Phil.	merchant	W. Southwk.
Solomon Eytinge	12	1792	?	?	dry goods merchant	High
Isaac Garritson	7	1795	1863	Nashville, TN	pawnbroker	W. Southwk.
Levi M. Goldsmit	9	1781	1849	Phil.	fancy goods store	N. Lib. 1
Leonard Goslin(g)	12	1793	1887	New York	?	N. Lib. 7
Moses I. Goldkop	9	1798	?	?	fancy goods store	Chestnut
Sarah Hart	6	1791	1863	Phil.	stationer	Walnut
Elias Hyneman	14	1765	1845	Phil.	merchant	Low. Dela.
Aaron Isaacs	7	1801	1878	Phil.	clothing store	N. Lib. 3
Abraham E. Israel	3	1773	1852	Phil.	Hebrew sexton	Low. Dela.
Jacob A. Jacobs	5	c.1785	1832	Phil.	dry goods merchant	Up. Dela.
Abraham Lazarus	3	1791	1865	Phil.	dealer	N. Lib. 1
Henry Myers	6	1783	1832	Phil.	dealer	W. Southwk.
Abraham L. Philip	7	c.1775	?	?	fancy store	Low. Dela.
Hyman Polock	10	1786	1870	Phil.	merchant	Spr. Gard.
Moses Semon	3	1796	1837	Phil.	secondhand clothing store	Moyamen.
Moses Spyers	2	1754	1837	New York	watchmaker	N. Lib. 1
Aaron Stork	7	1764	1842	Phil.	grocer, wine merchant	Dock
Herman van Beil	7	1799	1865	Phil.	pawnbroker	Pine
Myer van Collem	6	pre–1770	?	?	tailor	New Mark.

Source: Ira Rosenwaike, *On the Edge of Greatness: A Portrait of American Jewry in the Early National Period* (Cincinnati, 1985), 112–64.

137

Table 4.4
Jewish and Dutch Jewish Households, Philadelphia,
by Ward, 1830

Philadelphia	All Jews	Dutch Jews	% D	Suburban Districts	All Jews	Dutch Jews	% D
Cedar	0	0	0	Northern Liberties			
Chestnut	4	1	25	Ward 1	5	3	60
Dock	9	1	11	Ward 2	5	0	0
High	6	1	17	Ward 3	2	1	50
Locust	7	0	0	Ward 4	0	0	0
Lower Delaware	12	4	33	Ward 5	3	1	33
Middle	5	0	0	Ward 6	2	0	0
				Ward 7	2	1	50
New Market	9	2	22	Kensington	0	0	0
				Moyamensing	8	1	12
North	2	0	0	Spring Garden	4	1	25
North Mulberry	2	0	0	Southwark	3	3	100
Pine	3	1	33	Total Suburbs	34	11	32
South	2	0	0	GRAND TOTAL	105	24	23
South Mulberry	4	0	0				
Upper Delaware	3	2	67				
Walnut	3	1	33				
Total City	71	13	18				

Source: Compiled from Rosenwaike, *Edge of Greatness*, 124–27.

toward the fringe districts of the south and north ends, where nearly half lived in 1830. Across the entire city, the Dutch made up one-third of the Jewish population in the outlying districts and less than one-fifth in the central wards. Based on the average per capita tax assessments in the various wards in 1820, Dutch Jews lived in the middle economic strata. The heart of the city had the highest averages (around $3–4,000); the figures declined in the wards immediately to the north and south, and they declined even more (below $1,000) on the periphery (except for Wards 1 and 2 in Northern Liberties).[63]

The pioneer Dutch Jews in Philadelphia were well established by 1830. Two-thirds had lived in the city for ten to thirty years and all but four of the 1830 cohort lived out their lives within the city and died there. Of the few exceptions, two died in New York, one in New Orleans, and one in Nashville, TN. The age structure of the

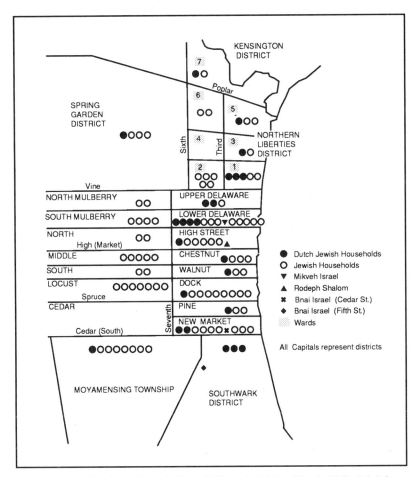

Fig. 4.1. Distribution of Dutch Jewish Households by Ward, Philadelphia, 1830. Adapted by permission from Ira Rosenwaike, *On the Edge of Greatness: A Portrait of American Jewry in the Early National Period* (Cincinnati, 1985).

Dutch household heads in 1830 also reveals a mature population: nine were over fifty years, five in their forties, nine in their thirties, and only one was below thirty (age 29).[64]

Between 1830 and 1860 Philadelphia became an urban melting pot plagued by labor strife and too rapid growth; population increased from 161,000 to 566,000. Yet, Philadelphia remained a small city geographically, confined between the Delaware River on the east and Schuykill River on the west. It was a walking city of homogeneous neighborhoods where almost every trade, nationality and religion lived "near every other," as Sam Bass Warner, Jr., has documented. The Germans, 44,000 strong in 1860, were concentrated on the northside, although they lived throughout the city, as did the Irish, who numbered 95,000 in 1860. Among both German and Irish immigrants, 60 percent lived on the ring region and 40 percent in the core city. Half of the Jews lived in the city proper and half in the outlying districts, mainly Moyamensing.[65] Dutch Jews in 1850 numbered only 148 persons, or 5 percent of the Jewish population. Clearly, the Dutch presence in the Jewish community declined sharply after 1830, when the wave of German Jewish immigration flooded in.

The center of the Dutch Jewish community had shifted southward by 1850 to the three southernmost districts where the new immigrants settled (Fig. 4.2 and Table 4.5). New Market in Ward 5 (immediately north of South Street) had thirty-eight Dutch, Southwark twenty-three, and Moyamensing thirty-nine. Two-thirds of the Dutch lived in these three wards, compared to only 18 percent of all Jews in the city. In Moyamensing, the Dutch Jews comprised nearly half (44 percent) of all Jews in the district, which was the highest concentration in the city. These were mainly new immigrants, attracted to South Philadelphia by the availability of cheap housing and jobs, although they tried to live at least several blocks away from the noxious docks and wharves. The Dutch in the central city wards (excluding New Market on the south fringe) and in the northernmost districts had greatly declined since 1830. Only one in seven Dutch lived in the northern suburbs, compared to 58 percent of the entire Jewish community. The Dutch Jews in 1850 thus were heavily concentrated in the three south end wards, which in 1820 had been near the bottom in average tax assessments, whereas the primary Jewish settlement was centered at the other end of town in the northern section. By contrast, in the central wards (excluding New Market), a smaller proportion (18 compared to 23 percent) of Dutch Jews lived than of all Jews (see Table 4.5).

From the 1840s through the 1870s the anchor of the south Philadelphia Dutch community was the Bnai Israel Synagogue, which in 1857 was relocated to Fifth Street at Catherine in Ward 4 (formerly Pine Ward). After this the Dutch became even more concentrated in Wards 4 and 5, which were the city's first slums. In 1860, 86 percent of all the Dutch Jews in Philadelphia lived in the four southside wards north and south of Cedar (South) Street: Ward 4 had 185 Dutch, Ward 5 (mainly in New Market), 107; Ward 3, 28; and Ward 2, 9 (Table 4.5 and Fig. 4.3). The total Dutch-born population by

Table 4.5
Dutch Jews* as a Percentage of Jewish Population, Philadelphia, by Ward, 1850, 1860 (1870 Dutch only)

Wards	1850 ALL	D	%D	1860 ALL	D	%D	1870 D
Southern Section							
1 Passayunk				82	0	0	0
2 Southwark	191	23	12	159	9	6	12
3 Moyamensing	89	39	44	100	28	28	16
4				605	185	31	247
Subtotal	280	62	22	945	222	23	275
	(10%)	(42%)		(14%)	(58%)		(77%)
Subtotal (incl. Wd. 5)	(19%)	(68%)		(19%)	(67%)		
City							
5 New Market, Pine, Dock Walnut	262	38	15	345	107	31	0
6 Upper & Lower Delaware, Chestnut, High St.	345	16	5	507	1	0	2
7 Cedar (Lombard)	42	2	5	82	0	0	23
8 South, Locust (Spruce)	93	6	6	143	0	0	0
9 North, Middle (Locust)	104	0	0	128	8	0	0
10 North & South Mulberry	89	3	3	143	0	0	18
Subtotal	935	65	7	1348	116	9	43
	(32%)	(44%)		(20%)	(31%)		(12%)
Subtotal (excl. Wd.5)	(23%)	(18%)		(15%)	(2%)		
Near North Section							
11				1148	7	1	5
12 Northern Liberties	1286	12	1	1127	3	0	0
16				841	34	4	0
13				661	32	5	14
14 Spring Garden	187	8	4	203	2	1	0
15				83	2	2	0
17				60	8	13	10
18 Kensington	195	0	0	34	0	0	0
19				103	0	0	10
20 Penn				258	0	0	0
Subtotal	1668	20	1	4518	88	2	39
	(57%)	(13%)		(66%)	(23%)		(11%)

Table 4.5 (Continued)

Wards	1850 ALL	1850 D	1850 %D	1860 ALL	1860 D	1860 %D	1870 D
Northern Section							
21 Kinsessing	15	1	0	19	0	0	0
22 Germantown	3	0	0	5	0	0	0
23	9	0	0	0	0	0	0
Subtotal	27 (1%)	1 (1%)	0	24 (3%)	0	0	0
Western Section							
24 West Philadelphia	9	0	0	7	7	100	0
GRAND TOTAL	2919	148	5.1	6842	428	6.3	357

*Includes Dutch-born and their children (either parent Dutch).

Sources: Compiled from Kenneth David Roseman, "The Jewish Population of America, 1850–1860: A Demographic Analysis of Four Cities," (Ph.D. diss., HUC, Cincinnati, 1971), Tables 1 and 5; Robert P. Swierenga, comp., *Dutch Households in U.S. Population Censuses, 1850, 1860, 1870: An Alphabetical Listing by Family Heads*, 3 vols. (Wilmington, DE, 1987).

1860 had risen to 428 including the second generation. This was still only 6.3 percent of the estimated Jewish population in greater Philadelphia of 13,500. Nevertheless, in the main Dutch wards (4, 5, and 3), they comprised one-third of the total Jewish population.[66]

The Civil War decade brought some dispersion, as the growing city expanded into suburban districts. The departure of Reverend Noot from the Dutch synagogue in 1862 undoubtedly hastened the dispersal. The core Dutch area remained near the Fifth Street Synagogue but some families (about one in ten) moved to the fashionable Uptown districts north of Callowhill. Already in the 1850s Jews began moving into better housing to the north, away from the waterfront districts where crime and prostitution flourished and their middle class sensibilities were offended. Nevertheless, in 1870 the south wards (1 through 5) still housed 77 percent of all Dutch Jews (84 percent if Ward 7 west of Seventh Street is included), but the remaining 23 percent were equally divided, with 12 percent in the central wards—Cedar on the southwest and South Mulberry on the northwest—and 11 percent north of Callowhill. The total Dutch Jewish community in 1870 numbered 357, down slightly from 1860. Thus, the Dutch community was no longer growing and it was

142

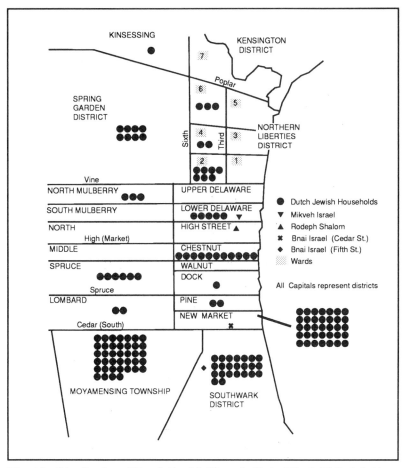

Fig. 4.2. Distribution of Dutch Jewish Households by Ward, Philadelphia, 1850. Compiled from Robert P. Swierenga, comp., *Dutch Households in U.S. Population Censuses, 1850, 1860, 1870: An Alphabetical Listing by Family Heads*, 3 vols. (Wilmington, DE, 1987).

breaking up. The suburban movement—especially to the south but also to the north—which began slowly in the 1860s, accelerated and hastened the integration of the Dutch into the greater Ashkenazic community.

The federal censuses also provide a social picture of the Philadelphia Dutch. Females outnumbered males in each census year whereas the total Jewish population had a large male surplus in 1850 (1.07) and the sexes reached parity by 1860.[67] The female Dutch

143

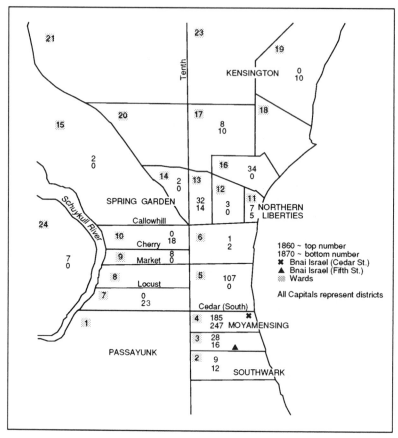

Fig. 4.3. Distribution of Dutch Jewish Households by Ward, Philadelphia, 1860, 1870. Compiled from Robert P. Swierenga, comp., *Dutch Households in U.S. Population Censuses, 1850, 1860, 1870: An Alphabetical Listing by Family Heads*, 3 vols. (Wilmington, DE, 1987).

ratio was 1.04 in 1850, 1.02 in 1860, and a very large imbalance of 1.22 in 1870. First-generation immigrants as a proportion of the total population was 53 percent in 1850, 55 percent in 1860, and 51 percent in 1870. The Dutch preferred to live in single-family homes. Eighty-five percent did so in 1850, compared to less than one-third among other Jews in Philadelphia.[68] But the percentage dropped twelve points by 1860 to 73 percent and 69 percent in 1870. This was still very much better than Jews generally, among whom a little over one-half (54 percent) resided in single-family dwellings in 1860. Meanwhile, the number of Dutch families residing in two-flats

Table 4.6
Dutch Jews with Non-Dutch Spouses by Generation,
Philadelphia, 1850, 1860, 1870

Census	First Generation			Second Generation		
	Total N	N	%	Total N	N	%
1850	29	8	28	5	5	100
1860	68	22	32	9	3	33
1870	66	20	30	13	8	62
Totals	163	50	31	27	16	59

Source: Swierenga, *Dutch Households in U.S. Population Censuses, 1850, 1860, 1870.*

and multifamily buildings increased. Seventeen percent lived in two-family dwellings in 1860, mostly shared with Dutch compatriots. By 1870 only 13 percent lived in two-flats (half shared with fellow Hollanders) and 10 percent were in larger dwellings of three or more families, of which one-third were exclusively Dutch Jews. That so many in these multifamily dwellings included Dutch families indicates their clannishness in Philadelphia. The proportion of Dutch Jewish roomers and boarders in non-Dutch families was only 8, 5, and 7 percent, respectively, for the three censuses. Clearly, Dutch young adults lived at home until marriage rather than "boarding out."

In choosing their mates, first-generation Dutch overwhelmingly married Dutch-born Jewish spouses, but the second generation (including those who immigrated as children) married non-Dutch Jewish spouses. Among those couples married at the time of immigration, the censuses reveal a consistent pattern of more than two-thirds with Dutch spouses. (The exact figures are 72 percent in 1850, 68 percent in 1860, and 70 percent in 1870.) For the second generation, however, 59 percent (sixteen out of twenty-seven) married non-Dutch spouses (see Table 4.6). This high rate of same nationality marriage in the first generation gives evidence of the strength of the Dutch Jewish communities in the Netherlands and London. But the low rate among the second generation also reveals much about rapid loss of Dutch identity in America.

The sex of the non-Dutch partner also shows a pronounced cultural pattern. In first-generation mixed couples, the wife was non-Dutch more than three-fourths of the time, and in second-generation mixed couples, the wife was always non-Dutch. This shows that Dutch Jewish sons outmarried but not daughters. Why

Table 4.7
Nationality of Non-Dutch Spouse, First- and Second-Generation Dutch Jews, Philadelphia, 1850, 1860, 1870

		Non-Dutch Wife										Non-Dutch Husband									
		Eng		Ger		Fr		Swi		USA		Eng		Ger		Fr		Sw		USA	
	N	F	S	F	S	F	S	F	S	F	S	F	S	F	S	F	S	F	S	F	S
1850	13	4	1	1				2		1	2	1									1
1860	25	9		3	2	2		1		3	1	1				2	1				
1870	28	4	1	6	3	1				4	4	1		4							

Source: Swierenga, *Dutch Households in U.S. Population Censuses, 1850, 1860, 1870.*

Dutch Jewish fathers refused to allow their daughters to marry German-, French-, or U.S.-born Jews is not clear since sons could do so freely. The Dutch pattern seems to derive from ethnic loyalties and the greater freedom of men compared to women rather than from demographic factors such as a shortage of Jewish women. There is no evidence that any of these Dutch Jews married Gentiles.[69]

The nationality of the non-Dutch spouses was mainly English until the 1860s because of the common practice of sojourning in England and the higher reputation of English Jews (Table 4.7). English mates outnumbered Germans by five to three, and French and Americans by four to three. By 1870, however, German-born spouses outnumbered English by two to one, and the second generation Dutch men selected German brides by three to one. During the 1860s, therefore, Dutch Jews in Philadelphia lost their perennial English orientation and became increasingly tied to the German Jewish community. This shift suggests that the Dutch Jews in Philadelphia suffered a cultural status decline in the Civil War era.

The increase in the number of recent immigrants with fecund families also lowered the economic status of the Dutch. Family size increased between 1850 and 1870. In 1850 Dutch Jewish families in the city averaged 2.1 children, in 1860 the average was 2.7, and in 1870 3.1. In twenty years the number of children per family increased by 40 percent. This could be expected, perhaps, since the average age of the Dutch Jewish population declined from 29.4 years in 1850 to 24.6 years in 1870. Younger couples have more children. Illiteracy rates are first available in the 1870 census; they show that the Dutch Jews in Philadelphia had a high rate of 22 percent compared to 13 percent for Dutch Gentiles. Out of 254 Dutch-

Table 4.8
School Attendance by Sex, Jewish Children Aged 5–19, Philadelphia, 1850, 1860, 1870

| Census | Dutch Jewish Children | | | Dutch Jews in School | | | | | All Jews* | | |
	M	F	N	All %	M N	M %	F N	F %	School N	School N	School %
1850	25	23	48	56	13	52	14	61	1103	605	55
1860	70	60	130	57	39	56	35	58	2485	1480	60
1870	63	83	146	57	38	60	45	54	NA	NA	NA
All Years				57		57		57			58

*Estimated

Source: Compiled from Roseman, "Jewish Population," Table 18; Swierenga, *Dutch Households in U.S. Population Censuses, 1850, 1860, 1870.*

born Jews and their children ten years and older, 55 could not read or write in any language. Dutch Jews comprised over three-quarters of all Dutch illiterates, but made up only two-thirds of those of Dutch birth or ancestry age ten and older. These Jewish rates of illiteracy are related to the occupational profile of the community and to the cultural values of parents who sent their youngsters out to work instead of allowing them to continue in school.

School attendance figures confirm this generalization and they are also available for all Jewish children. In 1850 only 55 percent of all Jewish children aged five to nineteen attended school; in 1860 the figure was only slightly improved at 60 percent (Table 4.8).[70] Dutch Jewish children in the city attended in nearly the same proportion: 56 percent on 1850, and 57 percent in both 1860 and 1870. The proportion of Dutch girls in school was higher than boys in 1850 and 1860 (61 to 52 percent in 1850 and 58 to 56 percent in 1860, respectively), but in 1870 the percentage of boys in school was higher than for girls (60 to 54 percent). When times were hard, families sent sons out to work earlier, so the low attendance rate for sons in the 1840s and 1850s suggests such economic necessity, which was largely obviated by 1870. These were, after all, new immigrant families for the most part. Age-specific attendance figures confirm the economic forces. Through age thirteen more than three-quarters of all Dutch Jewish youngsters attended school in the year preceding the censuses of 1850, 1860, and 1870. But only one-half of fourteen- and

147

fifteen-year olds were in school in these years, one in five sixteen-year olds, and only one in ten seventeen-year olds. No eighteen- or nineteen-year olds were in school.

Occupation

The Dutch, like other Jews in Philadelphia in the Jacksonian era, were almost entirely engaged in commerce or trade. The 1825 City Directory listed at least thirteen Dutch merchants. Their shops were mainly in the central business district, although one was on Callowhill Street at the north end and two on Cedar (South) at the south end. Tradesmen located near the city center between Front and Sixth streets and running north and south of Market Street for a block or two included David & Van Dyke dry goods, Abraham Lazarus dealer, and Goldsmit and Goldkop dry goods, all on North Second; Michael E. Israel merchant on Walnut; A. C. Peixotto merchant on South Fifth; Joseph Pereyra taper manufacturer on Bryans Court; Aaron Stork, grocer, wine and liquor merchant; and Barnet Eytinge, wholesale fancy goods, both on Front Street. The Callowhill shopkeeper was Moses Spyers, a dealer. The two south end tradesmen were A. B. Cohen, a carver and gilder, and the secondhand clothing shop of Herman van Beil, both along Cedar Street.[71]

The 1830 federal census, which is more comprehensive than the city directories but lacks street addresses, includes twenty-three Dutch Jewish household heads whose occupations are known; twenty (83 percent) were merchants (Table 4.9). They primarily owned dry goods and fancy goods stores and pawnshops, but there were also two dealers and a grocery, bookstore, watchmaker's shop, and stationery store. The two craftsmen, a tailor and a carver and gilder, were likely master craftsmen and also operated retail shops for their wares.[72] The preponderance of merchants was common among Jews generally; in Philadelphia 65 percent were merchants in 1830. Discrimination in Europe had forced Jews into mercantile pursuits. Their religious beliefs also led them into the types of shops and trades that would permit Saturday closings and would supply the needs of the community for kosher foods and clothing dictated by Mosaic law.[73]

The occupations of Philadelphia's Jews in 1850 and 1860 follows this standard picture (Table 4.9). In 1850 of 765 Jews in the labor force, over half (51 percent) were merchants, dealers, peddlers, and

Table 4.9

Occupations, Dutch Jews as a Percentage of All Jews, Philadelphia, 1830, 1850, 1860, 1870 (1870 Dutch only)

	1830			1850			1860			1870
	ALL	D	%	ALL	D	%	ALL	D	%	D
Professions										
accountant, bookkeeper	2	0	0	1	1	—	21	0	—	1
attorney	3	0	0	0	1	100	—	—	—	—
auctioneer	—	—	—	1	0	—	4	0	—	—
chemist	1	0	0	4	0	—	7	0	—	1
doctor, dentist, drug	1	0	0	9	2	22	13	1	8	—
engineer	—	—	—	1	0	—	1	0	—	—
minister, rabbi, sexton	2	1	50	3	0	—	4	1	25	—
musician	—	—	—	3	0	—	10	0	—	—
optician	—	—	—	3	1	—	4	0	—	—
student (law, med.)	—	—	—	2	1	50	0	0	—	1
teacher	—	—	—	0	0	—	8	0	—	—
other	—	—	—	1	0	0	7	1	14	1
Subtotal	9 (9%)	1 (4%)	11	28 (4%)	6 (13%)	21	79 (4%)	3 (3%)	4	4 (3%)

Table 4.9 (Continued)

	1830			1850			1860			1870
	ALL	D	%	ALL	D	%	ALL	D	%	D
Business										
agent, broker, dealer	15	2	13	61	5	8	143	46	32	12
bookbinder, publisher	—	—	—	8	3	37	0	0	—	1
bookseller	—	—	—	3	1	33	3	1	33	—
clerk, salesman/lady	—	—	—	52	0	—	183	3	2	10
clothier	3	2	67	19	0	—	58	2	3	5
collector	—	—	—	1	1	100	0	0	—	—
grocer	4	1	25	5	0	—	0	0	—	—
jeweler, watchmaker	2	1	50	9	1	11	39	0	—	1
manufacturer	6	0	0	5	1	20	12	0	—	—
merchant	15	3	20	128	4	3	162	3	2	3
pawnbroker	3	3	100	6	3	50	4	0	—	—
peddler	—	—	—	61	1	2	142	3	2	16
storekeeper	17	8	47	17	3	18	48	12	25	1
tavern, inn, hotel-keeper	2	0	0	8	0	—	35	1	3	—
trader	1	0	0	9	4	44	4	0	—	—
Subtotal	68 (65%)	20 (83%)	29	392 (51%)	27 (59%)	7	833 (45%)	71 (69%)	8	49 (39%)

Skilled

Skilled										
baker	—	—	—	9	0	—	8	0	—	—
barber	—	—	—	2	0	—	8	0	—	1
blacksmith	—	—	—	3	0	—	18	0	—	—
bricklayer	—	—	—	5	0	—	14	0	—	—
butcher	—	—	—	8	1	12	6	1	17	3
carpenter, cabinetmkr	1	0	0	8	0	—	23	0	—	—
carver & gilder	1	1	100	—	—	—	—	—	—	—
confectioner	—	—	—	6	0	—	3	0	—	1
cooper, tinner	—	—	—	2	2	100	6	1	17	—
cap & hatter, furrier	—	—	—	30	0	—	65	2	3	2
cigarmaker, tobacconist	—	—	—	21	2	10	92	9	10	26
dyesinker	1	0	0	—	—	—	—	—	—	—
machinist	—	—	—	10	0	—	16	0	—	1
painter	—	—	—	4	2	50	19	1	5	1
paperhanger	—	—	—	2	0	—	3	0	—	—
printer	—	—	—	10	0	—	25	0	—	—
seaman	—	—	—	1	0	—	2	0	—	—
shoemaker, cordwainer	—	—	—	36	1	3	109	0	—	1
tailor(ess), seamstress	1	1	100	84	3	4	247	10	4	15
weaver	—	—	—	6	0	—	4	0	—	—
misc.	—	—	—	53	0	—	89	5	6	4
Subtotal	4 (4%)	2 (8%)	50	300 (39%)	11 (24%)	4	757 (41%)	29 (28%)	4	55 (44%)

Table 4.9 (Continued)

	1830			1850			1860			1870
	ALL	D	%	ALL	D	%	ALL	D	%	D
Unskilled										
driver, coachman	—	—	—	2	0	—	14	0	—	—
drover	—	—	—	2	0	—	11	1	1	3
farmer, gardener	—	—	—	0	0	—	5	0	—	2
factory worker	—	—	—	3	0	—	6	0	—	5
household servant	—	—	—	0	0	—	95	0	—	5
laborer	—	—	—	24	1	4	22	0	—	—
janitor	—	—	—	0	0	—	2	0	—	—
porter	—	—	—	1	0	—	2	0	—	1
watchman	—	—	—	1	0	—	1	0	—	—
waterman	—	—	—	2	0	—	3	0	—	—
misc.	—	—	—	3	0	—	12	0	—	1
Subtotal	0	0	0	39 (5%)	1 (2%)	3	173 (9%)	1 (1%)	—	17 (14%)
Other										
gentleman/woman	15	0	0	6	1	17	24	0	—	0
retired, not given	9	1	11	0	0	—	1	0	—	0
Subtotal	24 (23%)	1 (4%)	11	6 (1%)	1 (2%)	17	25 (1%)	0	—	0
GRAND TOTAL	105	24	23	765	46	6	1867	104	5	125

Sources: Kenneth David Roseman, "Jewish Population of America, 1850–1860." Table 3-C "Occupational Distribution"; Swierenga. *Dutch Households in U.S. Population Censuses, 1850, 1860, 1870.*

the like; more than one-third (39 percent) were craftsmen, mainly in cigar making and clothing; 5 percent were unskilled workers; and 4 percent were professionals. By 1860 this occupational distribution had changed only slightly in a downward direction. The proportion of businessmen fell by 6 points (51 to 45 percent), which was a decline of 10 percent. Meanwhile, the proportion of skilled craftsmen increased slightly and unskilled wage laborers nearly doubled from 5 to 9 percent.

Dutch Jews in the antebellum decade when compared to all Jews in the city ranked higher on the occupational prestige scale. The Dutch had a higher proportion of businessmen and professionals and fewer skilled and unskilled wage earners. For all employed Jews in 1850, 51 percent were tradesmen compared to 59 percent for the Dutch. The percentage of Dutch professionals was three times higher than for Jews generally (13 and 4 percent, respectively). Among blue-collar workers, 24 percent of the Dutch were craftsmen compared to 39 percent for all Jews, and only 2 percent of the Dutch were unskilled compared to 5 percent of all Jews. By 1860 the Dutch Jews had further outdistanced Jews generally in the city; 69 percent were merchants and tradesmen in contrast to only 45 percent among all Jews, and only 29 percent of the Dutch were wage earners (skilled and unskilled) compared to 50 percent of all Jews.

Thus in the antebellum decade, Dutch Jews in Philadelphia advanced more rapidly up the occupational ladder than did other Jews. At a time when the proportion of Jews in business and trade declined by nearly 10 percent, Dutch Jews *increased* their proportion in business by nearly the same amount. Among skilled craftsmen, the percentage increased about 15 percent while other Jews remained the same. But among unskilled laborers and domestics, the percentage of all Jews nearly doubled, but only one Dutch Jew could be found in this lowly category in 1850 and 1860.

The Dutch advancement of the 1850s was only temporary. Throughout the middle decades of the nineteenth century they generally experienced a long-term decline in occupational status because of the arrival of large numbers of immigrants. In the 1840s the first major economic shift occurred. The number in business and trade declined while those in skilled crafts increased. Between 1830 and 1850, the percentage of tradesmen declined from 83 to 59 percent, and in the 1860s the number of businessmen fell sharply to only 39 percent. The number of skilled craftsmen tripled between 1830 and 1850 from 8 to 24 percent, and this proportion held steady in the 1850s. Professionals were always a small minority among Dutch Jews; there was only 1 in 1830 (4 percent), 6 in 1850 (13 percent), and 3 (3 percent) in 1870.

153

The second major downward occupational shift occurred in the 1860s when more Dutch were blue-collar workers, both skilled and unskilled, fewer owned businesses. By the time of the 1870 census, 44 percent of the city's Dutch Jews were craftsmen, 14 percent were unskilled day laborers, and only 42 percent were in the professions and business. Of the 17 unskilled workers—a rare group among Jews—5 were female domestics, 2 were factory hands, 3 were in gardening, and 5 were simply described as "laborer." Of the 49 in business in 1870, 16 were peddlers, 12 agents and dealers, and 10 clerks and retail sales persons.

Dutch Jewish merchants ranked near the bottom of the prestige scale in 1860 and 1870. Most were peddlers (designated as "dealers" in the 1860 census) or used-clothing dealers. The peddlers lived in the city's first slum area along South Street east of Sixth Street in the eastern division of Ward 4, and the clothing stores, both used and new, were farther west along the same street, in the western division of Ward 4. The eastern stretch of South Street was in the older section of Philadelphia near the docks and wharves of the harbor where the garment sweatshops were concentrated. It is unknown whether the peddlers traveled with a basket—the very poorest—or a trunk, pack, or even a horse and wagon (the aristocrats of the trade), but only a few reported any personal property, and that only $200 or less. One, however, reported $4,000 worth of personalty. This suggests that at least one Dutch Jewish peddler reached the ranks of the "aristocrats."[74]

Dutch Jewish artisans turned to the tobacco and garment trades. Philadelphia was the nation's textile center in the 1850s, employing over ten thousand, and Jewish clothiers dominated the business. Cigar making was just emerging as a true growth industry under the impact of protective tariffs during the Civil War and the soaring popularity of cigars after the war. Between 1860 and 1870 the number of Dutch cigarmakers, strippers, and tobacconists increased from nine to twenty-six; and the number of tailors, seamstresses, and dressmakers rose moderately from ten to fifteen. Thus in 1870 half the craftsmen worked with the weed and a third toiled in the garment industry. Except for the peddlers, the 1860s immigrants instead of becoming self-employed shopkeepers and dealers had to work for wages in the tenement house lofts and cellars of cigar and clothing manufacturers. Sweating meant long hours of tedious work for low wages in dank rooms, most of which were concentrated in the southside fringe area among the city's first slums.[75] The Dutch could easily walk downtown from their residences in the poor southern wards. Clearly, the economic status of Dutch Jewry in Philadelphia declined during the years after the Civil War.

The U.S. Census reports of real and personal property, although notoriously unreliable, show a leveling off in the 1860s after a sharp rise in wealth in the 1850s. In 1850 when real estate alone was recorded, only four Dutch Jewish families (out of forty-seven households in the labor force) reported realty valued from $1,500 to $14,000, for a total value of $25,000. In 1860 only six out of eighty-three employed households reported real estate ranging up to $30,000, for a total value of $53,000. By 1870 nine Dutch families owned realty, ranging up to $40,000, for a total value of $81,000.

These rates of Dutch households owning real estate appear low, but compared to all Jewish households in Philadelphia, the Dutch were favorably situated. The proportion of Dutch families owning realty in 1850 and 1860 was more than twice that of all other Jews. Excluding Dutch-headed households, in 1850 only 68 Jewish households reported realty, out of more than 2,500 Jewish households in the city. In 1860, 233 owned realty, out of more than 6,500 households.[76]

Personal property was more widespread. In 1860, twenty-seven Dutch households reported from $100 to $900, and eighteen had $1,000 or more, including three whose personalty exceeded $10,000. Of all Dutch Jewish households in 1860, forty-five owned personalty and thirty-eight did not. By 1870, the number of property owners held steady but the dollar value had risen; twenty-eight owned less than $1,000 and fifteen had more, including three (again) with $10,000 or more. Again the Dutch compared favorably. Their proportion of one-third of households owning personalty in 1860 was twice as great as among Jews generally.[77]

The total reported wealth of the Dutch thus rose from $25,000 in 1850 to $135,000 in 1860, to $162,000 in 1870. On a per household basis (including nonwealth holders), the average wealth of the Dutch Jews in 1860 was $1,626 and in 1870 $2,160. These figures are skewed by several extremely wealthy families. Two men at the top of the wealth pyramid were Herman van Beil, a merchant whose wealth increased from $14,000 in 1850 to $40,000 in 1860, and Hyman Polock, a jewelry merchant who was worth $50,000 in 1870. Three-fourths of the wealth of Van Beil and Polock was in real estate. Hyman's son, Moses Polock, a publisher and bookseller, was worth $11,000 in 1860 and $24,000 in 1870.

After 1850, a select few Dutch Jews filled the position of U.S. court interpreter in Philadelphia, where they interpreted and translated documents for immigrants. Probably because of an adeptness at languages, at least four Dutch in succession held the interpreter's post: David Eytinge (1850–1855), David A. Davis (1855–1862),

Herman van Beil (1862–1865), and Joseph Sanson (1861–1865 and again 1869–1894).[78] Merchandizing afforded the best opportunities for Dutch Jews to excel in Philadelphia in the postbellum years and several did very well. In the early 1860s Louis Hano (1823–1897) began a wholesale clothing business on Third and Market streets that he expanded into several retail outlets, the largest at Tenth and Market.[79] Leon Isaacs (1831–1889) owned a retail store for two decades and then with two of his sons built a prosperous business manufacturing steel writing pens.[80] Abraham Meyer Frechie (1831-post 1896), who emigrated in 1856, was a famed tobacco dealer. His skill in grading American-grown tobacco that rivaled Havana's best made him prominent in the trade throughout the United States. Major dealers and importers often sought his judgment on questions of grading and quality. Retiring in 1887 after thirty years in the business, Frechie sojourned in Paris where his wife's relatives were prominent bankers. He later returned to Philadelphia and began importing Cuban tobacco in partnership with a Cuban immigrant.[81]

The most successful Dutch merchants in Philadelphia history were the brothers Samuel D. and Jacob D. Lit, sons of Dutch-born David J. Lit. In 1891 the ambitious young men opened a small department store on Eighth Street, featuring ladies coats and hats. Their sign "Hats Trimmed Free of Charge" was familiar to every woman walking along this busy retail street. In 1893 in the teeth of a financial crisis, they bought a five-story building fronting on the northeast corner of both Eighth and Market streets, the prime retail corner in Philadelphia. Within three years, despite the depressed economy, Lit Bros. expanded from the lower into the upper floors and then quadrupled their space by demolishing five buildings on both sides and erecting an imposing Renaissance-design building of 118,300 square feet of display space and featuring French-plated display windows "with their various exhibits, bright in color and most artistically arranged," all brilliantly illuminated by hundreds of electric lights (see Fig. 4.4). The whole edifice "suggests to the beholder viewing the corner from an angle that the crystal palace has been transferred to Philadelphia," crowed a writer for the *Jewish Exponent*. "What a contrast to the humble little store in which the Litts [*sic*] cradled their earliest hopes!" declared the publicist. The huge enterprise employed 860 by 1897, all protected by a company-sponsored mutual benefit association. The Lit brothers attributed their success to "hard work, quick judgments, shrewd enterprise, liberal methods, up-to-date ideas, and a thorough appreciation of the wants of the public." In truth, they operated a modern discount store fea-

Fig. 4.4. Lit Bros. Department Store, Philadelphia, PA. Reprinted from the *Jewish Exponent* (Philadelphia), December 11, 1896.

turing the lowest prices and guaranteed customer refunds "if the article has not proved acceptable in every way. We never quibble about returning money; it is to be had for the asking," declared Samuel Lit.[82]

Philanthropy

In addition to the synagogue leadership, economically successful Dutch Jews were active in numerous Jewish benevolent, educational, and literary organizations, and a few were involved in politics. A dozen names appear again and again in Jewish institutional life. The most prominent among first-generation immigrants were Van Beil, Polock, De Boer, and Frechie. Noteworthy second-generation Dutch were Aaron Dropsie's son Moses A.

Fig. 4.5. Moses Aaron
Dropsie (1821–1905) of
Philadelphia, PA.
Courtesy of Maxwell
Whiteman.

(1821–1905) (see Fig. 4.5), Hyman Polock's son Moses (1817–1903), and Alfred T. Jones (1822–1888). Dropsie, the oldest son of Aaron, was the consummate Dutch Jew. Although his mother was Protestant, Moses at age fourteen chose Judaism as his religion and remained an ardent, Orthodox Jew for all of his long and productive life. He became a prominent attorney, traction magnate, philanthropist, and promoter of Jewish higher education—including Dropsie College.[83] Polock rose to prominence in the prestigious, old-line Philadelphia publishing house of McCarty and Davis, which he took over in 1853. One of his early ventures was to publish the first collected edition in 1857 of Charles Brockden Brown, America's first novelist. Polock retired early and followed his avocation as a rare book dealer and bibliophile.[84]

Jones, despite his English-sounding name, was born in Boston of a Dutch father, Andrew A. Jones. Young Jones left New York for Philadelphia in 1847 at age twenty and worked for over fifteen years in the wholesale clothing trade. In 1874 he established and edited, with Henry Morais, a successful weekly, the *Philadelphia Jewish Record*. When the Russian pogroms began in 1881, the *Record* took a special interest in raising an alarm and in organizing relief efforts. In 1884 Jones, with the help of Moses Dropsie and a few others,

158

formed the Association of Jewish Immigrants to help resettle Russian refugees in Philadelphia. Alfred Jones was renowned for this kind of leadership in Jewish communal life. The list of his activities is long: first president of the Association of Jewish Immigrants (1884–1888); founder, first president, and longtime director of the Jews Hospital (1866–1884); vice president and secretary of the Hebrew Education Society (1861–1867); recording secretary of the Jewish Publication Society (1845); president of his synagogue; president of the Philadelphia *Chebrah* (1863); director of United Hebrew Charities (1869); and active in B'nai B'rith and the Shekinah Masonic Lodge. For all this he died "full of honor" in 1888.[85]

The Hebrew Benevolent Society, the oldest charity in Philadelphia founded in 1813, had at least fifteen Dutch trustees and officers at various times in the nineteenth century. Hyman Polock worked in the society more than fifty years and served in the early years as president. Davis was secretary and Van Beil the faithful treasurer of the Hebrew Benevolent Fuel Society, which likewise had many Dutch officers. Five of twelve managers in 1861 were Dutch. These included Henry de Boer, Abraham Frechie, Abraham Hart, Louis Raines, and Judah Isaacs. Three Dutch were managers of the Hebrew Relief Association in the 1860s (De Boer, Dropsie, and Polock) and Dr. Philip de Young, the only Dutch Jewish physician in the city, provided free medical care.[86]

The United Hebrew Charities of Philadelphia, formed in the merger of six relief societies, had Moses Lazarus as the first assistant secretary and Abraham Goldsmith as one of the first managers; Moses Simons "rendered excellent service" as president from 1871 to 1875. Lazarus, a merchant born in the Netherlands in 1815, "rendered considerable aid to the Society by his knowledge of languages, which enabled him to see to the wants and necessities of individuals from different climes."[87] Goldsmith was the Philadelphia-born son of Levi M. Goldsmit, who emigrated in 1810. He was also a manager of the Jewish Foster Home of Philadelphia along with Dutch-born Mrs. George Cromelien. Simons was a peddler born in Holland about 1813. Dropsie promoted the Hebrew Charity Ball Association as a fund-raiser among the well-to-do in support of the United Hebrew Charities. The "celebrated Hebrew clergyman" Samuel M. Isaacs of New York's Shaaray Tefila Congregation gave the invocation at several balls. Abraham Hart, of German-Dutch parentage, presided over the association in the 1850s and was treasurer for many years.[88]

Jewish international unity and self-help were also close to the hearts of the Dutch. Dropsie was the third president of the Philadelphia branch of the Alliance Israélite Universelle serving from 1879 until at least 1894, and Frechie was treasurer. The alliance, headquartered in Paris, was the largest and most comprehensive international Jewish organization. Hart was the third president of the Board of Delegates of American Israelites, an association of Orthodox congregations that cooperated with Jewish societies in Europe in ameliorating conditions of Jewish poor in Palestine and other "benighted countries."[89]

Dropsie and Louis Hano helped found the Jews Hospital of Philadelphia in 1866, (forerunner of the Albert Einstein Medical Center) and in the early 1880s when Russian Jewish immigrants overwhelmed the existing charities, Dropsie also was a prime mover in establishing the Association of Jewish Immigrants in 1884, along with Frechie, a director and trustee (1884–1894). The association's agent met all steamers at the Philadelphia docks and aided Jewish newcomers. The agent also held the position of interpreter to the U.S. Commissioner of Immigration at Philadelphia in order to assist the new arrivals.[90]

In no work did the Dutch put more effort than in Jewish education. After the Reverend Isaac Leeser in 1843 first called for Jewish day schools in a stirring article in his *Occident*, which warned of the dangers in the "Gentile" schools, Dutch Jews in Philadelphia readily joined in the effort, spurred on by Leeser's ally Reverend Isaacs of New York, who endorsed Leeser's call.[91] Morris H. de Young spearheaded the attempts to found a Hebrew day school and at the first regular meeting of the Hebrew Education Society in 1848, Hart became secretary and Polock, Dropsie, and Van Beil were elected directors. In the next few years, De Boer and Moses vander Sluis (Slice) joined the directors' board.[92] Simon C. Noot, reader of Bnai Israel congregation, was Hebrew teacher in the 1850s, assisted by his son Isaac. Later Dutch teachers were 'Hayim Polano and Marcus Eliezer Lam. In 1854 when the society opened its new school building after three years in rented quarters, Dropsie gave the dedicatory address. Nearly forty years later, in 1891, after serving almost continuously as an officer or board member, Dropsie again had the honor of giving the dedication address when the school relocated into another new building. Lazarus was secretary in the 1860s and Lens, described as "a well-known member of the Hebrew community," served for many years as the collector and secretary of the board in the 1870s and 1880s. David van Beil was assistant secretary. Samuel Morais Hyneman and Andrew Kaas were directors and Myer Fleisher was president in 1892–1894.[93]

Higher education for Jews beyond the local area was not neglected either. Dropsie and Henry de Boer helped in 1867 to launch the first Jewish seminary, Maimonides College and Seminary of Philadelphia. Dropsie was president and Abraham Hart led the board of trustees, along with trustee Myer S. Isaacs of New York, son of Samuel M. Isaacs. The college failed in 1873 but not from any lack of effort by Dropsie. 'Hayim Polano, who was born in Holland in 1831, became a Hebrew instructor at the college. One of his prize students who taught at the Hebrew day school was Marcus Eliezer Lam, born in Amsterdam in 1854 and son of merchant Eleazer Lam.[94] In 1893 when Congregation Mikveh Israel received the large Hyman Gratz legacy to establish and maintain a Jewish college in Philadelphia, Dropsie again served as chair of the congregation's Permanent Committee, along with Frechie and Samuel Hyneman to make the dream a reality. He then became president of Gratz College from 1893 until his death in 1906.

Dropsie was passionately contemptuous of Reform Judaism and disappointed that a previous Jewish seminary (which failed) had been located in New York. He wanted in Philadelphia a conservative postgraduate school to study the sources of Judaism and rabbinic literature. His efforts and financial contributions, particularly $1 million bequeathed in his estate, made this possible in 1907. The governors named the college in his honor, Dropsie College for Hebrew and Cognate Learning. It was a specialized institution to train scholars rather than rabbis (because Dropsie was mildly anticlerical), and its admissions policy was nonsectarian, which the benefactor insisted on as an expression of respect to his Protestant mother.[95]

A minor aspect of Jewish educational efforts was an ambitious publication program to provide Jewish books in the English language. The American Jewish Publication Society (1845), Hebrew Literary Association (1850), and YMHA (1875) made such books available. Hart was the first president of the Publication Society and Leon Hyneman, son of Elias, was a founding trustee and manager. Solomon C. van Beil, Herman's son, was president of the Hebrew Literary Association in the early 1850s. He passed the Philadelphia bar in 1851 and died prematurely in 1853. E. Wolter, Samuel Hyneman, Benjamin W. Fleisher (the latter a grandson of Myer Fleisher) were active in the YMHA, and future rabbi Jacob Voorsanger was the association's librarian in the 1880s.[96]

Among third-generation Dutch, five sons of Isaac Hyneman, all leading businessmen, were active in Jewish affairs, three in Philadelphia and two in new York. Samuel's involvements have already been noted. Levi Leon Hyneman (1838–1899), a distillery commission merchant in Philadelphia, participated in Mikveh Israel Synagogue, Jewish charities, and the Mercantile Club.[97]

Only a few Dutch are known to have held political office, although a number of young men served in the Mexican and Civil wars. Attorney Moses A. Dropsie, son of Aaron, rose to the highest pinnacle in city politics and public affairs. In 1852 he ran for mayor of the Northern Liberties district on the Whig ticket and was an antislavery advocate. In 1856 he helped organize the Republican party in Pennsylvania. From 1856 to 1861 he was president of the Mercantile Club of Philadelphia, the highest honor the city elite could bestow. He was an early member of the Union League and supported President Abraham Lincoln. After the Civil War, when racists demanded that freedmen be barred from the Philadelphia street railways, Dropsie as a prominent president of several railways fought for their right to use public transport.[98] Other Dutch Jews known to hold public offices in Philadelphia were Abraham Kannewasser (? –1892), a special officer under Mayor Donald M. Fox, and Solomon Raines, a clerk in the Office of Prothonotary of the Court of Common Pleas in the 1890s. Both were Republicans.[99] One Jew of Dutch stock, Gabriel Dropsie, son of Aaron, fought in the Mexican war and at least eight others served in the Union army during the Civil War, including Elias Leon Hyneman, son of Benjamin, who paid the ultimate price of American citizenship: he died a prisoner of war in the hell-hole of Andersonville Prison. Ironically, his first cousin Jacob E. Hyneman fought in the Confederate army. Such is the nature of a fratracidal war.[100]

Conclusion

Philadelphia served as an early base for Dutch Jewish merchants who arrived during the Napoleonic wars, most coming directly from Amsterdam. These merchant families associated together in business, synagogue life, and their children married one another. Philadelphia Jews were also closely linked to family and friends in Baltimore, New Orleans, Richmond, and other commercial centers, and they moved freely back and forth.

The high point of Dutch Jewry in the city was in the 1830s when the Dutch comprised nearly 40 percent of the Jewish populace. But the heavy German immigration thereafter quickly made the Dutch a very small minority, concentrated in the southern part of the city near the Netherlandic synagogue. Although the first generation Dutch overwhelmingly married Dutch spouses, more than half the children married Germans and a few had English-born spouses.

162

This indicates a rapid loss of Dutch identity in favor of the dominant German Judaism.

But there are also evidences of continuing Dutch connections in the closing decades of the nineteenth century. Myer S. Frechie's daughter Melina married Eleazer Lam's son Samuel E. in 1891. In 1896 when Frechie's son S. M. Frechie married, ten of the thirteen couples on the guest list were Dutch, including the Fellermans, Lenses, Linses, Pereyras, Voorsangers, and Wolterses. Five of the eight pallbearers were Dutch at the funeral of Leon Isaacs, husband of Anna Hano. The Cremieux Lodge, No 83, International Order of B'nai B'rith was largely Dutch, including president Myer S. Frechie, vice president I. M. Goldsmit, secretary Isaac Pinheiro, treasurer Joseph Sanson, and warden S. van Mindes. Louis Hano and Eleazer Marcus Lam also were members.[101]

In synagogue life the Dutch were Orthodox and most affiliated with the German congregation, Rodeph Shalom, until they were able to found a Netherlands congregation in the early 1850s. A minority of pioneer families, however, remained with the prestigious Sephardic synagogue, Mikveh Israel. Wherever they worshiped, the Dutch held leadership positions, including ministers such as Simon Noot and Jacob Voorsanger, sextons such as John M. Davis, and synagogue presidents such as Henry de Boer and Abraham M. Frechie. They were also active in Jewish philanthropy and education, led by successful businessmen like Moses Dropsie.

Occupationally, the Dutch experienced several status shifts downward. The first came in the 1840s when the number of independent tradesmen declined and skilled craftsmen increased. The second was in the 1860s when a sweatshop army emerged in the tobacco and needle trades, which came to dominate the Dutch labor force. Nevertheless, compared to all Jews in the city, more Dutch relatively were businessmen and fewer were wage earners. Most Dutch businessmen, however, were peddlers and old clothes dealers, who ranked near the bottom of the prestige ladder.

Thus, both culturally and in their work, the Dutch Jews of Philadelphia in the decades after the Civil War became part of the larger German Jewish community. The closing of the Dutch synagogue in 1879 signified the completion of the transition.

Chapter 5

BOSTON: A CLOSE COMMUNITY

Boston's Dutch Jewish community flourished in the middle decades of the nineteenth century, totaling nearly 400 by 1870. Besides in New York and Philadelphia, only in Boston did the Dutch establish their own "Netherlandisch" synagogue. Under strong local leaders, especially the Reverend Markus Hamburger, the Boston Dutch maintained a conservative, close-knit community that intermarried and lasted for two generations. For decades the city's overall Jewish population remained comparatively small and was less than 2,500 in 1870. Its mainly Polish-Dutch constituency was religiously traditional and maintained a Hebrew school to train their youth. Occupationally, most Dutch peddled consumer goods or rolled cigars, but an elite group of diamond cutters made Boston the second center, behind New York, of the diamond trade.

Very few Jews lived in early New England, although many stopped there in trade. Boston's Jewish community did not take root until the 1840s when a wave of German Jews arrived.[1] Long before that time Boston had lost first place in population and ocean trade to New York City, but it developed into the manufacturing and distribution center of New England and its overseas trade spanned the globe.

Boston's Jews first met for worship in 1842. In the next few years they organized Congregation Ohabei Shalom (Lovers of Peace) and a mutual aid and charity society, hired a *hazan*, and built a synagogue. But the community remained small; the congregation numbered only seventy families in 1847.[2]

By the summer of 1850 the census taker numbered 360 Jews, about 110 families, nearly 75 percent of whom lived in the southern part of the city (Wards 10 and 12) and across the channel in South Boston. A number of merchants, however, owned shops at Beacon Hill in the north end business district and commuted daily a mile or more from their homes in the south. There were 2,300 Jews in the city in 1860, mainly living in row houses and apartments in the south end, although only a few yet remained in south Boston. Over 80 percent of Boston Jewry in 1860 resided in the area south of Boston Commons (in Wards 8, 9, 10, 11). However, nearly 10 percent had moved to the Beacon Hill business district, which was a precursor of future trends.[3]

Dutch Jews arrived in Boston in significant numbers in the 1840s and 1850s, although a few families settled there earlier—Isaac da Costa, Moses Michael Hays (1729–1805), Abraham Touro (1774–1822) and his brother Judah (1775–1854), William Pool, Andrew Abner W. Jones, and Aaron Isaacs (Van Brunt).[4] Da Costa came to America before 1762 with a lavish annual allowance of £200 from his wealthy father in Amsterdam. He settled in the pioneer Jewish community of Boston and purchased the Needham estate immediately outside of the city for £1,300. Later he developed 22,000 acres of raw land in Nova Scotia where he resided for a time in the mid 1760s before returning to Holland in 1768. His troubles began when he reemigrated to Revolutionary Boston late in 1777 to safeguard his estate, only to find himself briefly imprisoned and then summarily deported for refusing to take the Patriots' loyalty oath. His Massachusetts property was confiscated and all efforts to collect compensation from the British government failed, leaving him destitute.[5]

Moses Michael Hays moved from Newport to Boston during the Revolution and began a maritime insurance underwriting business on State Street. He was born in New York City to Judah Hays who had immigrated to New York in 1763 and became a prominent merchant and shipowner. Moses also engaged in banking and maritime shipping, including the China trade, at his base in Newport from 1769 until hostilities drove him out. The wealthy Hays held high positions in the Masons. He was grand master of the Massachusetts grand lodge from 1788 to 1792 while Paul Revere was deputy grand master. In 1784 Moses helped organize Boston's first bank, the predecessor of the First National Bank. He died in Boston in 1805 and his wife Rachel Myers, also of Dutch ancestry, died in 1810. Hays's younger sister Reyna, who married Rabbi Isaac Touro of New York's Congregation Shearith Israel, also came to Boston after her husband's death in 1783 and died in the city in 1787. Hays's nephews, Abraham and Judah Touro, surpassed in fame their uncle who gave them their start. Abraham remained in the city and became a successful businessman, while Judah moved to New Orleans in 1803 where he made his fortune.[6]

Descendants of the Hays and Touro families remained in Boston and prospered. In 1817 when Congregation Shearith Israel of New York issued a worldwide appeal to prominent merchants for donations for a new synagogue building, their who's who of leading Jews included only two men from Boston—Judah Hays and Abraham Touro. Touro's wealthy and influential uncle Moses Hays trained him well in the world of commerce. At his death in 1822 Touro left $50,000 to Hebrew philanthropies, plus $100,000 to his younger brother Judah that also went to Jewish charities eventually. Judah Hays, who became a founder of the Boston Atheneum, did not need the money since he had inherited his father's fortune.[7]

William Pool, who was probably of Rotterdam, was living in Boston in 1815 at the birth of his daughter, Mary A.; other Pool children were born in Boston in 1820 and 1834. Andrew A. Jones (1777–1850) was born in Amsterdam, a son of Jonah. His oldest daughter was born at the English Channel port of Sheerness in 1809, perhaps while the family was en route to London and eventually to the United States. After his wife's death, Jones remarried in 1821 at New York City to Miriam (Maria) Marks, widow of fellow Hollander Jonas Barnett. By 1822 the family had resettled in Boston where three children were born between 1822 and 1827. In that latter year Jones sent money from Boston to help New York's oldest Ashkenazic congregation, Bnai Jeshurun, to build a new synagogue. Later Andrew served for twenty years as assistant surveyor of the Port of New York. His only son Alfred Timons Jones (1822–1888) was born in Boston on July 4, 1822, and in 1842 moved to Philadelphia to engage in the wholesale clothing business.[8]

Aaron Isaacs of Amsterdam emigrated to Boston sometime before 1815. In 1824 he went to Richmond to marry a fellow Hollander, Esther Levy, and was back in Boston the next year when his first son Isaac Aaron was born. Thereafter, the family lived briefly in Atlanta, but by 1830 they had settled permanently in Philadelphia, where Aaron operated a large clothing shop in the central city for nearly five decades.[9]

A true Dutch Jewish community took shape after 1840 at the same time as the larger Jewish settlement developed. At least 13 Dutch Jewish men, 10 with families, came in the 1840s. They were joined in the 1850s by another 49 men, 46 with families. The 1850 census marshal recorded 22 Netherlandic Jews, or 6.1 percent of foreign-born Jews. The 1860 census included 115 Netherlands-born Jews, or 5.0 percent of all foreign-born Jews.[10] With the second-generation, the Dutch proportion increases dramatically. In 1850 there were 62 residents of Dutch Jewish birth or parentage, which increased to 269 persons in 1860. Between 1860 and 1870 the Dutch community increased by another 100 persons, totaling 374 in 1870, including wives and children.[11]

Religious Life

Initially, the Dutch joined the charter synagogue, Ohabei Shalom, located first on Washington Street and from 1863 on Warren Street near Tremont. Several held leadership positions, including Abraham Prince, an optician who arrived via England in the 1830s, and Levi Oldkerk, an embroidery shopowner and the wealthiest Dutch Jew in Boston in the Civil War era. Oldkerk's reported wealth was an impressive $17,000 in 1860. Prince served on the synagogue's three-man founding committee that drew up its constitution and bylaws in 1845, and he, along with Oldkerk, was among its first seven trustees in the 1840s.[12]

Several of these Dutch families migrated in stages, coming to Boston after stopping elsewhere for a time. This was a continuation of the earlier pattern of the Hays, Touro, and Jones families. Abraham Prince had a child born in England in 1835. Only Andrew Jones of the earliest group is known to have had a child born in England. Samuel Spear (Spier) and Solomon Cook had children born in Pennsylvania (probably Philadelphia) in the 1830s, as did Levi Oldkerk in 1845. A child of Eleaser Lazarus was born in Louisiana (probably New Orleans) in 1846, and Bernard Milkman had a son in New York in 1847. Other early arrivers were Benjamin de Young, whose daughter was born in Boston in 1843; Eliphalet Cook, whose daughter was born in 1845; Louis Goldsmith; Joel Hart; Morris Stern; and Solomon Isaac, who arrived in 1848 or 1849 with a wife and four children. Thus, Boston's Dutch immigrated from other American cities rather than from England. They were more like the Philadelphia than New York Hollanders.

Soon German and Polish Jews, along with Dutch Jews, settled in Boston and national rivalries began. The strife and factionalism between German and Polish Jews was particularly strong and led in 1854 to schism.[13] The Germans founded the new more liberal Pleasant Street synagogue. The Warren Street synagogue, mainly Polish and Dutch, maintained the strictly traditional worship. Oldkerk served as president and Bernard Milkman (Melkman) as secretary from 1854 to 1856. Prince succeeded Oldkerk as president from 1856 to 1857 and another Dutchman, Henry S. Spear (Spier), a merchant tailor born in Holland in 1822, followed Prince in 1858 and 1859. Milkman and William Block were two of the five synagogue trustees and Isaac Pachter (Pagter) was the kosher butcher. Prince and Spier in 1858 formed an ad hoc committee representing the Warren Street and Pleasant Street congregations, which drew up a resolution of commendation to the British government for granting Jews complete emancipation. So, Dutch Jews headed Boston's largely Polish synagogue during the 1850s after the Germans withdrew.[14]

To maintain its distinctiveness Ohabei Shalom opened a Hebrew school in 1854 with forty pupils. Oldkerk drew on his Dutch connections by having the congregation call the Reverend Simon E. Cohen Noot of New York to head the school. Noot had emigrated from Amsterdam in 1843 and was the noted Hebrew teacher and scholar of New York's Bnai Jeshurun Synagogue. Noot got the school underway during its first two years and then moved to Philadelphia to become the rabbi of Congregation Bnai Israel and principal of the Hebrew Education Society of Philadelphia. Milkman was secretary of the Hebrew school. The Reverend Samuel M. Isaacs declared in his *Jewish Messenger* in 1863 that this school "is probably the only real [Hebrew] Free School in the United States."[15]

The congregation also founded its own *Chevra* in 1854, the Hebrew Mutual Relief Society (less commonly known as the Hebrew Benevolent Association). Levi Oldkerk was the first president and Milkman and Prince were trustees. Besides these three, at least three other Dutch were among the thirty-nine trustees: William Block, Simon Levy, and Bernard Sugarman.[16]

Dutch Jews continued to take a leading role in Ohabei Shalom in the 1860s, which congregation according to the *Jewish Messenger*, "bids fair to become the first in the New England states." It had eighty members and forty seat holders in 1863. Abraham Prince was president and Isaac Pachter kosher butcher and custodian. He also preached on occasion in German, as on the second day of Rosh Hoshana in 1860. As a mark of its trust, the congregation in 1861 named Pachter to a three-man committee made responsible for undertaking regular collections for the Holy Land. Benjamin Hart, a clothier, and Isaac Buitenkant, a peddler, were trustees.[17] Even more important, the synagogue, after losing its rabbi in 1862, called to its vacant pulpit Reverend Simon C. Noot of New York, the former director of its Hebrew school. Noot accepted, returned to Boston after a six-year absence and served the congregation well as *hazan* for five years until his death in 1867. In September 1863, Noot conducted the dedication service of the new Warren Street Synagogue, assisted by son Isaac, the teacher of Hebrew in the Free School. President Abraham Prince gave an address recounting the twenty-five years of the congregation.[18] In 1865, Reverend M. H. Myers of Kingston, Jamaica, was elected as assistant rabbi.[19]

Beth Eil, the Dutch Synagogue

Although many of the pioneer Dutch continued to be involved in Temple Ohabei Shalom, the newer arrivals were sufficiently numerous by 1859 to secede and organize a pure Dutch synagogue, Beth Eil. This was the third congregation in the "Modern Athens." Like Boston's other immigrants in the mid-nineteenth century, Dutch Jews brought a sense of group identity that compelled them to segregate themselves in a worshiping community. As Oscar Handlin phrased it, the newcomers "strove to reweave on alien looms the sundered fabric of familiar social patterns." They created new institutions "to protect a vital cultural difference."[20]

Beth Eil's Hollanders and the few Englishmen who joined them were recent immigrants struggling for survival. "They are mainly men of limited means and dependent on their daily labor," the *Jewish Messenger* reported. Mark (Markus Jacob) Hamburger, a twenty-eight year old peddler with no theological training or ordination, was their leader and driving force, serving as the first president and perennial minister. When he died about 1890 after a long and active career, his monument in the Holland cemetery was a stone pulpit. Hamburger had emigrated from his native Amsterdam to New York in 1857 as a single young man of twenty-six. His father was a street seller and he became one too. By 1860 he had married Caroline Slocum, a daughter of Emanuel Slocum, a Dutch-born owner of a fancy goods store in Boston. Hamburger's younger brother, Meyer Jacob, immigrated from Amsterdam after the Civil War in 1865.[21]

Although no formal records are extant of Temple Beth Eil, Albert Ehrenfried, the chronicler of Boston Jewry up to 1900, identified about thirty-six member families. Most were Dutch-born, although a few had children born in England. Services followed the orthodox Ashkenazic ritual and the congregation met in a chapel on Gloucester Pike in the south end. Their cemetery in Melrose was purchased in 1860. In 1867 to save money they moved their place of worship to a small hall on the ground floor of the Mishkan Tefila Congregation on Orange Street. Four years later they moved again to a leased building on Dover Street between Albany Street and Shawmut Avenue. Trustees of the congregation in the early years, besides the Reverend Hamburger, were Nathan Goldsmith, Lewis Levy, Emanuel Slocum, and Louis Verveer. Simon Sugarman and Jacob Cornel were involved in the cemetery administration. Joseph Stockfish (Stokvis), a cigarmaker, succeeded Hamburger as minister, followed by Alexander Buitenkant, a son of former trustee Isaac Buitenkant, who was a clothing dealer and later importer of Dutch goods. All three ministers were Amsterdammers.[22]

The Dutch Jews of Congregation Beth Eil also founded their own *Hollandsche Chevra* or mutual aid society, called the United Brethren Association. The date of founding is unknown, but it was likely in 1859 because mutual aid societies were usually founded before or in conjunction with a new congregation.[23]

The Boston Hollanders, according to Ehrenfried, were a closely knit social group, who held themselves somewhat aloof from Jews of other nationalities. But in 1865 the *Jewish Messenger* countered this view by commending their benevolence. The Hollanders "are imbued with a Jewish spirit, and whenever the occasion demands it, they are always ready to extend a helping hand to their needy brethren."[24] As the years passed the Hollanders gradually became integrated into the broader Jewish religious and social community. Attendance at Beth Eil declined and the congregation finally had to give up its chapel on Dover Street, meeting only on high holy days in rented space at Red Man's Hall (near the corner of Dover and Tremont streets) or at Paine Memorial Hall. During the remainder of the year, the Dutch attended other synagogues, particularly Mishkan Tefila, a strictly traditional synagogue comprised mainly of East Prussians from Posen Province.

In the 1870s Congregation Beth Eil experienced a brief revival when its membership of seventy was augmented by accessions of dissatisfied conservatives from Congregation Ohabei Shalom, which was moving toward moderate Reform. In September 1875 the Dutch congregation consecrated a new synagogue at Gloucester

Place in a renovated former church. Cantor Hamburger sang the service before a "large assemblage" and led a voluntary male choir. The Reverend Isaac C. Noot, former Hebrew teacher at the Free School, returned from New York City to deliver the sermon. Noot urged his fellow Hollanders "to adhere with tenacity to the ancient ritual of the ancient creed, to beware of innovation, and to remain steadfast to the grand old forms of the faith." Despite the best intentions, revival could not be sustained. Few new Dutch immigrants arrived to nourish the congregation and modern trends militated against orthodoxy in religion. Eventually, declining membership forced the congregation to give up its synagogue and abandon all religious functions. Only the *Hollandsche Chevra*, which in March 1875 was incorporated with the congregation as Corporation Beth Eil, remained to conserve and maintain the mutual benefit society and Montrose Cemetery.[25]

There is a conflicting picture of Congregation Beth Eil in 1875, this from the pen of Rabbi Zvi Falk Vidaver, then minister of Ohabei Shalom. Writing in the Vienna (Austria) Hebrew Monthly *Ha Shakhar*, Vidaver described Beth Eil as "progressive in spirit, [but] these Jews nevertheless have done nothing to propagate the faith. They meet on Saturday and pray in Hebrew, though few of them understand their own prayers. They make no effort to sustain the principles of Judaism, nor do they exert themselves to transmit Jewish learning or loyalty to their children."[26] The Dutch synagogue was hardly atypical in this respect. None of the Jewish boys in Boston learned the Talmud or were taught to read and pray in Hebrew, according to a north end banker in 1875 writing in *Ha Shakhar* in reply to Rabbi Vidaver.[27]

Since the *Hollandsche Chevra*, which in 1909 had reorganized as the Netherland Cemetery Association, was still active in the 1950s —providing sick benefits and burial rites to Jews—one can conclude that the Dutch Jews maintained some sense of Dutchness for one hundred years. Other evidence is the Ladies' Mutual Beneficial Association founded in March 1872 by wives of the Hollanders' Shul. Elizabeth Cook was president, Marian (Mrs. Mark) Jacobs secretary, and Henrietta Slocum treasurer. Mrs. Jacobs, who was born in Holland, served as secretary for thirty-eight years. The society was an auxiliary of Congregation Beth Eil and the *Hollandsche Chevra* and it outlived them both. It disbanded temporarily in 1932, but in 1935 it was revived as the Ladies' Netherlands Association in affiliation with the Netherlands Cemetery Corporation.[28]

Boston's Dutch Jews, in conjunction with the English-Dutch Jews, in 1876 launched one other *chevra*—the United Hand-in-

Hand Society. Its leaders were more secular and Americanized Dutch, including some of the second generation. Moses van Dam, the president, had recently withdrawn from the Dutch synagogue. The society's cemetery was in Dedham on the West Roxbury line. It is reported to be the largest Jewish burial ground in Massachusetts. The society continues to provide burial services and sickness and death benefits to Jews "of good moral character not married contrary to Jewish law and custom."[29]

In the early nineties, a few of the Dutch and English Jews in Boston, mainly cigarmakers by trade, tried unsuccessfully to organize a congregation, the Baron de Hirsch Synagogue; and they purchased a burial ground in Montvale. The synagogue failed, but the Roxbury Mutual Society that the Temple formed in 1892 still flourished in the 1940s.[30]

Similar to Jews elsewhere in America, the religious life of Boston Jewry was weakened by rival nationalisms. All Jews, though they shared a common religion, were also Dutch, German, Polish, Prussian, Portuguese, or English. Each nationality group had their doctrinal diversities and unique culture. Dutch Jewry in Boston reflected the conservative, closed, familial society of the nineteenth-century Amsterdam Jewish Quarter and the London East End ghetto from which the immigrants came.

Economic Life

Boston's Jews, like Jews everywhere, worked primarily in the retail trades as self-employed merchants. Younger immigrants were clerks who graduated to peddling or merchandising as soon as they became somewhat acculturated. A minority were craftsmen in small cottage industries where they tailored or rolled cigars by piecework, which allowed them to retain a measure of autonomy and control over their schedules, as did independent artisans in the European tradition.[31]

Specifically, 42 percent of Boston's Jews in 1850 were tradesmen, which figure rose to 49 percent by 1860. The tradesmen included peddlers, traders, merchants, agents, brokers, and various dealers, all of whom varied only slightly except in the self-images of the respondents. The number of peddlers jumped from 40 percent (seventeen) to 60 percent (ninety-three) during the decade. The next largest group was tailors, clothiers, and cap- and hat-makers. These needle craftsmen totaled 35 percent in 1850 and 24 percent in 1860. Other

Table 5.1
Dutch Jewish Occupational Groups in Boston, 1850, 1860, 1870

	Mer-chant		Peddler/Trader		Profes-sional		Clerk/Sales		Skilled		Un-skilled		Total
Census	N	%	N	%	N	%	N	%	N	%	N	%	N
1850	1	8	9	69	1	8	0	0	2	15	0	0	13
1860	16	23	34	49	2	3	5	7	12	17	1	1	70
1870	33	28	17	14	2	2	12	10	52	43	4	3	120

Source: Compiled from Robert P. Swierenga, comp., *Dutch Households in U.S. Population Censuses, 1850, 1860, 1870: An Alphabetical Listing by Family Heads*, 3 vols. (Wilmington, DE, 1987).

Jews, ranging between 12 and 15 percent, were cigarmakers and jewelers and watchmakers. The only significant contingent in the service sector was that of ten Jewish barbers counted in the 1860 census. But only 6–7 percent of Boston Jews provided services between 1850 and 1860.

Like their compatriots, most of the Dutch Jews in Boston in the pre-Civil War decades were traders and peddlers, but soon retail merchants appeared, and even more important, cigarmakers later became prominent (Table 5.1). In 1850 there was only one Dutch clothing merchant, one optician, a shoemaker, and a cabinetmaker. Nine of thirteen family heads, or 69 percent, were peddlers. Thus, the Dutch had nearly twice as large a proportion in the retail trades as did the other Jews in Boston (77 percent compared to 42 percent). In 1860, thirty-four out of seventy Dutchmen, or 49 percent, were peddlers and traders; and there were also sixteen (23 percent) clothing and fancy goods merchants. Thus, throughout the 1850s the proportion of Dutch tradesmen held steady, being 72 percent in 1860. This compared to 49 percent tradesmen among other Jews in the city. The thirty-four Dutch peddlers alone comprised more than one-third of the ninety-three Jewish peddlers in Boston in 1860. Five Dutch Jews in 1860 were cigarmakers, plus one tobacconist. These were the first Dutch Jews in Boston to work in the tobacco industry, and they were harbingers of the future. Besides cigarmakers, there were several tailors and tailoresses, a cabinetmaker, and a coppersmith. A skilled class of artisans clearly was emerging. By 1870 fifty-two Dutch Jews were cigarmakers and skilled craftsmen, comprising 43 percent of the work force.

Protective tariffs had much to do with the rise of cigar making. As the U.S. cigar industry grew in the antebellum decades, it pressured Congress to erect tariff barriers against imported cigars, including the famous Dutch Masters. As a consequence, Dutch firms in Rotterdam, Amsterdam, and Zwolle established branch houses in Boston, New York, and Philadelphia, and they sent their cigarmakers to America to bypass the tariffs. A Dutch visitor, J. Jansen, noted that at the turn of the century, "Many cigar makers were in evidence" in Boston. They remained devoted to Holland, he added, because "many of them were above all tipplers of Schiedam's whoopee water." Schiedam, a Rotterdam suburb, was the center of the Dutch distillery industry, especially of gin (*jenever*).[32]

Given this tariff incentive, Boston's Dutch Jews "took naturally to cigarmaking." The turn-of-the-century chronicler Ehrenfried recalled, "Several old Boston Dutch families have manufactured cigars for decades."[33] There were only seventeen peddlers and traders (14 percent) in 1870, half the number in 1860 when peddlers comprised half of the Dutch work force. At least eight peddlers in 1860 had opened retail clothing or dry goods stores by 1870, which is the classic economic ladder for Jewish hucksters. One had become a clergyman (Mark Hamburger) and one was a diamond cutter. Only one of the 1860 peddlers was still plying that trade in 1870. Clearly, during the Civil War decade, new Dutch Jewish immigrants in Boston moved into the cigar trade, while the earlier arrivals who began as peddlers, hucksters, and traders advanced into the rank of retail merchants. The community lacked a professional group, but they also avoided unskilled laboring jobs. The 12 clerks and salesmen (10 percent), mostly young men, were at the bottom of the job scale, but they were learning the merchandising trade and poised to move up.

The most noteworthy contribution of the Dutch Jews was in the diamond-cutting trade beginning in the 1860s. Depression conditions in the Dutch diamond industry drove several craftsmen to America. Benjamin de Young arrived in Boston from Amsterdam in the late 1840s, single and in his early twenties. For a time he owned a secondhand clothing store, but with three other Hollanders, including Adam Keyser (Keizer), he set up a diamond-cutting shop. According to Ehrenfried, Keyser's descendants preserve an impressive gold medal (undated), which was presented to him in recognition of his service of introducing diamond-cutting into America.[34]

Keyzer was born in Amsterdam in 1818 and arrived with his wife and daughter in New York in the mid 1850s. In 1858 the family lived briefly in Connecticut, but by 1860 they had settled in Boston where Adam was a peddler.[35] Late in the year 1870 Keyzer chanced to enter the general store of Crossby, Moss and Foss in Boston, where the familiar sound of the polishing wheel in a back room caught his attention. To his surprise, he found co-owner Henry D. Moss bent over a primitive wooden disk trying to polish diamonds that one of Crossby's kin in Kimberly, South Africa, had sent in exchange for some food items.[36]

The firm, quick to spot an opportunity, offered Keyzer $60 per week to set up a modern, Dutch-type workshop with the latest technology such as metal disks. Keyzer knew of two former diamond craftsmen from Amsterdam, George van Herpen and Jacob de Boer, who as clothiers in Detroit occasionally traveled to Boston on buying trips. Keyzer hired them for $40 per week to relocate to Boston and resume their former calling as diamond polishers. For an instrument technician he found an older Hollander, H. Wiener, already living in Boston. Keyzer attracted more skilled cutters, polishers, and technicians directly from Amsterdam by offering the princely wage of $60 a week under two-year contracts. These included N. van Volen, H. Cohenno, and M. Streep, all Jews. Thus, an entirely Dutch diamond industry developed in Boston in the 1870s.

Since the rules of the diamond cutters' guild decreed that only sons and brothers of craftsmen could serve apprenticeships, the children of Keyzer, Van Herpen, De Boer, and Van Volen entered the craft, and Moss also learned the polishing art. The firm, on occasion, cut and polished South African gems for New York jewelers such as I. Herman. The great Boston fire of 1872 damaged part of the shop of Crossby, Moss and Foss, but Van Herpen saved the tools and diamonds and the business carried on.

The technology transfer from Amsterdam to Boston occurred on a smaller scale than anticipated because Boston was not strongly linked to Amsterdam and London importers, and gems manufactured in Europe had virtually free access to the American market. Moreover, the tremendous revival of the Dutch industry during the "Cape period" of the 1870s pulled most of the immigrant craftsmen back to Amsterdam when their contracts ended. Only a few remained. Cohenno, for instance, was the only polisher left in Boston by the 1880s.

The census reports on wealth-holding provide more evidence of the success of Boston's Dutch Jews. In 1860, of fifty-three households, all but ten owned reportable wealth of at least $50. Among all Jewish households only half reported any wealth.[37] The total Dutch wealth, mainly in personal property, amounted to $63,810, an average of $1,204 per household. By 1870 the total reported wealth had increased to $98,800; but the figure greatly underestimates the

Table 5.2
First- and Second-Generation Dutch Jews, Boston, 1850, 1860, 1870

Wards	1850			1860			1870		
	F	S	Total	F	S	Total	F	S	Total
1	3	2	5	1	4	5	1	4	5
2	6	3	9	—	—	—	6	9	15
3	—	—	—	11	11	22	6	1	7
4	—	—	—	6	4	10	—	—	—
5	—	—	—	3	6	9	8	7	15
6	—	—	—	—	—	—	—	—	—
7	—	—	—	1	5	6	85	70	155
8	—	—	—	1	0	1	6	22	28
9	1	4	5	19	24	43	12	10	22
10	3	5	8	80	53	133	35	41	76
11	19	16	35	8	12	20	5	9	14
12				9	11	20	—	—	—
13							4	10	14
14							2	5	7
15							10	7	17
Totals	32	30	62	139	130	269	180	195	375

Source: Compiled from Swierenga, Dutch Households in U.S. Population Censuses.

actual wealth because many merchants refused to provide the census marshals with wealth data. More than half (forty-one out of seventy-two) of the Dutch Jewish household heads reported no wealth in 1870. The cigarmakers likely had none to report, but the merchants and peddlers had obviously become wary of the tax man because of the Civil War income tax legislation.

The Social Picture

The size of the Dutch Jewish community grew from 62 in 1850 and from 269 in 1860 to 375 in 1870 (Table 5.2). About half of these were born in the Netherlands (32 in 1850, 139 in 1860, and 180 in 1870). First-generation Dutch outnumbered their American-born progeny at least until 1870, when 41 percent of the community was American-born. This was a result of the continuing immigration in the middle decades.

The Dutch Jewish settlement was concentrated around Beth Eil Synagogue in Ward 11 along the wharves and docks of south Boston Bay below Orange Street in the far south end. In 1850, more than half lived in this ward, squeezed between the bay on the east and the receiving basin on the west. Lesser Dutch concentrations were north of Orange Street in Wards 9 and 10, which also fronted on the docks, and in the far north end in Ward 1 along the Charles River wharves and on Ward 2 along east Boston Bay. This was the older part of the city.

Before the early 1850s the Dutch Jews lived on the fringes of the Jewish Quarter, but by 1860 they were squarely in the center of the city. Three-quarters of Boston's Jews in 1850 lived in Ward 10 and in south Boston (Ward 12), whereas the Dutch were to the southwest in Ward 11. By 1860, however, the city's Jewish Quarter had shifted to Ward 9, immediately south of Boston Common, and to Ward 10 along the Fort Point Channel. Two-thirds of all Jews in the city inhabited these two wards in 1860, where many had moved from isolated south Boston, which the Jews virtually deserted in the 1850s.[38]

In 1860 half of the Dutch Jews were also concentrated in Ward 10, which now included a small part of former Ward 11. There were small neighborhoods in Ward 9, in south Boston (Ward 12), and in the original settlement in Ward 11. In south Boston a few recent Dutch immigrants filled in some of the empty places left by the upwardly mobile Jews. In the north end, some Dutch moved into the upscale areas above Beacon Hill (Wards 3, 4, 5) near the city center. Forty-two percent of the Dutch by 1870 still lived along the Fort Point Channel in Ward 7 (Old Ward 10) and another 20 percent remained in the original core region in Old Ward 11 (Ward 10 by 1870). Thus, nearly two-thirds of the Dutch in 1870 yet remained in their primary zone in the southern regions of the city near their synagogue, although the remaining one-third were now widely scattered. A number of families had moved uptown to neighborhoods nearer the commercial and business center.

Dutch housing arrangements reflected an urban environment with tight demands on space. They also signify economic well-being. Fully one-quarter of the Dutch lived in single-family dwellings in 1860, which compares very favorably to the rest of the city's Jews, among whom only 20 percent lived in single-family homes.[39] Thus, the Dutch rate of single-family living surpassed that of all Jews by 25 percent. Nearly 70 percent inhabited multifamily buildings shared mainly with non-Dutch neighbors, although 11 percent were all-Dutch. Two-thirds of the multifamily dwellings included three or

Table 5.3
School Attendance by Sex, Jewish Children, Aged 5–19, Boston, 1850, 1860, 1870

	Dutch Children							All Jews		
				ALL	M		F		School	School
Census	M	F	N	%	M	%	F	%	N	N	%
1850	6	14	20	60	3	50	9	64	71	53	75
1860	45	49	94	78	38	84	35	71	381	310	81
1870	71	68	139	62	44	62	42	62	NA	NA	NA
All Years				68		70		66			79

Sources: Compiled from Swierenga, *Dutch Households in U.S. Population Censuses*; Kenneth David Roseman, "The Jewish Population of America, 1850–1860: A Demographic Analysis of Four Cities," (Ph.D. diss., HUC, Cincinnati, 1971), Table 18.

more flats, one-third contained only two flats. For the rest of the Jewish families, 79 percent lived in apartments in 1860, so the Dutch were slightly better off than the Jews generally.

Demographically, Dutch Jewish females outnumbered males in the city by a 60:40 ratio in 1850, whereas males outnumbered females by five points among all Jews in Boston.[40] But by 1860 Dutch males outnumbered females 53 to 47 percent, which was slightly above the Jewish norm but more balanced, and in 1870 there was a perfectly balanced sex ratio, which indicates a mature community. Married couples increasingly chose Dutch spouses. In 1850 only 55 percent had Dutch spouses, but by 1870 80 percent did so. The Dutch marriage pool had obviously increased by then to permit intragroup marriage. Some of the early settlers had English-born wives, perhaps of Dutch stock; but in Boston the Dutch preferred to marry fellow Hollanders. This marked clannishness is similar to that among the Calvinists, but in marked contrast to the high outmarriage rate among Dutch Roman Catholics, who also belonged to an international religious institution.

Boston's Jews were committed to education for their children, but the Dutch were slightly less financially able to do so. They needed the earnings of their children's labor. Seventy-five percent of all Jewish children aged 5 to 19 in 1850 attended school during the year, and 81 percent did so in 1860 (Table 5.3). But among the Dutch Jews, 60 percent attended in 1850, 78 percent in 1860, and 62 percent in 1870.[41] Comparable data for all Boston Jews in 1870 are not available, but the Dutch likely remained ten points or more below their fellow religionists.

Taking into consideration the sex of the children (data only available for Dutch Jews), in 1850 half the boys attended school and nearly two-thirds of the girls. In 1860, however, 84 percent of boys attended and 71 percent of girls. By 1870, 62 percent of each sex attended school. The higher female school attendance in the 1840s reflected the economic hard times of the Dutch families who needed the earnings of their sons. The more prosperous 1850s enabled them to send sons to school as well, but by the 1860s more than one-third of both sexes remained out of school. Almost all of the nonattenders were above 13 years of age. Between ages 5 and 12 almost every Dutch youngster was in school. Of 147 children in this age group, all but 4 attended school, and these were 7 years and younger. Two-thirds of 13-year-olds attended and over half the 14-year-olds, but among 15-, 16-, and 17-year-olds only 1 in 5 attended, and only 1 out of 21 18- and 19-year-olds. School leaving among Boston Dutch Jews began at age 13, increased at age 15, and was completed at age 17. Compared to the Philadelphia and New York Dutch Jews, however, more Boston children were in school, they began earlier (at age 5 compared to age 6), and they left later (at age 17 instead of age 16).

Conclusion

The Dutch Jewish community in Boston in the middle decades of the last century was small but dynamic. Ten families arrived in the 1840s, nearly fifty more families came in the 1850s and yet another twenty-five families were welcomed in the 1860s (Tables 5.4, 5.5, 5.6). This was a sufficient critical mass for them to establish their own synagogue and maintain it for a generation, to found the necessary mutual aid and burial societies, and to purchase cemeteries. The Dutch were a closely knit community that lived somewhat separately in the first decades, as is evidenced by the increasing rate of ingroup marriages. Even though the Dutch synagogue disbanded in the 1870s, the *Hollandsche Chevra* and Netherlands Cemetery Association continued for another hundred years. In service to the larger Jewish community, the Dutch, particularly the more integrated members of the mother synagogue, founded the first Hebrew school and called Simon Noot from New York to direct it.

In commercial life the Dutch were heavily overrepresented in the retail trades. In manufacturing activity, Dutch gem craftsmen brought diamond-cutting shops to Boston in the Civil War years

Table 5.4
Dutch Jewish Household Heads and Single Adults,
Boston, 1850

Name	Age	N in Family	Time of Immi- gration	Occupation	Ward
Eliphalet Cook	30	4	pre–1845	peddler	11
Solomon Cook	40	3	pre–1833	peddler	11
B. de Young	30	1	1836	peddler	2
Benjamin de Young	40	4	pre–1843	none	11
Louis Goldsmith	30	1	pre–1850	cabinetmaker	2
Joel Hart	42	5	pre–1845	peddler	9
Solomon Isaacs	33	6	1848–1850	peddler	11
Eleaser Lazarus	33	8	1842–1846	trader	11
Bernard Milkman	25	5	1842	trader	1
William Pool	84	4	pre–1820	none	2
Abraham Prince	50	4	pre–1835	optician	10
Simon Spear	45	7	1835	shoemaker	11
Morris Stern	21	1	pre–1850	peddler	11
M. Sugarman	30	1	pre–1850	peddler	2

Sources: Compiled from Swierenga, *Dutch Households in U.S. Population Censuses*; Robert P. Swierenga, comp., *Dutch Immigrants in U.S. Ship Passenger Manifests, 1820–1880: An Alphabetical Listing by Household Heads and Independent Persons*, 2 vols. (Wilmington, DE, 1983).

and this enabled the city to become a national center of the precious stones industry until New York supplanted it after 1900. The Dutch also contributed greatly to the cigar making business, and several Dutch families manufactured cigars for many decades. In the years after the Civil War, when cigar making became established in Boston, up to half of the entire Dutch Jewish labor force worked in the city's weed trade.

After thirty to forty years, in the 1870s and 1880s, when the third generation came of age, the Dutch self-identity weakened and their families became absorbed into the greater Jewish religious and cultural life. Some Netherlandic societies remained, but these were only a shadow of the Dutch institutions built by the pioneers, like the energetic peddler Mark Hamburger, who helped establish Congregation Beth Eil and led the Dutch for thirty years as minister and mentor.

Table 5.5
Dutch Jewish Household Heads and Single Adults, Boston, 1860

Name	Age	N in Family	Time of Immigration	Occupation	Realty $	Personalty $	Ward
Aaron Appel	24	2	pre-1860	tailor	—	—	3
Solomon Beage	41	7	1850–1853	coppersmith	—	—	9
A. H. Berthold	38	4	pre-1860	tobaccanist	—	1,000	11
William Block	40	5	1840–1844	fancy goods	—	3,000	1
David Buitenkant	51	4	1854	peddler	—	400	10
Louis Coene	26	1	1858	musician	—	—	8
Moses Coene	55	1	1858–1859	schoolteacher	—	—	9
Alexander Cook	37	11	pre-1847	peddler	—	100	10
Louis de Haan	28	2	pre-1860	cigarmaker	—	—	10
Benjamin de Young	35	5	1836	secondhand clothing	—	500	10
Samuel de Young	34	3	pre-1860	trader	—	100	12
Simon de Young	48	4	pre-1858	secondhand clothing	—	500	10
Eliza Green	67	1	pre-1860	none	—	—	10
Henry Green	38	2	pre-1860	peddler	—	60	10
Marcus Hamburger	30	2	1857	peddler	—	—	11
Benjamin Hart	38	3	1850–1858	clothing	—	1,000	3
Henry Isaacs	36	2	pre-1860	peddler	—	75	10
Samuel Isaacs	42	9	1849–1851	peddler	—	200	10
Jacob Jacobs	32	4	1842	peddler	—	—	10
Solomon Kaiser	33	5	pre-1851	peddler	—	—	11

Table 5.5 (Continued)

Name	Age	N in Family	Time of Immigration	Occupation	Realty $	Personalty $	Ward
Louis Keiser	57	3	pre-1860	peddler	—	1,700	10
Maurice Keiser	24	1	pre-1860	peddler	—	—	10
Aaron Keyser	40	6	1853–1856	peddler	—	—	10
Leonard Lamb	46	4	1855–1860	peddler	—	—	10
Ephraim Lamen	60	2	pre-1860	old clothes	—	—	10
Abraham Lamphery	36	6	pre-1850	cigarmaker	—	100	10
Teresa Lazarus (widow Eleaser)	41	7	1842–1846	fancy goods	—	500	3
Hannah Levi	28	1	pre-1860	none	—	—	10
Louis Levi	38	6	1851–1856	secondhand clothing	—	500	4
Simon Levi	40	7	1853–1855	peddler	—	200	10
Jacob Lewis	16	1	pre-1860	peddler	—	—	10
Bernard Milkman	35	9	1842	milliner	4,000	1,000	5
Barney Mock	35	6	1857–1860	peddler	—	150	10
Levi Oldkerk	49	2	pre-1860	embroidery	6,000	11,000	11
Cozia Pulo	28	3	pre-1860	butcher	—	—	8
Isaac Robles	35	7	pre-1851	cigarmaker	—	—	10
Philip Rose	44	6	pre-1851	peddler	—	500	10
Simon Rose	34	7	1849–1850	none	—	1,000	9
Solomon Scheriger	26	2	pre-1860	peddler	—	50	10

Name							
Harmen Simon	50	5	pre–1840	trader	—	200	12
Emanuel Slocum	58	7	1847–1860	fancy store	—	1,000	9
Isaac Solomon	40	4	1853	peddler	—	300	4
Henry S. Spear	38	1	1835	merchant tailor	—	3,000	9
Simon Spear	60	5	1835	fancy store	—	5,500	9
Mark Streep	26	2	pre–1860	peddler	—	50	10
W. Streep	36	1	pre–1860	peddler	—	—	9
H. Sugarman	27	3	pre–1860	peddler	—	—	9
Simon Sugarman	41	4	1850–1857	secondhand clothing	—	500	4
Moses van Dam	32	5	1855	trader	—	—	12
Moses I. van der Sluis	54	6	pre–1832	clerk	—	500	3
Isaac van Diner	48	7	pre–1850	peddler	—	75	10
Nathan van Outer	44	7	1854–1860	peddler	—	100	10
David van Praag	35	2	pre–1860	merchant	—	1,000	9
M. S. van Praag	30	2	pre–1860	merchant	—	15,000	9
Maas van Raalte	31	2	pre–1850	cigarmaker	—	200	3
Abraham Viping	36	2	pre–1860	peddler	—	—	10
Lewis Vorner	31	7	pre–1852	cigarmaker	—	200	11
Henry Weiner	21	1	pre–1860	clerk	—	—	10

Sources: Compiled from Swierenga, *Dutch Households in U.S. Population Censuses*; Swierenga, *Dutch Immigrants in U.S. Ship Passenger Manifests*.

Table 5.6
Dutch Jewish Household Heads and Single Adults, Boston, 1870

Name	Age	N in Family	Time of Immi-gration	Occupation	Realty $	Person-alty $	Ward
Nathan Beck	23	2	1865–1869	cigarmaker	—	—	7
Sol Bellefonter	30	4	1861–1866	cigarmaker	—	—	7
Kate Bloomendaal	65	1	1867	no occupation	—	—	7
Levie Bossie	35	6	pre–1861	cigarmaker	—	—	13
Barney Buisterman	39	5	1860–1864	retail clothier	—	—	10
Alex Buitenkant	32	5	1854	clothing dealer	—	500	5
David Buitenkant	73	2	1854	none	—	—	5
Joseph Cipp	48	7	1862–1864	clothing store	—	200	7
Clara Cohen	55	1	pre–1870	no occupation	—	—	7
Jacob Cohen	30	4	1860–1865	china peddler	—	—	7
Alexander Cook	45	9	1855–1859	trader	—	—	7
Jacob Cornel	62	3	1838	peddler	—	—	7
Moses de Groot	47	2	pre–1870	journeyman tailor	—	—	7
Samuel de Groot	27	6	1864	confectioner	—	300	7
Lewis de Haan	40	3	pre–1860	cigarmaker	—	—	7
Benjamin de Young	48	8	1836	clothing dealer	—	—	8
Isaac de Young	30	2	pre–1870	works confectionary	—	150	15
Simon de Young	45	6	pre–1858	clothing dealer	—	—	8
Isaac Frank	46	6	1859–1865	pawnbroker	5,000	1,000	3
Moses Felleman	59	5	pre–1848	peddler	—	10,000	11

Name							
Isaac Goldsmith	27	5	1860–1865	retail clother	600	—	10
John Goldsmith	32	4	1860–1865	retail cigarstore	500	—	10
Nathan Goldsmith	35	6	1855–1859	peddler	—	—	7
Lewis Goodheart	30	4	1868	business traveler	100	—	10
Eliza Green	70	1	pre–1852	no occupation	—	—	7
Henry Green	31	2	1860–1869	china peddler	—	—	10
Michael Green	45	3	1860–1869	china peddler	500	—	7
Michael Grishaver	30	3	pre–1865	cigarmaker	—	—	7
Morris Gussevan	52	6	1860–1869	huckster	—	—	7
John Hambri	28	7	1866–1869	tailor	—	—	10
Mordecai Hambri	54	5	1857	porter	—	—	10
Mark Hamburger	38	5	1857	clergyman	—	—	5
Moses Hamburger	25	1	1865	cigarstore	—	—	9
Benjamin Hart	55	3	1850–1858	clothing dealer	—	—	6
Isaac Isaacs	49	2	1860–1869	retail clothing	—	—	10
Mary Isaacs (w. Samuel)	46	4	1850–1859	keeping house	—	—	7
Moses Isaacs	28	2	1865–1869	dry goods peddler	—	—	7
Louis Jacobs	44	8	1857–1863	tailor	—	—	8
Solomon Jacobs	40	8	1850–1853	huckster	400	—	13
Abraham Joustman	36	6	pre–1854	cigarmaker	—	—	8
Aaron Keyser	52	6	1853–1855	diamond-cutter	400	—	7
Francis Keyser	35	8	1853–1859	peddler	400	—	10
Cornelius Lamb	50	4	pre–1870	no occupation	—	—	10
Leonard Lamb	55	4	1856–1859	secondhand clothing	1,000	6,000	7,10

Table 5.6 (Continued)

Name	Age	N in Family	Time of Immigration	Occupation	Realty $	Personalty $	Ward
Abraham Lamphery	46	5	pre–1851	cigarmaker	—	—	7
Louis Levi	47	7	1852–1855	clothier	—	—	2
Simon Levi	49	7	1853–1855	secondhand clothing	5,000	10,000	7
Isaac Lyons	60	6	pre–1853	jeweler	—	—	3
Solomon Mandall	40	3	1860–1862	iron moulder	—	—	7
Bernard Moch	46	4	1857–1860	secondhand clothing	—	—	7
Lewis Park	25	5	1860–1866	cigarmaker	—	—	7
Simon Park	56	4	1860–1866	cigarstore	—	500	7
Henry Paserline	15	1	1860–1869	appr. cigarmaker	—	—	10
Daniel Pinentel	24	2	1860–1869	cigarmaker	—	—	8
Abraham Prince	64	6	pre–1850	optician	5,000	2,000	14
Emanuel Slocum	68	2	1860–1866	retail dry goods	—	—	8
Isaac Slocum	48	6	1860–1869	fruit store	—	200	7
Michael Slocum	36	5	1860–1869	retail dry goods	—	—	8
Isaac Solomon	35	1	1853	merchant	—	—	11
Hannah Spinoza	61	4	1869	keeping house	—	—	7
Joseph Stokvis	26	2	1865–1869	cigarmaker	—	—	7
Mark Streep	36	3	1860–1862	retail clothes	—	500	10
Simon Sugarman	50	2	pre–1865	clothier	—	—	2
S. Suikerman	32	6	1860–1864	retail clothier	—	300	10

Simon Susan	26	4	1869–1870	cigarmaker	—	—	7
Abram Tudor	26	1	1860–1869	cigarmaker	—	—	10
Jacob van Dam	40	5	1860–1865	cigarmaker	—	—	7
Moses van Dam	41	5	1854	dry goods store	—	1,000	7
Isaac van Diner	58	9	pre–1853	fancy goods peddler	—	—	7
Aaron van Emden	32	5	1868–1869	cigarmaker	—	—	10
Nathan van Outer	52	7	1852–1859	retail clother	—	—	11
Solomon van Praag	57	6	pre–1848	importer WI goods	—	—	11
Stephen van Praag	45	2	1860–1869	merchant	—	—	9
Jacob van Raalte	62	1	1860–1864	at home	—	—	9
Joseph van Raalte	37	5	1860–1864	traveler	—	—	9
Lewis Vorner	41	11	1854–1856	cigarmaker	—	—	10
Abram Whiteboon	42	2	1860–1869	secondhand clothing	6,000	800	7
Samuel Whiteboon	32	4	1852	secondhand clothing	—	—	7
Joseph Woodhouse	22	2	1860–1869	pocketbook peddler	—	—	7
Alien Yanger	40	6	pre–1861	huckster	2,000	500	15
Maurice Ziske	30	4	1865–1868	cigarmaker	—	—	7

Sources: Compiled from Swierenga, *Dutch Households in U.S. Population Censuses*; Swierenga, *Dutch Immigrants in U.S. Ship Passenger Manifests*.

Chapter 6

〰️

BALTIMORE: THE FELLS
POINT SETTLEMENT

A Jewish merchant, David Ferera of New Amsterdam, came to Maryland in 1657 to trade tobacco, but the English navigation acts drove him away by 1661. A genuine Jewish community did not develop in Baltimore for another century. In the late 1770s Jews moved from nearby Philadelphia and Lancaster and from the West Indies to seize business opportunities in the rapidly growing Maryland port city whose population neared six thousand in 1775. The Baltimore Jewish community thereafter developed virtually as an adjunct of Philadelphia through family intermarriages and commercial ties. Growth was slow until after 1800. The city had only five Jewish families, with sixteen persons in 1790.[1] As the community took shape in the early nineteenth century, according to the reminiscence of an early pioneer, "nearly all those here were Dutch Jews, the Germans coming later."[2]

Forming the Community

One Holland native, the merchant Eleazer Lyons (1729–1816), was among the early arrivals, coming in 1779 from

188

Lancaster. He remained in Baltimore until at least 1786. By 1790 he had migrated to Surinam, but later returned to the United States and resided in Philadelphia until his death.[3] Lyons's sojourn in Surinam was part of the long-standing commercial ties between the port of Baltimore and the Caribbean Islands. As late as 1844, Jamaican Jews responded to an appeal of the Baltimore Hebrew congregation with a contribution for Baltimore's first synagogue.[4]

Another early Dutch Jew in Baltimore was Abraham Peters, an indentured servant. In 1775 Peters was the object of a newspaper advertisement by a Mr. Purdue offering a reward for the return of his escaped servant, who was described as a twenty-eight-year-old "bearded Jew, a cripple who spoke good Dutch."[5] Whether Peters was recaptured is not known, but his low status was typical of later Dutch Jewish settlers in the Maryland port.

A group of new immigrants, primarily from Amsterdam, found their way to Baltimore in the first decade of the nineteenth century. A few had stopped for some time in Philadelphia and New York before moving south. Abraham S. Schoyer (1773–1823), a peddler, was involved in a lawsuit in Baltimore in 1807, which documents his residence. By 1812 he was a grocer and in 1819 a merchant, located on Fleet Street in the Fells Point district of the city. His synagogue membership remained in the Rodeph Shalom congregation of Philadelphia in the years 1815–1818, but when he died in New York in 1823 his membership was at Shearith Israel of that city.[6]

Solomon Benjamin, like Schoyer, began as a peddler and by 1817 was the proprietor of a jewelry shop on Wilk Street. His estate at the time of his death in 1818 was worth almost $4,000, which was an impressive achievement. Benjamin's partner in peddling and in the jewelry shop was his fellow countryman, Jacob Moses. Because of economic reverses brought on by the business panic of 1819, Moses and Benjamin had a legal embroglio, and Moses again reverted to peddling temporarily. But there is evidence that by 1820 he was a jeweler in Philadelphia and a member of Congregation Rodeph Shalom.[7]

Other Amsterdam Jews in Baltimore were Hart Levi, a Fells Point peddler, trader, and cutlery-store owner; Andrew Levy (1779–1834), another Fells Point peddler in the 1810 and 1819 city directories, who died of cholera in 1834 while a member of Rodeph Shalom; and Alexander Wertheim (1775–1830), the most distinguished Baltimore Jew in the early decades. Wertheim was a medical doctor who first lived in New York around 1808. By 1810 his office was on Bond Street in the Fells Point district. Like the other Dutch Jews in Baltimore, he too moved to Philadelphia where he became clerk of the Board of Health.[8] But Wertheim returned to Baltimore several times; during the years 1818 and 1819 he performed eleven circumcisions there, which must have included all of the Jewish boys born in those years.[9]

Since Baltimore's Jewish population in 1810 consisted only of fifteen households, the five new Amsterdam immigrant families at Fells Point comprised one-third of the Jewish population. But the new immigrants were distinctly segregated from the ten Jewish families of early American stock (pre-1790 origin) who resided in the city proper. Fells Point, located in the newly created Ward 7, had developed independently of Baltimore. It lay along the waterfront red light district, inhabited by stevedores, shipbuilders, sailors, and prostitutes along with Dutch Jewish peddlers and shopkeepers. By contrast, the earlier Jewish residents of the central city were merchants, brokers, manufacturers, and proprietors. In effect, early Baltimore Jewry comprised two communities: (1) the native-born, propertied, well-assimilated families (e.g., the Ettings and Cohens) of eighteenth-century origin who lived in fashionable homes on Charles and Saratoga streets and owned slaves and freed black servants and (2) a new immigrant group clustered at Fells Point without capital and struggling to escape poverty. The two groups, both numbering about a dozen families, had such disparate life-styles that they could find no common ground to organize a congregation. It would be another two decades before the Baltimore Hebrew Congregation began and by then all but one of the early settlers had died or departed the city.[10]

Baltimore's Jewish population increased slowly in the early nineteenth century, and it was highly mobile and unstable. Although the Maryland port city ranked third in population in 1810, after New York and Philadelphia, the number of Jews there in the 1810s grew slowly from about fifteen families in 1810 to twenty-one in 1820.[11] Many others came and went, primarily to and from Philadelphia, but also New York, Richmond, New Orleans, and elsewhere.

Thirteen of the thirty known Jewish newcomers in the 1810s came from Amsterdam, many by way of Philadelphia.[12] Hollanders thus formed the nucleus of the growing Jewish settlement, centered in the lower-class district of Fells Point. The five men who remained at least a decade were Michael and Isaac de Young, Moses J. Millem, Levi Benjamin, and Leonard (Lazarus) Levi. Many more Dutch stayed only briefly or moved between Baltimore and Philadelphia. The two brothers Michael H. (1791–1854) and Isaac (1795–1868) de Young were born in Amsterdam and came to Philadelphia as youngsters with their parents, Joseph de Young and his wife in

1803. Both parents died in 1811 and the sons moved to Baltimore by the next year, where Michael ran a jewelry shop and comb factory, first in Fells Point and later on Baltimore Street in the city's newer commercial center, which move indicated his upward rise. That a free black servant lived with the family was also a status symbol. Isaac first joined the U.S. Army and fought in the Second War against Britain. After five years in service and several years working for his brother, Isaac opened a fancy goods store also on Baltimore Street. Both men became naturalized citizens in 1823. In 1827 Michael divorced his wife—the first Jew in Maryland to do so (according to the acts of the General Assembly), and he shortly thereafter married thirty-six-year old Amelia Morange, a French Catholic who was half his age. In the 1830s the brothers left Baltimore. Isaac in 1830 returned to Philadelphia and operated a fancy goods store there until his death. Michael four years later moved to New York and also opened a fancy goods store. But from 1837 on, he became a rolling stone, moving first to Saint Louis, then Texas, New Orleans, and Cincinnati. He died in 1859 enroute to San Francisco on a Mississippi River steamer above New Orleans and was buried in that city.[13]

Levy Benjamin (1783–1860) arrived via Annapolis from Holland in January 1815 with his wife and infant daughter and settled on Fleet Street in Fells Point among the other Dutch, where he began peddling. The depression of 1819, which was particularly severe in Baltimore, ruined him and he returned to the Netherlands for a year with his family. But in the summer of 1820 he remigrated with his wife and three young children, the youngest a daughter, Esther, born during the stay in Holland. She later married Samuel Leon, a fellow Dutch immigrant, and became well-known in the community. Levi Benjamin gradually climbed the ladder of economic success, first running a secondhand furniture store then becoming a pawnbroker and real estate investor. By 1837 he was so well-off that he donated a valuable lot at the corner of Harrison Street and Etna Lane for a new synagogue for the Baltimore Hebrew Congregation, of which he was a charter member. The 1850 federal census marshal recorded his occupation as speculator and the value of his real estate holdings at $26,000. He was the wealthiest Dutch Jew in the city at midcentury. His brother-in-law, Moses Millem (1786–1830), arrived in Baltimore from Amsterdam in 1816, a year after Benjamin. Millem became a successful watchmaker and real estate investor. Another watchmaker at Fells Point was Leonard Levy (1769–1843), who married in Baltimore in 1818. Levy later peddled for several decades, ultimately moving to Philadelphia.[14]

Some Dutch Jews lived in Baltimore intermittently or only briefly. Four who married there are Abraham Lazarus, Jacob Levy, Moses David van Wezel, and Solomon Hyman van Praag. Other merchants were David Phillips, Wolf (William) N. Polack, Maurice A. Cohen, and Marius Philipson. Lazarus (1793–1865) was born in Amsterdam, married in Baltimore in 1817, and was a peddler on Fleet Street in 1819. In 1820 he moved to Philadelphia where he became a naturalized citizen in 1823 and had a long career as a dealer.[15] Levy (1795–1832) married in Baltimore in 1819 where his son Levy was born the next year. By 1827 he was a peddler in New York and continued in that work until his early death. Van Wezel married in 1818 and was in Baltimore's Chancery Court four years later on a wife-beating complaint filed by spouse Rebecca Condley van Wezel. In 1825 Van Wezel first appeared in New York City directories as a dry goods dealer and was affiliated with Bnai Jeshurun Congregation. Van Praag (1798–1826) married in Baltimore in 1820 and likewise removed to New York where he died prematurely at age twenty-eight and was buried in the cemetery of Shearith Israel Congregation.[16]

David Phillips and Wolf Polack both lived in at least three Dutch Jewish centers: Baltimore, Philadelphia, and New York. Phillips (1791–1861) was a trader in Fells Point in the 1810s, where his sons Philip and Samuel were born and circumcised by Dr. Wertheim in 1816 and 1818. Phillips had some talmudic learning and performed marriages and other religious services for the Fells Point community as a quasi rabbi. By 1819 he was in Philadelphia and had joined Rodeph Shalom Congregation, but by the late 1830s he became the sexton of Shearith Israel until his death in 1861. Polack was a trader and dealer in Baltimore in the 1810s and in Philadelphia in the early 1820s, and then he moved to New York as a dry goods dealer. In Philadelphia he joined Rodeph Shalom, and in New York he was a trustee of the new German congregation Anshe Chesed. In 1835 he renounced his Dutch citizenship and became a naturalized American.[17]

Little is known of the other two Dutch transients, Morris Cohen and Marius Philipson. Cohen was a Fells Point watchmaker in 1819 and partner of fellow Hollander Leonard Levy in the firm of Cohen & Levy, located at 11 Market Street. Cohen later peddled, was a clothier, dealer, and then jeweler in Philadelphia. He moved several times between Baltimore and Philadelphia and was a member at various times of Rodeph Shalom and Baltimore Hebrew congregations. Philipson was yet another Fleet Street peddler in the late 1810s who moved to New York by 1820 and became a seatholder in Shearith Israel Congregation.[18]

These sketches of the Baltimore Dutch Jews in the 1810s reveal common patterns. All settled initially in the seedy Fells Point district, but they were a highly mobile lot, many leaving the city during the devastating economic depression of 1819 for Philadelphia, the financial capital of the nation. In the 1830s when Wall Street supplanted Chestnut Street as the financial hub, the Dutch went there. As traders and merchants they were sensitive to major economic shifts and new opportunities. Philadelphia, in turn, served as the southward staging area for Dutch Jews to Baltimore, New Orleans, and elsewhere.

Early Religious Life

During the 1820s Baltimore's Jewish population increased by 50 percent, from 100 to 150 by 1830. This compared to only 2 households in Boston and 1,150 in New York. Nearby Philadelphia had 750. Most Baltimore Jews in the 1820s came from Bavaria and England, but Hollanders were also well represented; 13 of 30 household heads were Dutch in 1830 (Table 6.1)—the same number as in 1820—and they still comprised 43 percent of the Jewish population. While many of the Dutch continued to live in the harbor area, the more prosperous had moved uptown to East Baltimore, where by the 1830s the majority of the city's Jews lived, centered around the intersection of Baltimore Street and Bel Air Market.[19] Secondary Jewish settlement centers, besides Fells Point, were small areas in West Baltimore around Lexington Market and in south Baltimore.

The first public Jewish worship on record began very belatedly in 1829. The reasons for the delay are related to the close relationship between Baltimore and Philadelphia Jewry and to the historical cultural division in Baltimore between Sephardim and Ashkenazim. The Baltimore Jews certainly had the required *minyan* (ten adult men) by 1810 or earlier. The 1820 census counted twenty-one family heads totaling one hundred persons. Nor did they lack a commitment to Judaism since most worshiped at synagogues in Philadelphia, New York, and wherever else they lived.

As was noted earlier, the Baltimore Jews were divided in the early years religiously, socioeconomically, and geographically. The native Sephardi lived in the city center and the immigrant Ashkenazi settled in Fells Point. But both communities maintained close ties to their respective Philadelphia hearth communities 100 miles distant.

Table 6.1
Dutch Jewish Household Heads and Single Adults, Baltimore, 1830

Name	Birth	N in Family*	Occupation	Place of Death	Death	Ward
Jacob Aaron	1799	6	secondhand clothing store	Balt.	1842	5
Levi Benjamin	1784	7	pawnbroker	Balt.	1860	2
Isaac de Young	1794	5	jewelry and comb fancy store	Phil.	1868	7
Michael de Young	1791	11	comb manufacturer, jewelry and fancy store	New Orleans	1854	9
Simon Eytinge	1788	6	pawnbroker	Balt.	1869	9
Solomon Hunt	1793	5	clothing store	Rich.	1846	9
Leonard Levy	1769	2	?	Phil.	1843	2
Moses Millem	1787	3	?	Balt.	1830	10
Wolf Myers	1797	2	victualler	New Orleans	1837	2
Joseph Osterman	1799	3	merchant	Galveston	1861	3
Emanuel Semon	1798	1	?	Phil.	1871	2
Lewis Silver	1798	3	pawnbroker	New York	1846	6
Samuel A. Waterman	1801	3	secondhand clothing store	Balt.	1872	7
		57				

*White persons only (typically, Dutch Jewish households in Baltimore included some black slaves and freed men as servants)

Source: Compiled from Rosenwaike, *On the Edge of Greatness: A Portrait of American Jewry in the Early National Period* (Cincinnati, 1985), 112, 140.

The old Sephardi families—Ettings and Cohens—retained their membership in Philadelphia's Mikveh Israel Congregation because they preferred the Sephardi rites of worship, and they frequently returned to the Quaker city to visit family and on business.[20]

The Ashkenazi, largely Dutch, immigrants in Baltimore had similar motives and practices. They too had initially landed at Philadelphia, had continuing family and business ties there, and preferred to worship according to the Dutch-German rite at Bnai Jeshurun. Scholars have overlooked the Philadelphia-Baltimore Dutch links and attributed the delay in beginning worship in Baltimore to the absence of a "sense of community" caused by the "high turnover of residents and the fluctuating economic circumstances."[21] But both the Sephardi and Ashkenazi in Baltimore experienced high outmigration in the early decades and both suffered from the periodic economic crises.[22]

The basic reason for the twenty-year delay in beginning formal religious services in Baltimore was the ethnocultural division between the assimilated Sephardi in the fashionable central district and the immigrant Ashkenazi Dutch in the Fells Point harbor district. This was a conflict endemic in all east coast immigrant centers between assimilated and unassimilated groups that divided the religious and ethnic populace during the great century of immigration. The separation was greater among Baltimore Jewry because the two communities were geographically divided and with a socioeconomic gulf as well.

Both communities also lacked strong religious leaders in the early years. David Phillips served the Dutch in Fells Point in the 1810s, but moved to Philadelphia in 1819. In the central city congregation, a chemist Joseph Jacobs, of whom little is known, acted as "priest of the Jews" (as described in the 1830 City Directory) for its first two years until 1831, when the elderly and well-respected German Jew Zalma Rehiné arrived from Richmond.[23] Another possible explanation for the delay was that Maryland was one of the last states to grant Jews legal equality and complete religious freedom. The Maryland legislature passed the "Jew Bill" in 1826 after an eight-year struggle and the bill only passed by a margin of one vote. The overt antisemitism and the closeness of the vote may explain why the Baltimore Jews waited three years to request a synagogue charter. The fear of rejection was well founded; the legislature nearly killed the charter bill in committee, and it passed only after the active intervention of one member.[24]

For all these reasons it was December 1829 before five Baltimore Jews, chosen from those attending the first *minyan*, petitioned the

Maryland legislature for a synagogue charter. Four of the five petitioners or electors were Dutch-born: Levi Benjamin, Joseph Osterman, Moses Millem, and Lewis Silver.[25] The petitioners finally received legislative permission in 1830 to organize their first synagogue, which they appropriately named Nidhei Israel (Dispersed of Israel), although it was commonly known as the Baltimore Hebrew Congregation. It was located in the Old Town sector (Wards 3 and 4) of the city at the corner of Bond and Fleet streets. Old Town lay between Fells Point and the newer commercial and residential area west of Jones Falls.[26]

Dutch Jews were prominent among the early membership of the Baltimore Hebrew Congregation. In 1832 more than one-third (eleven of the twenty-nine) of the members were Dutch-born.[27] Most had emigrated previously to the West Indies and Philadelphia and then came to Baltimore because of the intimate commercial relations between the areas. After 1835 many Bavarian Jews arrived and soon outnumbered the Dutch, but the congregation remained true for decades to the old Orthodox ritual adopted at its founding. Dutch Jews were nothing if not strictly Orthodox. Only in 1870 did the Baltimore Hebrew Congregation adopt Reform, and that after a bitter court fight.[28]

The Dutch provided numerous officers for the Baltimore congregation, especially at the beginning. Joseph Osterman was the first treasurer, followed by Simon Eytinge (1788–1869). Both had been members of Mikveh Israel of Philadelphia before coming to Baltimore.[29] Levi Benjamin served as the third treasurer from 1833 to 1840. Eytinge was the second president from 1834 to 1837, and he launched a national appeal for funds to purchase the first synagogue. Moses Millem was the first vice president. Benjamin in 1837 donated the lot on which the newly purchased, three-story brick synagogue stood on the corner of Harrison Street and Etna Lane. This was in the heart of Baltimore's German neighborhood known as *Klein Deutschland.* Abraham Rosenfeld was the fifth president from 1847 to 1849, and Solomon H. Lewyt served as secretary from 1850 to 1870.[30] Of the twenty-nine family heads in the Harrison Street Shul in 1832, at least eleven were Dutch.[31]

Baltimore Jews were poor struggling immigrants who as traders, merchants, and dealers gradually accumulated wealth. They lacked education and cultural graces. But they did build a magnificent $20,000 synagogue in 1845—the Lloyd Street Shul (on another lot donated by Levi Benjamin)—and followed the Orthodox rites under the leadership of their first rabbi, Abraham Joseph Rice (Reiss), who served from 1840 to 1849. Rice was the first ordained rabbi in

America, the leader of Orthodoxy, and was crowned unofficially as Chief Rabbi of the United States.[32]

A Dutch rabbi and teacher from New York, Reverend Samuel Myer Isaacs, participated in the synagogue dedication ceremonies along with Isaac Leeser of Philadelphia. Isaacs delivered the dedicatory sermon in impeccable English and thoroughly enthralled the congregation with his rhetorical gifts. This created a longstanding language controversy—"the battle of the tongue"—in the Baltimore Hebrew Congregation because Rabbi Rice, who was not yet proficient in English, spoke in the customary Yiddish. Those many members of the congregation who favored English resolved to engage Isaacs to give regular English sermons, whereas Rice would preach occasionally in Yiddish. But Isaacs declined the call, even though he had recently resigned his position at Bnai Jeshurun owing to a schism. Thus Yiddish remained the language of the services in Baltimore until 1847 when one English service per sabbath was introduced. By 1859 membership reached 175 (148 families) in the city's largest and wealthiest congregation, which stood in the Lombard sector of the city. Baltimore's Jewish population then stood at six thousand or fifteen hundred families.[33]

Fells Point Hebrew Friendship Congregation

The Baltimore Hebrew Congregation initially was the main focal point for all Jews in the city, the place where they aided one another to adjust to a strange land and to preserve their language, culture, and religion. But social, religious, and ethnic rivalries caused fissures. As early as 1838, newly arrived immigrants who remained in the dockside area on the city outskirts organized a second synagogue, the Fells Point Hebrew Friendship Congregation, Oheb Israel (Lovers of Israel), better known later as the Eden Street Shul. This synagogue was necessary because the distance to the city synagogue was greater than that permitted by Jewish law on Sabbaths and holy days. Of the six incorporators, two were Dutch, Mark Pollack and Jacob Gazan, both peddlers. Pollack had arrived from the Netherlands between 1835 and 1838 and Gazan between 1840 and 1843, judging from the ages and birthplaces of their children in the 1850 census.[34] The Eden Street Shul within two decades moved toward Reform and in 1859 elected their first Reform minister, Dr. Henry Hochheimer, who was ousted by the more Orthodox Baltimore Hebrew Congregation.[35]

Eden Street was not the first to espouse Reform. By 1842 a small Reform group who feared the "establishment of a Jewish hierarchy" and opposed the extreme Orthodoxy of the "Stadt Shul," organized a Reform synagogue, Har Sinai, of the German type. Of the six incorporators, only one was Dutch-born—Simon Eytinge, the former president of Baltimore Hebrew Congregation. Eytinge was a pawnbroker and merchant who lived in Baltimore until his death.[36]

In addition to the synagogues, Baltimore Jews organized several mutual aid and charitable societies to care for the poor and bury the dead. One such charitable organization was the Hebrew Society for Educating Poor and Orphan Children, of which Jacob Gazan was treasurer for many years. H. S. Lewyt, son of Solomon, was the director of the Hebrew Benevolent Society of Baltimore in 1891–1892. Solomon van Leer (1823–1898), who emigrated in 1854 from Gorredijk, Groningen Province, earned a reputation as "one of the most widely known and benevolent gentlemen in the city." He helped found Oheb Shalom Congregation and worked with the benevolent society, the Hebrew hospital, the orphan asylum, and free burial society. Bertha Weil, daughter of Elizabeth and the late M. H. Weil, was a leader in the Hebrew Ladies Sewing Society and the hospital and orphanage associations. Jews served the nation in other ways. During the Mexican War when President James Polk called for forty thousand volunteers, Baltimore Jews organized the First Baltimore Hebrew Guards in 1846. Two Hollanders, Levi Benjamin and Simon Eytinge, were among the five officers.[37]

This recital reveals that Dutch Jews provided religious and civic leadership to Baltimore Jewry in the first half of the nineteenth century. This despite the fact that in the 1820s and 1830s German Jews became totally dominant in the population.

Occupations

Baltimore became a booming city in the 1850s and 1860s. Nearly 125,000 German immigrants alone disembarked at Baltimore in the two decades. Many were Jews who remained in the city. East Baltimore became the major Jewish center until the 1920s, although the more prosperous moved to new upscale neighborhoods. The Dutch were quickly engulfed by these newcomers. There were only 15 Dutch Jewish families totaling 84 persons recorded in the 1850 federal population census (Table 6.2), out of approximately 700 Jewish families in the city. Thus, barely 2 percent of the Jews were Dutch. Most of these Holland Jews had immigrated in the 1820s and 1830s, and by 1850 they were widely scattered among the eight city wards. During the 1850s 6 or 7 new families arrived, and by 1860 there were 24 Dutch Jewish households, with 125 persons. This was the numerical high point of the community (Table 6.3). No more than 4 families came in the 1860s, which was less than the families leaving so that by 1870 there were only 21 Dutch Jewish families, totaling 100 persons (Table 6.4).

Although Baltimore's Dutch Jews were a very small part of the Jewish community, they comprised a sizable part of the Dutch-born in the city. One half (49 percent) of the Holland-born in Baltimore in 1850 were Jewish (41 out of 84 persons). In the next decades, this proportion declined rapidly, however, as Dutch Catholic immigrants increasingly found the city hospitable. By 1860 only 17 percent of the Baltimore Dutch-born were Jewish (41 out of 245), but in the 1860s the Jewish proportion briefly increased slightly to 24 percent by 1870 (43 out of 176). This was because Dutch Catholics had departed the city during the Civil War for Catholic centers in non-slave holding areas in the North. Apparently the Dutch Jews in Baltimore did not flee the War, although those in New Orleans and other centers did so.

Dutch Jews in Baltimore were mobile. At no time was there a clearly recognized Dutch-Jewish neighborhood in Baltimore. Of the thirteen household heads in the 1830 federal census, only five remained in the city until death. The other eight moved—three to Philadelphia, two to New Orleans, and one each to New York, Richmond, and Galveston.[38] Of the thirteen heads in the 1850 census, six were still in Baltimore in 1860 and at least two had died. Outmigration had slowed in the 1850s. But the persistence rate slipped again in the 1860s; only seven out of twenty in the 1860 census remained for ten years. The war years and immediate postwar era also saw a marked decline in new Dutch Jewish immigration to Baltimore. Only three families in the 1870 census had arrived from Holland during the 1860s. The main locale of Dutch Jewry, with one-third of the families, was in Ward 10 in 1860 and Ward 5 in 1870, although the Dutch lived among fellow Jews throughout the city.

Baltimore Jews made a living as peddlers, small shopkeepers, and craftsmen. As the city exploded in new growth, some Jews rode the rising tide as merchants, moneylenders, land speculators, and other lucrative pursuits.[39]

A careful analysis of the 170 Jews in given occupations listed in

Table 6.2
Dutch Jewish Household Heads and Single Adults, Baltimore, 1850

Name	Age	N in Family	Time of Immigration	Occupation	Address	Ward
Levi Benjamin	75	9	1815	speculator	Guy and Harrison	3
Joseph Dammelman	55	9	pre-1834	optician	Lombard and Charles	3
Benjamin de Wolf	32	8	pre-1840	clothier	11 Harrison	10
Jacob de Wolf	72	3	pre-1840	secondhand clothier	11 Harrison	10
Samuel Eytinge	31	6	pre-1840	furniture dealer		14
Simon Eytinge	60	5	1828	merchant	41 North Howard	14
Jacob Gazan	41	10	1834	peddler		5
Brendella Goldstone	36	2	pre-1838	none		5
Hartog (Henry) S. Hartogensis	21	1	1848	stationer		9
Ira Lanestreet	66	6	pre-1831	merchant		19
Samuel Leon	40	3	1837	clothing dealer		10
Solomon H. Lewyt	38	8	pre-1837	watch dealer	21 Harrison	5
Samuel Nyburg	30	5	c. 1834	clothier		9
Marcus L. Pollack	50	6	1835–1838	peddler		3
Samuel Waterman	49	3	pre-1823	dealer	39 Light	8
		84				

Sources: Compiled from Robert P. Swierenga, comp. *Dutch Households in U.S. Population Censuses, 1850, 1860, 1870: An Alphabetical Listing by Family Heads,* 3 vols. (Wilmington, DE, 1987); Robert P. Swierenga, comp. *Dutch Immigrants in U.S. Ship Passenger Manifests, 1820–1880: An Alphabetical Listing by Household Heads and Independent Persons,* 2 vols. (Wilmington. DE, 1983); Baltimore City Directories, 1819–1840, compiled by Lance Sussman, "The Economic Life of Jews in Baltimore as Reflected in the City Directories, 1819–1840" (unpublished paper, 1977), app. 1:5–7.

Table 6.3
Dutch Jewish Household Heads and Single Adults, Baltimore, 1860

Name	Age	N in Family	Time of Immigration	Occupation	Property Value Realty $	Property Value Personalty $	Ward
Louis Aaron	45	7	pre–1849	none	—	300	18
Esther Cohen	38	3	pre–1857	none	—	—	12
Louis J. Cohen	40	8	pre–1840	none	—	—	12
Benjamin de Wolf	46	11	pre–1840	jeweler	8,000	7,000	10
George Draer	50	1	pre–1860	rag dealer	—	—	10
Samuel Elzas	36	2	pre–1860	clothier	—	400	10
Edward Hartogensis	23	1	pre–1860	clothier	—	800	10
Henry Hartogensis	30	6	1848	bookseller	—	100	10
Jacob Gazan	51	4	1843	clothing store	1,000	7,000	2,5
Isaac Goldsmith	36	9	pre–1848	clothier	—	800	10
Sarah H. Goldsmith (widow of Samuel)	69	2	pre–1808	none	110,000	1,500	11
Brendella Goldstone	43	4	pre–1838	clothing dealer	—	2,000	10
Esther Leon (widow Leon)	41	6	pre–1840	dry goods dealer	—	500	11
Samuel Leon	50	7	1837	peddler	8,000	5,500	10

Table 6.3 (Continued)

Name	Age	N in Family	Time of Immigration	Occupation	Property Value Realty $	Property Value Personalty $	Ward
S. H. Levy (Lewyt)	50	10	pre–1839	peddler	—	1,000	5
Elias Lewis	40	6	pre–1841	clothier	—	500	7
Isaac Lobe	45	7	pre–1851	runs loan office	3,000	10,000	9
Sarah Lobe	75	1	pre–1850	none	—	—	9
Marcus Polk	60	4	pre–1841	collector	—	200	3
Jacob Rice	45	6	pre–1854	speculator	—	—	4
Abraham Rosenfeld	50	11	pre–1838	property agent	8,000	3,000	4
Wolf Springer	40	5	pre–1842	clothing store	—	1,000	4
Henry van Kirk	19	1	pre–1860	silversmith	—	—	10
James Waterman	60	3	pre–1823	peddler	1,200	150	8
		125					

Sources: Compiled from Swierenga, *Dutch Households in U.S. Population Censuses*; Swierenga. *Dutch Immigrants in U.S. Ship Passenger Manifests*.

Table 6.4
Dutch Jewish Household Heads and Single Adults, Baltimore, 1870

					Property Value		
Name	Age	N in Family	Time of Immi-gration	Occupation	Realty $	Person-alty $	Ward
Louis J. Cohen	50	8	pre–1842	store salesman	—	—	13
Jacob de Boer	32	4	pre–1866	peddler	—	—	20
Jacob Gazan	63	3	1834	retail merchant	20,000	600	5
Rachel Gutman	89	1	pre–1850	none	—	—	3
H. S. Hartogensis	46	8	1848	clothing	—	2,500	9
Joseph Judik	75	8	pre–1845	commission merchant	75,000	—	14
Moses Lappmann	47	3	pre–1859	secondhand furniture	—	500	15
Samuel Leon	62	7	1837	clothing	22,000	2,000	8
Louis Levy	73	3	pre–1850	schoolteacher	—	—	5
Solomon Lewyt	60	8	pre–1839	trader watches	5,000	1,600	4
Isaac Lobe	55	8	pre–1851	none	—	—	9
Aaron Marks	80	3	pre–1853	cigarmaker	—	—	5,6
Samuel Nyburg	52	5	1834	furniture dealer	—	1,500	16

Table 6.4 (Continued)

Name	Age	N in Family	Time of Immigration	Occupation	Property Value Realty $	Property Value Personalty $	Ward
Meyer Salabes	56	7	1844–1856	peddler	—	400	8
Jacob Schilt	49	5	pre–1853	peddler	—	300	5
Harmon Simon	60	6	pre–1855	peddler	—	125	8
Moses Stokvis	61	7	1867	peddler	—	—	5
Sarah Stokvis	21	1	1867	domestic servant	—	—	14
Mary Straus	42	4	pre–1854	saleslady	3,000	200	5
Elias van Loe	65	1	pre–1870	patient, Hebrew Hospital	—	—	7
Elizabeth Weil (wid. M. H.)	60	4	pre–1836	none	—	—	5
		104					

Sources: Compiled from Swierenga, *Dutch Households in U.S. Population Censuses;* Swierenga, *Dutch Immigrants in U.S. Ship Passenger Manifests.*

204

the Baltimore City Directories of 1819 to 1840 shows that the overwhelming majority (70 percent) were self-employed merchants and a few professionals. Of the remainder 26 percent were skilled craftsmen, mainly tailors and shoemakers, and only 4 percent were unskilled laborers. Most of the merchants were in clothing, dry goods and notions, and groceries, plus a few in furniture, jewelry and watches, and tobacco. At the lowest rung 10 percent were peddlers; another 7 percent were brokers, traders, and dealers. This was a typical Jewish occupational distribution in the nineteenth century, although craftsmen in Baltimore were overrepresented.[40]

Occupations of the Dutch Jews mirrored the Jewish population at large. As early as 1830, all ten Dutch household heads (whose occupations are known) were shopkeepers: three owned clothing stores, three were pawnbrokers, two operated jewelry and fancy goods stores, one was a merchant, and one a victualler (Table 6.1).[41] This pattern continued for decades, with the Dutch primarily being in the clothing business as wholesale dealers and retail merchants. Others dealt in other consumer products—jewelry, watches, shoes, books, furniture, and stationery. Those beginning the upward climb worked as peddlers, the traditional entry job.

In 1850 the Dutch continued in the earlier pattern (Table 6.2). Of fourteen employed household heads twelve were retail and wholesale merchants, especially in clothing and dry goods, while two were peddlers. In 1860, of nineteen employed family heads, fourteen were merchants, eight in clothing and two in jewelry (Table 6.3). By 1870, of seventeen employed heads of households, eight were merchants (four in clothing) and five were peddlers (Table 6.4). Three were sales clerks, one each a school teacher and cigarmaker. Clearly, the general prestige status of the Dutch Jewish community moved downward in the 1860s. The increase in the number of peddlers and concomitant decline in clothiers reflects a generational shift and also the negative impact of the depression of 1857–1860.

But the Dutch Jews continued to prosper in terms of wealth accumulation, if not in prestige jobs. In 1860 or in 1870, seven families reported combined real and personal property above $10,000, with one widow, Sarah H. Goldsmith, reporting in 1860 more than $110,000, and a commission merchant, Joseph Judik, reporting $75,000 in 1870. Seven families in these decennial years were worth from $1,000 to $10,000, ten owned less than $1,000, and fifteen (mostly widows) reported no property. One Hollander who gained economic independence the easy way, by inheritance, was Hartog Weinberg (c. 1852–1899). He emigrated as a teenager and happily received a legacy in the will of his close relative Adolph Sutro,

205

former mayor of San Francisco. Weinberg operated retail stores in Frederick and Hagerstown, MD, for many years until joining the Baltimore firm of Lowenstein & Weinberg.[42]

Henry S. Hartogensis

The most renowned Jewish Hollander in Baltimore in the second half of the nineteenth century was Henry (Hartog) S. Hartogensis. He was born in 1830 in 's Hertogenbosch, the capital of Noord Brabant Province in the Catholic southeastern Netherlands, the son of "Rabbi" Samuel Hartogensis, a banker, Talmudist scholar, and philanthropist. Nineteen-year-old Henry immigrated in 1848 to Baltimore via New York City to "earn a living" and escape the "financial crash owing to the impending French revolution." He first started a stationery and printing firm and later owned a large sporting goods store on East Baltimore Street. In 1849 he married a fellow Hollander, Rachel de Wolff, daughter of Jacob who had arrived in the 1830s. In the 1850s Henry's younger brother Eleazer (Edward) joined the growing family and worked as a clothier. After marrying he moved to Washington, D.C., opened a "dry goods emporium," and established that branch of the family.[43]

In religion, the Hartogensis brothers were strictly Orthodox. Edward helped found the Adas Israel Congregation in Washington and taught in its religious school. Henry frequently officiated as *hazan* at Baltimore Hebrew until the majority espoused Reform in 1870. He led the minority to start the Chizuk Amuno (Emunah) Congregation in 1871 and served as secretary for twenty years. He also helped fund and erect its new synagogue in 1876, located on Lloyd Street only a few doors from its nemesis, Baltimore Hebrew. When Chizuk Amuno moved uptown in 1892, Hartogensis financed a new Ashkenazic synagogue, Zichron Jacob, located near his home on Baltimore Street, where he served as president, *hazan*, and "chief mainstay (financial and otherwise)." Earlier, in 1887 Congregation Oheb Shalom's Society for the Education of the Poor elected him as its secretary. From 1904 until his death, Hartogensis affiliated with Shearith Israel Congregation (founded in 1879), which remained an ultra-Orthodox synagogue for a century. Again he served as reader at services and was much honored by the congregation.[44]

Following a lengthy vacation in the Netherlands in 1890, Hartogensis wrote a report for the Philadelphia *Jewish Exponent* extolling the virtues of Dutch religious Orthodoxy. Despite their achievements in the arts and literature, in sciences and statecraft, which "compares favorably with the best Israelites of other countries," Hartogensis boasted, "nowhere have I seen 'orthodoxy' so triumphant." The Dutch had no use for "modern innovations to devotion —viz. the family pew, the organ, the mixed choirs mainly composed of Christians, the mutilation of the prayer-book, and the desecration of the holidays. What we call 'conservative' congregations," Hartogensis added, "are unknown to Holland Jews." Despite the rising materialism of the young, he concluded with satisfaction, there "are not enough of them in the whole country to form a 'Reform' congregation."[45]

In addition to his religious leadership, Hartogensis took an active part in Jewish fraternal organizations such as the Hebrew Education Society and the Hebrew Free Burial Society, and even in a "nonsectarian" Masonic lodge, in which he helped purge the Christian underpinnings from its rituals and ceremonies.

Several of his seven children became even more prominent, notably son Benjamin Henry Hartogensis (1865-1939)—a leading lawyer, Jewish historian, and editorial columnist of the Baltimore *Sun*, the *Jewish Exponent*, and the Baltimore *American*—who advocated separation of church and state in "Christian America". Benjamin bequeathed more than $50,000 for Jewish and public charities and educational institutions, including Johns Hopkins University. When his young wife Grace died in 1900, his father read the burial service at Oheb Shalom Cemetery. Several sons moved to New York City, where S. A. Hartogensis (who shortened his name to Harte) established the Weiss Manufacturing Company.[46]

Conclusion

A few Sephardic Jewish merchants came to Baltimore in the Revolutionary era from Philadelphia and the Netherlands West Indies as a result of trade ties. In the first decades of the nineteenth century Ashkenazic families arrived directly from Amsterdam, or indirectly via Philadelphia, and settled in the waterfront district of Fells Point. These were poorer folk who peddled goods or opened small shops. Between 1810 and 1830 nearly one-half of Baltimore Jewry was Dutch, but this was the high watermark because German Jews soon overwhelmed them.

Dutch Jews were active in 1830 in the founding of the first congregation, Baltimore Hebrew Congregation, and they played a prominent part in the early life of the synagogue. In the mid1840s, those in Fells Point also helped found the Eden Street Shul. Never did the Dutch have sufficient numbers to establish a Netherlandic synagogue.

No homogeneous Dutch Jewish neighborhoods developed in Baltimore. There was an early concentration in Ward 7 (Fells Point) and a later center in Ward 5 in the city proper. Gradually, the Dutch became interspersed among the German Jews. The primary occupation was shopkeeping, mainly in the clothing trades. But many new immigrants first peddled for a few years and only gradually advanced into the middle ranks of the city. By midcentury the Dutch Jews in Baltimore were swallowed up in a sea of Germans, and they quickly lost their national identity. Of 930 marriages in Reverend Henry Hochheimer's "Record of Marriages" in Baltimore from 1850 to 1900, 25 (2.6 percent) included one spouse of Dutch stock, but only 2 couples were both Dutch. In Baltimore and in Boston, the Dutch marriage pool was simply too small to sustain ethnic boundaries.

Chapter 7

NEW ORLEANS:
A SECULAR LOT

Sephardic Pioneers Before 1800

Dutch Jews were a prominent part of the New Or-
leans business community from at least the 1750s. Although French
mercantile laws, the *Code Noir* (Black Code), supposedly barred foreign merchants and traders, Sephardic Jews established themselves
in the city nonetheless. But these were Jews of a different sort—
largely secularized merchants of the Caribbean basin, who worshiped Mammon rather than the God of Abraham, Isaac, and Jacob.
Unlike Dutch Jews in the Netherlands and in East Coast centers,
those in the Crescent City for many decades displayed no interest in
formal worship, in keeping kosher, or being buried in consecrated
ground. With little compunction they formed marriage alliances
with powerful French Catholic families and allowed their children
to be baptized. New Orleans Jewry was a selective immigration that
screened out the more devout young men and passed through those
who followed the main chance wherever it might lead.

The first documented Jews in New Orleans were Isaac Monsanto
and his family, who hailed from The Hague, and his father David
Rodrigues Monsanto, a native of Amsterdam. These pioneers settled in New Orleans in 1758 after a three-year stay in the Dutch

colony of Curaçao. David Monsanto suffered financial reverses in the Netherlands in the 1740s and became a pauper. After living for years on synagogue charity in The Hague and suffering the death of his wife, he agreed to accept a ƒ600 grant from the Jewish community to enable him to emigrate to Curaçao with his eldest son Isaac and Isaac's wife and eight children, plus several unmarried children. The ambitious Isaac clearly took the initiative in the decision to emigrate, although the pauper's subsidy went to David as the titular head of the family.[1]

Isaac Monsanto opened an export-import business in Curaçao and his brother Joseph did the same in Saint Domingue. But within three years, in 1757, Isaac moved the base of the clan's commercial activities to New Orleans, where he became a prosperous merchant, shipping magnate, and country banker for the next decade. The Great War for the Empire (1756–1763) created a scarcity of consumer goods and Isaac and his younger brothers imported the needed commodities. When the war ended, Monsanto provided British authorities in Mobile and Pensacola in 1764–1765 with supplies and equipment for a military expedition up the Mississippi River to take possession of the Illinois country.[2] But his fortunes soon turned for the worse because the Spanish gained control of New Orleans from the French (in exchange for turning Florida over to the British victors in the war). Spain never tolerated Jews in her American colonies and in 1769 New Orleans authorities expelled all Jews, including the influential Isaac Monsanto, who owned one of the largest firms in the city.[3] Monsanto had to liquidate his extensive business assets under duress and went into exile in British West Florida in desperate straits. He failed to rebuild his fortune and died in 1778 a broken man. But his three sons returned after the American Revolution to conduct business along the lower Mississippi River.[4]

The Monsanto family were secularists for whom Judaism had little meaning. All but one son and all the daughters married Christians. Nevertheless, Isaac Monsanto and his brothers and sisters were pioneers who succeeded for a time despite the French and even the Spanish prohibitions against Jews. They were the first to be forced from future American soil because they were Jews, but after the Revolution they restored permanent Jewish settlements in key cities: New Orleans, Baton Rouge, and Pointe Coupee, as well as Natchez, MS.[5]

Ashkenazic Pioneers, 1800–1815

Besides the Monsanto clan, there were only a few other Sephardic families in New Orleans under French and Spanish rule. The most famous was the second-generation Dutch immigrant Judah Touro (1775–1854), son of Rabbi Isaac Touro of Newport. Trained in business and maritime shipping by his uncle Moses Michael Hays of Boston, Touro struck out on his own and in 1802 he opened a general merchandise store in New Orleans. He prospered greatly in merchandizing, shipping, and real estate. After being seriously wounded as a volunteer in Andrew Jackson's army defending New Orleans in 1814–1815, Touro devoted more of his time to philanthropy on a vast scale, although he continued actively in business until his death. He was a nonpracticing Jew until his final days, but redeemed himself for American Judaism by his "munificent benefactions" for synagogues, missions, hospitals, and relief societies. In addition to many $10,000 donations over the years, he bequeathed $500,000 in his will. Touro was one of the greatest Jewish philanthropists of the nineteenth century.[6]

After the United States bought Louisiana territory in 1803, New York and Philadelphia Ashkenazic Jews sent relatives, often sons with capital, to open businesses in New Orleans and take advantage of the new opportunities. One of the earliest merchants of prominence was Maurice Barnett, who was born in Amsterdam in 1776, a son of Lazarus Barnett, a broker. Lazarus emigrated with his family to Philadelphia in 1782 or 1783. He went into business with another Dutch Jew, Lyon Moses, and joined Mikveh Israel Congregation. His business venture failed quickly and in 1784 Lazarus Barnett fled his bankruptcy creditors for London where he died in 1797. Maurice served in the British army and then emigrated to Baton Rouge with his younger brother Edward, who had been born in Philadelphia during the family's brief sojourn there. These were the first Jews in Baton Rouge, which was then part of Spanish West Florida. By 1805 Maurice operated a trading and merchandising business, but before 1812 he shifted his operations to New Orleans. In Baton Rouge, both Maurice and Edward married French Catholics. Interestingly, Maurice's five children all remained Jewish, but all four of Edward's children were baptized.[7] By the 1830s Maurice Barnett owned one of the best-known auction houses in New Orleans and he prospered greatly. He sold furniture, ships, houses, slaves, real estate, and "almost everything else imaginable." Maurice's two sons—Maurice Jr. and Louis—continued the family auction business throughout the second half of the nineteenth century after Maurice retired around 1850.[8]

Barnett was soon joined by other Dutch Jews. Salomon S. de Jonge (1780–1852), another Amsterdammer, was a commissioner and exchange broker and city constable as early as 1808. He advertised Philadelphia goods for sale, which reveals again the widespread trade links between Philadelphia and New Orleans. In the 1820s he briefly had a business associate from New York City via Richmond. Salomon's brother J. S. de Jonge died at New Orleans in 1822 at age twenty-three. De Jonge's brokerage house at the time was on Toulouse Street, but later he moved to Saint Philip Street. In 1838 Salomon became an incorporator of the New Orleans Philharmonic Society, which suggests his high status in the community.[9]

De Jonge had frequent commercial dealings with Asher Moses Nathan and Alexander Phillips, who were other prominent Amsterdammers active in New Orleans and Baton Rouge business life before 1810. Nathan was born in 1785 and emigrated about 1800, with a brief stay in London. He settled first in Charleston, SC, by 1804 and began shipping merchandise to New Orleans using Maurice Barnett's ships, boarding houses, and warehouses in the two cities. He soon moved to Baton Rouge and married a Catholic there in 1810; in 1813 he settled permanently in New Orleans, where he had close business ties with Barnett, De Jonge, and other Dutch Jews.[10]

Already during his London stopover, Nathan had formed a partnership with Alexander Hart, a Jew born in England probably of Dutch ancestry. Hart and Nathan went bankrupt in 1810 and Hart subsequently relocated in New York, where he became the cantor of Congregation Bnai Jeshurun. In 1836 Hart, recently widowed, married a Dutch Jewish widow from New Orleans, Betsy Kokernot (discussed later), and returned to the South with her, living there until his death in 1839. Nathan, like Maurice Barnett, married a Catholic, the daughter of a Baton Rouge government official. His successful commission and exchange brokerage was on Chartres Street. An R. G. Dun & Company credit report in 1853 described Nathan as "an old resident and one of the most respectable brokers in the city [who] belongs to the old school." Nathan was worth $50,000 at the time, but his estate at his death in 1864 was worth many times that amount.[11]

Another associate of Nathan was his brother-in-law, Hyam Harris, who had married Nathan's sister Catherine in London in 1799 and then emigrated with Nathan to Charleston by 1800. In 1825 Harris, unsuccessful in business, resettled his family of ten children in New Orleans, where Asher Nathan largely supported them. One of Harris's daughters married Nathan's associate Daniel Goodman of Amsterdam, and son Moses became a cotton factor and merchant banker at Mobile from 1837 to 1842 (with the backing of his prosperous uncle Asher Nathan).[12]

Alexander Phillips came to the United States in 1791 at age sixteen, possibly as an indentured servant. He had been an apprentice tinsmith but decided to emigrate after "enduring the numerous privations always attendant upon poverty," as he put it in his memoirs. Phillips settled in Pennsylvania, first in Harrisburg and then Philadelphia, where he advanced from peddler to merchant. By 1804 he was in partnership with two other Jews in the Quaker city, but in 1808 he had moved to Baton Rouge, where he joined Maurice Barnett and Asher Nathan as the only Jews in the city. Here in 1811 he married a Catholic. Several years later in 1815 after the War of 1812 ended, he resettled in New Orleans, where he specialized in the wholesale and retail grocery trade. In 1814 and 1819 he brought two younger brothers, Isaac and Asher, from Amsterdam. Isaac married a Protestant in Baton Rouge, and fought with General Andrew Jackson in the Battle of New Orleans. Asher's fiancée, a Jewish native of Rotterdam, joined him in 1820 and they were married in New Orleans. Both Isaac and Asher were in the clothing business and enjoyed some success, but not as much as their older brother. Alexander lived in the fashionable Chartres Street, was an active Mason, and served three terms as city alderman—the first Jew in New Orleans to hold elective office. Alexander had been a Second Lieutenant in Jackson's army and previously had served in Pennsylvania in the federal forces that quelled the Whiskey Rebellion in 1794. Several of his eight children became notable New Orleans merchants, attorneys, and wives of prominent men.[13]

The future spiritual leader of New Orleans Jewry, Manis (Menachem) Jacobs, the first "rabbi" of the Hebrew Congregation for eleven years, also arrived in the first wave, about 1809. He was born in Amsterdam in 1779 and had an illustrious business career in New Orleans as a jeweler, merchant, slave trader, and investor in city real estate until his death in 1839. Manis was a partner with Salomon S. de Jonge, Samuel Jacobs, and other Dutch Jews. His first wife, a Jewess, probably accompanied him from Amsterdam, and his oldest daughter, who was born in New Orleans around 1815, married a Jew. But when Manis was widowed, he remarried in 1826 with a French Catholic widow, although he refused to have a Catholic ceremony in Saint Louis Cathedral. Yet his new wife raised their son and daughter Catholic! Jacobs's funeral rites, however, were Jewish, "performed in a most solemn and impressive manner," and he was buried in the city's first Jewish cemetery. He also fulfilled the law of charity by contributing liberally for needy Jews in the city.[14]

Apart from his synagogue leadership, Jacob's intermarriage was typical of the early Jews in New Orleans. These pioneer merchants deliberately left Amsterdam, Philadelphia, Charleston, and New York—all places with large Jewish communities and synagogues—for a vibrant dynamic city that happened to be French Catholic. These largely secularized Jews owned slaves, fathered mulatto children, married Catholics (occasionally Protestants), and otherwise adopted the Creole way of life. When Andrew Jackson rallied the city to ward off the British invasion in 1815, ten or eleven of the fifteen Jewish men in the city served under him. All but two or three were Dutch Jews. Besides Maurice Barnett, Isaac and Alexander Phillips, and S. S. de Jonge, Simon M. Cohen also fought. Cohen arrived in New Orleans from Amsterdam in 1810 and ran a tobacco shop. He too married a Catholic and was baptized into this church on his deathbed in 1836.[15]

Ashkenazic Pioneers, 1815–1840

After the War of 1812, Dutch Jews continued to settle in the Crescent City, and by 1830 they comprised a majority of the Jewish populace (see Table 7.1). In 1820 four of ten Jewish household heads were Dutch and by 1830, 58 percent (89 of 153) of the persons in Jewish households lived in Dutch-headed households.[16] In 1817 Levi Moses Kokernot and his twelve-year-old son David Levi arrived from Amsterdam to establish a retail dry goods store. Levi's wife Betsy Levy vander Beugel and younger son Louis joined him early in 1820. This family was likely the first Jewish immigrant *family* in the city since all of the previous Jews arrived as bachelors. David was apprenticed to a ship captain and for several years sailed the oceans, occasionally buying merchandise for the family store in Hamburg and other European ports. Levi went bankrupt in 1828 and started over again, but he died by 1830. David moved to Texas, where he raised a family, fought with the American colonists in the war for independence from Mexico, and lived out his life a Texan.[17]

Between 1817 and 1820 Levi van Ostern and his family also emigrated from Amsterdam and established another dry goods store. Levi's sons, Benjamin, David, and Joseph also became merchants. The Van Ostern and Kokernot families were linked when Louis Kokernot married Levi's daughter Nancy and joined his father-in-law's business. Unfortunately, the couple was divorced in 1839 in

Table 7.1
Dutch Jewish Household Heads, New Orleans, 1830

Name	Birth*	Death	N in House-hold†	Occupation
Maurice Barnett	1776	1865	8	dry goods
Simon M. Cohen	1781	1836	1	tobacconist
Abraham H. de Jonge	?	?	1	?
Zachariah L. Florance	1766	1832	7	surgeon dentist
Daniel Goodman	1801	1858	2	dry goods store
Abraham Green	1785	1847	9	hat and dry goods store
Moses Harris	1808	1877	7	grocery
Levy Jacobs	1797	1855	8	slave trader
Manis Jacobs	1779	1839	6	slave trader, "rabbi"
Samuel Jacobs	1788	1855	3	dry goods
Aaron S. Kerkhan	1800	1851	3	?
Betsy Kokernot	1773	1863	8	dry goods
Alexander Phillips	1776	?	10	dry goods
Asher Phillips	1779	1839	6	dry goods and clothing
Isaac Phillips	1783	1851	7	dry goods
Abraham Plotz	1794	1881	3	dry goods
Judah Touro‡	1775	1854	3	merchant
Benjamin van Ostern‡	?	?	?	dry goods
Levi van Ostern‡	?	?	?	dry goods

*Birth year is estimated from age at death. All died in New Orleans, except Betsy Kokernot who died in New York.
†Black servants and slaves omitted.
‡Not included in 1830 census, but known to be in the city.

Sources: Ira Rosenwaike, *On the Edge of Greatness: A Portrait of American Jewry in the Early National Period* (Cincinnati, 1985), 146; Bertram Wallace Korn, *Early Jews of New Orleans* (Waltham, MA, 1969), 171.

what was probably the first divorce within the New Orleans Jewish community. By this time, Nancy's father Levi Kokernot had died and her mother, Betsy, had remarried Alexander Hart, who also brought her son Isaac into the now enlarged Kokernot dry goods business. The financial panic of 1837 severely hit the southern retail trade and in 1839, after Hart's death, all of these related families were squabbling in court over financial matters and business difficulties. Widow Kokernot lived to the ripe age of ninety (1863), continuing in the dry goods business with her son Louis for many years.[18] In 1831, widow Betsy Kokernot paid for the passage of her sister, widow Vander Beugel, aged fifty, and sons Philip and David who arrived in New Orleans from Amsterdam on the ship *Charles Beth* on May 18, 1831. The payment order to the ship captain apparently was lost according to a report in the *New Orleans Bee*, July 21, 1831.[19]

Another Amsterdam native and dry goods merchant in New Orleans was Daniel Goodman (b. 1801) who arrived in 1824 and four years later married Amelia Harris, daughter of Hyam Harris, the brother-in-law of Asher Nathan.[20] Goodman's first partner was Solomon Soher of Richmond and New York: he had come to New Orleans in 1822 to seek his fortune and first was a partner of S. S. de Jonge in a dry goods venture. Soher and Goodman, along with Goodman's brother-in-law, Abraham Hyam Harris, also owned a Mississippi River steamboat company for a half-dozen years as well as engaged in other ventures. Goodman employed Maurice Barnett, Jr., as clerk in his dry goods store for a time in the late 1820s. By 1834 Soher had left New Orleans for London after suffering financial difficulties. The panic of 1837 also bankrupted Daniel Goodman, who had overextended himself in western land investments and paper money speculations. But he rebuilt his fortunes and reputation, served in synagogue and chevra, and died "full of years and honor" in 1858.[21]

Less is known of other early Dutch Jews. Michael Soloman, who arrived from Surinam by 1823, opened a medical practice as a foot doctor. A few years later in 1827 or 1828 Dr. Zachariah Levy Florance, a dentist and dental surgeon who was born in the Netherlands in 1766, moved to New Orleans from Charleston, where he had practiced since 1802. Two of his sons, Jacob and William, had arrived in 1825 and two more sons, Benjamin and Henry, came in the early 1830s. Zachariah died in 1832, but his sons left their mark in various businesses such as the Florance House Hotel and in city politics (Jacob ran twice unsuccessfully for alderman) and in the Louisiana militia. Several of the brothers became wealthy and moved to North Philadelphia in the late 1840s or early 1850s. Abraham Green operated a hat and dry goods store in New Orleans from at least 1822 until his death in 1847. When the first Jewish synagogue was formed in 1828, he was elected junior warden.[22] Marcus Cohen, born in 1794 in Amsterdam, was a peddler who died in 1836. Perhaps he was a son of Simon M. Cohen, the tobacconist who also died in 1836. Abraham H. de Jonge came to New Orleans from Philadelphia in 1827, where he became a merchant but without much success; he went bankrupt in 1834 and again in 1837. He too joined the pioneer Congregation Shaarei Chesed (Gates of Mercy) in 1827.[23]

216

Other pioneers were Abraham M. Plotz, who was born in Amsterdam in 1794 and emigrated in the 1820s. He became a partner of Asher Barnett in 1829–1830, and then operated his own dry goods shop for many decades. He died in 1881 at age eighty-seven. Plotz was the junior warden in the first Jewish synagogue in 1828 and was elected president in 1835. Aaron Kerkhan emigrated to New Orleans in 1820 at twenty years of age. He joined the Jewish congregation and was a merchant until his death in 1851.[24] Other Dutch Jews were Emanuel Stern, a relative of the Van Ostern family, who arrived in 1824; Bernard Lejeune (le Jeune) of Rotterdam who came before 1828 and suffered a business bankruptcy in 1832; and Solomon Hunt from Amsterdam, whose wife Esther Millam Hunt was related to the Kokernot family and who died in 1836.[25] Joseph Solomons of Amsterdam, who by 1750 had settled in Charleston where his son Aaron was born in 1791, moved to New Orleans in the early 1820s along with Aaron and his family of five children. By 1829 Aaron Solomons was secretary pro tem of the Jewish congregation. Joseph Solomons's brothers and their families also moved from Charleston to New Orleans, where Israel Solomons went bankrupt in 1840. Lewis Solomons, a watchmaker, went bankrupt in 1832–1834, and Chapman Solomons died in 1849. Israel had seven children by 1820 and Chapman had four. We need to know more about the Solomons families in New Orleans and Georgetown, SC.[26]

At least four Dutch Jews settled in New Orleans in the 1830s. B. Voorsanger was a trustee of the Jewish congregation in 1835 and Abraham de Jonge held the same position in 1838. In 1836 Benjamin Samuel de Jonge, aged sixty, a merchant, arrived with his wife and son Meyer Benjamin de Jonge, age eighteen, from London aboard the *Grotius of Salem*. It is likely that they sojourned for a time in London after leaving Amsterdam. The next year Michael de Jonge (de Young), age thirty-five, and his wife and two-year-old son arrived directly from Amsterdam on the *Jonge Maria*, arriving on Christmas day.[27]

This recital of the pioneer Dutch Jews of New Orleans reveals that Sephardim arrived in the mid-eighteenth century and lived through the turmoil of the French-English war and then the American Revolution. The first Ashkenazim came after the infant United States purchased the Louisiana territory in 1803. Neither French nor Spanish authorities welcomed Jews, although the French were more lenient—thus Jews had to live in constant risk of expulsion.

Almost all of the Dutch Jews of New Orleans were born in Amsterdam. The Sephardim came via the large Jewish settlements in the Dutch West Indies and Charleston, SC, while most Ashkenazim

217

immigrated directly from Amsterdam or they came after stopovers in London, Philadelphia, or New York.

The Dutch were drawn to the Crescent City by business opportunities in this prosperous and cosmopolitan gateway to the Mississippi Valley and the Caribbean. Most were traders, dry goods storekeepers, and export merchants. Some found the financial success they sought, but only after surviving bankruptcies, political difficulties, and personal tragedies. Others died as failures or departed in despair for greener pastures elsewhere. Many became leaders in the business community and several held political offices—others barely left a trace of their lives.

The Jewish population of the city grew very slowly, partly because more devout Jews avoided cities without synagogues and partly because of upheaval caused by wars and cholera epidemics. As late as 1830, after more than forty years of Jewish settlement, the census marshal counted only thirty-five Jewish heads of households. The constitution of the first Jewish congregation in 1827 included thirty-five members, but some did not live in the city or were there only temporarily. The 1822 city directory listed twenty-five businessmen and the 1820 census counted only eleven Jewish households. Neither source is complete, but even a thorough count could hardly be expected to go beyond doubling the number.[28]

Synagogue Life

The early Jews of New Orleans were a religiously indifferent, mixed multitude of merchants who sought the main chance to financial success wherever it led. Most arrived as bachelors and married French Catholic women since no Jews were available, and their children grew up as Gentiles. This was hardly fertile ground for planting a congregation. Decades passed, even generations, before new Ashkenazic settlers founded a congregation in 1827. A newcomer, Jacob da Silva Solis, a devout Sephardic Jew from London, finally provided the impetus to do so. When he came to the Crescent City from New York City in 1827, he was appalled to find no unleavened bread for Passover. Within six months he created a congregation to remedy this and other deficiencies in the practice of pure Judaism.[29]

Solis and six others founded the Shaarei Chesed Congregation (later Touro Synagogue). Four of the seven incorporators were Dutch: Manis Jacobs, Isaac Phillips, Abraham Plotz, and Bernard

218

Lejeune. Isaac's brother Asher Phillips was one of the first officers (junior warden) and Jacobs, Sephardic like Solis, was elected as first president. Five of the seven first officers were Dutch and at least nine of the twenty-eight charter members, or one-third, were Dutch. Eleven other Dutch Jews were among the thirty-three nonmember "Israelite Donors." Solis returned to New York six months later and died there suddenly in 1829. The fledgling congregation in New Orleans was stunned by the news and profusely honored and praised him as their "Beloved member and first founder." Lejeune by 1830 had moved to Cincinnati and was among the successful petitioners to the legislature of Ohio for an act of incorporation of Congregation Bnai Israel.[30]

Although most of the members were Ashkenazic, the bylaws dictated the Sephardic ritual, at the insistence of Solis, Jacobs, and the other Sephardic leaders. That the German-Dutch majority acquiesced in this more prestigious rite of America's most successful Jews indicates the extent of their acculturation or perhaps of their indifference. This Americanization is further revealed by the unique proviso in the bylaws that permitted the burial of non-Jewish spouses, women as well as men, in the congregational cemetery. Shaarei Chesed was the only congregation in the nation to deviate from Jewish burial law. Indeed, the first president of the congregation was himself married to a Catholic. But the deviation did not continue for long because of the influence of more Orthodox Ashkenazic immigrants in the 1830s. The revised bylaws of 1841 changed the worship rite to the "rules and customs of German Israelites" and banned from membership those who intermarried with Gentiles. Nine years later the German-Dutch congregation built its first synagogue, eventually named after Judah Touro, its chief benefactor.[31]

During its first decade the spiritual and administrative leader of Shaarei Chesed after Solis's death was its first president Manis Jacobs. Manis performed the first documented Jewish wedding in New Orleans in 1828 between Hollander Daniel Goodman and Amelia Harris, daughter of Hyam Harris and niece of Asher Nathan (see Fig. 7.1). The first funeral three months later was that of Hyam Harris, the first to be interred in the newly purchased cemetery in distant Jefferson Parish. Jacobs expressed his Jewish identity by signing all notarized business papers in English, but he used his Hebrew name Menachem as a cachet or seal. By this unique act he publicized his identification with Judaism, even when no formal Jewish life existed in New Orleans. Jacobs was a successful trader, real estate investor, and promoter. At his death in 1839, he was eulogized as the Rabbi of New Orleans and a noted city philanthropist. For

Fig. 7.1. Hebrew Wedding Certificate of Daniel Goodman and Amelia Harris, 1828, New Orleans, LA. Reprinted by permission of the American Jewish Historical Society, from Bertram Wallace Korn, *The Early Jews of New Orleans* **(Waltham, MA, 1969).**

more than a decade he had conducted services, performed marriages and burials, and fulfilled the role of minister and reader. That a Hollander with a Catholic wife and no rabbinic training had the courage or audacity to give synagogue leadership for more than a decade is quite remarkable.[32]

Even more surprising is that New Orleans Jews waited so long to establish a synagogue and then it required the initiative of a Londoner. The Jewish pioneers in New Orleans were young entrepreneurs, more secular than Jewish. "They were willing to leave the protective shelter of a full Jewish life at home, in Frankfort, Ham-

220

burg, Amsterdam, London, or New York City, in order to find fortune and success on a frontier where Judaism did not exist." Men like Asher Nathan and Alexander Phillips valued fortune more than faith. Indeed, they may even have immigrated to New Orleans to break the tight bonds of Jewish separateness in Amsterdam or elsewhere. This separateness had for centuries marked Jews as different, even degraded. Of the fifteen Jews in New Orleans between 1800 and 1815, seven remained bachelors and eight married Gentiles. Jewish intermarriage rates of 50 percent were common into the 1830s. Many early New Orleans Jews married in the Saint Louis Cathedral and all of the children of these unions were lost to Judaism. When the Jewish congregation finally began, the wealthy pioneer Jews even refused to support it financially. Manis Jacobs had to appeal for a loan to more devout New Yorkers.[33]

New Orleans Jewry was truly a community with only a weak consciousness of their Jewishness. They were simply disinterested in religious life. Their French and Creole Catholic neighbors were equally indifferent to their religion. Many were second-generation immigrants, single young men who valued their Jewishness less than their material pursuits. There was clearly a selection process at work in their migration to New Orleans. The early Jews were highly acculturated and moved easily in Catholic and Protestant circles. But they were not assimilated. Their business partners and relationships were largely with fellow Jews, which confirms their mutual affinity. New Orleans Jews, including the Dutch, lived within a social and economic web of intimate relationships. This proved that an "irreducible residue of Jewishness" remained, according to the authority, Bertram Wallace Korn.[34]

Dutch Jews were more religious than most. They gave leadership to the two congregations in the antebellum decades. The names Van Ostern, Phillips, Plotz, Hyam, Voorsanger, Jacobs, and De Jonge repeatedly appear as officers of Congregation Shaarei Chesed. By the early 1840s the congregation had adopted the Ashkenazic rite when the Germans became dominant. One of the newcomers, Gershom Kursheedt of New York, a disciple of Isaac Leeser of Philadelphia, with Leeser's help in 1845 organized a Sephardic-rite congregation, Nefutzoth Yehudah (Dispersed of Judah). Judah Touro, the philanthropist, funded the remodeling of a church into a synagogue for the new congregation. Both religious and social reasons lay behind the schism. Besides the prestige factor, the Sephardi clearly desired to maintain their traditional worship rite, which had been abandoned in the late 1830s.

The first rabbi of Nefutzoth Yehudah was an Orthodox Dutch

Jew, Moses N. Nathan (1801–1883), a nephew of Asher M. Nathan, who had been serving Sephardic congregations in Jamaica and Saint Thomas in the West Indies from the mid 1830s until 1850. Before leaving Kingston for Saint Thomas in 1845, he was the coeditor in 1844 of *Bikkure Hayam* (First Fruits of the West), a monthly published in Kingston and one of the earliest Jewish periodicals in the Western Hemisphere. Rabbi Nathan accepted the New Orleans appointment on February 1850 and arrived in May, a few days before the dedication of the new sanctuary. Judah Touro agreed to pay his salary of $2,500 for two years. Only a few Dutch were among the forty men who joined the new congregation, specifically the Florance brothers, members of the Harris and Hyam families, and Daniel Goodman. Nathan was disappointed that the Dispersed of Judah Congregation did not prosper and in 1853, when the salary guarantee expired, he took a position in Charleston.[35]

Nathan's successor as temporary minister in 1853 was Benjamin da Silva, the congregation's sexton and also a Netherlander. Da Silva was born in Amsterdam in 1811 and had emigrated to New York in the 1830s before coming to Mobile, AL, in 1845 to become the first regular reader of the new Congregation Shaarai Shomayim (Gates of Heaven). From late 1845 until 1849 Da Silva conducted services at this pioneer synagogue of Alabama. He then moved to New Orleans where he sold jewelry and brokered real estate while holding the post of sexton. Da Silva remained active in Jewish affairs throughout the Civil War and Reconstruction eras and was buried with honors in the Canal Street Jewish Cemetery at his death in 1881.[36]

In 1850 some twenty-six men living in the adjacent town of Lafayette, most of whom belonged to Shaarei Chesed, organized the third synagogue in New Orleans, Congregation Shaarei Tefiloh (Gates of Prayer). Most members of this Orthodox group were Germans, but the first president was Dutch-born salesman Abraham H. de Jonge, who had lived in the city since the 1820s. De Jonge's was the first name on the congregation's charter document and the only Netherlander. During the Civil War de Jonge departed the Crescent City for a place safely under the Union Flag.[37]

Little is known of the unfortunate career of another Dutch cleric living in New Orleans in 1850 who had been an associate of Moses Nathan in the West Indies. This is Benjamin Cohen Carillon who was born in the Netherlands in 1810 and emigrated to London after 1836 with his wife and infant daughter. There he joined the recently organized Reform congregation, the West End Synagogue, even though the chief rabbinate of England had placed it under a ban of excommunication.[38]

In early 1842 one of the leaders of the renegade synagogue, Moses Mocatta, responded to a request to recommend a competent minister to serve the Sephardic congregation in Charlotte Amalie, Saint Thomas, in the Danish Virgin Islands, which was in transition from Orthodoxy to Reform. The congregation was large; the 1850 census counted five hundred Jews in Saint Thomas. The congregation desired a "minister of gentlemanly deportment, possessing a thorough knowledge of the English language, a strict Mosaic believer, a liberal man who does not place rabbinical writings on a level with the Pentateuch."[39] By letter, Mocatta recommended his London friend, Benjamin Carillon, then thirty-two years of age and probably living in New York. Mocatta also enclosed a copy of the abridged prayer book that he and the other leaders of London's West End Synagogue had authored. Nothing is known of Carillon's training for the ministry, but it likely was minimal since he lacked ordination. He spoke English fluently, of course, and may already have been known to the Saint Thomas congregation because in 1840 his son Aaron was born in the West Indies. Carillon had then moved to New York, where a daughter was born in 1842.

The Saint Thomas congregation, on Mocatta's endorsement, offered Carillon a contract of engagement as its minister, which he accepted and sailed for Saint Thomas later in 1842, probably from New York. When Carillon arrived at Charlotte Amalie, the congregation asked him to approve the new West End Synagogue prayer book, which they had happily received earlier that year. But, to their great surprise, the "liberal man" Carillon refused, on the grounds that the composer was not an ordained rabbi and thus lacked authority.

When challenged by the congregation, the Reverend Carillon submitted his opinion for publication in Isaac Leeser's influential Anglo-Jewish journal, the *Occident and American Jewish Advocate.* Carillon's views provoked a sharp rejoinder from a fellow Dutch *hazan*, the Reverend Henry Goldsmith of New York, a teacher of Hebrew at the Talmud Torah School of Congregation Bnai Jeshurun. This began a heated exchange of articles, which was joined by the Reverend Abraham Rice of Baltimore, the unofficial Chief Rabbi of the United States. Rice declared that both were in error, because the Reform cleric, Carillon, rejected the divine origin of the Talmud, and the Orthodox cleric, Goldsmith, accepted it. But the Talmud included both divine and rabbinic laws and yet it was authoritative, Rice declared.

Rabbi Carillon's tenure in Saint Thomas was understandably difficult and brief, lasting less than two years. Rejecting the Reform prayer book pleased the Orthodox party, who Carillon successfully prevented from seceding. But his ardent support of Danish King Frederick VII's edict that girls as well as boys must be confirmed by all religious communities satisfied the Reform faction as much as it displeased the Orthodox members. And this act led to his outright dismissal.

By 1844 Carillon, after receiving a "severance compensation" of $2,400 for breach of contract, had left Saint Thomas for Congregation Shaar Hashamayim (Gate of Heaven) in Montego Bay, Jamaica, in the British West Indies, where as *hazan* he preached regularly in English for several years. Three daughters were born in Jamaica—in 1844, 1846, and 1848. Fellow Hollander Moses N. Nathan, who was also in Jamaica in 1844 eventually replaced him at Saint Thomas in 1845 and turned the Charlotte Amalie congregation back to Orthodoxy. Trouble followed Carillon to Jamaica as well, and he was dismissed, this time without severance pay, "for attempting violent and unauthorized changes in the usual form of worship as current among Portuguese Jews." Carillon clearly did not well gauge the liturgical preferences of his congregations. In 1848 Carillon was one of four applicants for the vacant position of *hazan* of Charleston's Congregation Beth Elohim, but the search committee passed over him.[40]

Nathan and Carillon both departed the West Indies for New Orleans by 1850. Nathan arrived in May 1850 in response to a call to serve the Dispersed of Judah Congregation. Carillon's time of arrival is unknown but his family of eight were found in Ward 4 in June 1850 by the federal census marshal. Carillon's occupation in the census was "Jewish clergyman," but it is not known if he ever served any New Orleans congregation. A notation of the census marshal may provide a clue. He reported tragically that the forty-year-old Carillon was "insane." The family's history thereafter is yet unknown, but they were no longer in the city at the time of the 1860 census.[41]

Antebellum and War Decades, 1840–1870

In the antebellum decades a second smaller wave of Dutch Jews settled in New Orleans to augment the pioneer community. At least five new families arrived in the 1840s and seven in the 1850s, most coming directly from Amsterdam, although one had lived at least a decade in Missouri. Three other household heads (a Spaniard, German, and Pole) had Dutch wives. The high point of the Dutch Jewish settlement was around 1850 when the community totaled seventeen households (80 persons), including women and children (Table 7.2). By 1860, on the eve of the Civil War, the number of Dutch-headed families had declined slightly to fifteen, totaling 53 persons (Table 7.3). The severe yellow fever epidemic in the summer of 1858 carried off 150 Jews, including several Dutch. But the economic dislocation of the Civil War was far more devastating than disease. By 1870, the census marshal counted only four Dutch Jewish households: Abraham Plotz, a pioneer; Levi van Ostern's widow Nancy Kokernot; Fritz Jacobs, a tailor; and Geson Gerritsma, a jewelry dealer, who came early in the war (Table 7.4).[42]

The Civil War and defeat of the Confederacy obviously had a heavy effect on the New Orleans Jews. According to Rabbi Max Heller, "It revolutionized fortunes and homes, it profoundly affected institutional life, it tested patriotism and public spirit, [and] it forced a readjustment of civilization."[43] Almost all of the Dutch Jews left the city and no newcomers arrived, except Gerritsma in 1860. Since the booming economy of the Crescent City had attracted Jews in the first place, the city's financial demise in the war drove them away. Historically, Jews had been underrepresented in the city ever since, although reasons other than the war certainly account for this. In 1938 a careful demographic census of the city's Jews counted less than 6,500, or 2 percent of the populace, compared to 3.5 percent nationally. In relation to fourteen other cities of similar size in 1920, the proportion of Jews in New Orleans was the lowest by far. Nevertheless, New Orleans was the only southern city to have a sizable Jewish community at the time.[44]

The antebellum Dutch Jews in New Orleans had no single residential focal point to their community. In 1850, six families with twenty-four persons lived outside of the city in Orleans Parish; five families (thirty persons) were in Ward 7, four families (nineteen persons) were in Ward 4, and two families (seven persons) were in Ward 5. Wards 1 and 4 thus were the primary areas for the Dutch. The Orleans Parish residents were the blue-collar workers, while the city residents were merchants. In 1869, Orleans Parish had become Ward 11 of the city proper and five families (nineteen persons) yet lived there. The other Dutch were widely scattered throughout the city.

Occupations

The Jews of New Orleans, as Jews elsewhere, primarily were merchants and dealers. An analysis of the occupations of

Table 7.2
Dutch Jewish Household Heads and Single Adults, New Orleans, 1850

Name	Age	N in House-hold	Time of Immi-gration	Occupation	Property Value $	Ward
Benjamin Carillon	40	8	1848–1850	Jewish clergyman	—	N.O. 4
Levy Cohen	35	1	pre–1850	clerk	—	N.O. 4
Benjamin da Silva	34	6	pre–1838	sexton	—	Orleans Par.
M.A. de Bott	33	2	pre–1850	painter	—	Orleans Par.
P. H. de Jonge	64	1	pre–1850	painter	—	N.O. 4
Salomon S. de Jonge	70	3	pre–1808	landlord	5,000	N.O. 5
Daniel Goodman	45	12	pre–1824	salesman	12,000	N.O. 1
J. T. Guildemester	24	4	pre–1846	merchant	—	N.O. 5
Henry Hamburger	35	5	pre–1842	tailor	—	Orleans Par.
Louis Kokernot	48	10	1820	merchant	500	N.O. 1
Widow Levy Kokernot	32	9	pre–1832	none	—	N.O. 4
E. S. Mendels	33	6	pre–1838	clerk	—	Orleans Par.
Asher M. Nathan	64	2	1800	exchange broker	10,000	N.O. 1
Bernard Phillips	40	5	pre–1839	notary public	—	N.O. 1
D. M. Phillips	39	1	pre–1850	laborer	—	Orleans Par.
B. van Ostern	36	1	1817–1820	merchant	—	N.O. 1
Barnes S. Wolff	47	4	pre–1835	druggist	—	Orleans Par.
Total		80				

Source: Compiled from Robert P. Swierenga, comp., *Dutch Households in U.S. Population Censuses, 1850, 1860, 1870: An Alphabetical Listing by Family Heads,* 3 vols. (Wilmington, DE, 1987).

226

Table 7.3
Dutch Jewish Household Heads and Single Adults, New Orleans, 1860

Name	Age	N in House-hold	Time of Immi-gration	Occupation	Property Value Realty $	Person-alty $	Ward
H. Eckstein	46	5	pre–1840	drayman	—	175	11
Abraham de Jonge	59	1	pre–1830	salesman	—	400	1
Madeline de Jonge	60	7	pre–1839	none	—	3,000	1
Isaac Fedder	29	1	pre–1860	variety store	—	400	4
Aaron Green	25	1	pre–1860	clerk	—	—	5
C. E. Hamburger	60	2	pre–1860	none	—	—	10
Henry Hamburger	48	5	pre–1844	tailor	—	1,500	2
Widow B. Kokernot	67	1	1820	none	—	—	11
Jacob Liedwirth	44	1	pre–1860	none	—	—	3
R. O. Mesritz	30	6	1848	clothing store	—	1,000	5
Nanette Phillips (Widow Bernhard)	46	3	pre–1839	none	—	200	6
Abraham Plotz	62	6	pre–1830	speculator	—	4,500	6
J. Rusbane	37	6	pre–1846	carpenter	—	100	8
Moses Schreiber	27	3	pre–1855	peddler	—	200	11
E. W. C. Zadock	39	5	pre–1851	huckster	—	250	11
Total		53					

Source: Compiled from Swierenga, *Dutch Households in U.S. Population Censuses.*

Table 7.4
Dutch Jewish Household Heads and Single Adults, New Orleans, 1870

Name	Age	N in House-hold	Time of Immi-gration	Occupation	Realty $	Person-alty $	War
Geson Gerritsma	47	5	pre–1862	jewelry dealer	—	1,000	6
Fritz Jacobs	41	8	pre–1854	tailor	—	—	3
Nancy Kokernot	50	4	1817–1820	none	3,000	200	10
Abraham Plotz	76	2	pre–1830	none	—	150	5
Total		19					

Source: Compiled from Swierenga, Dutch Households in U.S. Population Censuses.

two hundred Jews listed on the city directories between 1811 and 1838 revealed that nearly two-thirds were proprietors, mainly retail shopowners in clothing and dry goods, plus a few brokers and manufacturers. Surprisingly, there was nary a peddler, although some merchants may have combined shopkeeping with peddling. Slightly less than one-fifth of the city's employed Jews were in the professions such as accounting, law, and medicine, and an equal number were skilled craftsmen in the building construction and needle trades. Unskilled laborers could hardly be found among the Jews.[45]

Prior to the 1840s, most Dutch Jews were also retail merchants. The 1830 census listed eleven of seventeen employed family heads operating dry goods stores. Two others were slave traders, one each operated a grocery and a tobacco shop, and one was a dental surgeon (Table 7.1). Thus, sixteen out of seventeen were merchants, which was a much higher proportion than among the city's Jews generally. Twenty years later, by 1850, the occupational profile had changed drastically. There were only three unspecified merchants, and barely half of the family heads were in trade and commerce, two as clerks and one a salesman (Table 7.2). Most had become wage earners. A cleric, synagogue sexton, and druggist comprised the professional group and two painters and a tailor the skilled trades. There was one unskilled laborer. Clearly, the socioeconomic status of the Dutch Jews had declined sharply in these decades but, unfortunately, there is no comparable study of the vast majority of other Jews in New Orleans in the middle decades from 1840 through 1870. Only four Dutch reported real estate ownership in 1850 and their holdings were substantial, but all were pioneer families.

On the eve of the Civil War, the Dutch Jews barely held to their middling status. Two were merchants running a clothing and variety store, along with a salesman, speculator, and clerk (Table 7.3). The speculator Abraham Plotz, with $4,500 in personal property, was the wealthiest Hollander; he was a pioneer who had arrived before 1830. The others were employed in the tailoring and carpenter crafts or were peddling. Except for the tailor, Henry Hamburger, who owned $1,500 in personalty, none reported personal property of more than $400 and none owned real estate. The Dutch were no longer merchants but peddlers and wage earners occupying the lower rungs of the middle class.

By 1870 most Dutch Jews had left the city, and only two merchants remained active—Geson Gerritsma, a jewelry dealer, and Fritz Jacobs, a tailor. Nancy Kokernot (widow Van Ostern) owned a home worth $3,000 and was the wealthiest Hollander after the Civil War (Table 7.4). This economic decline is a telling commentary on the negative impact of the war on the Dutch Jews.

Conclusion

Dutch Jews in New Orleans were always few in number, yet they played an important role in the economic and religious life of the city from the earliest times. The Monsanto clan and the De Jonge, Nathan, and Phillips families were mainstays of the mercantile community in the Revolutionary and Federalist periods. In the Jacksonian era, Dutch Jews like the Van Ostern and Kokernot families were heavily involved in the retail dry goods trade.

The Dutch were drawn to the Crescent City on the Mississippi delta by its business opportunities as a gateway to the Caribbean and the American interior. They remained only as long as economic conditions were favorable and departed when New Orleans lost its preeminent place during the Civil War era owing to the decline in North-South interregional trade and the devastation of the Confederate defeat.

Establishing Jewish congregations and synagogues in New Orleans was difficult because of religious indifference and the propensity of the Jewish pioneer men to marry French Catholic women. Outsiders from New York and Philadelphia finally became the needed catalysts to found congregations. Once the locals were motivated, however, Dutch Jews led in establishing the first congregations of Shaarei Chesed and Nefutzoth Yehudah. The Dutch trader

229

and promoter Manis Jacobs earned the accolade Rabbi of New Orleans because of his unstinting efforts, and Moses Nathan and possibly Benjamin Carillon served as *hazans*. While generally a secular lot, it appears that Dutch Jews were more religious than most and usually Orthodox, except for Carillon.

The apogee of the Dutch Jewish community in New Orleans came around 1850, but it lacked a critical mass to form a Dutch synagogue or even a Dutch neighborhood. The Hollanders were interspersed among the German Jews and hidden from view. By the time of the Civil War the pioneers had died off and the later comers moved to more promising mercantile centers in the North. The primary Dutch Jewish settlement in the South quietly came to an end.

Chapter 8

THE GREAT LAKES FRONTIER: THE RESTLESS ONES

The Reverend Samuel Myer Isaacs of New York journeyed to Chicago in 1851 to speak at the consecration of a new synagogue. While en route he was amazed by the infiltration of Jews into the Middle West. In a letter to the London *Jewish Chronicle*, he wrote: "It is remarkable that not a village on my route was without an Israelite, much less the towns, such as Detroit and Ipsilanti, each containing 20 families, Kalamazoo and Marshall 10, and others in proportion; and all these are destined to be congregations."[1] Most of these Israelites were young itinerants scratching for a start in life where competition was minimal.

Dutch Jewish peddlers and roving merchants also migrated throughout the growing midwestern cities, along with their German and east European coreligionists. They traveled to the interior as peddlers and petty clothiers, sponsored initially by family business houses in the East. With little capital but great initiative, they brought much-needed city consumer goods to the developing frontier regions.

Most of the Dutch settled first in eastern cities and then after establishing themselves they moved inland along the trade routes. New York City, Buffalo, and Pittsburgh were the main jumping off

231

points, with secondary staging areas being Cleveland, Toledo, Detroit, Chicago, Saint Louis, Milwaukee, Indianapolis, Cincinnati, and other interior cities. Before the Civil War, however, Chicago was a first-stop city for some Dutch Jews.

Buffalo—The Van Baalen and Boasberg Families

Buffalo initially in 1795 was called New Amsterdam and served as the western anchor of the 33 million-acre Holland Land Company tract laying west of the Genessee River, which was owned by four Dutch banking houses. When in the 1820s the Erie Canal opened and the mouth of Buffalo Creek on Lake Erie's eastern shore was deepened for lake vessels, Buffalo became a boomtown and attracted its share of Dutch immigrants, in competition with Cleveland, Pittsburgh, Detroit, and Chicago.[2]
German Jews first settled in Buffalo in 1835, but the earliest known Dutch Jews did not arrive until the 1840s and their numbers were never large. The Dutch were mainly merchants following the trade routes into the heartland of the Middle West that were spawned by westward immigration.

In the 1850 census, the Dutch numbered only three out of twenty-four Jewish families in the city. Two of these three families remained only a few years before moving west. The heads of the two families who stayed were related: Emanuel Israel van Baalen, an auctioneer, and Emanuel Joseph van Baalen, a peddler. They were joined by Emanuel Israel's brother, Joseph Israel van Baalen, also a peddler. All the Van Baalens were from Amsterdam. Auctioneer Emanuel's oldest daughter Rachel in 1848 married another young Hollander in Buffalo, Nathan Boasberg (1827–1910), also a peddler at the time, who became the most prominent Dutch Jew in Buffalo.

These Van Baalen (Van Balen) families, all clothing merchants, were a truly remarkable clan on the Great Lakes frontier. Their story can best be told here, although it also took place in Cleveland, Detroit, Pittsburgh, and Chicago.[3] The chain migration of the clan began in May 1842 with Emanuel Israel van Baalen, a peddler born in 1810. The family sailed on the *Fame* from Antwerp to New York, arriving on June 1, and included Emanuel, his wife Maria (or Mary), and three children. By 1850 the family had four more children.[4] Emanuel settled in Buffalo and by 1850 was an auctioneer; his oldest son Israel was a peddler. The family of nine lived in Buffalo's Fourth Ward, along with all the other Dutch Jews in the city.

Emanuel van Baalen used his sons and brother to create a network of clothing stores in Detroit, Cleveland, Pittsburgh, and Chicago. His oldest son Joseph Israel, born in the Netherlands in 1832 and known as Israel, married in 1853 to Rose Lit (b. 1828) of the Philadelphia Dutch merchant clan. After their first son's birth in Buffalo in 1854, Israel moved to Detroit by 1856 where he began as a dealer in old clothes. Two daughters were born to the couple in Detroit. Sometime after 1862 the family moved again to Chicago, where Israel first became a clothing merchant in the city center. By 1900 he was a fire insurance agent in the fashionable Hyde Park district. His married daughter Louisa lived in the same six-flat apartment building with her Dutch-born husband, Jacob Litt, a dry goods salesman and son of Solomon Litt, who was her mother's brother. So Louisa had married her cousin and kept the bloodline 100 percent Dutch. This also meant that the Philadelphia Lit (single "T") clan was linked with the Chicago Litt (double "T") clan.[5]

Emanuel's second son Morris van Baalen moved to Pittsburgh before 1864 where he married a Dutch Jewess, Betsy de Roy, who was born in Holland in 1846 as the daughter of Abraham Levie de Roy and Saartje Israel van Baalen of Amsterdam. Betsy was a sister of Hartog Israel van Baalen (discussed later). Hence, Morris married his cousin.[6] Abraham de Roy, who had been a storekeeper in Amsterdam's Jodenbreestraat, the heart of the Jewish Quarter, owned a secondhand clothing store in Pittsburgh. In 1868 Morris lived in Detroit, where his second son Emanuel was born, but by 1870 the family was back in Pittsburgh. Morris was then a salesman-clerk in his father-in-law's clothing store and lived with his in-laws in a two-family dwelling. His father-in-law's wealth in 1870 totaled $12,000, but Morris reported none.

Emanuel van Baalen's third son, Abraham, was born in Buffalo in 1844 and moved to Detroit sometime before 1867 and became a clothing dealer. His wife Sarah was also Dutch-born and the family had two children at that time. Emanuel's fourth son, Henry, enlisted in the Union Army at Buffalo in 1861 and was killed in action in 1864 at the very beginning of the Battle of the Wilderness in Virginia.[7]

In late 1849 Emanuel's unmarried younger brother Joseph Israel van Baalen arrived in Buffalo. He was born in Amsterdam in 1826, where he achieved middling economic status as a street seller before emigrating at age twenty-three. In Buffalo he resumed peddling and boarded briefly with his cousin Emanuel Joseph. He soon married a

German Jew, and in January 1851 the couple's first child, Israel, was born in Buffalo. By 1865 Joseph and his family had followed in the steps of his Boasberg and Van Baalen cousins and moved to Chicago. Here he raised his family and worked in merchandising. By 1900 he had become a widower and also lived in Hyde Park together with his unmarried son Israel (a traveling salesman) and two daughters (the older tended the house and the younger worked full-time as a stenographer).[8]

The second Van Baalen family from Amsterdam arrived in Buffalo in 1849. This was Emanuel Joseph, born in 1815, with his wife Hannah and their son Joseph.[9] Emanuel was a first cousin of Emanuel Israel van Baalen. Emanuel took up peddling in Buffalo, but soon moved with his family to Cleveland in the early 1850s. Late in the decade he went to Detroit. In both cities he continued to peddle notions and dry goods. He valued his inventory in 1860 at $500, which indicated he was moving up within the ranks of peddlers. By 1870 and still in Detroit he had, indeed, advanced in the usual career path of peddlers to become a retail clothing merchant. He now owned real estate worth $4,000 and personal property of $1,000.

The third member of Amsterdam's Van Baalen clan to emigrate was Willem van Baalen, who was born in 1828 and came to Cleveland with his wife in the early 1850s, and moved to Detroit by 1857, judging from the birthplaces of his children. Willem was a clothier with $2,500 in merchandise in 1860, but he greatly prospered in the Civil War years and by 1870 reported real estate worth $20,000 and merchandise of $10,000.

The fourth Van Baalen family to emigrate was Emanuel Israel's younger brother, Hartog Israel (Henry) van Baalen, an Amsterdam peddler of middling economic status, who sailed to New York in the summer of 1857 on the ship *William and Jane*, arriving at New York on July 15 with his wife and eight young children.[10] The family immediately left New York for Cleveland where Henry became a clothing merchant by 1860, in all likelihood as a representative of his older brother Emanuel's enterprise headquartered in Buffalo. His whereabouts thereafter are yet unknown, but his three oldest sons and one daughter were living in Detroit in 1870. Son Emanuel (or Mannes), was a clothier worth $5,000 and married with two children. Mannes's older brother Isaac and younger brother Joseph were clerking in his dry goods store and boarding with the family, along with Isaac's twin sister Esther.

Not only did the Van Baalens follow the typical pattern of chain migration but every male for at least two generations was a clothing

234

merchant. The persistence of close family ties also had an important economic function. The family fanned out in its mercantile pursuits along the Great Lakes corridor from Buffalo and Cleveland to Pittsburgh, Detroit, and Chicago. Detroit became the focal point, probably because of its central location. This merchant clan merits further study, including its background in Amsterdam. It is a microcosm of the Jewish economic network of clothing and dry goods retailers that spanned the nation by the 1850s.

Nathan Boasberg was the most renowned Dutch Jew in Buffalo and the Boasberg clan became prominent. Boasberg was born in Amsterdam in 1827 of Sephardic descent, graduated from Leiden University and then served in the navy. In 1840 he arrived aboard a Dutch man-o-war in New York City where an uncle persuaded him to jump ship. He went directly to Buffalo on an Erie Canal packet boat and took up peddling. In 1848 he married Rachel van Baalen, thereby uniting Buffalo's only two Dutch Jewish families. Boasberg became a naturalized citizen in 1854.[11]

Nathan Boasberg's younger brother Benjamin, who was born in Amsterdam in 1827, followed Nathan to Buffalo. In the mid-1850s Benjamin married a Buffalo-born Jewess, Sarah, who may have been the next younger sister of Rachel van Baalen. The young couple then lived briefly in Detroit where son Isaac was born in 1857. In 1860 the family had resettled in Chicago, where Benjamin was a clerk and living in the Second Ward among a half-dozen other Dutch Jewish families. By 1870 he owned one of the three secondhand clothing stores in Chicago and was a successful businessman.[12]

Benjamin Boasberg's son Isaac and grandson Benjamin carried on the family tradition in the clothing trade. Isaac became a traveling salesman who returned to Detroit in the late 1870s, married a Michigan-born daughter of Dutch Jewish parents (like himself). After son Benjamin was born in 1881, the family moved to Texas where a daughter was born in 1883. By 1900 the family had resettled on Chicago's northside in Ward 26, many miles from the core group of Dutch Jews in Hyde Park. Grandson Benjamin was then an eighteen-year-old stock keeper in a clothing store.

Nathan Boasberg remained in Buffalo and spent his long career in the clothing business. In 1860 he owned a secondhand store with $5,000 worth of goods, and his wife had a hired girl to help care for their four small children. The family lived near or above the store in the city center until the 1880s when they moved to the old westside. Before Nathan's death in 1910 the family had moved six times within the city, always following the shifting Jewish neighborhoods in Buffalo. His leadership in synagogue life is described later.[13]

Boasberg's children and grandchildren were active in Buffalo's business and professional life, although minimal information on the family is yet known. Oldest son Isaac (1852–1920) became a diamond broker and Democratic party activist. A number of Buffalo Jews specialized in the jewelry business and gave the city a reputation for this type of trade. Son Emanuel established the successful wholesale tobacco firm of Keiser and Boasberg in 1889, which continued until 1937. In 1925 Emanuel Boasberg endowed a chair in American history at the University of Buffalo, first held by the noted diplomatic historian Julius W. Pratt. Nathan's daughter Adele became a theater actress (under the stage name of Judith Berolde); another daughter, Margaret, taught Hebrew in the Buffalo public schools. Grandson Charles Boasberg in the 1950s became president of Warner Brothers, the famed motion picture distributing firm.[14]

Like the Van Baalens and Boasbergs, most of Buffalo's Dutch Jews were primarily peddlers in the early years and later clothiers and jewelers, plus a few cigarmakers (Table 8.1). They included haves and have-nots. A few gained sufficient wealth to move into upscale suburbs on the East Side, but many remained in the inner city Jewish neighborhoods on lower Main Street. Most prospered wherever they lived and participated in the city's business life. Several Dutch jewelers and goldsmiths in 1860 contributed to the city's growing jewelry business. These were Charles Loeser, William Schwartz, and Julius Felgenmacher. Lewis Goldsmith, who had lived in New York for more than a decade, was the city's first Dutch Jewish cigarmaker. Although he was the second wealthiest Dutch Jew in 1860, he had moved on by 1870. Emanuel Ferger took his place, having arrived from England, where at least two children were born.

The H. Oppenheimer family from the city of Dinxperlo in Gelderland Province, the Netherlands, near the German border, arrived in 1858. He was a street seller of middling social status who emigrated with his family of ten in the hope of economic betterment. He and two adult sons were working as laborers in 1860 and their reported personal wealth was only $200. The Oppenheimers began at the very bottom of Buffalo's economic ladder. Whether they achieved their goal of success in unknown since their whereabouts after 1860 are not yet determined.[15]

Three other newcomers by 1870 were the peddlers Salomon Koord and Abraham Elias, and the candy manufacturer Bernard Bierman (Berman). Elias was likely the father of Abraham J. Elias (1862–1933), who became a prominent Buffalo lumber dealer and Democratic party leader.[16] Berman was the wealthiest Dutch Jew in 1870 with $1,800 worth of real estate and $300 in personalty.[17]

Table 8.1
Dutch Jewish Household Heads and Single Adults, Buffalo, 1850, 1860, 1870

Name	Age	N in Family	Time of Immigration	Occupation	Property Value Realty $	Property Value Personalty $	Ward
1850							
Nathan Boasberg	23	2	1846	peddler	—	—	4
Emanuel Israel van Baalen	40	9	1842	auctioneer	—	—	4
Emanuel Joseph van Baalen	35	3	1848–1850	peddler	—	—	4
Joseph Israel van Baalen	24	1	1850	peddler	—	—	4
1860							
Nathan Boasberg	33	6	1846	secondhand clothes	—	5,000	8
Julius Felgenmacher	21	1	1845–1848	goldsmith	—	400	6
Joseph S. Goldberg	44	6	1848–1849	doctor	—	200	4
Lewis Goldsmith	42	3	pre–1845	cigarmaker	—	1,000	8
Charles Loeser	38	1	1850–1858	jeweler	—	100	7
Fred Loeser	16	1	1858–1860	none	—	—	7
H. (or A.) Oppenheimer	54	9	1858	laborer	—	50	7
Jacob Oppenheimer (H.'s son)	27	1	1858	laborer	—	—	7
William Schwartz	24	4	pre–1855	jeweler	—	100	7

237

Table 8.1 (Continued)

Name	Age	N in Family	Time of Immi-gration	Occupation	Property Value Realty $	Person-alty $	Ward
1870							
Bernard Bierman	45	2	pre–1865	candy manufacturer	1,800	300	5
Abraham Elias	45	11	1862	laborer	—	50	7
Julius Felgenmacher	31	1	1845–1848	works for jeweler	—	—	3
Emanuel Ferger	40	3	pre–1864	cigarmaker	—	—	2
Solomon Koord	28	4	pre–1865	peddler	1,500	200	5

*Excluding boarders and servants

Sources: Compiled from Robert P. Swierenga, comp., *Dutch Households in U.S. Population Censuses, 1850, 1860, 1870: An Alphabetical Listing by Family Heads*, 3 vols. (Wilmington, DE, 1987); Robert P. Swierenga, comp., *Dutch Immigrants in U.S. Ship Passenger Manifests, 1820–1880: An Alphabetical Listing by Household Heads and Independent Persons*, 2 vols. (Wilmington, DE, 1983).

Several Prussian Jews who lived for a time in the Netherlands and married there also arrived in Buffalo after 1860. Joseph S. Goldberg was a medical doctor who married Rachel Cohen in Holland in the late 1840s and raised three children born there. By the spring of 1860 the family had settled in Buffalo where another three children were born. By 1867 Dr. Goldberg had moved his medical practice to Cleveland where Rachel's parents were already living. An earlier "mixed" family to arrive in Buffalo was Bernhardus J. Rodenburgh, a cigarmaker, who emigrated to Buffalo between 1846 and 1849 with his Dutch-born wife and son. Another Prussian Jew, Lewis Israel, a retail clothing merchant, came to Buffalo in the early 1860s and married a Dutch Jew, as did Jacob Isaacs, also a merchant, who was a native New Yorker.[18]

This recital indicates that Buffalo Jews were a transient lot. The city at the terminus of the Erie Canal and later astride the New York to Chicago rail route was clearly a gateway to the Great Lakes. Dutch Jews came to Buffalo from New York City and Boston and then moved on to midwestern mercantile centers. In their residential patterns, they were always integrated into the larger Jewish community.

The Dutch were active in religious life as in business. Most of the thirty charter families of Congregation Beth El, which was organized in 1847, were Polish and German, but Emanuel van Baalen, the auctioneer, and son-in-law Nathan Boasberg were among the charter members; Boasberg later served as secretary, trustee, and president. He was long remembered for signing his name with a flourish and for his artistic script. At his death in 1910 he was the last of the charter members. Boasberg also served on the original board of directors in 1854 of the Hebrew Benevolent Society of Buffalo, a mutual-aid society founded to succor the sick and bury the dead. When Congregation Beth El dedicated its first synagogue in 1850, the Dutch-born Reverend Samuel Myer Isaacs of New York was the celebrant and orator. He chanted the customary Hebrew prayers and then delivered the dedicatory sermon in English, as he always did. This was the first vernacular sermon in a Buffalo synagogue.[19]

The first minister of Beth El was Isaac Moses Slatsky, from German Poland, whose wife Leah was born in the Netherlands in 1785. Slatsky served as *hazan*, kosher butcher, and circumciser, plus other needed functions in the small congregation. But his lack of proper training and his fiery temper and combative nature filled his twelve-year tenure with turmoil. Twice he was removed from office only to be restored again for want of another cleric.[20]

Early in the history of Beth El, nationality conflicts caused a schism. Beth El followed the Polish ritual and the Dutch and Germans were not satisfied. In 1851 a group of dissidents, led by Emanuel van Baalen, the auctioneer, seceded and established Beth Zion Congregation. Orthodox in its first fifteen years, in 1864 Beth Zion became the first Reform synagogue in Buffalo. Son-in-law Boasberg, however, remained a member of Beth El for nearly twenty years, in the hope of bringing liberal changes or perhaps out of a sense of loyalty. But finally in 1869 he too left Beth El for Beth Zion. Beth El at the time was beginning its gradual shift from Orthodoxy to Conservative Judaism.[21]

A leader in the conversion of Beth Zion from Orthodoxy into a moderate Reform congregation was Aaron Aarons, the president of the synagogue in the mid-1860s and a retail clothing merchant at 35 Exchange Street. Aaron was born in the Netherlands in 1805 and emigrated first to Boston and then to Buffalo. He was active in the Montefiore Lodge, B'nai B'rith, and other civic and charitable organizations. He died in honor in 1871 and his funeral was held in the Beth Zion Temple, which was a sign of special respect.[22]

Pittsburgh: The De Roys

The Jewish community in Pittsburgh was never large and grew slowly in the nineteenth century until the city finally gained a rail link in the early 1850s. Before that the city was off the beaten path to the West via the Erie Canal. By the late 1840s new flat-bottomed steamboats plied the Ohio River and its tributaries, including the Allegheny and Monongahela rivers, but the rivers froze in the winter and traffic ceased. An unfavorable location thus retarded economic growth and this, in turn, slowed the development of a Jewish merchant colony. Itinerant peddlers plied their trade in the area, however, from the early days and a few remained from the 1810s.[23]

Pittsburgh's Jewish community did not organize until 1847 when they began religious services and opened the first cemetery. The pioneer congregation, Shaare Shamayim (Gates of Heaven), was chartered in 1848. By 1850 two-thirds of the city's three dozen Jewish families were German and one-third Poles, mainly from German and Russian Poland. Forty percent owned retail clothing stores and many others ran dry goods shops. By 1860 Jewish newcomers expanded into dealing in liquor and livestock, but 50 percent were yet in clothing and notions houses, located mainly along

Market Street. In 1855 recently arrived German Jews founded a second Orthodox synagogue, Rodef Shalom (Pursuer of Peace), which congregation in 1860 was amalgamated with Shaare Shamayim. The combined body built a new, more lavish structure in 1862 on Eighth Street.[24]

At this very moment, when the pioneer era had passed and the Jews in Pittsburgh had pulled themselves together into a solid community, the first Dutch Jews arrived. The small colony began during the Civil War years when Pittsburgh prospered greatly and grew rapidly. More than ten Dutch Jewish families arrived from 1861 to 1865, and another ten came by 1870 (Table 8.2). Most had lived previously in Philadelphia, Buffalo, New York City, Detroit, and Cleveland, but several came directly from the Netherlands or via England. For example, Alexander Schenkan (1837–1904) and his wife Fanny, both born in Amsterdam, emigrated directly in 1865. George Cohen and Lewis (Louis) de Haan, however, had first stopped in England in the late 1840s and early 1850s. There they married English Jews and after a few years and the birth of a child or two, came on to New York and Philadelphia. Lewis de Haan served as an officer in the Dutch synagogue in Philadelphia, Bnai Israel.[25]

The most prominent newcomers were Abraham de Roy (de Rooy) and Philip and Louis Susman. Abraham Levie de Roy, the patriarch of that family, was born in Amsterdam in 1809 and became a storekeeper. He married Saartje (Sarah) Israel van Baalen, also of Amsterdam, a sister of Jacob Israel, Emanuel Israel, and Hartog Israel. Thus, the Pittsburgh De Roy family was linked to the Van Baalen families of Buffalo and Cleveland. The De Roys had six children, all born in the heart of the Amsterdam Jewish quarter.[26] The family emigrated to Pittsburgh in 1852 but soon moved temporarily to Cleveland where Abraham was a petty clothing merchant. Probably he was sent to establish an outpost in Cleveland for his brother-in-law Emanuel Israel van Baalen of Buffalo. De Roy's brother-in-law, Henry van Baalen, as already noted, was also a clothing merchant in Cleveland. These were the first and only Dutch Jewish families in the city in the 1850s.[27]

During the Civil War De Roy returned to Pittsburgh to stay. The next years were good ones for the family. By 1870 Abraham owned a secondhand clothing store with an inventory worth $8,000 and buildings valued at $4,000. His oldest son Levi described himself as a "gentleman" and second son Emanuel was a very prosperous pawnbroker with $10,000 in personal property and another $10,000 in real estate. Emanuel's younger brothers Israel and Joseph were

Table 8.2
Dutch Jewish Household Heads and Single Adults, Pittsburgh, 1870

Name	Age	N in Family	Time of Immigration	Occupation	Property Value		Ward
					Realty $	Personalty $	
Simon Bentelzer	39	3	pre–1861	retail clothing	—	500	5
Aaron Bernard	18	2	pre–1870	pawnbroker	—	—	6
George Cohen	48	6	pre–1854	pawnbroker	—	10,000	3
Moses Cohen	29	5	pre–1865	tobacco manufacturer	—	2,000	5
William Cohen	42	5	pre–1866	tobacco dealer	—	200	5
Frederick de Haan	50	5	pre–1855	bookkeeper	15,000	5,000	6
Lewis de Haan	55	9	1847	retail clothing	—	500	5
Abraham de Roy	61	2	1852	secondhand clothing	4,000	8,000	9
Emanuel de Roy	28	3	1852	pawnbroker	10,000	10,000	6
Israel de Roy	23	2	1852	pawnbroker	—	—	4
Joseph de Roy	20	1	1852	pawnbroker	—	—	4
Levi A. de Roy	34	6	1852	gentleman	—	—	17
Henry Gelder	24	1	pre–1870	peddler	—	—	5
Isaac Gelder	34	7	pre–1859	retail clothing	—	2,000	5
Abraham Green	32	4	pre–1864	peddler	—	100	6
Sam Oppenheimer	18	1	pre–1870	salesman	—	—	4
Isaiah Pachter	40	5	1865	teacher	3,000	200	7
Lena Phillips	60	1	pre–1861	at home	—	—	5
Henry Samuels	35	7	pre–1859	pawnbroker	—	500	5
Abraham Schenkan	32	4	pre–1865	pawnbroker	—	500	6

Jacob Schreiber	50	5	pre–1861	cigarmaker	—	200	5
Jacob (L.) Susman	24	1	1863	salesman	—	—	5
Louis Susman	48	3	1863	retail clothing	8,000	5,000	5
Philip Susman	52	3	1864	retail clothing	—	500	5
Morris van Baalen	38	6	1842	clothing salesman	—	—	9
Barnet van Holm	50	5	pre–1862	secondhand clothing	—	300	5
Abraham Weiler	25	1	pre–1870	tobacco dealer	—	10,000	6
Emanuel Weiler	27	2	pre–1870	tobacco dealer	—	10,000	6

Sources: Compiled from Swierenga, *Dutch Households in U.S. Population Censuses*; Swierenga, *Dutch Immigrants in U.S. Ship Passenger Manifests.*

also pawnbrokers in their brother's store, which in the 1860s and 1870s was located at 47 Smithfield. Levi lived nearby in 1875 at 145 Smithfield. Fellow Hollander George Cohen's pawnshop stood on the same street at 200 Smithfield. This minor clustering of Dutch Jewish shopkeepers on Smithfield Avenue in the 1860s and 1870s gives evidence of continuing ethnic ties.[28]

Philip and Louis Susman were born in Ludingwaeth, Hanover, Germany, in 1818 and 1822, respectively. Both migrated to Amsterdam, married Dutch Jewish wives, and fathered several children there. Louis, a portrait painter and artist, immigrated first in 1863 with his wife and twin children, taking passage from Hamburg to New York on the ship *Borussia*. But his grandson, Milton Susman, stated that Louis "owned a circus in Europe and continued it in the United States. Later he went into the clothing business on the northside."[29] Probably Louis's artistic talents were put in the service of his circus venture. Philip (born David Philip) Susman and his family followed his older brother to America the next year. Before emigrating Philip was a musician and very likely also a circus entrepreneur. In Pittsburgh Philip likely worked for, or was a junior partner in, Louis's secondhand clothing store. Louis in 1870 reported property worth $13,000 including $8,000 in real estate, but Philip only had $500 in personal property. By 1875 Louis had upgraded his store to a pawnshop.[30]

A half dozen more Hollanders arrived in Pittsburgh after 1865, including Morris van Baalen, a relative of the De Roys. In 1870 the Dutch Jewish families totaled about one-hundred persons or 10 percent of all Jews in Pittsburgh.[31] A number had non-Dutch wives: two English and six from various German states. Two also married Pennsylvania-born women who were likely from the Philadelphia Dutch Jewish community. Thus, Dutch male intermarriage with German women was most common, but only one Dutch woman had outmarried and that to a Polish Jew.

The Dutch Jews left the home country in poverty or narrowing economic opportunities, and thus they began in America at the bottom, as peddlers and secondhand clothing dealers. Both businesses required little capital and promised advancement. But the Dutch in Pittsburgh and elsewhere quickly moved up to retail clothing and pawnshops. In Pittsburgh they were mainly dealers, brokers, and retail merchants. Seven owned clothing stores and four worked as salesmen or bookkeepers. Seven others operated pawnshops, three were tobacco dealers, two peddled, and one each was a tobacco manufacturer, cigarmaker, and teacher (Table 8.2). This occupational profile mirrors that of Jews generally in the city. An analysis of the 1865–1866 city directory revealed that of 77 household heads known or thought to be Jewish, 73 percent were merchants, 13 percent dealers and salesmen, and 5 percent clerks.[32]

A few Dutch Jewish families in the city had gained considerable wealth by 1870, namely the De Roys, Cohens, De Haans, and Susmans. Emanuel de Roy, who had returned from Cleveland, and Frederick de Haan each reported owning real estate and personal property worth $20,000—they were the two wealthiest Hollanders; Louis Susman reported $13,000; Abraham de Roy $12,000; George Cohen, Emanuel and Abraham Weiler (partners in Weiler Bros. Tobacco Co. on First Street) $10,000 each; and Moses Cohen and Isaac Gelder each $2,000. Overall, the Dutch had done extremely well in Pittsburgh, compared to their kinsmen elsewhere on the Great Lakes frontier.

Religiously, Pittsburgh's Dutch aligned themselves solidly with the Orthodox congregation. When in 1863 Rabbi Isaac M. Wise, a founder of Reform, came to Pittsburgh and persuaded a majority of members of the only synagogue, Rodef Shalom, to reject Orthodoxy for Reform, and replace Yiddish-German with English in the worship services, many of the Dutch along with those of Lithuanian and Polish origin plus a few Germans resigned and formed in 1864 the new Orthodox congregation Etz Hayyim (Tree of Life). Julius van Raalte and Louis Susman served on the committee of five who drafted the new constitution, and in 1868 Isaac Gelder chaired the congregation's Hebrew school board. The Orthodox minority adopted *Minhag Poland* as their prayer ritual. It appears that the seceders were the less prosperous families in the Jewish community.[33]

One Hollander who became a leader at the pioneer Rodef Shalom Synagogue was the Reverend Isaiah Pachter (Pagter). In 1865 the congregation hired him as sexton and kosher butcher. A fulltime teacher, he also taught Hebrew and religion in the congregation's after hours Hebrew school, assisted in the large Sunday school program, and codirected the synagogue's mixed-voice choir.[34]

Thus, the Dutch were important mainly in the second phase of Pittsburgh's Jewish community. They arrived in the 1860s during the interlude after the pioneer period had passed but before the wave of East European Yiddish flooded the city in the 1880s. There was little continuing Dutch immigration to Pittsburgh after the influx of the 1860s, but several families, particularly the Susmans, Gelders, and Cohens, continued to live in the community for generations and today remain an integral part of the city's Jewish life.

Cincinnati—The Workums and Ezekiels

If the Reverend Samuel Isaacs had traveled inland down the Ohio River in 1851, instead of taking the northern route, he would have found a larger Dutch Jewish settlement in Cincinnati than in Pittsburgh. According to Rabbi David Philipson of Congregation Bene Israel, among the immigrant pioneers there was "quite a contingent of Dutch Jews who settled here after the first years had passed, such as the Le Jeunes, De Jongs, Workums, and others, who emigrated from the populous Jewish community of Amsterdam."[35] Actually, several of these families had first settled in New Orleans as merchants, and their business dealings took them up the Mississippi and Ohio River systems to Cincinnati.

The first Jews reached Cincinnati in 1817, coming mainly from England or east coast cities. By the time of the federal census in 1830, two of the sixteen Jewish families were Dutch and their thirteen family members totaled 10 percent of the 138 Jews in the city (Table 8.3).[36] The Dutch families were those of Bernard le Jeune (Lejeune) of Rotterdam and Jacob L. Workum of Amsterdam, each with families of six plus a boarder. Le Jeune had first lived in New Orleans before coming upriver to Cincinnati, and Workum had initially settled in New York. Both men were merchants in the central city. Workum's general store stood at the corner of Plum and West Row streets; Le Jeune's clothing store was at Sycamore and Broadway streets. The Workums lived up from the river front on South Street and the Le Jeunes resided in a heavily Jewish neighborhood on Front Street. Le Jeune died in Cincinnati prematurely in 1833 at age thirty-three after suffering a business bankruptcy in 1832. But Workum lived to a ripe old age, dying in Cincinnati in 1870 at age seventy-eight.[37]

In 1860 Workum, then sixty-seven years old, reported to the census enumerator owning $5,000 in real estate and $3,000 in personal property. Levi Joseph Workum and family, who resided in his parents' household, also reported realty of $5,000 and personalty of $13,000. The Civil War years were immensely profitable for this merchant family. By 1870 Levi was a liquor dealer who reported owning $100,000 in real estate and personal property of $300,000. This was a massive estate for this era, and one wonders if Workum had unduly overstated his wealth to the census enumerator for appearances sake. His recently widowed mother and aunt lived nearby.[38]

In the 1830s three Dutch Jews arrived, all via England. These were the young man Samuel Jacob de Young (de Jong), a clerk, and

Table 8.3
Dutch Jewish Household Heads and Single Adults, Cincinnati, 1830, 1850, 1860, 1870

Name	Age	N in Family	Time of Immigration	Occupation	Property Value		Ward
					Realty $	Personalty $	
1830							
Bernard le Jeune	29	6	pre-1830	merchant	—	—	3
Jacob L. Workum	38	7	pre-1830	clothing store	—	—	2
1850							
Michael de Young	59	10	pre-1830	dry goods merchant	—	1,500	2
1860							
Levi Cook	36	8	1847–1849	peddler	—	100	14
George Frank	50	1	1857	peddler	—	100	10
Philip Frank	61	1	1857	peddler	—	100	10
Levi Speelman	49	12	1854	secondhand clothing	2,000	400	14
Jacob Sugarman	30	4	1852	peddler	—	50	14
Levi Sugarman	23	4	1852	peddler	—	3,000	14
Solomon Sugarman	20	1	1852	peddler	—	0	14
Emanuel van den Berg	50	10	pre-1849	secondhand store	—	250	14
Abraham van West	30	3	1851	peddler	—	100	14
Jacob L. Workum	67	2	pre-1830	merchant	5,000	3,000	4
Levi Joseph Workum	38	3	born NY	merchant	5,000	13,000	4

Table 8.3 (Continued)

Name	Age	N in Family	Time of Immi-gration	Occupation	Property Value Realty $	Person-alty $	Ward
1870							
Henry Brearman	43	7	1861–1862	retail cloth store	—	500	10
Emanuel Frank	70	1	1857	peddler	—	3,000	10
Philip Frank	68	1	1857	peddler	—	2,500	10
Aaron Hamburger	46	10	1866–1869	cigarmaker	—	1,000	8
Solomon Kustner	38	2	1860s	cigar store	—	800	14
Helena Meyer	49	6	pre–1846	washerwoman	—	4,000	14
Solomon Pereira	56	6	1842	pawnbroker	9,000	3,000	14
Zadoc Prince	59	3	pre–1850	peddler	—	—	14
Herman Stearns	30	1	1860s	peddler	—	—	1
Levi Sugarman	35	7	1852	keeps store	—	1,000	14
Jacob Sugarman	40	8	1852	keeps store	—	3,000	14
Abraham van West	43	3	1851	peddler	—	200	14
Moses Waterman	57	2	1860s	at home	9,000	500	15
Levi Joseph Workum	47	10	born NY	liquor dealer	100,000	300,000	6

Sources: Compiled from Ira Rosenwaike, *On the Edge of Greatness: A Portrait of American Jewry in the Early National Period* (Cincinnati, 1985), 116, 144; Swierenga, *Dutch Households in U.S. Population Censuses*; Swierenga, *Dutch Immigrants in U.S. Ship Passenger Manifests*.

248

his brother Moses de Young with wife and family, plus Joseph Abraham. Within a short time, in 1837 or 1838, Abraham married Sarah de Young, Moses's daughter. By 1850 another relative, Michael H. de Young, a prosperous dry goods merchant temporarily joined the clan in Cincinnati with his wife and eight children.[39] He operated on a wide geographical scale.

Michael de Young was born in Amsterdam in 1791 and came to Philadelphia in 1803 as a teenager with his parents. Before 1830 he moved to Baltimore, married there, and opened a jewelry and comb shop. After a few years, he went on the road for the next twenty years as a traveling merchant throughout the Mississippi Valley, moving between New Orleans, Saint Louis, and Cincinnati. His children were born in New York City (1836), Saint Louis (1837), New Orleans (1840 and 1843), Saint Louis again (1845), and New Orleans again (1847 and 1849). In 1850 the family lived in Cincinnati but in 1854 Michael was back in New Orleans and filled with ambitious plans to go to San Francisco. The family set out that year aboard a Mississippi River steamer; but Michael died suddenly just above the city. His widow continued to their destination, where the three sons gained notoriety, if not fame, in the field of journalism.[40] All the other De Young families had left Cincinnati by 1850.

The character of Cincinnati's Dutch Jewish settlement changed in the 1850s. The pioneer merchants of the Mississippi River system had departed, except for the Workums, to be replaced by a lower class of peddlers and secondhand clothiers who had initially lived in Boston, Philadelphia, and New York City in the 1840s and 1850s. New York had been the port of entry for four families, Boston served for two, and one entered at New Orleans. Two unmarried brothers, Emanuel and Philip Frank, came directly in 1857 from Holland, one from Rotterdam and one from Bergen op Zoom in Noord Brabant. Both had been street sellers.[41] By 1860 there were eleven Dutch-born family heads or single adults in the Queen City (including forty-nine persons), seven of whom were peddlers and two operated used clothing shops, in addition to the Workum merchants (see Table 8.3). Most of the newcomers lived in Ward 14, which was on the city outskirts.

Ten years later, in 1870, fourteen Dutch Jewish households, numbering sixty-seven persons, resided in Cincinnati. Most remained centered in Ward 14 (Table 8.3). Three, and possibly as many as five, of the eight families arriving in the 1860s came directly from the Netherlands. The other three had lived previously in Rhode Island, Boston, and elsewhere in Ohio. The two Frank brothers, the Sugarman brothers, Abraham van West, and Levi Workum

249

were the only persisters from the 1850s. Workum and Jacob Sugarman both had advanced from peddling to storekeeping, while the Frank brothers continued peddling with considerable financial success.[42]

Several of the newcomers fared better, notably Soloman Pereira, a pawnbroker who came from Providence, RI, where he had lived for more than twenty years. He valued his property in 1870 at $12,000. Moses Abraham Waterman (1813–1881), who was retired, reported $9,500, which was primarily the value of his home. The average wealth of the thirteen households—excluding the very wealthy Levi Workum—was $2,885 in 1870, up from $678 in 1860 (again excluding the two Workums).[43]

Religiously, the Dutch Jews in Cincinnati were too few to consider their own nationality synagogue. At first most joined the Polish-German Congregation Bene Israel, founded in 1824 and the oldest Jewish congregation in the West. In 1830 when the congregation procured an Ohio state charter, Bernard le Jeune and Samuel de Young were among the seventeen incorporators. Le Jeune served in the first five-man vestry. Subsequently, Jacob L. Workum was a warden (1836–1839) and his son Levi later was a trustee and member of the building committee in 1867 for the Mound Street Temple, dedicated in 1869. Grandsons who were members in the early twentieth century included Abraham S., D. J., and Theodore Workum. Other Dutch members were Jacob Ezekiel; H. de Haan; Joseph Hamburger; Jacob, Albert, and S. Sugarman; S. Waterman; and Morris Vanberg. The merchant Ezekiel, who was prominently connected in American Jewry, arrived from Richmond in 1869 and joined Congregation Bene Israel. In 1873 he represented that body in the founding of the Union of American Hebrew Congregations. In 1876 he was elected a member of the board of governors of Hebrew Union College and served as secretary continuously for twenty-five years. Ezekiel's wife Catherine bore him eleven children. At her death in 1891 she was eulogized with the ultimate accolade "mother in Israel," as a "true wife, a devoted mother, a faithful Jewess, and a benefactor of the poor." Her oldest son Moses became a famed sculptor and a daughter Hannah kept the Dutch connection by marrying Levi J. Workum.[44]

In brief, the Dutch Jews in Cincinnati in the pioneer era left their mark but they failed to grow into a viable community. They numbered in 1870 less than 100 in an overwhelmingly German Jewish population of 8,000 and easily blended into Congregation Bene Israel.

Cleveland—The Peixottos and Isaacs

Cleveland was the second center of Jewish settlement in Ohio after Cincinnati. The first Jews arrived in the mid-1830s, nearly twenty years later than in Cincinnati, and by 1839 there were enough men to organize the first synagogue—the Israelite Congregation (later Anshe Chesed). A decade later, the Western Reserve settlement numbered between four hundred and five hundred. Cleveland's Jews came from German lands, particularly Bavaria, plus a few English Jews who were predominant in the Ohio Valley. In the 1850s Jews reached Cleveland in increasing numbers and from diverse backgrounds in Poland, Hungary, Switzerland, and Holland. By 1860 they totaled twelve hundred persons, 3.5 percent of the population. The three Jewish boarding houses also accommodated a transient population of itinerant merchants.[45]

The first Jewish family to live in the Western Reserve was Dr. Daniel L. M. Peixotto (1799–1843), who was born in Amsterdam of the famed Peixotto family. Peixotto obtained his education and established his family and career in New York City, after trying unsuccessfully in 1821 to be licensed to practice medicine in Curaçao. In 1823 he married Rachel M. Seixas while attending Columbia College, where he mastered Hebrew, Greek, and Latin, as well as French and Spanish, and earned B.A., M.A., and M.D. degrees. With this classical education and the special training under the renowned professor Dr. David Hosack of Columbia's medical faculty, the young doctor quickly gained distinction as a physician, lecturer, author, and medical society administrator. In 1835 these credentials convinced the trustees of the newly established Willoughby (Ohio) Medical College to name him president and professor of medicine at this pioneer institution in the Western Reserve. Dr. Peixotto's inaugural lecture, which was widely disseminated, appealed to Ohio Governor Robert Lucas for state funding for higher education. Peixotto returned to New York after four years in the post and in 1843 the college moved to Columbus, where it eventually became the Ohio State University College of Medicine. Dr. Peixotto was not only the first president of the college but the first Jewish professor and medical doctor in Ohio.[46]

In 1837 after two years in Willoughby, Dr. Peixotto moved his family of eight to Cleveland, where he practiced medicine and lectured frequently on civic, historical, and medical topics at such venues as the Cleveland Lyceum, the Old Stone Church on the Square, and the Ohio State Medical Convention in Cleveland in 1839. In mid-1839 the family returned to New York, stopping for a few months in Trenton, NJ, where Dr. Peixotto dabbled in politics and in journalism as coeditor of a Democratic newspaper, the *Daily True American*.[47] In New York Dr. Peixotto again practiced medicine until his untimely death at age forty-three in 1843. The tragedy left the widow and her eight children in financial straits, so the oldest child Judith, who was twenty years of age, began teaching in the public schools to support the family. She later became the first Jewish principal in New York city. The second son Benjamin Franklin (1834–1890) returned to Cleveland in 1847 and later contributed much to American Judaism there and in San Francisco. The youngest son Raphael (1837–1905), who was the first Jewish child born in Cleveland, became a successful merchant and philanthropist in San Francisco.

Benjamin F. Peixotto completed law school and in January 1856 and became associate editor of the Cleveland *Daily Plain Dealer*, a Democrat sheet with the highest circulation by far in the city.[48] J. W. Gray, the editor and proprietor, introduced Peixotto as a "young gentleman of decided talent as a writer and excellent literary taste." But this scion of an ardent Democrat and sometime law student of Illinois Democratic Senator Stephan A. Douglas was the "red-hottest kind of a Democrat." His biting editorials were hardly tasteful. He repeatedly castigated the opposition as "Black Republicans" for their anti-slavery leanings, and twitted them by recommending that they fuse with the nativist Know Nothing Party in the 1856 presidential contest.

Peixotto bid his readers adieu after only five months, having parlayed his brief editorial stint into a lucrative position as junior partner of George A. Davis, a successful wholesale merchant, under the rubric Davis, Peixotto and Company. Benjamin remained active in politics, supporting Douglas's presidential bid in 1860 and opposing Abraham Lincoln's reelection in 1864. But the Civil War soon converted Peixotto's political allegiance to the Republican Party as it did for many northern Democrats.[49]

Peixotto's civic involvements were extensive. He was president of the Cleveland Library Association and organized Jewish communal activities, notably the Jewish Orphan Asylum and the Solomon Lodge of B'nai B'rith, of which he was a moving spirit. In 1851 he was elected president of the Cleveland order and thereafter devoted most of his time and energy to the society. In 1863 at the youthful age of twenty-nine he became national president of B'nai B'rith, raising that body from a handful of members into a powerful organization. Peixotto also used his position to promote his pet project, the orphanage. At the 1863 national convention held in

Cleveland, Peixotto persuaded representatives of Grand Lodge No. 2, which included a fifteen-state region, to pledge a dollar a year per member to fund the orphanage. By 1868 $12,000 was collected, enough to build the facility on Woodlawn Avenue.[50]

Following the Civil War Peixotto went to New York City in 1866 and a year later he moved cross-country to San Francisco and established a lucrative law practice. The pogroms against Jews in Rumania aroused his ire and he became a champion of their cause. In 1870 President Ulysses S. Grant appointed him as U.S. consul general to Rumania. Before embarking he went on a speaking tour on behalf of Rumanian Jews, visiting Chicago, Louisville, Saint Louis, Cleveland, Baltimore, and finally New York. In Bucharest he used his influence to stem the persecutions and to gain minimal civil and political rights for Jews there.[51]

After a brief furlough in New York in 1876–1877, during which time Benjamin helped form the Union of Hebrew Congregations and worked for the election of Ohio's Rutherford B. Hayes; the new president named him in 1878 as U.S. consul at Lyons, France, where he served until 1885. In 1881 his eldest son, George D. M. Peixotto, a noted portrait painter who was born in Cleveland in 1859, joined his father in Lyons as viceconsul, being appointed by President James A. Garfield who was his father's boyhood friend from nearby Moreland Hills. Father and son returned to New York in 1885, and Benjamin practiced law and was active in Temple Israel and in such Jewish endeavors as founding the literary periodical *Menorah* as the organ of B'nai B'rith and aiding Rumanian and Russian émigrés. Peixotto advocated planting colonies for the flood of immigrants, but the advice went largely unheeded. When he died in 1890, a eulogist declared, "His death leaves a marked void among the foremost Jews of America." The Peixotto family, the Cleveland area's first Jewish family, well represented their Dutch heritage by holding religious and civic posts of distinction.[52]

Five years after the departure of the Peixotto family, from 1845 through 1847, several Dutch Jewish merchants arrived in Cleveland from New York and Philadelphia. These included the brothers Isaac A. and George Isaacs of Philadelphia (who were second-generation Dutch born in Boston), and from New York City Jacob H. Frank, Rowland R. Davies, and Louisa (Lieve) Cohen and her husband Frederick I. Cohen of Prussia (actually German Poland) (Table 8.4). While Frank peddled goods from his home on Bolivar Street and Cohen was a lumber merchant on River Street, the Isaacs brothers and Davies opened clothing shops in the city center on Superior Street.[53]

Table 8.4
Dutch Jewish Household Heads and Single Adults, Cleveland, 1860, 1870, 1880

Name	Age	N in Family	Time of Immigration	Occupation	Property Value		Ward
					Realty $	Personalty $	
1835–1839							
Daniel L. M. Peixotto	35	7	1807	medical doctor	—	—	—
1850							
Louisa Cohen	58	3	pre-1840	none; River St.	—	—	?
Joseph Davies	?	?	c. 1821	?	—	—	3
Rowland R. Davies	47	2	c. 1821	merchant 30 Superior St.	—	5,000	3
Jacob H. Frank	?	1	pre-1845	peddler 27 Bolivar St.	—	—	?
George A. Isaacs	20	1	born Boston	clothing merchant Superior St.	—	—	3
Isaac A. Isaacs	24	3	born Boston	clothing merchant Superior St.	—	—	3
1860							
Lieve (Louisa) Cohen	69	3	pre-1840	none	—	—	3
Abraham de Roy	51	6	1852	clothing	—	100	3
Isaac A. Isaacs	35	7	born Boston	clothing merchant	14,000	5,000	3
Henry van Baalen	48	10	1857	clothing	—	—	1

1870							
Lieve Cohen	75	1	pre–1840	none	—	—	1
Joseph S. Goldberg	52	9	1858–1859	physician	—	200	1
M. Meanden	36	6	1864–1867	cigarmaker	—	700	1
John Samuels	33	7	1861–1863	notions peddler	—	300	1
1880							
Lieve (Jennie) Cohen	90	1	pre–1840	none	—	—	1
Rosetta Goldberg	54	6	1858–1959	widow	—	—	1
John Samuels	43	12	1861–1863	clothing	—	—	1
Lucas Swaab (Schwab)	36	10	1873	peddler	—	—	4
Simon Swaab (Schwab)	43	4	1872	peddler	—	—	4
William Swaab (Schwab)	39	8	pre–1865	cigarmaker	—	—	4
Kalman van Goor	36	3	1874	paper/rag peddler	—	—	7

Sources: "Ante Bellum Cleveland Jewish Immigrants Database," WRHS, Cleveland: Cleveland City Directories, 1845–1860: Cuyahoga County and Jewish Synagogue Archives, Jewish Community Federation Records; compiled from Swierenga. *Dutch Households in U.S. Population Censuses*; Swierenga, *Dutch Immigrants in U.S. Ship Passenger Manifests*; Swierenga, "Dutch Households in Federal Manuscript Population Census," Cleveland, 1880 (unpublished computer file).

255

Isaac A. Isaacs and his younger brother George had learned the tailoring trade by working in their father's (Aaron Isaacs) large shop in Philadelphia.[54] They began a small clothing store for men on the north side of Superior Street in late 1845, stocked with goods brought from Philadelphia. Because of innovative business practices within ten years Isaac A. Isaacs could boast that his enterprise was the "largest department store west of New York City." Mass manufacturing, aggressive advertising, and customer oriented selling were his keys to success. He introduced Cleveland men to cheap, yet carefully crafted, ready-made suits. Custom tailors and clothiers resisted this threat to their livelihood from mass-produced goods and customers at first were wary of shoddy "eastern-made clothing," having been previously duped by unscrupulous dealers. Isaacs overcame the opposition and consumer resistance by establishing a reputation for the "best-made" clothes in Ohio at a "substantial" reduction from the "exorbitant prices" in effect before. In 1852 and again in 1855 his suits won first prize at the Ohio State Fair.

In October 1852 a massive fire along Superior, Union, and Water (now East Ninth) streets completely destroyed Isaacs's store and stock, which he had valued in 1860 at $14,000 and $5,000, respectively. But he managed to reopen a year later in an elegant new four-story brick building on the corner of Superior and Union streets, which he named Union Hall as a statement of his strong feelings against secession. The building covered 12,000 square feet and the ground floor retail showroom boasted seven superb gas chandeliers to illuminate the most modern furnishings. Guarding the front entrance were two giant male figures suitably clothed who "do the eyes of passers greet." The upper floors were crammed with wholesale goods for hundreds of his retail dealers. The firm employed three to five hundred tailors off-site to keep the store stocked. No wonder that Isaacs could claim in 1856 that he ran "the largest and most magnificent Clothing establishment west of New York City and the talk of the United States." As fellow Hollander Benjamin F. Peixotto of the *Cleveland Plain Dealer* admonished readers in a flattering story in 1856 honoring the Isaacs firm's tenth anniversary: "Let young men just entering upon business emulate Mr. Isaacs. Be industrious, persevering and honest; and above all, imitate his shrewdness, and advertise liberally and judiciously."[55]

Isaacs's skill as a clothier was equaled only by his clever self-promotion abilities. He wrote so many original verses and slogans for advertisements in newspapers, city directories, and for his own pamphlets that he earned the title of the Clothier Poet. It is claimed that he coined the phrase "The Buckeye Boys" in one of his rhymes.

An 1863 pamphlet typically reveals his often gauche, yet effective, verses. Its catchy title reads "The Terrifically Thrilling Poem of the 'Fair Inez': or The Lone Lady of the Crimson Cliff, a Tale of the Sea."[56] The pamphlet opens with an advertisement poem entitled "Union Hall," which begins as follows:

> In Cleveland there's a Warehouse known
> As Isaacs' Union Hall,
> Where the people who want Clothing
> Ready Made, are sure to call.
> For the stock there is the largest,
> And is made the very best,
> And is sold at prices lower,
> Than elsewhere in all the West.

Running borders around the pages carry verses such as this trite doggerel:

> Save your dollars, save your dimes,
> All are needed in these times;
> Where sales are quick, and profits small—
> You will Clothing find at Union Hall.
> In these lines, on every page,
> For boys of every age.

The poem itself, running for thirty-seven pages, recounts the tale of a Confederate pirate, Jeff Davis ("A traitor bold is he, but Uncle Sam will catch him soon"), and his captive maiden, "my sweet and fair Inez." Interspersed near the end of the poem's narrative, which is quite imaginative as a romantic piece, is another plug:

> The persons we've named in this romance,
> Are doing well, one and all,
> For they all of them purchase their Clothing
> At *Isaacs'* famed *Union Hall.*
> And now and then we are honored
> With a visit from Inez the Fair,
> Who brings all her boys and her husband,
> To buy Clothing of us, rich and rare.
>
> And so I leave them, dear reader,
> In the sunshine of prosperity,
> They all will live long and happy,
> As do all who buy Clothing of me:
> In my Clothing they all take great comfort,
> For 'tis all made to fit very nice,

It is fine, substantial and handsome,
And is sold at a very low price.

After the Union victory in the Civil War, the jubilant Isaacs
wrote a six-stanza verse for a space ad in the *Cleveland Plain Dealer*
of June 21, 1865, which ends with the following:

The boys who caught Jeff Davis,
We'll welcome one and all,
And treat them to a fine new suit
At Isaacs' Union Hall!
Huzzah! Huzzah! fling the starry banner out,
Our gallant boys are coming home,
Let all the people shout.

The punch line at the bottom of the ad declared, "Look out for the
giants."

How could such a colorful entrepreneur not succeed in a rapidly
growing metropolis. Nevertheless, around 1869 Isaacs closed his
store and moved his family, which included five children at the
time, to New York City, where he carried on the clothing business
for many years until his death in 1897. After his wife's death he remarried in 1877 and fathered seven more children. His children
married into many prominent Jewish families such as Seixas, Roth-
child, Raphael, and Hendricks. Younger brother George had left
Cleveland already before the war. Why Isaac Isaacs moved his base
of operations is not known, but he likely wished to do business in
the national center of the needle trades.[57]

In the 1850s two related Dutch Jewish families reached the north
coast city on Lake Erie. These were the in-laws Henry van Baalen
with his wife and eight children, who came directly from Amsterdam, and Abraham de Roy (De Rooy) and his wife and four children who had first lived in Pittsburgh for a few years.[58] Both men
were clothing merchants linked to the Buffalo Van Baalen clan, and
neither remained in Cleveland more than five or six years (see Table
8.4 above).

In the years immediately after the Civil War, several new families
came to Cleveland. One included Frederick Cohen's son-in-law Joseph S. Goldberg, a physician and a Prussian, who had married a
Dutch woman in the Netherlands around 1848 and fathered three
children there by 1858 before emigrating to Buffalo. His wife's
mother Lieve or Louisa Cohen was widowed by 1870 and lived with
the Goldbergs for more than a decade until her death. Goldberg's
sons, Isaac E., Abraham, and Lennie, became merchants in Cleve-

land in the 1870s and 1880s. A second Dutch Jewish family was a notions peddler from Holland, John Samuels, and his Dutch wife, who had lived in England for a few years—their oldest child was born there in 1860—and then they emigrated to New York where more children came. John's brother Henry Samuels was a Pittsburgh pawnbroker who had also lived in New York City during the Civil War. Henry went inland to Pittsburgh immediately after the war, but John Samuels opted for Cleveland. Both families lived in Ward 1 in 1870. John Samuels operated a clothing store in which five of his teenaged sons clerked.[59]

Four additional families, including three married brothers, arrived in Cleveland in the 1870s. The brothers exemplify the pattern of chain migration. William Swaab (Schwab), who was born in the Netherlands around 1841, emigrated with his Dutch wife to New York by 1865, and came to Cleveland in 1868. He was a cigarmaker. His older brother Simon (born in 1837) came to Cleveland with his wife in 1872 directly from the Netherlands. He took up peddling, as did his younger brother Lucas (born in 1844), who arrived from the Netherlands in 1873 with his wife and four children. Within ten years, therefore, all three Swaab brothers and their families settled in Cleveland.[60]

The fourth arrival of the mid-1870s was Kalman Levi van Goor, an old peddler from the interior city of Winterswijk on the German border. Van Goor's reported reason for emigrating, according to official Dutch records, was stated: "Alternative to jail sentence." Once in Cleveland Van Goor collected old rags with a pushcart and married a widowed Bohemian immigrant with a teenage daughter. Van Goor was clearly at the bottom of the Jewish social hierarchy in Cleveland. The Swaab brothers plus the Goldberg, Samuels, Van Goor, and Cohen families (forty-four persons in all) comprised all of the Dutch Jews in Cleveland in 1880. In addition, there were two youngsters, Philip van Baalen of Detroit and Edward Calisch of Toledo, who were wards of the Jewish Orphan Asylum on Sawhill Avenue.

Edward Calisch (1865–1946) bears special mention because he later became the renowned ultra-Reform rabbi for fifty-four years of Richmond's premier synagogue, Beth Ahabah. Edward was the son of Henry Calisch, a teacher of languages, and Rebecca van Noorden, both of Amsterdam. The couple migrated in the late 1850s to Detroit where their eldest son Solomon was born in 1863. They then moved to Toledo where Henry was born in 1865 and where the Van Noordens also settled. Subsequently, Calisch moved his family to Chicago, where the opportunities were greater to teach in the large

Jewish community. But when the Chicago fire disaster struck in 1871, Henry flung himself into the rebuilding effort with abandon, and being a frail man, within three years he died of physical exhaustion, leaving Rebecca and the family destitute. They returned temporarily to her parents in Toledo. Realizing that her son Henry was intellectually gifted, Rebecca in 1876 sent him to the Jewish Orphan Asylum of Cleveland.[61]

The new superintendent Samuel Wolfenstein encouraged the bright pupil to consider rabbinic training, and when Dr. Isaac M. Wise of Hebrew Union College, who regularly recruited at orphanages, heard Calisch's oration at the graduation ceremony in 1879, he reportedly declared, "I want that boy." Calisch enrolled in the preparatory department of the college and within eight years completed high school, college, and seminary training, earning the reputation as a wunderkind. He was the sole member of the 1887 graduating class and the twelfth student to be ordained by this first permanent rabbinic institution in the United States.

After ministering four years at Congregation Anshe Ameth in Peoria, IL, where Calisch also married and began a family, he accepted a call in 1891 to the prestigious 150-member Richmond congregation. This progressive group of first-generation immigrants, mainly Germans, desired to move rapidly toward Reform Judaism and demanded a native-born rabbi, "one whose first breath was drawn under Republican skies." The Reverend Edward Nathan Calisch filled the bill admirably and left an indelible mark in the Jewish community and in the city at large over the next half-century. A person of national prominence in religious and civic affairs, Calisch gained the admiration of Jew and Gentile alike for his scholarly attainments and ecumenical spirit.[62]

Most of Cleveland's Jews, like those in Richmond, spoke German and religious services were conducted in that language until after the Civil War. The few Dutch Jews necessarily were trilingual, using their native tongue at home, German in the synagogue, and English on the streets. The religious attitudes of the earliest Dutch Jews in Cleveland, like those throughout the midwestern frontier, were clearly inclined toward Reform. From 1845 to 1850, when the city had only one congregation, Anshe Chesed (People of Loving Kindness), all of the Dutch Jews belonged. Jacob Frank served as one of the first five trustees of the sixty-member congregation in 1845–1846. But in 1850 some twenty Reform-minded dissidents withdrew to form Tifereth Israel (Glory of Israel), now Temple Israel. Of forty-seven charter members, mostly Germans, at least five (11 percent) were second-generation Dutch, including Benjamin F.

Peixotto, Rowland and Joseph Davies, Isaac A. and George Isaacs, and Jacob Frank. By 1852 the much larger Congregation Anshe Chesed, now Fairmount Temple, also moved in the direction of Reform. Where the later Dutch newcomers affiliated is not known at present, but living in close proximity to the synagogue rather than views about proper liturgy and practice likely determined the choice since both of these major Ashkenazic congregations had adopted *Minhag America* by the 1860s. The mainly second-generation Ohio Dutch were more acculturated than their East Coast compatriots and accepted ecclesiastical change. For good reason, the Midwest became the stronghold of Reform Judaism, with Cincinnati as the headquarters city.[63]

Prior to the Civil War, Cleveland's Jews were peddlers and shopkeepers, and they quickly came to dominate the retail clothing business. Most of the Dutch Jews did not share in that familiar path of upward socioeconomic mobility. Only the Isaacs brothers and the in-laws De Roy and Van Baalen succeeded as clothing merchants but they had moved on by 1870. In the next two decades, of eight male household heads, four were peddlers and two cigarmakers. Only a physician and clothing merchant held a higher status position. The Dutch Jews in Cleveland were too few to form an ethnic enclave; they were primarily appendages of the New York, Philadelphia, and Buffalo-Pittsburgh communities.

Toledo—An Isolated Few

In the 1860s a small Dutch Jewish settlement consisting of eight families and single adults took shape in Toledo on the outlet of the Maumee River. These were primarily clothing merchants. Joseph van Ulm, a street seller from the Dutch village of 's Gravendeel (province of Zuid Holland), operated a ready-made clothing store with his sons Abraham and Jacob (Table 8.5). Other clothiers were W. D. Oosterman, Samuel and Louis van Noorden, Marcus Rosenbach, H. Salomon, and Julius Tano. Cigarmaker G. van Leeuwen and china peddler Philip Speelman rounded out the group. Oosterman, whose wife was English had lived in New York City for more than a decade. The prosperous Tano, who reported $18,000 in property in 1870, had emigrated first to England with his Dutch wife, where a son was born in 1862. Salomon likewise migrated via England, where four children were born between 1853 and 1860.

Table 8.5
Dutch Jewish Household Heads and Single Adults, Toledo, 1870

| | | | Time of | | Property Value | | |
| | | | | | | Person- | |
Name	Age	N in Family	Immi-gration	Occupation	Realty $	alty $	Ward
W. D. Oosterman	31	8	1850	clothing dealer	—	2,000	2
Marcus Rosenbach	28	1	1860s	clothing store	—	—	3
H. Salomon	42	9	1860–1866	clothier	—	1,000	4
Philip Speelman	40	2	1860s	china peddler	—	3,000	2
Julius Tamo	36	4	1862–1868	merchant	8,000	10,000	4
G. van Leeuwen	37	4	1850s	cigarmaker	—	1,000	2
Louis van Noorden	20	1	1860s	clerk, cloth store	—	—	3
Samuel van Noorden	25	1	1860s	clothing store	—	2,000	3
Joseph van Ulm	65	4	1857	retired	—	2,000	2

Sources: Compiled from Swierenga, *Dutch Households in U.S. Population Censuses*; Swierenga, *Dutch Immigrants in U.S. Ship Passenger Manifests.*

The Toledo Dutch Jews prospered. By 1870 their reported wealth, both real estate and personal property, totaled $29,000, for an average per family of $3,625. This was $740 on average higher than their countrymen in Cincinnati. But Toledo never attracted many Dutch Jews; they favored larger market centers like Detroit and Chicago.

Detroit—The Van Baalens Again

The Jewish community of Detroit, Michigan's largest city, began in 1843–1844 with the arrival of several traders from the Ann Arbor and Adrian areas. The German immigration in the late 1840s soon brought other settlers and by 1850 Jews numbered about sixty. That year they first had more than the required ten men to begin formal worship, and they organized Congregation Beth El (House of God), engaged a teacher and ritual slaughterer, established a relief society, and bought a burial ground. These steps, of course, were essential for devout Jews everywhere. The congregation was Orthodox until adopting Reform in 1861; the synagogue ritual was conducted in Hebrew and German (*Minhag Ashkenaz*) until 1865 when they adopted the English *Minhag America*. The congregation's elementary school in the 1860s used all three languages. The majority decision at Beth El to adopt Reform prompted a more Orthodox minority of seventeen members to secede and found Congregation Shaarey Zedek in 1861.[64]

By 1880 Detroit's isolated Jewish community totaled about 1,000, less than 1 percent of the city population. They were equally divided between the early Germans, who lived immediately north of the city center along fashionable Woodward Avenue, and the later-arriving eastern European community, which was located east of the city center among lower-class Germans along Hastings and Gratiot streets.[65]

Dutch Jews arrived in Detroit in the 1850s. Perhaps the first two were Solomon van Worck and Hughlius Ingerman. Van Worck, a clothier, married and lived in New York for six years before moving to Detroit between 1850 and 1853. Ingerman was a storekeeper; his oldest child was born in Detroit in early 1850. Neither family remained in Detroit until the time of the 1870 census (Table 8.6).[66]

Members of the Van Baalen tribe arrived next between 1856 and 1859. Israel van Baalen, the oldest son of Emanuel of Buffalo, came in 1856 and dealt in old clothes for a few years until moving to

Table 8.6
Dutch Jewish Household Heads and Single Adults, Detroit, 1860, 1870

Name	Age	N in Family	Time of Immigration	Occupation	Property Value Realty $	Personalty $	Ward
1860							
Aaron Davis	38	9	1857–1858	peddler	—	600	3
Hyman Davis	44	5	post–1849	clothier	—	600	2
Hughlius Ingerman	39	8	pre–1850	storekeeper	—	—	8
Emanuel Joseph van Baalen	36	6	1848–1850	peddler	—	500	4
Israel van Baalen	28	6	1842	dealer old clothes	—	500	5
Willem van Baalen	32	6	1851–1853	clothier	—	2,500	3
Solomon van Worck	40	8	pre–1845	clothier	—	—	3
1870							
Aaron (Eben) Davis	49	14	1857–1858	clothing dealer	—	600	5
Solomon du Bois	53	5	1863–1865	clothing dealer	—	750	5
David Hanaman	32	3	post–1860	peddler	—	500	3
Emanuel Joseph	31	6	1860–1865	cigarmaker	—	250	7
Michael Kohn	22	1	post–1860	tailor	—	—	5
Levi Lambert	31	2	1856–1862	peddler	—	1,000	3
Moses Lambert	44	6	1856–1862	cigarmaker	—	—	3
Assar Oppenheimer	35	4	1860–1868	cigarmaker	—	200	5
Matthew Oppenheimer	39	1	1860–1868	agent, clothing house	—	—	5
Israel Reens	19	1	1866	clerk, clothing store	—	—	3

Joseph M. Smit	32	6	1854	clothing dealer	—	—	5
Louis Smit	34	10	pre-1861	clothier	1,000	5,000	2
Rachel Solomon	44	1	?	none	—	—	3
Abr. van Baalen	26	4	born NY	clothing dealer	—	300	5
Emanuel Joseph van Baalen	46	7	1848–1850	clothing retail	4,000	1,000	5
Emanuel van Baalen	24	4	1857	clothier	—	5,000	2
Esther van Baalen	26	1	1857	none	—	—	2
Isaac van Baalen	26	2	1857	clerk dry goods	—	—	2
Joseph van Baalen	19	1	1857	clerk dry goods	—	—	2
Willem van Baalen	42	8	1851–1853	clothing merchant	20,000	10,000	3
George van Heussen	40	9	1862–1865	clothing dealer	—	150	5
Louis (Levi) Wolters	36	7	1853	peddler	—	500	4

Sources: Compiled from Swierenga, *Dutch Households in U.S. Population Censuses*; Swierenga, *Dutch Immigrants in U.S. Ship Passenger Manifests.*

265

Chicago after 1860. Willem van Baalen came from Cleveland by 1858, remained in the city, and thrived as a retail clothing merchant. In late 1859 or early 1860 another Van Baalen, Emanuel Joseph, came from Cleveland and took up peddling. He too prospered by operating a retail clothing store. Sometime after 1865 another Van Baalen family group reached Detroit from Cleveland. These were the four children of Henry van Baalen. Emanuel, who was born in Amsterdam about 1846, opened a clothing shop, probably as a branch of the Cleveland house; brothers Isaac and Joseph clerked in the store.[67]

Another family group, the Davis brothers Hyman and Aaron (Eben), also settled in Detroit in the late 1850s. Hyman, a clothier, immigrated directly from Amsterdam with his family of six. Aaron Davis and his family of seven first stopped in England for a few years where a daughter was born in 1857. Aaron began by peddling and then dealt in clothing on a small scale. Neither brother prospered. But Aaron's family had grown from seven to twelve children! His two adult sons, Israel and Soloman, were clerking, probably for their father. Hyman had left Detroit by 1870.[68]

Between 1860 and 1870 more than a dozen Dutch Jewish families and single adults settled in Detroit. By 1870 they totaled 103 persons, of whom 46, or nearly one-half, were Dutch-born. Since the total persons in all Dutch-headed families (including Gentiles) in 1870 was 385, the Jews comprised more than one-quarter (27 percent) of all Netherlanders in Detroit. For most, Detroit was a second-stage migration point, after initially settling in Buffalo, Philadelphia, Cleveland, or Pittsburgh. Nine families and single adults came directly from the Netherlands, judging from the 1870 census report, and three families stopped en route in England. The Dutch Jews lived separately from Dutch Gentiles, most of whom were Roman Catholics. The Jews were concentrated in Wards 2, 3, and 5; the Catholics were in Wards 6, 7, and 9. Only in Ward 5 did Dutch Catholics and Jews live in proximity. This ward had fifty-one Jews and thirty-two Catholic Hollanders.

Detroit's Dutch Jews, like their countrymen elsewhere, participated in synagogue life, but little is known of their specific activities. The scanty evidence that is available indicates that most were affiliated with the Reform congregation Beth El. Several were leaders at this prestigious synagogue. Levi Lambert served as secretary in 1864 and Emanuel Joseph van Baalen in 1867 was one of the four trustees. At the dedication of the new Washington Avenue (Boulevard) Temple in 1867, Sarah, Rachel, and Louisa van Baalen were among thirteen young women who led the clerical procession carrying floral wreaths. Sarah was the eldest daughter of Willem van Baalen, and Rachel and Louisa were the eldest daughters of Emanuel Joseph van Baalen. Both men were retail clothing merchants.[69] Willem van Baalen was the wealthiest Hollander in Detroit; he had amassed $30,000 in property by 1870.

In their occupational life, the Dutch Jews in 1870 were in trade and commerce (Table 8.6). Of twenty employed men, ten were clothing merchants, three each peddled, clerked, and were cigarmakers, and one was a tailor. The two-thirds in business was the same proportion as among all Jewish males in the city in 1880. Compared to the entire city work force, in which only 25 percent held white-collar jobs and only 2 percent were proprietors and managers, the Jews were heavily concentrated in retail merchandising.[70] The Dutch clothiers especially prospered. All clothiers benefited from the prosperity of the 1860s brought on by the push of government spending during the Civil War and the population growth spurt after the war owing to heavy foreign immigration. The peddlers of 1860 evolved into retail clothiers by 1870 and the clerks had opened their own stores.

Although Detroit had the largest Dutch Jewish population in the Midwest, except for Chicago, there is little evidence of an ethnic community. No Netherlandic congregation took shape and marriage between Dutch families was rare. The population barely reached one hundred in 1870; this was clearly an insufficient mass for the survival of an ethnic settlement.

Chicago—The Midwestern Dutch Jewish Center

Chicago by 1920 had the largest Jewish population of any interior American city. Given its commercial and mercantile pursuits, it was inevitable that Jews found Chicago very attractive. Its central location and spectacular population growth made the city the market of the Midwest, a hub of the nation's water and rail systems, and the jumping-off point for immigrants from Europe and the East Coast. By the 1860s Chicago harbor had become a vital place, receiving three hundred vessels a day carrying lumber from the northern forests, manufactured goods from the East, and agricultural produce from the surrounding farms. Chicago's seventeen grain elevators in 1870 bulged with 60 million bushels of grain, some of which went directly to Europe by ship. Its Union Stock-yards and industrial plants such as the McCormick Reaper and Mower Works provided jobs.[71]

The booming trade, transport, and manufacturing brought settlers to Chicago with unprecedented rapidity, giving the city the epithets of lightning city and exploding metropolis. Between 1850 and 1870 the population grew tenfold from 30,000 to 300,000. In the next decade it surpassed 500,000, by 1890 it topped 1 million, and by 1905 it reached 3 million. The city spread inland, but mainly southward; the northside and westside grew more slowly until after 1900. As the well-to-do moved into newer subdivisions, the workers and newcomers filled in the vacated areas around the city center and converted homes into crowded multifamily dwellings.[72]

The first Jews arrived in Chicago at least by 1832, a year before the small settlement around Fort Dearborn was incorporated as a town. By 1841 at least four Jews resided in Chicago, and some twenty men were found by 1844. Several of these newcomers were a group of Bavarians from New York City who had been part of a failed agricultural colony near Schaumburg, IL, some 20 miles west of Chicago.[73] The city's Jewish community mushroomed in 1849 with the arrival of a sizable contingent from the East. Chicago that year had emerged as a great rail center. Within ten years, by 1860, there were 1,500 Jews among Chicago's 109,000 inhabitants, or 1.4 percent. The largest part were Germans, followed by Posen (or Prussian) Poles and some eastern Europeans.[74]

Jewish businessmen were attracted by the overwhelming demands for goods and services by the city's bustling population. They were "fairly well situated," according to an early resident. In the antebellum decades, their stores lined the streets south of the Chicago River along Lake, Randolph, Washington, Wells, LaSalle, and Clark streets. "Some had dry goods stores, others clothing stores; many were engaged in the cigar and tobacco business, and there were already a plumber and joiner, and even a carpenter, here," the settler recalled. "Some—loading their goods upon a wagon, others upon their shoulders—followed the honorable vocation of peddling. . . . They made a good living for their families, and while gathering money, at the same time established a business that grew with the country."[75]

Religious life followed economic life. On the Day of Atonement (Yom Kippur) in October 1845 Chicago's Jews mustered a *minyan* and held their first High Holy Day service and formed the Jewish Burial Ground Society which purchased a cemetery north of the city limits. Two years later this society merged itself with the pioneer congregation Kehilath Anshe Maarab (Congregation of the Men of the West), known popularly as KAM, which was established in 1847 with fifteen paying members, all Germans, but quickly doubled to thirty. Five years later this mother synagogue of the Illinois region dedicated its first sanctuary in a solemn assembly with the Dutch cleric Samuel M. Isaacs of New York officiating in the English language to impress non-Jews in the audience.[76]

In the meantime, however, ethnic (and to a lesser extent religious) rivalries arose between the dominant group of strictly Orthodox Bavarians and the more liberal minority of Posen Poles. In 1849 some twenty Prussian Poles founded their own congregation, Kehilath B'nai Sholom (Congregation of the Children of Peace), known popularly as KBS. Officially, both pioneer synagogues were solidly Orthodox. The Poles resented the Bavarian dominance of KAM, and they preferred the familiar *Minhag Poland* over the *Minhag Ashkenaz* of KAM. Both services, however, were in German, English, and Hebrew. There were about 200 Jews in the city at this time.[77] By 1864 KAM boasted 125 members and KBS had 80. Two new Reform congregations, Sinai (1861) with 100 members and Zion (1964) with 60, nearly equaled in size the pioneer synagogues. These membership statistics may overstate the case. At least one critic, a conservative member of KAM, reported to the *Occident* in 1859 that Judaism was not flourishing. The Polish congregation in a typical Sabbath service is "mostly empty benches, since the majority of the members are attending to their business, and openly desecrate the day of rest." His own German congregation, meanwhile, was racked by turmoil over the introduction of Reform innovations by a "small but daring minority."[78] Such problems were typical of American Judaism at this time.

To the Germans and Poseners "should be added another small group known as 'Holland Jews,'" reported editor Hyman L. Meites in his *History of the Jews of Chicago*. The Hollanders in the 1850s and 1860s came from Amsterdam primarily, plus a few other Dutch cities. Some migrated in stages via England but most came directly. Once in Chicago, according to Meites, they "cast in their lot chiefly with the 'Polish' constituency either in its synagogue, B'nai Sholom, or in its *chevras* [benevolent organizations]. Among these 'Holland Jews' were many substantial and loyal Jewish families," Meites continued, "including the Andrews, the Van Gelders, the Van Praags, the Van Baalens, and others."[79] To this list Meites might have added the families Boasberg, De Wolf, Cohen, Litt, Greenburg, and Rosenbach among others (see Tables 8.7 and 8.8.). From seven families in 1860 totaling 24 persons, the number of Dutch Jewish families in

Name	Age	N in Family	Time of Immigration	Occupation	Realty $	Personalty $	Ward
Solomon Andrews	23	3	1858	secondhand clothing 192-1/2 S. Monroe 1861 CD 162 S. Wells 1867 CD	—	—	3
Benjamin Boasberg	31	4	1842	clerk secondhand clothing 1869 CD 253 S. Wells 1869 CD	—	170	2
Louis Cohn (Cohen)	29	5	pre–1849	tailor cigar manufacturer 1859 CD Harrison & Gurley Streets	—	—	8
Samuel de Wolf	27	2	pre–1857	secondhand clothing 13 N. Clark 1861 CD 183 S. Wells	—	1,000	8
Henry S. Haas	27	2	1850	clothing, wholesale and retail 155-1/2 S. Clark 1860 CD 161 S. Clark 1861 CD 157 S. Clark 1867 CD	—	2,500	2
Newman Levi (Levy)	35	5	1856–1857	storekeeper boots & shoes 1859 CD 311 S. Clark 1859 CD 269 S. Clark 1860 CD crockery 1861 CD 242 S. Clark 1861 CD clothing, tailor 1859–1861 CD corner Canal & Mather	5,000	200	2
Isaac Neever (Verveer)	42	3	pre–1852	secondhand clothing 269 S. Clark 1861 CD	—	1,000	2

Property Value spans *Realty $* and *Personalty $*.

Sources: Compiled from Swierenga, *Dutch Households in U.S. Population Censuses;* Swierenga, *Dutch Immigrants in U.S. Ship Passenger Manifests;* Chicago City Directories (CD), 1859–1869.

Table 8.8
Dutch Jewish Household Heads and Single Adults, Chicago, 1870

Name	Age	N in Family	Time of Immigration	Occupation	Property Value		Ward
					Realty $	Personalty $	
Aaron H. Andrews	45	2	1856	pawnbroker clothing 1867 140 S. Wells 1867–1870 CD 291 S. Clark 1876 CD	—	2,000	1
Andre Andrews	31	5	1860	pawnbroker 134 S. Wells 1869 CD 299 S. Clark 1876 CD	5,000	2,000	1
Leon Andrews	36	4	1862	pawnbroker pawnbroker 1876 CD secondhand clothing 1870 CD 170 S. Wells, 1870 CD 572 S. State 1876 CD	—	1,000	1
Solomon Andrews	33	4	1858	pawnbroker secondhand clothing 162 S. Wells 1868–1870 CD jeweler 798 S. Wabash 1876 CD	10,000	4,000	1
Morris Blom	31	3	?	cigarmaker 44 W. Randolph 1870 CD	—	500	10
Benjamin Boasberg	43	7	1842	clothier	—	—	2
Jonas A. Drielsma	38	7	pre–1860	merchant tailor, clothing 131 W. Randolph 1870 CD 397 S. Clark 1876 CD	—	700	11

Table 8.8 (Continued)

Name	Age	N in Family	Time of Immigration	Occupation	Property Value		Ward
					Realty $	Personalty $	
Jerome Frank	29	2	1868	clothing store	—	500	1
David Gelder	28	3	1864	cigarmaker	—	—	3
Isaac Gelder	33	3	1860	secondhand clothing 204 S. Wells	—	—	2
Jonas Gelder	39	10	1860	clothier 204 S. Wells	—	1,000	2
Abraham Greenburg	34	6	1863–1865	peddler 87 S. Canal 1876 CD	—	—	10
Clara Greenburg	59	4	1863–1865	secondhand clothing	—	500	10
Emanuel Greenburg	24	4	1863–1865	cigar manufacturer 86 W. Madison 1876 CD	—	2,000	10
Henry Greenburg	28	4	1863–1865	cigarmaker 123 W. Washington 1870 CD dry goods store 161 W. Randolph 1868 CD secondhand clothing 87 S. Canal 1876 CD	—	500	10
Simon Greenburg	32	2	1859	cigar & tobacco shop 240 W. Madison 1870 CD 403 W. Randolph 1872 CD	—	400	1
Henry S. Haas	38	5	1850	retail clothing merchant 161 S. Clark 1861 CD 157 S. Clark 1867 CD	12,000	25,000	3

Name				Occupation / Address			
Henry Henkel	38	5	pre–1858	retail dry goods	—	2,000	9
George Hetzel	27	1	1870	clerk in store	—	—	1
Martin Lam	32	1	?	tailor	—	—	1
Joseph Leveitzen	63	3	pre–1863	tailor	—	200	20
Jacob (S.) Litt	20	3	1852	clerk in store	—	—	2
Jacob T. Litt	59	9	pre–1855	clothing store	—	—	8
Solomon Litt	51	6	1852	pawnbroker 132 S. Wells 1870 CD	—	400	1
George S. Poppers	28	3	1852	pawnbroker watches & jewelry 1870 CD 443 S. Clark	—	3,000	3
Peter Regitz	29	3	pre–1866	fruit dealer	—	—	2
Benjamin Rosenbach	24	1	1867	clerk in cigar store	—	—	1
Joseph Rosenbach	27	4	1867	cigarmaker 174 W. Madison 1870 CD	—	450	1
Myer Rosenbach	19	1	1867	clerk in cigar store	—	—	1
Solomon Rosenbach	19	1	1867	cigarmaker	—	—	1
Mark Schneider	49	3	1866	clothier 214 S. Wells 1870 CD	—	200	2
Adrian A. Schockaert	34	6	pre–1860	cigar manufacturer 106 W. Randolph 1870 CD	—	450	10
Edward Sickel	50	6	pre–1855	commission merchant 212 Kedzie 1870 CD	20,000	3,000	19
Benj Speelman	47	1	?	tailor	—	—	1

Table 8.8 (Continued)

Name	Age	N in Family	Time of Immi- gration	Occupation	Property Value		Ward
					Realty $	Person- alty $	
Joseph Israel van Baalen	38	4	1842	clothing merchant 53 W. Randolph 1870 CD retired 755 S. Wabash 1876 CD	—	2,000	11
Joseph Israel van Baalen	45	5	1849	merchandizing 55 3rd Ave. 1869 CD	—	—	11
Joseph van Buren	44	11	pre-1850	retired	—	800	2
Levi D. van Gelder	55	7	1861–1865	lithographer 250 Townshend 1870 CD	2,500	500	18
Solomon van Straaten	44	5	1862–1868	china peddler clothing 1876 CD 11 Bremer 1876 CD	—	—	18
Samuel Voorsanger	32	2	1861	bookkeeper salesman 1876 CD 616 W. Butterfield 1876 CD	—	—	1

Sources: Compiled from Swierenga, *Dutch Households in U.S. Population Censuses*; Swierenga, *Dutch Immigrants in U.S. Ship Passenger Manifests*; Swierenga, "Dutch Households in Federal Manuscript Population Census, Chicago, 1900" (unpublished computer file); Chicago City Directories, 1861–1876.

1870 had increased to 40, totaling 166 persons. Surprisingly, none of the Dutch held leadership positions in the KBS Congregation.

These earliest Jews in Chicago, including the Hollanders, Meites explained, "not only spoke German in their daily intercourse but also transacted their various organized activities and heard their sermons preached in the language they had brought with them." There were German newspapers, theaters, and synagogue schools. "English slowly made inroads, however," says Meites, "and finally replaced the tongue that was heard practically throughout the Chicago Jewish community until the fire [1871] and for a few years thereafter."[80] If the Hollanders, perforce, spoke German in *shul* and shop, they assuredly spoke Dutch at home.

It is not known whether the Chicago Dutch ever contemplated founding a Netherlandic congregation based on the Amsterdam rite as their brethren did in New York, Philadelphia, and Boston. They had a sufficient population mass for a viable congregation and historical precedent was in their favor. By the late 1860s Chicago had ten nationality congregations, but none was Dutch.[81]

The factor that made the Chicago experience different was the nature of the migration. Chicago was primarily a second-stage destination. In the eastern centers Dutch Jews established congregations in the 1840s and 1850s. But Chicago's Dutch Jews did not arrive in strength until the 1860s after many had first lived in the east. A self-selection process was at work. The most assimilated ones tended to relocate in the West, while those who valued *Minhag Amsterdam* stayed put. Adult children went West but parents remained in the East.

Chicago's Dutch Jews joined with other Jews in religious life, particularly Germans. The process began already during immigration when at least seven Dutch families stopped in England in the 1850s and 1860s and married and had children there. In Chicago assimilation continued. From one-half to two-thirds of the married Dutch-born Jews had non-Dutch spouses; approximately one-half were German, one-quarter were English, and the remainder were other Europeans or Americans. In 1870 and 1880 three-fourths of these interethnic marriages involved Dutch men, but by 1900 more Dutch women than men had non-Dutch spouses (see Table 8.9).[82]

The timing of the migration was also critical. Meites notes that the various nationality groups "went their own way at first, but gradually their differences narrowed and eventually disappeared."[83] The Dutch Jews arrived after the Civil War and by then the process of amalgamation among Ashkenazic Jews in Chicago was well underway. By 1900 nearly three-fourths (110 of 153) of married couples of

Table 8.9
National Stock of Ethnically Mixed Dutch Couples,
Chicago, 1870, 1900

National Stock	Dutch Husbands		Dutch Wives	
	N	%	N	%
1870				
Germany	10	50	5	83
England	5	25	1	17
Other western Europe	2	10	0	0
United States	3	15	0	0
Totals	20	77	6	23
1880				
Germany	9	41	1	17
England	8	36	5	83
France	2	9	0	0
United States	3	14	0	0
	22	79	6	21
1900				
Germany	18	47	20	43
Austria-Hungary	2	5	3	7
Poland-Russia	1	3	6	13
England	10	26	7	15
Other western Europe	2	5	2	4
United States	5	13	8	17
	38	45	46	55

Sources: Compiled from Swierenga, *Dutch Households in U.S. Population Censuses*; Swierenga, *Dutch Immigrants in U.S. Ship Passenger Manifests*; "Federal Manuscript Population Census, Chicago, 1880," ibid., 1900.

Dutch Jewish birth or parentage had non-Dutch spouses. The percentage of Dutch husbands with English wives (26 percent) was nearly twice as great as for Dutch wives (15 percent), whereas the percentage of Dutch wives with eastern European husbands, especially Russians and Poles, was almost three times as great as for Dutch husbands (Table 8.9).

That the Dutch felt a greater affinity for the Polish Shul than for the Bavarian Shul is understandable. The Bavarians were in turmoil over adopting Reform and they were also ardently German, whereas the Prussian Poles clung to Orthodoxy, although they quickly adopted English in their worship services and generally assimilated more rapidly. Both the KAM and KBS congregations initially worshiped in rented quarters on Lake Street, just a few doors from each other, in upstairs rooms above Jewish retail shops. While KAM purchased their own building in 1851, KBS could not afford their first synagogue until 1864 after the arrival of new members in the Civil War years, some of whom were Dutch. They erected a magnificent brick building in the south loop on Harrison and Federal streets.[84]

As the Jewish pioneers prospered in the Civil War years, they moved out of the central city into newer neighborhoods. This dispersal lengthened the distance to the pioneer synagogues downtown and required the founding of new congregations. Russian-Polish Jews also came in growing numbers and desired their own congregations. As a result, by 1870 Chicago counted ten congregations, seven with synagogue buildings. Each served a particular nationality, neighborhood, socioeconomic, and religious group. It is estimated that two-thirds of the Jews in the city belonged to a congregation. Chicago had ten thousand Jews at the time, 3.3 percent of its population.[85]

The great fire of 1871 was a turning point in Chicago's history. The entire city center and northside was destroyed, including the homes and stores of five hundred Jews, the Jews Hospital on LaSalle Street, and five of the seven synagogues, including the Polish-Dutch Congregation KBS. The fire spared the KAM synagogue on the westside, but it fell to a large fire in 1874 that struck the surrounding East European Jewish quarter.[86] Jews were thus devastated by the fires, but they also benefited from the rebuilding from the ashes. Chicago thrived more than ever after the fire. Large commercial buildings and industries sprang up in the city center and residents moved to new neighborhoods in outlying districts.

The complexion of Chicago's Jewish community also changed after the fire. The various nationality groups became self-ghettoized and Russians soon outnumbered Germans. The poor Russian victims of the pogroms settled primarily on the westside, penetrating as far as the Lawndale district, whereas Polish Jews remained in their early neighborhood on Canal Street just west of the river. The wealthier Germans expanded southward and northward along fashionable Michigan and Indiana avenues to the south and along LaSalle Street to the north, forming the so-called golden ghettos. In the 1890s the poorer German Jews, who had remained in the west division, also made a mass exodus to the Hyde Park district near the University of Chicago on the southside. This included most of the

Dutch Jews as well. There were more than fifty Jewish congregations by 1900, including eleven German congregations, all Reform. By this time Yiddish fraternal lodges and clubs had become the center of social life; synagogues and their religious activities had lost their priority. By 1900 Chicago Jewry totaled 75,000 and boasted the second largest settlement after New York City.[87]

The Dutch Jews likewise increased in number. From 166 persons in 1870, they quadrupled by 1900 to 642 persons (see Table 8.10). They also joined in the population dispersal. In the 1850s and 1860s they lived above their stores and shops in a compact three-square block area in the western part of the city center along Wells, Clark, and Monroe streets. Twenty-five of the 39 Dutch Jewish residences and businesses in 1870 were along Wells and adjacent streets. Eleven families lived immediately west of the south branch of the Chicago River and four families lived along the north branch on the near northside. All except the families west of the river were completely burned out in 1871 and the westsiders lost everything in an 1874 fire.

The fire disasters scattered the Dutch, as it did the other Jews. Most westside Dutch moved into South Town (Wards 1-4) and Hyde Park (Ward 32) in the last quarter of the century. In 1900 36 percent lived in Hyde Park and 38 percent were in South Town (Table 8.10). Only ten families (forty-seven persons) remained on the westside (Ward 12) along fashionable Jackson Boulevard and other tree-lined avenues. A few clothiers and pawnbrokers retained their stores in the central business district and commuted to work. The two prestigious synagogues, KAM and KBS, were both situated by the 1890s in the southside golden ghetto.[88]

In Chicago, as elsewhere, the Dutch Jews did not mix with the larger Dutch Gentile population. In the 1850s and 1860s, while the Jews were concentrated in the city center districts among coreligionists, Dutch Calvinists and Catholics lived in outlying wards. In the heavily Gentile wards on the westside (7, 8, 9, 12, and 15), which in 1870 contained nearly fourteen hundred persons of Dutch stock, only two Dutch Jewish families (13 persons) could be found. By contrast, in the city center wards, all of the forty Dutch-stock persons in Ward 2 were Jewish, as were 61 percent in Ward 1 (Table 8.10). Only in the earliest years prior to the Civil War, when Chicago's residential areas were tightly packed in and around the city center, had Dutch Jews and Gentiles lived in proximity. But even then, if one could make a block-by-block analysis, Jews and Gentiles would be found clustered on different streets.

At the turn of the century residential segregation was even more

Table 8.10
Dutch Jewish Wards in Chicago, 1870, 1900

1870 Census

Ward	Jewish Stock	Column %	% of Dutch Stock*
1	37	22	61
2	40	24	100
3	11	7	13
8	9	5	5
9	5	3	1
10	27	16	40
11	16	10	57
18	12	7	52
19	6	4	14
20	3	2	9
Total	166	100	17

*Total Dutch stock in all wards in 1870 was 2,095, and Dutch Jews were 8 percent.

1900 Census

Ward	Jewish Stock	Column %	% of Dutch Stock†
1	27	4.2	29.7
2	5	0.8	10.2
3	48	7.5	48.5
4	161	25.1	82.6
5	2	0.3	0.8
7	10	1.6	9.5
8	3	0.5	1.5
11	13	2.0	6.0
12	47	7.3	8.3
13	5	0.8	0.9
14	9	1.4	0.9
15	6	0.9	2.2
17	9	1.4	52.9
18	3	0.5	7.9
20	9	1.4	11.1
21	19	3.0	23.2
22	10	1.6	30.3
23	6	0.9	15.4
24	5	0.8	7.2
26	4	0.6	2.3
30	6	0.9	0.5
32	233	36.3	70.2
34	2	0.3	0.0
Total	642	100.1	5.2

†Total Dutch stock in all wards in 1900 was 18,881, and Dutch Jews were 3.4 percent citywide.

Sources: Compiled from Swierenga, *Dutch Households in U.S. Population Censuses*; Swierenga, *Dutch Immigrants in U.S. Ship Passenger Manifests*; "Federal Manuscript Population Census, Chicago, 1900."

pronounced. Over 80 percent of the 642 Dutch Jews were concentrated in 1900 in only five wards (1, 3, 4, 12, 32), in two of which (4 and 32) they comprised 82.6 and 70.2 percent, respectively, of the entire Dutch population (Table 8.10). Two-thirds of the Dutch Calvinists and Catholics, on the other hand, resided on the westside (Wards 9, 10, 12, and 13) and in the southern suburbs of Englewood and Roseland (Wards 30, 31, and 34).

Occupationally, Chicago's Jews like all Jews were mainly storekeepers and merchants, with a sprinkling of professionals and tradesmen. As soon as they learned to speak English, most went into business for themselves. Since Chicago excelled as a dry goods market second nationally only to New York City by the time of the Civil War, its Jews became prominent in dry goods merchandizing as well as all aspects of the clothing trade—manufacturing, wholesaling, and retailing. Their shops lined the streets of the central business district until the Great Fire of 1871 caused a wider dispersal. More prosperous shopkeepers were located in the southern fringes and later arrivals gravitated to the cheaper western edge of the city center.[89]

The Dutch Jews in Chicago dealt primarily in clothing, both new and used, but a number operated pawnshops and cigar stores (Table 8.11). In 1860, of the seven family heads, three owned secondhand clothing outlets, one had a retail and wholesale clothing store, and one ran a dry goods store. These were young men (average age of 30.6 years) who were at the outset of their business careers and starting with little or no capital.

Newman Levi (Levy), a storekeeper on South Clark Street, was the wealthiest Dutch Jew in 1860. He had emigrated in 1856 or 1857 and by 1860, despite the hard time following the financial crash of 1857, he reported owning real estate valued at $5,000, plus $200 worth of personal property. Levi was the only Dutch contributor in 1861 to the fund for equipping a Jewish company from Chicago in the Civil War. He had departed the city by 1870 for destinations unknown.[90]

The wealthiest in that year was Henry S. Haas whose retail and wholesale clothing store stood until the Great Fire in the 100 block of South Clark Street. His merchandize, which he valued at $2,500 in 1860, had increased tenfold by 1870 to $25,000, plus real estate (likely his store and home on South Wabash Street) worth $12,000. For many years in the 1860s he served as the consular agent of the Dutch government in Chicago. In 1866 he contributed $50 to a fund to build a veterans hospital in Chicago. After the fire, which destroyed his business, nothing more is heard of Henry Haas. Presumably he left the city.[91]

Table 8.11
Occupations, Actively Employed Dutch Jewish
Household Heads, Chicago, 1860, 1870, 1880, 1900

	1860		1870		1880		1900		1900*	
Occupation	N	%	N	%	N	%	N	%	N	%
White-Collar										
Professional	0	0	0	0	2	5	2	3	3	2
Merchant, Storekeeper	5	71	27	68	21	54	33	46	50	39
Clothing, Dry Goods	(5)		(14)		(7)		(3)		(6)	
Cigar and Tobacco	(0)		(7)		(1)		(9)		(11)	
Pawnbroker	(0)		(6)		(9)		(0)		(1)	
Other					(4)		(21)		(32)	
Dealer, Agent, Salesman, Peddler	0	0	3	8	11	28	17	24	39	31
Clerk, Bookkeeper	1	14	5	12	1	3	5	7	7	6
Blue-Collar										
Skilled Crafts	1	14	5	12	4	10	10	14	23	18
Cigarmaker	(0)		(1)		(3)		(4)		(8)	
Tailor	(1)		(3)		(1)		(2)		(8)	
Factory foreman	(0)		(0)				(1)		(1)	
Other			(1)				(3)		(6)	
Unskilled	0	0	0	0	0	0	4	6	5	4
Totals	7	99	40	100	39	100	71	100	127	100

*All Dutch stock, including second generation.

Sources: Compiled from Swierenga, *Dutch Households in U.S. Population Censuses*; Swierenga, *Dutch Immigrants in U.S. Ship Passenger Manifests*; "Federal Manuscript Population Censuses, Chicago, 1880," ibid., 1900.

Not so with Solomon Andrews, Benjamin Boasberg, and the two Joseph Israel van Baalens, who were just beginning long careers in Chicago. Andrews sold used clothing on West Monroe Street until 1870 when he upgraded himself to a pawnshop on South Wells Street. By 1876 he advanced further and owned a jewelry store in the more affluent section on South Wabash Avenue. Solomon Andrews was one of four Andrews families in the city in 1870. Perhaps they were brothers. All were pawnbrokers with stores almost side by side on South Wells Street (at building numbers 134, 140, 162, and 170). They likely collaborated and perhaps specialized in different merchandize, such as Solomon becoming a jeweler. One can hardly imagine that they were competitors.[92]

Benjamin Boasberg (of the Boasberg and Van Baalen clans of Buffalo) arrived in Chicago in the late 1850s and after clerking in a clothing store for a few years, opened his own used-clothing outlet by 1869 located on South Wells Street. This was the same business his older brother Nathan Boasberg operated in Buffalo.[93]

Boasberg's brother-in-law, Joseph Israel van Baalen, known as Israel, came to Chicago via Buffalo and Detroit and by 1870 was a prosperous clothing merchant on West Randolph Street with an inventory of $2,000. As noted earlier, he had married into the prosperous Philadelphia Lit merchant family. Israel's son Emanuel clerked in the family store. The great fire wiped out the business and Israel became a fire insurance agent. By 1900 he lived on the fashionable South Prairie Avenue. His uncle and namesake, Joseph Israel van Baalen, who also lived nearby, came to Chicago from Buffalo in 1865 and engaged in merchandizing until the fire destroyed his property and pushed him into early retirement. His three middle sons in 1875 were all clerks in downtown retail stores while his oldest son was a hatter and his youngest son a watchmaker.[94]

In 1870 the census marshal recorded the occupations and wealth of forty Dutch Jewish households (Table 8.11). The fourteen clothiers and dry goods storekeepers still dominated, but seven men ran cigar stores and six were pawnbrokers. Five were clerks and bookkeepers, and three were peddling. Together, these commercial persons totaled 88 percent. The three tailors and the cigarmaker, who made up the other 12 percent, may also have run their own businesses. None of the Dutch were unskilled workers. Ten years later, in 1880, the proportion of merchants and storekeepers declined (except for pawnbrokers), and salesmen, peddlers, and dealers increased threefold (Table 8.12).

The occupational distribution in 1870 was similar to that of Chicago Jewry generally, as Table 8.13 shows, but the Dutch had more merchants (both upper and lower levels); no professionals, and only half as large a proportion in the blue-collar crafts. The Dutch, therefore, were concentrated in the middle of the Jewish occupational prestige ladder.[95]

Reported property values likewise point to men at the middle rungs of respectability. Only the Andrews clan, Henry Haas, Edward Sickel, Israel van Baalen, and Levi van Gelder could boast of substantial wealth. Solomon Andrews in 1870 reported a total of $16,000, Andre Andrews $7,000, Aaron Andrews $2,000, and Leon Andrews $1,000. Sickel, a produce commission merchant on Kedzie Avenue at the western city limits, reported $23,000 mostly in real estate. Van Baalen was a downtown clothier worth $2,000 and Van

Table 8.12
Dutch Jewish Household Heads and Single Adults, Chicago, 1880

Name	Age in 1880	N in Family	Occupation	Enum. Dist.	Ward
Aaron Andrews	61	3	pawnbroker	3	1
Leon Andrews	48	9	pawnbroker	8	2
H. Arends	42	7	secondhand clothing	8	2
Gertrude Boas	19	1	servant	105	11
Rebecca Calisch	50	4	—	24	4
Abraham Cappell	42	11	cigar manufacturer	12	2
James Cohen	46	12	clothing store	101	10
Henry de Young*	27	4	pawnbroker	8	2
Abraham Diamond	58	3	clerk	4	1
Solomon Diamond	25	4	—	4	1
Lena Drielsma (widow Jonas A.)	42	7	—	8	2
David Eckstein	49	5	keeps store	194	RD
Louis Elzas	52	9	diamond dealer	12	2
John Frisco	33	6	—	6	1
Isaac Gelder	44	12	pawnbroker	15	3
Jonas Gelder	48	11	pawnbroker	8	2
Emanuel Greenburg	33	6	pawnbroker	93	9
Simon Greenburg	41	3	pawnbroker	101	10
Leo Herschel	35	4	clothing dealer	12	2
Jacob Hessmer	23	4	peddler	12	2
M. C. Isaacs	37	6	treas. Steel & Iron Co.	21	4
F. H. Jacobs*	32	2	dry goods store	95	9
Myer Jacobs*	45	9	commercial trader	20	3
Louis Kesner	39	8	cigarmaker	12	2
Elias Koekkoek	33	3	peddler	12	2
Samuel Jamelt	73	1	clothing dealer	12	2
Levi Judah	28	6	huckster	65	7
Martin Levi	50	5	butcher shop	131	13
Jacob Litt	69	10	none	124	13
Sarah Lyons	43	8	none	4	1
Raphael Prince, Jr.	38	5	shoe dealer	28	4
Benjamin Rosenbach	34	4	tailor		
Joseph Rosenbach	37	6	liquor store	95	9
Myer Rosenbach	31	5	pawnbroker	101	10

Table 8.12 (Continued)

Name	Age in 1880	N in Family	Occupation	Enum. Dist.	Ward
I. B. Scheffer	41	4	works dry goods	124	13
Simon Scheffer	40	3	cigarmaker	12	2
Mark Schneider	60	9	clothier	8	2
J. B. Siegers	29	1	Chicago Club	8	2
Ed Speelman	31	5	traveling salesman	15	3
L. D. Stoover	34	4	agent wholesale co.	12	2
Louis van Baalen	30	1	traveling salesman	8	2
William van Buren	28	9	peddler	12	2
Alexander van Ellen	36	4	peddler	12	2
David van Gelder	38	7	retail stationery	12	2
Abraham van Praag	48	4	cigarmaker	12	2
Charles van Straten	60	1	pawnshop salesman	101	10
Frank Wynberg	18	1	—	1	1

*Second generation of Dutch parentage.

Source: Compiled from Swierenga, "Dutch Households in Federal Manuscript Population Census, Chicago, 1880."

Gelder was a lithographer worth $3,000. Sixteen family heads, 40 percent of all families, reported no property. The median wealth was $900.

Between 1870 and 1900 the many Dutch Jewish newcomers broadened the occupational distribution. The proportion of merchants declined by thirteen points (from 68 to 55 percent) while the number of salesmen and dealers more than doubled (from 8 to 20 percent). Two physicians comprised the only professionals among the Dutch in 1900. The two persons in the unskilled category were a janitor and a department store packer (Table 8.14).

The foregoing discussion includes only Dutch-*born* household heads. If the group is expanded to include the second-generation Dutch Jews in 1900, the occupational distribution widens, but it is not changed substantially. The distribution remains skewed toward small businessmen and salesmen, particularly in tobacco, clothing, and jewelry. Fewer than one in five were blue-collar workers and only three were professionals. Specifically, of 127 persons of Jewish stock in the labor force, merchants comprised 39 percent; salesmen, agents, and dealers 31 percent; and clerks 6 percent. Together, these petty businessmen totaled 76 percent of the work force. Skilled

Table 8.13

Occupational Categories, Dutch Jews, and a Sample of All Jews in 1870 Census and 1870 Chicago City Directory

Occupations	Dutch		All Jews	
	N	%	N	%
White-Collar	35	88	474	76
Professional	(0)	(0)	(45)	(7)
Merchant	(27)	(68)	(413)	(66)
Agent, Dealer	(3)	(8)	(16)	(3)
Clerk, Bookkeeper	(5)	(12)	(0)	(0)
Skilled Crafts	5	12	135	22
Miscellaneous			15	2
Totals	40	100	624	100

Sources: Compiled from Swierenga, *Dutch Households in U.S. Population Censuses*; Swierenga, *Dutch Immigrants in U.S. Ship Passenger Manifests*; Michael Charney, "An Analytical Study of the Economic Life of the Jews in Chicago, 1870–1872" (unpublished paper, HUC, 1974), 4.

craftsmen made up 18 percent and unskilled workers only 4 percent. In sum, in the period 1850–1900 the Dutch Jewish economic profile became more diverse. Retail clothing stores gave way first to pawnshops and then by 1900 to cigar sweatshops and retail outlets.

One reason for the relative economic success of the Chicago Dutch Jews was their residential longevity in the city. They were not transient in terms of outmigration, although they moved frequently within the city into better neighborhoods. Of the seven families in 1860, three remained in 1870. Of the forty families in 1870, 29 or nearly three-fourths were yet represented in the city thirty years later in 1900. The notable clans who matured with the city were the Andrews, Gelders, Greenburgs, Litts, Rosenbachs, and Van Baalens. Single families that persisted were those of Benjamin Boasberg, Jerome Frank, George Hetzel, George Poppers, Mark Schneider, William van Buren, Levi van Gelder, Solomon van Praag, and Samuel Voorsanger.

Solomon van Praag, a saloon keeper on Wabash Avenue, is the only Dutch Jew known to be politically active, but there were doubtless others. Van Praag belonged to the Democratic party and represented Cook County in the Illinois state legislature in 1891–1892.[96]

Table 8.14
Dutch Jewish Household Heads and Single Adults, Chicago, 1900

Name	Birth	Year of Immi-gration	N in House-hold	Occupation	Enum. Dist.	Ward
Aaron H. Andrews	1825	1856	2	illegible	11	1
Alexander Andrews	1838	1861	3	merchant	24	1
Leon Andrews	1832	1862	5	none	60	3
Samuel Andrews	1856	1858	1	jewelry salesman	11	1
Sarah Boasberg	1840	1842	4	widow	1023	32
William Boas	1844	1862	6	store manager	94	4
Abraham Cappell	1847	1856	2	cigar manufacturer	10	1
Jacob Capples	1853	1866	8	tobacco merchant	74	3
James V. Cohen	1834	1856	5	merchant	104	4
Jacob de Bruin	1853	1870	3	hotel keeper	11	1
Simon de Bruin	1874	1894	4	tin can maker	331	12
David de Roos	1840	1892	2	store packer	682	22
Abraham Diamond	1829	1861	6	retired	711	24
Jacob Doornheim	1864	1866	7	janitor	1017	32
William Edelman	1870	1885	5	storekeeper	184	7
Nathan S. Frank	1851	1868	6	merchant store	994	32
John Fresco	1846	1865	2	cigar manufacturer	1006	32
Abe Gans	1876	NA	1	stenographer	103	4
Haddie Gans	1874	1898	3	salesman	580	18
Leopold Gans	1867	1872	4	auctioneer	994	32

Name						
Samuel Gans	1842	1872	3	capitalist	992	32
David Gelder	1841	1864	5	cigar manufacturer	1007	32
Henry Gelder	1850	1861	11	cigar dealer	22	1
Isaac Gelder	1837	1860	3	storekeeper	35	1
Jonas Gelder	1831	1860	3	tailor	1006	32
Nathan Green	1876	?	1	?	1013	32
Albert Greenburg	1849	1870	2	merchant	77	3
Simon Greenburg	1865	1875	6	jewelry store	1016	32
John Hartog	1864	1882	4	provisions export	1031	32
Elias Herschel	1845	1872	6	clerk millinery store	322	11
George Hetzel	1845	1870	6	clerk city government	1027	32
Edward Hirsch	1847	1870	4	printer-secretary	78	3
Henry Hirsch	1843	1870	2	insurance solicitor	78	3
Jacob Isaacson	1873	1892	3	bookkeeper	200	8
Frank H. Jacobs	1847	1873	2	furnishing goods	100	4
Jacob Kaplan	1840	1891	5	doctor	176	7
Julia Kesner	1824	1868	2	widow	1006	32
Louis J. Kesner	1841	1876	5	cigar manufacturer	995	32
Henry Levy	1849	1889	3	cigarmaker	34	12
D. Litt	1830	1852	4	hat & cap salesman	1013	32
Jacob Litt	1852	NA	2	dry goods salesman	1014	32
Joseph Litt	1850	1860	4	tree salesman	1039	32
Abram Mendelssohn	1854	1894	5	provisions export	1031	32
Moses Morisco	1833	1865	4	landlord	423	14
Arnold Nathan	1861	1898	9	bookkeeper	368	12
Esther Nathan	1835	1888	1	none	368	12
Abraham Peres	1843	1851	6	manager	81	4

Table 8.14 (Continued)

Name	Birth	Year of Immigration	N in Household	Occupation	Enum. Dist.	Ward
Jacob Polack	1849	1851	5	foreman, glass factory	625	20
George S. Poppers	1842	1852	6	merchant	364	12
Raphael Prince	1840	1860	5	mail order business	93	4
Israel Reens	1852	1866	3	clothing manufacturer	1027	32
William Reens	1870	1890	1	physician	366	12
Herman Robbe	1871	1895	1	receiving clerk	103	4
Joseph Robbe	1870	1889	3	illegible	103	4
William Robbe	1876	1900	1	packer department store	103	4
Benj. Rosenbach	1845	1867	5	jeweler	82	4
M. D. Rosenbach	1850	1858	3	jewelry store	1014	32
Nathan Ruit	1846	1865	9	merchant	95	4
Isaac Scheffer	1856	1876	7	clothing cutter	102	4
Mark Schneider	1821	1866	6	cigarmaker	91	4
Henry Schwartz	1867	1891	2	florist	119	5
Joseph Smit	1830	1854	4	agent	626	20
Louis Soltz	1862	1886	6	rag peddler	698	23

288

Henry Starr	1843	1860	5	clothing business	103	4
Morris Stokvis	1878	1894	1	shoe salesman	311	11
Abraham Strauss	1859	1882	10	cigarmaker	542	17
Marcus Strauss	1858	1886	11	cigarmaker	650	21
William Tausig	1847	NA	7	tobacco wholesaler	1030	32
Joseph Israel van Baalen	1826	1849	4	none	1029	32
Joseph Israel van Baalen	1832	1842	3	fire insurance agent	1014	32
William van Buren	1842	1861	8	at home	91	4
Van Eggers	1858	1882	5	manufacturer	1031	32
Benjamin van Emden	1855	1881	5	cigarmaker	678	22
Morris van Gelder	1861	1882	7	mattress manufacturer	330	12
Solomon van Praag	1856	1860	3	saloon keeper	52	2
Van Praag	1832	1885	1	cigar manufacturer	91	4
Mary van Ulm (W.Barend)	1824	1857	1	widow	11	1
Samuel Voorsanger	1836	1861	9	stationery store	93	4
Jac. Weinburg	1840	1861	9	landlord	94	4
Henry Wever	1857	1884	7	cigar manufacturer	1028	32

Sources: Compiled from Swierenga, "Dutch Households in Federal Manuscript Population Census, Chicago, 1900."

Saint Louis, a Way Station

The bustling gateway city to the West attracted a "large body" of Jews in the mid-nineteenth century, but very few Dutch settled there to capitalize on its thriving business opportunities.[97] They preferred Chicago.

The Dutch Jews of Saint Louis, as elsewhere in the Middle West, were merchants and shopkeepers (Table 8.15). Several became very wealthy and all generally prospered, but few remained in the city for as long as ten years. Unlike the stability of the Chicago Dutch, those in Saint Louis resembled Jews in Detroit and Cleveland. The first Dutch Jew was Solomon Segaar, a widower. He and his family of eight adult children, all born in the Netherlands, had emigrated in the early 1840s. The oldest son, J. Solomon, married a Dutch wife after arriving, and three children were born in Saint Louis between 1845 and 1848. The father and two unmarried sons were peddling in 1850 and the elder son operated a clothing business. The family must have been poor in the Netherlands. Solomon and four of five adult children were illiterate. But there were two signs of economic betterment in Saint Louis. The youngest daughter, aged thirteen, was able to attend school and the married son could afford to hire an Irish girl as a live-in domestic.[98]

The Segaar families left Saint Louis by 1860 and four other Dutch Jewish families took their places, two of whom came via London. These included Simon Drooker, a pawnbroker who had migrated from Holland to London in the early 1830s, married there, and raised seven children. Between 1853 and 1860 the family reached Saint Louis, probably coming by way of New Orleans. Drooker was the only Dutch Jew to remain in the city more than a decade. Abraham S. Jacobs had also lived in London for a time and married there before coming to the Gateway City, where three children were born between 1851 and 1855. Jacobs returned to London with his family; his fourth child was born there in 1857. But the family was back in Saint Louis by 1860, accompanied by an English-born sister-in-law or niece. An Irish servant girl also lived in. Jacobs was a very wealthy man with real estate holdings worth $40,000 in 1860. The enumerator left Jacobs's occupation designation blank on the census form, but he was likely a successful land investor.[99]

By 1870 all of these families had left Saint Louis, except for Drooker, whose pawnshop had given way to a clothing store. But six new families replaced them, raising the number of Dutch Jews to forty-four. Most notable were the hardware merchant Moses Meyer and the pawnbroker Henry Smith (Smit). Meyer had lived in Mis-

Table 8.15
Dutch Jewish Household Heads and Single Adults, Saint Louis, 1850, 1860, 1870

Name	Age	N in House-Hold	Year of Immi-gration	Occupation	Property Value		Ward
					Realty $	Person-alty $	
1850							
J. Segaar	31	5	1841	clothing business	—	—	2
Soloman Segaar	50	7	1841	peddler	—	—	3
1860							
Simon Drooker	56	10	pre-1836	pawnbroker	—	—	5
Louis Eichel	28	1	pre-1860	variety store	—	500	5
Abraham Jacobs	48	6	pre-1851	—	40,000	800	4
Lawrence Wolff	36	8	pre-1849	clothing	—	3,000	8
1870							
Seymour Blitz	34	7	1843	secondhand clothing dealer	—	5,000	8
Simon Drooker	70	5	pre-1836	clothing store	—	500	5
Moses Meyer	45	6	pre-1860	hardware merchant	30,000	10,000	8
Henry Smith	44	5	1850–1870	pawnbroker	—	50,000	8
Philip Spier	42	6	1831	clerk-clothing store	—	1,000	6
Isaac Truman	57	6	pre-1852	tailor	—	5,000	12
B. A. Wolff	40	9	pre-1855	cigarmaker	—	—	2

Sources: Compiled from Swierenga, *Dutch Households in U.S. Population Censuses;* Swierenga, *Dutch Immigrants in U.S. Ship Passenger Manifests.*

souri for at least twelve years and by 1870 had accumulated a whopping estate of $40,000. Smith had even greater wealth. He valued his property at $60,000 in 1870, making him one of the wealthiest men in the city. His adult sons, Saul and Morris, clerked in the pawnshop. When the family emigrated is unknown, but all five members were Dutch-born, including the youngest child Morris, age twenty-one.[100]

Three other newcomers in 1870 had also accumulated property. Solomon Blitz, a secondhand clothing dealer, reported $5,000 in personal property, as did the tailor and clothier Isaac Truman, who had lived in Canada for at least five years between 1848 and 1852. Blitz resided in New York City in 1860 and was a tailor. His move to Saint Louis was advantageous. The third family was that of Philip Spier, a clerk in a wholesale clothing store, who come from Boston via New York, where he was a dry goods merchant. Another recent arrival in 1870 was truly a rolling stone. B. A. Wolff, a cigarmaker without property, and his Dutch wife had six children who were born (in order) in Saint Louis (1855), England (1857 and 1859), Canada (1865), and Illinois (1867 and 1868). His mother-in-law, also born in the Netherlands, lived with the family.[101]

Intermarriage with non-Dutch immigrants was common among the Saint Louis Dutch Jews. In 1870 eight had Dutch-born spouses and seven (three men and four women) did not; most of the latter married Germans. Most had wed in East Coast centers before coming to Saint Louis, although at least three couples were married in Holland. This was a highly mobile populace on the path of assimilation into the larger Jewish population and acculturated to American life. Saint Louis was merely a stop on their way up.

Conclusion

Dutch Jewish merchants in New York, Philadelphia, and other cities penetrated the Great Lakes frontier in the antebellum decades to provide consumer goods and services to the rapidly growing region. Every major market center attracted some Dutch, but only Chicago developed a substantial stable settlement.

The Van Baalen and Boasberg clans of clothiers typified the business networking that led to the establishment of branch houses from their Buffalo base in Pittsburgh, Cleveland, Detroit, and Chicago. Isaac A. Isaacs had first shown the way in the 1840s by introducing ready-made suits to Clevelanders from his father's shop in Philadelphia. Within a decade Isaacs boasted of owning the largest store west of New York City.

The Dutch Jews in the Midwest were a transient lot except for those in Chicago. Nowhere did they coalesce into a definable group, but rather they amalgamated into the larger German Jewish community. Chicago's Hyde Park district had the largest concentration of Dutch Jews in 1900. Since this area was a major Jewish neighborhood, the Dutch here too blended in.

Religiously, the Dutch in the interior cities were more open to the liberal transition within Judaism than were those in the East. The explanation is twofold. These migrants were typically young men whose attachment to the Orthodox tradition was not strong. They were willing to leave the shelter of the ethnoreligious centers in the East and venture out on their own. Second, the Midwestern Dutch Jews were mainly second-generation immigrants who were well on the way to acculturation. The burgeoning cities of the interior offered them tickets to success.

Chapter 9

SAN FRANCISCO:
AN INSTANT ELITE

Dutch Jews in San Francisco were a transient lot of less than a hundred persons, but several joined the "instant elite" and rose to leadership positions in journalism, business, and religion. The De Young brothers Charles and Michael founded the *San Francisco Chronicle*, Isaac Magnin and Raphael Peixotto built prosperous businesses, and Jacob Voorsanger became the leading Jewish rabbi in the West Coast. But as a group the Dutch blended into German Jewry.

The Pacific port of San Francisco became an instant metropolis following the discovery of gold in northern California in 1848. Within five years the city bustled with nearly 60,000 inhabitants who poured in from all over the world. Jewish merchants from the East Coast and Midwest joined the throng to supply the city and nearby mining camps with goods. By the 1870s San Francisco was the second Jewish city in the United States with a population of 15,000 to 18,000, substantially ahead of Philadelphia's 10,000 to 12,000, but far below New York's 75,000 to 100,000.[1]

The earliest Jewish arrivals came from Charleston, New Orleans, Saint Louis, and New York City.[2] While most originated in the German lands of central Europe, all nationalities were represented. As the famed Dutch Jewish rabbi of San Francisco, Jacob Voorsanger,

294

later noted: "English and French Jews 'bunked' side by side; the Hollander and the Pole, the German from Hanover and Bavaria, the semi-Pole from West-Prussia and Galicia, the Russian from Lithuania and Bessarabia, all met together and bravely faced the difficulties of the new environment."[3]

Religious services began in the fall of 1849 when some thirty Jews met on Rosh Hashanah. By Yom Kippur the group grew to nearly fifty. A year later more than one hundred gathered for worship, and they opened a cemetery and formed the First Hebrew Benevolent Society. A Dutch Jew, Emanuel Hart, raised the funds to buy two city lots for the cemetery.[4]

Whatever feelings of unity existed in the first days, by the High Holy Days of late 1850 the more conservative Poles refused to worship with the more liberal Germans. Within a few months two congregations had formed—the mostly Bavarian and reformist-minded Emanu-El (God with Us) and the mostly Polish and traditional Shearith Israel, which also included some Englishmen and Poseners. By late 1860 the larger German congregation, which numbered over two hundred member families, had hired a full-time rabbi, raised its first synagogue in the North Beach residential district where many Jews lived, and moved far along the road to Reform. Shearith Israel had also erected their synagogue by 1860 and two new small congregations had formed.[5]

The economic life of San Francisco Jewry revolved around merchandising in the central financial district.[6] At the top were an elite group of pioneer German clothing and dry goods manufacturers, such as Levi Strauss and Henry Seligman, who intermarried like European royalty and worshiped at the lavish Sutter Street Temple of Congregation Emanu-El. Ten members of the temple in the mid-1870s were together reputedly worth $45 million. But the vast majority of the 1,167 Jews identified in the city directors between 1861 and 1865 were of the middle class. Two-thirds (64 percent) were dealers and merchants (mostly in clothing, dry goods, and tobacco), and another 15 percent were salesmen, clerks, and bookkeepers in their employ. Skilled craftsmen (mainly tailors and shoemakers) comprised 10 percent, professionals numbered 4 percent, and day laborers and draymen 6 percent.[7]

Pioneer Dutch

When the first Dutch Jew reached San Francisco is unknown, but Emanuel Hart was among the earliest in 1849. Eleven

295

years later the city had nine Dutch-headed Jewish households totaling thirty-five persons (Table 9.1). Dutch Jewry grew to fifteen families and single adults (fifty-six persons) by 1870 and to thirty-one
families and singles (eighty-five persons) by 1880. Almost one in ten
Dutch-born in the city were then Jewish. Their residences were scattered across the city in the early decades, but by 1880 they had con-
gregated near Market Street between Third and Sixth streets. Some
were below Market in Ward 10 while others were above it in Ward 8
near the Sutter Street Synagogue.

The small Dutch contingent were rapidly being Germanized,
judging from the nationality of their spouses. Of the seven married
men in 1860, three wives were German (from Prussia and Hanover), one was Polish, and only three were Dutch. One German Jew
was married to a Dutch wife. In 1870 of eleven married men, five
wives were German (three Prussian and one each from Hanover
and Baden), two were Irish, one English, one Polish, and only two
Dutch. Also two Germans and a Russian Jew were married to
Dutch wives. By 1880 seven of thirteen Dutch Jewish men had outmarried, two choosing English brides, and one each women from
Prussia, Würtemburg, Posen, France, and Maine. Six of seven married Dutch women had also outmarried: five husbands were Prussian or German and one Polish. Such mixed nationality marriages
could be expected in the heavily German Jewish community, although Dutch men married Dutch wives more than did Dutch
women. This was the same pattern discovered in New York City
and other eastern centers.[8]

Based on the children's birthplaces, at least ten Dutch families
had first settled in the East, primarily in New York City, but also in
New Orleans, Philadelphia, and the states of Texas, Virginia, Ohio,
and Wisconsin. Two families came directly from England. Isaac
Levy arrived via Cape Horn by 1870 after marrying and fathering
four children in London between 1858 and 1868. Isaac Magnin and
his family of seven children, all born in England, similarly rounded
the Cape to San Francisco in 1876. About one-third of the couples
began their families in San Francisco. This was a transitory group.
Only the three wealthiest of ten families in 1860 remained in the city
ten years later.

The pioneer Dutch in the Bay City were a cut below the larger
Jewish community. Of the nine employed family heads and single
adults in 1860, four were merchants or manufacturers, one a collector, and two lowly cartmen (Table 9.1). Only the bookmaker, Bernard Bouwman, was wealthy; Bouwman reported more than
$20,000 in real estate. By 1870 the Dutch had improved their status

Table 9.1
Dutch Jewish Household Heads and Single Adults, San Francisco, 1860–1880

Name	Age	N in House-hold	Time of Immi-gration	Occupation	Property Value		Ward
					Realty $	Person-alty $	
1860 Census							
Bernard Bouwman	46	4	1846–1852	bookmaker	20,500	200	7
L. A. de Groot	32	1	1850	collector	—	—	6
Jacob de Roos	50	3	1856	hand cartman	—	200	7
Morris de Young	61	8	pre-1833	commission merchant	—	—	4
Morris Hitz	34	2	1850s	teamster	—	600	7
Solomon Jacobs	29	6	pre-1853	dry goods merchant	—	600	7
Isaac Mails	50	6	pre-1840	merchant	—	400	8
E. S. Mendels	48	4	1837	none	—	300	6
B. E. van Straten	28	1	1850s	drayman	—	1,250	6
1870 Census							
Theodore Blitz	45	4	pre-1852	clothing dealer	1,500	1,000	4
Bernard Bouman	57	6	1846–1852	bookmaker	18,000	3,000	11
Herman Commissans	51	3	pre-1851	merchant's clerk	—	1,500	2
Louis Dees	36	4	pre-1860	baker	—	—	4
Jacob de Solla	52	5	1845–1852	singing teacher	—	1,000	2
Henry Lamis	30	3	1860s	pawnbroker	3,500	500	1
Isaac Levy	34	7	1868–1869	clothing dealer	5,000	6,000	4
Isaac Mails	62	5	pre-1840	upholsterer	—	1,000	8

Table 9.1 (Continued)

Name	Age	N in Household	Time of Immigration	Occupation	Property Value Realty $	Property Value Personalty $	Ward
Morris Meyer	35	7	1850–1859	glazier	5,000	1,500	11
Joseph A. van Praag	55	1	pre–1870	clerk in store	—	—	8
Samuel van Praag	45	3	1860–1866	cigar dealer	—	500	4
B. E. van Straten	36	6	1850s	express wagon	—	1,000	12
J. H. van Straten	31	1	1865	pawnbroker	—	—	1
A. Zeehandelaar	29	1	1860s	secretary	—	—	12
1880 Census							
Henry Blankman	38	4	1860s	dentist	—	—	8
David Davis	45	5	pre–1872	teacher	—	—	10
Hans Davis	20	1	1870s	store clerk	—	—	10
Max Davis	19	1	1870s	store clerk	—	—	8
David D'Ancona	52	7	1850–1852	furrier	—	—	8
Jacob de Roos	75	1	1856	retired	—	—	10
Leon de Roos	21	1	b. SF	traveling agent	—	—	10
Esther M. de Solla	56	1	1845–1853	widow—at home	—	—	3
Amelia de Young	71	2	pre–1833	widow—at home	—	—	8
Lewis de Young	38	1	b. NYC	stockbroker	—	—	11
Michael H. de Young	34	1	b. Balt.	journalist	—	—	8
Rosa de Young	66	3	pre–1832	widow—at home	—	—	11
Jeanette Ezekiels	50	4	pre–1865	secondhand clothing	—	—	11
J. Gordon	37	1	1870s	clothing dealer	—	—	1

Name			Occupation			
Louis Green	48	7	merchant	1860s	—	10
Edward Hartog	55	2	lawyer	1854	—	8
Fanny Lam	37	1	tailoress	b. Maine	—	10
William Lam	34	3	bookkeeper	b. SF	—	8
Francois Levi	70	1	retired	?	—	10
Isaac Levy	44	6	wholesale clothier	1868–1869	—	12
Louis Levy	33	2	shoe dealer	1870s	—	2
Isaac Magnin	34	9	keeps fancy bazaar	c. 1850	—	10
Tookey Mendels	62	1	laborer	1837	—	10
Samuel Meyers	27	2	cigarmaker	1870–1880	—	10
Leon van Collem	65	5	clockmaker	pre-1850	—	8
John van der Berg	25	1	store porter	1870s	—	10
Samuel van Praag	41	3	merchant's solicitor	1860–1966	—	11
George Waters	33	3	salesman	b. Balt.	—	8
Henry Witveld	52	3	gilder	b. NYC	—	10
Felix J. Zeehandelaar	32	1	store clerk	1860s	—	8

Sources: Compiled from Robert P. Swierenga, *Dutch Households in U.S. Population Censuses, 1850, 1860, 1870: An Alphabetical Listing by Family Heads,* 3 vols. (Wilmington, DE, 1987); Robert P. Swierenga, comp., *Dutch Immigrants in U.S. Passenger Manifests, 1820–1880: An Alphabetical Listing by Household Heads and Independent Persons,* 2 vols. (Wilmington, DE, 1983); Robert P. Swierenga, comp., "Dutch Households in Federal Manuscript Population Census, San Francisco, 1880" (unpublished computer file).

slightly, but their average wealth slipped from $3,900 in 1860 to $3,571 in 1870. The occupations in 1870 were more middle class. Theodore Blitz and Isaac Levy were clothing dealers. Samuel van Praag was a tobacco dealer, Henry Lamis and J. H. van Straten operated pawnshops, Isaac Mails ran an upholstery shop, and Morris Meyer a glazing shop. Only three of the fourteen in the 1870 cohort remained in San Francisco ten years later, but the continuing mercantile focus of the newcomers is clear. Of twenty-five actively employed Dutch Jews in 1880, one-third were merchants, primarily in wearing apparel, and another one-third were brokers, agents, salesmen, and store clerks. Three professionals, four craftsmen, a store porter, and a common laborer rounded out the group. Two of the Dutch businessmen quickly rose to prominence in the city. These were the department store magnate, Isaac Magnin, and Michael de Young, the owner and publisher of the *San Francisco Chronicle*, whose stories are told later. Other success stories were those of Isaac M. and Abraham M. de Solla, sons of Jacob, a singing teacher. In 1900 Abraham was president of his own company, De Solla Deussing Co., which manufactured pipe and boiler coverings. Isaac was a partner in a liquor store. David E. Davis, who had started as a teacher, became the cantor at Congregation Shearith Israel. His son Max in 1900 was the senior partner in a ladies' and children's wear store.[9]

Dutch Gentiles far outnumbered Jews in San Francisco in these years, but many were mariners and seamen who happened to be in port during the census. Sixty-five out of 138 Dutch-born in 1860 were seamen. Deleting these, Jews comprised nearly one-fifth (thirteen out of seventy-three) of the Dutch-born populace. Ten years later only sixteen of 190 Dutch-born in the city were mariners; Jews then comprised less than 10 percent (eighteen of 174) of the Dutch population, or half of the 1860 proportion.

Charles de Young, Editor

Following the pioneer generation of 1849 to 1870, several Dutch Jews and their offspring earned fame and power in San Francisco, but at least one gained ignominy. He was Charles de Young, the brainy and brash editor and publisher of the *San Francisco Chronicle*, who in 1880 at age thirty-five was murdered in his office at the newspaper by the son of the city's mayor.[10] Charles was the eldest of three sons of Baltimore merchant Michael H. de Young of the Netherlands and his French Catholic wife, Amelia Morange, whose father was Dutch-born. Charles was born in 1845 in Natchitoches, LA, where his father was a roving merchant. In 1854 the family headed for California but the father died en route. The widow continued on to San Francisco with her three sons and a daughter. Charles, then only seventeen years of age, opened a printing shop and brother Michael Henry became a clerk.

Three years later Charles, with the minor help of his youngest brother, Gustavus, who borrowed the firm's startup capital of $500, began publishing the San Francisco *Daily Dramatic Chronicle*, a theatrical paper with reviews and advertisements for the city's avid theater patrons. Using an early version of yellow journalism, De Young built up readership with spicy personal items. In 1868 he converted his paper for a general readership into the *Daily Morning Chronicle*. The initial circulation of 10,000 reached 16,000 by the end of 1869.

But De Young's upstart brand of sensational and often unflattering stories about local elites earned him many enemies. By 1871 he had accumulated a dozen criminal libel suits, most of which he won, and he had been caned in the street by an irate federal judge. Michael, who like his brother was slight of build, was beaten and shot by an angry municipal judge who weighed 240 pounds. Fortunately, Michael escaped with only a superficial head wound. The brothers thereafter armed themselves with pistols. In 1874 all three brothers together attempted to kill a former employee who had defamed their mother and sister in a rival newspaper. Their shenanigans only drove the circulation of the *Chronicle* up to thirty thousand, while they somehow escaped punishment in the courts.

In the mid-1870s after a triumphal tour of the International Exposition in Paris, Charles de Young decided to align the *Chronicle* behind the radical Workingmen's party of California, whose agenda included a new prolabor state constitution. De Young's broader goal was to become a state power broker as the boss of the New Constitution party. When Democratic politicos tried to block his bid for control, De Young launched a withering editorial attack. This brought a return volley of invective in the *San Francisco Bulletin* so biting that Charles attempted to assassinate his political foe, a Baptist clergyman. The rival miraculously recovered from two bullets to the chest and abdomen and went on to win election as mayor. A few weeks later, in April 1880, the mayor's son succeeded in assassinating Charles De Young. The escalating cycle of violence had trapped its participants.

Michael de Young continued to publish the steadily growing *Chronicle* in comparative quiet for another forty-five years. He later was the director general of the Panama-Pacific International Exposition held in San Francisco.[11] He died in 1925 and received last rites in the Catholic church. This was in contrast to his assassinated brother, whose funeral had been conducted by Rabbi Elkan Cohn of Emanu-El Temple, although Charles was a nonpracticing Jew.[12] The M. H. De Young Memorial Museum in San Francisco is a legacy to this lapsed Jewish publisher and civil leader.

The Peixotto Family

San Francisco attracted several members of the notable Peixotto family who traced their roots for over four hundred years from Portugal to Amsterdam (1599), to New York (1800), to Cleveland (1836), and finally to San Francisco (1869). The patriarch of the American clan was Moses Levi Maduro Peixotto, a merchant who was appointed *hazan* of New York's historic Congregation Shearith Israel. Moses's son Dr. Daniel L. M. Peixotto was a renowned physician in New York and Ohio. Daniel's oldest son Benjamin Franklin Peixotto succeeded in the Cleveland mercantile world before practicing law in San Francisco from 1867 to 1872, after which he held U.S. diplomatic posts in Rumania and France.[13]

Raphael Peixotto, Daniel's younger son, was born in Cleveland in 1837 and after his father's early death in 1843, he had to leave school and go to work. He joined the firm of his older brother Benjamin F., who was in partnership with the English Jewish immigrant George A. Davis. In 1863 Raphael married George's daughter Myrtilla J., in New York's Synagogue Shearith Israel. Six years later, in 1869, he moved to San Francisco with his wife and four children.[14]

The business opportunities in San Francisco attracted Raphael Peixotto and he prospered there greatly. This allowed time for self-education through intensive reading. As Rabbi Jacob Voorsanger observed; "[Peixotto was] a merchant by day and a student by night." His first love was education and he devoted much time to teaching the youth in Temple Emanu-El's Sunday school. He also served a stint as president of the congregation in the late 1890s and was active in many Jewish institutions in the city. He died in San Francisco in 1905.[15]

Several of Raphael Peixotto's children distinguished themselves. Edgar practiced law in San Francisco, served as assistant district attorney, rose in national Republican party circles, and joined the city's elite clubs. Oldest daughter Dr. Jessica Peixotto was a professor at the University of California who, in A. W. Voorsanger's words in 1916, was "one of the most distinguished Jewish women the West has yet produced." Sidney founded and led for many years the Columbia Park Boys' Club of San Francisco and youngest son Ernest studied in Paris and was an artistic painter.[16]

Jacob Voorsanger, Rabbi

In 1886, six years after Charles de Young's demise, another Hollander arrived in San Francisco to begin an illustrious career. This was Jacob Voorsanger (1852–1908) of Amsterdam, rabbi of Congregation Emanu-El and mentor of the brilliant Judah Magnes, the Western region's first native-born rabbi (Fig. 9.1). Voorsanger, a man of extraordinary ability and energy, rose to the very pinnacle of renown on the Pacific Coast as the leader for twenty years of the largest and wealthiest congregation in the West. Temple Emanu-El's membership in 1902 exceeded five hundred families, or more than three thousand souls.[17]

The Voorsanger family had lived in Amsterdam for several generations and Jacob's father Wolf was a diamond cutter. After the completion of his Hebrew parochial high school program, young Jacob, not yet twenty years of age, left Amsterdam for London to seek his future.[18] After three months he left for Philadelphia where he arrived in 1873. Even as a young man Jacob had a commanding presence, imposing in stature and a forceful personality. Using the resources of the ethnoreligious community, Voorsanger within a few months gained a position as librarian of the YMHA and was appointed assistant cantor by the struggling Netherlandic Congregation Bnai Israel. He then embarked on an extended self-study program to become a rabbi.[19]

Voorsanger left Philadelphia after three years and went on to become one of the most talented and powerful Jewish Reform preachers and journalists in America. He next served one year each as cantor at the Orthodox Adas Israel Congregation of Washington, DC, and then at the Sons of Israel and David Congregation of Providence, RI, which had recently adopted a moderate Reform liturgy. That year (1877) Voorsanger returned to Philadelphia as a delegate to the gathering of the Union of American Hebrew Congregations, a new unity association that tilted toward Reform and eventually became wholly Reform. These activities presaged his gradual shift from Orthodox reader to Reform rabbi. In 1878 Congregation Beth

Fig. 9.1. Rabbi Jacob Voorsanger (1852–1908) of Congregation Emanu-El, San Francisco, CA. Reprinted by permission of Congregation Emanu-El from Fred Rosenbaum, *Architects of Reform: Congregational and Community Leadership, Emanu-El of San Francisco, 1849–1980* (1980).

Israel of Houston recognized his growing pulpit skills and appointed him rabbi for the first time. Here he studied privately with a retired rabbi and read assiduously, all of which prepared him for his appointment in June 1886 as junior and in 1889 as senior rabbi of the predominantly German Temple Emanu-El of San Francisco, the leading congregation of the city and the most influential west of the Rocky Mountains.

In his writings and preaching, or more accurately lecturing, Voorsanger identified with the Reform movement's radical second generation leaders who would truck no compromise with Orthodoxy or even Conservative Judaism. His hyper-rationalistic theology was based on Darwinian evolutionary naturalism. As a consequence, the Dutchman attacked Orthodoxy and rejected the traditional Jewish doctrine of the supernatural revelation of the law and the prophets. According to Voorsanger, "God grew in history only as the capacity of men's minds grew to accommodate him." He praised the French Revolution for the "good it accomplished then, unwittingly or intentionally, and the benefits which the world enjoys now from its workings."[20]

The implications of this "religion of reason" for mundane religious life were great. Voorsanger despised "legalism," rabbinism," and "orientalism" in all its forms, including the kosher system, traditional liturgies, ministerial garb, and the Yiddish language. In his first year he moved the Friday evening services to Sunday morning. He read most of the liturgy at the magnificent Sutter Street Temple in English, bareheaded, and without the usual tallith. But there were limits even to his latitudinarian views. He refused to accept rapproachment between Judaism and Christianity, nor would he condone the Sunday Sabbath, both of which were advocated by a few Reform leaders.[21]

Rabbi Voorsanger's social and political views were as conservative as his theology was radical. He became a thoroughgoing "American Israelite," a one hundred percenter, who adopted middle-class values and called for the "complete assimilation" of Jews into the American melting pot. He condemned women's suffrage, unrestricted immigration, labor strikes, anarchism and socialism, the Democratic party, popular spectator sports such as prizefighting and bicycle races, and even the new-fangled automobile, which he deemed a "terror." Voorsanger attacked Zionism as a delusion and labeled as "the wildest of all wild dreams" a return to the "Turk-ridden land" of Israel. Above all, as a militant Americanist he denounced in the strongest terms every Orthodox Jewish custom and tradition that he deemed oriental and nonwestern. The growing Russian Jewish immigrant ghetto in San Francisco drove him to distraction. In keeping with his cosmopolitan views, the Dutch rabbi helped found Jewish employment and educational organizations and settlement houses, with the intent to hasten the assimilation of San Francisco's Russian Jews.[22]

In addition to his rabbinical successes, Voorsanger was an educator, journalist, and social activist. In 1894 he began regular lecturing (until his death in 1908) on a voluntary basis in the Semitic Department of the University of California, Berkeley, and annually he lectured on the Hebrew Bible at Stanford University. In 1895 he founded and edited for thirteen years with his brother A. W. Voorsanger the San Francisco periodical *Emanu-El*, which promoted the cause of ultra-Reform and became "one of the most articulate weeklies in North American Jewish life." He contributed to leading Jewish journals, including the *American Israelite*, and he had previously edited the New Orleans *Jewish South* (1881 to 1883), the Cincinnati *Sabbath Visitor* (1883 to 1886), and the San Francisco *Jewish Progress* (1893 to 1895). His admirers noted that he wrote "with remarkable fluency in a direct, terse style, for he had acquired the English idiom with great rapidity and seldom showed the influence of the Dutch or the German language."[23] Voorsanger published a biography of Moses Mendelssohn and a history of Emanu-El Temple that included a reasoned defense of Reform. He assisted in translating the biblical books of Obadiah and Jonah for the 1917 English-language Old Testament of the Jewish Publication Society, and he wrote articles on Palestine after his visit there.[24] Voorsanger served on countless religious, philanthropic, and civic organizations including the vice presidency of the California Red Cross, which he helped establish. For a man who lacked formal religious training, these were brilliant accomplishments.

Even more important to Judaism over time was Voorsanger's tutoring of the gifted teenage scholar Judah L. Magnes of Oakland, who as the founder and first president of The Hebrew University in Jerusalem was the greatest California-born rabbi and one of the outstanding public figures of the modern world. On the recommendation of Oakland's first rabbi, Myer Solomon Levy, Voorsanger in the early 1890s agreed to tutor Magnes in the sacred Hebrew texts. Throughout his high school years Magnes regularly crossed the bay by ferry to learn all he could from his Dutch mentor. In 1894 HUC admitted Magnes, in part because of Voorsanger's glowing recommendation, and Voorsanger corresponded regularly with his protégé in Cincinnati, taking a fatherly interest in his academic progress.

Following Magnes's ordination in 1900, Voorsanger invited him to preach at Temple Emanu-El. "Never have I felt so happy or proud as I do in making way for this lad," Voorsanger told his congregation, "whom I sent away with a benediction and who now

306

comes back a rabbi in Israel." Voorsanger even arranged for a stipend for Magnes to begin doctoral study in Germany.[25] "I have always hoped great things for you, and your going to Europe has always been part of my plans," Voorsanger declared to his understudy shortly before his ordination at Cincinnati. Hebrew Union College trained ministers and not scholars, Voorsanger noted, but the "pew is outgrowing the pulpit in intellectuality." Only "eminent scholars" can reach the young Jewish intelligentsia, the Rabbi continued. "I want you to become a scholar. I want you to have these years in Germany and a Ph.D. degree, and if possible a *Semicher* [diploma] from a European college."[26]

Magnes revered Voorsanger and was deeply affected by his intellect and wide community involvements. But the intellectual father and son gradually parted ways in the following years when Magnes committed himself to the Zionist cause. Voorsanger was much chagrined but gave Magnes his lukewarm blessing: "You have the future before you. If Zionism is your aim, concentrate." While the dream of a Jewish homeland is "chimerical" and "in no wise moral," yet "Jews in America need this vigorous touch of association. . . ." Zionist organizational efforts might give American Judaism "the great lever of ambition and loyalty" that it desperately needed. "I cannot be a Zionist," Voorsanger declared, "but I can admire . . . the persistency that seeks to regenerate Israel, to resuscitate its soul, to restore its honor, to rejuvenate its inheritance and I will quarrel with no adjectives in my anxiety to do honor to the man or men who will achieve this hope." The American Israel was Voorsanger's concern, not Palestinian Israel. Moreover Magnes's more conservative views and his incisive critiques of ultra-Reform Judaism for its vapid assimilation of American culture implicitly condemned life at Temple Emanu-El.[27]

Voorsanger's pulpit appointments, university lectures, and other work increasingly required proper credentials for the self-taught rabbi. Isaac Mayer Wise of HUC, the leading Reform rabbi in America, arranged in 1895 for the college to award him the unusual honorary degree of Bachelor of Theology. This brought Voorsanger a new five-year contract from Emanu-El Temple at an annual salary of $6,000.[28]

The rabbi's finest hour followed the 1906 San Francisco earthquake and fire that destroyed the heavily Jewish eastern part of the city. Ten thousand Jews lost their homes, and leading merchants and shopkeepers suffered fire losses in the tens of millions of dollars. Several synagogues and other Jewish institutions were destroyed, including the majestic Sutter Street Temple, which at the time was considered the seventh most beautiful synagogue building in the world. Through his tears at the loss of the synagogue and the venerated Torah scroll which had been donated by Moses Montefiore, as well as the loss of his prized library and all of the temple records and minute books, Rabbi Voorsanger immediately went to work. He organized relief efforts and reconstruction projects, and issued appeals for an estimated $100,000 in Jewish aid that he believed would be needed.

To his chagrin and frustration, American Jewry failed to respond to the disaster. In part this was the result of a report greatly downplaying Jewish homelessness by Judah Magnes, who had been sent to San Francisco by the National Conference of Jewish Charities to assess the damage to Jewish property by the quake and fire. Voorsanger publicly rebuked his former student, but the damage was done. The San Franciscans had to rebuild mainly with local funds. For visible and prestigious projects, these funds were obviously adequate and wealthy persons stepped forward. The merchants had recovered quickly and were soon doing a brisk business at new locations on swank midtown avenues such as Van Ness.[29] Emanu-El's membership after the fire actually increased to four hundred families and the entire experience of rebuilding restored the sense of mission of the pioneer years. This was Rabbi Voorsanger's theme at the rededication service of the temple. He concluded: "So shall this beautiful edifice, reconsecrated to its high mission, serve indeed as a sacred emblem of the redeemed city by the Gate, its beauty restored, its sins purged, its temple rebuilt, its children reunited in [their] mission."[30]

Voorsanger's vigorous relief efforts physically exhausted him and aggravated a cardiac problem. The unexpected death of his beloved wife, Eva, the next year further drained him. The following year, in April 1908, while vacationing at the Hotel Del Monte in Monterey, CA, he suffered a fatal heart attack. He was fifty six. From inauspicious beginnings as a poor teenaged immigrant without formal theological training, Voorsanger had parlayed his charismatic gifts and impressive innate abilities to reach the front ranks of the American rabbinate. In keeping with his mature status as the leading rabbi of the West Coast and as one of the most important spiritual leaders of American Reform Judaism in the first decade of the twentieth century, HUC had in 1903 very appropriately awarded him an honorary degree of Doctor of Divinity.[31]

Voorsanger's final bequest to American Jewry was his estimable sons, Dr. William C., Leon M., and Rabbi Elkan C. Voorsanger, although they ranked far below his intellectual protégé, Magnes.

William graduated in 1899 from the Stanford University Medical College, then known as Cooper's Medical College, and after studying for two years in Berlin and Vienna, he returned to San Francisco to practice his specialty, the treatment of tuberculosis. Leon engaged in the flavoring-extract business in the city. Both were members of Congregation Emanu-El. Rabbi Jacob Voorsanger's special concern fell on his youngest son Elkan who he patiently prepared for the rabbinate. Elkan was ordained by HUC and became a Junior Rabbi of a congregation in Saint Louis until May of 1917, when after the United States declared war on Germany, he volunteered as a military chaplain and left for France. Elkan Voorsanger was commissioned in the field as the first Jewish chaplain of the American Expeditionary Force. He thereby became the first ordained rabbi to receive rank in the U.S. Armed Forces. He advanced in rank from private to captain by the war's end and was decorated for bravery in combat with the Purple Heart. Elkan stayed on in Europe following the armistice as head of the first Joint Distribution Committee in Poland to assist war refugees. Subsequently, he returned to the United States and for many years served as executive director of the Jewish Welfare Federation of Milwaukee, a service organization for war veterans. He died in 1963 after a life of public service. Although never active in the pulpit, he was always a "rabbi at heart."[32]

The Magnin Clan, Clothiers and a Rabbi

Just as Rabbi Jacob Voorsanger dominated West Coast Judaism at the turn of the century, another rabbi of Dutch ancestry, Edgar Fogel Magnin of Los Angeles's B'nai B'rith Congregation (Wilshire Boulevard Temple since 1929), became the spiritual leader of Reform Judaism in southern California in the twentieth century. Magnin was born in 1890 in San Francisco into the well-known family of Dutch clothing merchants and, later, department store magnates. Like Jacob Voorsanger, he became a rabbi, lecturer, author, and civic leader.[33]

Isaac Magnin (Moeijen), the patriarch of the clan, was born in 1842 in Groningen, the oldest son of a Russian father and Dutch mother. When Isaac was eight years old, his parents emigrated to the United States.[34] As a teenager Isaac was an itinerant merchant in Texas and New Mexico until he enlisted in the army during the Civil War. After he was mustered out at war's end, he emigrated to London, where he opened an arts goods store, married the Dutch-born

Mary Ann Cohen in October 1865 at the Great Synagogue, and began a family. A decade later, in 1876, he returned with his wife and seven young children to the United States, coming directly to California by way of Cape Horn.

The family settled temporarily in Oakland, where Isaac took a menial job as a woodcarver at Solomon Gump's mirrors and picture framing shop, and Mary Ann, a skilled seamstress, made fine baby clothes at home. At her insistence Isaac quit his job and began peddling clothes from a backpack, while she continued her needlework. Soon the family moved across the bay to San Francisco where Mary Ann opened her first store to sell elegant women's and children's clothing. As a dutiful Jewish wife, she gave the store her husband's name. The inventory included her handmade silk blouses and bridal trousseaus stitched from the finest imported fabrics. She did her own purchasing and supervised garment cutting, sewing, and alterations. Her timing was as good as her taste in fabrics. I. Magnin became the major provider of luxury women's clothing in the San Francisco area in the prosperous years after the Gold Rush.[35]

One gets no hint of Mary Ann's role from the 1880 federal census report in which Isaac's occupation is listed as keeps a fancy bazaar, while Mary Ann is merely keeping house and raising seven young children. Fourteen-year-old Samuel, the oldest son, was an apprentice tailor working under his mother's watchful eye. When the younger sons Joseph and Emanuel John finished their schooling, their parents likewise introduced them to the business, which remained a family affair for at least three generations. Mary Ann Magnin's seminal part in the business was typical of the Jewish economy in the Netherlands, in which married women working at home happily helped cut diamonds, prepare tobacco, or sew garments for their husbands' petty trades. Among the Dutch, only Jews appreciated women's work and Jewish women alone wished to be business partners even when there was no urgent need.[36]

Out of these inauspicious beginnings came the Golden Lady of the West, the renowned I. Magnin and Co. Department Store of San Francisco, located on Market Street, the young city's main thoroughfare. It was the first retail store in the city to display merchandise in beautiful cabinets and showcases accented with gilded mirrors. Isaac and Mary Ann were also among the first in California to realize the potential of branching out, and they opened a store in Los Angeles in 1893. As the business grew the Magnins established their own buying office in New York City in order to keep abreast of the latest fashion trends and stay ahead of the competition. Emanuel John became president of the company in 1907 on Isaac's death, and he headed the New York City office of the firm. Younger son Victor A. was a salesman for the business. The oldest son Joseph, formerly a factory manager for the firm, had already established his own store in San Francisco, J. Magnin and Co. The youngest son, Grover A., and only child born in the city (in 1886), was by 1916 vice president of the company, manager of the San Francisco store, and in command of all California operations.

Although Mary Ann Magnin had retired from day-to-day operations by 1900, she kept an active hand in policy decisions and general oversight. For many years her chauffeur drove her from her home in the Saint Francis Hotel for her daily rounds of the store, which after the 1906 earthquake and fire was rebuilt at the corner of Grant and Geary streets. Business historian Milton Moskowitz reports that in later years her maid pushed her up and down the aisles in a wheelchair, and she is reputed to have come to the store near the end of her life by ambulance and stretcher.[37]

The Magnin family were among the most prominent in San Francisco. Progenitor Isaac had joined the Masonic Order in London and rose to the highest rank in the United States. The family affiliated with the prestigious Temple Emanu-El.[38] During the Second World War, Grover Magnin was treasurer of the American Council for Judaism, an anti-Zionist organization. The Magnin family, like the Voorsangers, indeed, the majority of Emanu-El Temple's members, strongly opposed Jewish nationalism. The Magnin men were all upwardly mobile American businessmen who were active in the Masons and belonged to the prestigious country clubs. But they also maintained minimal Jewish involvements, notably the San Francisco Federation of Jewish Charities. Eventually, the I. Magnin and Co. Department Stores passed to Isaac's grandson, Cyril Magnin, who was born in 1899 and continued in the business into the 1970s. By 1980 I. Magnin and Co. operated twenty-four stores across America and had become part of the giant Federated Department Stores chain.[39]

Rabbi Edgar Fogel Magnin (1890 to 1985) was the most illustrious member of the family in the third generation. Son of Isaac's oldest son Samuel, he studied at HUC along with Elkan Voorsanger, for whom he later wrote a glowing memorial tribute. After his ordination in 1914 he accepted the call of Reform Congregation Temple Israel in Stockton, CA, where he served for a year before being elected in 1915 as associate rabbi of Congregation B'nai B'rith in Los Angeles. In 1919 he assumed full leadership of the congregation.[40] During his rabbinate of more than fifty-three years at Wilshire Boulevard Temple, this congregation became one of the largest and most influential synagogues in the United States. Described as "outspoken, colorful, forceful," Magnin for decades led the Jewish community through many of its key institutions—the Los Angeles Jewish Community Council, Cedars-Sinai Medical Center, B'nai B'rith, Hillel Council, the University Religious Conference, and the California School of HUC. He wrote columns for the *Los Angeles Herald Examiner* and the Anglo-Jewish weekly *Heritage* and lectured at the University of Southern California. Later he became an adjunct professor of homiletics at the HUC Jewish Institute of Religion. He developed a close friendship with Richard Nixon who chose him to deliver the prayer at his presidential inaugural in 1969 and in 1973 he spoke at a White House ecumenical worship service.[41]

Conclusion

San Francisco's Dutch Jews had joined the American mainstream. They were thoroughly assimilated second- and third-generation immigrants who rejected old-fashioned ways in religion and culture. Jewish nationalism and Zionism had no appeal whatsoever, nor did Orthodox traditionalism in the synagogue. They were Masons, Republicans, country club members, and businessmen who participated in Jewish affairs mainly through charitable activities. This is in marked contrast to their conservative coreligionists in the East, who preferred Netherlandic synagogues of the Orthodox stripe and who married fellow Hollanders whenever possible. San Francisco was farther than 3,500 miles from New York, but it was light years apart culturally for the Holland Jews.

Chapter 10

THE "ESSENCE" OF DUTCH JEWRY IN AMERICA

This close view of the local histories of Dutch Jews in North America reveals a surprising pattern in their settlement. Where one might expect from their relatively small number and double identity a quick and traceless absorption into American Jewry; nevertheless, they held on to their Dutchness into the second generation at least. The story began in the 1650s with the Jews who came from the Netherlands and Dutch colonies in Latin America to New Amsterdam. They were in pursuit of commercial dealings throughout the Atlantic world under the aegis of the WIC. These forerunners opened the way for Jewish settlement in North America by securing legal and property rights for Jews. Over the next 150 years, other Dutch found their way to the thriving Jewish commercial centers of Newport, Charleston, Richmond, and Philadelphia. In every Jewish center at least one Dutch family or group of families contributed in a significant way to synagogue life, charitable societies, and business activities.

By the middle decades of the nineteenth century, from 1850 to 1870, when there exists a nearly complete listing of Dutch households in the federal population censuses, one-half of the Dutch Jews lived in New York City and Brooklyn, and one-fifth were in Philadelphia and Boston (Table 10.1).[1] In 1850 New Orleans had

Table 10.1
Dutch Jewish Urban Population, 1850, 1860, 1870*

State	City	1850		1860		1870	
		N	%	N	%	N	%
CA	San Francisco	0	0	41	2	65	2
IL	Chicago	0	0	39	2	166	4
LA	New Orleans	178	18	98	4	33	1
MD	Baltimore	103	10	167	7	121	3
MA	Boston	62	6	269	12	375	10
MI	Detroit	0	0	49	2	103	3
MO	Saint Louis	13	1	26	1	85	2
NJ	Newark	5	0	40	2	54	1
NY	Buffalo	17	2	32	1	37	1
NY	Brooklyn	0	0	43	2	196	5
NY	Rochester	0	0	24	1	23	1
NY	New York	429	43	792	35	1676	45
NY	Troy	0	0	18	1	23	1
OH	Cleveland	4	0	27	1	27	1
OH	Cincinnati	12	1	74	3	97	3
OH	Toledo	0	0	0	0	34	1
PA	Philadelphia	148	15	428	19	357	10
PA	Pittsburgh	0	0	0	0	123	3
WI	Milwaukee	0	0	20	1	14	0
	Other cities	23	2	49	2	146	4

*The totals include all persons of Dutch stock, including spouses of non-Dutch. Hence, these numbers may exceed the household totals in the tables listing "Dutch Jewish Household Heads and Single Adults."

Source: Compiled from Robert P. Swierenga, comp., *Dutch Households in U.S. Population Censuses: 1850, 1860, 1870*, 3 vols. (Wilmington, DE, 1987).

one-fifth, but only a few families remained by 1870. Baltimore's share likewise declined, from 10 percent in 1850 to only 3 percent in 1870, while Boston's share increased from 6 to 10 percent and Chicago's climbed to 4 percent by 1870. Some twenty-five other cities from Newark to San Francisco had the remaining one-fifth, but none had more than 3 percent. The nuclear family was the norm everywhere; over 90 percent of Dutch Jews lived with their immediate family members. Half of the small remainder lived in extended families and half boarded out. While families lived separately they were not isolated because they increasingly resided in multifamily dwellings. In the censuses of 1850, 1860, and 1870, households living in flats and apartments increased sharply from 31 to 44 to 59

Table 10.2
Dutch Jewish Occupational Distribution: 1850, 1860, 1870

	1850		1860		1870	
	N	%	N	%	N	%
Professional	7	3	9	1	11	1
Managerial	10	4	23	4	72	6
Petty Merchants	146	61	317	53	478	42
Skilled/Semiskilled	70	29	228	38	518	46
Unskilled	6	3	26	4	49	4

Source: Compiled from Robert P. Swierenga, comp., *Dutch Households in U.S. Population Censuses.*

percent. Conversely, those in single family dwellings decreased from 56 to 49 to 39 percent. The percentage boarding out decreased from 12 to 7 to 5 percent. The evidence is clear that Dutch Jews lived at home until marriage. Their young people seldom boarded out except in times of dire financial need shortly after immigration.

The Dutch Jewish immigrants were neither poverty stricken nor affluent but middling in economic status.[2] The very poorest could not afford to emigrate and the wealthiest had little incentive to do so. According to the U.S. federal censuses, only 10 percent of male household heads reported owning real estate worth $500 or more, but 47 percent reported owning personal property, half worth less than $500 and half more. This low rate of owning property should not be surprising since 85 percent were first-generation immigrants and the average age of the entire Dutch Jewish population was only twenty-two years. Occupationally, half were petty businessmen, including a few professionals and managers. Most of the remainder were skilled or semiskilled craftsmen, including a smattering of unskilled laborers (Table 10.2).

In addition to their Jewish identity, Dutch Jews in America were a product of two cultures—that of their homeland and that of their adopted country. As their host societies changed under the forces of modernization, they changed as well. The Netherlands and the United States had similar legal structures.[3] Both had democratic governments where minorities were in theory protected by law. The American Bill of Rights of 1790 and the Netherlands Emancipation Law of 1796 assured these seminal rights and freedoms. Each citizen thus had the ostensible freedom to seek their own identity. But while public policy in both countries *permitted* cultural pluralism, governments actively promoted acculturation and even total assimilation. Dutchification in the Netherlands found its counterpart in Americanization in the United States. Thus, the pressures to integrate into the majority culture were strong, but yet it was possible for Jews to retain their identity. They could in Jonathan Sarna's words "be active Jews and active citizens at the same time."[4]

Their culture was a synthesis, the product of a felt need both to preserve their Jewish identity and to survive in a dominant Gentile society. Traditionalists and integrationists clashed over which moves and practices to preserve and which to jettison. Defenders of Orthodoxy such as the Reverend Samuel Myer Isaacs and committed Americanizers such as Rabbi Jacob Voorsanger set the outer limits, but most followers chose a middle course. They balanced their Jewishness, which came from within, and their European or American culture, which came from without.

What was the "essence" of Dutch Jewry in the nineteenth century? J. Michman defines the essence as their "attachment to and solidarity with Judaism."[5] Were Jews in Holland both Jews and Europeans? Were the immigrants to the United States both Jews and Americans? What was the Dutch part of their Jewry? The Jewish part? The American part? In the Netherlands the watershed event was the Napoleonic conquest. The French regime transformed the Netherlands from a particularistic republic to a centralized and bureaucratic nation-state, and subsequent Dutch monarchs continued the process of Hollandization begun in 1795.

How did Dutch Jewry fare under the forces of homogenization? Although the largely illiterate and impoverished Ashkenazi masses continued to rely on imported German leaders for their synagogues and schools, nevertheless their community remained very cohesive. The vast majority clung to traditional Orthodoxy, even if somewhat petrified, and rejected anything "new" in science or religion. Such rigidity made Dutch Jewish customs and patterns of thought brittle and unable to withstand the onslaught of secular socialism in the late nineteenth century. But for many decades they assimilated more slowly than did Jews in Germany, Austria, France, and Italy because of the highly segmented nature of Dutch society which evolved into a formal religio-political segregation or pillarization (*verzuiling*) in the late nineteenth century.[6]

The Jews did not take advantage of the system and establish separate religious day schools like the Calvinists and Roman Catholics, but they did maintain social solidarity, even while becoming increasingly cosmopolitan and secular in their way of life, values, and occupations. Especially in Amsterdam many spurned the synagogue, openly desecrated the Sabbath, and ignored *kashrut* (kosher laws), but in the pivotal life passages of birth, marriage, and death, they maintained strong links with their heritage. They had their infant sons circumcised by the *mohel*, they married in the synagogue, and were buried in consecrated ground. Amsterdam also remained the administrative center of fund-raising for Jews in Palestine and Dutch Jews participated in international movements such as the Alliance Israélite Universelle (1870s) and Zionism (1890s), although they eschewed the World Union of Progressive Judaism (1920s).[7]

Whether traditional Jewish society in the Netherlands broke down gradually, as M. H. Gans maintains, or suddenly in the 1870s as a result of the expansion of the diamond trade, as Jozeph Michman asserts, Jews and Gentiles in the Netherlands seldom mingled.[8] The majority culture with its utilitarian ethic tolerated Jews for their economic contributions while they continued to discriminate against them socially. The Jews perforce formed their own societies, associations, and newspapers, even as they accepted the Dutch cultural imperative "Do as we do" in language, dress, housing, and even in values. Some went so far as to abandon all things Jewish and to blend into Netherlandic Gentile society. Dutch Jews espoused Dutch bourgeois values of utility and social justice.[9]

It was this special Jewish adaptation to the Dutch national character that inspired Sigmond Seeligmann to designate them as "species hollandia judaica." Dutch Jews always considered themselves as different from German Jews, as having a separate development from the rest of European Jewry. The Emancipation Law brought this "unique coloration," this independent character, to Dutch Jews in the period after 1825 and the subsequent government policy of religious pillarization enabled them to preserve their identity, despite the social pressures for Hollandization.[10]

The changes in Netherlandic Jewry in the course of the nineteenth century from Yiddish to Dutch, from Orthodox to socialist, from ghettoized to acculturated, and from tradesmen to craftsmen are all reflected in the American immigrants. The very early arrivals during the Napoleonic wars, 1790–1825, were preemancipation Jews, in the sense that the 1796 law had little impact in their lives. They were Europeanized Jews from the higher social strata and accustomed to international business activities in Germany, England, and the Caribbean islands. They had developed a strong self-identity during several centuries as a minority group, one that easily blended into Ashkenazi Jewry in North America and the Caribbean basin. They were not ethnically segregated but lived among other Jews and also Gentiles.

The second wave from 1825 to 1870 were postemancipation Jews who, while still Orthodox and probably Yiddish-speaking, were increasingly Dutch in language and culture. They were products of government day schools, petty merchants imbued with middle-class values, who clung to Orthodoxy more for its practice than substance. Emanuel Goldsmith (Goudsmit) of New York City described their sterile Orthodoxy in his 1848 letter to a friend in Amsterdam: The observant Dutch are "ignorant just like the English Jews and devout"; he continues, the rest are "no Jews at all."[11] It was this devout group who sought to maintain the pure Amsterdam worship rites by founding Netherlandic congregations in New York, Philadelphia, and Boston in the 1840s and 1850s. But the synagogue records of Bnai Israel of New York were kept in English from the beginning in 1847. The immigrants also established Dutch cemeteries and benevolent societies. That they succeeded in forming congregations only in three cities testifies more to their lack of sufficient members than to their ardent desires. Even these successes were short-lived. After two generations, in the 1890s, the time for nationality synagogues seemed to be over. Even the ardently Orthodox Reverend Samuel Myer Isaacs in 1875 accepted the idea of a common simplified worship rite for all American synagogues: "The badge we all should have proudly worn is that of American Jews," he declared.[12] In family and business affairs there is much evidence that parents arranged marriages with other Dutch families whenever possible, even linking families in distant cities. Similarly, Dutch Jewish businessmen created partnerships with fellow countrymen.

The third wave from 1870 to 1915 represented the proletariat who were increasingly secular in religion, socialist in politics, and worked as wage earners in the new tobacco and diamond trades. They still practiced the rites of passage of Judaism—the ceremonies of circumcision, *bar mitzvah*, marriage, and burial—but Jewish clubs, societies, and lodges took the place of the synagogue in their daily lives. The Orthodox Netherlandic synagogues particularly had no appeal. These liberals rejected traditional religion with its "ghetto existence" that was so "materially and spiritually suffocating." They had literally been swept away by the "revolutionary secularization process" that permeated liberal circles in the Netherlands after midcentury.[13]

For each of these immigrant waves, the London stopover of as many as a quarter of the migrants was of inestimable importance in hastening Americanization. In London the Dutch Jews learned the English language and culture, they intermarried with English and other Jews, they established commercial ties, and they adapted to the more westernized worship style of the London synagogues that as early as 1817 included regular preaching in English.

Although it is difficult clearly to differentiate the Dutch, Jewish, and American parts of Dutch Jewry in America, some characteristics can be identified. The Dutch part brought a commitment to Amsterdam Orthodox traditionalism and resistance to Reform. The Dutch prized social justice and fought for civil rights. They willingly interacted socially with Gentiles without feeling threatened in their Jewishness. They were family oriented and looked to the extended family for assistance in migration, in business dealings, and for perpetuating the Dutch cuisine, such as Mrs. Gompers's Dutch kitchen. Dutch craftsmen also brought special skills such as diamond-cutting and polishing.

The Dutch influence largely explains why Dutch Jews in America were so little attracted to Reform Judaism and its Americanizing practices of worship. First, Reform was not indigenous in the Netherlands. It originated in Germany and the Dutch always considered it as a foreign corruption. Jewish religious leaders also actively resisted Reform. As a result, it barely penetrated Netherlands Jewry until the twentieth century. Second, Dutch Jewish immigrants to America in the 1870s and 1880s were a largely secularized proletariat for whom socialism had more appeal than Judaism of any stripe. Samuel Gompers and his fellow cigarmakers put their trust in the American labor movement. Even Reform Judaism, which had gained ground rapidly in America, was too conservative politically and socially for the sweated workers. Reform appealed to upwardly mobile businessmen and professionals who belonged to Jewish Masonic lodges and B'nai B'rith.

The Jewish contribution to Dutch Jewry was the Yiddish language and literature, a confident self-identity as a tiny minority in a Gentile culture, the flexibility to adapt to Protestant America in order to survive (as they had done in Protestant Holland), and the reliance (and even preference) for lay religious leaders and lay control of the congregation and synagogue. The Dutch demonstrated their thoroughgoing Jewish identity by their impassioned response to worldwide antisemitic incidents in the mid-nineteenth century. The Damascus Affair of 1840, the protests in the 1850s against the U.S. government's proposed diplomatic recognition of Switzerland, and the Mortara "kidnapping" case in Italy in 1859 all found Hollanders acting in concert with American Jewry in the international crusades spawned by these events. The Reverend Samuel Myer Isaacs and other Dutch Jews served on protest committees, and Isaacs joined with leaders such as Isaac Lesser to use these political movements as a vehicle to galvanize American Jewry.

319

The American contribution to Dutch Jewry was the English language, public day school education with all of its social and cultural overtones of American nationalism, and a wide open business environment that allowed Jewish entrepreneurs to flourish. But conditions in the American job market also transformed many an unskilled immigrant into a sweatshop worker. In religion, the Jews took on the trappings of American Protestantism in worship style and congregational life. They had ministers to represent the body to the general public and to preach weekly topical sermons, and they ran Sunday schools. Dutch Jews demonstrated their American nationalism by supporting the Revolutionary cause, the Second War with England, the Mexican War, and the Union side in the Civil War. Their sons fought in each of these conflicts, while the fathers invested in government bonds, sold military supplies, and otherwise supported the cause. Most Dutch Jews voted the Republican ticket, as did Jews generally, from 1860 until after the Great Depression. They were influenced by Protestants in their politics as in their religious practices.

In sum, the early national period was the Dutch era in American Jewry when Dutch Jewish immigrants from Amsterdam provided leadership in synagogue, school, and society. But over the middle decades Dutch Jewish homogeneity and Orthodoxy gave way to the heterogeneity and heterodoxy that characterizes modern Jewry. Although the rate varied, depending on the distinct character of the individual city settlement, within two generations the Dutch Jews had lost first their Dutchness and then their Orthodoxy. Like the English, Polish, and even German Jews to some extent, they were absorbed into the greater Jewish-American community that, in turn, had accommodated itself to Protestant voluntarism and denominationalism by espousing German Reform. The Dutch were so successful at blending into American Jewry that they were all but invisible by the end of the century. Now one hundred years later, the story of their lives has been retold and they will not be forgotten again.

APPENDIX I:
IMMIGRATION STATISTICS

The actual number of Dutch Jewish overseas emigrants in the nineteenth century is unknown and must be estimated indirectly from data of the receiving countries. Official Netherlands government statistics, which are available annually for the years 1847 to 1880 are totally inadequate. They total only 285 households and single adults, or 572 persons.[1] This is a yearly average of only 19 persons, which is unreasonable given the Jewish population of 70,000 in these years.[2]

That the official statistics greatly understate the true overseas emigration in these years is attested by a tally of Dutch-born Jews in the U.S. manuscript population censuses. Table AI.1 provides the actual and estimated number of Dutch-born Jews for each census from 1800 through 1880. From these figures I computed the immigration during each decade using the method of Pieter R. D. Stokvis: immigration equals the sum of the decadal increase in Dutch-born plus the sum of the death rate per thousand average decadal population in the Netherlands, plus the estimated 5 percent remigration rate until 1880.[3] Based on this formula, sixty-five hundred Dutch Jews emigrated to the United States from 1800 to 1880. For the shorter period 1850 to 1880, the total estimated immigration was fifty-three hundred, or nearly ten times the official total.

Besides the sixty-five hundred Dutch Jews who went to the United States at least ten thousand went to England in the nineteenth century. Between 1800 and 1880 Jews in England increased from twenty thousand to sixty thousand; and many were immigrants

Table AI.1
Dutch Jewish Immigration Estimated from U.S.
Census Data, 1800–1880

Census Year	No.	C_1+C_2 C_2-C_1	2	Est. Mortality*Deaths	Est. Net Migration	Est. 5% Remigration	Est. Immigration per Decade
1800	100†	100	105	0.309	32	137	7	144
1810	110†	10	115	0.309	35	150	8	158
1820	120‡	10	120	0.284	34	154	8	162
1830	320‡	200	220	0.279	62	282	14	296
1840	350†	30	335	0.269	90	425	21	446
1850	400	50	375	0.276	103	478	24	502
1860	1,000	950	700	0.258	181	881	44	925
1870	1,500	500	1,250	0.249	311	1,561	78	1,639
1880	2,000†	500	1,750	0.243	425	2,175	109	2,284
Totals					1,273	6,243	313	6,556

*Ten times the average death rate in the Netherlands during the preceding decade, from E. W. Hofstee, *Korte Demografische Geschiedenis van Nederland van 1800 Tot Heden* (Haarlem, 1981), Table 1, 122–23.
†Estimated.
‡Excludes children ten years and under, and black servants in Dutch-headed households.

Sources: Compiled from Ira Rosenwaike, "The Jewish Population of the United States as Estimated from the Census of 1820," *American Jewish Historical Quarterly* 53 (Dec. 1963): 131–78; Ira Rosenwaike, *On the Edge of Greatness: A Portrait of American Jewry in the Early National Period* (Cincinnati, 1985), 112–64; Robert P. Swierenga, comp. *Dutch Households in U.S. Population Censuses, 1850, 1860, 1870: An Alphabetical Listing by Family Heads*, 3 vols. (Wilmington, DE, 1987). The methodology is derived from Pieter R. D. Stokvis, "Dutch International Migration 1815–1910," in Robert P. Swierenga, ed., *The Dutch in America: Immigration, Settlement, and Cultural Change* (New Brunswick, NJ, 1985), 57–60, Table 2.6.

from Holland, northern Germany, and Poland.[4] One scholar noted that the numerous Dutch arrivals "helped to give a pronounced Dutch cast to a large part of English Jewry."[5] One can, therefore, accept the ten thousand figure as a lower-bound estimate. Many Dutch Jews in England migrated to the United States after a residence in London of up to ten years. Others emigrated to the Caribbean, especially to the Dutch colonies of Curaçao and Surinam, although this stream dwindled after 1800. Thus, overseas migration of Dutch Jews was endemic in the nineteenth century.

Why was Jewish emigration missed by Dutch officialdom? The main reason was the common pattern of cross-Channel movement, which was viewed simply as international business travel or labor migration, not true emigration. When some of these migrants moved on to the United States, Dutch officials had no interest. Second, one-fourth of the emigrants (seventeen hundred) departed the Netherlands before 1847 when official registration began for overseas emigrants. Third, previous record-linkage studies, based on nominal records of the United States and the Netherlands, demonstrate that urban migrants more likely departed for overseas destinations without registering with local officials, as Dutch law required. Such urban emigrants were also most likely to escape notice by local government functionaries.[6] Dutch Jewish emigrants fit this urban profile of unregistered emigrants; most lived in the crowded Amsterdam Jewish Quarter.

APPENDIX II:
DUTCH JEWISH HOUSEHOLD HEADS AND WORKING ADULTS IN NEW YORK: 1850, 1860, 1870 CENSUSES

Name	Ward	Year	Ward	Year	Ward	Year
Aarons, Jacob	7	1870				
Abrams, Jacob	11	1870				
Abrahams, Joseph	13	1870				
Abrahams, Samuel	13	1870				
Adam, Jacob	11	1870				
Anderson, Israel	11	1860				
Appel, Maurits	11	1870				
Aslone, Emanuel	20	1860				
Assenheim, Joseph	6	1860				
Bache, Solomon	6	1860				
Bamberger, Aaron	11	1870				
Barbara, Moses	6	1850				
Baruch, David	17	1870				
Barzilli, Emanuel	8	1870				
Beck, Isaac	11	1870				
Belyne, Bernard	11	1870				
Bismuntil, Joseph	11	1870				
Blankenstein, Levy	13	1870				
Blitz, Aaron	11	1870				
Blitz, Solomon	11	1860				
Block, William	20	1870				
Boas, William	11	1870				
Bosing, Joseph	11	1870				
Bossie, Jacob	14	1860				

Name	Ward	Year	Ward	Year	Ward	Year
Broek, Abraham	17	1850				
Broek, Moses	11	1870				
Bult, Philip	11	1870				
Camik, Abe	21	1870				
Canis, Isaac	14	1860				
Canter, Alexander	6	1850	16	1860	16	1870
Canter, David	22	1870				
Canter, Morris	6	1870				
Canter, Solomon	16	1860	16	1870		
Casner, Levi	11	1870				
Caspers, William S.	13	1870				
Charles, Samuel	11	1870				
Citters, Rosa	7	1870				
Cohen, A. A.	2	1850				
Cohen, Alexander	11	1870				
Cohen, Elisha	11	1870				
Cohen, Hannah	6	1860				
Cohen, Herman	4	1860				
Cohen, H.	4	1860				
Cohen, Louis	11	1860	11	1870		
Cohen, Lyon	11	1870				
Cohen, Matthew S.	14	1850				
Cohen, Moses	6	1850				
Cohen, Moses	11	1870				
Cohen, M. S.	17	1870				
Cohen, William	14	1860				
Cohn, Barney	11	1870				
Cohn, Jacob	11	1870				
Cohn, Louis	10	1870				
Cole, Henry	11	1870				
Coleman, Moses	9	1850				
Cooper, Isaac	11	1870				
Copeler, Levy	6	1860				
Corlander, Eleazer	7	1870				
Costman, Abraham	8	1870				
Couse, Barnard	7	1870				
Cuntz, Isaac	21	1870				
Dammers, Rachel	8	1860				
Davidson, David	20	1870				
Davis, John M.	4	1850				
Debane, Abraham	7	1870				
de Bowen, Abraham	11	1870				
de Bruin, M.	4	1850				
de Brus, Hart	7	1870				
Decasseres, Isaac	7	1870				
de Graff, Levi	11	1870				
de Groot, Rebecca	6	1860				
de Groot, Louis	1	1870				
de Kan, Elizabeth	11	1870				

Name	Ward	Year	Ward	Year	Ward	Year
de Koehena, David	17	1870				
de Leeuw, Simon	16	1870				
de Leeuw, William	17	1870				
de Lerden, Morris	17	1860				
Delmond, Jacob	13	1870				
de Marks, Solomon	9	1850				
de Markus, Lucius	22	1870				
Demeza, David	9	1870				
Demprez, Abram	6	1860				
de Sapia, Barth	14	1850				
Desendorf, L. E.	21	1870				
de Silva, Moses	9	1870				
de Vos, Aaron	9	1850				
de Vos, Isaac	14	1850	6	1860	10	1870
de Vries, George G.	13	1870				
de Vries, Jacob	11	1870				
de Weiser, Moses	7	1860				
de Wolf, Moses	12	1860	10	1870		
de Wolf, Wolf	6	1850				
de Young, Emanuel	7	1850	22	1870		
de Young, Israel	8	1860				
de Young, John	13	1870				
de Young, Joseph	4	1850				
de Young, Joseph	6	1850	11	1870		
de Young, Solomon	9	1860	16	1870		
Dillon, Moses	22	1870				
Disseldorf, Allen	6	1850				
Dressen, Jacob	14	1870				
Dreyfus, Albertus	9	1860				
Dreyfus, B.	21	1860				
Dreyfus, Moses	11	1870				
Edesheim, Louis	13	1870				
Elias, Emanuel	4	1850				
Emilburg, Richard	11	1870				
Ephraim, Henry	11	1850				
Ernst, Abraham	13	1870				
Ernst, Joseph	12	1870				
Ernst, John M.	9	1860				
Feddelson, Abraham	17	1850				
Feddelson, William	17	1850				
Fellerman, Edward	4	1850	20	1870		
Fellerman, Israel	4	1850				
Fellerman, Levi	4	1850	4	1860		
Fellerman, Moses	4	1850				
Fellerman, S.	4	1860				
Ferraris, Jacob	6	1860				
Finian, Aaron	11	1870				
Finkburg, Lydia	17	1850	9	1860		
Fleisher, M.	4	1860				

Name	Ward	Year	Ward	Year	Ward	Year
Fles, Henry	11	1860				
Fles, Isaac	11	1870				
Fleshen, M.	4	1860				
Folenhofer, Sam	11	1870				
Frank, Ignatz	7	1860				
Frank, Isaac	11	1870				
Frank, Jacob	7	1860				
Frankfort, Julius	11	1870				
Freiber, Vove	13	1870				
Freich, Isaac	6	1850				
Frenchman, J.	17	1870				
Frenchman, Moses	11	1870				
Gabay, Henry A.	8	1870				
Gabay, Raphael	10	1870				
Gans, Isaac	17	1870				
Garritson, David	13	1870				
Gendering, William	13	1870				
Gerrits, Solomon	6	1870				
Goedhart, Michael	6	1860	11	1870		
Goedhart, Morris	21	1870				
Goedhart, Samuel	11	1870				
Goldberg, Myer	11	1870				
Goldfish, Abram	11	1870				
Goldfish, George	11	1870				
Goldfish, Louis	11	1870				
Goldsmit, Emanuel	4	1860				
Goldsmit, Isaac	14	1860				
Goldsmith, Gerald	19	1870				
Goldsmith, Henry	8	1850	20	1860	20	1870
Goldsmith, John	17	1870				
Goldsmith, Morris	20	1870				
Goldstein, Israel	11	1870				
Gompers, Solomon	11	1870				
Gomperts, Louis	4	1850				
Gomperts, Moses	13	1870				
Gomperts, Samuel	11	1870				
Gosling, Leonard	1	1850	9	1860		
Gottlieb, Hyman	20	1870				
Gottschalk, George	11	1870				
Granders, Matthew	14	1860				
Gratz, Aaron	17	1860				
Green, Matthew	11	1860				
Greenberg, Abraham	21	1870				
Haan, Eleazer	10	1870				
Hacker, Elkan S.	16	1870				
Hacker, Henry	11	1860				
Halberstadt, Isaac	7	1870				
Halpster, Elias A.	14	1850				
Hamburg, Elkan	11	1870				

Name	Ward	Year	Ward	Year	Ward	Year
Hamburger, Charles	11	1870				
Hamburger, Julius	6	1850				
Hamel, Israel	7	1870				
Hamel, Moses	11	1870				
Harmon, Meyer	4	1850				
Harris, Amelia	16	1860	20	1870		
Hart, Benjamin	6	1850				
Hart, Henry	9	1850				
Hart, L. J.	7	1870				
Haym, John	7	1860				
Herman, Abram S.	11	1860				
Herzog, Frederich	21	1860				
Hess, Jacob	16	1860				
Heyman, Emanuel	7	1860				
Holstein, Moses	7	1870				
Honing, Ben	11	1870				
Horowitz, W. L.	21	1860				
Hurtz, Benjamin	18	1860				
Hurtz, Jacob	18	1860				
Hyman, Esther	6	1860				
Hyman, Henry	8	1860	21	1870		
Hyman, Sophia	8	1860				
Hymans, Henry	9	1860				
Isaacs, Aaron	17	1870				
Isaacs, Isaac	16	1860				
Isaacs, Joel	6	1850	16	1860		
Isaacs, Lena	7	1860				
Isaacs, Myer S.	4	1860				
Isaacs, Samuel M.	15	1850	8	1860	22	1870
Israel, Samuel	16	1870				
Israels, Lehman	16	1860	16	1870		
Jackson, Isaac	10	1870				
Jacobs, Abraham	13	1870				
Jacobs, Isaac	13	1870				
Jacobs, Julia	13	1870				
Jacobs, Morris	4	1850				
Jacobs, Philip	7	1860	7	1870		
Jacobs, Samuel	6	1860	13	1870		
Jacobs, Solomon	11	1870				
Jacobs, Wolf	8	1870				
Jacobson, Joseph	10	1870				
Jacobson, Leon	18	1860				
Jessurun, Joshua	22	1870				
Joseph, Samuel	16	1870				
Kan, Jacob	11	1870				
Kan, Morris	11	1870				
Kandler, Moses	11	1870				
Karelsen, Ephraim	14	1860				
Karsten, Joseph	13	1870				

Name	Ward	Year	Ward	Year	Ward	Year
Kasner, Levi	11	1870				
Kaufman, Nathan	11	1870				
Keizer, David	6	1850				
Keyzer, Michael	14	1860				
Kese, Kasper	17	1850				
Kingsburg, Henry	11	1870				
Kingsburg, Solomon	11	1870				
Knockel, Meyer	10	1870				
Kohen, Jacob	17	1870				
Kohen, Myer	20	1860				
Kohn, Henry	11	1870				
Korper, Louis	6	1870				
Krauss, Jacob	10	1870				
Kuhn, Henry	11	1870				
Kuhnsberg, Moritz	17	1870				
Kuit, Nathan	11	1870				
Ladifelt, Philip	13	1870				
Lampert, Jacob	13	1870				
Lampert, M.	4	1850				
Lampert, Sarah	6	1870				
Lamsteen, Jacob	9	1860				
Lamel, Morris	9	1870				
Lang, Arthur	7	1860				
Lansburg, Johannes	9	1860				
Lazarus, Solomon	16	1870				
Lazard, Isaac	17	1870				
Lebaur, Israel	14	1860				
Leman, Edward J.	8	1860				
Leman, Michael	4	1850	4	1860	7	1870
Linse, Isaac	20	1860				
Linse, Solomon	6	1860				
Leon, Abram	4	1850				
Leon, Benjamin	6	1860				
Leon, Esther	16	1870				
Leon, Isaac	4	1850	8	1860		
Leon, Israel	4	1850				
Leon, James	8	1850				
Leon, Joseph	22	1870				
Leon, Morris J.	9	1860	21	1870		
Leonard, Isaac	22	1870				
Lippman, Isaac	11	1870				
Leversteyer, Jacob	14	1850				
Levi, Phillip	6	1850				
Levy, Alexander	10	1850				
Levy, Barnet	4	1850	14	1870		
Levy, Betsy	6	1850				
Levy, David	10	1850	13	1870		
Levy, Hart	4	1850				
Levy, Esther	10	1870				

Name	Ward	Year	Ward	Year	Ward	Year
Levy, Isaac	22	1870				
Levy, Jeda	5	1860				
Levy, Joseph	6	1860				
Levy, Marcus	19	1870				
Levy, Markus	4	1850	11	1870		
Levy, Mordecai	1	1850	20	1870		
Levy, Morris	11	1870				
Levy, Moses	10	1850				
Levy, Simon	14	1860				
Lewis, Jacob	6	1860				
Lichtenberg, Ben	11	1870				
Lopez, Grietje	6	1860				
Lopez, Mayer	11	1870				
Lopez, Moses	11	1870				
Lyons, Emanuel	11	1850				
Lyons, Theodore	12	1870				
Magnus, Louis	7	1860				
Manus, Meyer	9	1860	15	1870		
Manus, Solomon	14	1860				
Marks, David	13	1850				
Marks, Jacob	9	1850				
Marx, Isaac	12	1870				
Matthysse, Solomon	11	1870				
Mendels, E. S.	8	1870				
Mendels, Emanuel	15	1870				
Mendes, Bendix	11	1870				
Menich, Solomon	10	1870				
Messers, Hyman	10	1870				
Metz, Eleazer	17	1850				
Meyer, Harmon	4	1850				
Meyer, Hyman	10	1870				
Meyer, Jacob	13	1870				
Meyer, Levinsti	11	1870				
Meyers, Godfried	11	1870				
Meyers, Henry E.	10	1850				
Missquita, Henry	11	1870				
Mitkus, Isaac	6	1860				
Mitkus, Solomon	6	1860				
Morell, Emanuel	4	1850				
Morris, Isaac	7	1870				
Mulder, Maurice	7	1870				
Myers, Henry	10	1850	22	1860	7	1870
Myers, James	19	1870				
Nekelsburg, Michael	13	1870				
Noot, Isaac	11	1870				
Noot, Simon C.	17	1850				
Nunes, Moses	22	1870				
Nykerk, Ezekiel	13	1870				
Oostermans, Margaret	7	1870				

Name	Ward	Year	Ward	Year	Ward	Year
Oostermans, Mauritz	7	1860	13	1870		
Oostermans, Wolf	4	1850				
Oppenbach, Solomon	7	1870				
Pardo, Abe	11	1870				
Payer, Moses	11	1870				
Pereira, David	11	1860				
Pero, Servis	11	1870				
Phillips, George	4	1850				
Phillips, Moses	6	1850				
Phillips, Myer	14	1850				
Pike, David R.	6	1850	7	1860	15	1870
Pike, Emanuel B.	4	1850				
Pike, Henry B.	13	1870				
Pike, Israel B.	8	1850				
Pike, Louis B.	13	1870				
Pike, Moses P.	8	1850				
Pike, Samuel	22	1870				
Pinto, Rose	8	1860				
Pohler, Philip	11	1870				
Polak, Jacob	14	1860	10	1870		
Polak, Joseph	11	1870				
Polak, Louis	6	1860	11	1870		
Polak, Samuel	14	1870				
Poppers, Nathan	13	1870				
Poppers, Solomon	17	1860				
Post, Judah	17	1860	7	1870		
Praeger, Emil	10	1870				
Praer, Jacob	11	1870				
Pray, Elias	22	1870				
Prince, Hart	7	1860	3	1870		
Prince, Joachim	9	1860				
Prince, Maurice	16	1850				
Prince, Raphael	20	1870				
Prince, Robert	8	1860				
Prowler, Moses	11	1860				
Radestein, Ephraim	18	1870				
Rempe, Louis	7	1860				
Revere, Joel	11	1870				
Rinaldo, Markus	4	1870				
Robles, Isaac	11	1870				
Rosenberg, Marius	17	1870				
Rose, Cosman	19	1870				
Rose, Samuel	11	1870				
Rosenthal, Aaron	10	1870				
Ruper, Leonard	13	1870				
Sammis, William	14	1860				
Sanders, Henry	11	1870				
Samson, Ber	22	1870				
Schaefer, Louis	11	1870				

Name	Ward	Year	Ward	Year	Ward	Year
Schilt, Esther	13	1870				
Schilt, Fred	17	1870				
Schilt, Louis	6	1850	7	1860	7	1870
Schinberg, Leon	4	1850				
Schneider, Moses	10	1870				
Schoolmeister, Isaac	14	1860	11	1870		
Schroyer, David	17	1850				
Schulfish, Moses	11	1870				
Schurysman, Jacob	6	1850				
Schurysman, Simon	6	1850				
Schwartz, Marcus	13	1870				
Schwiezer, Meyer	11	1860				
Seligman, Isaac	17	1870				
Seligman, Jacob	17	1870				
Sharp, Abraham	11	1870				
Sharp, George	11	1870				
Sharp, Morris	13	1870				
Sheal, Jacob	11	1870				
Sieres, Henry	17	1870				
Simons, Louis	14	1850	8	1870		
Simons, Nathan	11	1870				
Simson, Edward	16	1860				
Simson, Louis	8	1860				
Simson, Solomon	17	1860				
Sloe, Morris	2	1850				
Sofer, Abraham	6	1850				
Solomon, Abraham	7	1860				
Solomon, Hanby	11	1870				
Solomon, Henry	10	1870				
Solomon, Jonas	12	1860				
Solomon, Julius	22	1870				
Solomon, Levi	8	1860				
Solomon, M.	7	1870				
Solomon, Rachel	19	1870				
Solomon, Sarah	6	1860				
Solomon, William	20	1860				
Solomon, Solomon	6	1850	6	1860	16	1870
Solomons, Abraham	7	1860				
Solomons, Benedict	8	1860				
Solomons, Daniel B.	5	1850				
Solomons, Hart B.	8	1860	16	1870		
Solomons, Joseph	13	1870				
Spiers, Nathan	12	1860				
Spiers, Philip	8	1860				
Spiers, Simon H.	16	1870				
Stokvis, Jacob	12	1870				
Stodell, Abraham	13	1870				
Stoilskey, Bernard	10	1870				
Strauss, Abel	18	1860				

Name	Ward	Year	Ward	Year	Ward	Year
Strauss, Herman	18	1870				
Streep, Myer	7	1860	7	1870		
Streep, Samuel	20	1870				
Sugarman, Samuel	13	1870				
Tableporter, Joseph	11	1870				
Taleman, J. A.	11	1870				
Teerman, Jacob	18	1860				
Telohuis, Myers	6	1860				
Tencoorn, Abraham	11	1870				
Tencoorn, Ephraim	11	1860				
Thoesen, Philip	18	1870				
Troelsch, Leon	17	1870				
van Been, Louis	7	1870				
van Blaricum, Moses	22	1870				
van Buren, William	20	1870				
van Collem, Leon	7	1850				
van Coulter, Leon	7	1850				
van den Berg, Abraham	13	1870				
van der Burgh, Emanuel	11	1870				
van der Maas, Joseph P.	6	1850				
van der Nut, Abraham	6	1860				
van der Nut, Marcus	6	1860				
van der Poorten, Simon	11	1870				
van der Velden, Aaron	6	1860	14	1870		
van der Wiele, Isaac	19	1870				
van Gelder, Jacob	20	1870				
van Gelder, Marcus	17	1850	6	1870		
van Gelderen, Wolf	13	1870				
van Gelgan, William J.	6	1850				
van Groot, Rebecca	6	1860				
van Moppes, Morris	13	1870				
van Nesten, D.	22	1870				
van Noorden, Moses	11	1860	11	1870		
van Praag, Aaron S.	9	1860	22	1870		
van Praag, Abraham	20	1870				
van Praag, Elias	22	1870				
van Praag, Jacob	17	1870				
van Praag, Victorina	18	1860				
van Praag, Wolf	6	1870				
van Pratt, Louis	11	1870				
van Raalte, Benjamin	17	1870				
van Raalte, Moses	11	1870				
van Ulm, Abram	6	1860				
Verlence, Isaac	6	1870				
Vos Benjamin	4	1850				
Vreeland, Levy	12	1860				
Waitzfelder, Morris	9	1860	16	1870		
Wallach, Abraham	14	1870				
Wessel, Henry	7	1870				

Name	Ward	Year	Ward	Year	Ward	Year
Wienhuis, Philip	11	1870				
Wind, Aaron	7	1860				
Wind, Isaac	7	1870				
Wind, Rufus	13	1870				
Wind, Solomon	7	1870				
Winkel, Joseph	11	1870				
Winkel, Simon	6	1860	13	1870		
Wisma, Isaac	6	1860				
Wolff, James	14	1860				
Wolff, Peter	11	1870				
Wolfstein, Wolf	11	1870				
Young, Edward	11	1870				
Young, Henry	22	1870				
Young, Israel	11	1870				
Young, William	22	1870				
Zeldenrust, Morris	10	1860	7	1870		

Source: Compiled from Robert P. Swierenga, comp. *Dutch Households in U.S. Population Censuses, 1850, 1860, 1870: An Alphabetical Listing by Family Heads*, 3 vols. (Wilmington, DE, 1987).

APPENDIX III:
DUTCH JEWISH HOUSEHOLD HEADS AND WORKING ADULTS IN PHILADELPHIA: 1850, 1860, 1870 CENSUSES

Name	Ward	Year	Ward	Year	Ward	Year
Aarons, Aaron	NL	1850	16	1860		
Aarons, Markus	7	1870				
Alexander, Israel	4	1870				
Alexander, Simon	4	1860				
Bear, Myer	4	1870				
Bernheim, Moses	5	1860				
Betstein, Bernard	6	1870				
Blaauw, Levi	5	1860				
Blaauw, Samuel	5	1860				
Blitz, Solomon S.	NM	1850	3, 5	1860		
Bloom, Marcus B.	5	1860				
Boekbinder, Ludmil	4	1860				
Boekbinder, Manuel	4	1860				
Boekbinder, Mary	4	1870				
Boekbinder, Simon	4	1870				
Boloca, Hyman	13	1870				
Boutelje, Eleazer	4	1860				
Boutelje, George	4	1860				
Boutelje, Leonard	4	1860				
Boutelje, M.	2	1870				
Boutelje, Rudolf	4	1860				
Boutelje, Samuel	2	1870				
Boutelje, Simon	4	1860				
Cohen, Abraham	NM	1850				

Name	Ward	Year	Ward	Year	Ward	Year
Cohen, Daniel	16	1860				
Cohen, Hart	4	1860				
Cohen, Servis J.	NM	1850				
Cooper, Alexander	4	1860	4	1870		
Cooper, Philip	3	1870				
Cromelien, Washington	NL	1850				
D'Ancona, Thomas	5	1860				
Davis, David A.	4	1860				
de Boer, Henry	MO	1850	3	1860	7	1870
de Boer, Israel	4	1870				
de Boer, Jacob	7	1870				
de Bruin, Abraham	4	1860	4	1870		
de Bruin, Morris	NM	1850				
de Haan, Abraham	4	1860				
de Haan, Betsy	4	1870				
de Haan, Jane	4	1870				
de Haan, Johan	4	1860				
de Haan, Louis	MO	1850	5	1860		
de Haan, Moses	4	1870				
Dekker, Solomon	MO	1850				
de Vis, A.	5	1850				
de Vis, Elizabeth	10	1870				
de Wolf, Samuel	6	1870				
de Wolfe, Henry	MO	1850				
de Wolfe, Hyman	5	1860				
de Young, David	7	1860				
de Young, Isaac	CH	1850	13	1860		
de Young, Joseph	NL	1850				
de Young, Philip	NL	1850				
de Zwaan, Jacob	11	1870				
Dressen, David	4	1860				
Dropsie, Ann	NL	1850				
Dropsie, Gabriel	NL	1850				
Dropsie, Moses A.	NL	1850				
Eytinge, Anna M.	NM	1850				
Eytinge, Bernhard	NM	1850				
Faasen, Abraham	4	1870				
Fellerman, Abraham	MO	1850	4	1860	4	1870
Fellerman, George	4	1860	4	1870		
Fellerman, Matilda	4	1870				
Fellerman, Sarah	4	1870				
Fish, Levi	4	1860				
Fisherman, Louis	4	1870				
Fleisher, Myer	5	1860				
Frank, Nathan	13	1870				
Frank, Philip	13	1870				
Frechie, Abraham M.	4	1860				
Frechie, Andrew	4	1870				
Gerrits, Moses	NM	1850				

Name	Ward	Year	Ward	Year	Ward	Year
Gerson, David	4	1870				
Goodman, Rachel	NM	1850				
Gross, Henry	11	1870				
Gross, Myer	5	1860				
Haanke, Simon	4	1870				
Hano, Simon	9	1860				
Hart, Sarah (widow Abr.)	5	1860				
Helmstaadt, Abraham	MO	1850				
Hoffman, Henry	11	1870				
Hollander, Abraham	3	1870				
Hollander, Isaac	MO	1850				
Hond, Jacob	3	1860				
Hond, Samuel	4	1860	4	1870		
Isaacs, Aaron	16	1860				
Isaacs, Alfred	4	1860				
Isaacs, Eleazer	MO	1850	5	1860		
Isaacs, Henry	MO	1850	10	1860		
Isaacs, Isaac	5	1860				
Isaacs, Jeremiah	17	1860				
Isaacs, Judah	7	1870				
Isaacs, Levi	13	1870				
Isaacs, Markus	SO	1850	16	1860	13	1870
Isaacs, Solomon	16	1860				
Isard, Abraham	MO	1850				
Israel, Abraham E.	LD	1850				
Kannewasser, Abraham	4	1860				
Kannewasser, Jacob	4	1870				
Keyser, Jacob	2	1870				
Krieger, Levi	4	1860				
Lam, Eleazer	4	1860	4	1870		
Lam, Fanny	12	1860				
Lam, John	12	1860				
Lam, Levi	5	1860				
Lantman, Frederick	1	1870				
Lazarus, Moses	LD	1850				
Levy, Aaron	NM	1850				
Levy, Augustus	5	1860				
Levystein, Rosetta	SG	1850				
Linse, Elias S.	MO	1850	4	1860	4	1870
Linse, Elizabeth	4	1870				
Linse, Rebecca	4	1870				
Linse, Solomon	4	1870				
Lipper, David	17	1860				
Lit, David J.	9	1860				
Lit, Joseph J.	3	1860				
Loeyer, L. T. (age 40)	4	1860				
Loeyer, L. T. (age 27)	4	1860				
Louis, Samuel	14	1860				
Marcus, Jacob	9	1860				

Name	Ward	Year	Ward	Year	Ward	Year
Meyer, Abraham	4	1870				
Nathan, Emil	24	1860				
Noot, Simon C	4	1860				
Perez, Isaac	16	1860				
Pereira, Abraham	4	1870				
Pereira, Emanuel	4	1870				
Pereira, Isaac	4	1870				
Pereira, Jane	4	1870				
Pereira, Judah	4	1870				
Pereira, Moses	4	1860	4	1870		
Pereira, Samuel	4	1870				
Philips, P.	4	1860				
Pinheiro, Isaac	4	1860				
Pinheiro, Rina	4	1870				
Ploy, Abraham	4	1860	4	1870		
Ploy, Emma	SO	1850				
Polano, Hyman	4	1870	13	1870		
Polock, Hyman	SG	1850	13	1860	13	1870
Polock, Moses	13	1860	13	1870		
Poons, Simon	4	1870				
Portner, Hyman	4	1870				
Primtella, Joseph	4	1860				
Rachuykesel, Luskmar	4	1860				
Raines, Louis	5	1860	4	1870		
Sanson, Emanuel	3	1870				
Sanson, Jacob S.	3	1870				
Sanson, Joseph	2	1860				
Sanson, Samuel	4	1870				
Sanson, Solomon	4	1870				
Schreiber, Theodore	3	1850				
Segaar, Isaac	4	1860				
Shreck, Benjamin	4	1860				
Siek, Isaac	SO	1850				
Simons, Jacob	4	1870				
Simons, Moses	4	1860	4	1870		
Sinkel, Levi	4	1860				
Slaugh, Emma	SO	1850				
Sluizer, Myer	4	1860	4	1870		
Snoek, Isaac	4	1860				
Snoek, Myer	4	1860				
Spelman, Philip	4	1860				
Stern, Levi	4	1870				
Stork, Elizabeth	PI	1850				
Stork, Henry	15	1860				
Swaab, Benjamin	4	1870				
Swaab, Mark	4	1870				
Swaab, Solomon	4	1870				
Tokes, Simon	4	1860				
van Beil, Herman	SO	1850	13	1860		

Name	Ward	Year	Ward	Year	Ward	Year
van den Heuvel, Colen	NM	1850				
van der Sluis, Moses	NM	1850				
van Gelder, Isaac	4	1860				
van Loon, David	5	1860				
Visch, Ariel	4	1870				
Visch, Levi W.	4	1860	4	1870		
Voorsanger, Caroline	7	1870				
Voorsanger, Elizabeth	2	1860				
Voorsanger, Jane	2	1860				
Voorsanger, Nathan	7	1870				
Voorsanger, Sarah	7	1860				
Waas, Abraham	4	1860				
Waas, Henry	4	1870				
Walvisch, Abraham	4	1860	4	1870		
Walvisch, Mann	4	1870				
Weaver, Henry	4	1870				
Weaver, Mary	4	1870				
Weaver, Philip	4	1870				
Willing, Elizabeth	4	1870				
Wolf, Hyman S.	13	1870				
Wolters, Betsie	4	1870				
Wolters, E.	4	1860				
Wolters, Levi	4	1860				
Wolters, Lyman	4	1860				
Wolters,Sarah	4	1860	4	1870		
Wolters, Wolf	4	1860	4	1870		

Township Codes: CH=Chestnut, LO=Locust, LD=Lower Delaware, MO=Moyamensing, NL=North Liberties, NM=North Mulberry, PI=Pine, SG=Spring Garden, SO=Southwark

Source: Compiled from Robert P. Swierenga, comp. *Dutch Households in U.S. Population Censuses, 1850, 1860, 1870: An Alphabetical Listing by Family Heads*, 3 vols. (Wilmington, DE, 1987).

NOTES

Chapter 1

1. Ivo Schöffer, *A Short History of the Netherlands* (Amsterdam, 1973), 77–79. A brilliant analysis of the culture is Simon Schama's *The Embarrassment of Riches: An Interpretation of Dutch Culture in the Golden Age* (London, 1987).
2. Wilhelmina Chr. Pieterse, "The Sephardi Jews of Amsterdam," in R. D. Barnett and W. M. Schwab, eds., *The Sephardi Heritage*, (Grendon, Northants, Eng., 1989), 2:75–76; Karin Hofmeester, "Ashkenazic-Jewish Immigrants in the Netherlands, 1600–1914" (unpublished paper, 1990), 1–2.
3. Mozes Heiman Gans, *Memorbook: History of Dutch Jewry from the Renaissance to 1940* (Baarn, Neth., 1971), 5, 274 (Asher quote), 8–22; Jozeph Michman, "Historiography of the Jews in the Netherlands," in Jozeph Michman and Tirtsah Levie, eds., *Dutch Jewish History: Proceedings of the Symposium on the History of the Jews in the Netherlands November 28—December 3, 1982, Tel-Aviv—Jerusalem* (Jerusalem, 1984), 7–8. The 1982 symposium volume should be supplemented by reports of succeeding symposia: Jozeph Michman, ed., *Dutch Jewish History: Proceedings of the Fourth Symposium on the History of the Jews in the Netherlands 7–10 December, Tel-Aviv—Jerusalem, 1986*, vol. 2 (Assen/Maastricht, Neth., 1989); M. P. Beukers and J. J. Cahen, eds., *Proceedings of the Fifth International Symposium on the History of the Jews in the Netherlands [1988]*, in *Studia Rosenthaliana*, 23 (Fall 1989) Special issue.
4. Gans, *Memorbook*, 15–272; J. Michman, *Jews in the Netherlands*, 9–14; "Amsterdam," *Jewish Encyclopedia* 1:537–45; "Amsterdam," *Universal Jewish Encyclopedia* 1:284–88; "Holland," *Universal Jewish Encyclopedia*, 5:421–41; "The Netherlands," *Encyclopaedia Judaica*

12:973-94; Pieterse, "Sephardi Jews of Amsterdam," 75-99; Robert Cohen, "Passage to the New World: The Sephardi Poor of Eighteenth Century Amsterdam," in Lea Dasberg and Jonathan N. Cohen, eds., *Neveh Ya'akov Jubilee Volume Presented to Dr. Jaap Meijer on the Occasion of His Seventieth Birthday* (Assen, Neth., 1982), 31-42. An excellent brief overview of Dutch Jewish history is Ivo Schöffer, "The Jews in the Netherlands: The Position of a Minority Through Three Centuries," *Studia Rosenthaliana* 15 (Mar. 1981): 85-100. A revisionist analysis of the Sephardi and Marrano immigration is that by Jonathan I. Israel in "Sephardic Immigration into the Dutch Republic, 1595-1672," *Studia Rosenthaliana* 23 (Fall 1989): 45-53. A companion piece is Yosef Kaplan, "Amsterdam and Ashkenazic Migration in the Seventeenth Century," *Studia Rosenthaliana* 23 (Fall 1989):22-44. On Marranos, see Cecil Roth's *A Life of Menasseh Ben Israel: Rabbi, Printer, and Diplomat* (Philadelphia, 1945) and his *A History of the Marranos* (Philadelphia, 1932).

5. J. Michman, *Jews in the Netherlands*, 11-15.
6. "Amsterdam," *Encyclopaedia Judaica* 1:900-901; "Amsterdam," *Universal Jewish Encyclopedia* 1:287; "Baruch De Spinoza," *Encyclopaedia Judaica* 15:275-84; Gans, *Memorbook*, 88-92.
7. Committee for the Demography of the Jews, "Dutch Jewry: A Demographic Analysis, Part One," *Jewish Journal of Sociology* 3 (1961): 206 (table 3).
8. J. Michman, *Jews in the Netherlands*, 16-21; E. Boekman, *Demografie van de Joden in Nederland* (Amsterdam, 1936), 21, 31; E. Boekman, "De Verspreiding der Joden over Nederland, 1830-1930," *Mens en Maatschappij*, Jubileumnummer 1925-1975 (1975): 77-99 (repr. from vol. 10, 1934, 174-96). See also J. A. de Kok, *Nederland op de breuklijn Rome-Reformatie* (Assen, Neth., 1964), 292-95, 325; Philip van Praag; "Demografische ontwikkeling van de Joden in Nederland sinds 1830," *Mens en Maatschappij* 47, no. 2 (1972): 169; Philip van Praag, "Between Speculation and Reality," *Studia Rosenthaliana* 23 (Fall 1989): 175; Karin Hofmeester, *Van Talmoed tot Statuut: Joodse Arbeiders en Arbeiders-Bewegingen in Amsterdam, London, en Parijs, 1880-1914* (Amsterdam, 1990), 15.
9. Robert Cohen, "Boekman's Legacy: Historical Demography of the Jews in the Netherlands," in J. Michman, *Dutch Jewish History*, 2:521-23; and Robert Cohen, "Family, Community and Environment: Early Nineteenth Century Dutch Jewry," *Studia Rosenthaliana* 19 (Oct. 1985): 321-41.
10. Herman Diederiks, "Residential Patterns: A Jewish Ghetto in Amsterdam Around 1800?" (unpublished paper, University of Leiden), 1-4. The figure of 12 percent Portuguese is derived from table 2. See also Diederiks, *Een stad in verval: Amsterdam Omstreeks 1800* (Amsterdam, 1982). Gans, *Memorbook*, 326-27, 362; Hofmeester, *Van Talmoed*, 21-22.

11. Diederiks, "Residential Patterns," 10–11; Gans, *Memorbook*, 831–32, 318.
12. E. J. Fischer, "Jews in the Mediene: Jewish Industrial Activities in the Cotton Industry in Twente, 1795–1900," *Studia Rosenthaliana* 19 (Oct. 1985): 249–57; and more definitively, Benjamin W. de Vries, *From Pedlars to Textile Barons: The Economic Development of a Jewish Minority Group in the Netherlands* (Amsterdam, 1989).
13. H. Daalder, "Dutch Jews in a Segmented Society," *Acta Historiae Neerlandica* (Studies on the History of the Netherlands) 10 (1978): 175–94, esp. 178–79; Gans, *Memorbook*, 274–314. Two documents from the 1796 debate on Jewish emancipation that show that the civil liberties Jews enjoyed in the United States influenced the Dutch decision are printed in Joseph L. Blau and Salo W. Baron, eds., *The Jews of the United States, 1790–1840: A Documentary History*, 3 vols. (New York and London, 1963), 1:78–80.
14. Adolf Kober, "Holland," *Universal Jewish Encyclopedia*, 5:435; Marylin Bender, "In Amsterdam: 300 Years of Jewish Life," *New York Times*, August 14, 1988, sec. 8, p. 20; Daalder, "Dutch Jews," 176–81; Schöffer, "Jews in the Netherlands," 89–90.
15. H. Beem, *De Joden van Leeuwarden* (Assen, Neth., 1974), 89–92; "Amsterdam," *Jewish Encyclopedia* 1:542; "Amsterdam," *Universal Jewish Encyclopedia* 1:287. Felix Libertate had less than one hundred members, one-third of whom were non-Jews, but the French overlords touted their efforts. Gans, *Memorbook*, 274–76, 281.
16. Daalder, "Dutch Jews," 181; Beem, *Joden*, 114–17; Kober, "Holland," *Universal Jewish Encyclopedia* 5:436; Gans, *Memorbook*, 293, 296. The forced reorganization combined eleven synagogues into four, under the direction of Paris. For a "liberal" and sympathetic picture of Louis Napoleon, see "Amsterdam," *Jewish Encyclopedia* 1:542; S. E. Bloemgarten, "De Amsterdamse Joden gedurende de eerste jaren van de Bataafse Republiek (1795–1798)," *Studia Rosenthaliana* 1 (Jan. 1967): 66–96; (July 1967): 45–70; 2 (Jan. 1968): 42–65; and D. S. van Zuiden, "Lodewijk Napoleon en de Franse Tijd," *Studia Rosenthaliana* 2 (Jan. 1968): 66–88. On the religious conflict caused by Louis Napoleon's policy, see Jozeph Michman, "The Conflicts Between Orthodox and Enlightened Jews and the Governmental Decision of 26th February, 1814," *Studia Rosenthaliana*, 15 (Mar. 1981): 20-36, esp. 26; Jozeph Michman, "De stichting van het Opperconsistorie" (in three parts), Studia Rosenthaliana 18 (Jan. 1984): 41–60; (Sept. 1984): 143–58; 19 (May 1985): 127–58. A critique of this literature is A. H. Huussen, Jr., "De emancipatie van de Joden in Nederland: Een discussie bijdrage naar aanleiding van twee recente publicaties," *Bijdragen en mededelingen betreffende de geschiedenis der Nederlanden* 94 (1979): 75–83.
17. Jews in all of the lands of French hegemony responded reluctantly to the enforced naming. See Lee M. Friedman, *Pilgrims in a New Land*

(New York, 1948), 203–7. For an analysis of Dutch Jewish naming patterns under the July 20, 1808, decree, see H. Beem, "Joodse namen en namen van Joden," *Studia Rosenthaliana* 3 (Jan. 1969): 82–95.

18. J. Michman in "Conflicts Between Orthodox and Enlightened Jews," 25–26, cites at least one example of a prosecution for "rebellious behavior."

19. Diederiks, "Residential Patterns," 3.

20. Beem, *Joden*, 114–15; "Amsterdam," *Jewish Encyclopeidia* 1:542. The two Jewish battalions had 883 men each.

21. Beem, *Joden*, 117; S. Kleerekoper, "Het Joodse Proletariaat in het Amsterdam van de 19e Eeuw," *Studia Rosenthaliana* 1 (Jan. 1967): 97–108, (July 1967): 71–84; Fischer, "Jews in the Mediene," 251.

22. This abandonment of Europe was a new phenomenon. Dutch and other European Jews had for 150 years migrated between the large Ashkenazic centers or within the Sephardic Diaspora in northwestern Europe, moving generally to England by way of Holland. Dan Michman, "Migration Versus 'Species Hollandia Judaica': The Role of Migration in the Nineteenth and Twentieth Centuries in Preserving Ties Between Dutch and World Jewry," *Studia Rosenthaliana* 23 (Fall 1989): 57–58. Because the first official census of the Netherlands was in 1830, there are no specific figures on the Jewish population or the extent of early overseas emigration. In any case, the outflow was not sufficient to reverse the gradual Jewish population growth. Amsterdam Jewry increased from an estimated 23,000 in 1795 to 30,000 in 1809, during which time the overall city population decreased from an estimated 210,000 to 180,000. The amount of internal migration of Jews to Amsterdam is unknown however, but this may explain the Jewish increase. See Bloemgarten, "Amsterdamse Joden," 50.

23. Albert Ehrenfried, *A Chronicle of Boston Jewry: From the Colonial Settlement to 1900* (Boston, 1963), 278–81; Michman, "Conflicts Between Orthodox and Enlightened Jews," 30–33.

24. Daalder, "Dutch Jews," 178–79; Gans, *Memorbook*, 331; O. Vlessing, "The Jewish Policy of King William I," in J. Michman, *Dutch Jewish History*, 2:177–88, esp. 186–87.

25. Kleerekoper, "Joodse Proletariaat, 1," (Jan. 1967): 99, 105; "Joodse Proletariaat, 2," (July 1967): 83.

26. J. Michman, "Conflicts Between Orthodox and Enlightened Jews," 21–23; Gans, *Memorbook*, 310–11, 325.

27. Vlessing, "Jewish Policy of King William I," 188; Gans, *Memorbook*, 325.

28. Daalder, "Dutch Jews," 182; the *Jewish Messenger* Aug. 21, 1868; Sept. 15, 1876; Ira Rosenwaike, *On The Edge of Greatness: A Portrait of American Jewry in the Early National Period* (Cincinnati, 1985), 36; Hofmeester, *Van Talmoed*, 21; Gans, *Memorbook*, 325. In 1817, 21.9 percent of all Noord Holland inhabitants were on the dole, which was twice the rate in Zuid Holland. See H. J. Prakke, *Drenthe in Michigan*

(Grand Rapids, 1983), 30–31. A socioeconomic analysis of the Amsterdam elite in 1813 finds the Jewish element almost entirely absent. Of the 245 highest taxed persons in 1813 in Amsterdam, Rotterdam, and The Hague, only four Jews are listed, all in The Hague. See Herman Diederiks, "The Amsterdam Elite at the Beginning of the Nineteenth Century," in Heinz Schilling and Herman Diederiks, eds., *Burgerlich Eliten in den Niederlande und in Nordwestdeutschland* (Cologne and Vienna, 1985), 445–57.

29. Arend Lijphart, *The Politics of Accommodation: Pluralism and Democracy in the Netherlands*, 2nd ed. (Berkeley, 1975); and Michael Wintle, *Pillars of Piety: Religion in the Netherlands in the Nineteenth Century, 1813–1901* (Hull, Eng., 1987), 62–68.
30. Daalder, "Dutch Jews," 183, 189, quotes 178, 185; Schöffer, "Jews in the Netherlands, 85–100, esp. 89, 98. On the process of assimilation, see Carolus Reijnders, *Van 'Joodsche Natie' tot Joodse Nederlanders* (Amsterdam, 1969).
31. Frederique P. Hiegentlich, "Reflections on the Relationship Between the Dutch *Haskalah* and the German *Haskalah*," in J. Michman and Levie, *Dutch Jewish History*, 207–18, quotes 213, 215; Gans, *Memorbook*, 300, 274–76, 286, 307.
32. J. Michman, *Jews in the Netherlands*, 25–26, 32–33; Gans, *Memorbook*, 370–80.
33. Daalder, "Dutch Jews," 180–81; Gans, *Memorbook*, 312.
34. Daalder, "Dutch Jews," 185–86, 191; Schöffer, "Jews in the Netherlands," 94–98; Gans, *Memorbook*, 331, 404, 307.
35. Schöffer offers this profound insight in "Jews in the Netherlands," 97–98. Cf. Gans, *Memorbook*, 380-82, 328-30, 831-34.
36. Daalder, "Dutch Jews," 184–90; "Amsterdam," *Jewish Encyclopedia* 1:542–44; H. Heertje, *De diamantbewerkers van Amsterdam* (Amsterdam, 1936), 66–67.
37. Gans, *Memorbook*, 557.
38. The article is in *Simonsens Festschrift* (*Festskrift i Anledning af Professor David Simonsens 70-Aairge Fødseldag*) (Copenhagen, 1923), 253–57.
39. Jozeph Michman, "The Jewish Essence of Dutch Jewry," in J. Michman, *Dutch Jewish History*, 2:2–5.
40. Ibid., 6–22; Gans, *Memorbook*, 639.

Chapter 2

1. Although the "first" Jew anywhere is seldom the first, an anonymous clipping in the *Boston Jewish Advocate*, Tercentenary issue (Jan. 27, 1955), p. 7, states that a Moses Simonson "from the Jewish settlement of Amsterdam" arrived in Plymouth Colony in 1621 on the ship *For-*

tune (cited in Morris A. Gutstein, *To Bigotry No Sanction: A Jewish Shrine in America 1658–1958* [New York, 1958], 20, 161). Simonson's daughter Rebecca married John Soule, whose father George sailed on the *Mayflower*. Rebecca's son married Sarah Standish, daughter of Miles Standish and also of John Alden. Since Puritans were not known for their religious tolerance, this account of acceptance and even intermarriage is suspect. Either Moses Simonson was a Christian convert or he was not a Jew. The latter is the adamant contention of Jacob R. Marcus in *The Colonial American Jew, 1492–1776*, 3 vols. (Detroit, 1970), 3:1193, 1428. The first known Jew in the Bay Colony, according to Marcus, was Solomon Franco, a ship's supercargo from Holland who arrived in Boston in the late 1840s and was left behind when the ship departed. The authorities sent him packing on the next vessel to Holland ten weeks later. Franco lived most of his life in London, first as a "rabbi" and after his conversion to Christianity in 1668 as a theological writer (ibid., 300–1).

2. Isaac S. Emmanuel and Suzanne A. Emmanuel, *History of the Jews of the Netherlands Antilles*, 2 vols. (Cincinnati, 1970), 1:37–50; Jonathan I. Israel, *Empires and Entrepots: The Dutch, the Spanish Monarch, and the Jews, 1585–1713* (London and Ronceverte, WV, 1990), 385–86, 431, 437, 106–7, 139, 155–56, 161–62, 176–77; Anita Novinsky, "Sephardim in Brazil: The New Christians," and Aubrey Newman, "The Sephardim of the Caribbean," both in R. D. Barnett and W. M. Schwab, eds., *The Sephardi Heritage* (Grendon, Northants, Eng., 1989), 2:431–73; Marcus, *Colonial American Jew*, 1:69–79; Gutstein, *To Bigotry No Sanction*, 23–24.

3. David De Sola Pool and Tamar De Sola Pool, *An Old Faith in the New World: Portrait of Shearith Israel, 1654–1954* (New York, 1955), 3–13. An excellent historical overview is "New York History," *Encyclopaedia Judaica* 12:1062–1127; Abraham J. Karp, *Haven and Home: A History of the Jews in America* (New York, 1985), 4–5.

4. Jonathan I. Israel, *European Jewry in the Age of Mercantilism, 1550–1750* (Oxford, 1985), 177. Israel's *Empires and Entrepots* (417–47) argues that Dutch Sephardi Jewry "functioned as one of the vital components of the imposing ediface of Holland's global commerce" in the eighteenth century (418). See also R. A. J. van Lier, *Frontier Society: A Social Analysis of the History of Surinam* (The Hague, 1971), 25, 32–33, 85–95; Marcus, *Colonial American Jew*, 1:144–56.

5. Emmanuel and Emmanuel, *Netherlands Antilles*, 1:37–50; Newman, "Sephardim of the Caribbean," in Barnett and Schwab, *Sephardi Heritage*, 2:459–63; Marcus, *Colonial American Jew*, 1:174–201: G. Herbert Cone, "The Jews in Curaçao," *Publications of the American Jewish Historical Society* (hereafter *PAJHS*) 10 (1902): 141–57. Cone contains errors and must be used with caution.

6. Emmanuel and Emmanuel, *Netherlands Antilles*, 1:51–61; Cone, "Jews in Curaçao," 140–47.

7. Emmanuel and Emmanuel, *Netherlands Antilles*, 1:62–70; 2:618–19, 681, 758; 2:1036–45; Cone, "Jews in Curaçao," 146–47 (quote). For trade patterns generally, see Jacob Price, "Economic Function and the Growth of American Port Towns in the Eighteenth Century," *Perspectives in American History* 8 (1974): 123–86; and Franklin W. Knight and Peggy K. Liss, eds., *Atlantic Port Cities: Economy, Culture and Society in the Atlantic World, 1650–1850* (Knoxville, 1991).

8. Marcus, *Colonial American Jew*, 1:95–140, esp. 99–100, 123.

9. Newman, "Sephardim of the Caribbean," in Barnett and Schwab, *Sephardi Heritage*, 2:461; Moses Rischin, review of Jacob R. Marcus, *The Colonial American Jew, 1492–1776* (1970), in *William and Mary Quarterly* 30 (Apr. 1973): 353–55.

10. Ira Rosenwaike, *On the Edge of Greatness: A Portrait of American Jewry in the Early National Period* (Cincinnati, 1985), 1–3; Isaac S. Emmanuel, *Precious Stones of Jews of Curaçao: Curaçaon Jewry, 1656–1957* (New York, 1957).

11. Emmanuel and Emmanuel, *Netherlands Antilles*, 1:279–80; 2:1066–67; Newman, "Sephardim of the Caribbean," in Barnett and Schwab, *Sephardi Heritage*, 2:462.

12. Rosenwaike, *Edge of Greatness*, 2–3, 15–16. For reliable population estimates by city and state, see Jacob Rader Marcus, *To Count a People: American Jewish Population Data, 1585–1984* (Lanham, MD, 1990).

13. Alan D. Corré, "The Sephardim of the United States of America," in Barnett and Schwab, *Sephardi Heritage*, 2:389.

14. Quotes cited in Ira Rosenwaike, *Population History of New York City* (Syracuse, 1972), 4. The best overview is Marcus, *Colonial American Jew*, 1:215–48, 306–10. But Marcus curiously overlooked the salience of Dutch Jewry in eighteenth century North America (ibid., 1:260–61; 3:1423).

15. Abraham Vossen Goodman, *American Overture: Jewish Rights in Colonial Times* (Philadelphia, 1947), 77–80; Albion Morris Dyer, "Points in the First Chapter of New York Jewish History," *PAJHS* 3 (1895): 43–45; Max J. Kohler, "Phases of Jewish Life in New York Before 1800," *PAJHS* 2 (1894): 77–79, 3 (1895): 73–76.

16. Seven of 167 shareholders were Jewish, each investing more than 6,000 guilders. Goodman, *American Overture*, 81; George L. Smith, *Religion and Trade in New Netherland: Dutch Origins and American Development* (Ithaca, 1973), 213–15, 244–46; Morris U. Schappes, ed., *A Documentary History of the Jews in the United States, 1654–1875* (New York, 1950), 2–13. The latter includes copies of the petition and subsequent directives of the WIC.

17. "Abraham de Lucena," *Universal Jewish Encyclopedia* 7:228–29. Abraham's brothers Jacob and Moses de Lucena accompanied him. The list of freedmen is in Max J. Kohler, "Civil Status of the Jews in Colonial New York," *PAJHS* 6 (1897): 101–3. Marcus, *Colonial Ameri-*

can Jew, 1:252, 287, 292, notes that the Jewish community had almost vanished by 1664 in favor of Curaçao and Surinam.

18. Information on early Dutch Jews can be found in Malcolm H. Stern, comp., *First American Jewish Families: 600 Genealogies, 1654–1977* (Cincinnati, 1978), 7, 44, 56, 106, 110, 131, 218–19, 250; Joseph R. Rosenbloom, *A Biographical Dictionary of Early American Jews; Colonial Times Through 1800* (Lexington, KY, 1960), 6, 28–29, 58–59, 61, 72, 101, 126, 128, 143–44; David De Sola Pool, *Portraits Etched in Stone: Early Jewish Settlers, 1682–1831* (New York, 1952), 5–9, 215–16, 243–45, 272–74, 300–301, 309, 379, 453–54, 459–60, 471–74, 489; Pool and Pool, *An Old Faith*: 20–23, 26, 41, 46, 114, 159–61, 244, 270–71, 305, 320–21, 473, 479–84; Samuel Rezneck, *Unrecognized Patriots: The Jews in the American Revolution* (Westport, CT, 1975), 15–16, 141–42, 112, 120–21, 60, 51, 48; Goodman, *American Overture*, 75–85, 96; "Uriah Hendricks," *Universal Jewish Encyclopedia* 5:314. Isaac Adolphus was born in Bonn, Germany, but lived in the Netherlands for many years before emigrating. For Myers see Jeanette W. Rosenbaum, *Myer Myers, Goldsmith, 1723–1795* (Philadelphia, 1954).

19. Pinto's compendium and calendar survive only in manuscript. H. P. Solomon, "Joseph Jesurun Pinto 1729–1782: A Dutch Hazan in Colonial New York," *Studia Rosenthaliana* 13 (Jan. 1979): 18–29; Pool and Pool, *An Old Faith*, 165–67; S. Gaon, "Some Aspects of the Relations Between Shaar Hashamayim of London and Shearith Israel of New York," in Aubrey Newman, ed., *Migration and Settlement: Proceedings of the Anglo-American Jewish Historical Conference Held in London . . . July 1970* (London, 1971), 7–9. This and the following two paragraphs rely on these sources.

20. Compiled from Ira Rosenwaike, "An Estimate and Analysis of the Jewish Population of the United States in 1790," *PAJHS* 50 (Sept. 1960): 37–38; Ira Rosenwaike, "The Jewish Population of the United States as Estimated from the Census of 1820," *American Jewish Historical Quarterly* 53 (Dec. 1963): 153–57.

21. Rosenwaike, "An Estimate . . . in 1790," 23–35; Rosenwaike, "Census of 1820," 131–49; Rosenwaike, "Demographic Characteristics of the Jewish Population of the United States and Philadelphia in 1830," *Proceedings of the American Philosophical Society* 133 (June 1989): 333–38; Rosenwaike, *Edge of Greatness,*: 1–3; Werner Keller, *Diaspora: The Post-biblical History of the Jews* (New York, 1966), 459.

22. Rosenwaike, "Census of 1820," 34; Rosenwaike, "Demographic Characteristics," table 1, 334; Rosenwaike, *Edge of Greatness*, 31.

23. Gutstein, *To Bigotry No Sanction*, 24–26, 162–63, makes the case that Habib Ben-Am and his group reached Newport 5 to 6 years before the customary "first arrival" date of 1658 agreed on by "all authorities." A scholar who fixed a later date of 1677 is Goodman, *American Overture*, 37–38.

24. Gutstein, *To Bigotry No Sanction*, 25–26 (quote), 31–35, 163–65. See

also Gutstein, *The Story of the Jews of Newport: Two and a Half Centuries of Judaism, 1658–1908* (New York, 1936), 28, 46, 53–56; Gutstein, "Newport," *Universal Jewish Encyclopedia* 8:213–15; Max J. Kohler, "The Jews in Newport," *PAJHS* 6 (1897): 61–80; S. Broches, *Jews in New England: Six Historical Monographs*, vol. 1, *Historical Study of the Jews in Massachusetts (1650–1750)* (New York, 1942), 12, 23; Goodman, *American Overture*, 37–46.

25. Leon Huhner, *The Life of Judah Touro (1775–1854)* (Philadelphia, 1946), 10, 15–20; Gutstein, "Jews of Newport," 72–73; Rosenbloom, *Biographical Dictionary*, 169–70. Gutstein, *To Bigotry No Sanction*, 44–50, notes that the place of Touro's birth and his route to Newport "cannot be determined with certainty" (ibid., 46).

26. Gutstein, "Jews of Newport," 81–97, 112–17, 125, 153; Gutstein, *To Bigotry No Sanction*, 52–73, 83.

27. Touro married Reyna Hays, sister of Michael Moses Hays. There is disagreement in the sources about when Hays moved between New York, Newport, and Boston during the war years. See Harry Smith and J. Hugo Tatsch, *Moses Michael Hays, Merchant—Citizen—Freemason, 1739–1805* (Boston, 1937), 28–35; Huhner, *Life of Judah Touro*, 18–19; M. H. Stern, *First American Jewish Families*, 104; Rosenbloom, *Biographical Dictionary*, 59; "Hays," *Universal Jewish Encyclopedia* 5: 257–58; Gutstein, "Jews of Newport," 76, 169, 186, 193–94; Gutstein, *To Bigotry No Sanction*, 47–49. On the loyalty oath see Rezneck, *Unrecognized Patriots*, 137; Goodman, *American Overture*, 58.

28. Gutstein, "Jews of Newport," 168–72, 193–94; Gutstein, *To Bigotry No Sanction*, 87–92.

29. Gutstein, "Jews of Newport," 181–82, 188–89, 229.

30. Gutstein, "Jews of Newport," 230–48; "Isaac Touro" and "Judah Touro," *Universal Jewish Encyclopedia* 10:284–86. The quote is in Rabbi I. Harold Sharfman, *The First Rabbi: Origins of Conflict Between Orthodox and Reform: Jewish Polemic Warfare in Pre-Civil War America, A Biographical History* (Malibu, CA, 1988), 73.

31. Abraham Touro left $80,000 in his will, but Judah bequeathed $500,000! Gutstein, "Jews of Newport," 256–67. For the legal fight with Shearith Israel over the Touro synagogue's emancipation, see Gutstein, *To Bigotry No Sanction*, 104–18. The second minister of the reorganized Congregation Jeshuat Israel from 1894 until his death in 1899 was the Sephardi David Baruch of Amsterdam (1847–1899), who conducted services in the traditional Sephardi rite (ibid., 271–74).

32. Barnett A. Elzas, *The Jews of South Carolina; From the Earliest Times to the Present Day* (Philadelphia, 1905; repr. 1972), 106, 133, 279, 288, 290–92; Marcus, *Colonial American Jew*, 1:344–45, 287, 464; 2:533, 581, 674. Valentine was a brother-in-law of Asser Levy of New York.

33. Another South Carolina Dutch Jew was Levi Aaron van Blitz of Haarlem, who died in Black Mingo, SC, in 1792. For documentation see M. H. Stern, *First American Jewish Families*; Rosenbloom, *Biographical*

Dictionary; Elzas, *Jews of South Carolina*; Rezneck, *Unrecognized Patriots*, 48, 151.

34. M. H. Stern, *First American Jewish Families*, 84, 277; Elzas, *Jews of South Carolina*, 133–40, 167–72; Rosenwaike, "Census of 1820," 167–77; Rosenwaike, *Edge of Greatness*: 141–45; L. C. Moïse, *Biography of Isaac Harby, With an Account of the Reformed Society of Israelites of Charleston, SC, 1824–1833* (Charleston, SC, 1930), 33, 71–72. Possible Dutch-stock charter members were I. C. and Jacob Moses, I. S. Tobias, and Henry and Joseph H. Goldsmith.

35. Edwin Wolf 2nd and Maxwell Whiteman, *The History of the Jews of Philadelphia from Colonial Times to the Age of Jackson* (Philadelphia, 1956), 10–12; Abraham S. Wolf Rosenbach, "Notes on the First Settlement of Jews in Pennsylvania, 1655–1703," *PAJHS* 5 (1897): 191–98.

36. Secondary sources published since Isabella H. Rosenbach and Abraham S. Wolf Rosenbach's "Aaron Levy," *PAJHS* 2 (1894): 157–63, give Amsterdam as his birthplace, but his modern biographer, Sidney M. Fish, *Aaron Levy: Founder of Aaronsburg* (New York, 1951), notes that Levy's birthplace is unknown and that it may have been in Poland or Germany. Nathan M. Kaganoff confirmed Levy's Polish origin in a recently discovered inscription in Levy's own hand in the flyleaf of one of his prized books. It reads, "Aaron the son of Aaron from the holy community of Lissa [Leszno] in Poland, 1797" followed by his signature in English. See Kaganoff, "New Discoveries on Aaron Levy," *American Jewish History* 79 (Summer 1990): 505–6.

37. Rosenbloom, *Biographical Dictionary*, 91, 93, 87, 103; Marcus, *Colonial American Jew*, 1:261.

38. Rezneck, *Unrecognized Patriots*, 44, 125; Hyman Polock Rosenbach, *The Jews in Philadelphia Prior to 1800* (Philadelphia, 1883), 29.

39. Wolf and Whiteman, *History of the Jews of Philadelphia*, 171, 429, nn.30–32, 412 n.60; Rosenbloom, *Biographical Dictionary*, 10; Rosenwaike, "An Estimate . . . in 1790," 41.

40. The Jews numbered 29 households (about 100 persons) out of a total population of 2,282 whites in Richmond in 1790. Myron Berman, *Richmond's Jewry, 1769–1976: Shabbat in Shockoe* (Charlottesville, VA, 1979), xi, 29–30; Rosenwaike, "An Estimate . . . in 1790," 30–31, 63–65; Herbert T. Ezekiel and Gaston Lichtenstein, *The History of the Jews of Richmond from 1769 to 1917* (Richmond, 1917), 35, 236–57.

41. Rosenbloom, *Biographical Dictionary*, 126–29; M. H. Stern, *First American Jewish Families*, 218. Thus, two of Myer Myers's daughters married two of Moses Michael Hays's sons while both were fellow officers in King David's Lodge of New York City.

42. For this and the following paragraph see Malcolm H. Stern, "Moses Myers and the Early Jewish Community of Norfolk," *Journal of the Southern Jewish Historical Society* [Richmond] 1 (Nov. 1958): 5–13; Rezneck, *Unrecognized Patriots*, 51, 174.

43. Other members of the Myers clan from Amsterdam included Levy J.

Myers (1782–1835) and Jacob Myers (b. c. 1780), see M. H. Stern, *First American Jewish Families*, 104, 218; J. W. Rosenbaum, *Myer Myers*, 25–26, 31–33, 40; and Ezekiel and Lichtenstein, *Jews of Richmond*, 36, 57–62, 79, 92, 105, 133, 306–7.

44. M. Berman, *Richmond's Jewry*, 127–29.
45. Rosenwaike, "Census of 1820," 164–65; Ezekiel and Lichtenstein, *Jews of Richmond*, 239–40. The five Dutch in Richmond were Abraham Levy, M. M. Myers, Samuel Myers, and Isaac and Simon Solomon; the two Dutch in Norfolk were Moses Myers and his son Samuel Myers.
46. Ezekiel and Lichtenstein, *Jews of Richmond*, 202, 72–73, 35; M. H. Stern, *First American Jewish Families*: 70; letter of Ralph F. Colton, Chicago, to the author, September 19, 1991.
47. Moses Levy left Richmond on a Southern trip after his wife died. While in New Orleans in 1835 he became interested in Texan independence and joined a volunteer group as a surgeon for some two years. He participated in storming the Alamo in December 1835 when the Texan forces captured the fort from the Mexicans and was cited for bravery during the assault. Saul Viener, "Surgeon Moses Albert Levy: Letters of a Texas Patriot," *PAJHS* 46 (Dec. 1956): 101–13; 49 (Mar. 1960): 202–7.
48. Ezekiel and Lichtenstein, *Jews of Richmond*, 143, 201–2, 89, 91–93, 241–42, 309; M. H. Stern, *First American Jewish Families*, 162.
49. Abraham Levy, Sr., died in Richmond in 1852. See Ezekiel and Lichtenstein, *Jews of Richmond*, 201–2, 112–15, 71, 301.
50. Rachel Solomon, Simon's wife, died in 1847 at age 83. Ibid., 81, 89–90, 97, 133, 312–13, 67–69.
51. Ibid., 24, 117–20; M. Berman, *Richmond's Jewry*, 126–27; Joseph Gutmann and Stanley F. Chyet, *Moses Jacob Ezekiel: Memoirs from the Baths of Diocletian* (Detroit, 1975). Jacob Ezekiel's obituary is in the Philadelphia *Jewish Exponent*, May 19, June 2, 1899; as is a lengthy professional résumé of his son Moses (Oct. 27, 1899): "Sir Moses has probably the greatest reputation, both abroad and in this country, of any American sculptor, and his works are certainly more widely distributed, besides occupying prominent positions in public places, museums, art galleries, and in notable private collections."
52. Ezekiel and Lichtenstein, *Jews of Richmond*, 50, 93, 136, 202, 230, 117–18; see also *Jewish Exponent* (Philadelphia), Nov. 10, 1897; March 30, 1899.
53. Ezekiel and Lichtenstein, *Jews of Richmond*, 74, 93, 114, 149–50, 173, 186, 227, 242.
54. Ibid., 242, 92, 287; M. H. Stern, *First American Jewish Families*: 69, 219, 306; Rabbi David Philipson, *The Oldest Jewish Congregation in the West: Bene Israel, Cincinnati* [One Hundredth Anniversary 1824–1924, Rockdale Avenue Temple] (Cincinnati, 1924), 13–14, 27, 60–73.
55. Ezekiel and Lichtenstein, *Jews of Richmond*, 144, 308; M. H. Stern,

First American Jewish Families, 69–70; Gutmann and Chyet, *Moses Jacob Ezekiel*, 81–82, 122.

56. Ezekiel and Lichtenstein, *Jews of Richmond*, 95–99, 256, 275, 315, 227–28.

57. M. Berman, *Richmond's Jewry*, 241–83.

58. Rosenwaike, *Edge of Greatness*, 35; L. Hershkowitz, "Some Aspects of the New York Jewish Merchant in the Colonial Trade," in Newman, *Migration and Settlement*, 101; V. D. Lipman, *Social History of the Jews in England, 1850–1950* (London, 1954), 5–9. Compare Rosenwaike's figure of 60,000 in 1880 with Cecil Roth's 35,000 in 1870. Roth (*A History of the Jews in England* [Oxford, 1964], 268–69) excluded the majority of native-born Jews.

59. Todd M. Endelman, *The Jews of Georgian England, 1714–1830: Tradition and Change in a Liberal Society* (Philadelphia, 1979), 170–74, 199–200; Roth, *History of the Jews in England*, 242–43; Aubrey Newman, *The United Synagogue, 1870–1970* (London and Boston, 1976), 1–16.

60. M. Dorothy George, *London Life in the Eighteenth Century* (London, 1925, repr. 1965), 132–37.

61. Roth, *History of the Jews in England*, 239–40, 243, 250–51, 255, 259. For other prominent Dutch Jewish families in London see Cecil Roth, *The Great Synagogue of London, 1690–1940* (London, 1950), 196–201.

62. Lloyd P. Gartner, *The Jewish Immigrant in England, 1870–1914* (Detroit, 1960), 17, 33.

63. In the Bevis Marks Aliens List of 1803, 41 of 138 alien members were Dutch: 38 from Amsterdam, 2 from The Hague, and 1 from Middelburg. Leaders were Rabbi Moses Myers of the New Synagogue (1759–1804), Portuguese teacher Solomon Jeshurun of the Jews Asylum, and the beadle of Bevis Marks, Nathan Pinedo. See V. D. Lipman, "Sephardi and Other Jewish Immigrants in England in the Eighteenth Century," in Newman, *Migration and Settlement*, 37–63. An example from the 1880s is Levie Eleazer Wijzenbeek of Culemborg, Utrecht Province, who in the 1870s traveled to Manchester to buy English drapery. See Ineke Brasz, "The Influence of Economic and Demographic Developments of a Small Jewish Community Between 1870 and 1930," in Jozeph Michman and Tirtsah Levie, eds., *Dutch Jewish History: Proceedings of the Symposium on the History of the Jews in the Netherlands November 8–December 3, 1982, Tel-Aviv—Jerusalem* (Jerusalem, 1984), 544.

64. Dan Michman, "Migration Versus 'Species Hollandia Judaica': The Role of Migration in the Nineteenth and Twentieth Centuries in Preserving Ties Between Dutch and World Jewry," *Studia Rosenthaliana* 23 (Fall 1989): 54–76, esp. 60; Lipman, *Social History*, 107–8, 115.

65. Hans Winkel, *Genealogie van de familie Winkel* (Amsterdam, 1982), 13–14; Lipman, *Social History*, 97; George, *London Life*, 76–77, 131–37.

66. Israel Zangwill, *Children of the Ghetto: A Study of a Peculiar People*, 3rd ed. (New York, 1895), 14.

67. Ibid., 13–14.

68. Rosenwaike, *Edge of Greatness*, 35–36.

69. *Allgemeine Zeitung des Judenthums* 10 (1846): 448–49. This report was kindly supplied by Avraham Barkai and is quoted from his book, *Branching Out: German-Jewish Immigration to the United States, 1820–1914* (New York, 1994), xxx.

70. Rosenwaike, *Edge of Greatness*, 3–14.

71. Probable Sephardi families were Boas, Peixotto, and Touro. In the colonial period, of course, the proportion of Sephardi was greater, perhaps one-third by 1750.

72. Rosenwaike, *Edge of Greatness*, 38. Although they are incomplete, death records in the period 1821–1829 reveal that 12 percent of Charleston's Jewish populace was Dutch (six out of fifty-two deaths) and that 6 percent of New York Jewry was Dutch (four out of sixty-two deaths). Savannah recorded no Dutch Jewish deaths and Philadelphia death records do not state place of birth. See Ira Rosenwaike, "Jewish Deaths Included in the Vital Records of American Cities, 1821–1829," *American Jewish Historical Quarterly* 58 (Mar. 1969): 360–75.

73. Rosenwaike, *Edge of Greatness*, table 7, 39; 140–64. The figures are slightly adjusted upward to include other known Dutch.

74. Rosenwaike gives a breakdown by city of the most prominent Jewish occupations, as follows: New York—merchants nineteen, clothiers eight, pawnbrokers six, brokers six; Philadelphia—merchants fifteen, dealers eight, dry goods eight, brokers six; Charleston—dry goods thirteen, clothing ten; New Orleans—dry goods nine; Cincinnati—merchants five, dry goods five; Baltimore—no predominant groups (*Edge of Greatness*, 23–28, 95–102, 140–64.

75. Figures compiled from Rosenwaike, *Edge of Greatness*, 140–64. The craftsmen were a carder, carver, quill dresser, spectacle maker, tailor, and watchmaker. Occupations of thirty-eight household heads were not given, but almost all were merchants in southern centers like Richmond.

76. Ibid., 23–27, 95–102, 140–64.

77. Ibid., 75.

78. Ibid., 43–49.

79. Ibid., 31–33.

80. Ibid., 17–19.

81. Marcus, *Colonial American Jew*, 3:1249–1326; Rezneck, *Unrecognized Patriots*, 6, 135, 141–42; Cecil Roth, "Some Jewish Loyalists in the War of American Independence," *PAJHS* 38 (Sept. 1948): 81–107, based on Loyalist claims in the Public Record Office, London.

Chapter 3

1. Moses Rischin, *The Promised City: New York's Jews, 1870–1914*, 2nd ed. (Cambridge, MA, 1977), vii, 94; Ira Rosenwaike, *Population History of New York City* (Syracuse, 1972), 54, 87.

2. David De Sola Pool, *Portraits Etched in Stone: Early Jewish Settlers, 1682–1831* (New York, 1952), 272–74; Malcolm H. Stern, comp., *First American Jewish Families, 600 Genealogies, 1654–1977* (Cincinnati, 1978), 110.

3. Jeanette W. Rosenbaum, *Myer Myers, Goldsmith, 1723–1795* (Philadelphia, 1954), 23–49.

4. Jonathan Israel, "Sephardic Immigration into the Dutch Republic, 1595–1672," *Studia Rosenthaliana* 23 (Fall 1989): 53; Stern, *First American Jewish Families*, 251; Pool, *Portraits Etched in Stone*, 340–43, 248; David De Sola Pool and Tamar De Sola Pool, *An Old Faith in the New World: Portrait of Shearith Israel, 1654–1954* (New York, 1955), 222, 310, 356, 359.

5. "Peixotto Family," *Jewish Encyclopedia* 9:582–84; "Dr. Daniel Levy Maduro Peixotto" typescript, in Abraham Lincoln Nebel (1891–1973) Collection, Cleveland Jewish Miscellany, 1831–1971, WRHS, Cleveland; Pool, *Portraits Etched in Stone*, 428–32; Pool and Pool, *An Old Faith*, 503, 216, 244, 267, 355.

6. The data in this and the next two paragraphs are from Robert P. Swierenga, comp., *Dutch Households in U.S. Population Censuses, 1850, 1860, 1870: An Alphabetical Listing by Family Heads*, 3 vols. (Wilmington, DE, 1987).

7. In 1850 sixteen Dutch had English spouses, eleven German, and one each Polish and French. In 1860 twenty-one Dutch had German spouses, sixteen English, and one each from France, Belgium, Poland, Ireland, Brazil, and "Africa." In 1870 forty-eight Dutch had German spouses, thirty-three English, four French, and one each Spanish, Polish, and Curaçaon. Of the German spouses in 1870, 15 were Prussian and the rest were widely scattered: Baden, Bavaria, Hanover, Hesse-Cassel, Hesse-Darmstadt, Saxony, and Würtemberg.

8. Jacob R. Marcus, "The American Colonial Jew: A Study in Acculturation" in Jonathan D. Sarna, *The American Jewish Experience* (New York, 1986), 6–17; Jacob R. Marcus, "The Periodization of American Jewish History," in Jacob R. Marcus, *Studies in American Jewish History: Studies and Addresses* (Cincinnati, 1969), 3–9; Israel Goldstein, *A Century of Judaism in New York, B'nai Jeshurun 1825–1925: New York's Oldest Ashkenazic Congregation* (New York, 1930), 63; Ronald Sanders, "A History of the Jews in America," in Werner Keller, *Diaspora: The Post-biblical History of the Jews* (New York, 1966), 455–93. Kenneth David Roseman asserts that the ethnic balance shifted from Sephardic to Ashkenazic as early as the 1720s. See his "The Jewish Population of America, 1850–1860: A Demographic

Analysis of Four Cities" (Ph.D. diss., HUC, Jewish Institute of Religion, Cincinnati, 1971), 9.

9. Pool and Pool, *An Old Faith*, 35, 39; Hyman G. Grinstein, *The Rise of the Jewish Community of New York, 1654–1860* (Philadelphia, 1946, repr., 1976), 4–5.

10. Among the fifteen Bnai Jeshurun petitioners in 1825, who comprised the Committee of Israelites meeting at Washington Hall, were at least four Hollanders: Joseph Davies and his son John M. Davies, David Cromelien, and Elias L. Philips. Joseph Davies immigrated to New York in 1798 with his wife and son Rowland. Rowland and his brother John Myer married daughters of Ansel Cohen Cromelien, Betsy and Mary, in 1822 and 1824, respectively, at Synagogue Shearith Israel. Minutes of Shearith Israel Congregation, Oct. 25, 1825, and Shearith Israel Vital Records, abstracted in Rowland Davies File, Abraham Lincoln Nebel (1891–1973) Collection, Cleveland Jewish Miscellany, 1831–1971, WRHS.

11. Grinstein, *Jewish Community*, 5–6, 11–13, 40–41, 49; Adolph H. Fink, "The History of the Jews in New York City: 1654 to 1850" (Rabbinic thesis, HUC, Jewish Institute of Religion, 1930), 130, 132; Rabbi I. Harold Sharfman, *The First Rabbi: Origins of the Conflict Between Orthodox & Reform: Jewish Polemic Warfare in Pre-Civil War America, a Biographical History* (Malibu, CA, 1988), 408–12.

12. Grinstein, *Jewish Community*, 51, 17–20, 414–65.

13. E. Yechiel Simon, "Samuel Myer Isaacs: A Nineteenth Century Jewish Minister in New York City" (Ph.D. diss., Yeshiva University, 1974), 1. This section relies heavily on Simon's work. See also the obituary of Samuel's brother David Myer Isaacs (1810–1879), rabbi of the Liverpool and Manchester synagogues, in the *Jewish Messenger*, May 10, 1878; Moshe Davis, *The Emergence of Conservative Judaism: The Historical School in Nineteenth Century America* (Philadelphia, 1963), 340–42; H. Beem, *De Joden van Leeuwarden* (Assen, Neth., 1974), chaps. 14, 17, 18.

14. Mortgage Documents in Germeentearchief, Leeuwarden: Aug. 31 and Nov. 12, 1807; July 25 and Aug. 11, 1810 (Hypotheek 173/83 and 173/91). Rabbi David Myer Isaacs (1810–1879), in 1841 was the first to preach in English at London's Great Synagogue at a special service honoring Sir Moses Montefiore's return from his Damascus mission. See Cecil Roth, *The Great Synagogue of London, 1690–1940* (London, 1950), 259.

15. Goldstein, *A Century of Judaism*, 76, 80–81, 92–93. An incomplete, but useful, genealogical tree of Samuel M. and Jane Isaacs is in M. H. Stern, *First American Jewish Families*, 110.

16. Lance J. Sussman, "Isaac Leeser and the Protestantization of American Judaism," *American Jewish Archives* 38 (Apr. 1986): 8–10; "Preaching," *Encyclopaedia Judaica* 13:1002–7. This extensive article does not mention Samuel Isaacs or Isaac Leeser. Only an occasional

prayer had been recited in English before Isaacs' sermon. On the fiftieth anniversary of the event in 1889, Rabbi De Sola Mendes of Shaaray Tefila recalled the fact in his sermon (the *Jewish Messenger*, Oct. 4, 1889).

17. This sorry affair is fully documented in the *Occident and American Jewish Advocate*, including an exchange of letters containing charges and countercharges, Rabbi Isaacs's statement, and the full text of the New York court's decision. Despite the documentation of the power struggle for control of the congregation, there is no mention of underlying causes, which may have been a case of oldtimers against newcomers, natives versus immigrants, or even nationalistic rivalries (see the *Occident*, 3 (1845): 255–60, 300–5, 357, 408–15, 478–80). Sharfman describes the schism as an English versus German conflict (*First Rabbi*, 169–70). Goldstein (*A Century of Judaism*, 92–94) refers to "two opposing parties in the Congregation" before 1844, but does not explain the reason for the decision. On this point see Jonathan Sarna, "The Debate over Mixed Seating in the American Synagogue," in Jack Wertheimer, ed., *The American Synagogue: A Sanctuary Transformed* (New York, 1987), 376.

18. The Baltimore Congregation called Rabbi Isaacs within days of his stirring address in English at the consecration of their new Lloyd Street synagogue. Isaacs declined, said Isaac Leeser, who was also a participant in the dedication, because of "his attachment for his present flock." See Leeser's report in the *Occident* 3 (1845): 361–67, quote on 367; Sharfman, *First Rabbi*, 176.

19. Grinstein, *Jewish Community*, 49–50; Simon, "Samuel Myer Isaacs," 13; Simon Cohen, *Shaaray Tefila: A History of Its Hundred Years 1845–1945* (New York, 1945), 6–7. Known Dutch Jewish seatholders and members in 1845 were Simon Content, Andrew M. Davis, John M. Davis, Benjamin M. Davis, Isaac de Young, Levi Hamburger, Benjamin I. Hart, Philip Pike, S. Rode, and J. L. Simmons.

20. Sussman, "Isaac Leeser," 1–21.

21. M. Davis, *Emergence*, 134–38, 340; the *Occident* 5 (1847): 382–94. For the plaintive cry of a pious young clerk who wrote a "letter to the editor" explaining that he had to violate his conscience and work on the Sabbath in order to keep his job, see the *Jewish Messenger*, Dec. 21, 1860.

22. The *Occident* 3 (1845):87–93, quote on 89; 4 (1847): 542, 239; S. Cohen, *Shaaray Tefila*, 9; Grinstein, *Jewish Community*, 340, 342.

23. Sharfman, *First Rabbi*, 145–46.

24. The *Occident* 2 (1844): 284.

25. The *Jewish Messenger*, July 1, 1864; Jan. 24, 1873. Isaacs returned from Liverpool on the ship *Africa*, arriving in New York April 10, 1851. Robert P. Swierenga, comp., *Dutch Immigrants in U.S. Ship Passenger Manifests, 1820–1880: An Alphabetical Listing by Household Heads and Independent Persons*, 2 vols. (Wilmington, DE, 1983), 1:448.

26. The *Jewish Messenger*, Nov. 7, 1862; Sept. 18, 1863. The spirit of rivalry between the Greene Street and Wooster Street congregations is clearly evident in the very frank personal diary entries of 1863 by the young Myer S. Isaacs, eldest son of Rabbi Isaacs, who accuses the "Greene Street people" of "mischief," "contemptible conduct," and playing a "trick" in their plans to relocate to the same vicinity on Thirty-fourth Street where Shaaray Tefila planned to move, and for supposedly blocking attempts by Shaaray Tefila to purchase lots on that street. See "Myer S. Isaacs Diary, 1863 and 1868, New York, N.Y.," 2 vols., typescript, AJA, Cincinnati, 1:59–61, 66, 68, 76. Nevertheless, the Dutch shared in Bnai Jeshurun's Cypress Hills Cemetery on Long Island.

27. The Forty-fourth Street synagogue occupied four building lots covering over 10,000 square feet, with an alley on each side. The architectural style was Byzantine, and the building had seating for 400 on the main floor and 320 in the galleries (the *Occident* 26 [1868]: 93).

28. S. Cohen, *Shaaray Tefila*, 18–26. Rowland Davies was a trustee in 1861–1863 (the *Jewish Messenger*, Nov. 15, 1861). Isaac Bildersee's obituary is in ibid., Feb. 2, 1872. In 1850 Samuel Myer Isaacs and his wife Jane lived with their four children at 669 Houston Street between De Paw Place (Thompson Street) and Laurens Street in Ward 15. By 1857 the family, then with five children, had moved their eight children into a bigger house at 649 Houston, and in 1865 they moved their eight children to the fashionable Uptown district, living at 145 West Forty-sixth Street near Broadway. In 1869 the Shaaray Tefila Congregation had moved Uptown also to their Forty-fourth Street synagogue at Sixth Avenue (Ward 22). In the 1870 census, Samuel reported the value of his home at $30,000. Simon, "Samuel Myer Isaacs," 7–9; Swierenga, *Dutch Households*, 1:484–85; S. Cohen, *Shaaray Tefila*, 22–25; Goldstein, *A Century of Judaism*, 63–96; Simon, "Samuel Myer Isaacs," 43; the *Jewish Messenger*, Apr. 28, 1865. For evidence that Rabbi Isaacs's eldest son, Myer, shared his father's fervent concern for Orthodoxy, see "Myer S. Isaacs Diary, 1863 and 1868," esp. the 1868 volume.

29. The *Jewish Messenger* began publication on Jan. 2, 1857, as a vehicle for young writers, but Rev. Isaacs always wrote the editorials from the journal's office in his home. His son Abram S. joined the editorial team in July, 1857. Titles of editorials readily convey the tenor of the sheet: "Orthodoxy," "The Synagogue," "Religious Education," "What is to be Done for our Poor?" "Judaism," "The Sabbath," "A Hebrew College," "A Jewish Foster Home." See also Grinstein, *Jewish Community*, 216–17, 366–67.

30. M. Davis, *Emergence*, 162–65.

31. Ibid., 165–67, 431–32, 298, 308.

32. The *Jewish Messenger*, Mar. 25, Apr. 1, 8, 29, May 13, 1859; Nov. 20, 1857; Feb. 26, 1858; May 31, 1878; Grinstein, *Jewish Community*, 160–61, 436; M. Davis, *Emergence*, 60–64, 70, 78, 129–30.

33. Grinstein, *Jewish Community*, 446–47; the *Occident* 10 (1852): 170, 263; 11 (1854): 503–4; 18 (1860): 202–3.

34. Grinstein, *Jewish Community*, 440–47, describes the history of this relief agency. See also Sharfman, *First Rabbi*, 121, 484–507. For the Lehren family see Mordechai Elian, "R. Akiva Lehren: The Man and His Work," in Jozeph Michman, ed., *Dutch Jewish History: Proceedings of the Fourth Symposium on the History of the Jews in the Netherlands, 7–10 December, Tel-Aviv—Jerusalem, 1986* (Assen/Maastricht, Neth., 1989), 2:207–17; and Mozes Heiman Gans, *Memorbook: History of Dutch Jewry from the Renaissance to 1940* (Baarn, Neth., 1971), 348–49.

35. The minutes of Bnai Jeshurun refer to a "Rabbi Aaron" in Amsterdam who purchased scrolls and prayer books for the congregation. This was likely Aaron Mendes Chumaceiro, a member after 1838 of the rabbinic court of the Portuguese synagogue (Grinstein, *Jewish Community*, 414, 417, 270–71). Rabbi Aaron Chumaceiro became chief rabbi in Curaçao in 1860 ("Amsterdam," *Jewish Encyclopedia*, 1:542). Isaacs was "intimately acquainted" with Dr. Nathan Adler, the chief rabbi of London (1845–1890); Adler pushed Jewish education, founded the Jews' College in London, and defended "unflinching orthodoxy." See Grinstein, *Jewish Community*, 498, 446; "Nathan Marcus Adler," *Jewish Encyclopedia* 1:198–99; Goldstein, *A Century of Judaism*, 75.

36. The *Occident* 1 (1843): 470–73; Cohen, *Shaaray Tefila*, 2; Grinstein, *Jewish Community*, 231–34, 244–45; "Samuel Myer Isaacs," *Jewish Encyclopedia* 6:635; M. Davis, *Emergence*, 38.

37. The *Jewish Messenger*, July 31, Aug. 14, 1857; Jan. 21, 1859. The classic article on Jews in public schools is Lloyd P. Gartner, "Temples of Liberty Unpolluted: American Jews and Public Schools, 1840–1875," in Bertram Wallace Korn, ed., *A Bicentennial Festschrift for Jacob Rader Marcus* (New York, 1976), 157–89. Cf. Isaac Leeser, "The Jews of the United States—1848," *American Jewish Archives*, 7 (Jan. 1955): 82–84; Alvin Irwin Schiff, *The Jewish Day School in America* (New York, 1966), 22–23.

38. Myer S. Cohen and M. R. de Leeuw were the first principals and Isaac C. Noot and Louisa R. Bildersee were teachers. The *Occident*, 23 (1865): 190, 238; the *Jewish Messenger*, Feb. 3, Mar. 24, 31, June 23, 1865; May 11, June 1, Sept. 21, 1866; Mar. 15, 1867; May 8, 1868; Apr. 9, 1869.

39. The *Occident* 7 (1849): 137–39; Simon, "Samuel Myer Isaacs," 107, 131–32; Morris U. Schappes, ed., *A Documentary History of the Jews in the United States 1654–1875* (New York, 1950), 555, citing the *Jewish Messenger* editorial of July 19, 1872.

40. Sharfman, *First Rabbi*, 687–88.

41. The *Jewish Messenger*, Oct. 8, 13, Dec. 3, 10, 24, 1858.

42. Grinstein, *Jewish Community*, 217, 430–35, 594 n.16; the *Occident* 17 (1859): 83, 86–87, 193–94, 218–20; the *Jewish Messenger*, Jan. 20, Feb.

13, 1857; Feb. 4, 11, 25, May 6, 13, June 17, 24, July 1, 22, Oct. 28, Dec. 2, 16, 1859; Feb. 16, 24, Mar. 2, May 11, 1860; Apr. 14, 1861. These numerous citations show the importance of the Board of Delegates to Isaacs. The best history is that of Allan Tarshish "The Board of Delegates of American Israelites (1859–1878)," *PAJHS* 49 (Sept. 1959): 16–32, which rests on the author's rabbinical thesis at HUC. Cf. Sharfman, *First Rabbi*, 603–4; and M. Davis, *Emergence*, 99–108.

43. The *Occident* 3 (1845): 526; 4 (1847): 224; 7 (1849): 614; Bertram Wallace Korn, *Eventful Years and Experiences: Studies in Nineteenth Century American Jewish History* (Cincinnati, 1954), 50–51, 57.

44. Bertram Wallace Korn, "American Jewish Life in 1849," in Korn, *Eventful Years*, 50–51, 57; Schappes, *Documentary History*, 637.

45. The *Jewish Messenger*, Jan. 25, 1861; Oct. 26, 1860; May 17, June 25, 1861. Other Isaacs's editorials on the sectional conflict were published on Sept. 21, Nov. 16, Dec. 7, 28, 1860; June 14, 1861. Isaacs's editorial, "Stand by the Flag," (Apr. 26, 1861) is reprinted in Schappes, *Documentary History*, 436–39. See also Max J. Kohler, "Jews and the American Anti-Slavery Movement," *PAJHS* 9 (1901): 51.

46. The *Jewish Messenger*, Jan. 25, 1861; Apr. 28, 1865; M. Davis, *Emergence*, 110–11; Kohler, "Jews," 51–52.

47. The *Occident* 3 (1845): 526; 4 (1847): 224. The Shreveport resolution is reprinted in Schappes, *Documentary History*, 439–41.

48. For an obituary, tributes by his sons and Rev. Isaac Noot, congregational resolutions of sympathy, and an account of the funeral and address by Rev. S. Morais, see the *Jewish Messenger*, May 24, 31, June 6, 21, 1878. The key to Isaacs's claim is the word *Ashkenazic*. Prior to Isaacs, Sephardic clerics in America preached in English: Gershom Mendes Seixas of Shearith Israel beginning in 1768, Jacob de la Motta in Charleston and Savannah from 1785, and Isaac Leeser of Mikveh Israel in Philadelphia beginning in 1830. Leeser was actually the first Jewish minister to preach regular Sabbath sermons in English. See Leon A. Jick, The *Americanization of the Synagogue, 1820–1870* (Hanover, NH, 1976), 10–11, 60–61; Sharfman, *First Rabbi*, 169, 175–76; Sussman, "Isaac Leeser," 8–10. Sharfman erroneously described Isaacs as "the Englishman" (169) and a "native of England" (170; cf. 622, 624, 654). He likely followed M. Davis, *Emergence*, who made the same error (78, 82, 101).

49. Simon, "Samuel Myer Isaacs," 1; M. Davis, *Emergence*, 2. See the *Occident* 3 (1845): 361–67; 5 (1847): 225; 6 (1848): 142, 371; 8 (1850): 198, 312, 619; 19 (1861): 190; 21 (1863): 479–80, for reports of some of these appearances at Baltimore, Albany, Elmira, Rochester, New York City, Buffalo, and Chicago. A synopsis of the address at Newark's new synagogue in 1857 is in the *Jewish Messenger*, Sept. 25, 1857.

50. Isaacs's obituary, *New York World*, May 21, 1878; the *Jewish Messenger*, May 31, 1878.

51. S. Cohen, *Shaaray Tefila*, 28–35; the *Jewish Messenger*, May 31, 1878;

Apr. 9, Sept. 10, 1880. Isaacs hired de Sola Mendes upon the strong recommendation of the Rev. Dr. Nathan Marcus Adler (1803–1890), Chief Rabbi of Great Britain. Isaacs found the preaching of the young assistant very satisfactory.

52. The *Jewish Messenger*, June 21, 1872, provides the only brief history of the congregation, a speech by Myer S. Cohen, son of a charter member and president of the body at its twenty-fifth anniversary. Gosling died in New York in 1887 at the age of ninety-five. De Young's obituary is in ibid., Oct. 5, 1894.

53. "Amsterdam," *Jewish Encyclopedia* 1:540–42; Jacques Goldberg, "Amsterdam," *Universal Jewish Encyclopedia* 1:284–88.

54. Grinstein, *Jewish Community*, 49, 170; Fink, "Jews in New York City," 138–39; the *Occident* 5 (1847): 206–9, 370; 8 (1850): 575.

55. Grinstein, *Jewish Community*, 597. No synagogue souvenir booklet is listed in Alexandra Shecket Korros and Jonathan D. Sarna, eds., *American Synagogue History: A Bibliography and State-of-the-Field Survey* (New York, 1988). The only sources are occasional news items in the *Jewish Messenger*, 1857–1903, cited below; and in the *Occident* 5 (1847): 206–9, 317, 370, 400–407, 560; 6 (1848): 155; 7 (1849): 614; 8 (1850): 575; 9 (1851): 117; 10 (1852): 265; and the *Asmonean* 3 (1851): 188; 4 (1852): 165.

56. Grinstein, *Jewish Community*, 570 n.49, 585 n.2; the *Occident* 5 (1847): 370.

57. Fink, "Jews in New York City," 139; Grinstein, *Jewish Community*, 322, 491–92; the *Jewish Messenger*, June 21, 1872, July 24, 1885.

58. Fink, "Jews in New York City," 138–39, wrongly implies that Bnai Israel constructed their own synagogue on Williams Street. Fink cites Myer Stern, *The Rise and Progress of Reform Judaism: Embracing a History Made from the Official Records of Temple Emanu-el of New York* (New York, 1895), 25; and the *Occident* 5 (1847): 370; 8 (1850): 575. The Chrystie Street dedication on the second day of Passover is reported in the *Occident* 9 (1851): 117; and in the *Asmonean* 3 (1851): 188.

59. Grinstein, *Jewish Community*, App. 5, 486–87; the *Occident* 5 (1847): 207, 560; 8 (1850): 575; 10 (1852): 265; 11 (1853): 464; 12 (1854): 116; 17 (1859): 83, 218–20; 22 (1864): 93; 23 (1865): 190; Grinstein, *Jewish Community*, 107, 553 n.27.

60. The *Jewish Messenger*, Dec. 7, 1860; Oct. 9, 1863; Jan. 29, May 6, Oct. 28, 1864; Feb. 2, May 11, Oct. 12, 1866; Nov. 8, 1867. Emanuel de Young, Morris I. Leon, Solomon Gerrits, Louis Phillips, Solomon Rose, and A. van Kamerik were trustees; Isaac de Brave was secretary.

61. Report of the National Council of Jewish Communities, 1842, Library no. O-1339, Gemeentearchief Amsterdam, states that Simon Noot had a middle teaching certificate; Henry Samuel Morais, *The Jews of Philadelphia: Their History from the Earliest Settlements to the Present Time* (Philadelphia, 1894), 84–85; the *Occident* 1 (1843): 60; 5 (1847): 206; 7

(1849): 614; Grinstein, *Jewish Community*, 546–47. One of Noot's sermons at the Williams Street synagogue is reprinted in the *Occident* 5 (1847): 400–407.

62. The *Occident* 5 (1848): 506; 10 (1853): 506. For one of the advertisements see ibid., 2 (1844): 264.

63. Grinstein, *Jewish Community*, 283; Letter of Simon C. Noot, New York, to Isaac Leeser, Philadelphia, May 25, 5614 [1853]. Noot noted in the letter that he had first seen the expensive gilded bibles at Reverend Isaacs's home, but a cheaper version would sell better. "I must not conceal of you that the general opinion of your bibles is 'they are too dear.' I could perhaps sell more were they cheaper, try what you can do. I am determined to enlarge my business, which might lead to a more better sale of your books." This and several other Noot letters were disposed of by Dropsie College more than thirty years ago. Maxwell Whiteman of Elkins Park, PA, in a letter to the author, Nov. 19, 1991, provided a xerox copy of the originals.

64. The *Occident* 5 (1847): 317, 370. For a report on the school by A. Benjamin dated April 23, 1852, see ibid. 10 (1852): 158–60. Simon Noot also advertised as a tutor of Hebrew at his home at 258 Williams Street (ibid. 5 [1847]: 5A).

65. President Aaron S. van Praag of Bnai Israel strongly promoted the Green Street Hebrew School. The *Occident* 10 (1853): 573; 11 (1853): 232–33, 465; 12 (1854): 115, 165–66. See also Goldstein, *A Century of Judaism*, 115–19.

66. The *Occident* 10 (1853): 506; the *Jewish Messenger*, Oct. 13, 1871.

67. Letter of Simon C. Noot to Isaac Leeser, Jan. 4, 5613 [1852].

68. Albert Ehrenfried, *A Chronicle of Boston Jewry: From the Colonial Settlement to 1900* (Boston, 1963), 356–57, 59; Morais, *Jews of Philadelphia*, 108.

69. Morais, *Jews of Philadelphia*, 159. Simon Noot's salary was $500 per annum (the *Occident* 15 [1857]: 240). Isaac Noot's early career is documented in the *Jewish Messenger*, May 13, Oct. 28, 1864; June 23, 1865; June 1, Oct. 12, 1866; Apr. 19, June 21, Aug. 9, 1867.

70. The *Jewish Messenger*, June 22, Aug. 10, 1860. De Leeuw served thirty-four years (until 1900) as sexton of Bnai Jeshurun. He was a director of the Young Men's Hebrew Association (ibid., June 3, 1892; May 11, 1888; Oct. 19, 1900.)

71. The account of the relocation and dedication service is in the *Jewish Messenger*, Aug. 3, 10, 1860; the *Occident* 18 (1860): 124. Officers of the congregation at the time were : Victor Freibourg (1793–1884), president; Johannes Lansburg, vice president and treasurer; S. de Jonge, secretary; and trustee Dr. Lyon Berhard, Myer S. Cohen, and H. Lazar. Isaac Goldsmith chaired the Dedication Committee. Besides the Germans Freibourg and Berhard, M. I. Friedlander served in 1861 as secretary and Isaac Wertheimer was active on the Sunday School committee (the *Jewish Messenger*, June 24, Oct. 28, Dec. 2, 1859; Nov. 30, 1860; Apr. 12, 1861; May 16, 1884).

72. The *Jewish Messenger*, Aug. 10, 1860.
73. Ibid., Nov. 30, Dec. 28, 1860; Feb. 1, 1861; Feb. 14, May 2, Dec. 12, 1862; May 15, 29, 1863; Nov. 11, 1864. Rev. De Leeuw superintended the school and the school committee consisted of Myer S. Cohen, Lyon Berhard, and Isaac Wertheimer. Teachers included De Leeuw, M. B. Abrahams, A. S. Cohen, Samuel R. Davis, Rose Cohen, Sarah Lewin, Bertha Leopold, Priscilla Ezekiels, Fannie Berlyn, and Rose Sidenberg.
74. Ibid., Oct. 17, 1861; Apr. 28, June 9, Dec. 2, 1865.
75. Ibid., Jan. 29, Sept. 16, 24, 1864; Dec. 12, 1862 (quote).
76. Bnai Israel also participated in a city-wide meeting of twenty-three congregations to discuss Sabbath observance. Ibid., May 15, June 26, Apr. 17, 1863; May 4, 11, 1866; June 26, 1868.
77. The *Jewish Messenger*, Nov. 18, 1870; Jan. 13, Feb. 3, Apr. 21, Sept. 8, Oct. 13, 1871; May 10, 24, June 21, Nov. 1, 1872; Apr. 11, July 11, 1873; Apr. 24, Sept. 18, 1874; Sept. 14, 1877; June 6, 1878, June 13, 1879; Dec. 15, 22, 1882; Mar. 12, 1886. Leaders at Bnai Israel in the 1870s and 1880s—besides Noot and Cohen—were Dr. Lyon Berhard, G. B. Berlyn, Isaac de Brave, Dr. David Brekes, Benjamin S. de Young, Isaac Fles, Isaiah Frankfort, Michael E. Goodhart, I. Jacobson, Samuel Joseph, Jacob E. Kan, Joshua Kantrowitz, Morris I. Leon, Herman Levey, L. Lipman, Louis Osterman, S. Joseph Osterman, Joseph Polak (*shamas*), K. Rose, Myer Rosenthal, Lewis I. Schilt, E. vander Beugel, and J. vander Velden. Leon's obituary in the *Jewish Messenger*, May 29, 1891, described him as a "familiar figure in business and social life . . . [who] took a prominent part in benevolent and synagogue work when the workers were but few."
78. Noot advertised the auction in the New Orleans *Morning Sun*, June 14, 1848, as cited in Sharfman, *First Rabbi*, 498. Bnai Israel also appointed a committee to raise additional monies, composed of M. S. Cohen, M. R. de Leeuw, Isaac de Brave, Emanuel de Young, and Philip Levy (Grinstein, *Jewish Community*, 588–89 n. 31; the *Occident* 11 [1853]: 369).
79. The *Occident* 6 (1848): 155; 23 (1865): 177–80, 470; 26 (1868): 156; the *Jewish Messenger*, Dec. 2, 1859; Jan. 25, 1878; Oct. 14, 1881; Mar. 12, 1886; Grinstein, *Jewish Community*, 593 n. 7. Myer S. Cohen and Lyon Berhard were Bnai Israel's delegates to the first Board of Delegates meeting; E. Ezekiels was the delegate in 1865. Jacob E. Kan and Isaac Fles helped launch the Seminary in 1886.
80. The *Jewish Messenger*, Feb. 26, 1868; June 24, Oct. 28, 1859; Feb. 12, 17, 1861; Nov. 17, 1865; Nov. 2, 30, 1866; Aug. 23, 1867; Sept. 23, 1870. Ladies active in the benevolent society were the wives of Jacob Davis, E. M. Ezekiels, George Berlyn, M. Rosenthal, S. Assenheim, Myer S. Cohen, S. Marks, A. Samson, Michael E. Goedhart (Goodhart), Mark Isaacs, Solomon Rose, and Emanuel de Young.
81. The *Jewish Messenger*, June 21, 1878, states that the Society was formed "thirty years ago." Thus, it may have been the successor of

congregation Bnai Israel's burial and mutual aid society of 1848. In 1885 the Tree of Life Society had ninety members and capital of $3,000 (ibid., Jan. 30, 1885; Oct. 30, 1891; Sept. 1, 1895). The Netherland Israelitisch Sick Fund, a significant organization, was rediscovered only recently by Joël Cahen, "Een eigen ziekenfonds voor joden in New York," *Nieuw Israëlitisch Weekblad*, Nov. 15, 1985, pp. 145–46 (Jubilee number). The issue includes a 1985 interview with Nathan Fish, secretary of the NISF, whose archives are located at the funeral enterprise of the NISF, Hirsch & Sons, 1225 Jerome Avenue, The Bronx, New York. A notarized "Certificate of Incorporation" of NISF, dated February 17, 1866, was filed with the city and county of New York on February 26, 1866. The brief document, containing original signatures of the seven trustees, is in the incorporation records of the New York County Division of Records, and is also available in photocopy form at American Jewish Historical Society, Waltham, MA.

82. Simon Winkel (1826–1917) was one of the first three directors of the fund and for many years was secretary. A Son of David Winkel, a merchant in The Hague and 's Hertogenbosch, Simon emigrated to London in 1854 with his older brother, married there and then after the birth of his second child in 1857 emigrated to New York. He worked as a cigarmaker in Manhattan and later opened a cigar store in The Bronx. The family lived at 738 Kelly Street. Simon died in New York City in 1917 after a long career of service to the Dutch Jewish community. Hans Winkel, *Genealogie van de familie Winkel* (Amsterdam, 1982), 11, 15, 37, 76; obituary, *New York Times*, May 1, 1917, p. 9.

83. Goldstein, *A Century of Judaism*, 385. In the post- 1960s the NISF bought two additional cemeteries—Beth Israel in Woodbury, NJ, and Beth David in Elmont, Long Island, NY.

84. Cahen, "Een eigen ziekenfonds," 145; the *Jewish Messenger*, June 27, 1873. The oldest tombstones at the Acacia Cemetery in Queens contain the following names of New York Dutch Jews: De Vries, Winkel, Polak, Cahen, Cohen, Mossel, Robles, Pereira, Van Dam, Van Praag, Sanders, Van der Poort, Handlooper, Scheffer, Lewin, Van der Poorten, Fleeschdrager, Wolfers, Prins, Van Gelder, Lipman, Benjamin, Rue Levy, Van den Berg, Waas, Mekelburg, Bossie, Hamel, Wagenhuisen, Gomperts, Jacobs, Kingsburg, Keit, Karelsen, Montezinos, Patto, Loon, Van Vest, Decesseres, Frenchman, De Leeuw, Vollenhoven, Mesritz, Hymans, Back, Spiero, Slap, Drucker, De Haan, Reens, Swart, Simons, Saphier, Poons, and Heertje.

85. The *Jewish Messenger*, Aug. 16, Sept. 27, 1877; Jan. 31, June 13, 1879.

86. Ibid., Sept. 5, 12, 1879.

87. Ibid., Feb. 13, Apr. 1, 30, May 14, Oct. 8, Dec. 3, 1880; Mar. 25, Apr. 8, 22, June 10, Oct. 14, Dec. 23, 1881; June 2, Sept. 8, Dec. 15, 22, 1882; Dec. 21, 1883; Jan. 4, 1884.

88. The *Jewish Messenger* of Sept. 2, 1887, states: "the Rev. I. C. Noot will continue to give conscientious care to the old-time Dutch congrega-

tion, Bnai Israel." In 1891 or 1892 Noot left Bnai Israel to become principal of the Sunday school at the uptown Temple Rodeph Shalom (the *Jewish Messenger*, Sept. 19, 1890; Sept. 9, Dec. 9, 1892). Bnai Israel moved to 229 East Seventy-ninth Street (ibid., Oct. 15, 1897).

89. The *American Hebrew* 60 (Dec. 31, 1896): 258; the *Jewish Messenger*, Mar. 30, 1866; Jan. 13, 1880; Oct. 5, 1894. Van Praag (1806–1880) of Leiden emigrated in 1826 to New York City after completing his training in dentistry at the University. He practiced until retiring in 1873. He was a founder of Congregation Bnai Jeshurun and vice president of its Green Street School, and an officer in the Adelphi Lodge. He led the protest movement against the Mortara kidnapping. As the perennial president of the Gemileth Chesed Society, in 1866 he received a medal at a testimonial dinner in his honor after twenty-five years of leadership. His funeral at the Thirty-fourth Street Synagogue was a large affair.

90. See Isaac Leeser's comments in the *Occident* 3 (1845): 462; cf. Bernard H. Puecker, "Immigrant Aid Within the Jewish Community, 1780–1860" (unpublished ms., n.d., AJA, Cincinnati). Also Grinstein, *Jewish Community*, 106–7; Goldstein, *A Century of Judaism*, 68–70; the *Jewish Messenger*, Mar. 25, 1859; May 7, 1860; Jan. 4, 1861.

91. Grinstein, *Jewish Community*, 232, 256, 547 n.43, 552 n.19, 592 n.30; the *Jewish Messenger*, June 12, 1868; the *Occident* 1 (1843): 395–97, 550–51; 2 (1844): 94–96, 237–40; 3 (1845): 21; 5 (1847): 206–9; 6 (1848): 262; 7 (1849): 517; legal advertisements in the *Jewish Messenger*, 1860–1864. Goldsmith's teaching pedagogy was innovative (Grinstein, *Jewish Community*, 256).

92. Grinstein, *Jewish Community*, 120–22, 485–87, 574 n.40, 575 n.42, 150, 157, 431, 552 nn.19 and 22, 553 nn.26 and 27, 555 n.44, 592 n.31; Ira Rosenwaike, "The Jewish Population in the United States as Estimated from the Census of 1820," *American Jewish Historical Quarterly*, 53 (Dec. 1963): 156; Goldstein, *A Century of Judaism*, 62, 69, 73, 84, 167; the *Jewish Messenger*, July 2, Aug. 27, 1858; May 13, 1859; June 20, 1862; Sept. 15, 1871; Oct. 5, 1894. Another Hollander, Isaac de Casseres, acted as unpaid minister and Hebrew teacher in 1866 of the new eastside Portuguese Congregation on Orchard Street (ibid., Aug. 31, 1866).

93. Peixotto's oldest daughter Judith S., wife of David Hays, was the first Jewish public school principal in New York (Ward School for Girls No. 10 on James Street), as reported in the *New York Sun*, April 18, 1851. One of her great-grandsons, Arthur Hays Sulzberger (1891–1968), became publisher (1935–1961) of the *New York Times*. Peixotto's son Moses L. M. (1826–1890) served as a Union officer in the Civil War and then had a long career as a New York City pharmacist. "Hendricks," *Universal Jewish Encyclopedia*, 5:314; Grinstein, *Jewish Community*, 220, 566 n.51; Ira Rosenwaike, *On the Edge of Greatness: A Portrait of American Jewry in the Early National Period* (Cincinnati,

1985), 150, 122; M. Stern, *First American Jewish Families*, 241; the *Occident* 19 (1861): 431; 23 (1865): 190; "Moses Levy Maduro Peixotto," *Jewish Encyclopedia*, 9:584; Schappes, *Documentary History*, 181–85. "Dr. Daniel Levy Maduro Peixotto" typescript, in Abraham Lincoln Nebel Collection, erroneously gives Daniel's birthplace as Curaçao rather than Amsterdam.

94. Charles Reznikoff, "Isaacs," *Universal Jewish Encyclopedia* 5:594–95; "Isaacs," *Encyclopaedia Judaica*, 9:39–40; Isaac Markens, *The Hebrews in America* (New York, 1888; repr. 1975), 219–21; the *Occident* 17 (1859): 218–20; 25 (1867): 214; 26 (1868): 134; "Myer S. Isaacs Diary, 1863 and 1868;" *Jewish Exponent* (Philadelphia), Oct. 14, 1887; Dec. 16, 1887; Feb. 24, 1893; the *Jewish Messenger*, Dec. 2, 1856; Mar. 8, 1889; Oct. 21, 1891.

95. Markens, *Hebrews in America*, 214–15.

96. Ibid., 264–65; Goldstein, *A Century of Judaism*, 118; the *Occident* 21 (1863): 361; 23 (1865): 190.

97. J. J. Lyons died in August 1877. He was president of Sampson Simpson's Theological Seminary Society; he edited a valuable Jewish calendar, and authored a "History of the Jews of America" (the *Jewish Messenger*, Aug. 17, 1877). Solomon Lyons's sister, Rebecca, married John Moss, Sr., of Philadelphia, who was born in England, and in 1804 she gave birth to Joseph Lyons Moss. Asher was another brother. See Morais, *Jews of Philadelphia*, 285, 444; Sharfman, *First Rabbi*, 498.

98. Grinstein, *Jewish Community*, 169–71.

99. *Allgemeine Zeitung des Judenthums* 10 (1846): 448–49. This quote was kindly provided by Avraham Barkai, from his book, *Branching Out: German-Jewish Immigration to the United States, 1820–1914* (New York), xxx.

100. Grinstein, *Jewish Community*, 170, 207–9.

101. In 1845 Goldsmith served with Isaac B. Kursheedt and four others to rule on a dispute at the Shearith Israel Congregation regarding who was qualified to read from the Torah scrolls in worship services. In 1858 Goldsmith, along with Samuel M. Isaacs and C. M. Levy, moderated a contract dispute over Jewish law involving a matzoh bakery. In 1860 Goldsmith chaired a committee, again with S. M. Isaacs, to honor the Prague rabbi Solomon L. Rapaport. Goldsmith's mediation roles are described in Grinstein, *Jewish Community*, 220, 284, 677 n.64. The *Jewish Messenger*, Aug. 31, 1860, is the only source that identifies Goldsmith as "rabbi" of the Bnai Israel Congregation. Goldsmith emigrated to New York around 1842, having followed his children who preceeded him (see his obituary in ibid., Nov. 22, 1872).

The original of Goldsmith's letter is in the Jewish Historical Museum in Amsterdam. Cahen published the letter in Dutch, "Een eigen ziekenfonds," in the *Nieuw Israëlitisch Weekblad*, November, 15, 1985. Dr. Adriaan de Wit (Professor of Romance Languages, Kent State University) translated the letter, and two authorities on Judaism,

Dr. Herbert Hochhauser (Professor of Germanic Languages, Kent State University) and Rabbi Abraham Liebtag of Akron's Temple Israel, explained the meaning of the numerous religious phrases.

102. Swierenga, *Dutch Households*, 2:484–85; the *Jewish Messenger*, May 2, 1862. In 1866 Emanuel Goldsmith and his wife sponsored a lavish celebration to mark the silver wedding anniversary of Moses Cohen and his daughter Betje. Y. P. de Young made a presentation of a silver pitcher and goblet on behalf of Congregation Bnai Israel and the Reverend S. M. Isaacs again spoke, as did the Reverend M. R. de Leeuw (the *Jewish Messenger*, May 11, 1862).

103. Grinstein, *Jewish Community*, 41. Emanuel Goldsmith's membership in Bnai Jeshurun is inferred from his letter, which states: "There are 11 synagogues here: large as no other is the English synagogue to which we belong. Then follows the Portuguese synagogue [Shearith Israel]. The remainder are German and Polish ones and two temples." Bnai Jeshurun was the largest synagogue in terms of membership, reaching nearly 150 in 1850. See Goldstein, *A Century of Judaism*, 67.

104. The initials in the original handwritten letter are likely L. G., referring to Leonard Gosling, Esq., the first President of Bnai Israel. See the *Occident* 5 (1847): 207, 560.

105. The *Occident* 14 (1857): 553–61, quote on 561.

106. Ibid., 9 (1851): 437–39.

107. The *Jewish Messenger*, July 26, 1867. The flag was designed by the noted A. Millner.

108. Grinstein, *Jewish Community*, 528–29 n.10; the *Occident* 14 (1857): 584; 15 (1858): 575; 16 (1859): 592. In 1862 only 4 of 562 patients (0.7 percent) admitted to the Jews Hospital were Dutch (the *Occident* 21 [1863]: 138–39).

109. The only account of the colony is in Gabriel Davidson, *Our Jewish Farmers and the Story of the Jewish Agricultural Society* (New York, 1943): 196–204, which is reprinted from an article, "The Tragedy of Sholem," published in the *Jewish Tribune*, June 16, and 23, 1922. See also Grinstein, *Jewish Community*, 119–22, but this account has numerous discrepancies.

110. Samuel Rezneck, *Unrecognized Patriots: The Jews in the American Revolution* (Westport, CT, 1975): 61; the *Occident* 1 (1843): 214. Hays was the only subscriber in Westchester County.

111. The *Occident* 16 (1858): 363–64; Nathan Ricardo, "Reuben Etting," *Universal Jewish Encyclopedia*, 4:188. On the Etting family of Baltimore and Philadelphia, see Isaac M. Fein, *The Making of an American Jewish Community: The History of Baltimore Jewry from 1773 to 1920* (Philadelphia, 1971), 13–21.

112. Rosenwaike, *Edge of Greatness*, 146–51, 119–23; Jerome C. Rosenthal, "A Study of Jewish Businessmen in New York City as Reflected in the City Directories, 1776–1830" (unpublished paper, HUC, Cincinnati, 1977).

113. Beverly Hyman, "New York Businessmen, 1831–1835" (unpublished paper, HUC, Cincinnati, 1977); "Hendricks," *Universal Jewish Encyclopedia* 5:314; "New York City," *Encyclopaedia Judaica* 12:1071; Stephen Birmingham, *"Our Crowd": The Great Jewish Families of New York* (New York, 1967), 30. Less helpful, because a listing of names is omitted, is Kerry M. Olitzky, "An Economic Profile of New York City Jews: 1835–1840" (unpublished paper, HUC, Cincinnati, 1979).

114. The primary sources are Samuel Gompers, *Seventy Years of Life and Labor: An Autobiography* (New York, 1925); Stuart B. Kaufman, ed., *The Samuel Gompers Papers*, vol. 1, *The Making of a Union Leader, 1850–86* (Urbana and Chicago, 1986). Secondary sources are Bernard Mandel, *Samuel Gompers: A Biography* (New York, 1963); Florence Calvert Thorne, *Samuel Gompers—American Statesman* (New York, 1957); Rowland Hill Harvey, Samuel Gompers, *Champion of the Toiling Masses* (Stanford, 1935).

115. Kaufman, *Making of a Union Leader*, 3, and Gompers, *Seventy Years*, 2–3.

116. Gompers, *Seventy Years*, 13. In a 100 square yard area 240 families lived in squalid conditions. The Gompers family with twelve children lived in a one-room tenement that doubled as Solomon's cigar workshop (see Gans, *Memorbook*, 668–69).

117. Gompers, *Seventy Years*, 2–3.

118. Ibid., 5–7; Kaufman, *Making of a Union Leader*, 4.

119. Gompers, *Seventy Years*, 23, 17, 21–22.

120. Ibid., 24.

121. Mandel, *Samuel Gompers*; Kaufman, *Making of a Union Leader*; Thorne, *American Statesman*; Harvey, *Champion of the Toiling Masses*.

122. The discussion of Dutch diamond workers is condensed from Jacob van Hinte, *Netherlanders in America: A Study of Emigration and Settlement in the Nineteenth and Twentieth Centuries in the United States of America*, Robert P. Swierenga, gen. ed., Adriaan de Wit, chief trans. (Grand Rapids, MI, 1985): 615, 835–39; H. Heertje, *De diamantbewerkers van Amsterdam* (Amsterdam, 1936), 61, 127, and passim; Th. Van Tijn, "Geschiedenis van de Amsterdamse diamanthandel en-nijverheid, 1845–1897," *Tijdschrift voor Geschiedenis* 87 (1974): 16–69, 160–200. The definitive history of the colonial trade is Gedalia Yogan, *Diamonds and Coral: Anglo-Dutch Jews and Eighteenth-Century Trade* (Leicester, Eng., 1978). The 1860 date for the inception of the firm of Groen and De Bruyn in the *Jewish Messenger* (Nov. 2, 1860) corrects Van Hinte, who placed the date at 1872 (*Netherlanders in America*, 836).

123. "Tariff Act of October 1, 1890," in Robert G. Proctor, *Tariff Acts Passed by the Congress of the United States from 1789 to 1897* (Washington, DC, 1898), 357, 361. The Tariff Act of March 3, 1883, is reprinted on p. 300.

124. "Tariff Act of August 27, 1894," in Proctor, *Tariff Acts,* 437; Heertje, *Diamantbewerkers,* 178, 144.

125. Van Hinte, *Netherlanders in America,* 837–38.

126. Ibid., 838–39; Heertje, *Diamantbewerkers,* 54–58.

127. Editor S. M. Isaacs applauded the nonsectarian policy in the *Jewish Messenger,* Dec. 21, 1866.

Chapter 4

1. Edwin Wolf 2nd and Maxwell Whiteman, *The History of the Jews of Philadelphia from Colonial Times to the Age of Jackson* (Philadelphia, 1956), 82–84, 110; Henry Samuel Morais, *The Jews of Philadelphia: Their History from the Earliest Settlements to the Present Time* (Philadelphia, 1894), 22–30.

2. Wolf and Whiteman, *History,* 62–63, 80, 134. An English translation and the original in cursive Judeo-German of Phillips's letter is reprinted in Samuel Oppenheim, "Letter of Jonas Phillips," *PAJHS* 25 (1917): 128–31.

3. *Seventy-Five Years of Continuity and Change: Our Philadelphia Jewish Community in Perspective* (Supplement of the *Jewish Exponent* (Philadelphia), Friday, March 12, 1976). The list of charter members and early history is in Morais, *Jews of Philadelphia,* 11–21. Possible Dutch members were Abraham van Etting, Isaac da Costa, Isaac da Costa, Jr., Samuel da Costa, Naim van Ishac, Colonoms van Shelemah, and Cushman Polock.

4. Morais, *Jews of Philadelphia,* 19–20, 43–45.

5. Wolf and Whiteman, *History,* 223–24.

6. Quoted in Morais, *Jews of Philadelphia,* 69. Since Judaism lacked rabbinical authority in the early years, synagogues facing difficult questions had to appeal to higher authorities in Europe, usually in London or Amsterdam. When Mikveh Israel needed a legal interpretation (*Din Torah*) concerning a member who had blatantly disregarded the judgment of the synagogue, they sent a question (*she' elah*) for an interpretation to Rabbi Saul (Löwenstamm) of the Ashkenazic community of Amsterdam. It is noteworthy that Mikveh Israel was Sephardic and yet appealed to an Ashkenazic rabbi because of his Orthodoxy and rabbinical knowledge. Similarly, in 1823 the German congregation of Philadelphia requested the advice of Ashkenazic rabbis in London and Amsterdam regarding a religious problem.

7. Edward Davis, *The History of Rodeph Shalom Congregation, Philadelphia, 1802–1926* (Philadelphia, 1926) 12; Jeanette W. Rosenbaum, "Hebrew German Society Rodeph Shalom in the City and County of Philadelphia (1800–1950)," *PAJHS* 41 (Sept. 1951): 83–93.

8. Wolf and Whiteman, *History,* 184, 225–26, 447 n.17; Henry Berkow-

itz, "Notes on the History of the earliest German Jewish Congregation in America," *PAJHS* 9 (1901): 123–27, quote 125; Morais, *Jews of Philadelphia*, 70–72; E. Davis, *Rodeph Shalom*, 23. The ten Dutch members were Abraham B. Cohen, Jacob de Lange, Levi M. Goldsmit (Goudsmit), Elias Hyneman, Abraham Eleazer Israel, Abraham Lazarus, Abraham Schoyer, Moses Spyers, Aaron Stork, and Isaac Stuttgart.

9. Wolf and Whiteman, *History*, 249–52; E. Davis, *Rodeph Shalom*, 27.

10. Jacob Rader Marcus, *To Count A People: American Jewish Population Data, 1585–1984* (Lanham, MD, 1990), 147–48, 193–95.

11. The names of the immigrants and their vessels are listed alphabetically in Michael H. Tepper, ed., *Passenger Arrivals at the Port of Philadelphia, 1800–1819: The Philadelphia "Baggage Lists"* (Baltimore, 1986).

12. Joseph de Young's residence in Montgomery County, PA, in 1809 is known by the birth of his son Philip there. The scant information of this family can be pieced together from Morais, *Jews of Philadelphia*, 427–28, 440, 460; Tepper, *Passenger Arrivals*, 169; Wolf and Whiteman, *History*, 288–89; 469; Ira Rosenwaike, *On the Edge of Greatness: A Portrait of American Jewry in the Early National Period* (Cincinnati, 1985), 138, 140, 164; E. Davis, *Rodeph Shalom*, 14, 142. Davis is richly detailed but must be used with caution.

13. Morais, *Jews of Philadelphia*, 259–62. Morais relied on the "Autobiography of Jacob Ezekiel, 1812–1896," in Joseph L. Blau and Salo W. Baron, eds., *The Jews of the United States, 1790–1840: A Documentary History*, 3 vols. (New York and London, 1963), 3: 871–993. Tobias Ezekiel (1786–1832) served in the Richmond Blues in 1807 (see M. H. Stern, comp., *First American Jewish Families, 600 Genealogies, 1654–1977* [Cincinnati, 1978], 69–70).

14. Tepper, *Passenger Arrivals*, 346. The journal of Abraham Eleazar Israel's trip to America, in the possession of Maxwell Whiteman (co-author of *History of the Jews of Philadelphia*) as of this writing, states that he embarked from Amsterdam on June 13, 1804. Hence the trip took more than three months.

15. Wolf and Whiteman, *History*, 233, 449 n.66.

16. Ibid., 255, 457 n.78, 370, 499 n.54, 447 n.17, 302, 476 n.63. See also Jacob Ezekiel's "Autobiography" in Blau and Baron, *Jews of the United States*, for more details.

17. Morais, *Jews of Philadelphia*, 274–75; Wolf and Whiteman, *History*, 230.

18. Wolf and Whiteman, *History*, 226, 445, 352–54, 491–94, 365, 447, 497; *Jewish Exponent*, Nov. 10, 1897; Mar. 30, 1899. Hyneman's grocery first was at 210 Sixth Street and then on Fourth Street north of Arch. Spyers's business in 1810 was located at 66 Callowhill. For Stork and Hyneman see M. H. Stern, *First American Jewish Families*, 99, 123; and Joseph R. Rosenbloom, A *Biographical Dictionary of Early American Jews: Colonial Times Through 1800* (Lexington, KY, 1960), 166.

19. Wolf and Whiteman, *History*, 353, 490 n.106, 497 n.25. Ezekiel refers in a letter to his two uncles, Abraham E. Israel and Levi M. Goldsmit, which indicates that Goldsmit and Israel were brothers-in-law. E. Davis, *Rodeph Shalom*, 37–38. Goldsmit and Goldkop's store in 1825 was at 68 North Second Street.

20. Wolf and Whiteman, *History*, 230, 267, 269–70, 463 n.47; Morais, *Jews of Philadelphia*, 294–95; *Jewish Exponent*, Oct. 27, 1899. Sarah's siblings were Mrs. A. M. Wolf, Mrs. I. Binswanger, Mrs. M. Rosenbach, and Moses Polock, all of Philadelphia. Rosenbach was Dutch.

21. Tepper, *Passenger Arrivals*, 192; Wolf and Whiteman, *History*, 240–41. An analysis of Jewish exogamy by Malcolm H. Stern, "The Function of Genealogy in *American Jewish History*," is found in Jacob Rader Marcus, ed., *Essays in American Jewish History* (New York, 1975), 82–97.

22. Rosenwaike, *Edge of Greatness*, 152, 140; Rosenwaike, "The Jewish Population of the United States as Estimated from the Census of 1820," *American Jewish Historical Quarterly* 53 (Dec. 1963): 158–61; Wolf and Whiteman, *History*, 353, 492 n.129; Robert P. Swierenga, comp., *Dutch Immigrants in U.S. Ship Passenger Manifests, 1820–1880: An Alphabetical Listing by Household Heads and Independent Persons*, 2 vols. (Wilmington, DE, 1983), 1:276. David Eytinge, listed as Louis D. Eytinge on the manifest, sailed on the *Salem* from Liverpool to New York, arriving March 15, 1828, with stated destination New York. Simon Eytinge and family arrived at New York on June 19, 1828; Robert P. Swierenga, comp., *Dutch Households in U.S. Population Censuses, 1850, 1860, 1870: An Alphabetical Listing by Family Heads*, 3 vols., (Wilmington, DE, 1987), 1:322.

23. Wolf and Whiteman, *History*, 354, 493 n.139; the *Occident* 23 (1865): 528; 16 (1858): 65; 17 (1859): 41; 17 (1860): 252; 18 (1861): 304; Morais, *Jews of Philadelphia*, 45, 53, 72, 255; Swierenga, *Dutch Immigrants*, 2:1111. Other Dutch-born trustees of Beth-El Emeth in 1859–1861 were P. Goldsmith and Henry and Joseph Newhouse.

24. For Hart see Wolf and Whiteman, *History*, 377, 352–53, 478 n.96, 491 n.111, nn.115–17.

25. Van Amring later married a Christian wife and his four children (George, Samuel, Augustus, and Rachel Sophia) were raised as non-Jews. In the 1820s the three sons operated a chain of three grocery stores in Philadelphia under the name Augustus Van Amringe & Co. (see Wolf and Whiteman, *History*, 226, 445 n.3, 493 n.140).

26. E. Davis, *Rodeph Shalom*, 25–26, 37; Rosenwaike, *Edge of Greatness*, 152–55; Wolf and Whiteman, *History*, 439, 447, 466, 492–94.

27. Wolf and Whiteman, *History*, 226–27, 231, 447 n.18.

28. Compiled from the list of families of Mikveh Israel in Morais, *Jews of Philadelphia*, 68. I counted twenty-one out of seventy- eight families, or 27 percent: Cohen, Cromelien, Baruch, Da Costa, D'Ancona, De Casseres, De Young, Dropsie, Frechie, Hart, Hond (Hunt), Hyneman,

Israel, Isaacs, Levy, Peixotto, Polock, Phillips, Wolf, Pereyra, and Shoyer.

29. Abraham M. Frechie and Simon Hano's son Louis, a wholesale clothier, served as president in the 1870s and 1880s, and Samuel M. Hyneman, son of Isaac and grandson of Elias, was vice president of the Board of Adjunta in 1887. Morais, *Jews of Philadelphia*, 45, 53, 72, 255; *Jewish Exponent*, Apr. 22, 1887; May 27, 1887; Nov. 19, 1897.

30. Morais, *Jews of Philadelphia*, 407; E. Davis, *Rodeph Shalom*, 30–34, 136–47, 152–55.

31. E. Davis, *Rodeph Shalom*, 35, 55–57, 70; Morais, *Jews of Philadelphia*, 72; Rosenwaike, *Edge of Greatness*, 152.

32. E. Davis, *Rodeph Shalom*, 32–35, 38, 47, 57, 141–47.

33. Idid., 55–62, 152–57; Morais, *Jews of Philadelphia*, 71–72.

34. Morais, *Jews of Philadelphia*, 84–85.

35. Ibid., 84–88; the *Occident and American Jewish Advocate* 1 (Apr. 1843): 60, 357; 17 (1859): 228; 17 (1860): 23; the *Reformed Advocate* (Chicago), Sept. 22, 1894.

36. The *Occident* 7 (1849): 106–8. The Philadelphia City Directory of 1858 is quoted in Morais, *Jews of Philadelphia*, 85.

37. At least one Dutch member in the later years was Julius Blankensee, a trustee in 1894. Morais, *Jews of Philadelphia*, 85–87.

38. The *Occident* 11 (1853): 326.

39. Ibid., 9 (1851): 437–39.

40. Ibid., 11 (1853): 326; Morais *Jews of Philadelphia*, 108.

41. The *Occident* 14 (1852): 546; 16 (1858): 31.

42. Noot was born in Amsterdam in 1809 as the oldest son of Eliazer Philip Noot, a fish merchant, and Beletje Simon. The family was living in the Jodenkerkstraat (Nieuwe Kerkstraat) on May 20, 1812, when Eliazer assumed the family name Noot, according to the Amsterdam Name-Taking Register (vol. E, p. 43). Siblings were Philip, born in 1811, and Katje, born in 1808. Noot married on November 14, 1832, at Amsterdam to Susanna Snoek of Amsterdam, the twenty-three-year old daughter of Marcus Abraham Snoek, a tailor, and Judie Isaac de Leeuw (Amsterdam Civil Marriage Registers 1832, vol. 4, p. 81). I am indebted for this information to Odette Vlessing, archivist, Gemeentearchief Amsterdam.

43. The *Occident* 1 (1843): 60, 357; 2 (1844): 107; 12 (1854): 469; 14 (1856): 309, 453.

44. Ibid., 14 (1856): 453; 14 (1857): 546; E. Davis, *Rodeph Shalom*, 76.

45. The officers of Bnai Israel in 1856–1857 were Abraham Solomons, president; Henry de Boer, treasurer; and trustees Solomon Blitz, Isaac Goldsmit, Isaac Cohen, L. A. de Haan, and B. Munchweiler. The building committee was composed of Cohen, De Boer, Munchweiler, and Matthew Kaas; the fund-raising committee was made up of Cohen, De Boer, Goldsmit, and Kaas plus Simon Alexander, Moses Simons, and Isaac van Gelder. All were Dutch but Munchweiler. Some of these per-

sons are identified in the federal censuses. Solomon Blitz was a clothier, De Boer a dealer in old clothes, De Haan and Simons dealers, Alexander and Van Gelder clothes dealers, and Kaas a pawnbroker. The most property that any of these persons owned was $1,000. Alexander, Van Gelder, and Kaas were younger than thirty years of age in 1857. Solomon Blitz emigrated at age twenty-two from his birthplace of Amsterdam in 1857; he was the middle son of Solomon Blitz, a clothes buyer, according to the Amsterdam Population Registers (Bevolkingsregisters).

46. The *Occident* 18 (1861): 280; 20 (1862): 328–29, 381–82; the *Jewish Messenger*, May 30, Sept. 19, 1862.

47. Ibid., 19 (1861): 140–42. The 1860 federal census lists the Noot family as living in Ward 4, the Western Division, and it included Simon age fifty-one, listed incorrectly as a "Methodist minister" with personal property valued at $500, wife Suzanna (earlier records give his wife's name as Jane) age fifty-two, daughter Elizabeth twenty-eight, and six sons: Lewis twenty-one, no occupation; Isaac twenty, teacher; Philip eighteen, cigarmaker; Abraham fourteen, no occupation; Myer thirteen and Joseph eleven attending school. Abraham, Myer, and Joseph were born in New York and all the others were born in Holland. Swierenga, *Dutch Households*, 2:733. Isaac Noot became a noted New York City rabbi and in 1887 was a delegate and read the Scripture at the regular spring meeting of the Jewish Ministers' Association of America, meeting in Philadelphia. *Jewish Exponent*, Apr. 29, 1887.

48. The *Occident* 18 (1861): 280; 25 (1867): 523. G. M. Goldsmit was appointed the new sexton. He was likely a son of Levi M. Goldsmit, who operated a fancy goods store in the 1820s.

49. Auditors of the treasurer's books were Joseph Davis, a son of John; Simon Alexander; Moses Symons (Simons), and Jacob Segar (Segaar), both dealers; and Simon Alexander, who later became treasurer (the *Occident* 18 [1861]: 280; 20 [1862]: 382). Abraham Solomons, who may be a son of Dutch pioneer Benedict Solomons, was a trustee in 1860. The non-Dutch trustees appear to be German or Polish. Eleazer Gerrit Boutelje was born in Amsterdam in 1834, son of Gerrit Eleazer Boutelje, a *venter* or peddler, and immigrated on July 25, 1852, at eighteen years of age, then a cigarmaker. Eleazer's father and mother emigrated a year later (July 20, 1853), and his younger brother followed the next year (October 3, 1854). It was a typical chain migration that brought the entire family to America (see Amsterdam Population Registers).

50. The *Occident* 15 (1857): 240.

51. Ibid., 18 (1861): 293–294; 23 (1865): 40–43. Bnai Israel in 1865 contributed $25, compared to $100 for Rodeph Shalom and Beth Israel and $200 for Mikveh Israel.

52. In the ceremony of Halizah, a widow whose husband died and left her childless, took off the shoe of her brother-in-law and thereby released him from the Levitical obligation to marry her and give her a child (see *Jewish Encyclopedia*, 6:170–74).

53. The *Occident* 18 (1861): 292.
54. Ibid., 22 (1864): 425–29, 479–80, 513–18.
55. Ibid., 24 (1866), 334.
56. Ibid., 24 (1866): 333–34; 25 (1868) : 625; 26 (1868): 428. Officers of the choir, elected for one year, were Myer de Bear [De Boer], president; I. Hays, vice president; W. Wolters, treasurer; Abraham Pereira, a twenty-year-old cigarmaker, musical director; Simon Boutelje, a forty-year-old dealer in secondhand clothes, treasurer and director Augustus Levy, a forty-six-year-old ivory turner; J. Levy; E. Wolters; and Rudolph Boutelje, a thirty-year-old dealer. Ages and occupations are derived from Swierenga, *Dutch Households*.
57. In Fellerman's obituary in the *Jewish Exponent* (Apr. 22, 1887), he is described as a "well-known Jewish citizen . . . especially popular in the southern section of the city, having resided there for a lengthy period." He died at age sixty. George Goldsmit died in 1897 at age sixty-three (ibid., Dec. 31, 1897). I. M. Goldsmit in 1887 reported glowingly in the *Jewish Exponent* (May 27, 1887) on the sevenieth birthday visit of King Willem III of the Netherlands to the Jewish Quarter in Amsterdam. Moses Simon(s) in 1892 resigned from the vice presidency of United Hebrew Charities because of failing health (ibid., Apr. 8, 1892).
58. The *Occident* 23 (1865): 174–77; 24 (1866): 331; 25 (1868): 139–40, 608–9.
59. Voorsanger and his wife Eva Corper raised seven children. Voorsanger's parents, who never emigrated, were Wolf Voorsanger and Alicia Pekel, both of Amsterdam. Voorsanger's life and career, which has yet to be studied in detail, is sketched briefly in the *American Hebrew and Jewish Messenger* 82 (May 1, 1908), p. 660; 69 (Nov. 1, 1901), p. 610; Kenneth C. Zwerin and Norton B. Stern, "Jacob Voorsanger: From Cantor to Rabbi," *Western States Jewish Historical Quarterly* 15 (Apr. 1983): 195–202; Morais, *Jews of Philadelphia*, 108–9, 167.
60. Morais, *Jews of Philadelphia*, 156.
61. Rosenwaike, "Census of 1820," 137, 157–61; Rosenwaike, *Edge of Greatness*, 40, 49.
62. Rosenwaike, *Edge of Greatness*, 45; Morais, *Jews of Philadelphia*, 71; Wolf and Whiteman, *History*, 233.
63. Stuart Blumin, "Mobility and Change in Ante-bellum Philadelphia," in Stephan Thernstrom and Richard Sennett, eds., *Nineteenth-Century Cities: Essays in the New Urban History* (New Haven and London, 1969), 186–88, esp. fig. 1.
64. Data compiled from Rosenwaike, *Edge of Greatness*, 124–27, 152–55; Rosenwaike, "Census of 1820," 157–61.
65. Kenneth David Roseman, "The Jewish Population of America, 1850–1860: A Demographic Analysis of Four Cities" (Ph.D. diss., HUC–Jewish Institute of Religion, Cincinnati, 1971), 52–57; Sam Bass Warner, Jr., *The Private City: Philadelphia in Three Periods of Its Growth* (Philadelphia, 1960), 56–57.

66. Roseman, "Jewish Population of America," table 1 "Overall Population Summary"; table 5 "Residential Distribution, Philadelphia."
67. Ibid., table 6 "Distribution by Sex."
68. Ibid., table 16 "Housing."
69. In the modern era Jewish men have twice the rate of marriage with Gentiles as Jewish women. Bernard Farber, Charles H. Mindel, and Bernard Lazerwitz, "The Jewish American Family," in Charles H. Mindel and Robert W. Habenstein, eds., *Ethnic Families in America: Patterns and Variations* (New York, Oxford, Amsterdam, 1976), 362.
70. Roseman, "Jewish Population of America," table 18 "Literacy;" and Swierenga, *Dutch Households*, passim.
71. Morais, *Jews of Philadelphia*, 445–48.
72. Data compiled from Rosenwaike, *Edge of Greatness*, 152–54; Swierenga, *Dutch Households*, passim.
73. Nathan Goldberg, *Occupational Patterns of American Jewry* (New York, 1947), 10.
74. Warner, *Private City*, 59; Allan Tarshish, "The Economic Life of the American Jew in the Middle Nineteenth Century," in Marcus, *Essays in American Jewish History*, 264–65.
75. The best social history of the tobacco industry is Patricia A. Cooper, *Once a Cigar Maker: Men, Women, and Work Culture in American Cigar Factories, 1900–1919* (Urbana and Chicago, 1987); discussion in this paragraph, see 10–17. A source that identifies Jewish clothiers, who comprised about one-third of all city clothiers, is Bruce L. Gottlieb, "Jews in the Clothing Industry in Philadelphia, 1850–1860" (unpublished paper, 1980, HUC, Cincinnati). See also Lee M. Friedman, *Jewish Pioneers and Patriots* (Philadelphia, 1948), 324–41, 405–11; Warner, *Private City*, 57–60.
76. Roseman, "Jewish Population of America," table 14 "Real Estate Ownership." Roseman only compiled data from the 1850 and 1860 censuses.
77. Ibid., table 15 "Personal Estate Ownership." In 1860, 973 Jewish households owned personalty, 27 of whom were Dutch. There were 6,579 Jewish households in the city, excluding 257 Jews in institutions.
78. Morais, *Jews of Philadelphia*, 411. Sanson was born in Amsterdam in 1825 and emigrated to Philadelphia in 1839.
79. Hano emigrated from Holland at age thirteen (c. 1836) to Baltimore where he apprenticed as a watchmaker. He then moved to Philadelphia and practiced his trade at a small store on Front Street in the 1840s and 1850s. Shortly before the Civil War he switched into the clothing business. By the 1890s he was president of a Boston book manufacturing firm, the Samuel Hano Co. Twice married, Hano at his death in 1897 left fifteen children and twenty-nine grandchildren. The family belonged to the Mikveh Israel Congregation (obituary in *Jewish Exponent*, Nov. 19, 1897).
80. Isaacs's parents emigrated about 1844 from Leiden to New York. He

married Anna Hano (perhaps Louis Hano's sister) and left four daughters and three sons at his death in 1889. He belonged to several Masonic lodges (Ibid. Sept. 1889).

81. Ibid., Apr. 22, 1887; May 27, 1887.
82. Ibid., Dec. 4, 1896; Feb. 5, 1897.
83. Morais, *Jews of Philadelphia*, 255–59; "Moses Aaron Dropsie" *Jewish Encyclopedia*, 5:3; "Moses Aaron Dropsie," *Universal Jewish Encyclopedia*, 3:602. The name Dropsie appears only once in the Amsterdam Name-Taking Registers, that is on December 9, 1811 (vol. B, p. 37) when Gimpert Mozes (probably Aaron's brother), residing at Prinsengraght 43 opposite the workhouse, having no children or grandchildren, adopted the family name of Dropsie according to genealogist John Verdonk of Hoogland, The Netherlands, and archivist Odette Vlessing. Maxwell Whiteman of Elkins Park, PA, kindly provided the author with copies from his private collection of the military inscription document of Aron Mozes Dropsie into the Netherlands National Infantry battalion, Tenth Section, dated January 19, 1816, and also the inscription document of Gompet (Gompert) Moses Dropsie on January 30, 1825, both of Amsterdam.
84. "Moses Polock," *Universal Jewish Encyclopedia*, 8:584.
85. Rosenwaike, *Edge of Greatness*, 148; Albert Ehrenfried, A *Chronicle of Boston Jewry: From the Colonial Settlement to 1900* (Boston, 1963), 316–17; Edwin Wolf 2nd, "The German Jewish Influence in Philadelphia's Jewish Charities," in Murray Friedman, ed., *Jewish Life in Philadelphia, 1830–1940* (Philadelphia, 1983), 131–32, 135; Morais, *Jews of Philadelphia*, 112, 131–32, 145, 155, 158, 175.
86. Those active were Samuel Dellevie, Elias S. Lens, Henry de Boer, David A. Davis, Abraham Eleazer Israel, Elias Hyneman and his sons Isaac and Leon, David A. Philips, A. Nachman, Hyman Polock and his son Magnus, Myer A. van Collem, Herman van Beil, and Abraham Frechie. See Morais, *Jews in Philadelphia*, 145, 294–95; the *Occident* 23 (1865): 174–77; 24 (1866): 331; 25 (1867): 95; the *Jewish Messenger*, Apr. 26, 1861. Philip de Young (1809–1880) was born in New Hanover Township, Montgomery County, PA and graduated from the University of Pennsylvania Medical School in 1838 (Morais, *Jews of Philadelphia*, 427–28, 440). Dr. Hendrikus de Young of Philadelphia, who married in 1887, may be a son of Philip (*Jewish Exponent*, Dec. 23, 1887).
87. Morais, *Jews of Philadelphia*, 312.
88. The *Occident* 24 (1868): 132; Morais, *Jews of Philadelphia*, 136–38.
89. Morais, *Jews of Philadelphia* 57, 141. A concise history of the board is that of Allan Tarshish, "The Board of Delegates of American Israelites (1859–1878)," *PAJHS* 49 (Sept. 1959): 16–32.
90. Morais, *Jews of Philadelphia*, 118, 131–35; Maxwell Whiteman, "The Philadelphia Group," in Friedman, *Jewish Life in Philadelphia*, 165–66.

91. The *Occident* 1 (1843), 411, 469–473; Lloyd P. Gartner, "Temples of Liberty Unpolluted: American Jews and Public Schools, 1840–1875," in Bertram Wallace Korn, ed., *A Bicentennial Festschrift for Jacob Rader Marcus* (New York, 1976), 167–69.

92. The *Occident* 5 (1847): 47–48; 6 (1848): 57–58, 213, 262–63; 7 (1849): 101–4. For an analysis of the Jewish school movement in the early days, see Gartner, "Temples of Liberty Unpolluted," 157–89, esp. 164–78. Bavarian-born Isidore Binswanger, who also was elected to this first board, married Hyman Polock's daughter Elizabeth the following year (Wolfe, "German Jewish Influence," 128–29; Morais, *Jews of Philadelphia*, 250–51).

93. The *Occident* 25 (1867): 213, 458–60; 26 (1868): 31–33, 134; 24 (1866): 283–86; Morais, *Jews of Philadelphia*, 156–57, 435. Polano in the 1890s assisted Dr. Morais in midweek services at Mikveh Israel Synagogue (*Jewish Exponent*, Sept. 22, 1893).

94. Marcus Lam later became a merchant. His father Eleazer, who died in 1889 at age seventy-three, was a longtime member of Mikveh Israel and was "well-known in the southern section of our city" (*Jewish Exponent*, Sept. 30, 1889); the *Jewish Messenger*, Nov. 18, 1864.

95. Morais, *Jews of Philadelphia*, 69; Maxwell Whiteman, "Philadelphia Group," in Friedman, *Jewish Life in Philadelphia*, 164; "Moses Aaron Dropsie," *Jewish Encyclopedia* 5:3; "Moses Aaron Dropsie," *Universal Jewish Encyclopedia* 3:602; "Dropsie College for Hebrew and Cognate Learning," ibid., 3:600–01.

96. The *Occident* 3 (1845): 421–28; Morais, *Jews of Philadelphia*, 162–64, 412, 166–67, 175, 265. Solomon van Beil married Rebecca Hyneman (also Dutch) in 1852 (see M. H. Stern, *First American Jewish Families*, 123).

97. Levi L., Jacob E., and Samuel M. Hyneman lived in Philadelphia; Augustus and Herman N. were in New York (*Jewish Exponent*, Mar. 30, 1899; Apr. 22, 1887; Nov. 10, 1897).

98. In 1868 Dropsie ran unsuccessfully in the Republican primary for district attorney and in 1870 he presided over the commission in charge of building a bridge across the Schuykill River. The *Jewish Messenger*, June 5, 1868; Whiteman, "Philadelphia Group," in Friedman, *Jewish Life in America*, 170; "Moses Aaron Dropsie" *Universal Jewish Encyclopedia* 3:602; Morais, *Jews of Philadelphia*, 407. In 1888 Dropsie resided at 1316 N. Broad Street (*Jewish Exponent*, Jan. 6, 1888).

99. Morais, *Jews of Philadelphia*, 407.

100. Hyneman died in prison on January 7, 1865. Other Union servicemen of Dutch stock included Solomon Pinheiro, son of Isaac; Solomon Asher, son of Michael; Jacob da Silva Cohen, a Navy surgeon; Washington R. de Young and Charles de Young, grandsons of Joseph; Benjamin B. Goodman; and Myer Fleisher, among others. See Morais, *Jews of Philadelphia*, 463, 476–77, 490–91, 530; the *Occident* 23 (1865): 192.

101. *Jewish Exponent*, Mar. 27, 1891; Sept. 4, 1896; Sept. 13, 1889; July 10,

30, 1887; Nov. 19, 1889. The Dutch pallbearers of Isaacs were M. Voorsanger, Joseph Sanson, Eli Goodman, Joseph Isaacs, and 'Hayim Polano.

Chapter 5

1. Albert Ehrenfried, *A Chronicle of Boston Jewry: From the Colonial Settlement to 1900* (Boston, 1963), 320–36; S. Broches, *Jews in New England: Six Historical Monographs* Vol. 1 *Historical Study of the Jews in Massachusetts (1650–1750)* (New York, 1942); Jacob R. Marcus, *The Colonial American Jew, 1492–1776,* 3 vols. (Detroit, 1970), 1:297–305.

2. Ehrenfried, *Chronicle of Boston Jewry,* 339, 341. The community lived within an area bordered by Boyleston, Washington, Indiana, and Church streets. Cf. Lee M. Friedman, *Jewish Pioneers and Patriots* (Philadelphia, 1948), 116–30.

3. Jacob Rader Marcus, *To Count a People: American Jewish Population Data, 1584–1984* (Lanham, MD, 1990) 92; Kenneth David Roseman, "The Jewish Population of America, 1850–1860: A Demographic Analysis of Four Cities" (Ph.D. diss., HUC, Jewish Institute of Religion, Cincinnati, 1971), 42–43, 46–47, 148.

4. Joseph R. Rosenbloom, *A Biographical Dictionary of Early American Jews: Colonial Times Through 1800* (Lexington, KY, 1960) 28–30; Ira Rosenwaike, "An Estimate and Analysis of the Jewish Population of the United States in 1790," *PAJHS* 50 (Sept. 1960): 25–27, 36; Malcolm H. Stern, comp., *First American Jewish Families: 600 Genealogies, 1654–1977* (Cincinnati, 1978), 44, 137; *Universal Jewish Encyclopedia* 3:115, 118, 444; Barnett A. Elzas, The *Jews of South Carolina: From the Earliest Times to the Present Day* (Philadelphia, 1905; repr. 1972), 32, 106.

5. Cecil Roth, "Some Jewish Loyalists in the War of American Independence," *PAJHS* 38 (Sept. 1948): 98–103; Ehrenfried, *Chronicle of Boston Jewry,* 246, 248–49.

6. Harry Smith and J. Hugo Tatsch, *Moses Michael Hays: Merchant—Citizen—Freemason, 1739–1805* (Boston, 1937), 34–67; Isaac M. Fein, *Boston—Where It All Began: An Historical Perspective of the Boston Jewish Community* (Boston, 1976), 10–15; Rosenbloom, *Biographical Dictionary,* 58–60, 129–30; M. H. Stern, *First American Jewish Families,* 104; Clarence I. Freed, "Hays," *Universal Jewish Encyclopedia* 5:257; Morris A. Gutstein, "George Washington," *Universal Jewish Encyclopedia* 10:470–71; "Boston," *Universal Jewish Encyclopedia* 2:481; "Massachusetts," *Universal Jewish Encyclopedia* 7:404; Samuel Oppenheim, "The Jews and Masonry in the United States Before 1810," *PAJHS* 19 (1910): 5; Joseph Lebowich, "The Jews in Boston Till 1875," *PAJHS* 12 (1904): 104, 107.

7. David De Sola Pool and Tamar De Sola Pool, *An Old Faith in the New World: Portrait of Shearith Israel, 1654–1954* (New York, 1955), 49; "Abraham Touro," *Universal Jewish Encyclopedia* 10:285; Freed, "Hays," *Universal Jewish Encyclopedia* 5:257; Leon Huhner, *The Life of Judah Touro (1775–1854)* (Philadelphia, 1946), 64–66; Morris U. Schappes, ed., *A Documentary History of the Jews in the United States 1654–1875* (New York, 1950), 660.

8. Ehrenfried, *Chronicle of Boston Jewry*, 316–17; M. H. Stern, *First American Jewish Families*, 137. In Philadelphia Alfred T. Jones became a communal leader, active in Shekinah Lodge, first president of Jewish Hospital, and founder and editor of the major weekly *The Jewish Record.*

9. Aaron Isaacs (1801–1878) lived in the far northern Philadelphia suburb of Northern Liberties in 1830 and in city Ward 21 in 1860. But his clothing shop was located in the city center at 511 N. Second Street. Ira Rosenwaike, *On the Edge of Greatness: A Portrait of American Jewry in the Early National Period* (Cincinnati, 1985), 125, 153; Bruce L. Gottlieb, "Jews in the Clothing Industry in Philadelphia, 1850–1860," unpublished paper, HUC, Cincinnati, 1980; see also the Isaac A. Isaacs Papers, especially the typescript, "Isaac A. Isaacs, Largest Department Store West of New York City," in the Abraham Lincoln Nebel (1891–1973) Collection, Cleveland Jewish Miscellany, 1831–1971, WRHS, Cleveland; and "Ante Bellum Cleveland Jewish Immigrant Database," also at WRHS. The family tree is in M. H. Stern, *First American Jewish Families*, 124. Aaron's grandfather Gatzel Isaac Pront (Van Brunt) of Amsterdam signed on during the American Revolution in 1779 as a contract surgeon on the famed American ship *Bon Homme Richard* when it docked in Amsterdam. Descendants presently own an advertising agency in New York City with the family name Van Brunt.

10. Ehrenfried, *Chronicle of Boston Jewry*, 342, reports that Boston in 1851 had 120 Jewish families, with 80 male members of the synagogue. Roseman identified 332 Jews in the 1850 federal census and 1,159 in 1860, "Jewish Population of America," 46–47. Doubtless, there were some that he missed. I identified 62 Dutch or Dutch-American Jews in the 1850 census and 269 in 1860. Thus, the percentages are 18.7 in 1850 and 23.2 in 1860. Marcus (*To Count a People*, 92) estimates the 1873 total at 2,500, the 1878 total at 7,000, and the 1900 total at 40,000.

11. These figures are compiled from Swierenga, *Dutch Households in U.S. Population Censuses, 1850, 1860, 1870: An Alphabetical Listing by Family Heads*, 3 vols. (Wilmington, DE, 1987); and Roseman, "Jewish Population of America," table 12, "Place of Birth."

12. Ehrenfried, *Chronicle of Boston Jewry*, 339, 343. According to the 1845 Boston City Directory, Prince lived at 9 Shawmut and his office was at 295 Washington Street. Oldkerk in 1843 lived at 30 Common Street and in 1844 at 27 Oak Street. In 1846 the city directory located his lace shop at 163 Washington and his residence at 103 Pleasant (see Ehrenfried, *Chronicle of Boston Jewry*, 324–25.)

13. Ibid., 345–46.
14. Ehrenfried, *Chronicle of Boston Jewry*, 347–52, 356, 369–70; *Jewish Messenger*, Oct. 8, 1858. Also in 1858 President Prince wrote his friend, Samuel M. Isaacs of New York, to verify the credentials of a Palestine fundraiser. Isaacs replied in the *Jewish Messenger* urging all contributions to be sent directly to Palestine or via Sir Moses Montefiore in London (July 30, 1858).
15. Ehrenfried, *Chronicle of Boston Jewry*, 350, 356–57; the *Jewish Messenger*, June 19, 1863. Isaacs gave the school ceremonies extensive coverage (ibid., June 26, July 2, 1863).
16. Ehrenfried, *Chronicle of Boston Jewry*, 466–67.
17. Ibid., 351–52, 355–56, 370; the *Jewish Messenger*, Nov. 2, 1860; May 23, 1862; Feb. 23, 1863; Swierenga, *Dutch Households*, 1:141). Isaac Buitenkant is listed as David Buitenkant.
18. The *Jewish Messenger*, June 19, Sept. 25, 1863. During the construction of the new Ohabei Shalom Synagogue, Reverend Noot wrote Rabbi Joseph Moses Aaronson, the author of an early book of American responsa published in Jerusalem, requesting approval to place the ark on the southwest side of the synagogue so worshipers would turn toward the Holy City of Jerusalem. Rabbi Aaronson gave temporary approval, pending geographical verification of the relative degrees of latitude of the two cities (see J. D. Eisenstein, "The Development of Jewish Casuistic Literature in America," *PAJHS* 12 (1904): 144–45).
19. Ehrenfried, *Chronicle of Boston Jewry*, 357–59; the *Occident* 18 (1860), 196; 22 (1865), 563; the *Jewish Messenger*, Feb. 3, 1865. The congregation advertised in the *Occident* for a first and second minister in 1862 (20 [1862], 141–42). Noot's son Isaac C. became Hebrew teacher at the Hebrew Free School No. 1 in New York City at its founding in 1865 and he also served twenty years as minister of the Dutch congregation Bnai Israel (the *Jewish Messenger*, May 13, Oct. 28, 1864; June 23, 1865). Son Myer of Providence, Rhode Island, became the first Jewish justice of the peace in the state. He was recorder and financial secretary of the Jewish congregation and spearheaded efforts to organize the Redwood Lodge in Newport (ibid., Mar. 29, 1878). The youngest son, Joseph C. Noot, was a Chicago neckwear manufacturer in 1900. See Swierenga, "Dutch Households in Federal Manuscript Population Census, Chicago, 1900."
20. Ehrenfried, *Chronicle of Boston Jewry*, 427–29; the *Jewish Messenger*, Nov. 30, 1860.
21. The *Jewish Messenger*, Oct. 20, 1865. Mark Hamburger sailed on the ship *William and Mary* from Amsterdam to New York, arriving on July 15, 1857. See Robert P. Swierenga, comp., *Dutch Immigrants in U.S. Ship Passenger Manifests, 1820–1880: An Alphabetical Listing by Household Heads and Independent Persons*, 2 vols. (Wilmington, DE, 1983), 1:364; Swierenga, *Dutch Households*, 2:400, 3:900. The Amsterdam population registers (Amsterdam Bevolkingsregisters) show Mar-

kus Jacob Hamburger was born on Jan. 30, 1831, as the oldest son of Jacob Meyer Hamburger, age twenty- six years, without occupation, and Sara Marcus Polak, age thirty years. His father had been born in Maarsserveen, Utrecht Province, and his mother's family was from Amsterdam. Meyer Jacob Hamburger was born April 1, 1836, in Amsterdam. Both brothers were without occupation when they immigrated.

22. Ehrenfried, *Chronicle of Boston Jewry*, 425, 428.
23. Ibid., 472.
24. Ibid., 428; the *Jewish Messenger*, Oct. 20, 1865. The congregation's committee on benevolence in 1865 included M. J. Hamburger, D. M. Davis, Lewis Levi, B. L. Cohen, and M. Fonseca. Hamburger and Levi are known to be Dutch-born; the others may be Dutch or English.
25. The *Jewish Messenger*, Sept. 24, 1875; Ehrenfried, *Chronicle*, 428–29, 472–73. Charter members of Corporation Beth Eil in 1875 were L. Bronkhorst, Isaac Buitenkant, Isaac Frank, Louis Goedhart, Isaac Grishaver, M. J. Hamburger, M. Isaacs, Louis Park, Solomon Sugarman, and Samuel Whitebone (Witteboon).
26. Quoted in Ehrenfried, *Chronicle*, 430.
27. Ibid., 431.
28. Ibid., 473–74. The first directors of the Netherland Cemetery Association in 1909, then still commonly called the *Hollandsche Chevra*, were Samuel Goldsmith, chair; Maurice Levy, vice chair; David Abraham, clerk; Solomon Grishaver, treasurer; Solomon Jacobs, collector; Aaron van Emden; Isaac Hyman; Isaac Verveer; and Solomon Berg. Moses van Dam was treasurer for more than forty years. He had emigrated from Amsterdam in 1855 and owned a dry goods store (Swierenga, *Dutch Households*, 3:1021). Samuel Fischer of Needham, MA, an officer in the Jewish Cemetery Association of Massachusetts, presently maintains the records of the Netherlands Cemetery Association. Letter of Miriam Drukman (administrator, Jewish Cemetery Association of Massachusetts) to the author, Jan. 20, 1993.
29. Ehrenfried, *Chronicle*, 476–77. Dutch-born charter members were: David Block, Joseph Davis, Moses de Groot, Simon de Young, Louis Jacobs, Louis L. Jacobs, Lazarus Levi, David Levy, Isaac Park, Lewis Park, and Moses van Dam.
30. Ibid., 480.
31. Roseman, "Jewish Population of America," 89–95 and table 13 "Occupational Distribution."
32. Jacob Van Hinte, *Netherlanders in America: A Study in Emigration and Settlement in the Nineteenth and Twentieth Centuries in the United States of America*, Robert P. Swierenga, gen. ed.; Adriaan de Wit, chief trans. (Grand Rapids, MI, 1985), 615, citing J. Jansen, "Een verblijf in America," *Vragen van den Dag* 36 (Aug. 1920): 628.
33. Ehrenfried, *Chronicle of Boston Jewry*, 297.
34. *Boston Globe*, Mar. 25, 1940, in ibid., 297–98. There are other claim-

ants to the title of first diamond-cutter. According to the obituary of Jacob de Young (1859–1940), his brother Simon, who had been born in Amsterdam about 1825 and immigrated to Boston in the 1850s, had started the first diamond-cutting shop in America in Boston with three partners. Later, this group associated itself with Henry Moss, of whom it was said that he "revolutionized the process of diamond cutting." The 1860 census, however, lists Simon De Young and his older brother Benjamin (who was born in Amsterdam about 1822) as owners of a secondhand clothing shop, each owning $500 in personal property in 1860. Again, in the 1870 census, the brothers were retail clothing dealers. Thus, when Simon and Benjamin became diamond-cutters, it was after 1870 and they were above fifty years of age. It seems more likely that Adam Keyser was the pioneer diamond-cutter in America.

35. Aaron Keyser was living in Ward 10 in 1860 in a four-family apartment with fellow Dutch Jews, and he gave his occupation as peddler. His wife Emma (or Anna) and oldest daughter, Jeannette, age seven, were born in the Netherlands, but four-year-old Fanny was born in New York. This sets the time of emigration between 1853 and 1856. Daughter Julia (two years) was born in Connecticut and daughter Matilda (one year) was born in Massachusetts. In 1870, Keyser lived in Ward 7 and listed his occupation as diamond-cutter, with personal property worth $400. He was renting a flat in a two-family dwelling. He and Anna (or Emma) had one new child, a son Herman, born in 1862 or early 1863 (Swierenga, *Dutch Households*, 2:531).

36. Van Hinte, *Netherlanders*, 835–36, 1085 n 56, for this and the following paragraphs.

37. Roseman, "Jewish Population of America," table 14 "Real Estate Ownership"; table 15 "Personal Estate Ownership." Unfortunately, the total wealthholding in dollars for Boston is not reported, nor is the per family average computed.

38. Ibid., table 2 "Residential Distribution."

39. Ibid., table 16 "Housing."

40. Ibid., table 6 "Distribution by Sex."

41. Ibid., table 18 "Literacy"; and Swierenga, *Dutch Households*.

Chapter 6

1. Isidor Blum, *The Jews of Baltimore: An Historical Summary . . .* (Baltimore and Washington, 1910), 3–8; Jacob Rader Marcus, *The Colonial American Jew, 1492–1776*, 3 vols. (Detroit, 1970), 1:336–37; Ira Rosenwaike, "The Jews of Baltimore to 1810," *American Jewish Historical Quarterly* 64 (June 1975): 291–320, esp. 291–93, 313; Ira Rosenwaike, "The Jews of Baltimore: 1810 to 1820," ibid. 67 (Dec. 1977): 101–24, esp. 102, 104.

2. Recollections of Jonas Friedenwald, *Jewish Exponent* (Philadelphia), Sept. 20, 1889.

3. Rosenwaike, "Jews of Baltimore to 1810," 299.

4. Adolf Guttmacher, *A History of the Baltimore Hebrew Congregation, 1830–1905* (Baltimore, 1905), 22–23; Rose Greenburg, *The Chronicle of Baltimore Hebrew Congregation, 1830–1975* (Baltimore, 1976), 1, 15. A detailed genealogy of the Eleazer Lyons family is in Malcolm H. Stern, comp., *First American Jewish Families, 600 Genealogies, 1654–1977* (Cincinnati, 1978), 182. The links between Dutch Jews in Baltimore and in the West Indies were particularly strong, according to Greenburg. On this point see also Rabbi I. Harold Sharfman, *The First Rabbi: Origins of Conflict Between Orthodox & Reform: Jewish Polemic Warfare in Pre-Civil War America, a Biographical History* (Malibu, CA, 1988), 79.

5. Isaac M. Fein, *The Making of an American Jewish Community: The History of Baltimore Jewry from 1773 to 1920* (Philadelphia, 1971), 11.

6. Rosenwaike, "Jews of Baltimore to 1810," 315–16.

7. Ibid., 316–17.

8. Ibid.; Rosenwaike, "Jews of Baltimore: 1810 to 1820," 102.

9. Rosenwaike, "Jews of Baltimore: 1810 to 1820," 118, citing "Wertheim Circumcision Book."

10. Rosenwaike, "Jews of Baltimore to 1810," 318–20.

11. Rosenwaike, "Jews of Baltimore: 1810 to 1820," 101–3.

12. Ibid., table 1, 103–4, 108.

13. Ibid., 108–9.

14. Ibid., 109–11, 120 n.68; Fein, *Making of an American Jewish Community*, 47, 49; *Jewish Exponent*, Nov. 21, 1890; Robert P. Swierenga, comp., *Dutch Households in U.S. Population Censuses, 1850, 1860, 1870: An Alphabetical Listing by Family Heads*, 3 vols. (Wilmington, DE, 1987), 1:51. Leon Levy died at age 74 in 1843 and was buried in the German Hebrew Cemetery. His watchmaking venture as "Cohen & Levy, Watchmakers, 11 Market, F.P." is conjecture. Four sons survived Rachel Leon at her death in 1890— Isaac, Levi, Benjamin, and Jacob.

15. Rosenwaike, "Jews of Baltimore: 1810 to 1820," 111; Rosenwaike, *On the Edge of Greatness: A Portrait of American Jewry in the Early National Period* (Cincinnati, 1985), 153.

16. Rosenwaike, "Jews of Baltimore: 1810 to 1820," 112.

17. Ibid., 112–13. Polack (1783–1854) died in New York (*New York Herald*, Dec. 11, 1854).

18. Rosenwaike, "Jews of Baltimore: 1810 to 1820," 120.

19. Rosenwaike, *Edge of Greatness*, 31, 112, 140; Fein, *Making of an American Jewish Community*, 36, 38.

20. Rosenwaike, "Jews of Baltimore: 1810 to 1820," 123–24; Fein, *Making of an American Jewish Community*, 13–25.

21. Rosenwaike, "Jews of Baltimore: 1810 to 1820," 124.

22. Ibid., 122, states that all of the Jews of early American stock had "either died or moved away during the 1820s," leaving only three native-born families in 1829.
23. Rosenwaike "discovered" Joseph Jacobs and corrected erroneous information about Zalma Rehiné in "The Founding of Baltimore's First Jewish Congregation: Fact vs. Fiction," *American Jewish Archives* 28 (Nov. 1976): 119–25.
24. Fein, *Making of an American Jewish Community*, 25–44.
25. Ibid., 42–44; Rosenwaike, *Edge of Greatness*, 140; Guttmacher, *Baltimore Hebrew Congregation*, 11–18; Rosenwaike, "Baltimore's First Jewish Congregation," 125. Five of fifteen electors who agreed to purchase the burial ground in 1831 were also Dutch (*Baltimore Hebrew Congregation*, 121). Joseph Osterman (c. 1799–1861), born in Amsterdam, moved his household for health reasons to Galveston, Texas, in 1839 and thereby became the city's first Jewish family. His wife Rosanna Dyer Osterman was born in Baltimore to German Jewish parents and died in Mississippi by drowning in 1866. She bequeathed large legacies to Jewish synagogues and charities in Texas and elsewhere (*Baltimore Hebrew Congregation*, 31–32). See also M. H. Stern, *First American Jewish Families*, 62.
26. Guttmacher, *Baltimore Hebrew Congregation*, 16–21; Fein, *Making of an American Community*, 43–44; Sharfman, *First Rabbi*, 76–77, 79. The name reflected the influence of the Caribbean Hollanders, who had difficulty with the guttural Hebrew pronunciation and transliterated the Hebrew name, Nidhei Israel as Nidche Israel, which later German Jewish arrivals corrected (*First Rabbi*, 78).
27. Blum (*Jews of Baltimore*, 7) provides the membership list for 1832, as does Guttmacher, *Baltimore Hebrew Congregation*, 21.
28. Guttmacher, *Baltimore Hebrew Congregation*, 23, 43–45.
29. Fein, *Making of an American Jewish Community*, 271 n.9.
30. Guttmacher, *Baltimore Hebrew Congregation*, 20–21, 55, and photo facing p. 30; the *Occident and American Jewish Advocate* 18 (1860): 232. Sharfman (*First Rabbi*, 79) incorrectly calls Levi Benjamin a "Bohemian Jew," but he was born in the Netherlands (see Rosenwaike, *Edge of Greatness*, 140).
31. These were Jacob Aaron, Levi Benjamin, Joseph Dammelman, Michael de Young, Simon Eytinge, Solomon Hunt, Moses Millem, Joseph Osterman, Lewis Silver, and Samuel A. Waterman. A. Kookegay was also possibly Dutch. Guttmacher, *Baltimore Hebrew Congregation*, 21–22; Rosenwaike, *Edge of Greatness*, 140.
32. Sharfman's *First Rabbi* is a brilliant 1988 biography of Rabbi Rice and his fight against Reform Judaism.
33. Fein, *Making of an American Jewish Community*, 59–61; Sharfman, *First Rabbi*, 81–82. Sharfman uses the term *Judeo-German* (81), which is sometimes used by scientific writers to designate Yiddish (see "Yiddish," *Universal Jewish Encyclopedia*, 10:598).

34. Fein, *Making of an American Jewish Community*, 61–62; Sharfman, *First Rabbi*, 80; Guttmacher, *Baltimore Hebrew Congregation*, 20. Fein gives 1847 as the founding date of the Eden Street Congregation, which is the year the Maryland legislature authorized the incorporation of the synagogue (Fein, *Making of an American Jewish Community*, 274 n.72).

35. Sharfman, *First Rabbi*, 620.

36. Guttmacher, *Baltimore Hebrew Congregation*, 27–28; Rosenwaike, *Edge of Greatness*, 140; Fein, *Making of an American Jewish Community*, 105.

37. Fein, *Making of an American Jewish Community*, 75; the *Occident* 17 (1859): 168; *Jewish Exponent*, Feb. 13, 1891; Nov. 5, 1897; Feb. 11, 1898. Bertha Weil died in 1897 at the home of her mother. Van Leer was in the wholesale clothing business until 1893 with Henry Sonneborn & Co. His son Charles van Leer became "well-known in the musical world."

38. Rosenwaike, *Edge of Greatness*, 140.

39. Fein, *Making of an American Jewish Community*, 76–77; Lance Sussman, "The Economic Life of the Jews in Baltimore as Reflected in the City Directories: 1819–1840" (unpublished paper, HUC, Cincinnati, 1977).

40. Compiled from Sussman, "Economic Life," app. 1, 5–7.

41. Rosenwaike, *Edge of Greatness*, 140.

42. *Jewish Exponent*, Nov. 10, 1899.

43. A brief history by a family genealogist is Flora B. Atkin, "Dutch Treats on My Father's Side: Discoveries in Preparing a Toledotaynu of the Hartogensis Family," *Avotaynu: The International Review of Jewish Genealogy* 7 (Winter, 1991):23–27; Blum, *Jews of Baltimore*, 281; "Record of Marriages by Dr. [Henry] Hochheimer," 1850–1900, Baltimore, MD, in AJA, Cincinnati. See also H. S. Hartogensis, letter to the editor, the *Jewish Messenger*, Aug. 2, 1878.

44. Blum, *Jews of Baltimore*, 281; Fein, *Making of an American Jewish Community*, 116–19, 110, 186; *Jewish Exponent*, Oct. 21, 1887; the *Jewish Messenger*, Aug. 25, 1876; July 29, 1878; July 12, 1889.

45. *Jewish Exponent*, Nov. 7, 1890.

46. Blum, *Jews of Baltimore*, 203, 281, 285; obituary clippings from various Baltimore newspapers, American Jewish Archives, Cincinnati; "Benjamin Henry Hartogensis," *Universal Jewish Encyclopedia*, 5:234; Ezekiel J. Londow, "Benjamin Henry Hartogensis," *PAJHS* 37 (1947): 469–70. Benjamin H. Hartogensis, "Denial of Equal Rights to Religious Minorities and Non-Believers in the United States," *Yale Law Review* 39 (Mar. 1938): 659–81. Another son A. Jacob was a Baltimore jewelry jobber and commission traveler for the firm of Hartogensis & Co. until his premature death in 1893 at age thirty-two. Sons Jacob and Morris also moved to New York by the 1880s. See *Jewish Exponent*, May 15, 1900; Mar. 17, 1893; May 6, 1887. In 1889 a Dr. A. E.

Hartogensis was elected president of the new Moses Montefiore Congregation in Uptown New York City (the *Jewish Messenger*, Sept. 27, 1889). He may have been the third brother to emigrate from 's Hertogenbosch.

Chapter 7

1. Bertram Wallace Korn, *The Early Jews of New Orleans* (Waltham, MA, 1989), 9–14.
2. Ibid., 20–23.
3. Ibid., 23–35.
4. Ibid., 35–40; Elliott Ashkenazi, *The Business of Jews in Louisiana* (Tuscaloosa, AL, and London, 1988), 5, 182.
5. Korn, *Early Jews of New Orleans*, 40–54, 66–67.
6. Leon Huhner, *The Life of Judah Touro (1775–1854)* (Philadelphia, 1946); "Judah Touro," *Universal Jewish Encyclopedia* 10:285–86; Korn, *Early Jews of New Orleans*, 196–97, 70–94, 247–58; Leon A. Jick, *The Americanization of the Synagogue, 1820–1870* (Hanover, NH, 1976), 54–55. The text of Touro's famous will is in Morris U. Schappes, ed., *A Documentary History of the Jews in the United States, 1654–1875* (New York, 1950), 333–41.
7. Korn, *Early Jews of New Orleans*, 104–5, 297; the family tree is in Malcolm H. Stern, comp., *First American Jewish Families: 600 Genealogies, 1654–1977* (Cincinnati, 1978), 16. Maurice Barnett died in 1806. Barnett's only daughter Helene married Sol Audler. Stern does not report the names of Barnett's sons' wives, but none were baptized.
8. Korn, *Early Jews of New Orleans*, 105–10, quote on 109.
9. Ibid., 135–36. The New York-Richmond associate was Solomon Soher, also likely Dutch-born.
10. Nathan Phillip's ancestor Nathan Nathan had been the scribe (*sofer*) of Amsterdam (ibid., 136–42); M. H. Stern, *First American Jewish Families*, 228. Stern notes that Nathan lived for a time in Paris.
11. Korn, *Early Jews of New Orleans*, 141.
12. Hyam Harris died in penury in 1828, one of the first buried in the cemetery of the new Hebrew congregation located just beyond the city in the suburb of Lafayette in Jefferson Parish. Korn, *Early Jews of New Orleans*, 138, 140–41, 205; Isaac Markens, *The Hebrews in America* (New York, 1888, repr. 1978), 89–90; M. H. Stern, *First American Jewish Families*, 94; Joseph R. Rosenbloom, A *Biographical Dictionary of Early American Jews; Colonial Times Through 1800* (Lexington, KY, 1960), 49–50; Bertram Wallace Korn, "The Jews of Mobile, Alabama, Prior to the Organization of the First Congregation, in 1841," *Hebrew Union College Annual*, 40–41 (1969–1970): 494. Moses's brother Aaron worked with him for a time.

13. Korn, *Early Jews of New Orleans*, 142–44, 155, 163, 309; M. H. Stern, *First American Jewish Families*, 248. Alexander was the oldest son of Abraham Phillips and Ella Mateman of Amsterdam.

14. Korn, *Early Jews of New Orleans*, 199–203, quote from Jacobs's obituary in the *New Orleans Bee*.

15. Ibid., 153–57, 144, 166, 312 n.118.

16. The four Dutch Jews in the 1820 federal census were Simon Cohen, A. M. Nathan, Alexander Phillips, and Judah Touro. See Ira Rosenwaike, "The Jewish Population of the United States as Estimated from the Census of 1820," *American Jewish Historical Quarterly* 53 (Dec. 1963): 177.

17. Korn, *Early Jews of New Orleans*, 138–39, 170–71, 306–7 n.84.

18. Ibid., 170–71. Ira Rosenwaike, On the *Edge of Greatness: A Portrait of American Jewry in the Early National Period* (Cincinnati, 1985), 146; M. H. Stern, *First American Jewish Families*, 146. David L. Kokernot died in Gonzales County, Texas, in 1892. Louis died in New Orleans in 1864.

19. Korn, *Early Jews of New Orleans*, 316 n.24, and Robert P. Swierenga, comp., *Dutch Immigrants in U.S. Ship Passenger Manifests, 1820–1880: An Alphabetical Listing by Household Heads and Independent Persons* 2 vols. (Wilmington, DE, 1983), 1:32.

20. Korn, *Early Jews of New Orleans*, 205–6.

21. Ibid., 109–10, 138, 141, 172–73; *Jewish Messenger*, Dec. 3, 1858. Daniel Goodman's son A. B. Goodman (1838–1888) and his daughters Hannah (1837–1914) and Virginia (1843–1903) lived much of their lives in Richmond and are buried in the Hebrew Cemetery there. Herbert T. Ezekiel and Gaston Lichtenstein, *The History of the Jews of Richmond from 1769 to 1917* (Richmond, 1917), 292–93, 146, 228.

22. Korn, *Early Jews of New Orleans*, 177, 319 n.37, 324 n.7; Rosenwaike, *Edge of Greatness*, 146.

23. Korn, *Early Jews of New Orleans*, 238–39, 336 n.6., 198, 306 n.82. J. L. and William Florance were managers of the Jewish Foster Home Society of Philadelphia in 1859 (*Jewish Messenger*, Feb. 25, 1859). William's wife Myrtilla, a daughter of Rev. Gershom Seixas of Philadelphia, died in the city in 1859 (ibid., Feb. 18, Mar. 11, 1859).

24. Korn, *Early Jews of New Orleans*, 196–98, 237, 324 n.6, 326 n.21.

25. Ibid., 206, 198, 325 n.9, 326 n.19. Lejeune's father Isaac was a native of Amsterdam (Schappes, *Documentary History*, 627).

26. Korn, *Early Jews of New Orleans*, 194–96, 198, 326 n.22, 327 nn.29, 36; Rosenwaike, "Census of 1820," 171, 173, 178. No male Solomon family members are listed in the 1850, 1860, or 1870 federal censuses of New Orleans. But Aaron died there in 1851. Most of the family had moved to Georgetown and Charleston, SC, and other southern cities. See M. H. Stern, *First American Jewish Families*, 277–78; Rosenbloom, *Biographical Directory*, 163; Barnett A. Elzas, The *Jews of South Carolina: From the Earliest Times to the Present Day*

(Philadelphia, 1905; repr. 1972), 90–91, 139, 243, 279. Rosenbloom states that Joseph Solomon died in Charleston in 1808, in which case he cannot be the person Korn states was in New Orleans in the 1820s.

27. Korn, *Early Jews of New Orleans*, 237–38; Swierenga, *Dutch Immigrants*, 1:185–86, 188, 239.

28. Korn, *Early Jews of New Orleans*, 158–59.

29. Ibid., 192–93.

30. Ibid., 198, 324–27, 194–95. The full constitution is reprinted in Leo Shpall, "The First Synagogue in Louisiana," *Louisiana Historical Quarterly* 21 (Apr. 1928): 518–31. The officers, besides Jacobs, were the junior wardens Abraham Plotz, Abraham Green, Asher Phillips, as well as Isaac Phillips, treasurer. Of the nineteen Dutch Jewish household heads listed in Table 7.1, only Cohen and the Van Osterns were not members or contributors to the synagogue.

31. Korn, *Early Jews of New Orleans*, 247–58; Jick, *Americanization of the Synagogue*, 54–55; Leo A. Bergman, *A History of Touro Synagogue, New Orleans* (New Orleans, 1968), 1.

32. Korn, *Early Jews of New Orleans*, 199–205.

33. Ibid., 210 (quote), 212–14, 207–8.

34. Ibid., 215–16, 221–22, 229–33 (quote on 229).

35. Nathan returned to Kingston in 1858 to resume the teaching post of religious instructor. Korn, *Early Jews of New Orleans*, 237, 245–53; *Jewish Messenger*, Jan. 7, 1859; Schappes, *Documentary History*, 661; Rabbi I. Harold Sharfman, *The First Rabbi: Origins of Conflict Between Orthodox and Reform: Jewish Polemic Warfare in Pre-Civil War America* (Malibu, CA, 1988), 84, 175, 650; Henry P. Silverman, "Kingston," *Universal Jewish Encyclopedia* 6:393–95; Hugo Bieber, "Virgin Islands," *Universal Jewish Encyclopedia* 10:425–26. Gershom Kursheedt was likely attracted to New Orleans by his sister's husband, Benjamin Florance, son of Dutch-born Zachariah Florance, with whom he was associated in the brokerage business (Korn, *Early Jews of New Orleans*, 177, 247). Florance in 1857–1859 was a trustee of Congregation Nefutzoth Jehudah, along with fellow Hollander Daniel Goodman. Florance served on its building committee and was treasurer of the Jewish Widows and Orphans Relief Society. Goodman in 1858 was a "worthy and esteemed" officer of the Hebrew Benevolent Society. See *Jewish Messenger*, Mar. 27, 1857; Aug. 13, Dec. 13, 31, 1858; Apr. 29, 1859.

36. Korn, "Jews of Mobile," 499–502. During Da Silva's tenure at Mobile, this Ashkenazic congregation had to tolerate his Portuguese mode of reading the service.

37. De Jonge was born about 1801 and was first recorded in the 1830 census. In the 1860 census, the last in which his name is found, he was living alone in Ward 1, age fifty-nine (see Tables 7.1 and 7.3). For some reason he was not reported in the 1850 census, and he had left the city before the 1870 census (Swierenga, *Dutch Households*, 1:208). Nathan-

iel S. Share's "History of the Congregation" is in *Centennial Volume: Congregation Gates of Prayer, January 13–15, 1950, New Orleans, La.* (New Orleans, 1950), 2–3.

38. The information about Carillon is in Sharfman, *First Rabbi*, 135–37, 176, 219–21, 281; Bieber, "Virgin Islands," *Universal Jewish Encyclopedia*, 10:426; Federal Manuscript Population Census, New Orleans, 1850, Ward 4. Carillon's wife was Rebecca age thirty-five, and his daughter was Marian age sixteen. All were born in the Netherlands. Carillon was likely a son (or brother) of the Aaron C. Carillon who in 1840 published in Amsterdam a little book on the Damascus Affair, in which he praised the Amsterdam banker Zevi Hirsch Lehren as a "brave man of Israel" (Mozes Heiman Gans, *Memorbook: History of Dutch Jewry from the Renaissance to 1940* [Baarn, Neth., 1971], 349).

39. Quoted in Sharfman, *First Rabbi*, 135. Cf. Bieber, "St Thomas," *Universal Jewish Encyclopedia* 10:425–26.

40. Sharfman, *First Rabbi*, 219–21; Elzas, *Jews of South Carolina*, 216.

41. Korn, *Early Jews of New Orleans*, 251; Sharfman, *First Rabbi*, 176; Federal Manuscript Population Census, 1850, New Orleans, Ward 4.

42. *Jewish Messenger*, Dec. 17, 1858. Isaac Leeser's Philadelphia-based journal, the *Occident and American Jewish Advocate*, reports several Dutch Jews in New Orleans not included in the federal censuses. Isaac Loperman, age fifty-five, from Holland, died in the city of yellow fever on October 12, 1858, and was interred in the Jewish Cemetery on Jackson Street (16 [1859]: 592). On September 8, 1867, the Reverend H. S. Jacob married Moses Aletrino of Amsterdam and Melanie, daughter of Solomon Ries of New Orleans (25 [1867]: 359).

43. Rabbi Max Heller, *Jubilee Souvenir* (New Orleans, 1922), 3 as cited in Leo Shpall, *The Jews of Louisiana* (New Orleans, 1936), 11.

44. Julian B. Feibelman, "A Social and Economic Study of the New Orleans Jewish Community," (Ph.D. diss., University of Pennsylvania, 1941), 3, 8.

45. Thomas J. Friedman, "A Study of Jewish Businessmen in New Orleans as Reflected in the City Directories of 1811 to 1840" (unpublished paper, HUC, Cincinnati, 1977). The best general survey of Jewish economic contributions is Allan Tarshish, "The Economic Life of the American Jew in the Middle Nineteenth Century," in Jacob Rader Marcus, ed., Essays in *American Jewish History* (New York, 1975), 263–93.

Chapter 8

1. Albert Ehrenfried, *A Chronicle of Boston Jewry: From the Colonial Settlement to 1900* (Boston, 1963), 404 n.4.

2. Selig Adler and Thomas E. Connolly, *From Ararat to Suburbia: The*

History of the Jewish Community of Buffalo (Philadelphia, 1960), 10–11.

3. The history of the Van Baalen family has not been told but one can piece together some details from government records in the Netherlands and the United States. See Robert P. Swierenga, comp., *Dutch Emigrants to the United States, South Africa, South America, and Southeast Asia, 1835–1880: An Alphabetical Listing by Household Heads and Independent Persons* (Wilmington, DE, 1983), 259; Robert P. Swierenga, comp., *Dutch Immigrants in U.S. Ship Passenger Manifests, 1820–1880: An Alphabetical Listing by Household Heads and Independent Persons*, 2 vols. (Wilmington, DE, 1983), 2:934–35; Robert P. Swierenga, comp., *Dutch Households in U.S. Population Censuses, 1850, 1860, 1870: An Alphabetical Listing by Family Heads*, 3 vols. (Wilmington, DE, 1987) 3:1010–11; Robert P. Swierenga, comp., "Dutch Households in Federal Manuscript Population Census, Chicago, 1900" (unpublished computer file).

4. John Verdonk of Hoogland, the Netherlands, a noted genealogist, kindly searched the Amsterdam population, marriage, and death registers and found that Emanuel Israel van Baalen was a son of Israel Emanuel van Baale(n) (1789–1849), a peddler, and Sapora Drittman, both residing in Amsterdam. Emanuel, also a peddler, married twice before emigrating; first at age eighteen to Klaartje Benjamin Couzijn and after her death to Maartje van Kleef in 1833 at age twenty-four (Marriage Registers 3:183, 2:191), Gemeentearchief, Amsterdam. Hence, Israel was a son of his first wife and Sarah and Morris were born to his second wife. Emanuel's father, son of Emanuel Joseph van Baalen of Amsterdam, died in 1849 in Noordwijk-Binnen, Province of Noord Holland (Death Registers 6:69), Gemeentearchief, Amsterdam.

5. The head of the Lit (Litt) families was Jacob Lit of Amsterdam. Some of Jacob's children in the United States were Joseph J. (b. 1811), David J. (b. 1815), Solomon J. (b. 1819), and Rosa (b. 1828). Joseph married Delphina (b. 1831), also Dutch-born, and their children were Henry (born in Buffalo in 1855), John (born in Cleveland in 1857), David (born in Philadelphia in 1859), Jonke (born in Detroit in 1865), Rosa (born in Detroit in 1865), and Isaac (born in Detroit in 1867). The family had moved to Chicago's Ninth Ward by 1870. David was a tailor in Philadelphia at 902 Market Street in 1850 and 1710 Market Street in 1860. David married Henrietta (b. 1811), also Dutch-born, and the couple moved to Chicago by 1900. Solomon married Mary (b. 1817) in the Netherlands, emigrated in 1852 with at least three children: Isaac, Joseph, and Jacob, and settled in Detroit where Henrietta was born in 1857. Son Jacob married Anna (also Dutch-born) in Detroit, and the couple had a daughter born there in 1869. By 1870 Solomon and family resided in Chicago's First Ward. Rosa married Joseph Israel van Baalen of the Buffalo Dutch clan and this couple also were in Chicago by 1870. The Litts are a very close-knit Dutch Jewish family. See Federal

Manuscript Population Census, Chicago, 1900, Ward 32, ED 1014; Swierenga, *Dutch Households*, 2:627; Federal Manuscript Population Census, Philadelphia, 1860; Philadelphia City Directory, 1860. Note that birth dates are derived from age reported in the census and may vary by plus or minus one year.

6. The information on the De Roy family is from the Amsterdam Population Registers (Bevolkingsregisters) of the 1850s.

7. Adler and Connolly, *Ararat to Suburbia*, 79.

8. Swierenga, *Dutch Households*, 3:1010; Federal Manuscript Population Census, Chicago, 1900, Ward 32, ED 1029. Joseph's wife Hannah died in Chicago in 1891 (see *Jewish Advocate* [Chicago], Dec. 5, 1891).

9. Emanuel Joseph van Baalen's name is variously recorded in the Federal Manuscript Population Censuses as Amanuel in 1850, N, in 1860, and El (perhaps an abbreviation of Emanuel) in 1870. There is no explanation for the first initial N. in 1860, but the names and ages of the wife and children offer a nearly perfect match between 1850, 1860, and 1870. Emanuel Joseph van Baalen was the oldest son of Amsterdam cattle drover and peat dealer Joseph Emanuel van Baalen (c. 1776–1844) and Rachel Alexander Polak, living at Jodenkerkstraat 3 in 1812–1815 and subsequently at Jodenbreestraat 91. Joseph was a brother of Israel Emanuel van Baalen. Marriage Registers 3:185, 6:6, 4:175; Death Registers 6:62, Gemeentearchief, Amsterdam.

10. Hartog (Henry) van Baalen was born in 1811 and his wife Clara in 1812. Genealogist John Verdonk reported that Hartog van Baalen, age twenty-four, a peddler, son of Israel Emanuel van Baalen and Sara Hartog (second wife), both of Amsterdam, married in 1836 to Klaartje (Clara) Isaacs Speijer, a seamstress, twenty-six years, also of Amsterdam (Amsterdam Marriage Registers, 3:185).

11. Selig and Connolly, *Ararat to Suburbia*, 56–57.

12. Swierenga, *Dutch Households*, 2:820, 831. Boasberg is incorrectly listed as Roasberg in 1850 and Roseberg in 1870.

13. This large amount of personal property seems to belie the undocumented assertion of Selig and Connolly, *Ararat to Suburbia*, 57, that Boasberg "was never very successful" at his business. In the early 1850s Boasberg moved from the old westside to the northwest sector on Ashland Avenue. Buffalo *Evening News*, September 6, 1900; and Buffalo *Express*, June 3, 1867.

14. Selig and Connolly, *Ararat to Suburbia*, 174–75, 238, 348, 134, 264, 355, 368.

15. Swierenga, *Dutch Emigrants*, 191. The religion of the family was Nederlands Israelite, not Nederlands Reformed, as erroneously indicated. The census data are in Swierenga, *Dutch Households*, 2:747.

16. Selig and Connolly, *Ararat to Suburbia* 126, 134; Swierenga, *Dutch Households*, 1:313, 2:566.

17. Bierman may be the father of Barney (Barnet) Berman, a leader of Buffalo's Hasidic congregation Anshe Emes Beth Zion Synagogue, and

later president of Temple Emanu-El. See Selig and Connolly, *Ararat to Suburbia*, 196, 327, 329; Swierenga, *Dutch Households*, 1:63.

18. Selig and Connolly, *Ararat to Suburbia*, 95; Swierenga, *Dutch Households*, 1:369; 2:485, 483. Rachel Cohen's parents were Frederick Cohen, a lumber merchant born in Prussia around 1804, and mother Louisa, born in the Netherlands around 1801. Their younger daughter Hannah was born in New York in 1840, which indicates they had emigrated much earlier and perhaps also settled in Buffalo (Swierenga, *Dutch Households*, 1:161).

19. Selig and Connolly, *Ararat to Suburbia*, 46–47, 52–53, 56–57; the *Jewish Messenger*, July 12, 1861; the *Occident and American Jewish Advocate* 6 (1848): 620; "Buffalo," *Encyclopaedia Judaica*, 4:1465; Temple *Beth El*, *Temple Beth El's First Century: Centennial Souvenir Book 1847–1947* (Buffalo, 1947), 13, 15, 30.

20. Selig and Connolly, *Ararat to Suburbia*, 57–58.

21. Ibid., 68, 98–99, 102.

22. Ibid., 93, 110.

23. Jacob S. Feldman, *The Jewish Experience in Western Pennsylvania: A History, 1755–1945* (Pittsburgh, 1986), 8–11, 21; "Pittsburgh," *Encyclopaedia Judaica*, 13:568.

24. Feldman, *Jewish Experience*, 18–25, 28–29; Feldman, "The Pioneers of the Community: Regional Diversity Among the Jews of Pittsburgh," *American Jewish Archives* 32 (Nov. 1980): 119–24; Steven Abrams, "An Economic Survey of the Jews in Pittsburgh, Pennsylvania, 1860–1880" (unpublished paper, HUC, Cincinnati, 1979).

25. Data derived from Swierenga, *Dutch Households*; and Swierenga, *Dutch Emigration*.

26. The Amsterdam home address of the De Roys was Jodenbreestraat 2. Their children's birth years were Levi A. (1836), Emanuel (1841), Bloemen or Betsy (1843), Israel (1847), Joseph (1849), and Rachel (1852). See Amsterdam Population Registers (Bevolkingsregisters), 1850–1860, Book Q1.4; Swierenga, *Dutch Emigrants*, 259.

27. Swierenga, *Dutch Households*, 1:246; 3:1011.

28. Ibid., 3:1010–11; Abrams, "Economic Survey of the Jews in Pittsburgh," chart 3. In 1875 Israel de Roy lived at 57 Webster and Joseph de Roy resided at 87 Logan.

29. The *Borussia* arrived in New York on February 26, 1863; (Swierenga, *Dutch Immigrants*, 2:887). The family name is listed as Suissman on the manifest. See also Ida Cohen Selavan, ed., *My Voice Was Heard* (New York, 1981), 34.

30. Philip Susman married Edelina Loude of Oude Pekela, Groningen (born 1819), also Jewish, and the couple had two children born in Amsterdam: Frederika (1847) and Edward (1852) (Amsterdam Population Registers [Bevolkingsregisters], 1850–1860 Book R1.157; Swierenga, *Dutch Households*, 3:953). Philip Susman and family have not yet been identified in the U.S. Ship Passenger manifests. Louis Susman lived

next door to his pawnshop at 14 Wylie, according to the city directories of 1865–1866 and 1874–1875 (see chart 3 of Abrams, "Economic Survey of the Jews in Pittsburgh").

31. Compiled from the Federal Manuscript Population Census, Pittsburgh, 1870. Of the one hundred, forty-four were Dutch-born and the remainder American-born children or non-Dutch spouses. Jacob S. Feldman in "The Early Migration and Settlement of Jews in Pittsburgh, 1754–1894" (unpublished paper, United Jewish Federation of Pittsburgh, 1959), 30, gives the total of one thousand.

32. Compiled from chart 1 in Abrams, "Economic Survey of the Jews in Pittsburgh." The breakdown for the 1874–1875 city directory is 75 percent merchants, 11 percent dealers and salesmen, 5 percent clerks, 7 percent artisans (chart 2).

33. Feldman, *Jewish Experience*, 43–44; *Tree of Life Congregation Anniversary Booklet, 1864–1952* (Pittsburgh, 1952), 4–5; Selavan, *My Voice Was Heard*, 34.

34. Feldman, *Jewish Experience*, 45, 48. It is unclear if Pachter was a full-time teacher in the congregation's school or the public school system.

35. Rabbi David Philipson, *The Oldest Jewish Congregation in the West, Bene Israel, Cincinnati [One Hundredth Anniversary 1824–1924, Rockdale Avenue Temple]* (Cincinnati, 1924), 17; see also Ann Deborah Michael, "The Origin of the Jewish Community of Cincinnati, 1817–1860," *Cincinnati Historical Society Bulletin* 30 (Fall-Winter 1972): 155–82, esp. 155. A masterful history of early Cincinnati is Stephan G. Mostov, "A 'Jerusalem' on the Ohio: The Social and Economic History of Cincinnati's Jewish Community, 1840–1875" (Ph.D. diss., University of Cincinnati, 1981).

36. Compiled from Ira Rosenwaike, *On the Edge of Greatness: A Portrait of American Jewry in the Early National Period* (Cincinnati, 1985), 116, 144.

37. For data from the early Cincinnati City Directories, see Judy Lewis, "Cincinnati Businessmen, 1818–1840" (unpublished paper, HUC, 1977), 7–8; Rosenwaike in *Edge of Greatness* (116, 144) gives the place and dates of death. Morris U. Schappes, ed., *A Documentary History of the Jews in the United States, 1654–1875* (New York, 1950), 627, gives Le Jeune's death date as 1843. Workum's wife Sarah Levy was born in the Netherlands in 1798 and died in Cincinnati in 1883. See Malcolm H. Stern, comp., *First American Jewish Families: 600 Genealogies, 1654–1977* (Cincinnati, 1978), 306–7.

38. Swierenga, *Dutch Households*, 3:1241, 1278. The family is incorrectly listed as Werkman.

39. Isaac Markens, *The Hebrews in America* (New York, 1888, repr. 1975), 101–2; Rosenwaike, *Edge of Greatness*, 112, 140. Samuel de Young may have arrived a decade earlier, since the 1825 Cincinnati City Directory lists a Samuel J. de Young from England (see Philipson, *Oldest Jewish Congregation*, 10).

40. Ira Rosenwaike, "The Jews of Baltimore: 1810 to 1820," *American Jewish Historical Quarterly* 67 (Dec. 1977): 101–24, esp. 102, 104; Rosenwaike, *Edge of Greatness*, 116, 144; Swierenga, *Dutch Households*, 1:214.
41. Swierenga, *Dutch Emigrants*, 88.
42. Swierenga, *Dutch Households*, 1:343; 3:952, 1160, 1278.
43. Ibid., 2:756; 3:1230.
44. Henry Samuel Morais, *The Jews of Philadelphia: Their History from the Earliest Settlements to the Present Time* (Philadelphia, 1894), 259–62; "Jacob Ezekiel," *Jewish Encyclopedia* 5:318; Philipson, *Oldest Jewish Congregation*, 13–14, 27, 60–73, contains a complete list of members, as does Joseph Jonas, "The Jews in Ohio," an autobiographical account, December 25, 1843, in Schappes, *Documentary History*, 228. See also the *Jewish Messenger*, Sept. 12, 1873; Herbert T. Ezekiel and Gaston Lichtenstein, *The History of the Jews of Richmond from 1769 to 1917* (Richmond, 1917), 24, 117–20; *Jewish Exponent* (Philadelphia), May 19, 1899; June 2, 1899. For the Waterman genealogy see M. H. Stern, *First American Jewish Families*, 303. Catherine Ezekiel's obituary is in the *Jewish Messenger*, July 17, 1891.
45. Lloyd P. Gartner, *History of the Jews of Cleveland* (Cleveland, 1978), 10–14; "Cleveland," *Encyclopaedia Judaica* 5:606–7; Congregation Tifereth Israel, *The Temple, 1850–1950* (Cleveland, 1950), 9–10; Allan Peskin, *This Tempting Freedom: The Early Years of Cleveland Judaism and Anshe Chesed Congregation* (Cleveland, 1973), 1–9.
46. This and the following paragraphs rely on "Peixotto Family," *Jewish Encyclopedia* 9:582–84; Isaac S. Emmanuel and Suzanna A. Emmanuel, *History of the Jews of the Netherlands Antilles*, 2 vols. (Cincinnati, 1970), 1:1076–77; "Dr. Daniel Levy Madura Peixotto" typescript, in Abraham Lincoln Nebel (1891–1973) Collection, Cleveland Jewish Miscellany, 1831–1971, WRHS, Cleveland.
47. David Naar, a brother-in-law of Dr. Daniel Peixotto's sister Sarah, who married Benjamin Naar, purchased the *Daily True American* in 1853 and edited it until 1905 after which nephews owned it ("Dr. Daniel Levy Maduro Peixotto" typescript, WRHS).
48. This and the following paragraph rely on Cleveland *Daily Plain Dealer*, Jan. 4–May 26, 1856; A. W. Voorsanger, *Western Jewry: An Account of the Achievements of the Jews and Judaism in California Including Eulogies and Biographies* (San Francisco, 1916), 132; and "Benjamin Franklin Peixotto," *Jewish Encyclopedia*, 9:582–8; Benjamin F. Peixotto obituary in *Jewish Exponent* (Philadelphia), Sept. 26, 1890; Archer H. Shaw, *The Plain Dealer: One Hundred Years in Cleveland* (New York, 1942), 124–26. After his political apostasy, the *Plain Dealer* refused to acknowledge that Peixotto had ever been its editor. "It would puzzle the astutist to discover why he has since changed his creed," opined the editor in 1877.
49. Gary E. Polster, "'To Love Work and Dislike Being Idle': Origins and

Aims of the Cleveland Orphan Asylum, 1868–1878," *American Jewish Archives* 39 (Nov. 1987): 127–55. Gustav Adolf Danziger, "The Jew in San Francisco: The Last Half Century," *Overland Monthly* 25 (Apr. 1895): 399.

50. The *Jewish Messenger*, Nov. 11, Dec. 16, 1870. As Peixotto's eulogist declared in 1890, "By his knowledge and diplomacy he succeeded in quelling the persecutions of his unfortunate co-religionists and there was only one serious outbreak . . . during his incumbency." Subsequently, he encouraged European governments to convene conferences in Brussels and Berlin in 1878 to press for an end to the Rumanian pogroms. In addition to diplomacy, Peixotto sought to lessen antisemitism in Rumania by pushing the Jews there to abandon their traditional garb for modern Western dress and to try to blend in as good citizens. *Jewish Exponent* (Philadelphia), Sept. 26, 1890; Schappes, *Documentary History*, 545–46, 728.

51. *Jewish Exponent*, Apr. 15, 1887; May 20,1887; the *Jewish Messenger*, Sept. 19, 26, 1890; Congregation Tifereth Israel, *The Temple*, 18. Burial was in the Portuguese Cemetery Cypress Hill.

52. Various printed and manuscript sources cited in "Ante Bellum Cleveland Jewish Immigrant Database," WRHS; Swierenga, *Dutch Households*. All these Dutch Jews lived in Ward 3, except Frank.

53. Aaron Isaacs (van Brunt) and Esther Levy were born in Amsterdam and emigrated to Boston in 1825, where Isaac A. (1825–1897) was born. The family moved briefly to Atlanta, but by 1830 they had settled permanently in Philadelphia, where most of their thirteen children, including George (1830–?), were born. See Rosenwaike, *Edge of Greatness*, 125, 153; Swierenga, *Dutch Households*.

54. "An Instance of Business Success," *Cleveland Weekly Plain Dealer*, January 30, 1856; and "Isaac A. Isaacs, Largest Department Store West of New York City" typescript, in the Abraham Lincoln Nebel (1891–1973) Collection, Cleveland Jewish Miscellany, 1831–1971, WRHS, Cleveland.

55. "An Instance of Business Success."

56. A copy of this rare pamphlet published by Isaac A. Isaacs at Union Hall in 1863 is in the possession of WRHS. The quoted portions are, respectively, on the fourth page (unnumbered) following the title page, the copyright page, and numbered page 35. The Buckeye Boys claim is in "Isaac A. Isaacs, Largest Department Store West of New York City," typescript, WRHS.

57. "Isaac A. Isaacs, Largest Department Store West of New York City," typescript, WRHS. The last Cleveland City Directory listing a Union Hall advertisement was that of 1869–1870. In the 1870 census, Isaacs was listed in New York City.

58. Swierenga, *Dutch Households*, 3:1011, 1:246.

59. A third family, whose Jewishness is likely but not confirmed, was M. Meanden, a cigarmaker, and his wife Rebecca, both Dutch-born, and

their four children, also in Ward 1. The family had migrated in stages; the oldest child was born in England, the second in Ireland, the third in New York, and the fourth in Cleveland in May, 1870. By 1880 they had departed the city. See Swierenga, *Dutch Households*, 1:369, 2:664, 845; Robert P. Swierenga, comp., "Dutch Households in Federal Manuscript Population Census, Cleveland, 1880" (unpublished computer file).

60. The Schwab families in 1880 lived in Ward 4 on Orange and Broadway streets. Swierenga, *Dutch Households*, 3:950; Swierenga, "Federal Manuscript Population Census, Cleveland, 1880."

61. This section relies on Myron Berman, *Richmond's Jewry, 1769–1976: Shabbat in Shockoe* (Charlottesville, VA, 1979) 241–89, 316–23, 381–88. See also Swierenga, "Federal Manuscript Population Census, Chicago, 1880."

62. Quote in Berman, *Richmond's Jewry*, 246. Calisch was president of the Central Conference of American Rabbis from 1921 to 1923 and authored the *Jew in English Literature* (1908), *Methods of Teaching Biblical History* (1914), and *Book of Prayers* (1893). He earned his Ph.D degree from the University of Virginia in 1908. (See *Universal Jewish Encyclopedia* 2:646–47).

63. Gartner, *Jews of Cleveland*, 15; "Cleveland," *Encyclopaedia Judaica*, 5:606–8; *The Temple*, 13–21. Peixotto was elected trustee of Tifereth Israel in 1858 and treasurer in 1860 (the *Jewish Messenger*, Oct. 15, 1858; Aug. 3, 1860).

64. Robert A. Rockaway, *The Jews of Detroit: From the Beginning, 1762–1914* (Detroit, 1986), 11–13, 31–32; Irving I. Katz, *The Beth El Story: With a History of the Jews in Michigan Before 1850* (Detroit, 1955), 50–78; the *Occident* 10 (1852); 58; "Detroit," *Encyclopaedia Judaica* 5:1567–8; *Congregation Shaarey Zedek, 1861–1981* (Southfield, MI, 1982), 19–23; Leo M. Franklin, "Jews in Michigan," *Michigan History Magazine* 23 (Winter 1939): 78–80; cf. also David E. Heineman, "Jewish Beginnings in Michigan Before 1850," *PAJHS* 13 (1905): 47–70; "A Call to Detroit—1869," *American Jewish Archives* 19 (Apr. 1967): 34–40.

65. Rockaway, *Jews of Detroit*, 20, 22–23 (map).

66. Swierenga, *Dutch Households*, 3:1162, 1:235. Ingerman is incorrectly listed as Den Engelsman.

67. Ibid., 3:1010–11. Emanuel H. and brother Henry van Baalen were active in Montefiore Lodge, Free Sons of Israel (the *Jewish Messenger*, Dec. 20, 1889).

68. Swierenga, *Dutch Households*, 1:260, 268. Aaron Davis is incorrectly listed as Devries and Hyman Davis is incorrectly listed as Dewit.

69. Katz, *Beth El Story*, apps. 10, 11. Mrs. J. Joseph of the Ladies' Society may be the wife of Emanuel Joseph (76). Emanuel Joseph van Baalen is known as Joseph van Baalen.

70. Rockaway, *Jews of Detroit*, 18–21.

71. Harold M. Mayer and Richard C. Wade, *Chicago: The Growth of a Metropolis* (Chicago, 1969), 30–54; "Chicago," *Encyclopaedia Judaica* 5:410–14.

72. Mayer and Wade, *Chicago*, 138–50.

73. Herman Eliassof, "The Jews of Chicago," *PAJHS* 11 (1903): 117–19; Jeffrey Ira Langer, "White-Collar Heritage: Occupational Mobility of the Jews in Chicago, 1860–1880" (M.A. thesis, University of Illinois, 1976), 19–20. The story of this agricultural colonization society was first recounted by Rabbi Bernhard Felsenthal of Chicago's Sinai Congregation, "On the History of the Jews of Chicago," *PAJHS* 2 (1894): 21–27. At least one Dutch Jewish garden farmer lived in the Chicago area in 1870. This was Jacob Heyligers of Rotterdam, who emigrated in 1854, lived in New York until at least 1863, and by 1870 was farming in Waukegan, Lake County, Illinois. (See Swierenga, *Dutch Emigrants*, 106; Swierenga, *Dutch Households*, 1:420).

74. Hyman L. Meites, ed., *History of the Jews of Chicago* (Chicago, 1924), 113. Bernhard Felsenthal reported 3,000 Jews in the city in 1863 ("A Contribution to the History of the Israelites in Chicago," unpublished paper, October 1863, AJA, Cincinnati). Langer estimated that 293 Jewish families resided in Chicago in 1860, with 437 employed ("White-Collar Heritage," 63).

75. Leopold Mayer, "Recollections of Chicago in 1850–1851," in Schappes, *Documentary History*, 310–11; Morris A. Gutstein, A *Priceless Heritage: The Epic Growth of Nineteenth-Century Chicago Jewry* (New York, 1953), 21–24, 30; Mayer and Wade, *Chicago*, 150; "Chicago," *Encyclopaedia Judaica* 5:410–11.

76. Gutstein, *Priceless Heritage*, 24–27; the *Occident* 5 (1847): 14–15; Bernhard Felsenthal and Herman Eliassof, *History of Kehillah Anshe Maarabh: Semi-centennial Celebration, November 4, 1897* (Chicago, 1897), 11–20. A report of Isaacs's dedication address is in the *Chicago Daily Journal*, June 14, 1851.

77. Gutstein, *Priceless Heritage*, 27–29; Bernhard Felsenthal, *The Beginnings of the Chicago Sinai Congregation* (Chicago, 1898), 9; Morton Mayer Berman, *Our First Century, 1852–1952: Temple Isaiah Israel* (Chicago, 1952), 11.

78. The *Occident* 22 (1864): 188–91, 285; 23 (1865): 95–96; Felsenthal and Eliassof, *History of Kehillah Anshe Maarabh*, 38. The report, signed "H," is in the *Occident* 17 (1859): 65–66.

79. Meites, *Jews of Chicago*, 113–14. The complete membership list of KAM, 1847–1897, is in Felsenthal and Eliassof, *History of Kehillah Anshe Maarabh*, and includes only three (or possibly four) Dutch Jews among its 485 members. These were Isaac Gelder, Jonas Gelder, Henry S. Haas, and possibly Lewis Cohen.

80. Gutstein, *Priceless Heritage*, 28. M. M. Berman, *Our First Century*, 13, also asserts that the Dutch Jews were "German-speaking." The Dutch assuredly learned the German worship rites, but their vernacular tongue was Dutch.

81. Gutstein, *Priceless Heritage*, 37.
82. The total Dutch-born Jews in 1870, 1880, and 1900 were 39, 67, and 150, respectively, of which 36 (66 percent), 28 (46 percent), and 66 (56 percent) had non-Dutch spouses (compiled from sources cited in Table 8.9).
83. Meites, *Jews of Chicago*, 114.
84. Gutstein, *Priceless Heritage*, 29–30, 53, 69. A report in the *Occident* 17 (1859): 65–66, from a member of the German congregation, signed H., noted that neither *shul* was flourishing.
85. Gutstein, *Priceless Heritage*, 31–32, 37, 45, 47, 71; Langer, "White-Collar Heritage," 22.
86. Gutstein, *Priceless Heritage*, 38–39, 72–74.
87. Ibid., 39–41, 47, 49–50, 75, 92. The nationality breakdown was twenty thousand German, five thousand Austro-Hungarian, and fifty thousand Russo-Polish, see Eliassof, "Jews of Chicago," 130.
88. Gutstein, *Priceless Heritage*, 78, 82.
89. Langer, "White-Collar Heritage," 12–13, 20. A more limited occupational study of the higher-class Jews is that of Ronald Klotz, "An Economic View of Chicago Jewry, 1879–1881" (unpublished paper, HUC, Cincinnati, 1974).
90. Swierenga, *Dutch Households*, 2:619, 717; 1:270; Chicago City Directory, 1861; Meites, *Jews of Chicago*, 90.
91. Swierenga, *Dutch Households*, 1:390; Chicago City Directories, 1860, 1861, 1867; Meites, *Jews of Chicago*, 103–4.
92. Leon Andrews had also moved south by 1876 to 572 South State Street. Swierenga, *Dutch Households*, 1:13; 3:1010–11; Chicago City Directories, 1861, 1867, 1869, 1876.
93. Benjamin Boasberg and his wife had thirteen children, ten of whom were still living in 1900, although he was deceased. Widow Sarah Boasberg and her sons Herman, Joseph, and daughter Adaline lived in Ward 32 at 4628 South Langley Avenue. Israel and his wife Bertha lived a block away at 23 East Forty-eighth Street. Herman was a printer, Joseph a clothing cutter, and Israel a trimmer tailor. The other children had departed the city. (See Swierenga, "Federal Manuscript Population Census, Chicago, 1900"; Chicago City Directory, 1869.)
94. The oldest son Israel, who was born in Buffalo in 1851, resided on West Lake Street with his first cousin, Emanuel van Baalen, now a clothing cutter. (Joseph) Israel van Baalen lived in Ward 11 in 1870. His store was at 53 West Randolph Street. Joseph van Baalen was not found in the 1870 census but he is recorded in the Chicago City Directories of 1869 and 1875, living at 55 Third Avenue in 1869 and 755 South Wabash Avenue in 1875. In 1900 both families lived in Ward 32. See Swierenga, *Dutch Households*, 3:1011; Swierenga, "Federal Manuscript Population Census, Chicago, 1900."
95. Langer in "White-Collar Heritage," 64, is therefore incorrect in his speculation that Dutch Jews in Chicago "did not possess the same pro-

pensity for white collar employment" as his sample of 103 German Jews (24 percent of all employed Jews in 1860) "carried over from their homeland." His sample, which is based on membership in the two most prestigious synagogues (KAM and Sinai) and the elite Standard Club, reveals that 80 percent were white collar, 13 percent skilled, and 6 percent semi- and unskilled in 1860 (compiled from ibid., Table 3.4, p. 32). Six of the seven Dutch Jews (85 percent) in 1860 and thirty-five of forty (88 percent) in 1870 were in white-collar positions, and there were no semi- or unskilled workers in either year.

96. John Clayton, comp., *The Illinois Fact Book and Historical Almanac, 1673–1968* (Carbondale and Edwardsville, IL, 1970), 249. Philip P. Bregstone, *Chicago and Its Jews: A Cultural History* (Chicago, 1933), 314, incorrectly reports that Van Praag served in the 1887–1888 legislature. Van Praag was born in the Netherlands in 1856 and came to America as a youngster in 1860. He reached Chicago in the years immediately after the great fire and by 1875 operated a clothing store at 597 South State Street. By 1900 he lived with his wife and daughter at his saloon at 440 South Wabash Avenue. See Chicago City Directory, 1875; Swierenga, "Federal Manuscript Population Census, Chicago, 1900."

97. The quote is from a correspondent of the *Occident* 10 (1852): 55–57.

98. Swierenga, *Dutch Households*, 2:609, 892. J. Segaar is listed incorrectly as Legar.

99. Swierenga, *Dutch Households*, 1:291, 2:486, 1:310, 3:1274.

100. Swierenga, *Dutch Households*, 2:682, 3:907–8.

101. Swierenga, *Dutch Households*, 1:69; 3:998, 922, 925; 3:1274. Spear was incorrectly listed as Spiers.

Chapter 9

1. Moses Rischin and John Livingston, eds., *Jews of the American West* (Detroit, 1991), 333–36; Jacob Rader Marcus, *To Count a People: American Jewish Population Data, 1585–1984* (Lanham, MD, 1990), 28, 194, 150.

2. Jacob Voorsanger, *The Chronicles of Emanu-El: Being an Account of the Rise and Progress of Congregation Emanu-El, Which Was Founded in July, 1850* (San Francisco, 1900), 14–15. See also Martin S. Meyer, "The Jews in California," in A. W. Voorsanger, *Western Jewry: An Account of the Achievements of the Jews and Judaism in California Including Eulogies and Biographies* (San Francisco, 1916), 5–29.

3. J. Voorsanger, *Chronicles of Emanu-El*, 15; A. W. Voorsanger, *Western Jewry*, 46–47.

4. J. Voorsanger, *Chronicles of Emanu-El, 15, 17*; Fred Rosenbaum, *Architects of Reform: Congregational and Community Leadership,*

Emanu-El of San Francisco, 1849–1980 (Berkeley, 1980), 2–3, 15; Meyer, "Jews of California," in A. W. Voorsanger, *Western Jewry*, 16–17.

5. J. Voorsanger, *Chronicles of Emanu-El*, 18–20, 59–61; F. Rosenbaum, *Architects of Reform*, 6–7, 23, 26, 15.

6. Meyer, "Jews in California," in A. W. Voorsanger, *Western Jewry*, 7–15; F. Rosenbaum, *Architects of Reform*, 14–15; Peter R. Decker, "Jewish Merchants in San Francisco: Social Mobility on the Urban Frontier," *American Jewish History* 68 (June 1978): 396–407; and Decker, *Fortunes and Failures: White-Collar Mobility in Nineteenth-Century San Francisco* (Cambridge, MA, and London, 1978), 238–39, 258. According to the 1860 federal census the prominent wholesale tobacco merchant, Joseph Brandenstein, was born in Holland, but this doubtless is an error. His wife, Jane Rosenbaum, was likely Dutch, but Brandenstein was born near Cassel, Germany, according to A. W. Voorsanger, *Western Jewry*, 80–81.

7. F. Rosenbaum, *Architects of Reform*, 32–37; Decker, *Fortunes and Failures*, 81–84. The occupational data were compiled from Seth Bernstein, "The Economic Life of the Jews in San Francisco During the 1860's as Reflected in the City Directories," *American Jewish Archives* 27 (Apr. 1975): 72–73.

8. This and the next three paragraphs rely on Robert P. Swierenga, comp., *Dutch Households in U.S. Population Censuses, 1850, 1860, 1870: An Alphabetical Listing by Family Heads*, 3 vols. (Wilmington, DE, 1987); and Robert P. Swierenga, comp., "Dutch Households in Federal Manuscript Population Census, San Francisco, 1880" (unpublished computer file).

9. *San Francisco City Directory*, 1899.

10. The full story is recounted by Irving McKee, "The Shooting of Charles de Young," *Pacific Historical Review* 16 (Aug. 1947): 271–85; see also Gustav Adolf Danziger, "The Jews in San Francisco: The Last Half Century," *Overland Monthly* 25 (Apr. 1895): 404.

11. Danziger, "The Jews in San Francisco," 404; Meyer, "Jews in California," in A. W. Voorsanger, *Western Jewry*, 11.

12. F. Rosenbaum, *Architects of Reform*, 34.

13. A. W. Voorsanger, *Western Jewry*, 132; "Benjamin Franklin Peixotto," *Jewish Encyclopedia* 9:582–83.

14. A. W. Voorsanger, *Western Jewry*, 132.

15. Ibid., 133; *San Francisco City Directory*, 1899, 50.

16. A. W. Voorsanger, *Western Jewry*, 133. Jessica Peixotto was the second woman to earn the PhD degree at the University of California. See "Raphael Peixotto," "Jessica Blanche Peixotto," "Sidney Peixotto," and "Ernest Peixotto," *Jewish Encyclopedia* 9:582–84.

17. Accurate biographical details are in Kenneth C. Zwerin and Norton B. Stern, "Jacob Voorsanger: From Cantor to Rabbi," *Western States Jewish Historical Quarterly*, 15 (Apr. 1983): 195–202. Voorsanger's reli-

gious, social, and theological views are described cogently by Marc Lee Raphael, *Profiles in American Judaism: The Reform, Conservative, Orthodox, and Reconstructionist Traditions in Historical Perspective* (San Francisco, 1984), 20–32; and Raphael's earlier "Rabbi Jacob Voorsanger of San Francisco on Jews and Judaism: The Implications of the Pittsburgh Platform," *American Jewish Historical Quarterly* 63 (Dec. 1973): 185–203. Voorsanger's career at Emanu-El Temple is described in detail in F. Rosenbaum, *Architects of Reform*, 43–68; and for his relationship with Judah Magnes see Rischin and Livingston, *Jews of the American West*, 42–43.

18. There is considerable confusion in the literature about Voorsanger's education and ancestry. See Zwerin and Stern, "Jacob Voorsanger," 195–196. Voorsanger vaguely claimed to have received his Jewish education in Amsterdam (see obituary in the *American Hebrew and Jewish Messenger*, 82 (May 1, 1908): 660. His brother, A. W. Voorsanger, in his book *Western Jewry* stated that Jacob earned his rabbinate degree at the Jewish Theological Seminary of Amsterdam. This is also stated in Jacob Voorsanger's earlier biographical sketch in *The American Jewish Year Book, 5664 [1903]* (Philadelphia, 1903), 104. Zwerin and Stern, however, after a thorough search of the seminary records, which are in the Amsterdam Municipal Archives, can find no record of a student named Jacob Voorsanger, nor were there any rabbinical examinations at the Seminary in 1871 or 1872, when Jacob would have graduated ("Jacob Voorsanger," 195–96). A. W. Voorsanger also claimed that their paternal and maternal grandfather and great-grandfather were "well-known rabbis in Germany." Zwerin and Stern are unable to document this fact in the Municipal Archives of Amsterdam (ibid., 196).

19. F. Rosenbaum, *Architects of Reform*, 64.

20. Ibid., 46; Raphael, *Profiles in American Judaism*, 21–24. Voorsanger's 1887 lecture, "The Contrast of the Century," praising the French Revolution, is reported in the *Jewish Exponent* (Philadelphia), May 20, 1887.

21. F. Rosenbaum, *Architects of Reform*, 48–49.

22. Ibid., 50–51, 53–54, 62; Raphael, *Profiles in American Judaism*, 23–32.

23. *American Hebrew and Jewish Messenger*, 82 (May 1, 1908): 660; Raphael, *Profiles in American Judaism*, 20–21; Meyer, "Jews in California," in A. W. Voorsanger, *Western Jewry*, 21.

24. The defense of Reform is in J. Voorsanger, *Chronicles of Emanu-El*, 61–94; cf. Raphael, "Rabbi Jacob Voorsanger," 185–203. The complicated story of the Jewish Publication Society is told in Jonathan Sarna, *JPS: The Americanization of Jewish Culture* (Philadelphia, 1989).

25. William M. Brinner and Moses Rischin, eds., *Like All the Nations? The Life and Legacy of Judah L. Magnes* (Albany, NY, 1987), 19–24; Rischin and Livingston, *Jews of the American West*, 41–42.

26. J. Voorsanger to J. L. Magnes, January 3, 1900, Voorsanger Papers, Western Jewish History Center, Berkeley, quoted in Rischin and Livingston, *Jews of the American West*, 41–42, 46–47.
27. J. Voorsanger to J. L. Magnes, October 19, 1905, Voorsanger Papers, quoted in Rischin and Livingston, *Jews of the American West*, 42, 47; Brinner and Rischin, *Like All the Nations*, 24–26.
28. Zwerin and Stern, "Jacob Voorsanger," 200–1. These authors note that HUC awarded only one other Bachelor of Theology degree in its history. They suggest that Rabbi Isaac Mayer Wise arranged this award to credential Voorsanger for his congregational work and university teaching and to enhance the Reform movement generally.
29. F. Rosenbaum, *Architects of Reform*, 55–58; "San Francisco," *Universal Jewish Encyclopedia* 9:356.
30. F. Rosenbaum, *Architects of Reform*, 59–61, quote 61.
31. Ibid., 65; Raphael, "Rabbi Jacob Voorsanger," 185; Zwerin and Stern, "Jacob Voorsanger," 200–1.
32. A. W. Voorsanger, *Western Jewry*, 244; F. Rosenbaum, *Architects of Reform*, 68; Edgar F. Magnin, "Elkan C. Voorsanger," *Central Conference of American Rabbis Yearbook 1963, Memorial Tributes* (New York, 1963), 140–41.
33. M. V., "Edgar Fogel Magnin," *Encyclopaedia Judaica*, 7:718–19; "Abbreviated Biography of Rabbi Edgar F. Magnin," typescript, Western Jewish History Center, Berkeley, CA.
34. See Wilber Leeds, comp., "Isaac Magnin Family Tree," typescript, 1973, Western Jewish History Center, Berkeley, CA; Voorsanger, *Western Jewry*, 125. Voorsanger states that Isaac "came to America from Holland, his birthplace, at the age of eight." In the "Dutch Households in Federal Manuscript Population Census, San Francisco,1880," the family lived in Ward 10 at 236 Third Street. By 1900 they had moved up to 1337 Laguna Drive. See *San Francisco City Directory*, 1899, 1103.
35. Milton Moskowitz, Michael Katz, Robert Levering, *Everybody's Business, an Almanac: The Irreverent Guide to Corporate America* (Cambridge, MA, 1980), 325–26; "San Francisco," *Universal Jewish Encyclopedia* 9:358.
36. Selma Leydesdorff, "The Policy of the Amsterdam Municipality Towards the Jewish Proletariat in the 1930s," in Jozeph Michman, ed., *Dutch Jewish History: Proceedings of the Fourth Symposium on the History of the Jews in the Netherlands, 7–10 December—Tel-Aviv—Jerusalem, 1986, vol. 2 (Assen/Maastricht, Neth., 1989) 237–38*.
37. Moskowitz, Katz, and Levering, *Everybody's Business*, 326.
38. A. W. Voorsanger, *Western Jewry*, 125–26, 208–9; F. Rosenbaum, *Architects of Reform*, 33, 59, 70, 137, 140.
39. F. Rosenbaum, *Architects of Reform*, 136–37; A. W. Voorsanger, *Western Jewry*, 208–10; Ruth Kelson Rafael, comp., *Guide to Archival and Oral History Collections*, (Berkeley, 1987) 153; Moskowitz, Katz, and Levering, *Everybody's Business*, 324, 328–29.

40. Magnin, "Rabbi Elkan C. Voorsanger," 140–41; A. W. Voorsanger, *Western Jewry*, 62, 67–68; Wilshire Boulevard Temple, *Seventy-Fifth Anniversary, Wilshire Boulevard Temple, Congregation B'nai B'rith, 1862–1937* (Los Angeles, 1937).
41. "Edgar Fogel Magnin", *Encyclopaedia Judaica* 7:718–19; F. Rosenbaum, *Architects of Reform*, 140.

·

Chapter 10

1. Robert P. Swierenga, comp., *Dutch Households in U.S. Population Censuses, 1850, 1860, 1870: An Alphabetical Listing by Family Heads, 3 vols.* (Wilmington, DE, 1987). The total Dutch Jewish household members and independent persons is 1,016 in 1850, 2,269 in 1860, and 3,839 in 1870.
2. Netherlands emigration records 1847–1880 reveal that 60 percent of Jewish households and single adults were of middling status, 10 percent were well-to-do, and 20 percent were in poverty. A greater proportion of Dutch Jewish immigrants were needy and fewer were affluent than Dutch Reformed and Roman Catholics.
3. The Netherlands legal system was based on the Code Napoléon, while the United States followed English common law as codified by Sir William Blackstone.
4. Jonathan Sarna, "The Spectrum of Jewish Leadership in Ante-bellum America," *Journal of American Ethnic History* 1 (Spring 1982); 63.
5. Jozeph Michman, "The Jewish Essence of Dutch Jewry," in Jozeph Michman, ed., *Dutch Jewish History: Proceedings of the Fourth Symposium on the History of the Jews in the Netherlands, 7–10 December, Tel-Aviv—Jerusalem, 1986*, vol. 2 (Assen/Maastricht, Neth., 1989), 2.
6. J. Michman, "Jewish Essence," in J. Michman, *Dutch Jewish History*, 3–8.
7. Ibid., 1–22; Dan Michman, *Het liberale Jodendom in Nederland, 1929–1943* (Amsterdam, 1988). J. Michman, "Jewish Essence," in J. Michman, *Dutch Jewish Jewry*, 4–5, cites statistics in the period 1930–1941. In Amsterdam in 1934 all but thirty-nine Jewish sons of Jewish fathers and of non-Jewish fathers and Jewish mothers were circumcised, 92 percent of Jewish marriages were solemnized in Jewish rites, and 100 percent of Jewish dead were buried in Jewish cemeteries. In 1941 only 7.1 percent of Jewish marriages in Amsterdam were mixed. The Dutch national average rose from 6 percent in 1930 to 18 percent in 1941, but the latter figure was much below the general European rate. In Berlin in 1930, 64 percent of Jewish marriages were mixed, and the national rate was 54 percent. The rate of religiously solemnized marriages in the Netherlands surpassed that among Dutch Catholics and Protestants. In 1934 in Amsterdam, 92 percent of Jewish marriages

were solemnized compared with 76 percent for Catholics and only 31 percent for Protestants. One might question, however, whether these rites of passage signify the "essence" of Jewry, if active synagogue worship and the Mosaic Law are completely disregarded.

8. J. Michman, "Jewish Essence," in J. Michman, *Dutch Jewish History*, 7–8; M. H. Gans, "The Jews in the Netherlands," in J. Michman, *Dutch Jewish History*, 390–93.

9. Gans, "Jews in the Netherlands," in J. Michman, *Dutch Jewish History*, 395–96.

10. Dan Michman, "Migration Versus 'Species Hollandia Judaica': The Role of Migration in the Nineteenth and Twentieth Centuries in Preserving Ties Between Dutch and World Jewry," *Studia Rosenthaliana*, 23 (Fall 1989): 54–55.

11. Letter of Emanuel L. Goudsmit of New York to S. L. Kyser of Amsterdam, April 4, 1848, portion printed by editor Meyer Roest in *Israëlietische Nieuwsbode*, April 30, 1886, under the title "Letter from New York, 1848: Americans Are Ignorant."

12. Moshe Davis, *The Emergence of Conservative Judaism: The Historical School in Nineteenth Century America* (Philadelphia, 1963), 163.

13. J. Michman, "Jewish Essence," in J. Michman, *Dutch Jewish History*, 7.

Appendix I

1. Netherlands Landverhuizerslijsten, 1847–1880, compiled by Robert P. Swierenga, and published as *Dutch Emigrants to the United States, South Africa, South America, and Southeast Asia, 1835–1880: An Alphabetical Listing by Household Heads and Independent Persons* (Wilmington, DE, 1983).

2. J. A. de Kok, *Nederland op de Breuklijn Rome—Reformatie* (Assen, Neth., 1964), 292–93.

3. Pieter R. D. Stokvis, "Dutch International Migration, 1815–1910," in Robert P. Swierenga, ed., *The Dutch in America: Immigration, Settlement, and Cultural Change* (New Brunswick, NJ, 1985), 57–60, esp. Table 2.6.

4. V. D. Lipman, *Social History of the Jews in England, 1850–1950* (London, 1954) 65; Salmond S. Levin, ed., *A Century of Anglo-Jewish Life, 1870–1970* (London, 1970), 3; Lloyd P. Gartner, *The Jewish Immigrant in England, 1870–1914* (Detroit, 1960), 17, 33.

5. Gartner, *Jewish Immigrant in England*, 33.

6. Robert P. Swierenga, "Dutch International Migration Statistics, 1820–1880: An Analysis of Linked Multinational Nominal Files," *International Migration Review*, 15 (Fall 1981): 445–70.

BIBLIOGRAPHY

I. Archival and Public Sources

Abbreviated Biography of Rabbi Edgar F. Magnin. Typescript. Western Jewish History Center, Berkeley, CA.

Abraham Eleazer Israel Travel Journal, 1804. Private Collection of Maxwell Whiteman, Elkins Park, PA.

Abraham Lincoln Nebel (1891–1973) Collection, Cleveland Jewish Miscellany, 1831–1971. Western Reserve Historical Society, Cleveland, OH.

Amsterdam Bevolkingsregisters (Population Registers), 1840–1880. Gemeentearchief Amsterdam.

Amsterdam Civil Marriage Registers. Gemeentearchief Amsterdam.

Amsterdam Death Registers. Gemeentearchief Amsterdam.

Amsterdam Name-taking Registers, 1808–1815. Gemeentearchief Amsterdam.

Ante Bellum Cleveland Jewish Immigrant Database. Western Reserve Historical Society, Cleveland, OH.

Chicago City Directories, 1860, 1861, 1867, 1869, 1870, 1875, 1876, and 1970.

Cleveland City Directories, 1845–1860.

Cuyahoga County and Jewish Synagogue Archives, Jewish Community Federation Records. Western Reserve Historical Society, Cleveland, OH.

Daniel Levy Maduro Peixotto (Dr.) Papers. See Abraham Lincoln Nebel (1891–1973) Collection.

Federal Manuscript Population Census, 1850, New Orleans.

Isaac A. Isaacs Papers. See Abraham Lincoln Nebel (1891–1973) Collection.

Leeds, Wilber, comp., "Isaac Magnin Family Tree." Typescript (1973). Western Jewish History Center, Berkeley, CA.

Magnin Family Papers. Western Jewish History Center, Berkeley, CA.

Military Inscription Records, the Netherlands, of Aron Mozes Dropsie and

403

Gompert Moses Dropsie. Private Collection of Maxwell Whiteman, Willow Grove, PA.

Morais, S. to S. M. Isaacs. Correspondence, 1867–1869. Anneberg Research Institute, Philadelphia, PA.

Mortgage Documents, 1807, 1810 (Hypotheek 173/83 and 173/91). Gemeentearchief Leeuwarden.

"Myer S. Isaacs Diary, Vols. I and II, 1863 and 1868, New York, N.Y." 2 vols. Typescript. American Jewish Archives, Cincinnati, OH.

Nederlands Israelitisch Ziekenfonds (NISF) Incorporation Papers. American Jewish Historical Society, Waltham, MA.

Obituary clippings. American Jewish Archives, Cincinnati, OH.

"Record of Marriages by Rev. Dr. [Henry] Hochheimer," 1850–1900. Baltimore, MD, American Jewish Archives, Cincinnati, OH.

Report of the National Council of Jewish Communities, 1842. Library no. O-1339. Gemeentearchief Amsterdam.

Rowland Davies File. See Abraham Lincoln Nebel (1891–1973) Collection.

San Fransisco City Directories, 1899–1900.

Swierenga, Robert P., comp. "Dutch Households in Federal Manuscript Population Census, Chicago, 1880." Unpublished computer file.

———, comp. "Dutch Households in Federal Manuscript Population Census, Chicago, 1900." Unpublished computer file.

———, comp. "Dutch Households in Federal Manuscript Population Census, Cleveland, 1880." Unpublished computer file.

———, comp. "Dutch Households in Federal Manuscript Population Census, San Francisco, 1880." Unpublished computer file.

Synagogue histories and anniversary booklets. Hebrew Union College, Cincinnati, OH, and Library of Congress.

II. Periodicals and Newspapers

American Hebrew and Jewish Messenger. 1901, 1908.
Asmonean. 1851–1853.
Cleveland *Plain Dealer* (daily and weekly). 1856.
Jewish Exponent (Philadelphia). 1887–1902.
Jewish Messenger. 1857–1903.
Occident and American Jewish Advocate. 1843–1870.
Reform Advocate (Chicago). 1891–1900.

III. Books and Articles

Adler, Selig, and Thomas E. Connolly. *Ararat to Suburbia: The History of the Jewish Community of Buffalo.* Philadelphia: Jewish Publication Society of America, 1960.

American Jewish Yearbook, 5664 [1903]. Philadelphia: Jewish Publication Society of America, 1903.

Ashkenazi, Elliott. *The Business of Jews in Louisiana*. Tuscaloosa, AL, and London: University of Alabama Press, 1988.

Atkins, Flora B. "Dutch Treats on My Father's Side: Discoveries in Preparing a Toledotaynu of the Hartogensis Family." *Avotaynu: The International Review of Jewish Genealogy* 7 (Winter 1991): 23–27.

Barkai, Avraham. *Branching Out: German-Jewish Immigration to the United States, 1820–1914*. New York: Holmes & Meier, 1994.

Barnett, R. D., and W. M. Schwab, eds. *The Sephardi Heritage, vol. 2*. Grendon, Northants, Eng.: Gibralter Books, 1989.

Beem, H. *De Joden van Leeuwarden*. Assen, Neth.: Van Gorcum, 1974.

———. "Joodse namen en namen van Joden." *Studia Rosenthaliana* 3 (Jan. 1969): 82–95.

Bender, Marylin. "In Amsterdam: 300 Years of Jewish Life." *New York Times*, August 14, 1988.

Bergman, Leo A. *A History of Touro Synagogue, New Orleans*. New Orleans: Touro Synagogue, 1968.

Berkowitz, Henry. "Notes on the History of the Earliest German Jewish Congregation in America." *PAJHS* 9 (1901): 123–27.

Berman, Morton Mayer. *Our First Century, 1852–1952, Temple Isaiah Israel*. Chicago: Temple Isaiah Israel, 1952.

Berman, Myron. *Richmond's Jewry, 1769–1976: Shabbat in Shockoe*. Charlottesville, VA: University Press of Virginia, 1979.

Bernstein, Seth. "The Economic Life of the Jews in San Francisco During the 1860's as Reflected in the City Directories." *American Jewish Archives* 27 (Apr. 1975): 70.

Beukers, M. P., and J. J. Cahen, eds. *Proceedings of the Fifth International Symposium on the History of the Jews in the Netherlands [1988]*. In *Studia Rosenthaliana*, 23 (Fall 1989). Special issue.

Birmingham, Stephen. *"Our Crowd": The Great Jewish Families of New York*. New York: Harper & Row, 1967.

Blau, Joseph L., and Salo W. Baron, eds. *The Jews of the United States, 1790–1840: A Documentary History*, 3 vols. New York and London: Columbia University Press, 1963.

Bloemgarten, S. E. "De Amsterdamse Joden gedurende de eerste jaren van de Bataafse Republiek (1795–1798)." *Studia Rosenthaliana* 1 (Jan. 1967): 66–96; (July 1967): 45–70; 2 (Jan. 1968): 42–65.

Blum, Isidor. *The Jews of Baltimore: An Historical Summary (. . .)*. Baltimore and Washington: Historical Review Publishing Company, 1910.

Boekman, E. *Demografie van de Joden in Nederland*. Amsterdam: Menno Hertzberger, 1936.

———. "De Verspreiding der Joden van Nederland, 1830–1930." *Mens en Maatschappij*, Jubileumnummer 1925–1975 (1975): 77–99 (repr. from vol. 10, 1934, 174–96).

Bregstone, Philip P. *Chicago and Its Jews: A Cultural History*. Chicago: 1933. Privately published.

Brinner, William M., and Moses Rischin, eds. *Like All the Nations? The Life and Legacy of Judah L. Magnes.* Albany: State University of New York Press, 1987.

Broches, S. *Jews in New England: Six Historical Monographs, vol. 1. Historical Study of the Jews in Massachusetts (1650–1750).* New York: Bloch Publishing Company, 1942.

Cahen, Joël. "Een eigen ziekenfonds voor joden in New York." *Nieuw Israëlitisch Weekblad* (November 15, 1985), pp. 154–55. Jubilee issue.

"A Call to Detroit—1869." *American Jewish Archives* 19 (Apr. 1967): 34–40.

Clayton, John, comp. *The Illinois Fact Book and Historical Almanac, 1673–1968.* Carbondale and Edwardsville: Southern Illinois University Press, 1970.

Cohen, Robert. "Family, Community and Environment: Early Nineteenth Century Dutch Jewry." *Studia Rosenthaliana* 19 (Oct. 1985): 321–41.

Cohen, Simon. *Shaaray Tefila: A History of Its Hundred Years 1845–1945.* New York: Greenberg, 1945.

Committee for the Demography of the Jews. "Dutch Jewry: A Demographic Analysis, Part One." *Jewish Journal of Sociology* 3 (1961): 195–242.

Cone, G. Herbert. "The Jews in Curaçao." *PAJHS* 10 (1902): 141–57.

Congregation Shaarey Zedek, 1861–1981. Southfield, MI: Congregation Shaarey Zedek, 1982.

Cooper, Patricia A. *Once a Cigar Maker: Men, Women, and Work Culture in American Cigar Factories, 1900–1919.* Urbana and Chicago: University of Illinois Press, 1987.

Daalder, H. "Dutch Jews in a Segmented Society." *Acta Historiae Neerlandica* (Studies on the History of the Netherlands) 10 (1978): 175–94.

Danziger, Gustav Adolf. "The Jew in San Francisco: The Last Half Century." *Overland Monthly* 25 (Apr. 1895): 381–410.

Dasberg, Lea, and Jonathan N. Cohen, eds. *Neveh Ya'akov Jubilee Volume Presented to Dr. Jaap Meijer on the Occasion of his Seventieth Birthday.* Assen, Neth.: Van Gorcum, 1982.

Davidson, Gabriel. *Our Jewish Farmers and the Story of the Jewish Agricultural Society.* New York: L. B. Fischer, 1943.

Davis, Edward. *The History of Rodeph Shalom Congregation, Philadelphia, 1802–1926.* Philadelphia: Rodeph Shalom Congregation, 1926.

Davis, Moshe. *The Emergence of Conservative Judaism: The Historical School in Nineteenth Century America.* Philadelphia: Jewish Publication Society of America, 1963.

Decker, Peter R. *Fortunes and Failures: White-Collar Mobility in Nineteenth-Century San Francisco.* Cambridge, MA, and London: Harvard University Press, 1978.

———. "Jewish Merchants in San Francisco: Social Mobility on the Urban Frontier." *American Jewish History* 68 (June 1978): 396–407.

de Kok, J. A. *Nederland op de breuklijn Rome-Reformatie.* Assen, Neth.: Van Gorcum, 1964.

de Vries, Benjamin W. *From Pedlars to Textile Barons: The Economic Development of a Jewish Minority Group in the Netherlands.* Amsterdam: North Holland, 1989.

Diederiks, Herman. "The Amersterdam Elite at the Beginning of the Nineteenth Century," in *Burgerlich Eliten in den Niederlande und in Nordwestdeutschland,* 445–57, edited by Heinz Schilling and Herman Diederiks. Cologne and Vienna: Bohlan Verlag, 1985.

———. *Een stad in verval: Amsterdam omstreeks 1800.* Amsterdam: University of Amsterdam, 1982.

Dyer, Albion Morris. "Points in the First Chapter of New York Jewish History." *PAJHS* 3 (1895): 41–60.

Ehrenfried, Albert. *A Chronicle of Boston Jewry: From the Colonial Settlement to 1900.* Boston: 1963. Privately printed.

Eisenstein, J. D. "The Development of Jewish Casuistic Literature in America." *PAJHS* 12 (1904): 139–47.

Eliassof, Herman. "The Jews of Chicago." *PAJHS* 11 (1903): 117–30.

Elzas, Barnett A. *The Jews of South Carolina: From the Earliest Times to the Present Day.* Philadelphia: Lippincott, 1905. [Repr. Spartanburg, SC: Reprint Co., 1972.]

Emmanuel, Isaac S. *Precious Stones of Jews of Curaçao: Curaçaon Jewry, 1656–1957.* New York: Bloch Publishing Co., 1957.

Emmanuel, Isaac S. and Suzanne A. Emmanuel. *History of the Jews of the Netherlands Antilles,* 2 vols. Cincinnati: American Jewish Archives, 1970.

Encyclopaedia Judaica, 16 vols. Jerusalem and New York: Macmillan, 1971.

Endelman, Todd M. *The Jews of Georgian England, 1714–1830: Tradition and Change in a Liberal Society.* Philadelphia: Jewish Publication Society of America, 1979.

Ezekiel, Herbert T., and Gaston Lichtenstein. *The History of the Jews of Richmond from 1769 to 1917.* Richmond: Herbert T. Ezekiel, 1917.

Fein, Isaac M. *Boston—Where It All Began: An Historical Perspective of the Boston Jewish Community.* Boston: Boston Jewish Bicentennial Committee, 1976.

———. *The Making of an American Jewish Community: The History of Baltimore Jewry from 1773 to 1920.* Philadelphia: Jewish Publication Society of America, 1971.

Feldman, Jacob S. *The Jewish Experience in Western Pennsylvania: A History, 1755–1945.* Pittsburgh, PA: Historical Society of Western Pennsylvania, 1986.

———. "The Pioneers of the Community: Regional Diversity Among the Jews of Pittsburgh." *American Jewish Archives* 32 (Nov. 1980): 119–24.

Felsenthal, Bernhard. *The Beginnings of the Chicago Sinai Congregation.* Chicago: Chicago Sinai Congregation, 1898.

———. "On the History of the Jews of Chicago." *PAJHS* 2 (1894): 21–27.

Felsenthal, Bernhard, and Herman Eliassof. *History of Kehillah Anshe*

Maarabh, Semi-Centennial Celebration, November 4, 1897. Chicago: KAM Temple, 1897.

Fischer, E. J. "Jews in the Mediene: Jewish Industrial Activities in the Cotton Industry in Twente, 1795-1900." *Studia Rosenthaliana* 19 (Oct. 1985): 249–57.

Fish, Sidney M. *Aaron Levy: Founder of Aaronsburg.* New York: American Jewish Historical Society, 1951.

Franklin, Leo M. "Jews in Michigan." *Michigan History Magazine* 23 (Winter 1939): 78–92.

Friedman, Lee M. *Jewish Pioneers and Patriots.* Philadelphia: Jewish Publication Society of America, 1948.

———. *Pilgrims in a New Land.* New York: Farrar, Straus, 1948.

Friedman, Murray, ed. *Jewish Life in Philadelphia, 1830-1940.* Philadelphia: ISHI Publications, 1983.

Gans, Mozes Heiman. *Memorbook: History of Dutch Jewry from the Renaissance to 1940.* Baarn, Neth.: Bosch & Keuning, 1971.

Gartner, Lloyd P. *History of the Jews of Cleveland.* Cleveland: Western Reserve Historical Society, 1978.

———. *The Jewish Immigrant in England, 1870-1914.* Detroit: Wayne State University Press, 1960.

George, M. Dorothy. *London Life in the Eighteenth Century.* London: Kegan Paul, Trench, Trubner and Co., 1925; repr. Penguin ed., 1965.

Goldberg, Nathan. *Occupational Patterns of American Jews.* New York: JTSP University Press, 1947.

Goldstein, Israel. *A Century of Judaism in New York, B'nai Jeshurun 1825-1925: New York's Oldest Ashkenazic Congregation.* New York: Congregation B'nai Jeshurun, 1930.

Gompers, Samuel. *Seventy Years of Life and Labor: An Autobiography.* New York: E. P. Dutton, 1925.

Goodman, Abraham Vossen. *American Overture: Jewish Rights in Colonial Times.* Philadelphia: Jewish Publication Society of America, 1947.

Greenburg, Rose. *The Chronicle of Baltimore Hebrew Congregation, 1830-1975.* Baltimore: Baltimore Hebrew Congregation, 1976.

Grinstein, Hyman G. *The Rise of the Jewish Community of New York, 1654-1860.* Philadelphia: Jewish Publication Society of America, 1946; Porcupine Press ed., 1976.

Gutmann, Joseph, and Stanley F. Chyet. *Moses Jacob Ezekiel: Memoirs from the Baths of Diocletian.* Detroit: Wayne State University Press, 1975.

Gutstein, Morris A. *To Bigotry No Sanction: A Jewish Shrine in America 1658-1958.* New York: Bloch Publishing Co., 1958.

———. *A Priceless Heritage: The Epic Growth of Nineteenth-Century Chicago Jewry.* New York: Bloch Publishing Company, 1953.

———. *The Story of the Jews of Newport: Two and a Half Centuries of Judaism, 1658-1908.* New York: Bloch Publishing Co., 1936.

Guttmacher, Adolf. *A History of the Baltimore Hebrew Congregation, 1830-1905.* Baltimore: Lord Baltimore Press, 1905.

408

Handlin, Oscar. *Boston's Immigrants, 1790–1880*, rev. ed. New York: Atheneum, 1968.

Harvey, Rowland Hill. *Samuel Gompers: Champion of the Toiling Masses*. Stanford: Stanford University Press, 1935.

Hartogensis, Benjamin H. "Denial of Equal Rights to Religious Minorities and Non-Believers in the United States," *Yale Law Review* 39 (Mar. 1938): 659–81.

Heertje, H. *De diamantbewerkers van Amsterdam*. Amsterdam: D. B. Centen's Uitgevers, 1936.

Heineman, David E. "Jewish Beginnings in Michigan Before 1850." *PAJHS* 13 (1905): 47–70.

Hofmeester, Karin. *Van Talmoed tot Statuut: Joodse Arbeiders en Arbeiders-Bewegingen in Amsterdam, London, en Parijs, 1880–1914*. Amsterdam: IISG, 1990.

Hofstee, E. W. *Korte demografische geschiedenis van Nederland van 1800 tot heden*. Haarlem: Fibula-Van Dishoeck, 1981.

Huhner, Leon. *The Life of Judah Touro (1775–1854)*. Philadelphia: Jewish Publication Society of America, 1946.

Huussen, A. H., Jr. "De emancipation van de Joden in Nederland: Een discussie bijdrage naar aanleiding van twee recente publicaties." *Bijdragen en mededelingen betreffende de geschiedenis der Nederlanden* 94 (1979): 75–83.

"An Instance of Business Success." *Cleveland Daily Plain Dealer*, January 30, 1856.

Isaacs, Myer S. "Sampson Simson." *PAJHS* 10 (1902): 113–14.

Israel, Jonathan I. *Empires and Entrepots: The Dutch, the Spanish Monarchy, and the Jews, 1585–1713*. London and Ronceverte, WV: Hambledon Press, 1990.

———. *European Jewry in the Age of Mercantilism, 1550–1750*. Oxford: Clarendon Press, 1985.

———. "Sephardic Immigration into the Dutch Republic, 1595–1672." *Studia Rosenthaliana* 23 (Fall 1989): 45–53.

Jewish Encyclopedia, 12 vols. New York: KTVA Publishing House, 1901.

Jick, Leon A. *The Americanization of the Synagogue, 1820–1870*. Hanover, NH: University of New England Press, 1976.

Kaganoff, Nathan M. "The Jewish Landsmanshaften in New York City in the Period Preceding World War I." *American Jewish History* 76 (Sept. 1986): 56–66.

———. "New Discoveries on Aaron Levy." *American Jewish History* 79 (Summer 1990): 505–6.

Kaplan, Yosef. "Amsterdam and Ashkenazic Migration in the Seventeenth Century." *Studia Rosenthaliana* 23 (Fall 1989): 22–44.

Karp, Abraham J. *Haven and Home: A History of the Jews in America*. New York: Schocken Books, 1985.

Katz, Irving I. *The Beth El Story: With a History of the Jews in Michigan Before 1850*. Detroit: Wayne State University Press, 1955.

Kaufman, Stuart B., ed. *The Samuel Gompers Papers*, vol. 1, *The Making of a Union Leader, 1850–86*. Urbana and Chicago: University of Illinois Press, 1986.

Keller, Werner. *Diaspora: The Post-biblical History of the Jews*. New York: Harcourt, Brace & World, 1966.

Kellner, Jacob. "Formative Years of Jewish Social Welfare (1842–1869)." *Journal of Jewish Communal Service* 53 (1977): 228–34.

Kleerekoper, S. "Het Joodse Proletariaat in het Amsterdam van de 19e Eeuw." *Studia Rosenthaliana* 1 (Jan. 1967): 97–108; 2 (July 1967): 71–84.

Knight, Franklin W., and Peggy K. Liss, eds. *Atlantic Port Cities: Economy, Culture and Society in the Atlantic World, 1650–1850*. Knoxville: University of Tennessee Press, 1991.

Kohler, Max J. "Civil Status of the Jews in Colonial New York." *PAJHS* 6 (1897): 81–106.

———. "Jews and the American Anti-slavery Movement." *PAJHS* 9 (1901): 44–52.

———. "The Jews in Newport." *PAJHS* 6 (1897): 61–80.

———. "Phases of Jewish Life in New York Before 1800." *PAJHS* 2 (1894): 77–100; 3 (1895): 73–86.

Korn, Bertram Wallace. *The Early Jews of New Orleans*. Waltham, MA: American Jewish Historical Society, 1989.

———. *Eventful Years and Experiences: Studies in Nineteenth Century American Jewish History*. Cincinnati: American Jewish Archives, 1954.

———. "The Jews of Mobile, Alabama, Prior to the Organization of the First Congregation, in 1841." *Hebrew Union College Annual* 40–41 (1969–1970): 494.

———, ed. *A Bicentennial Festschrift for Jacob Rader Marcus*. Waltham, MA: American Jewish Historical Society, 1976.

Korros, Alexandra Shecket, and Jonathan D. Sarna, eds. *American Synagogue History: A Bibliography and State-of-the-Field Survey*. New York: Markus Wiener, 1988.

Lebowich, Joseph. "The Jews in Boston Till 1875." *PAJHS* 12 (1904): 101–12.

Leeser, Isaac. "The Jews of the United States—1848." *American Jewish Archives* 7 (Jan. 1955): 82–84.

"Letter from New York, 1848: Americans Are Ignorant." *Israelietische Nieuwsbode*, April 30, 1886.

Levin, Salmond S., ed. *A Century of Anglo-Jewish Life, 1870–1970*. London: United Synagogue, 1970.

Lijphart, Arend. *The Politics of Accommodation: Pluralism and Democracy in the Netherlands*, 2nd ed. Berkeley: University of California Press, 1975.

Lipman, V. D. *Social History of the Jews in England, 1850–1950*. London: Watts & Co., 1954.

Londow, Ezekiel J. "Benjamin Henry Hartogensis." *PAJHS* 37 (1947): 469–70.

Magnin, Edgar F. "Elkan C. Voorsanger." *Central Conference of American Rabbis Yearbook 1963, Memorial Tributes*. New York: Central Conference of American Rabbis, 1963, 140–41.

Mandel, Bernard. *Samuel Gompers: A Biography*. New York: Antioch Press, 1963.

Marcus, Jacob R. *The Colonial American Jew, 1492–1776*, 3 vols. Detroit: Wayne State University Press, 1970.

———. *To Count a People: American Jewish Population Data, 1585–1984*. Lanham, MD: University Press of America, 1990.

———. *Studies in American Jewish History: Studies and Addresses*. Cincinnati: Hebrew Union College Press, 1969.

———, ed. *Essays in American Jewish History*. New York: KTAV Publishing House, 1975.

Markens, Isaac. *The Hebrews in America*. New York: Isaac Markens, 1888; repr. Arno Press, 1975.

Mayer, Harold M., and Richard C. Wade. *Chicago: The Growth of a Metropolis*. Chicago: University of Chicago Press, 1969.

McKee, Irving. "The Shooting of Charles de Young." *Pacific Historical Review* 16 (Aug. 1947): 271–85.

Meites, Hyman L., ed. *History of the Jews of Chicago*. Chicago: Jewish Historical Society of Illinois, 1924.

Michael, Ann Deborah. "The Origin of the Jewish Community of Cincinnati, 1817–1860." *Cincinnati Historical Society Bulletin* 30 (Fall-Winter 1972): 155–82.

Michman, Dan. *Het liberale Jodendom in Nederland, 1929–1943*. Amsterdam: Van Gennep, 1988.

———. "Migration Versus 'Species Hollandia Judaica': The Role of Migration in the Nineteenth and Twentieth Centuries in Preserving Ties Between Dutch and World Jewry." *Studia Rosenthaliana* 23 (Fall 1989): 54–76.

Michman, Jozeph. "The Conflicts Between Orthodox and Enlightened Jews and the Governmental Decision of 26th February, 1814." *Studia Rosenthaliana* 15 (March 1981): 20–36.

———. "De stichting van het Opperconsistorie" (in 3 parts). *Studia Rosenthaliana* 18 (Jan. 1984): 41–60; (Sept. 1984): 143–58; 19 (May 1985): 127–58.

———, ed. *Dutch Jewish History: Proceedings of the Fourth Symposium on the History of the Jews in the Netherlands, 7–10 December, Tel-Aviv—Jerusalem, 1986*. vol. 2. Assen/Maastricht, Neth.: Van Gorcum, 1989.

Michman, Jozeph, Hartog Beem, and Dan Michman. *Pinkas: History of the Jewish Community in the Netherlands*. Amsterdam: Ede, 1992.

Michman, Jozeph, and Tirtsah Levie, eds. *Dutch Jewish History: Proceedings of the Symposium on the History of the Jews in the Netherlands November 28—December 3, 1982, Tel-Aviv—Jerusalem*. Jerusalem: Tel-Aviv University, 1984.

Mindel, Charles H., and Robert W. Habenstein, eds. *Ethnic Families in*

America, Patterns and Variations. New York, Oxford, Amsterdam: Elsevier, 1976.

Moise, L. C. *Biography of Isaac Harby with an Account of the Reformed Society of Israelites of Charleston, SC, 1824-1833*. Charleston, SC. Reformed Society of Israelites, 1930.

Morais, Henry Samuel. *The Jews of Philadelphia: Their History from the Earliest Settlements to the Present Time*. Philadelphia: Levytype Company, 1894.

Moskowitz, Milton, Michael Katz, and Robert Levering. *Everybody's Business, an Almanac: The Irreverent Guide to Corporate America*. Cambridge, MA: Harper & Row, 1980.

Newman, Aubrey. *The United Synagogue, 1870-1970*. London and Boston: Rutledge & Kegan Paul, 1976.

————, ed. *Migration and Settlement: Proceedings of the Anglo-American Jewish Historical Conference Held in London . . . July 1970*. London: Jewish Historical Society of England, 1971.

Oppenheim, Samuel. "The Jews and Masonry in the United States Before 1810." *PAJHS* 19 (1910): 1-94.

————. "Letter of Jonas Phillips." *PAJHS* 25 (1917): 128-31.

Peskin, Allan. *This Tempting Freedom: The Early Years of Cleveland Judaism and Anshe Chesed Congregation*. Cleveland: Anshe Chesed Congregation, 1973.

Philipson, David. *The Oldest Jewish Congregation in the West, Bene Israel, Cincinnati*, [One Hundredth Anniversary 1824-1924, Rockdale Avenue Temple]. Cincinnati: Rockdale Avenue Temple, 1924.

Polster, Gary E. "'To Love Work and Dislike Being Idle': Origins and Aims of the Cleveland Orphan Asylum, 1868-1878." *American Jewish Archives* 39 (Nov. 1987): 127-55.

Pool, David De Sola. *Portraits Etched in Stone: Early Jewish Settlers, 1682-1831*. New York: Columbia University Press, 1952.

Pool, David De Sola and Tamar De Sola Pool. *An Old Faith in the New World: Portrait of Shearith Israel, 1654-1954*. New York: Columbia University Press, 1955.

Prakke, H. J. *Drenthe in Michigan*. Grand Rapids: Wm. B. Eerdmans, 1983.

Price, Jacob. "Economic Function and the Growth of American Port Towns in the Eighteenth Century." *Perspectives in American History* 8 (1974): 123-86.

Proctor, Robert G. *Tariff Acts Passed by the Congress of the United States from 1789 to 1897*. Washington, DC: Government Printing Office, 1898.

Rafael, Ruth Kelson, comp. *Guide to Archival and Oral History Collections*. Berkeley, CA: Western Jewish History Center, 1987.

Raphael, Marc Lee. *Profiles in American Judaism: The Reform, Conservative, Orthodox, and Reconstructionist Traditions in Historical Perspective*. San Francisco: Harper & Row, 1984.

————. "Rabbi Jacob Voorsanger of San Francisco on Jews and Judaism: The Implications of the Pittsburgh Platform." *American Jewish Historical Quarterly* 63 (Dec. 1973): 185-203.

Reijnders, Carolus. *Van 'Joodsche Natie' tot Joodse Nederlanders.* Amsterdam: Sloterweg, 1969.

Rezneck, Samuel. *Unrecognized Patriots: The Jews in the American Revolution.* Westport, CT: Greenwood Press, 1975.

Rischin, Moses. *The Promised City: New York's Jews, 1870–1914.* Cambridge, MA: Harvard University Press, 1962, 2nd ed. 1977.

———. Review of *The Colonial American Jew, 1492–1776. William and Mary Quarterly* 30 (Apr. 1973): 353–55.

Rischin, Moses, and John Livingston, eds. *Jews of the American West.* Detroit: Wayne State University Press, 1991.

Rockaway, Robert A. *The Jews of Detroit: From the Beginning, 1762–1914.* Detroit: Wayne State University Press, 1986.

Rosenbach, Abraham S. Wolf. "Notes on the First Settlement of Jews in Pennsylvania, 1655–1703." *PAJHS* 5 (1897): 191–98.

Rosenbach, Hyman Polock. *The Jews in Philadelphia Prior to 1800.* Philadelphia: Edward Stern & Co., 1883.

Rosenbach, Isabella H., and Abraham S. Wolf Rosenbach. "Aaron Levy." *PAJHS* 2 (1894): 157–63.

Rosenbaum, Fred. *Architects of Reform: Congregational and Community Leadership, Emanu-El of San Francisco, 1849–1980.* Berkeley, CA: Western Jewish History Center, 1980.

Rosenbaum, Jeanette W. "Hebrew German Society Rodeph Shalom in the City and County of Philadelphia (1800–1950)." *PAJHS* 41 (Sept. 1951): 83–93.

———. *Myer Myers, Goldsmith, 1723–1795.* Philadelphia: Jewish Publication Society of America, 1954.

Rosenbloom, Joseph R. *A Biographical Dictionary of Early American Jews: Colonial Times Through 1800.* Lexington: University of Kentucky Press, 1960.

Rosenwaike, Ira. "Demographic Characteristics of the Jewish Population of the United States and Philadelphia in 1830." *Proceedings of the American Philosophical Society* 133 (June 1989): 333–38.

———. *On the Edge of Greatness: A Portrait of American Jewry in the Early National Period.* Cincinnati: American Jewish Archives, 1985.

———. "An Estimate and Analysis of the Jewish Population of the United States in 1790." *PAJHS* 50 (Sept. 1960): 23–67.

———. "The Founding of Baltimore's First Jewish Congregation: Fact vs. Fiction." *American Jewish Archives* 28 (Nov. 1976): 119–25.

———. "Jewish Deaths Included in the Vital Records of American Cities, 1821–1829." *American Jewish Historical Quarterly* 58 (Mar. 1969): 360–75.

———. "The Jewish Population of the United States as Estimated from the Census of 1820." *American Jewish Historical Quarterly* 53 (Dec. 1963): 3–178.

———. "The Jews of Baltimore to 1810." *American Jewish Historical Quarterly* 64 (June 1975): 291–320.

————. "The Jews of Baltimore: 1810 to 1820." *American Jewish Historical Quarterly* 67 (Dec. 1977): 101–24.

————. *Population History of New York City.* Syracuse: Syracuse University Press, 1972.

Roth, Cecil. *The Great Synagogue of London, 1690–1940.* London: Edward Goldstein & Son, 1950.

————. *A History of the Jews in England.* Oxford: Clarendon Press, 1964.

————. *A History of the Marranos.* Philadelphia: Jewish Publication Society of America, 1932.

————. *A Life of Menasseh Ben Israel: Rabbi, Printer, and Diplomat.* Philadelphia: Jewish Publication Society of America, 1945.

————. "Some Jewish Loyalists in the War of American Independence." *PAJHS* 38 (Sept. 1948): 81–107.

Sarna, Jonathan D. *The American Jewish Experience.* New York: Holmes & Meier, 1986.

————. *JPS: The Americanization of Jewish Culture.* Philadelphia: Jewish Publication Society, 1989.

————. "The Spectrum of Jewish Leadership in Ante-bellum America." *Journal of American Ethnic History* 1 (Spring 1982): 59–67.

Schama, Simon. *An Embarrassment of Riches: An Interpretation of Dutch Culture in the Golden Age.* London: William Collins Sons, 1987.

Schappes, Morris U., ed. *A Documentary History of the Jews in the United States, 1654–1875.* New York: Citadel Press, 1950.

Schiff, Alvin Irwin. *The Jewish Day School in America.* New York: Jewish Education Committee Press, 1966.

Schilling, Heinz, and Herman Diederiks, eds. *Burgerlich Eliten in den Niederlande und in Nordwestdeutschland.* Cologne and Vienna: Bohlan Verlag, 1985.

Schöffer, Ivo. "The Jews in the Netherlands: The Position of a Minority Through Three Centuries." *Studia Rosenthaliana* 15 (March 1981): 85–100.

————. *A Short History of the Netherlands.* Amsterdam: Albert de Lange, 1973.

Selavan, Ida Cohen, ed. *My Voice Was Heard.* New York: KTAV Publishing House, 1981.

Seventy-five Years of Continuity and Change: Our Philadelphia Jewish Community in Perspective. (A Supplement of the *Jewish Exponent*, Friday, March 12, 1976).

Share, Nathaniel S. "History of the Congregation." in *Centennial Volume: Congregation Gates of Prayer, January 13–15, 1950, New Orleans, La.* New Orleans: Congregation Gates of Prayer, 1950.

Sharfman, Rabbi I. Harold. *The First Rabbi: Origins of the Conflict Between Orthodox and Reform: Jewish Polemic Warfare in Pre-Civil War America, a Biographical History.* Malibu, CA: Pangloss Press, 1988.

Shaw, Archer H. *The Plain Dealer: One Hundred Years in Cleveland.* New York: Alfred A. Knopf, 1942.

Shpall, Leo. "The First Synagogue in Louisiana." *Louisiana Historical Quarterly* 21 (Apr. 1928): 518–31.

―――. *The Jews of Louisiana.* New Orleans: Steeg Printing & Publishing Co., 1936.

Simonsens Festschrift (Festskrift i Anledning af Professor David Simonsens 70-Aarige Fødseldag). Copenhagen: Hertz's bogtr., 1923.

Singer, Steven. "The Anglo-Jewish Ministry in Early Victorian London." *Modern Judaism* 5 (Oct. 1985): 279–99.

Smith, George L. *Religion and Trade in New Netherland: Dutch Origins and American Development.* Ithaca, NY: Cornell University Press, 1973.

Smith, Harry, and J. Hugo Tatsch. *Moses Michael Hays: Merchant—Citizen—Freemason, 1739–1805.* Boston: Moses Michael Hays Lodge, 1937.

Solomon, H. P. "Joseph Jesurun Pinto 1729–1782: A Dutch Hazan in Colonial New York." *Studia Rosenthaliana* 13 (Jan. 1979): 18–29.

Staten van de Bevolking der Steden en Gemeenten van het Koningrijk der Nederland, 1 Januari 1840. The Hague, 1841.

Stern, Malcolm H., comp. *First American Jewish Families: 600 Genealogies, 1654–1977.* Cincinnati: American Jewish Archives, 1978.

Stern, Myer. *The Rise and Progress of Reform Judaism: Embracing a History Made from the Official Records of Temple Emanu-El of New York.* New York: Myer Stern, 1895.

Sussman, Lance J. "Isaac Leeser and the Protestantization of American Judaism." *American Jewish Archives* 38 (Apr. 1986): 1–21.

Swierenga, Robert P. "Dutch International Migration Statistics, 1820–1880: An Analysis of Linked Multinational Nominal Files." *International Migration Review* 15 (Fall 1981): 445–70.

―――, ed. *The Dutch in America: Immigration, Settlement, and Cultural Change.* New Brunswick, NJ: Rutgers University Press, 1985.

―――, comp. *Dutch Emigrants to the United States, South Africa, South America, and Southeast Asia, 1835–1880: An Alphabetical Listing by Household Heads and Independent Persons.* Wilmington, DE: Scholarly Resources, 1983.

―――, comp. *Dutch Households in U.S. Population Censuses, 1850, 1860, 1870: An Alphabetical Listing by Family Heads,* 3 vols. Wilmington, DE: Scholarly Resources, Inc., 1987.

―――, comp. *Dutch Immigrants in U.S. Ship Passenger Manifests, 1820–1880: An Alphabetical Listing by Household Heads and Independent Persons,* 2 vols. Wilmington, DE: Scholarly Resources, Inc., 1983.

Tarshish, Allan. "The Board of Delegates of American Israelites (1859–1878)." *PAJHS* 49 (Sept. 1959): 16–32.

Temple Beth El's First Century: Centennial Souvenir Book, 1847–1947. Buffalo: Temple Beth El, 1947.

The Temple, 1850–1950. Cleveland: Congregation Tifereth Israel, 1950.

Tepper, Michael H., ed. *Passenger Arrivals at the Port of Philadelphia, 1800–1819: The Philadelphia "Baggage Lists."* Baltimore: Genealogical Publishing Company, 1986.

Thernstrom, Stephan, and Richard Sennett, eds., *Nineteenth-Century Cities: Essays in the New Urban History*. New Haven and London: Yale University Press, 1969.

Thorne, Florence Calvert. *Samuel Gompers: American Statesman*. New York: Philosophical Library, 1957.

Tree of Life Congregation Anniversary Booklet, 1864–1952. Pittsburgh: Tree of Life Congregation, 1952.

Universal Jewish Encyclopedia, 10 vols. New York: Universal Jewish Encyclopedia Company, 1948.

van Hinte, Jacob. *Netherlanders in America: A Study of Emigration and Settlement in the Nineteenth and Twentieth Centuries in the United States of America*. Robert P. Swierenga, gen. ed.; Adriaan de Wit, chief trans. Grand Rapids, MI: Baker Book House, 1985.

van Lier, R. A. J. *Frontier Society: A Social Analysis of the History of Surinam*. The Hague: Martinus Nijhoff, 1971.

van Praag, Philip. "Between Speculation and Reality." *Studia Rosenthaliana* 23 (Fall 1989): 175–79.

———. "Demografische ontwikkeling van de Joden in Nederland sinds 1830." *Mens en Maatschappij* 47 (no. 2, 1972): 167–83.

van Tijn, Th. "Geschiedenis van de Amsterdamse diamanthandel en-nijverheid, 1845–1897." *Tijdschrift voor Geschiedenis* 87 (1974): 16–69, 160–200.

van Zuiden, D. S. "Lodewijk Napoleon en de Franse Tijd." *Studia Rosenthaliana* 2 (Jan. 1968): 66–88.

Viener, Saul. "Surgeon Moses Albert Levy: Letters of a Texas Patriot." *PAJHS* 46 (Dec. 1956): 101–13; 49 (Mar. 1960): 202–7.

Voorsanger, A. W. *Western Jewry: An Account of the Achievements of the Jews and Judaism in California Including Eulogies and Biographies*. San Francisco: Emanu-El, 1916.

———. *The Chronicles of Emanu-El: Being an Account of the Rise and Progress of Congregation Emanu-El, Which Was Founded in July, 1850*. San Francisco: Congregation Emanu-El, 1900.

Warner, Sam Bass, Jr. *The Private City: Philadelphia in Three Periods of Its Growth*. Philadelphia: University of Pennsylvania Press, 1960.

Wertheimer, Jack, ed. *The American Synagogue: A Sanctuary Transformed*. New York: Cambridge University Press, 1987.

Wilshire Boulevard Temple. *Seventy-Fifth Anniversary, Wilshire Boulevard Temple, Congregation B'nai B'rith, 1862–1937*. Los Angeles: Wilshire Boulevard Temple, 1937.

Wilson, Edmund. *A Piece of My Mind: Reflections at Sixty*. New York: Farrar, Straus, 1956.

Winkel, Hans. *Genealogie van de familie Winkel*. Amsterdam: 1982. Privately printed.

Wintle, Michael. *Pillars of Piety: Religion in the Netherlands in the Nineteenth Century, 1813–1901*. Hull: Hull University Press, 1987.

Wolf, Edwin 2nd, and Maxwell Whiteman. *The History of the Jews of Phila-*

delphia from Colonial Times to the Age of Jackson. Philadelphia: Jewish Publication Society of America, 1956.

Yogan, Gedalia. *Diamonds and Coral: Anglo-Dutch Jews and Eighteenth-Century Trade.* Leicester, Eng.: Leicester University Press, 1978.

Zangwill, Israel. *Children of the Ghetto: A Study of a Peculiar People,* 3rd ed. New York: Macmillan, 1895.

Zwerin, Kenneth C., and Norton B. Stern. "Jacob Voorsanger: From Cantor to Rabbi." *Western States Jewish Historical Quarterly* 15 (Apr. 1983): 195–202.

IV. Unpublished Works

Abrams, Steven. "An Economic Survey of the Jews in Pittsburgh, Pennsylvania, 1860–1880." Unpublished paper, Hebrew Union College, Cincinnati, OH, 1979.

Charney, Michael. "An Analytical Study of the Economic Life of the Jews of Chicago, 1870–1872." Unpublished paper, Hebrew Union College, Cincinnati, OH, 1974.

Diederiks, Herman. "Residential Patterns: A Jewish Ghetto in Amsterdam Around 1800?" Unpublished paper, University of Leiden, Neth., n.d.

Feibelman, Julian B. "A Social and Economic Study of the New Orleans Jewish Community." (Ph.D. diss., University of Pennsylvania, 1941.)

Feldman, Jacob S. "The Early Migration and Settlement of Jews in Pittsburgh, 1754–1894." Unpublished paper, United Jewish Federation of Pittsburgh, 1959.

Felsenthal, Bernhard. "A Contribution to the History of the Israelites in Chicago." Unpublished paper, American Jewish Archives, Cincinnati, OH, 1863.

Fink, Adolph H. "The History of the Jews in New York City: 1654 to 1850." Cincinnati: Rabbinic thesis at Hebrew Union College—Jewish Institute of Religion, 1930.

Friedman, Thomas J. "A Study of Jewish Businessmen in New Orleans as Reflected in the City Directories of 1811 to 1840." Unpublished paper, Hebrew Union College, Cincinnati, OH, 1977.

Gottlieb, Bruce L. "Jews in the Clothing Industry in Philadelphia, 1850–1860." Unpublished paper, Hebrew Union College, Cincinnati, OH, 1980.

Hofmeester, Karin. "Ashkenazic-Jewish Immigrants in the Netherlands, 1600–1914." Unpublished paper, Amsterdam, 1990.

Hyman, Beverly. "New York Businessmen, 1831–1835." Unpublished paper, Hebrew Union College, Cincinnati, OH, 1977.

Klotz, Ronald. "An Economic View of Chicago Jewry, 1879–1881." Unpublished paper, Hebrew Union College, Cincinnati, OH, 1974.

Langer, Jeffrey Ira. "White-Collar Heritage: Occupational Mobility of the Jews in Chicago, 1860–1880." (M.A. thesis, University of Illinois, 1976.)

Lewis, Judy. "Cincinnati Businessmen, 1818–1840." Unpublished paper, Hebrew Union College, Cincinnati, OH, 1977.

Mostov, Stephan G. "A 'Jerusalem' on the Ohio: The Social and Economic History of Cincinnati's Jewish Community, 1840–1875." (Ph.D. diss., University of Cincinnati, 1981.)

National Council of Jewish Communities. 1842 Report. Amsterdam: Gemeente Archief Amsterdam, Library no. O–1339.

Olitzky, Kerry M. "An Economic Profile of New York City Jews: 1835–1840." Unpublished paper, Hebrew Union College, Cincinnati, OH, 1979.

Puecker, Bernard H. "Immigrant Aid Within the Jewish Community, 1780–1860." Unpublished paper, Hebrew Union College, Cincinnati, OH, n.d.

Roseman, Kenneth David. "The Jewish Population of America, 1850–1860: A Demographic Analysis of Four Cities." (Ph.D. diss., Hebrew Union College—Jewish Institute of Religion, Cincinnati, 1971.)

Rosenthal, Jerome C. "A Study of Jewish Businessmen in New York City as Reflected in the City Directories, 1776–1830." Unpublished paper, Hebrew Union College, Cincinnati, OH, 1977.

Simon, E. Yechiel. "Samuel Myer Isaacs: A Nineteenth Century Jewish Minister in New York City." (Ph.D. diss., Yeshiva University, 1974.)

Sussman, Lance. "The Economic Life of the Jews in Baltimore as Reflected in the City Directories, 1819–1840." Unpublished paper, Hebrew Union College, Cincinnati, OH, 1977.

Note on Sources

Dutch Jews in North America have been virtually ignored by Jewish scholars and by historians of Dutch immigration and settlement. Neither of the two major monographs on the Dutch in America make any mention of the Dutch Jews. These are the twelve hundred-page tome by the Netherlands scholar Jacob van Hinte (1928) and the five hundred-page monograph by the Dutch-American Henry Lucas (1955) in America.

Primary sources are also extremely limited for the story of Dutch Jewry in America, except for the nineteenth century when census records are available. No records survive of the three Dutch Jewish synagogues, and only one of the many charitable and burial societies still exists, that of the Netherland Israelitish Sick Fund of New York City. Dutch Jews were not able to support a Dutch language newspaper or periodical. Surprisingly, no more than a half dozen immigrant letters and diaries have yet been found, although one might hope that others will yet appear since the Dutch were a highly literate people. Because the lettristic sources are so limited, primary reliance is placed on behavioral records compiled by governments. Netherlands emigration records (1847–1880) and U.S. population census manu-

418

scripts (1790–1900) document the geographical distribution, demographic profile, occupational structure, and social status of Dutch Jewish immigrants and their children. (See the published compilations by Swierenga listed in the Bibliography, Sections I and III.) But the third and subsequent generations cannot be traced in the censuses without detailed family reconstitution based on birth, marriage, death, synagogue, and cemetery records.

The Netherlands emigration lists fortunately designate religion, but federal censuses, of course, do not. This presents the perennial problem faced by all scholars of American Jewry. Who is a Jew? Which Dutch-born persons in the manuscript census are Jewish? Nominal record linkage between the federal censuses and Dutch emigration lists is the obvious solution for the period 1847–1880. But less than 10 percent of Dutch Jewish emigrants were dutifully reported in the Netherlands records (see App. I). So American sources must be used. First I abstracted Dutch-born persons and their families in the manuscript population censuses of 1850, 1860, and 1870, plus selected cities (Chicago, Cleveland, and San Francisco) in the 1880 and 1900 censuses. Altogether, these computer files include the complete census information for nearly 160,000 persons of Dutch birth or ancestry living throughout the United States. These names were then cross-checked with the extant Netherlands emigration records and with American Jewish sources such as synagogue souvenir booklets and congregational histories as well as published chronicles and histories of Jews in various cities. The most detailed of the city histories are those of Hyman G. Grinstein for New York, Edwin Wolf 2nd and Maxwell Whiteman for Philadelphia, Albert Ehrenfried for Boston, Isidor Blum and Isaac M. Fein for Baltimore, and Bertram Wallace Korn for New Orleans.

I also consulted unpublished course papers of undergraduate students in Professor Jacob Rader Marcus's American Jewish History courses at Hebrew Union College, which are preserved in the American Jewish Archives, also in Cincinnati. These papers, completed in the 1970s, identify Jews in major American cities in the period 1776–1881 by cross-checking city directories with synagogue membership lists and other Jewish records. For the early censuses, 1790, 1810, 1820, and 1830, Ira Rosenwaike's lists of Jews are virtually complete. As a final check, Rabbi Malcolm H. Stern, the noted Jewish genealogist, also perused my list and indicated persons likely to be non-Jewish. In most cases I accepted his advice and deleted the names. In the end, when record linkage failed I designated as Dutch Jews in the censuses those whose family and given names and occupations were typically Jewish, although this is very problematic because Jews sometimes had Christian-sounding names and Christians had Jewish-sounding names, as Grinstein has observed. A related question concerned the children of Dutch Jewish mothers and non-Dutch Jewish fathers. Usually, I excluded these children in the totals of Dutch Jews, although the influence of the typical Jewish mother may have made them more Dutch than those with Dutch fathers and non-Dutch mothers.

419

INDEX

Aaron, Jacob, 194, 382 n 31
Aaron, Louis, 201
Aarons, Aaron, 240, 335
Aarons, Jacob, 324
Aarons, Markus, 335
Aaronsburg, PA, 48
Aaronson, Joseph Moses (Rabbi), 378 n 18
Abraham, David, 379 n 26
Abraham, Sarah de Young, 249
Abraham Touro Fund, 45
Abraham(s), Emanuel, 47
Abraham(s), Joseph, 47, 249, 324
Abrahams, M. B., 367 n 73
Abrahams, Samuel, 324
Abrams, Jacob, 324
Acacia Cemetery, Queens, NY, 96, 362 n 84
Academy of the Beginning of Wisdom, New York City, 91
Adams, Joseph, 324
Adar Israel Congregation, Washington, DC, 303
Adler, Nathan Marcus (Rabbi), 357 n 35, 359 n 51
Adolphus, Isaac, 39, 347 n 18
Africa, 355 n 25
Agriculture, Jews in, 106–7, 268, 395 n 73

Alamo, battle of, 350 n 47
Aletrino, Melanie, 387 n 42
Aletrino, Moses, 387 n 42
Alexander, Israel, 335
Alexander, Simon, 132, 335, 370–71 nn 45, 49
Alliance Israèlite Universelle, 95, 160, 317
America, 120
American Hebrew (New York City), 100
American Israelite, 306
Americanization, 313, 315–17; in Boston, 172; in Cleveland, 261; in New Orleans, 219, 221; in New York, 101–6; in Philadelphia, 135. *See also* Intermarriage, with Gentiles
American Jewish Archives, Cincinnati, 419
American Jewish Historical Society, Waltham, MA, 362 n 81
American Jewish Publication Society, Philadelphia, 161
American Revolution, and Patriot Jews, 36, 38–39, 44–45, 47–51, 63–64, 107–8, 118, 126, 165–66, 229, 320, 377 n 9; and Loyalist Jews, 47

421